W9-CRP-786

BETTELHEIM

BETTELHEIM

a *Life*

---❋---

and a *Legacy*

NINA SUTTON

*Translated from the French by David Sharp,
in collaboration with the author*

WestviewPress
A Division of HarperCollins*Publishers*

All rights reserved. Printed in the United States of America. No part of this publication may be reproduced or transmitted in any form or by any means, electronic or mechanical, including photocopy, recording, or any information storage and retrieval system, without permission in writing from the publisher.

Copyright © 1996 by Nina Sutton

Paperback edition published in 1997 in the United States of America by Westview Press, 5500 Central Avenue, Boulder, Colorado 80301-2877, and in the United Kingdom by Westview Press, 12 Hid's Copse Road, Cumnor Hill, Oxford OX2 9JJ

First Published in France in 1995 by Éditions Stock

Library of Congress Cataloging-in-Publication Data
Sutton, Nina
     [Bruno Bettelheim, une vie. English]
          Bettelheim, a life and a legacy / Nina Sutton; translated
    by David Sharp, in collaboration with the author.
      p. cm.
  Includes bibliographical references and index.
   ISBN 0-8133-9099-0
   1. Bettelheim, Bruno. 2. Psychoanalysts—United States—Biography. I. Title
RC438.6.B48S8813 1996
618.92'89'0092—dc20
[B]

95-44421
CIP

The paper used in this publication meets the requirements of the American National Standard for Permanence of Paper for Printed Library Materials Z39.48-1984.

10   9   8   7   6   5   4   3   2

To Emilie,
to Louise

Contents

Part II
"Dr. B"

Preface

In July 1990, when I undertook to write this biography, Bruno Bettelheim was for me the brilliant inventor of a unique method of treating autism in children, the first educator to have practiced total milieu therapy based on the teachings of Sigmund Freud, and as such a pioneer of psychoanalysis.

I was also aware that Bettelheim, after growing up in Freud's Vienna, had witnessed the takeover of the city by Adolf Hitler, and that before emigrating to the United States he had been interned in the Nazi camps of Dachau and Buchenwald.

I was intrigued by this Jew who seemed to reject the inevitability of the Holocaust, daring to criticize, for example, Anne Frank's father. I was touched by the enlightened lover of fairy tales—a man who, despite his forbidding exterior, had remained close enough to the little boy he had once been to delve into and explain the true roles played by those weird and wonderful characters that populate our childhood.

But most of all, this noble old gentleman had always impressed me, in his television appearances and press articles, by the loftiness, rigor, and yet the simplicity of his ideas. What he was saying—or at least what I was hearing him say—was that insanity does not exist as such. The unorthodox forms of behavior that we view as insane in fact make up a language, the best one available for those whose suffering is too great to express itself in any other way. It is up to us to decipher that language. In order to break through the walls of such people's "empty fortresses," one needs to be intuitive, totally available, cease-lessly vigilant concerning one's own motives, and patient. And last but not least, Bettelheim said that, whether "crazy" or not, children must always be respected.

I feel it necessary to recall the above because, in the four and a half years I spent tracking Bruno Bettelheim's footsteps from Vienna to Los Angeles, via Chicago, Basel, and Sydney, I heard so many terri-ble things that at times I forgot what my starting point had been. The question "What made you decide to write this book?" was asked so often—not least by myself—that I felt it should be answered one last time for the reader who has chosen to seek with me that unruly bun-dle of truths that makes up the life of a man—in this case, a man of rare complexity.

In France, where I live, Bruno Bettelheim has a particularly strong image. In 1974, French TV viewers had the rare privilege of discover-ing the Sonia Shankman Orthogenic School of the University of Chicago from the inside, thanks to a documentary which, because French television staff happened to be on strike that evening, was broadcast simultaneously in prime time on all the three channels then in existence. It made a big impression.

Filmed in 1973, just before Bettelheim retired from his post as director, Daniel Karlin's stunning four-hour documentary has the feel of a testament. And yet it has never been shown in the United States. The French director had to accept that ban, imposed by the need to protect the privacy of Bettelheim's young charges, before being allowed to take a movie camera into the school.[1]

A year earlier, Bettelheim's reputation in France had already been shaped by the publication of *La folie des autres* (Other People's Mad-ness), the writer Geneviève Jurgensen's account of her two years as a counselor at the Orthogenic School.[2] It is a very lively book that also provides a glimpse into daily life at the institution, even though its author never claims to do more than describe her experiences as a young Frenchwoman thrown into an unknown world. Yet, for the same reasons as for Karlin's documentary, its publication in the United States was stopped by the school's lawyers.

Finally, and without getting prematurely involved in a debate to which we will return in chapter 10, it should be noted that since psy-choanalysis was hounded out of Vienna by the Nazis in 1938, it has evolved differently in France and in the United States. To sum it up roughly, in the United States the notion of therapeutic efficiency rapidly took precedence over all other aspects of psychoanalysis, whereas in France the view of psychoanalysis as an investigatory process, which was always very precious to Sigmund Freud, has retained its importance. This may explain why Bettelheim's message has been interpreted by the French in a more dispassionate, less result-oriented way.

It was a life spanning eighty-six and a half years, sixteen published books, a considerable number of essays and articles on weighty subjects (insanity, anti-Semitism, parent–child relations, mass society); thirty years spent trying to save troubled young people. Running through it was an almost magical idea: that from an absolute evil—Nazism—could be drawn the salvation of mentally ill children. When I started out on this investigation, my subject had all the trappings of a saint.

Very rapidly, however, the flesh-and-blood man, with his little lies and major bouts of rage, began to emerge from behind the idealized image. As is no doubt the lot of most biographers, I started to feel a measure of disappointment, of irritation at the way reality was failing to live up to my image of it. And I was just beginning to familiarize myself with my subject when what might be called "the Bettelheim affair" broke out, disrupting the getting-acquainted process with a vengeance.

I use the word *affair* advisedly, since the scandal that erupted in the United States in the six months following Bettelheim's death in March 1990 was unprecedented in its suddenness, violence, and excess, particularly in the worlds of academe and psychoanalysis. By December 1990, I no longer had any idea who Bruno Bettelheim was. I was by no means alone: most of the people I had interviewed over the previous two months, people who had known him well, had betrayed their own confusion by asking me more questions about him than they gave me answers. One of them, although quite close to him at the end of his life, asked for time to think before seeing me because, he confessed, "I no longer know what to think of him."

This was hardly surprising: In the space of six months, not a single stone of the Bettelheim monument had been left standing.

The man had always had his detractors, and even enemies. He was provocative, he had firm opinions on a whole range of controversial subjects, he could easily be curt or condescending, he did not suffer fools gladly. He was, all told, not the kind of person who generates a calm consensus about himself. But this was something else. In just a few months, as if by magic, every facet of his reputation had come under attack. The psychoanalyst was nothing more than a charlatan, the benevolent pedagogue who understood children so well was really a sadistic brute, and even the respected author of several international bestsellers was no more than a common plagiarist.

Fortunately, Paris is a long way from Chicago, and after an initial trip to the United States, a spell at home allowed me to get things back in perspective. Far from the fury of the scandal, I reread my notes, played back the taped interviews, compared different accounts of the same incidents. And I began to hear what was being said along-side the actual words. This allowed me to go back to the States and listen to the stories I was told with the necessary distance.

I was then struck by how each person who had known, loved, or even hated Bettelheim was eager to learn more, to finally understand the man as a whole. He had always remained very discreet about him-self, despite the handful of anecdotes about his past that he would readily trot out to illustrate an idea, set people thinking, or make a point. He could carry on parallel relationships, equally intense but very different, with a wide range of people, many of whom did not even suspect the others' existence.

There were those in whose eyes he sought a reflection of the admirable man he would have liked to have been. There were those, more often than not women, to whom he served as father figure, teacher, guru. There were some whom he treated with condescension, since he always knew what made them tick better than they did them-selves. There were rivals, peers against whom he liked to score points. There were those, usually men, to whom he turned for the few robust certainties that helped him fight the depression that pursued him throughout his life. There were others, women usually very dear to him, in whose gaze he sought confirmation of what he believed to be his ugliness. There were some rare people to whom he confessed his weaknesses. And then there were his own children; to exist next to a man like Bettelheim, they had no choice but to focus their lives else-where.

In almost all these people I felt that same curiosity, that same desire at last to get a grip on the truth of the man, be it to hate or love him all the better. And after spending four and a half years listening to them, I am now convinced of one thing: Even if he had remained for the rest of his life the lumber merchant that the death of his father condemned him to be for a good dozen years in Vienna, a plausible if unlikely proposition, the true Bruno Bettelheim would still be difficult to apprehend, because, as his younger daughter Naomi remarked: "When my father said things, there were always at least two, and sometimes three levels. So people who heard Level One reacted one way; people who heard Levels One and Two reacted another way. They saw the same things, but read them differently."

Muddying the waters even more is the fact that Bettelheim chose the field of mental disorders for his life's work—a world of distorting mirrors in which every gesture and word has meaning only in relation to the understanding of the other person.

I hesitated for a long time over the best way to approach the scandal. Several people, particularly in Paris, recommended mere disdain. All this hubbub, they said, is much ado about nothing; it was whipped up by the media in the first place and will just as quickly be forgotten. It is but a parasite feeding on Bettelheim's teachings. Others, mostly in the United States, clamored for me to take sides. "So you're writing Bettelheim's biography," they would say. "Will it be for or against?"

Rather than seeking to answer that question, I tried to imagine what Bettelheim himself would have thought of it all. It was the least I owed him after going through his correspondence, checking his public statements against various records, prying into his every reaction, and quizzing those who had worked for him about his slightest idiosyncrasies—after violating the privacy of a man who guarded it so jealously during his lifetime.

Taking a leaf from Freud's book, Bruno Bettelheim was no great believer in biographies. Even if he read a few with obvious relish, he most definitely did not want anyone to write his own. He said this time and time again, publicly in reviews of Ernest Jones's biography of Sigmund Freud,[3] and privately in a number of letters to which I was granted access. Toward the end of his life, he finally yielded to the entreaties of an old friend and admirer with whom he had worked for many years, and agreed to answer a few questions into a tape recorder. But even that effort weighed heavily on him, as he was to remark gloomily on the day before his death.

This is without a doubt the reason he took advantage of the three moves to new homes that punctuated the last years of his life to destroy so many papers, depriving his future biographers of much precious material. But that was something Freud also had done to some extent[4]—and yet he allowed Jones to get on with his work as official biographer. As for Bettelheim, while ostensibly covering his tracks,[5] he kept on dropping little white pebbles along his path, just like little Hansel in his favorite fairy tale. Whoever is really determined to do so can follow the signs to almost every aspect of his life—including his lies. This, I feel, was his ultimate way of expressing himself on "at least two and sometimes three levels" at once.

Having chosen to defy the prohibition of Level One ("Thou shalt not write my biography"), it seemed to me that I at least owed it to Bettelheim to respect the ideal of rigor of Level Three. It is a rigor that allows for no softheartedness, that is often brutal, as was Bettelheim himself. Beyond appearances, it constantly seeks out, if not the truth, at least the reality of each person. It is stern, obstinate, and uncompromising, utterly devoid of any of the Viennese frills and flourishes that Level Two handles so adroitly.

I realized early on that it would be impossible to undertake an objective study of Bettelheim's life as long as I had not dealt with the scandal. It was there, standing in the way of my research, coloring everything I learned. I therefore decided, three years ago, to write it all down in a kind of introduction, knowing that it could always be moved elsewhere later. Today, it is quite intentionally that I leave the description here. It is its rightful place. The scandal is not part of the chronological story of Bettelheim's life, because when his accusers came forward he was no longer around to reply. But it is not just a postscript either, for I am now convinced that behind the posthumous blows that rained down on his memory, some of them quite vicious, one can discern not only Bruno Bettelheim's weaknesses, but also what made him a truly great therapist. And that is what this book is all about.

I have tried not to ignore any of the accusations leveled against Bettelheim after his death. Since the most serious of these accusations were made not by outsiders but by some of the children who were once in his care, they are an integral part of his life. Whether true or false, they have a place in his story because they express suffering born of the relationships that he had developed with those children, and because he unilaterally and abruptly brought those relationships to an end on the night of March 12, 1990, when he took his own life. And that, alas, is something he is not yet through paying for.

Acknowledgments

Researching and writing this book has brought me a great deal. But, over five years, it has also weighed heavily on those closest to me. Someone very dear to Bettelheim once told me: "It was a real meeting of minds between you. It is impossible to understand Bruno if one hasn't suffered." Maybe . . . I only wish I could have spared my family the experience. Thanks to all of them for having stayed strong, even when there seemed to be no light at the end of the tunnel.

Friendship also played a major role in this endeavor. Without my friends' support, I certainly could not have completed it. Some offered me shelter, in the United States, Israel, and Austria. Others saw me through tight spots. Some generously put their knowledge at my disposal, letting me decide how to use it. Several listened patiently, as I struggled with doubts and oversimplistic judgments. Some read and reread, helping me find the right words to express often difficult ideas. In short, they were there whenever I needed them. My warmest thanks to Helga Abraham, Marie-Ange d'Adler, Anne Albertson, Gordon Anderson, Thérèse Binchet, Danièle Braunschweig, Jean-Michel Braunschweig, Frank Browning, Faye and Charles Carey, Marie-Pierre Carretier, Shalom Cohen, Simone Conrad-Eybesfeld, Marie-Odile Fargier, Micheline Faure, Anita Frankel, Danièle Granet, Jean-Guy Gourson, Mark and Carol Hosenball, Rony Koven, Catherine Lamour, Martine Ledieu, Marie-José Lepicard, Danièle Lévy, Charles Lutz, Katia Lutz, Denise Mairey, René Major, Marie-Charlotte Maupas, Andrée Mazzolini, Jean-Michel Normand, Nora Pouillon, Pierre Pouillon, Renée

Shiponi, Mary Sills, Michèle Slung, Noreen Taylor, Christiane Tenenhaus, Bénédicte Thiéfine, Micheline Weinstein, Paul Zimmerman.

My deep gratitude also goes to all those who, having known Bettelheim, believed in my capacity to bring to life some of his true spirit. To Naomi and Eric Bettelheim, first of all, who acquiesced to most of my requests without ever demanding anything in return. Their generous and noninterfering attitude helped me recover the respect for their father that, at one point, I had started to lose. And to all the others: Etti Andreani, Ronald Angres and his parents, Hans Bandler, Bill Blau, Heda Bolgar, Heidi Braham, Stuart Brent, Heidi and Willy Brown, Jean Brown, Steve Cahodes, Madeleine Chapsal, Leslie Cleaver, Bert Cohler, Mary Ellen Cowan, Lee Cronbach, Preston Cutler, Gayle Donovan, Ronnie Dryvage, Nechama Edelman, Eliott Eisner, Kurt Eissler, Rudi Ekstein, Alex Elsen, Ernst Federn, Seymour Feschback, David James Fisher, Maurie Formigoni, Ugo Formigoni, Charlotte Fowler, Seymour Fox, Ljuba Frankenstein, Elio Fratteroli, Marilyn Garner, Desy Gerard, Jakob Getzel, Gilo Goetzl, Myles Gordon, Sue Gotschall, Joëlle de Gravelaine, Richard Grossman, Leah Hadoumi, Nina Helstein, Candace Hilldrup, Aimee Hornton, Roland Humery, Katherine Isenstadt, Gayle Shulenberger Janowitz, Geneviève Jurgensen, Diana Grossman Kahn, George and Cathy Kaiser, Jeremiah Kaplan, Linda Kaplan, Daniel Karlin, Connie Katzenstein, Jerry Kavka, Moshe Kerem, Oliver Kerner, Shelton Key, Charles Kligerman, Don Kofall, Robert Koff, Maria Kramer, Adrian Kuypers, Gretel Lowinski, Kathy and Marc Lubin, Patsy Lyne, Augusta Wallace Lyons, Tom Lyons, Jacky and Alan Manne, Ruth Marquis, Rahel Messinger, Leo and Ruth Nedelsky, Bernice Neugarten, Eva Neurath, Tom Neurath, Julie Newman, Joseph Noshpits, Heather Ogilvie, Nell Pekarsky, Charles Pekow, Patty Pickett McKnight, Eleonor and Gerard Piel, Maria Piers, Bettylou Pingree Rellahan, George Pollack, Albert Reiss Jr., Jacquelyn Sanders, Louis Shapiro, Edward Shils, Edwin Shneidman, Judy and Lee Shulman, Ada Skyles, Johanna Tabin, Ralph Tyler, Fae and Bob Tyroler, Jane Ullman, Annie Urbach, Emmi Vischer-Radanowicz, Charles Walton, Saul Wasserman, Gina Weinmann, Clifford Wilk, Miriam Williams, Wanda Willig, Josette Wingo, Ben Wright, Luitgard Wundheiler, Richard Younker, Karen Zelan. Some were more enthusiastic than others in talking to me. Some trusted me immediately, others were more wary. Some even became real friends. But all contributed to shaping in my mind the image of a complex man I had never met. That is no less true of those who do not appear in the following pages than of those who do.

Many thanks also to those who, without having known Bettelheim well, helped me to understand some aspects of his life. First of all to Laurence Dahan-Gaida, whose knowledge of Vienna—and reading of Bettelheim's dissertation—proved invaluable. And to Elisabeth Badinter, Ralph Bettelheim, Werner Bettelheim, Howard Buten, Marie Cardinal, René Diatkine, Alan Dundes, Ellen Fine, Peter Gaida, André Green, Russell Jacoby, Betty Looram, Paul Marcus, Jeffrey M. Masson, Léon Poliakov, Michael Pollak, Jean-Bertrand Pontalis, Jean Pouillon, Paul Roazen, Alan Rosenberg, Elisabeth Roudinesco, Claudine Vegh, Annette Wieviorka. Thanks to Herbert Belch, Edith Buxbaum's executor, who let me read a few pages of her unpublished memoirs. Thanks also to the many archivists and librarians who helped me, many of them well beyond the call of duty, notably at the University of Chicago's Regenstein Library, the Centre de Documentation Juive Contemporaine, the Dachau Memorial, the Vienna Freud Haus, the Albertgasse Bundesrealgymnasium, the Israelitische Kultusgemeinde, the Ford Foundation, the Rockefeller Archives, the Franklin D. Roosevelt Library, Columbia University's Lehmann Library, the Chicago Psychoanalytic Institute, the American Library in Paris, and many others, including the Singer Company archives.

This English-language edition owes a great deal to David Sharp, who translated the French version as I was writing it—no easy task.

And many thanks to my publishers, Claude Durand, Jo Ann Miller, and Robin Baird-Smith, for having been so patient.

Paris, February 1996

PROLOGUE

---✶---

The "Bettelheim Affair"

Not even the most tempting probability is a protection against error; even if all the parts of a problem seem to fit together like the pieces of a jig-saw puzzle, one must reflect that what is probable is not necessarily the truth, and that the truth is not always probable.

—*Sigmund Freud,*
Moses and Monotheism

---※---

March 13th, 1990: The well-known child psychoanalyst Bruno Bettelheim was found dead this morning at his home in Silver Spring, Maryland. According to the medical examiner, his death was the result of suicide by asphyxiation. The body of Dr. Bettelheim was found by the janitor of the retirement home he had recently moved into. His head was covered with a plastic bag . . .

Voice One:	Voice Two:	Voice Three:

Voice One:

"Bruno Bettelheim dead? . . . No! I don't believe it. It's not true . . . It's another of his tricks . . .

. . . Besides, he doesn't even live around here; he's in California. I know it; I read it in the paper . . .

. . . So, he killed himself, the son of a bitch. Good riddance! That's the best thing he ever did. No more lectures, no more lies, no more torture . . .

. . . And there's no way anyone can blame it on me; I haven't spoken to him in years. Sure, he drove me mad. And for good reasons: he damaged me for life . . . But that's the past. I've got my own life to lead now! . . .

. . . There wasn't anything wrong with me when I first went to that school. Not a thing! He did it all. He wrecked me. And now he's done it to himself. So, you see . . . He's responsible. I had nothing to do with it . . . "

Voice Two:

"*S.U.I.C.I.D.E . . . He killed himself . . . Him! . . . Dr. B has killed himself . . . He's abandoned us . . .*

How could he have done that to me? . . . I trusted him. I thought he meant it when he said there was always a chance for a new beginning. When he said that harm could be undone, that life would always have something to offer. When he insisted that I never give up . . .

. . . I believed him when he said he loved me, when he said I was worthy of love . . .

Lies, that's what it was. All lies. He was doing his job, that's all . . . Just proving his theories . . . Love is not enough? That's for sure! When you really love people, you don't leave them . . . Not like that!

True, he was old, and he'd been sick . . . After all, it was his life, not mine . . . What he gave me, I can keep. That's mine . . . yes, mine; I can do whatever I want with it. And if he's not here to see it, it's his problem! . . . Still, I'll miss him."

Voice Three:

"A plastic bag? A nursing home? That's . . . that's crazy! . . .

. . . That's right, it's crazy! I tell you, it's crazy . . . HE was crazy. Sure, he was crazy . . . I knew it, I knew it all along! . . .

I should have known! He was a paranoiac . . . Of course . . . That lousy temper! All those crazy threats . . . God! When I think how much he hurt me . . .

The great Dr. B was nuts! That's too funny for words! . . . And to think that my mother thought of him as a genius! What will she say now?

A plastic bag, you've got to be kidding! . . . I have to talk to the others. He was crazy! . . . When I think of all he said to me! And all that time, HE was the crazy one . . . Do you hear? He was mad, NOT ME."

The first letter appeared in the *Reader*, a free Chicago weekly, on April 6, 1990, less than three weeks after Bettelheim's death. It was unsigned. It described an unpredictable Bettelheim, prone to rages during which he beat and cruelly insulted the children. In particular, it told how the correspondent, then age fifteen, had been taking a shower when "Dr. B.," as everyone used to call the director of the Orthogenic School, suddenly burst into the bathroom, grabbed her by the hair, and dragged her naked and dripping out into a dormitory room full of people, where he proceeded to beat her. Far worse than the physical pain, the writer stressed, was the terrible humiliation she had felt. To this day, she added, she had not the slightest idea what she had done to deserve such abuse.

Two weeks earlier, a unanimous press had been paying tribute to Bruno Bettelheim as a "pioneer in treating childhood mental disturbances,"[1] known for his "warmth and wisdom."[2] That letter threw open the floodgates. Soon the letters-to-the-editor page of the *Reader* was hosting an animated debate between former patients and counselors of the Orthogenic School, a residential facility offering intensive therapy, with Bettelheim being sometimes depicted as a monster. The debate was further enlivened by contributions from a number of outsiders who were all too eager to point out the contradictions between the man's high-sounding pronouncements and the allegations now leveled against him.

The "antis" deployed more firepower than the "pros." They congratulated one another on their courage, often referring to each other's texts as if they had never met, much less been brought up together. In the trenches on the other side, most of Bettelheim's defenders were fighting with one arm tied behind their back, being unable for reasons of professional ethics to reveal what they knew, as former counselors or therapists, about their patients. Their replies to the barrage of criticism more often than not seemed lame, appearing at best beside the point, at worst a cover-up.

Soon the ranks of the combatants were swelled by the enemies of psychoanalysis who had always fought Bettelheim, by arguing that mental illnesses had nothing to do with family environment or upbringing, but were attributable only to physical, even chemical factors. Chicago quickly became the scene of an all-out, no-holds-barred battle. The hostility, incomprehension, and bitterness involved were commensurate with the role Bettelheim had played in the city for more than three decades. People who had known each other for years took to avoiding one another. Some sank into a despairing silence, while others poured out their feelings for all the world to hear.

On August 26 the controversy finally brimmed over into a wider arena. Charles Pekow, a freelance journalist who had spent eleven years as a student at the Orthogenic School, finally managed to get a piece into the Sunday edition of the *Washington Post*. It appeared under the headline "The Other Dr. Bettelheim: The Revered Psychologist Had a Dark, Violent Side." After briefly recalling the glowing tributes paid to Bettelheim in the obituaries, Pekow proceeded to list the charges against him. Not only had Dr. B been a sadistic brute, he asserted, he had also been a racist, since there had been no black kids at the Orthogenic School. Bettelheim had above all been a charlatan, whose fame enabled him to cover up his mistaken diagnoses and abuses of power; in short, his most noteworthy talent had been for self-promotion.

To back up his indictment, Pekow cited Alida Jatitch, by now revealed as the anonymous writer of that first letter to the *Reader:* "Those who were going through normal adolescent pains were labeled psychotic . . . What bothered me the most, more than the beating, insults, whatever, [was that] throughout my adolescence I was basically treated like I was a two-year-old," Jatitch said. On this point, Pekow noted that students at the school were prohibited from taking music lessons or engaging in other such extracurricular activities on the theory that they needed all their available time for "personality rebuilding." Pekow also quoted Bill Blau, a former counselor: "I would characterize the atmosphere at the Orthogenic School, at that time (1949–50), as the beginnings of a cult, with 'Dr. B' as the cult leader." That statement was echoed by a quote from Jacquelyn Sanders, who had run the Orthogenic School since Bettelheim's departure in 1973, after having worked under him for thirteen years as a counselor: "I believed blindly in him, and I don't like to think of myself as the type of person who would believe blindly in anything."

Some might find it surprising to see Sanders being quoted in an article so hostile to Bettelheim. Her reply would be that she never refused to talk to a former student, be it Charles Pekow or anyone else. One might, however, have expected a more spirited defense of the man who had been her teacher for so long, and who later picked her to succeed him. But this was not to be the last occasion on which

Jacquelyn Sanders's statements betrayed her ambivalence toward Bruno Bettelheim. In September 1990, for example, she wrote a letter to the editor of the *Chicago Sun-Times* in which, while ostensibly protesting a hostile article, she conceded: "I have long felt that Bettelheim did a disservice to the field by not discussing more thoroughly the issue of discipline." The letter also stressed that as director of the Orthogenic School Sanders had expressly forbidden any use of corporal punishment whatsoever. It also noted that she had long since stopped admitting autistic children. Finally, Bettelheim's successor asked the paper's readers not to hold it against him that "a powerful and brilliant man made some powerful and brilliant mistakes."

The scandal was now spreading beyond the confines of the United States, as Pekow's article was reprinted by the *International Herald Tribune*, the *Guardian* in London, and other foreign publications. It was received with amazement, and often with a measure of skepticism, throughout the world. In France, in particular, most observers dismissed the allegations out of hand as yet another example of transatlantic hyperbole, of how Americans were forever tearing down yesterday's idols, as undiscerning in their debunking as they had formerly been in their adulation.

The secrecy in which Bruno Bettelheim had shrouded the Orthogenic School contributed powerfully to the attention the scandal attracted in the United States. For everyone except those who had lived and worked there, the institution had always remained a mystery. Insisting that the children had to be protected from all intrusions, and that the slightest change in their daily routine could prove traumatic, Bettelheim had allowed hardly a single visitor to pass the famous firedoors that separated the reception area from the residential quarters. In later years, even when professionals such as psychiatrists, doctors, or psychoanalysts had come to visit, they had seldom been invited to go any further than the staffroom. Thus those who had known the school from the inside could say what they liked about it without fear of being challenged, except by others whose information was every bit as subjective—not to say defensive, in the case of counselors who were accused of abuse. Previously the secrecy surrounding the school had allowed outsiders to see it as a paradise; now that same secrecy let them project onto it the image of a living hell.

The wider it spread, the more the debate became reduced to almost comic-strip simplicity. Pretty soon it boiled down to one "yes–no" question: Did Bruno Bettelheim, who in his books and lectures had so often condemned corporal punishment, beat the children placed in his care? Just as quickly, the answer became obvious to all but the most uncritical: Yes, he did on occasion hit them. Sometimes, it seemed, Bettelheim was trying to force a reaction from a child who was completely shut off from the outside world, but more often the gesture appeared to be simply one of ill-controlled anger. He had in fact practically answered the question himself back in 1984, when a reporter had put it to him bluntly. "That's between me and the children," Bettelheim had replied.[3]

But that half-admission, published long before in a small New England paper, was hardly enough to satisfy the morbid curiosity that had now been aroused by the controversy. On the contrary, the accusations of brutality were only amplified by the whiff of hypocrisy. The wall between Bettelheim's detractors and his apologists grew even higher. One was either for or against; there was no middle ground.

"Beno Brutalheim?" The level the scandal had reached could be gauged by this headline in *Newsweek* less than six months after the same magazine ran a glowing obituary. Following an ostensibly balanced appraisal of Bettelheim's work, the article concluded that "Bettelheim's experiences in the concentration camps probably affected his methods." The argument was all the more damning in that it was backed up by a quote from one of the dead man's most faithful friends: "He had seen a dictator who destroys people, and he became a dictator who wanted to rescue people."[4]

In October it was the turn of former Orthogenic School student Ronald Angres to go public, in the October 1990 issue of the conservative Jewish magazine *Commentary*. His account, titled "Who, Really, Was Bruno Bettelheim?" had a livelier, less acrimonious tone than Charles Pekow's, showing both more distance and more personal feeling. It was even more damaging. Angres, described in the magazine as a graduate student in international affairs at George Washington University, started by inverting one of Bettelheim's pet quotes, speaking of the "shock of non-recognition" that he, like Charles Pekow, had experienced on reading the newspaper obituaries.[5]

Ronald Angres was almost seven when he entered the school and nineteen when he left it. Running through his text the careful reader once again detects agonizing yet unasked questions: "Why was I sent there? Was I really sick the way they said I was?" ("they" in his case being his psychoanalyst father, his mother, Bettelheim, and others). "Am I still sick today?" The questions were all the more haunting for Angres in that he had been one of the "autistic" children whose treatment had brought fame to Bettelheim—at least, he had been presented as such by his counselor of seven years, Jacquelyn Sanders, in the master's dissertation she had written about his case in 1964.[6]

Initially, at least, even a lay reader was sure to conclude that if the young man really had been autistic, and if he was now capable of pursuing graduate studies and writing the article published in *Commentary*, there could be no better tribute to the work of Bettelheim— even if Ronald Angres had nothing good to say about him. No parent or counselor of an autistic child could wish for a more spectacular result. And this was precisely the argument put forward by many readers of the article to counter Angres's damning testimony. The problem with that line of defense was the apparent ease with which Angres contested the original diagnosis, reached in 1959 when the definition of infantile autism was vaguer than it is today. As the article unfolded, the open-minded reader found the natural suspicions aroused by a patient's assessment of his own illness gradually dissolving. And as the original diagnosis began to appear questionable, so did all the rest.

Angres gave a host of examples of the "tyranny" exercised by Bettelheim, who, he wrote, made him live for twelve years "in terror of his beatings, in terror of his footsteps in the dorms—abject, animal terror." He recounted how his comic books were confiscated, how the little toy train he had brought from home, and which for that reason was dear to him, was dismissed as a "stupid toy." He also recalled how Bettelheim had on one occasion accused him of being a "megalomaniac" simply because he had chosen to sit apart in an armchair while waiting for a meal, rather than join the other children on an overcrowded bench, how Bettelheim slapped him during a game for hitting the ball too hard so it landed on a fellow-student's head, and so on. It was a long list of miseries, and it was all the more shocking for those readers who were aware of how Bettelheim had described the Orthogenic School in his books as a world in which the golden rule was to leave the children free to do as they pleased, within the limits of physical safety, in order to allow the language of their "madness" to be deciphered, with each symptom being seen as part of a puzzle.

Some of Angres's less serious accusations could, however, be seen in perspective by the informed reader. An example: having read in Bettelheim that it was essential to accept a child's bedwetting to make him realize that one loved him for himself,[7] and that a counselor should put a higher priority on the child's treatment than on the school's hygiene, the reader was not unduly surprised to find Ronald Angres complaining about the smell of urine permeating the junior dormitories.

There were also incidents that such a reader could easily see from both the therapist's and the child's point of view. Describing his first encounter with Bettelheim, Angres wrote:

> I drew for him a picture of a man. I don't remember now if he asked me to, but all psychologists seemed to crave such pictures, and I may have tried in this fashion to break the ice.
>
> "What a stupid and ugly picture," he snapped. (I did not yet know that he fancied himself an art connoisseur.) "You did not draw his hands!"
>
> "They're behind his back," I explained.
>
> "You just did that because you can't draw hands! Do you know what it means when a boy can't draw hands?"
>
> I did not. I still don't. To appease him, I redrew the picture and added some hands, carefully showing all five fingers.
>
> "Preposterous! You drew the hands entirely out of proportion! They're bigger than his head!"
>
> Once more he scowled darkly, as if I were expected to know the sinister significance of such a reversal of normal proportions.[8]

Angres was articulate and obviously highly intelligent—the psychologists who examined him before he entered the Orthogenic School at the age of six and a half credited him with an IQ of 168—and his indictment of Bettelheim was devastatingly effective, whatever comments could be made about it by a psychiatrist. Indeed, even though his article stressed the beatings, his main complaint was the constant "analytical" scrutiny to which his every act had been subjected while he was at the school. As an example, Angres told how he had given up playing baseball after a few years, even though his physical awkwardness was one of his major problems: "They kept us from forming teams, from deciding with whom we would play, from keeping score," he explained. (Bettelheim believed that competitiveness was damaging and that it diverted his charges from their key task at the school, which was the reconstruction of their egos.) But worst of all, "Every ball that hit a child was regarded as an intentional assault, requiring punishment. Needless to say, the intent did not have to be 'conscious' . . . Most of us were clumsy, if not 'spastic,' " he wrote, quoting the adjective he said Bettelheim often used to deride his physical performances. However, "our 'unconscious' was credited with superhuman skill and with the single determination to bean other kids with tennis balls."

The account may have been tinged with paranoia; it was nevertheless disturbing. Angres, whose father was a psychoanalyst, was able to quote Freud, draw parallels between Bettelheim and Wilhelm Reich, and in general come across as knowledgeable and credible. His description of how he had suffered as a little boy and an adolescent from having his every gesture, drawing, or utterance minutely observed and analyzed gives the lay reader a picture that is a far cry from the "home for the heart" of Bettelheim's writings.

It is easy to see how Ronald Angres's testimony would become grist for the mills of the foes of psychoanalysis. His article already betrayed signs of the phone conversations he had had with Jeffrey Masson, fallen angel of psychoanalysis who was then at the forefront of the anti-Freudian forces in the United States. Masson, a trained analyst, had risen spectacularly in the psychoanalytic community to become deputy director of the Freud Archives with the blessing of Kurt Eissler, the director, and to a lesser extent of Anna Freud herself. Having challenged Sigmund Freud's integrity, Masson had been cast out in disgrace just as suddenly as he had risen to fame.[9] For a time, Masson was to find himself the rallying point for some of Bruno Bettelheim's lost children, in search of someone who would listen to their stories. Soon he was writing to Jacquelyn Sanders to ask for biographical data about Bettelheim, to amend the article about him in his anthology of psychoanalysis!

In the meantime, a group of fourteen former counselors and teachers from the Orthogenic School had replied to Charles Pekow's attacks in the *Washington Post*. Their letter[10] was signed by two of Bettelheim's most trusted colleagues, notably Karen Zelan, with whom he had co-authored a book about reading.[11] Zelan had been the counselor of "Marcia," one of the three cases of autism described in Bettelheim's *The Empty Fortress*. The other signatory, Fae Tyroler, had acted as counselor to "Joey the mechanical boy," the most famous case in the same work.

This was heavy artillery, and could have been expected to strike a major blow for the Bettelheim camp. Strangely, however, the letter seemed almost to miss the point, as though it were replying to accusers other than Pekow and Angres. This was all the more obvious since the *Post* chose to publish it beneath a second letter from Pekow—a reply to yet another former counselor who had sought to defend Bettelheim. The correspondence had become such a regular feature of the *Post's* op-ed page that it ran under the heading "The Bettelheim We Knew (Cont'd)."

Karen Zelan and her associates remained too aloof to score any points against Bettelheim's critics, either directly or implicitly. Their text appeared dry and awkward in contrast with the anger, suffering, and anxiety expressed by the accusers. The letter did not even try to address the specifics of the accusations, and it also failed on the broader level of principles. It simply did not mesh with Bettelheim's own oft-published view that warmth and personal commitment were the most essential traits of a good counselor or educator. Such traits were conspicuously absent from the letter, and that could only reinforce the reader's suspicion that a yawning gulf between theory and practice had existed in Bettelheim's institution. Rather than lifting the debate to a higher plane, the text seemed merely defensive.

The first argument used by Zelan et al. rested on the worldwide reputation of the University of Chicago—of which the Orthogenic School is a part. "Is the public to believe that [Bettelheim] concealed the existence of this 'concentration camp' environment within one of the world's great research universities?" they asked. And without stooping to discuss a single one of the everyday details that had made the accusations so effective, the writers simply vouched for "Bettelheim's contribution to the understanding and treatment of children who otherwise would have been considered untreatable." Finally, in an all-too-brief paragraph, they evoked some of the emotions that filled their daily lives at the school: "Bettelheim was deeply moved by the inner chaos, rage, misery and terror of the children, which was often manifest in extreme behavior, ranging from endangering themselves or others, to the ludicrous or puzzling. Of course, he responded with a range of feeling and action. There was a great deal to be upset about, and sufficient to enjoy with good humor." Nevertheless, they added: "Bettelheim exhorted us never to give up in our efforts, because even the most hateful or bizarre behavior could be understood and perhaps remediated."

Meanwhile, Charles Pekow continued to pull no punches in his campaign, even seizing on the looming war in the Persian Gulf to compare the Orthogenic School to Saddam Hussein's Iraq! Neither side in the debate appeared to be making any impact on the other, but to the lay reader, seeking an immediate and therefore simplified view of events, the score was clearly not running in favor of the defense. By late fall of 1990 the anti-Bettelheim wave had made it impossible even to mention the man's name without sparking an impassioned debate, fraught with humiliation for all its participants: for the memory of Bruno Bettelheim and for his defenders, of course, but also for his former students/patients, whose every word and action was being subjected to the full glare of public scrutiny.

"Why wait until Bettelheim was dead to say all this?" his accusers were asked. "Because up until then nobody would believe us." The answer was as painful and bitter as the question was obvious. Charles Pekow, for example, had once tried to persuade another journalist to write an article about the Orthogenic School. Although fascinated by his story, the reporter had dropped it after talking to his editor. What does the testimony of a former mental patient count for against that of an innovative thinker respected throughout the world?

"Because an estate can't sue" was the frank admission made by one of the reporters covering the story. But the most obvious reason for the media's postmortem interest in Bruno Bettelheim was best summed up by former counselor Bill Blau: "No doubt the fact that Bettelheim committed suicide, and the way he did it, played right into our hands."[12]

Some reporters, their curiosity aroused by the accusations, started rummaging around in what had up until then been virgin territory: Bettelheim's childhood, education, and his eventual deportation by the Nazis. On November 11, 1990, the *Chicago Tribune* set off new ripples by revealing that not even those who had worked most closely with Bettelheim were able to say exactly what academic degrees he had. One witness was even quoted as saying that in Vienna Bettelheim had mainly been known as an ambitious businessman, and not at all as a psychologist.

The writer of the article, Ron Grossman, was a former college teacher, and Ronald Angres had been one of his students. Angres's *Commentary* article had come as no surprise to him; indeed, he had already read a portion of it, in a longer and less structured version, several years earlier. As a student, Angres had at first been incapable of producing the slightest essay; Grossman had spent weeks trying to get through to this obviously gifted young man. Then one day, out of the blue, Angres had dumped his report about the Orthogenic School on his teacher's desk. From that day, he had been able to complete his assignments like any other student. The incident had so intrigued Grossman that he became fascinated by Bettelheim. His *Tribune* article was the best documented so far, with a real attempt having been made to sound out the views of all sides. Grossman had talked to nineteen former students of the Orthogenic School and at least as many of Bettelheim's former colleagues. He had also interviewed psychoanalysts and even Ralph Tyler, the former head of the University of Chicago's Department of Education who back in the 1940s had given Bettelheim his first job in the United States. The Bruno Bettelheim that emerged from all these contradictory statements was part genius, part Svengali, a remarkably intelligent but also an extremely ambitious man, not very scrupulous, and something of a dandy.

By this point, Bettelheim's writings were the only part of his life's work that had not yet come under attack—or at least not directly. It was only a matter of time; in February 1991 he was accused of plagiarism. Writing in the *Journal of American Folklore*, a Berkeley professor of anthropology charged Bettelheim with having purely and simply lifted some of the ideas for his best-selling book *The Uses of Enchantment* from the thesis of a little-known teacher of psychiatry, Doctor Julius Heuscher.[13] The only consolation for Bettelheim's supporters in the spate of articles that ensued was the response of Heuscher himself. Questioned by reporters, he stated that when he had read *The Uses of Enchantment* upon its publication fifteen years previously, he had not at all felt he was being plagiarized. Specifying that he had not known Bettelheim personally, he added: "We all plagiarize. I plagiarize. Many times, I am not sure whether it came out of my own brain or if it came from somewhere else . . . Poor Bruno Bettelheim! I did not always agree with him. But I would not want to disturb his eternal sleep for this. I'm only happy that I would have influenced [him]."[14] Thanks to this simple and eminently sensible statement, the fuss died down almost as quickly as it had flared up, leaving only a slight whiff of fraud to blend in with the earlier allegations.

And this leads to a final question: Why had Bettelheim's most effective defenders in this posthumous scandal been people who had not known him well? Why did those who had known and admired him, those who had worked with him and who therefore suffered most from the distorted image created after his death defend him so feebly? They too could have come up with simple and sensible arguments, words that most people would have found convincing. Without violating their former patients' privacy, they could, for instance, have pointed out that Charles Pekow, Ronald Angres, Alida Jatitch, and most of the others who publicly attacked Bettelheim after his death all knew one another, since they all belonged to the same generation of Orthogenic School kids. It was the last generation that Bettelheim had worked with, and undoubtedly one that he had somewhat neglected, absorbed as he had been then with the engineering of his own tricky succession. Most important, it was the generation that he had abandoned by retiring.

Not much more would have been needed to get across the message that nothing occurring in the Orthogenic School, not even the slapping, should be viewed out of context, that nothing in the relationship between therapist and patient is ever clear-cut, and that interested outsiders should therefore avoid rushing to judgment. It seemed, however, that the Bettelheim faithful were simply unable, even eighteen years after his departure from the Orthogenic School, to strike the right tone when talking about him, to treat him just as a man, with human strengths and weaknesses.

They had been the privileged witnesses of his powerful clinical intuition; they had seen him find just the right words to pacify a terrified child after everyone else had tried and failed. They had also experienced the illuminating effect of some of his analyses, and all of them could remember the relief they had felt when Bettelheim had got them out of a tight spot with a child by helping them identify the painful memory it evoked in them. But they had also seen him lose his self-control, and knew how hurtful some of his interpretations could be. Most of them had been very young when they had met him. They owed him a great deal, but they were often unable to say exactly what. The Orthogenic School had been such a strange place; its atmosphere was so difficult to describe. They had not just worked there, they had lived there twenty-four hours a day. Elsewhere, psychotics are parked in hospitals, and the staff leave at the end of the day. Or else patients return to their families in the evenings. In Chicago, they had shared the everyday life of their young patients, in some cases for many years. It had not always been clear to them exactly what differentiated them from the children, since Bettelheim was continually encouraging them to examine their own motives in their relationships with them. Interminable working days, and practically no life outside the school—how could one get all that across to outsiders?

And how to communicate one's experience of a man who was at once learned, generous, attentive, and caring, but also unpredictable, temperamental, and intellectually domineering? The years spent at the school were buried inside each former counselor like a rare secret, something almost impossible to talk about. During those years, they had shared in the dream of an extraordinary man. Extraordinary for his ambition—to cure those said to be incurable—but also for his excessive personality. A man from another age, another world, one that they as Americans had never completely understood.

PART I

The Formative Years

1

---✴---

Vienna:
Once Upon a Time . . .

Vienna, occupied by the Nazis in 1938, then shattered by Allied bombing and besieged by the Soviets, is not the ideal place to search for someone's roots, particularly if that person is a Jew. A few documents can be retrieved, almost by chance, from the mounds of dusty archives. The visitor will locate a few addresses, only to be told by the current occupants, "Oh, it's changed a great deal, you know," or even worse, "You can't get much of an idea from this place; it was rebuilt after the war." There is a handful of memories, passed on to the next generation. And there are Bruno Bettelheim's writings.

His ancestry does not seem to have loomed very large among his concerns. He mentions it only briefly, in *Freud's Vienna and Other Essays.* Along with practically all the other Bettelheims whose opinions I was able to solicit, he apparently subscribed to the belief that the whole family could be traced to a single origin in the city formerly known as Pressburg. Now Bratislava, the capital of Slovakia, it is practically Vienna's backyard, being only some thirty miles distant.

The Bettelheims are less unanimous, however, on the etymology of their name. Many of them believe it to be simply a corruption of Bethlehem. But Bruno advanced another theory when discussing his paternal grandfather, Jakob Morris Bettelheim: "He never talked about his parents, either because he was orphaned at such an early age that he knew nothing about them or because he was born out of wedlock and deserted by his mother to cover her shame."[1] The implication was that Jakob, who was born in 1825, had been assigned his surname by the orphanage, which was run by a prominent Jewish family. At the beginning of the nineteenth century, when the Austro-Hungarian Empire's Jews were granted the right to a civil identity, the family was said to have quite naturally recorded the name under which it had been known until then, a contraction of the words *Bettler* (beggar) and *Heim* (home).

In support of the theory, Bruno Bettelheim cited the many efforts made later by his uncles, the brothers of his by-then dead father, to establish their kinship with the prominent family, which had died out leaving no known heir. Their quest had been in vain, however, because according to family legend Jakob Morris Bettelheim had destroyed all documents pertaining to his birth. The reason for that, it was whispered, was that he was in fact the bastard child of an aristocrat, and did not wish his real father to suffer opprobrium.

A fine tale indeed, and one that would certainly have appealed to the art historian and psychoanalyst Ernst Kris. In the 1930s, at the time when Sigmund Freud was examining the possibility that Moses could have been an Egyptian prince,[2] Kris was showing how in most great artists' biographies, the origins of at least one ancestor are always shrouded in mystery, thus allowing a myth of noble, or even royal, extraction to spring up behind a real-life situation of misery.[3]

Nevertheless, the records of the Vienna Jewish community are clear: Jakob Morris Bettelheim was born not in Pressburg but in the Hungarian city of Pest, on March 21, 1825. His father, Markus, and mother, Lewia, must even have been fairly well known there, since Markus pursued the respectable profession of notary, to a Jewish community so large and flourishing that the Hungarian capital was soon to be nicknamed "Judapest."[4] As for Pressburg, it is true that the family name can be traced there to at least the start of the eighteenth century, first as Betlehem, then Bethlehem, and finally as Bettelheim.[5] But although the city was then under Hungarian administration, I was unable to find any indications as to when or why Jakob would have been placed in an orphanage there.

Among the various hypotheses put forward by Bettelheim, only two are consistent with existing records. The first was that one or both of Jakob's parents died when he was very young, and that the other members of his family had then refused to take care of him.

The second was that Jakob Morris was the fruit of an adulterous union on the part of his mother, who abandoned him out of shame. Bruno Bettelheim obviously tended to give more credence to the second version (it was the only one which left his origins shrouded in mystery), even though it implied not only that his great-grandmother had sinned, but also that the surname he bore was in fact usurped.

Bettelheim's brief account of how both his grandfathers went up to Vienna and made their fortunes has all the ingredients of the fairy tales he was so fond of. In both cases, the story starts out in misery and misfortune and finds a happy ending in the good city of Emperor Franz Josef. Bettelheim himself stressed the fairy-tale quality of the story by including it in an essay called "The Child's Perception of the City," for his aim was to underline the rose-tinted image of Vienna that his mother had handed down to him, and in which he long believed.

"Happy as a Jew under Franz Josef" was a stock phrase at the time. The new ruler took the throne in 1848, and shortly thereafter Vienna became a glittering magnet for all Jews who aspired to emerge from their shtetls, or ghettos, across the Austro-Hungarian Empire.[6] Up until then, even though their lives had been far less harsh than those of the Russian Jews, who were still subject to regular pogroms, the Austro-Hungarian Jews had not been allowed to buy property in the imperial capital without a special permit. (Even Anselm von Rothschild, the emperor's banker, was for many years forbidden to buy a house in Vienna.) Faced with an upsurge in nationalist movements that threatened to tear apart the fragile patchwork of his empire, Franz-Josef, who had taken over from his uncle during the heat of the 1848 revolution, soon realized how useful it would be to have the Jews on his side.

Austria, a feudal, baroque, and deeply Catholic country, had until then managed to remain untouched by the ideas and reforms inspired by the Enlightenment. The young sovereign decided to give reform a chance. His natural allies in this were the liberals, who belonged to the German-speaking urban elite. As for the Jews, who were scattered across the length and breadth of the multinational empire, united primarily by common traditions rather than by geographical origins, they also spoke German or, in the ghettos that were farthest from Vienna, Yiddish, a dialect of German with some Hebrew and a few local Slav expressions thrown in. Gaining their allegiance therefore made sense for the young Habsburg emperor, whose central concern was to hold together what remained of the Germanic Holy Roman Empire.

In 1868, having tried to head off revolt in Hungary by having himself crowned king in Budapest, Franz Josef granted the Jews full citizenship rights, allowing them to practice any profession they wished and abolishing the special tax they had previously been subjected to. As the new constitution also proclaimed freedom of movement for all citizens of the empire, the reforms unleashed a huge tide of emigration toward the capital. Between 1857 and 1890 the percentage of Jews in the Viennese population rose from less than 2 to more than 12. They in fact made up quite a heterogeneous group. Generally, the farther away from the capital they originated, the less likely they were to be assimilated. But once they had made Vienna their home, it took no more than two or three generations for even the most traditionalist among them to cast off the long black caftans, round hats, and sidelocks which made them stand out so much on the city streets. Although some resisted assimilation, there have been few periods in Jewish history when the desire for integration, and the opportunities for accomplishing it, have been as great as they were in Vienna during the second half of the nineteenth century.

The trend was in complete harmony with a general change in European attitudes. Everywhere religion had lost ground and faith was being supplanted by rationalism. The Napoleonic armies had carried the ideals of the French Revolution, and had emancipated the Jews, wherever they had passed—not out of any affection for them, but from a desire to make them into ordinary citizens.[7] At the same time, the ideas of the Enlightenment had made inroads among the Jews themselves, discrediting the purely religious content of Judaism and inciting the most adventurous souls to leave their shtetls and become full-fledged citizens.

The social geography of assimilation in Vienna can be easily traced on maps of the period. The ghetto, the neighborhood in which Jews made up around a third of the population at the beginning of this century, was Leopoldstadt, the 2nd district.[8] It forms a long strip between two branches of the Danube, to the east of the old town. To the north is the 20th district, into which moved many of the families from Galicia and Bukovina (today part of Poland, Romania, and Ukraine). It was home to the most orthodox Jews, and although some of its streets were very poor, others were quite fashionable, in particular the ones bordering the Augarten and Prater parks. These were royal lands that

Emperor Josef II had opened to the public, and they were favorite haunts of the aristocratic horse-and-carriage set.

The Prater was Vienna in a nutshell: It had a part for the aristocracy with avenues for horses, a working-class area with a large amusement park, and above all a range of middle-class attractions, such as cafés and bandstands, where Strauss and his waltzes were all the rage. The park was a favorite site for Sunday walks *en famille*, a rendezvous for lovers, and a meeting place for intellectuals. Even vagrants were allowed to sleep in it as long as their behavior remained "decent"—a cherished Viennese notion. It was a courteous, tolerant city, in which one greeted one's equals and left room for everyone else. Its residents were prone to hypocrisy, and felt secure in the belief that they inhabited one of the world's two most civilized cities, the other being of course Paris.

From Leopoldstadt one only had to cross the canal to be in the 1st district, the heart of the city, with its old town, imperial palace, opera house, and Saint Stephen's Cathedral. It was also the home of the main Jewish institutions, including the grand synagogue. The existence of a "Jews' street," just behind the cathedral, was a reminder that before Vienna grew to its modern dimensions, the ghetto was right in the city center. At the end of the nineteenth century the proportion of Jews in the 1st district was still relatively high, between 10 and 24 percent. The same was true in the 9th, just to the north, where many doctors lived. But as one moved outward from the Ringstrasse, the majestic loop boulevard which was being built around the old town at that time, the proportion of Jews fell, to less than 5 percent in the city's outer areas.

In his memoir *The World of Yesterday* the Austrian novelist and playwright Stefan Zweig describes the city into which Bruno Bettelheim was born in 1903. Its center was the imperial palace, around which

the palaces of the Austrian, the Polish, the Czech, and the Hungarian nobility formed as it were a second enclosure . . . Then came "good society," consisting of the lesser nobility, the higher officials, industry, and the "old families," then the petty bourgeoisie and the proletariat. Each of these social strata lived in its own circle, and even in its own district, the nobility in their palaces in the heart of the city, the diplomats in the third district, industry and the merchants in the vicinity of the Ringstrasse, the petty bourgeoisie in the inner districts—the second to the ninth—and the proletariat in the outer circle.[9]

At the dawn of the twentieth century, Jews were thus represented in every stratum of Vienna society. Whether true or not, the beguiling stories Bettelheim told about his forebears are totally in keeping with the spirit of the age. They are stories that are worth studying, if only because, as their author was to point out on many occasions, the psychological life of a child begins with its grandparents.

Adolf Seidler, his maternal grandfather, was born in 1847 in Redschkau, Bohemia; his mother died giving birth to him. He then found himself in a Cinderella situation, with a stepmother who was determined that her own natural children get the lion's share of the household's meager resources. Adolf's father was a peddler who spent the weekdays making the rounds of local villages, returning home only on Friday evening and then, being a devout Jew, spending most of the Sabbath at the synagogue. The stepmother was eventually able to persuade the well-meaning but weak father to throw the boy out. At the age of thirteen, Adolf Seidler thus found himself on the road, with nothing more than the clothes on his back—his bar mitzvah suit— and a five-guilder coin his father had been able to slip him as he left (worth, Bettelheim says, around $2.50). "To protect his only pair of shoes, the boy walked barefoot the hundred miles from his village to the big city, Vienna. There, in a very hard struggle, he eventually managed to make a great fortune," Bettelheim concludes.[10]

In private, Bruno Bettelheim was somewhat more forthcoming about exactly how his grandfather had made that fortune. Again, the story has a fairy-tale quality to it, but in this case, not a very moral one. On arriving in Vienna, the young Seidler was taken in and given a job as an apprentice by a distant cousin, a mechanic. The family was so poor that the boy had to sleep in the workshop, but he learned fast and had a sharp mind. When the first Singer sewing machines appeared in Vienna, Seidler was quick to grasp their potential, and he resolved to become the company's distributor in the city. From the distant United States, the reply came back that he would need to prove he had a workshop and capital of around 10,000 florins. Neither Seidler nor anyone in his circle possessed such a large sum, but he did not let this deter him. He managed to persuade not only his cousin but also a large number of other people, impressed by his talent, and also no doubt by his chutzpah, to show up at the bank and deposit their savings in an account in his name for just the time it took him to get certification of the deposit—after which, Bettelheim added, the contributors all rushed to take their money out again, not

trusting either each other or their enterprising friend. By this stratagem (Bettelheim was on occasion to call it a "fraud") Adolf Seidler
was able to open the first Singer sewing machine store in Vienna.

That was only the beginning, however, for Seidler soon hit upon a
technique that was to make the business a runaway success. As he
could not at first afford to import more than a few machines at a time,
he tried to choose clients who looked as though they would be incapable of keeping up the monthly payments. As soon as they defaulted,
he would recover the merchandise, keeping the deposit and the
installments and then refurbishing the machine to sell it again as new.
This could happen with the same sewing machine two or three times
in a row; Bettelheim's mother could even remember, as a little girl,
hearing her father raging when too many of his customers managed
to make their payments!

The received family version of events is contradicted by official
records on only one point. Adolf Seidler did start out by selling American sewing machines, but they were labeled not Singer but Neuest.
He indeed opened a shop, in 1875, at the age of twenty-eight, but he
had a partner, a certain Adolf Gizidi. (The latter, probably his cousin
with the workshop, disappears from the commercial records three
years later.) It is, however, indisputable that Adolf Seidler possessed
considerable business acumen, and that he quickly became very rich.
Ten years after setting up shop, he had added jewelry and silverware
to his sewing-machine business, and three years after that he became
head of a construction company. He subsequently worked as a registered real estate dealer and even invested some money in a locksmith's
firm. His home was on Lerchenfeldstrasse, a quiet bourgeois street in
the city's 7th district.

In the same year that he founded his business, Adolf Seidler
entered into an arranged marriage with a young woman from the
Bohemian city of Luk. She first had a son, and then in December 1877
she gave birth to Pauline, who would be Bruno Bettelheim's mother.

The story of how Jakob Morris Bettelheim, the other grandfather,
made his money is more uplifting. Bruno Bettelheim's version is as
follows. Jakob soon impressed his teachers with his great intelligence,
and they decided he should become a rabbi. At the same time, Baron
Anselm von Rothschild—"the richest man of the realm," writes Bettelheim—was looking for a tutor for his three sons. Jakob was brought

to his attention, and in the twinkling of an eye the young man was propelled "from living in desperate poverty into the grand palace of the Rothschilds in Vienna. There he educated his charges, who grew so fond of him and were so impressed by his brilliance that when they became leaders of the Rothschild bank, they put him in charge of many of its operations. In consequence, he not only became very rich but exercised great influence over the social life of the Jewish community of Vienna."[11] The gratitude of the Rothschild sons extended to the whole family, Bruno Bettelheim told his children; they promised to have at least one of Jakob's descendants always among their inner circle of employees.

Anselm von Rothschild was to die in 1874, leaving his position as chairman of the family firm to his youngest son, Albert, then age thirty. The records show that Jakob Morris Bettelheim, who was then forty-nine, did become his *Gütterdirektor*, or estate manager, which is logical given that in the meantime he had already been in business as a lumber merchant, and that the Rothschilds owned vast forests.[12] As for the Rothschild bank, it was not Jakob but one of his sons, Richard, who was later to hold the post of *Prokurist*, or officer with power of attorney.[13] Around the same time, Jakob was elected to the honorary title of *Kommerzialrat*, (commercial adviser) and thus became a member of the chamber of commerce. His residence was one of the fine buildings on Glockengasse, in the well-off part of the 2nd district. In 1859 he had married one Eleonor Frankl, who was twelve years his junior and who came, as he did, from Pest. Bruno Bettelheim often expressed admiration for his grandmother, who underwent no less than sixteen pregnancies to produce eleven children, all but one of them boys. Anton, Bruno's future father, was born on April 4, 1869, the Bettelheims' fifth child.

Anton too was to go into the lumber trade, for when he was fourteen tragedy struck the family with the death of his eldest brother Morris, ten years his senior, in a duel.[14] Morris had been a law student, and duels were common at the university. "I did not bring up my sons for them to be killed by goyim," Jakob exclaimed, according to his grandson. As a result, Jakob decreed that no more of his children would go to the university, thus crushing Anton's hopes of an education.

The story does not tell whether or not Morris Bettelheim knew Theodor Herzl, who some twelve years later was to found the Zionist movement, but it is quite probable. The two were the same age, they both had roots in the Jewish bourgeoisie of Budapest, and both were studying law at Vienna University. At that time, the early 1880s, the city's students were particularly affected by the rising tide of anti-Semitism that accompanied the influx of Jews into Vienna. It was not long before Jewish students found themselves banned from taking part in duels and from membership in the main student clubs. Herzl's first awareness of his own Jewishness is generally believed to have been sparked by these developments.[15]

In this fin-de-siècle period, anti-Semitism was on the rise all over Europe. Berlin saw a long series of anti-Jewish riots, and in 1880, when Nietzsche's brother-in-law called for a special census of Jews and their eviction from all teaching and civil service jobs, he was able to collect 250,000 signatures in a matter of weeks. In the same year, the first mass anti-Semitic political parties were born in Vienna: notably, the Christian Social Union of the wildly popular and populist Karl Lueger, known to his supporters as "handsome Karl." In 1897, Lueger was to be triumphantly elected mayor of Vienna, after Emperor Franz Josef had tried twice to veto his appointment.[16] In the meantime, the Dreyfus affair in Paris had served as a reminder that, even in the country that had once promoted the emancipation of the Jews, they had not yet become ordinary citizens.

While both Morris Bettelheim and Theodor Herzl were busy pursuing law degrees, the future playwright and novelist Arthur Schnitzler was studying medicine, the other discipline open to Jews at Vienna University. His autobiographical notes show very clearly what kind of impact the rising tide of hatred must have had on the first generations of post-assimilation Jews. In an opening commentary on his diaries, made some years later, Schnitzler was to write:

> In these pages a lot will be said about Judaism and anti-Semitism, more than may at times seem in good taste, or necessary, or just. But when these pages may be read, it will perhaps no longer be possible to gain a correct impression (at least I hope so), of the importance, spiritually almost more than politically and socially, that was assigned to the so-called Jewish question when these lines were written. It was not possible, especially not for a Jew in public life, to ignore the fact that he was a Jew; nobody else was doing so, not the Gentiles and even less the Jews. You had the choice of being counted as insensitive, obtrusive and fresh; or of being oversensitive, shy and suffering from feelings of persecution. And, even if you managed somehow to conduct yourself so that nothing showed, it was impossible to remain completely untouched.[17]

The Vienna into which Bruno Bettelheim was born in 1903, twenty years after the death of his uncle Morris, had made ambiguity toward the Jews into a fine art, although unlike Schnitzler, many of them preferred not to notice the fact. It was indeed the Vienna of legend, described by the pamphleteer Karl Kraus as the "weather station of the world's end," a multinational ferment of thought in which all the great ideas that were to shape the twentieth century were being tried out and refined, under the benevolent yet autocratic rule of an aging monarch. But if Jews, half-Jews, and former Jews (converts to Christianity) were preponderant among the prime movers in this "Joyful Apocalypse" (to use the phrase coined by the novelist and essayist Hermann Broch), that fact was due much more to their own desire for assimilation than to any acceptance of that process on the part of those around them.[18]

Some, like Arthur Schnitzler, Sigmund Freud, and Theodor Herzl, accepted their own Jewishness while rejecting Judaic ritual as something from another age, while the likes of Gustav Mahler, Hugo von Hofmannsthal, and Karl Kraus believed they had put their origins behind them by converting to, or marrying into, Christianity. All may have thought that their science or their art transcended the contingency of their origins. Yet their compatriots saw them first and foremost as Jews, whatever was said openly. And at the end of the nineteenth century, it was being spelled out more and more often.

This phenomenon is studied in a considerable body of remarkable works; a detailed examination would be beyond the scope of this biography.[19] But Jewishness, anti-Semitism, and "ghetto thinking" all loom too large in Bruno Bettelheim's life and work for us to ignore what life was like for an assimilated Jew growing up in Vienna in those days. Bettelheim's feelings about the city of his birth were shot through with a deep ambivalence, for which anti-Semitism was the main reason. The idealized image of the city he projected in *Freud's Vienna* contrasts harshly with the many disillusioned and even cruel remarks he made to friends and also, when on visits there, in interviews and lectures.[20] In a 1957 review of Ernest Jones's biography of Freud (1953–57), Bettelheim states: "Freud's supposed 'hatred' of Vienna was probably the expression of a deep early love that became frustrated by anti-Semitism in the early twentieth century, a frustration the more keenly felt as the earlier love was never given up."[21] It is not difficult to see how much of his own feelings the writer is putting into this passage, especially if one compares it to the rags-to-riches stories of his two grandfathers, which Bettelheim chose to include in the same collection of essays.

As Arthur Schnitzler notes, the type of anti-Semitism that prevailed in turn-of-the-century Vienna was neither social nor economic in nature. In spite of the huge wave of immigration, the fundamental issue was not a question of population thresholds, of Jews suddenly becoming too visible in the imperial capital, even though some politicians exploited such fears, notably the explicitly anti-Semitic Karl Lueger, much supported by small shopkeepers. But for Jews born and bred in Vienna during this period, that was not the main problem. Much more important, it seems to me, was the interaction during this period (from around 1880 to 1920), between the types of questions that artists, writers, and philosophers were asking in Vienna and the content of anti-Semitic discourse itself. It was not yet purely race-based, as it was to become later. "I decide who's a Jew," Mayor Lueger was fond of saying. Nor was anti-Semitism founded purely on religion, in that strongly rationalistic and positivist era— even though the charge that Jews had murdered Christ was often used to express it.

The main accusation leveled against the Jews did not so much relate to what they believed in as to the way they thought, and even the way they felt. Against a backdrop of rampant nationalism, they stood accused of being a rootless, "cosmopolitan" group (an idea which conveniently overlooked the fact that until the start of the nineteenth century Jews were obliged to live in shtetls). But above all, the anti-Semitism of the period, co-opting an ill-digested version of Nietzsche's ideas, painted a picture of the "Jewish mind" as the great corrupter of the valorous Germanic soul. Many anti-Semites found inspiration in the way Richard Wagner, toward the end of his life, took to decrying the influence of "Judaism in Music."[22] The composer ascribed what he saw as "the sterility of the age in musical art" to "the Jewish mind," for which he stated his "invincible antipathy."[23] Fin-de-siècle anti-Semites attacked Jews both for being oversensitive and for harboring negative ideas. Their number-one defect in their eyes was not the shape of their noses but their habit of always asking questions. That was what anti-Semites saw as the corrupting influence that deprived the German people of its natural vigor, of the strength that only a direct relationship to the earth could foster. The charge concealed a measure of admiration, and in the case of Wagner one could even say of jealousy. Anti-Semites imagined that Jews possessed superior powers of handling abstract concepts which, when added to their supposed gift with money, made them all the more "dangerous." Their influence was seen as insidious, their intelligence as aimed only at undermining what others had built—as could be expected from people with no fixed roots, living in a state of perpetual exile.[24]

The period was one of great upheaval, with philosophers and scientists questioning the blithe certainties that had formed the very foundations of nineteenth-century thought. Belief in progress, reason, and science was under attack. Vienna was not the only city in which this process was taking place, but it was one of its main centers, with artists and scientists joining in a quest that found its most complete expression in Robert Musil's unfinished three-volume novel *The Man Without Qualities* (1930–32).[25] Most of all, in Vienna this effervescence in the world of ideas was set against the backdrop of the breakup of Europe's oldest empire. By contrast, Berlin was the capital of a rapidly expanding state, while France had weathered the disasters of the Napoleonic wars without losing its national identity. The Viennese, however, looked on helplessly as the various peoples of Austria-Hungary drifted apart. Only now did they realize to what extent those peoples had served to define Viennese identity. Changes which in Paris were giving birth to the Belle Epoque and art nouveau took on the appearance of an "apocalypse" in Vienna.[26]

Nothing seemed certain anymore. The empire was coming apart at the seams, and so was the individual. Light itself broke up into a mass of dots on canvases, and Sigmund Freud had exposed the human soul as an explosive cocktail of contradictory forces. What is inside and what is outside? Where are the limits between me and the world? How does one know about reality? Can I trust my senses? Is there any truth except in words? Human identity seemed less and less sharply defined; even the frontier between the sexes was being thrown into doubt. Man or woman, who am I? And what exactly is an Austrian— a German, a Moldavian, a Moravian, a Ruthenian?

For anti-Semites, one thing, at least, was clear: The fact that such questions were being asked was the surest sign that the culture had fallen under the baleful influence of Judaism. Jews certainly made up a high proportion of the actors in this intellectual revolution, and the reasons for that have been studied elsewhere.[27] Our concern here is to understand how this atmosphere could affect a young Jew born and raised in it, to see how a world that was apparently filled with excitement and stimulation, teeming with potential role models in all avenues of intellectual and artistic endeavor, could at the same time appear to confirm the expressions of contempt and even hatred that were part of his everyday life.

It was by no means uncommon to find Jews themselves joining in the chorus of anti-Semitism. A key reason was the mind-set that went along with assimilation, which by definition involved rejecting all outward signs of religious identity as being backward. Psychological reactions of fear, shame, or anxiety could be sparked by reminders of ancestral traditions which, long since rejected by one's parents, were only heard mentioned in negative terms. Although they are rare, traces of such suffering can clearly be detected in the writings of Bruno Bettelheim. In a 1963 article on the subject of race relations in the United States, he wrote: "In Vienna there was a 'Carl' with whom I walked to school every day, who was my friend, and who nevertheless suddenly hit me one day, announcing that we were quits from now on because my people had killed Jesus. There were the boys who extorted money: who beat us if we handed it over because we were dirty cowards, and who beat us if we didn't, because we were miserly Jews . . . It was the natural fate of the Jew."[28]

This incident appears to have taken place around 1910, a time when, according to most historians, the wave of anti-Semitism in Vienna had subsided somewhat (it was to reach new heights in the closing years of World War I). For those of us whose only experience of anti-Semitism is the watered-down form in which it has been forced to express itself since the discovery of Hitler's extermination camps, an effort of imagination is required to understand the powerful effect it could have on a child at that time, particularly one who had hardly emerged from the protective cocoon of his family, and who had been all the less prepared for the shock because of his parents' heavy investment in assimilation. It was a shock that each individual had to deal with as best as he or she could, and the process of adaptation could easily lead to what, since the philosopher Theodor Lessing, has been widely referred to as "Jewish self-hatred."[29] It should also be noted that the discovery of the anti-Semitism that pervaded the world outside the family was likely to affect the image a child had of his father.

Self-hatred can take many forms, but all result from the young Jew's attempts to dissociate himself from the negative image projected by the anti-Semites. Paradoxically, by so doing he to some degree makes that negative image his own.[30] As a result he finds himself, consciously or unconsciously, mounting an attack on everything inside himself that seems "Jewish," everything that serves to remind him of his fore-bears' existence in the shtetl. Some young people's way of dealing with the problem led them to affect elaborate dress, and even become dandies, as was the case for both Herzl and Schnitzler. Others would adopt a superior, condescending tone when speaking of their Ortho-dox brethren. But almost all were especially concerned to achieve perfect mastery of German, for "Jewish patter" had come to symbol-ize all the imagined defects associated with Jewishness, as can be seen in the following passage from *The Man Without Qualities*, in which Count Leinsdorf says:

> I have a banker, of the Mosaic faith of course, whom I've been seeing regularly for years. And at first his intonation always used to bother me a bit, so that I couldn't quite keep my mind on the business in hand. The fact is, the way he talks is exactly as if he were trying to convince me he's my uncle. I mean it's just as if he'd only got out of the saddle a moment earlier or had just come in from a day's grouse-shooting, exactly the way our own sort of people talk, if I may put it that way. Well, to cut a long story short, now and then when he's carried away he can't keep it up, and then, to make no bones about it, he falls into a very marked Jewish sing-song. It used to bother me a great deal, as I think I said before, because, the point is, it always happened at the most impor-tant moments from the business point of view, so that I couldn't help waiting for it, and finally I became quite incapable of paying attention to what he was saying or else simply believed I was listening to some-thing important the whole time. But then I found the way to get round it. Every time he began to talk like that, I simply said to myself: Now, he's talking Hebrew. And I only wish you could have heard how attrac-tive it sounded! Positively enchanting. The point is, it's a liturgical lan-guage. Such a melodious chanting—I'm very musical, you know—in a word, from then on he had me lapping up complicated calculations in compound interest or discount positively as if he were at the piano singing it to me.[31]

This passage sums up perfectly the "benign" anti-Semitism of the enlightened aristocracy of the period. Jewishness here is a question of accent, of music, money, and complicated interest-rate calculations, the subtext being that Jews, while talented people, should above all refrain from trying to ape their betters. Before this speech, Count Leinsdorf has been railing against civil servants, whom he blames for "a piece of impertinence" toward the old nobility: having assigned aristocratic names, such as Rosenberg, Rosenthal, Löw, Glelb, Blau, and Rot, to Jews once emancipation made such registrations possible. He adds, "The whole so-called Jewish question would disappear in a twinkling if the Jews would only make up their minds to speak Hebrew, go back to their old Hebrew names, and wear Oriental garb."

In some cases Jewish self-hatred could lead to extreme reactions, as in the case of the young writer-philosopher Otto Weininger. His suicide in August 1903, a week after Bruno Bettelheim's birth, was to send a shock wave through Vienna's intelligentsia.[32] Weininger, a pure product of Vienna's Jewish bourgeoisie, was to achieve spectacular, albeit posthumous, success with his *Sex and Character*, an adaptation of his doctoral thesis that was to run through no less than twenty printings between 1904 and 1920. He had for a while associated with the "Young Vienna" school of writers, before rejecting their ideal of art for art's sake as evidence of a decadent culture. Then, only twenty-three but already feted as an up-and-coming writer, Weininger abruptly underwent a mystical conversion. He opted not for the Catholicism of Austria and the Hapsburgs, however, but for Protestantism, the creed of Kant and the all-conquering Prussians. A few weeks later, the tortured young man rented the house in which Beethoven had died, on Schwarzspanierstrasse (a few hundred yards from where it changes its name to become Berggasse, the street where Freud lived) and went there to put a bullet through his head.

Sex and Character is a work that sums up many of the anxieties of the age. For Weininger, the decadence and instability he detected all about him had two causes: the predominance of what he called the feminine principle in Viennese society, and the influence of Jewish ways of thinking. Weininger saw bisexuality as being the basic nature of all individuals, and argued that human existence on both the individual and the social levels was governed alternately by the masculine and the feminine principle.[33] The latter, characterized by sensuality and what Freud was to call the pleasure principle, was the common fate of mankind. To transcend it required renunciation, mental power, and even genius, the masculine qualities that alone could save society from decadence. As for the Jews, they basically had the same effect as the feminine principle, sapping the foundations of society with their mercantile and hedonistic ethos. The main difference between women and the Jews was, for Weininger, that women at least believed in something—to wit, men—whereas the Jews were devoid of any beliefs whatsoever.[34]

Although cited by many authors as the epitome of Jewish self-hatred, Otto Weininger is, however, too extreme a case to provide a clear understanding of the overall phenomenon, which affected practically all the assimilated Jews of the period, even those who were apparently the best integrated.[35] Nevertheless, *Sex and Character*, a work that drew grudging admiration even from those, such as Sigmund Freud, who were most shocked by it, at least had the merit of clearly defining the terms of the problem: mind–body, man–woman, Gentile–Jew—with, in the background, the idea of a redeeming nature characterized by authentic roots and virile regenerative power. Such ways of defining humanity were to leave their mark on all the Viennese Jews of the period. Bruno Bettelheim was no exception.

Like Schnitzler, Bettelheim was fully aware of the prevailing anti-Semitism, and made no attempt to play it down. He nevertheless displayed a tendency to choose his anti-Semites. In his review of the Ernest Jones biography of Freud, for example, he criticizes in particular the author's failure to point out that "the leading aristocracy was strongly opposed to the lower-middle-class anti-Semitism of Lueger."[36] While it was true that the Viennese nobility tended in general to be more open to the Jews' upward mobility than the petty bourgeoisie were, this was no doubt because they felt much surer of their status and privileges. As is shown by Musil's Count Leinsdorf, their anti-Semitism would emerge whenever they perceived that some Jew, however rich, talented, and intelligent, was trying to be like them. Even in the world of the arts, where the great Jewish families had gradually taken over the role of patron formerly played by the aristocracy, admiration expressed by non-Jews for Jews was rarely free of undertones. It is significant for instance that Gustav Mahler, when writing his application to become head of Vienna's Imperial Opera in 1897, considered it necessary to state: "Given the current situation in Vienna, I feel it is worth pointing out that, in line with a long-standing plan, I converted to Catholicism a long time ago."

Several critics have detected traces of self-hatred in Bettelheim's denunciation of "ghetto thinking."[37] Others have noted that when he decided to go into analysis he chose Richard Sterba, one of the very few non-Jews among the psychoanalysts then practicing in Vienna. Still others have expressed indignation at the fact that even though many of the students at the Orthogenic School were Jews, the institution celebrated Christmas but not the Jewish religious holidays.

All these signs certainly show that Bettelheim felt a degree of ambivalence about his Jewishness. Depending on one's point of view, they can be read as indications of liberal thinking or as evidence of an implicit rejection of his origins. At no point during his life, however, did he ever deny his Jewishness. He accepted that he had been born Jewish, and continued to do so very explicitly until the end of his life, when it was unfashionable, and even when it was dangerous. In 1987, in an interview published at the time Kurt Waldheim was elected president of Austria, Bettelheim was quite candid about it:

> "I think that, if it hadn't been for Hitler, Austrian and German Jews would have been assimilated within three or four generations . . . Freud, in his optimism, believed that religion, that illusion, would eventually disappear completely. But on the other hand he wrote 'Moses and Monotheism.' Here you have all the ambivalence of the assimilated Jew. You can't get out of it; you are Jewish."
>
> "What about you, did you ever want to get out of it?"
>
> "No . . . in fact, no. That's what I am, that's my history, my evolution. As a psychoanalyst, I know very well that one can never free oneself from one's parents."[38]

Bettelheim's parents showed little or no interest in Judaism; according to him, they never set foot inside a synagogue. In the Jewish section of Vienna's main cemetery, the tombstones of both Anton and Jakob Morris Bettelheim are extremely simple, and bear no inscriptions in Hebrew. However, both do feature a small, elongated jug, the symbol of the Levys, the second tribe of Israel and the servants of the temple. Although Bruno Bettelheim could hardly have had any influence over the tombstone chosen for his grandfather, who died before he was born, he must have had some over that selected for his father, of whom he was the only son. That small symbol is therefore also to be taken into account when assessing the complex relationship Bettelheim had to his own Jewishness.

There is another significant clue, even though it relates to a memory cited by Bettelheim toward the end of his life, and then almost in passing. In an article written in 1987, and then included in *Freud's Vienna*, he confirms how the pain and injustice felt by young Viennese Jews as a result of the regular irruption of anti-Semitism in their lives was aggravated by the fact that they knew so little about Judaism. Brought up to be "just like everyone else," they had but a dim understanding of the reasons behind the attacks made on them. Discussing the books that had most influenced his life, Bettelheim relates how in late adolescence he discovered the works of Martin Buber, a Zionist writer who was both agnostic and mystical and who favored Jewish–Christian dialogue. Buber had been raised in an ultra-Orthodox family of Hasidic Jews, and while he rejected all the dogmatic aspects of their faith, he strongly believed that it was necessary to preserve Jewish culture in the form of its myths, the stories that circulated in the shtetls. A large part of Buber's work consisted of recording those stories. Bettelheim wrote about him:

> As I tried to fight free of the world of my parents, more haphazardly than by design, I encountered books by Martin Buber which told about the world of the Hasidim, a world as strange and exotic as those in the utopian novels I read during my efforts to escape reality. But this was a world of my ancestors, and yet not even a glimmer of it was left in the life of my parents, although they were barely two generations away from the world about which Buber was writing. Because of the assimilated life of my entire family, all I knew about being a Jew was that I and my closest friends, most of whom were also Jewish, had to suffer from the taunts, the rejection, and occasionally the open aggression of some of our gentile schoolmates and even some of our teachers. Now, suddenly, my Jewishness had a positive content.[39]

2

One Big Family

> Those who, like Korczak, single-mindedly devote themselves to making this a better world for children are usually motivated by their own unhappy childhoods. What they suffer then makes such a lasting impression that all their lives they try to come to terms with it by working to change things so that other children will not have to suffer a similar fate.
>
> —*Bruno Bettelheim,*
> *"Janusz Korczak: A Tale for Our Time"*

Anton Bettelheim was nearly twenty-nine years old when, in February 1898, he wed Pauline Seidler, who had just turned twenty. It was an arranged marriage. He was then employed in a sawmill, where he was completing his training as a wholesale lumber merchant.[1] Whatever the truth about Jakob Morris Bettelheim's fortune, he obviously saw to it that his sons were not spoiled. It is difficult, however, to gain a clear idea of the surroundings in which Bruno Bettelheim spent his early childhood since, unlike most middle-class Viennese at the time, his parents seem to have moved a great deal in those years.

At both the time of their marriage and that of Bruno's birth, Pauline and Anton Bettelheim are listed as living at no. 3 Rampengasse, in the 19th district. But when their daughter Margarethe was born, between those two events, the Jewish community records a different address, in the more elegant 3rd district. There follow another two locations, one in the 5th and the other in the 7th, with the family only settling down in 1911, by which time Bruno was almost eight. One possible explanation for this unsettled existence could be the severe financial setback Anton suffered at the start of the marriage, when he lost his wife's dowry in an ill-conceived lumber trade investment. Another explanation could have been the real estate activities Adolf Seidler was getting involved in at the time of his daughter's marriage.

Rampengasse, the street where Bettelheim was born, is a tiny alley running into a small footbridge over the Danube Canal just above Leopoldstadt. The street's location between the river and a railroad line suggests a possible link to the lumber trade practiced by both Anton and his father before him, but this is only a guess: the neighborhood was razed during the war, and is now home to warehouses.

To illustrate just how stable and influential a place Vienna was at the time of his birth, Bettelheim harks back to the sixteenth century and the reign of Hapsburg emperor Charles V.[2] The imperial city he describes, with its serenity, comfort, and warmth, conjures up the opening passages of Stefan Zweig's *World of Yesterday:* "When I attempt to find a simple formula for the period in which I grew up, prior to the First World War, I hope that I convey its fullness by calling it the Golden Age of Security. Everything in our almost thousand-year-old Austrian monarchy seemed based on permanency, and the State itself was the chief guarantor of this stability."[3]

Paula, as she was known to everyone in the family, brought Bruno into the world on August 28, 1903. The birth occurred at home, as had been the case four years earlier for Bruno's sister. The young mother was "comforted and helped in her labor by a midwife," as her son was later to write, adding regretfully that to his knowledge, he was the last member of the entire family to have been born in such surroundings, far from the antiseptic atmosphere of a medical institution.[4] As was common in bourgeois families at the time, the baby was handed over to a wet nurse, a German peasant girl who had left her own infant in the care of her mother. According to Bettelheim, she was very inexperienced, and often somewhat drunk—but all the more affectionate for that: She had heard that beer helped keep the milk flowing, he explained.

He would no doubt have preferred to have been nursed by his mother. As a child development expert, Bettelheim was, after all, a strong proponent of breastfeeding, and he was aware of the contradiction. But although he described his wet nurse in one interview as "a strong-smelling woman, who staggered," and in another as "a young sexual delinquent" who had abandoned her own child, he generally portrays her in *A Good Enough Parent* as an attentive and gentle young woman. He explains that he was her only charge, and that she had a compelling incentive to look after him well, as a successful wet nurse would traditionally be rewarded with a generous gift. "The respect my nurse had for my parents and her happiness at being part of our home (it was very important to my parents that she should be healthy and happy, so that she would have plenty of good milk, and enjoy taking care of me, so she received excellent care) were important elements in convincing me how lucky I was that this was my home."[5] His mother's social obligations prevented her from giving him as much attention as did his nurse, who, as Bettelheim notes, was "entirely devoted to my care." The overall picture of his first years of life is a happy one, and it is difficult to find, in four hundred pages of a book scattered with personal anecdotes illustrating the upbringing of children, a single incident to show that Bettelheim's own parents were not "good enough."[6]

The nurse was to be succeeded by a nanny, and then by maids. But each time young Bruno fell ill, it was Paula who took care of him. "She spent many hours caring for me and entertaining me, and she fed me all my meals," he writes. It was also his mother who told him fairy tales at bedtime. And if sleep would not come, there would always be one or the other of his parents to hold him in their arms until he finally dropped off. If a nightmare woke the little boy up, Paula did not appear worried or strained; she would go and sit at the side of his bed, talking calmly to him, playing or telling him stories until he fell asleep again.

As Bettelheim tells it, his parents appear to have known instinctively what their son would later devote so much energy to trying to drill into the minds of his American audience: that their own anxiety, rather than any external event, was likely to spark anxiety in their children. Bettelheim recalls, for example, the night when he was six years old that the house opposite theirs burned down. As the street was narrow, the firefighters sprayed not only the burning house but all the ones nearby as well to stop the blaze from spreading. Bruno was sleeping in a room at the other end of the house and his parents, far from panicking, "woke me up and took me to the window to watch the unusual and exciting spectacle. Since they were calm and talked with me about the varying colors and forms of the flames, it did not occur to me to be afraid." Once the fire was out, the little boy went quietly back to sleep, and never felt worried by what he had seen: "During the following months, whenever I left our house I was confronted by the ruins across the street. I never felt anxious; it never occurred to me that I might have been in danger, or that our house might go up in flames. All I thought was that it had been a most unusual experience, and that I had been fortunate to witness it."[7]

What comes through most clearly in Bettelheim's writings about his childhood, maybe more than the gentleness and understanding of his parents, is the happiness he felt at belonging to a large family. One of the main criticisms he would later level at the American way of life was that it split families up. "I grew up in a big family. My father had ten living brothers and sisters and my mother had four. And even if everything was not perfect all of the time, even if there were fights and jealousy, we were a family. Here [in America], we are very alone, and so are our children."[8]

Each year, on the occasion of Eleonor Bettelheim's birthday, all her grandchildren gathered at her house to put on a show they had rehearsed in secret. Bruno's pride at taking part in the collective effort was to remain one of his strongest early memories. Other favorite moments came on Sundays, when the Bettelheim clan gathered.

> Among the happiest memories of my childhood are the times when I and the cousins near my age—we were called "the little ones"—played under the huge table around which a dozen or more adult members of the family had gathered, often forgetting that we were literally underfoot. We would play together in the cozy darkness, hidden by the huge tablecloth that hung down nearly to the floor; as we played we listened to the talk and arguments of those we called "the big ones." We and they, each group on its own level, thus had a grand time every Sunday.[9]

Among Bruno's many cousins was a boy who suffered from schizophrenia. Although he was not dangerous, he spoke and acted strangely. One day Bruno, who saw the boy frequently and was puzzled by his behavior, asked his aunt what she thought of it. "Listen, my boy, I have ten children. One out of ten, that's not a bad average," she replied. Bettelheim saw this answer as a good example of the wisdom often found in the parents of large families, in contrast to the anxieties and obsession with perfection of parents with only one or two children.[10]

A large family also offers mutual support. As an example of the latter, Bettelheim cited another of his cousins who "went astray" when Bruno was a child. "Naturally this was viewed as a terrible misfortune, but in those times, nobody blamed his parents." On the contrary, the two dozen or so families that made up the clan got together to provide comfort, and decide what could be done to help the wayward boy. Money was found to send him to the United States, where he could start a new life. The result was that, "encouraged by the unexpected support he had received from so many relatives, my cousin took heart, and soon succeeded where he had failed before. Because his parents had also received emotional support from the wider family when they needed it most, it was easier for them to send their son away with blessings rather than recriminations."[11]

Another bygone custom Bettelheim valued was the family death ritual. "My paternal grandparents were the last members of my family who died at home in their beds, surrounded by all their children. My other relatives died either in hospitals or at home, but neither their children nor their grandchildren were present; the family assembled after they had died for their funerals. Thus the emphasis has shifted from the rite of passage in which the death of a loved one is actually witnessed to the comforting of survivors."[12]

This nostalgia for old rites and customs, with its idealized vision of close-knit kin working hard and helping one another, in which character was formed and respect was forged as sons learned their crafts by watching their fathers or uncles on the job, can be detected all through Bettelheim's work, even when, pointing a finger at the negative role played by parents, he would recommend that a child be cut off from all contact with his family for a year or more. As Bettelheim got older, the nostalgia came more and more to the surface, and *A Good Enough Parent*, a book he found very difficult to write because he saw it as a kind of summing-up of his life and work, can be read as a veritable ode to the past, to a time when parents, without needing to ask why, reared their children in line with all the strictures of modern psychology.

This contradiction between a stern and censorious Bettelheim, scourge of possessive and ill-loving modern mothers, and the man haunted by nostalgia for a time when father and son worked shoulder-to-shoulder, is of course symptomatic of the wounds of exile, which never completely healed. But it also betrays other scars, even deeper and better-hidden.

"When I was four years old I nearly died of dysentery at the same time as my father contracted a deadly disease of which he knew that he would die. This projected him and my mother into a state of deep anxiety which was not lost on my sister and me—only she had at least eight good years before it all happened. From this moment on the life of my parents was a nightmare for them which they kept hidden from everybody, even their parents and siblings. But they suffered quietly."[13]

Bruno Bettelheim spoke and wrote very little about the wounds he suffered in early childhood, referring to them only briefly in private correspondence late in life, when he could no longer get the better of his depression. In four years of research, I unearthed only one letter referring explicitly to the question, and even that, from which the above quote is taken, omits a key detail. It dates from November 1986, precisely when Bettelheim was reworking *A Good Enough Parent*, because his publisher was demanding that he make deep cuts: The book, into which Bettelheim had poured a lot of himself, was considered too stern in its prescriptions for an American public.

Carl Frankenstein, to whom the letter was addressed, was a German-born Israeli psychoanalyst and educator who late in Bettelheim's life had become a close friend. By the standards of Bettelheim's correspondence, this letter is extraordinarily intimate. What is said in it, as well as what is not said, provides a number of clues to the fear, anxiety, and suffering that lay behind the idyllic picture of a model Viennese family—suffering that was no doubt at the root of the remarkable insight Bettelheim would later bring to bear as a healer of sick children.

First, there were all the illnesses. Bruno Bettelheim must have been a sickly child indeed, to judge from the catalogue of maladies he reels off: "scarlet fever, diphtheria, measles, mumps, and other ailments, not to mention several bouts of influenza and tonsillitis, which kept me in bed for many weeks at a time."[14] And then there was the attack of dysentery, which was clearly no ordinary illness. "I was very sick and was rushed to [the doctor's] office, where he instantly bedded me down on the couch of his living room, adjacent to his office. In his own home he cared for me for four days and nights, going back and forth between me and his consulting room till the danger was past."[15] It is impossible to know for sure whether the young Bettelheim's life-and-death struggle against dysentery really did coincide with his father's discovery that he was suffering from an incurable illness. The essential fact remains that the two incidents were linked in his mind.

Depressive is the word most commonly used to describe the Bettelheim household by the very few witnesses still living (all of whom visited it at a somewhat later date). Paula Bettelheim was not yet thirty when she learned that she could at any time find herself widowed with two young children to care for. She nevertheless kept her household going, caring for her sick husband and shielding the children from his ailment. And she dealt with the disaster on her own, refraining from seeking help from her parents. When she visited them, which she did almost every day, she acted as if everything was all right, avoiding any mention of Anton's illness. One of Bettelheim's cousins commented: "I remember her husband's death was kept secret from my grandparents, because they were old and sick. I don't know who imposed this secrecy on her, but to imagine the cruelty! These types of secrets and hypocrisies were the rule in our families, all in the name of protecting somebody's feelings."[16]

The atmosphere in the Seidler household was indeed strained enough not to need aggravating by the news of Anton Bettelheim's illness. Adolf Seidler, who remained very rich at least up until World War I, had a truly awful temper. His marriage was an unhappy one, and he bullied everyone in the family so much that, with the exception of Paula, they all fled from him. Although he seems to have been one of their favorites, the young Bruno hated visits to his grandparents' home. Even when the couple were not fighting, the tension between them made him uneasy. His grandmother had gradually taken refuge in violent attacks of asthma, which gave her an excuse, once her children were grown, to flee Vienna and her despotic husband for health spas several months each year. The family's younger daughter, Jenny, followed suit, Bettelheim recounted, adding that his aunt's chronic and supposedly serious heart trouble vanished as if by magic once she set foot in the United States!

Adolf Seidler's abiding chagrin was that none of his three sons had a head for business. As Bruno Bettelheim pointed out, if Seidler had not terrorized them so much they might have fulfilled themselves in their chosen fields, which were artistic. Instead, he was continually spending large sums to set them up in one business or another, with invariably disastrous results. Thus, in 1908, did he agree to give Anton Bettelheim another sum equal to Paula's ill-fated dowry, on condition that he take Seidler's youngest son, Rudolf, on board as a partner.

Bruno got on well with his Uncle Rudolf, who was a great connoisseur of Wagner and the only Seidler son to have made a happy marriage. But he proved to be such a bad businessman that Anton soon began to resent him, the more so in that he was unable to break the partnership. Anton would pour out his bitterness about the situation to his wife; Bruno Bettelheim later told his children that although his parents were not very happy together, the only open fights he ever witnessed were those over Rudolf. The partnership was dissolved along with the company, which vanished from the business records at the start of World War I. Later, Bruno Bettelheim would say that his uncles had tried to wrest his father's company away from him after Anton's death in 1926.

Information on Paula Bettelheim is scarce. People who knew her in Vienna do not have much to say; in general they portray her as kindhearted, discreet, brave, and very protective of her "menfolk," especially when they were sick. Indeed, Bruno Bettelheim writes that his mother would on occasion spend the entire night at his bedside, sponging his burning forehead and applying cold compresses. Given the frequency of his illnesses, he was certainly a coddled child. His first wife recalls with some irony how, when she spent a summer with the family in the Italian Alps, Bruno's mother would, after eating her own breakfast with her daughter-in-law while her son still slept, carefully lay out his place setting, even putting a cushion on his chair.

Basically, Paula comes across as someone who did not count for very much. One acquaintance recalls that she was a good cook, another that she took to learning Italian late in life. But there is nothing substantial to go on, no way of distinguishing between what could have been her true personality and the clichés that tended to define women at that time. Housewives and mothers were by definition not very interesting. And yet one would like to know more about the woman behind the man who was later to prove such a stern judge of the maternal function.

In comparison with the rather colorless picture of Paula Bettelheim one gets from her son's writings and from the memories of his friends, the image he handed down to his children was of a woman of character. Paula, who was born sixteen months after Adolf's first son, is shown as very much her father's daughter. A brilliant student, she would have liked to have gone into business, which at the time was

the only career avenue open to an ambitious young woman, Bettelheim stressed. For Adolf Seidler, however, the scholastic successes of
his daughters (Jenny also was a good student) served only to underline the failings of his sons. He forbade the girls to continue their
studies, and married them off as soon as he could. Being a devoted
daughter, Paula knuckled under, marrying the man her father had
chosen for her and later, when Seidler fell ill, going religiously to her
parents' home five afternoons a week to care for them. The only
breaks in that routine came on Fridays, when she had coffee with her
circle of friends, and Sundays, when the Bettelheims gathered.

The few people who encountered Paula Bettelheim in Chicago,
when she went there to visit her son, have memories of a rather
imposing, stern-faced lady, with a very strong accent. "She looked
like the queen of Rumania," says one. To complement a sketchy picture, I have only two other clues. One is the last letter Paula sent to
her son, and the only one he still had in his possession at the time of
his death. Written in Old German in an elongated, spare hand not
unlike Bruno's, it is couched in language of great purity and conci-
sion. Paula Bettelheim, behind the role life thrust upon her, must have
been a cultured and intellectually rigorous woman. The other clue is
somewhat at odds with the image of a mother concerned above all
with the well-being of her children. It was provided by Joan Little
Treiman, an early counselor at the Orthogenic School. Toward the end
of the 1940s during a visit to New York, she attended with a colleague
one of Bettelheim's first public lectures. When he stood up to speak,
the two young women, who knew him well from working alongside
him every day in Chicago, noticed his nervousness, and his evident
embarrassment at his faltering, accented English. An elderly lady
entered the lecture hall as he was speaking, and rather than taking
the first available seat, she walked right across the hall to a place in
the front row, which irritated Joan somewhat. When her companion
whispered that the lady was Dr. B's mother, it occurred to Joan that
Bettelheim's relations with her could not have been simple.

Despite her attentiveness when he was ill, Bettelheim resented the
fact that his mother did not spend more time caring for him. He
refers explicitly to this in a letter to the editor published in the *New
York Times Magazine* in 1970, written to refute a widely circulated
story about him. According to the story, Bettelheim, who had gained
a reputation as an autocratic professor, had sharply rebuked a student in the front row who was knitting during his lecture. "Miss,

don't you know that knitting is a substitute for masturbation?" he purportedly said. And the young woman shot back: "Dr. Bettelheim, when I masturbate, I masturbate, but when I knit, I knit."[17] In his letter, Bettelheim denied the story but explained the origins of the supposed link between knitting and sexuality, noting that similar anecdotes had frequently been cited about other psychoanalysts.[18] He went on:

> But something did indeed happen in one of my classes, when I had just started teaching at the University of Chicago. One young lady was sitting in a front row knitting, which distracted my attention. I pondered whether to say anything about it, but decided that if I wanted my students to acquire self-knowledge, I certainly had to be the first to apply this principle to myself. So I asked her whether she would be so kind as to refrain from knitting in my class, because it distracted my attention from my teaching, due to a childhood experience which I obviously had not yet fully mastered. When [I was] a little boy, my mother often concentrated on her embroideries, knitting, etc., when I wanted her to play with me, or otherwise give me her full attention.[19]

He also had to share her attention with his sister, Margarethe, described by sources who knew her then as an independent, ambitious, rather spoiled child, subject to mood swings; she would, for instance, throw a tantrum on receiving a birthday present she did not like. There was strong rivalry between the two children, and their relationship was fraught with conflict. Bruno's best childhood friends were two of his cousins, Kitty and Edith. Kitty, who was the same age as Bruno, was the daughter of his uncle Adolf Bettelheim and Edith, a year older, that of his mother's sister, Jenny Buxbaum. "We grew up together like brother and sister," Edith explained shortly before her death. "His older sister Margarethe did not get along with him at all and wrote me only when she needed me as an ally against him . . . But Bruno and I were very close."[20]

There is now nobody alive to testify to that period in Bettelheim's life. The only available sources are two of his close friends who visited his parents' home much later on. The picture they reveal is of an inward-looking, rather mournful household, where one would be well received, but had to be careful where one trod. There was also, apparently, some shouting and door-slamming, mostly by Margarethe, but also by Bruno. Although generally calm and reserved, he was prone to sudden bursts of temper that always left him feeling upset. On one occasion, when he was around ten, he found a few coins lying on a dresser, forgotten there by someone he does not identify. On a sudden whim, he pocketed the money. As Bettelheim tells the story, he spent the remainder of that day "fearing that the theft would be discovered, and that it would be apparent that I was the culprit, but also hoping it would, so that the matter would be settled." Twenty-four hours later, however, he put the money back where he had found it. "I was greatly relieved, but now I wondered more and more why I had stolen it in the first place, since I had had no intention of spending it. I gradually became angry that I had been led into temptation by someone who, moreover, was so careless that he didn't even realize the money was missing. And then, young as I was, I realized that I had wanted to punish him for tempting me, that this had been my motive."[21]

Another childhood memory reported in *A Good Enough Parent* throws some light on his relations with his parents.

> I forget what I was annoyed about, but I said something offensive to my mother. She was shocked and hurt, but she said and did nothing. When she told my father about it, he was visibly upset. He asked me in a very firm voice, "Do I really have to punish you for you to watch the way you speak to your mother?" This was all, but it made a deep impression on me, a much greater one, I believe, than any punishment could have made. The idea that he might have to punish me obviously distressed my gentle father. And so I worried, not that I might be punished—I never was—but that I had upset and worried my father to such a degree.[22]

What is striking about this anecdote is that the only regrets expressed by Bettelheim relate to his father. Although he says himself that his mother was "shocked and hurt," he shows no remorse at his "offensive" outburst. It is almost as if his mother's feelings were of no importance, as if it were assumed that she was strong enough to take it, whereas Anton had to be protected in his role as the family's moral authority. This imbalance in Bettelheim's treatment of his parents can be found in practically everything he said about them. Any reference to his mother usually relates to services she provided him, rather than to their relationship. As for Anton, however, the few comments Bettelheim makes give the impression of a cozy and affectionate complicity between father and son. Many of the personal memories Bettelheim used to illustrate his educational precepts related to his father.

Anton was fond of playing cards. Bruno was often allowed to watch, on condition that he kept quiet, and when his father won, he would get a share of his winnings. On rainy days Anton would occasionally entertain his children by playing card games with them too. On such occasions, however, his attitude would be completely different, even though the games involved were the same ones he played with his adult friends. It would be the attitude "of a parent who enjoys what he is doing because it is enjoyable to his children . . . When parent and child, each for his very own reasons, are engrossed in the same play, this can form a bond between them that is truly *sui generis*," Bettelheim comments, in a chapter devoted to the role of play in personality development.[23]

Furthermore, when Bettelheim mentions a mistake his father made, he does not identify him. Of his own early interest in carpentry, no doubt to be expected in the son of a lumber merchant, he writes: "Before I was permitted to build anything . . . I had to learn to make perfect joints. It took me a few months to be able to make those joints well. By then I had lost all interest in carpentry, due to the drudgery involved in learning to make joints . . . Fortunately, we no longer make such mistakes in teaching carpentry." The passage appears in an article on teaching children to read.[24]

On the rare occasions when Bettelheim refers to his mother, however, the image is flat, inert, frozen, and he never quotes her directly. In four years, I found only one exception to that rule, in an anecdote which he cited, for instance, when he was interviewed by Geneviève Jurgensen in 1986.[25] Although clearly at ease with the former Orthogenic School counselor, Bettelheim suddenly turned to her photographer, who had been snapping away at him from all angles. "You are very talented, young man, but that's enough pictures. Don't waste any more film; I'm an impossible subject. When I was born, my mother exclaimed: 'Thank God it's a boy!'" This surprising statement was uttered in the self-mocking tone of one who has resolved to make the best of a bad situation and treats his misfortune as a joke. But the pain Bettelheim was also expressing in the anecdote, which he told on occasion throughout his life, stands out behind the humor.

At first sight, for a mother at the start of this century, having already produced one girl, to exclaim "Thank God it's a boy!" may not seem remarkable, particularly for the granddaughter of a religious Jew, whose required daily prayers contained the phrase "Blessed art thou,

O Lord our God, who hast not made me a woman." For Bruno Bettelheim, however, it was clear that the utterance was a reaction to his ugliness. Regardless of how he came to know of his mother's supposed exclamation, the wound was a deep one, which remained with him until the very end of his life. Eighty-five years after the event, a depressed and suicidal Bettelheim would still be ruminating on what he saw as his unredeemable ugliness when confiding in a fellow-psychoanalyst in Los Angeles.

The anecdote also surfaced on happier occasions, however, as in the short speech Bettelheim delivered in 1977 on accepting the National Book Award's prize in Contemporary Thought, for *The Uses of Enchantment:*

> Once upon a time, in a faraway land across the big sea, there was a very old city. Some thought of it as a fairy-tale city . . . It bordered on some woods and there, in a little house close to them, many many years ago, a boy was born. His mother had wanted another child, and was very glad . . . She was a woman who loved poetry, but she also had a healthy, down-to-earth sense of reality. So when . . . her son was shown to her, she took in his appearance carefully and then breathed a deep sigh of relief. "Thank God," she said, "it is a boy."
>
> This mother told her children many fairy tales. And since they lived at the most remote edge of the German land, she told the tales of the Brothers Grimm, not those of Hans Christian Andersen. Thus the boy never got the idea that an Ugly Duckling could turn into a beautiful Swan. This was fortunate, and saved him from disappointment, because his looks remained very much the same as they had been when his mother first beheld him.

In 1911, the Bettelheims moved into a spacious and comfortable apartment on the Neubaugasse, in Vienna's 7th district, where Paula was to remain until after the Anschluss in 1938. The move came two years after Bruno had started primary school, at age six. "The first day of school for the child is not just another new experience along the lines of many, often startling ones he has met in the past. Instead, it adds a new dimension to his life, which will never again be the same."[26]

It was around this time that Bettelheim was roughed up by his non-Jewish pal on his way to school (see chapter 1). As he would stress later, starting school is the discovery of a whole new world outside the family.

In his case, it meant primarily being faced with anti-Semitism—and thus with his own Jewishness. In spite of the fact that his parents were confirmed atheists, he had to attend religious education classes. Even much later, when he was preparing for his *Matura*, or school-leaving exam, he still had two semesters of compulsory religious instruction. Half a century later, on discovering Israel, he found it very difficult to accept that Hebrew could have become a living language.

Bruno Bettelheim was a short, puny, sensitive daydreaming pupil, the exact opposite of a schoolyard tough. He enjoyed kicking a ball around with his friends, but was no good at sports. Being both very nearsighted and astigmatic, he often did not see the ball until it was too late, even with his glasses on. He was to find out ten years later that he had not been given the right type of lenses; in the meantime, he suffered from a permanent feeling of clumsiness. The transition from the cozy world of home to the cold, impersonal classroom environment was a shock. Each evening, he insisted on sitting next to his mother to do his homework. He was serious and hardworking, a good pupil.

Bettelheim was later to come out very strongly against methods of teaching children to read and write that centered exclusively on technical skills rather than on awakening the child's interest in the subject matter. He was speaking from personal experience. "When I went to school I was taught penmanship in all the primary grades. Now I'd say that my handwriting is, by and large, a little more legible, maybe even a little prettier, than [that of] the children we educate nowadays. On the other hand, I didn't get any social studies, and very little natural history. And, you know, I'm so terribly deficient in some of the natural sciences, because the time was spent on penmanship . . . the point is that everything has a price."[27] But he had also learned early on how to use his head: "In former times, when learning to read was much more exclusively the central issue in early education, the main way—often the only way—to gain the pleasure of receiving the teacher's attention and praise was to learn to read well. It was this reward that made learning to read a sensible reason . . . to be in school."[28]

In September 1914, Bruno Bettelheim entered high school, the Albertgasse *Bundesrealgymnasium* in Vienna's 8th district. It was a mere ten minutes' walk from his home, and next door to the school his cousin Edith Buxbaum was attending. Bruno's high school, opened in 1905, was the most modern in the whole city. Unlike the five "noble schools," as the most exclusive Vienna institutions were called, the *Bundesrealgymnasium* stressed such forward-looking subjects as mathematics and foreign languages. There were so many Jews among its students that after World War II, when the school principal tried to gather information on alumni, he found that entire classes had been wiped out.[29]

No less than fifty-four students were in Bruno's class, among them Hans Willig and Walter Neurath, who in spite of Hitler and exile were to remain among his closest friends until the end of their lives. But he hated the *Gymnasium.* German-style education, with its overcrowded classes, harsh discipline, and authoritarian and needlessly boring teaching methods, would become for Bettelheim the model of how not to teach children. He was also to come out strongly against the tendency of many parents to push their children at school, turning them into exam-passing machines to the detriment of their overall maturity and the development of their critical faculties, and he condemned special schools for gifted children, which he saw as educational ghettos, cutting their pupils off from their peers.[30]

Plans for educational reform were indeed being aired at the time Bettelheim was at school. The general cultural upheaval under way in Vienna, including advances in psychology and psychoanalysis, had led many intellectuals to start looking at education from a point of view nobody had previously considered: that of the child itself. The process was to lead in 1918, when the Socialists took control of the city council, to a vast reform aimed at making schools more accessible to children from all social classes, banning religion in any form, and catering to the child's personal development as well as intellectual performance.

Already the reform movement was causing ferment in circles close to the Social Democrats, and particularly in youth groups, of which there were many in Austria at that time. Bettelheim was in his early to mid-teens when he joined one such organization, the Jung Wandervogel (literally, "young migratory bird"), at the suggestion of Hans Willig and Edith Buxbaum.[31] The main activity of the group, whose membership varied between fifty and a hundred, was hiking and picnicking in the forests and mountains around Vienna on Sundays. This above all provided an excuse for the young people to talk, and much of the talk was about what kind of world awaited them. Although the Jung Wandervogel had been born in Germany as a conservative and nationalist group at the turn of the century, in

Austria it was very close to the Social Democratic Party. This meant, as Bettelheim himself stresses, that it was pacifist (World War I was by then in full swing), socialist, and anti-monarchist.[32] But why did Bettelheim and most of his friends choose a group that on its foundation in 1901 had explicitly declared itself to be *Judenrein*, or "cleansed of Jews"? Because the only alternatives for young socialistically inclined atheists like them were the Zionist movements, and they were assimiliationist.

Those Sundays with the Jung Wandervogel played an important role in the lives of Bettelheim and his friends. The long outings were an opportunity not only for intense discussion, but for the first contacts between young men and women outside the family setting. They saw their love of the great outdoors and the simplicity of their clothes as a form of rebellion—"our locus for emancipating ourselves from our parents," Edith Buxbaum would write later. The jolly member of Bruno's group was Walter Neurath. "Hans and Bruno were the serious types," recalls the woman who would later become Hans Willig's wife. "They spent all their time talking."[33]

While Sundays were spent discussing how to change things, notably through Socratic methods of teaching based on respect for the individual, weekdays at the *Gymnasium* were given over to dealing with the all-too-real world. In the first year, Bruno was at the top of his class; the next year, he was outdistanced by his friend Neurath. The only really serious act of insubordination Bruno committed during his school years—one that produced "such a deep impression on me that it has stayed vividly in my mind for the more than sixty-five years which have passed since"—occurred around his fourth year at the *Bundesrealgymnasium*.

I was a very good student, a quiet, introspective, even subdued youngster. But one day the behavior of one of our schoolmasters, which I had found annoying all along—as had most of my fellow students because it was so unlike that of all our other masters, past or present—provoked me so much that suddenly, without forethought, I laid hands on him and, with a couple of other boys, whom my example enticed to help me, pushed him out of the classroom. As soon as we had accomplished it, I was shocked by what I had done; it was so unlike my usual behavior in school and out. I only knew that I had felt so outraged that I had had to do *something*; but of what specifically triggered my action, what motives other than rage had been at work in me, I had not the slightest idea; nor did I know what had caused my rage.[34]

The chapter in which Bettelheim relates this anecdote is titled "The Question 'Why?' " In it, he stresses that parents are often wrong in insisting that their child explain a shocking attitude or action, because "there is always the possibility that the child doesn't know his reasons, as I didn't [in this case]."[35] However strange it may seem, any action on the part of a child always has a meaning, and it is always the best response that the child is capable of giving at that particular time and in those particular circumstances. That idea was to become the cornerstone of Bettelheim's teaching and work as a therapist.

Fortunately for the errant schoolboy, Bruno's parents did not ask the reasons for his attack on the teacher, at least as far as he could remember when he wrote about the incident. Instead, on the evening after the event, they had a calm talk with him about where he could go if he were expelled. The following morning the principal showed up in the classroom, which was a rare occurrence. The whole class was made to stand at attention while the principal gave a short, sharp speech, singling out Bruno, but also the companions who had failed to hold him back, for harsh criticism. Bruno was particularly wounded at hearing himself described as a hypocrite, on the grounds that he had always behaved like a good boy. Indeed, up until this incident his conduct record had been exemplary. But then, instead of the expected punishment, he was astounded to hear the principal acknowledging that the teacher in question was simply not up to the job. "Tomorrow you will stay for two hours, after school, working on your own on studies which Dr. X should have made so interesting that there would have been no place for such behavior," he concluded.

Bettelheim was understandably relieved, and also impressed by the principal's ability to admit making a mistake. He nevertheless spent most of the following night wondering what he would have said if he had been asked to explain his act. He simply could not comprehend what had gotten into him. It was to be a quarter-century before understanding would finally come—on a psychoanalyst's couch.

———— ❁ ————

To return to Bettelheim's revealing letter of 1986: After referring to his own dysentery and to his father's illness, as well as to the oppressive silence that had descended on the household, he comments:

Part of the trouble was that our parents were good parents and tried to shield us from the family tragedy, which meant that we could not be angry at them.

When I was thirteen, my father had, as a consequence of his illness, a severe stroke. He could not move or talk for nearly two weeks. Another trauma for me who at this age did not understand what went on. He recovered to some degree, but lived the next ten years as a wreck till he died when I was twenty-three, much too early for me . . .

Even in this unusually intimate letter to a close friend, written just three and a half years before his own death, Bettelheim could still not bring himself to actually name his father's illness. Two years later, however, depression had won out over discretion.

The scene takes place on November 24, 1988, in Los Angeles, a city that epitomized everything Bettelheim hated about America. He saw it as the capital of superficial glitter, of show-business and shrinks for movie stars, of egotism and slavery to the sole god of money. He was now living there alone; he felt physically diminished and was obsessed by thoughts of suicide. Connie Katzenstein, a former University of Chicago student who had since become a therapist, was fully aware of Bettelheim's condition, as she regularly accompanied him on outings, to the doctor or sometimes to concerts. Worried at seeing him so miserable, she tried to cheer him up by inviting him to her Thanksgiving dinner. This well-meaning gesture was a disaster from the outset. Bettelheim proved unable to clamber up the steep wooden stairs leading to her house and had to be half carried by Connie's husband, which enraged the old man. He found himself wondering what on earth he, who normally loved meaningful celebrations, was doing at this party, far from his own children and surrounded by people who knew practically nothing about him, except that he was a celebrity of some sort. Bettelheim, seated in front of the huge turkey of which he was unable to partake due to an ailing esophagus, glowered and remained obstinately mute. Connie Katzenstein, seeing her star guest casting a pall over the proceedings, was at her wits' end.

After he had rejected a number of attempts to get him involved in the conversation, the other guests continued talking without paying much attention to him. Almost inevitably, the conversation drifted toward the number-one fear of the moment: AIDS, and how to avoid getting it. It was then that Bettelheim's gruff voice suddenly boomed out. "I was four years old when my father found out that he had syphilis. For the next twenty years, he never touched my mother again. AIDS patients can do the same thing!"

Leaving the old man aside for a moment, let us visualize the thirteen-year-old, just out of bed and set to leave for school, running as usual to say goodbye to his parents and finding his father silent and inert, unable to understand or even recognize him. Then fighting back his fear and leaving for the *Gymnasium*, to spend the day acting as if nothing had happened, telling no one. How much pain was tied up in that dinner-table growl!

Anton's condition remained stable for a week after that attack, and then it began to improve. The family doctor, the same one who had treated Bruno for his dysentery and for whom the boy had the greatest respect, then told him that if his father recovered from his stroke he would be able to lead a more or less normal life for another ten years. At age thirteen, Bettelheim had obviously not been informed that his father's illness was syphilis, the most terrifying affliction of the age.[36] As he would later explain to others, however, a child always understands whatever his parents think they are hiding from him, particularly when it causes them anxiety. Thirteen is an age when one does not know much, but when one can guess a lot, a time when ignorance only amplifies the fears generated by a budding sexuality. It is an age at which the reproachful silence of a mother and the ill-disguised guilt of a father can lead one to imagine the worst.

This was especially true for a boy brought up in bourgeois Vienna at the start of the twentieth century. One need only flip through a few pages of Stefan Zweig's memoir—his generation was halfway between that of Anton and that of Bruno—to realize the extent to which the blanket censorship of all things sexual served only to sharpen young people's curiosity and fantasies. In the Middle Ages, sexuality had been seen as "the sting of the devil," Zweig wrote, noting that this was at least a form of recognition of sensual desire. But the enlightened bourgeoisie of late-nineteenth-century Vienna no longer believed in the devil. "A silent pact was reached, by which the entire bothersome affair was not mentioned in school, in the family, or in public, and everything which brought its existence to mind was suppressed." Nothing could be more effective in stirring a young man's curiosity than this clumsy attempt at disguising human nature. "There was scarcely a fence or a privy that was not besmeared with obscene words and drawings, hardly a bathing pool in which the wooden wall of the women's quarters was not bored full of peepholes . . . 'Art' and nude photographs in particular were offered to half-grown boys for sale under the table by peddlers in every café."[37] Not to mention the dimly lit backstreets just behind the glittering Ring, where, if one bumped into an acquaintance, one pretended not to recognize him.

In such an atmosphere, the fear of syphilis was never far from anyone's mind. The disease was widely seen as a form of divine punishment visited upon sinners. Vienna's suburbs were dotted with small clinics where middle-class families hid their afflicted members. The shame was all the greater in that in its terminal phases syphilis causes disfigurement and dementia. Is it really conceivable that Bruno Bettelheim, a sensitive and observant child who was clearly imbued with the moral values professed by his family, could not have suspected what was wrong with his father—particularly given that Anton often had to return to the hospital, since his treatment was not proving effective?[38]

In a syphilitic's home, the fear of contagion meant obsessive concern about such things as "a badly washed towel, toilet seats, razor blades, cups and cutlery . . . coins that one holds in the mouth, and all the daily gestures of household and working life, such as using spittle to clean a small child's face, or simply kissing. Scientific treatises were dotted with warnings about such things," one historical work on the subject notes.[39] Worse, experts at that time were seriously considering the possibility that syphilis, and the progressive degeneration of the central nervous system it caused, was hereditary. This idea had already found its way into popular songs and literature, which depicted mentally retarded and malformed children on whom had been visited, in a literal sense, the sins of the fathers. Indeed, in 1914, two years before Anton suffered his first major stroke, the Austrian Ministry of War had decreed that the French play *Les avariés* (literally, The Damaged Ones) by Eugène Brieux, about the transmission of the disease from parents to their offspring, be performed in all the empire's military academies.[40]

How long did Bruno know the truth without being sure of it, hope against hope that he was mistaken, without daring to confide in anyone? When did he begin to see his many illnesses as signs of a possible contamination? There can be no definitive answers to those questions, although some impressions may be gleaned from the articles he was later to write about adolescence. For example: "Like adolescents, we must all learn to live in a continuous state of insecurity."[41] Discussing the awakening of sexuality that accompanies puberty, Bettelheim says it is a mistake to believe that the adolescent is simply frustrated at not being able to fulfill his or her desires immediately. "The truth is that most adolescents are terrified by anything grossly sexual," he writes, adding that what the adolescent needs most of all is reliable information, because what the young person does not know, he will seek to find out. And "the starting point for this sex exploration is unfortunate; since he was not told, he is not supposed to know. Therefore he feels guilty about his attempts to learn."

Bettelheim cites two types of pathological reaction to the anxieties generated by puberty, exemplified by the "rigid" and the "explosive" adolescent. The former strives to deny the existence of his inner struggle, while the second, refusing to grow up, chooses to let his tensions burst out. Bettelheim recommends that such adolescents be encouraged to master their problems intellectually. This will prevent them from being "immediately overwhelmed by [their] conflicts." At the same time, "intellectualization . . . gives [the adolescent] the prestige and strength of ego that he badly needs." He adds that the required intellectual effort can take several forms, which may include daydreaming. But whatever the form, it is better than trying to act out the problems. "Thinking strengthens the adolescent's ego, while action usually weakens it by defeat because he cannot yet act successfully with regard to his most pressing problems."

Bettelheim made no mention of his father's syphilis in any of his books and articles. He told his son, Eric, that Anton had been infected by a prostitute one summer while Paula and the children were vacationing in the Alps: certainly the most acceptable type of explanation he could have given the young man. Prostitution, to quote Stefan Zweig, was at the time the "dark underground vault over which rose the gorgeous structure of middle-class society with its faultless, radiant facade."[42] As for the effect the uncertainty and suspicions about his father's ailment must have had on Bettelheim as a young man, one can note the vehemence with which he was later to denounce the hypocrisy of Vienna and its bourgeoisie. It was a city in which, he once wrote, it was common to see little mirrors suspended outside the windows of middle-class houses, allowing their occupants to observe what was going on in the street without themselves being seen. More tellingly, he offered the following anecdote in another article: "When I was a young man of good intentions, I objected to legalized prostitution. But my Victorian father told me: 'It is these girls who protect nice women like your mother from the danger of being raped.' " *But not from the worst of all venereal diseases!* one could imagine the young Bettelheim thinking, and it is certainly no coincidence that this anecdote should be cited in an article titled "Children Should Learn About Violence," aimed at warning parents against giving their children an overidealized, sugar-sweet view of the world.[43]

Bruno Bettelheim was clearly deeply attached to his father, a man who was described by all those who knew him as charming, kind, and gentle. How could this love cohabit with the perception of the syphilitic as "a web of desire, shame, confusion and even of despair"? On the intellectual plane too, the father–son relationship must have been undermined by fearful doubts. Syphilis, which was widespread in literary and artistic circles at the end of the nineteenth century, was often presented as a mark of genius by those who suffered from it. This myth gained currency from the symptoms of the disease itself, which in its later stages could include "intellectual exaltation, ideas of grandeur and hyper-activity."[44]

One cannot but wonder how much of himself Bettelheim put into his portrait of the great Polish educator Janusz Korczak.[45] After the passage quoted as an epigraph at the start of this chapter, he writes:

> In all external respects, [Korczak's] early life was spent in very comfortable circumstances, in the well-to-do upper-middle-class home of his parents. Yet he was familiar with emotional difficulties from an early age on—his father held often grandiose and unrealistic notions of the world, and had a poorly developed ability to relate to reality . . .
>
> When Henryk [Janusz's real name][46] was only eleven years old, his father began to suffer from serious mental disturbances, which eventually required his placement in a mental institution. He died there when Henryk was eighteen years old . . . From then on, Henryk had first to contribute to the family's livelihood and later to provide for it.[47]

According to Korczak's American biographer, the educator suspected that his father was suffering from syphilis.[48] The two men's early lives had enough in common for Bettelheim to have been tempted to identify with the admirable Korczak, who had passed up the opportunity to escape from the Warsaw Ghetto in order to stay with the little orphans he was taking care of there, and thus died with them in the Nazi death camp at Treblinka.

Bettelheim's first bout of serious depression came shortly after Anton's first stroke. But being his mother's son, Bruno knew how to keep up appearances and go through the motions of normal life. He attended school and continued to see a few friends; he even got good grades. He "functioned," as he was later to tell his children, but mechanically and joylessly. On returning home from school he would shut himself up in his room and spend hours sitting in darkness doing nothing. As he recalled, he was not suicidal but simply depressed, convinced that life had nothing to offer him. He was to remain in that state for eighteen months to two years.

It could well have been around the age of fifteen, the time of his apparently inexplicable outburst of rage at the incompetent school-teacher, that Bettelheim began consciously to formulate his suspicions about his father's illness. This is the explanation he was later to give for the classroom incident, based on insights gained in his psycho-analysis. "Dr. X had been a simpering fool who spoke with the voice of a eunuch . . . We boys were at an age when we had anxious doubts about our budding masculinity and needed suitable masculine figures with which to identify. Dr. X, far from offering a suitable image for identification, increased our anxieties that we might not make it as male adults; he presented us with our worst fears about ourselves." The anxiety was aggravated for the young Bettelheim by his father's recent attack of paralysis. Bruno was "confronted with the possibil-ity—as the only other male in the family—that I might have to step into my father's shoes. This was a terrifying prospect to an insecure teenager already wracked by doubts about his masculinity and afraid he lacked male assertiveness. My father's severe illness . . . made me fear that I might turn into someone like Dr. X. This was an intolera-ble thought."[49]

A father who did not touch his wife for twenty years (one wonders how Bettelheim obtained that piece of information!), a teacher whose effeminate manner made his lessons unbearable, a young man whose mother had not only told him on numerous occasions that he would soon be called upon to shoulder his father's responsibilities, but treated him as though this was already the case[50]—to anyone schooled in Freud's ideas, this is probably enough to explain the young Bettel-heim's depression, and his anger. But there is no need to delve into the Oedipus complex to understand what Bettelheim is trying to say when he refers to the "personal bent" that lay behind his interest in autis-tic children: "What first disturbed me and aroused my interest in these children was how deliberately they seemed to turn their backs on humanity and society."[51]

That oppressive society, shot through with hypocrisy and prejudices, was deeply mistrusted by its young people. "A single untruthfulness on the part of teachers and parents inevitably leads a young person to regard his entire surroundings with a suspicious and therefore a sharper eye," noted Stefan Zweig. And such adolescent crises "brought about an awakening in another sense: for the first time it taught us to observe more critically the social world in which we had grown up, and its conventions," he added.[52]

Trapped between a family tragedy made worse by the shameful secrecy surrounding it and the rigors of an authoritarian teaching system that stressed intellectual abstraction above all, Bettelheim found solace in books, becoming an insatiable reader. It so happened that one of his best friends, Walter Neurath, also entertained doubts about his father: his mother lived openly with her lover in the family apartment, while his father slept in a separate room on the same premises. Amid such contradictions the younger generation dreamed of a better, more just and joyful world, in which people's actions would be at one with the principles they professed. Neurath was soon to become a militant Marxist. Bettelheim was more of a skeptic. Along with adventure stories, he devoured history and philosophy books.

"Personal experiences within my family and my adolescent turmoil combined with a terrible war to make me feel deeply pessimistic about life and myself." In the light of what we know of Bettelheim's childhood, his essay "Essential Books of One's Life" is a moving document.[53] "The belief in progress which my parents had instilled in me, and which the teachings of history in school had solidified, could not be maintained in view of what was now happening in the world," he adds, going on to explain the influence that the works of Theodor Lessing, F. A. Lange, and Hans Vaihinger had on him. From Lessing he learned that "history is not an account of man's progress over time, but that this progress and the meaning of historical events are only projections of man's wishful thinking."[54]

In Vaihinger's *The Philosophy of "As If"* (1911), however, Bettelheim discovered that his own pessimism, far from being destructive, could in fact give him the moral strength to go on living. Lessing, Bettelheim writes, had taught him to see fiction as a means of making life bearable, and to bet on the hypothesis that the cosmos did have some kind of order; Vaihinger showed him how to use hypotheses he knew to be false to help him act.[35] "Together these two authors provided the guidance I needed most of all: how one may manage to live a meaningful life despite one's inner doubts."

To defeat the causes of suffering by the sheer force of intellect; to make sense of whatever happened to him and his environment, through the greatest joys or the sharpest pain—such was to be Bruno Bettelheim's main mental activity from that point on. As he writes in the opening pages of his essay "Surviving": "In times of trouble . . . it seems that if we could just grasp life's deeper significance, then we would also comprehend the true meaning of our agony—and incidentally that of others—and this would answer the burning question of why we have to bear it, why it was inflicted on us." Any time his "inner doubts" got the better of him, suggesting a gloomy, pessimistic view of events, he would call on his moral sense or, if that failed him, on his imagination to nevertheless find a positive interpretation and pass it on to others. He would go on doing so until age and solitude overwhelmed him, and he could no longer keep up the effort.

It was around this time that Bettelheim first discovered Martin Buber and his Hasidic tales, which must have both awakened his interest in the Jewish traditions his parents had rejected, and helped him interpret some of the harsh realities of his everyday life. Not only did they provide him with a sense of belonging that had eluded him up until then, they also echoed, in a more realistic tone, the beautiful and reassuring fairy tales his mother used to tell him. Indeed, the gap between fairy tales and Jewish stories is not all that great. Simply remove the princesses' crinolines and replace the castles with the narrow streets of the shtetl and you will find the same cast of characters: wise old men and foolish youngsters, witches bent over their cauldrons and pretentious young girls. Take out some of the miracles and replace them with a good measure of humor, and you will find the moral is often the same.[36]

The Bettelheim family drama was being played out against the backdrop of a worldwide disaster. Bruno was not yet eleven when, in June 1914, Archduke Franz Ferdinand of Austria was assassinated in Sarajevo. A month later the aged emperor, his uncle, was obstinately and arrogantly to strike the first blow in a world war of which his own empire was to be the first victim. The loyalty of the empire's Jews to Franz Josef was such that, along with most other Austrians, they blindly supported his foolish obstinacy, underwriting his war loans and gladly accepting mass mobilization.[57]

A mere two years later, when the emperor breathed his last in the same Schönbrunn Castle where he had been born eighty-six years earlier, the atmosphere was very different. The empire's industrial backwardness had proved a terrible handicap right from the start of the war. Military defeats were piling up, while production was sagging dangerously for lack of manpower. The unresolved national questions sapped the morale of the imperial troops, while galloping inflation undermined that of the civilians. Although a host of Jews, among them the young Bruno with his father and grandfather, turned out for the emperor's burial at Saint Stephen's Cathedral on November 21, 1916, many of them, including both Anton Bettelheim and Adolf Seidler, had by then been ruined by the collapse of the Austrian war loans. "That my father lost a great fortune at the beginning of World War I did not improve matters, because up to then he was convinced that even if he died soon, his family would be well off. 1914 changed all that," Bettelheim wrote in the 1986 letter to his friend Carl Frankenstein.

The empire had begun to break up well before the end of the war, and the death of the emperor, who had been the last symbol holding the disparate entity together, hastened the process. One by one the Hungarians, Czechs, Slovaks, Serbs, Croats, Poles, and Italians were to break away, either to found new states of their own or to seek incorporation into other existing states. By 1919 Austria had become a huge head with no body left to keep it alive. As a French periodical described it, "What is now referred to as 'Austria,' since the secession of the Czecho-Slovaks and the Yugo-Slavs, since the Hungarian Revolution, is a modest entity of six million inhabitants, too small for a too-large capital, submerged in central Europe and left to its own devices . . . Ruined, with no trade or industry, threatened with Bolshevism, [Austria] will only survive if it is given a status which provides it with outlets and reliable protection."[58]

Starting in the autumn of 1918, Vienna suffered full-scale famine. In 1913 its citizens had consumed 900,000 liters of milk daily; in 1919 the figure was a mere 100,000. In October 1918, rations for each Viennese amounted to a mere 40 grams (1.4 ounces) of fat and 1 kilogram (2.2 pounds) of potatoes a week, and a few months later even that meager allotment had been cut back by half. Bread was so adulterated as to be practically uneatable, and a loaf cost fifteen times more than before the war. There was no coal at all, and only half a liter of kerosene weekly per household. Like other Viennese families, the Bettelheims shivered with cold throughout the winter, and had to spend hours waiting in line to buy even a tiny loaf of the bad bread. In the early days of the war, Anton had been able to get food from the countryside via his business connections, but with the advance of the Russian troops, who burned down sawmills and cut off the roads to Vienna, the supplies ended. The family now inhabited a hungry world of anarchy and *sauve-qui-peut*, where the legend of Vienna as a beacon of civilization was but a distant and absurd memory. The following incident, reported in the *Reichpost* newspaper on April 19, 1919, during a period of social unrest, gives a good idea of the deprivation suffered by the city's inhabitants:

> During a wave of shooting, a policeman's horse was hit, bringing the animal down and wounding the policeman in the process. In the wink of an eye, the crowd rushed at the fallen horse, and a sailor finished it off with his knife, encouraging his fellows to help themselves to a cheap roast. The horse was instantly torn to pieces by the crowd, with men and women fighting over the remains. A few minutes later people could be seen running away, clutching still-steaming chunks of meat.

For Bettelheim, the chaos in the world outside could not but amplify his internal conflicts.

> It is hard to revolt against a parent whose whole world has suddenly fallen shattered to pieces. Revolt is the less avoidable because the adolescent feels even more betrayed at suddenly realizing that the parent he thought an oppressive but protective hero is just a clay god. He can no longer test his new values against those of his parents . . . All of a sudden he feels deprived of the firm support, not of his parents, but of the values they instilled in him; and this happens just when he needs them most as a safe harbor from which to venture on his new and anxious moves into semi-adult independence.[59]

Bettelheim was often to write that his father never recovered from the ruin into which the war plunged him. And, even worse, Anton had never been able to grasp the fact that a page of Austria's history had been turned, and that the world in which he had grown up was gone forever.

Up until the end of his life, Anton Bettelheim was to seek compensation for the losses he had suffered during the war. But the provinces conquered by the Russians had in the meantime become Communist, and he was never to recover a single cent. He did not give up, however. In January 1919, with famine still raging in Vienna and strikes paralyzing all of southern Austria, Anton Bettelheim registered a new wholesale timber company, with himself as director and a new partner in place of his brother-in-law: a certain Hans Schnitzer, age twenty. Their offices and warehouses were located at no. 3A Gaudenz-dorfergürtel in the 12th district, on the main road leading to Graz. It was there, at the age of twenty-three, that Bruno would step into his father's shoes.

Meanwhile, Bruno's outings with the Jung Wandervogel did him a lot of good and helped him over his depression. Led on by his cousin Edith Buxbaum, who had now become his constant companion, he started taking a keen interest in the social and political situation. He lost his fear of public speaking, and was even to head one of the discussion groups to which the Wandervogel gave rise toward the end of the war. The young people, fired by concern for the new world that would necessarily emerge from the ruins that surrounded them, discussed everything: politics, art, literature, even sex. Unsurprisingly, they saw peace as the number-one precondition for accomplishing their aims. Bruno Bettelheim would later tell his son how in his early teens he and his Socialist friends had gone out to greet with pacifist slogans soldiers returning from the front, asking them to hand over their guns before entering the city.

The monarchy was not to survive the war. On October 17, 1918, Emperor Karl I, grandnephew and heir to Franz Josef, signed a document transforming Austria into a federation of national states. On October 21, the German members of parliament declared a "Provisional National Assembly of the autonomous State of Austrian Germans" (*Deutschösterreich*), considering themselves to have the same right to self-determination as the Poles, Czechs, Slovaks, and other nationalities. On November 11 the emperor abdicated, and the next day the Provisional National Assembly declared an Austrian German Republic.

For Bettelheim and his peers, the fate of that other great prewar European empire, czarist Russia, at the hands of the Bolsheviks served to underline all the more starkly the dramatic collapse of the old world. Soon, with shortages spreading, the situation in Vienna became explosive. In general, however, Austrians were not much given to violence, and their strain of Socialism remained a moderate one. Having chosen democracy rather than revolution, the Austrian Social Democrats agreed to take part in the new coalition government, and social reform was to get under way even before the first republican elections. Legislation was passed to create an eight-hour workday and a system of unemployment benefits, and to ban child labor.[60] And then in December 1918, the government embarked on the major plan for educational reform that Bruno Bettelheim and his friends had been dreaming of.

But prejudices still ran deep, and since 1916, anti-Semitism had been on the rise again. During the war, Jews had been accused of avoiding combat:[61] after it they were held to be profiteering.[62] Eternal scapegoats for society's ills, they found their situation made even more difficult by the sudden arrival in Vienna of some 100,000 dispossessed *Ost juden*, Jews who had fled the empire's eastern provinces before the advancing Russian troops. Unlike preceding generations of immigrants, these eastern Jews had come against their will, seeking not assimilation into Viennese society but simply a safe haven.

Providing an easily identifiable target for the anti-Semites, the new arrivals could not have come at a worse time from the point of view of the assimilated Viennese Jews, whose contradictions and fears were thus heightened even more. They often counted themselves among the most pro-German of the "Austrian Germans," and indeed some of them firmly believed that only by uniting with Germany could Austria become a modern state.[63] Most of them felt they had nothing whatsoever in common with the recent immigrants. The latter were religious, and observed customs viewed as medieval by the Viennese Jews, most of whom were freethinkers. Not even their language united them: Most Viennese Jews considered German their native tongue, and even Theodor Herzl had never imagined the inhabitants of his planned Zion speaking anything else. Nevertheless, when in 1919 the regional governor, caving in to pressure, ordered the expulsion of the *Ost juden* immigrants from Vienna (an order that was never carried out, for lack of transportation), the young Bruno Bettelheim, who had only recently discovered the world of the Hasidim in the works of Martin Buber, could not but have felt concerned.

Outside, a world bursting apart like a rotten fruit, shedding seeds that could promise a better future, but still reeking with the stench of old prejudices. In the family home, an unmentionable disaster, with a father fighting courageously against irreversible physical decay to go on supporting his family. Such was the environment in which Bruno Bettelheim completed his secondary schooling, not before plunging once again into depression, although only for a short time, at age seventeen. The spring of 1921 found him studying for his final high school exams in the company of his cousin Edith and her best friend, Annie Pink. He helped the two girls with their mathematics; the following year, at the university, Edith was to repay the debt by helping him with his Latin. On July 12, 1921, Bruno received his high school diploma, with good grades. He had done very well, receiving honorable mentions in German, mathematics, geography, English, and French.

When asked the inevitable question, "What do you want to do later?" he replied "Philosophy," as if he were leading an affluent, trouble-free life, and expected to have all the time in the world to read, study, and become a distinguished man of letters. Sixty-five years later, however, he was to sum up the story of his childhood as follows:

> My parents obviously suffered, and tried their very best to be very good parents, tried even to make up for it all to us. So we could not blame them, and if we occasionally questioned their depressive way of life, we had to feel guilty because they were good parents, tried to be, beyond their ability caused by conditions.
>
> . . . So there you have the story of my life, and also the explanation why I could devote it so single-mindedly to work strenuously to help children overcome the damages their childhood experiences did to them.[64]

3

❖

Gina

Gina Weinmann, née Altstadt, cannot remember exactly where she first met Bruno Bettelheim. At an exhibition, a concert maybe . . . What she knows for sure, is that she was never at any time in love with him. "He was always homely, you know," she says, almost apologetically, "but I liked his voice, his manners . . ."[1]

He was maybe nineteen, and she two and a half years younger. They shared a passion for beautiful things, art, and theater. She was impressed by his culture, intelligence, and lordly manner; he was fascinated by this petite young woman with exquisite legs, whose independent mind and sharp judgment he could sense behind her apparent frailty. Coquettish and always impeccable, Gina Altstadt was more than pretty, she had class. She was also proud, neurotic, demanding, and something of a tease. Totally under her spell, he showered her with gifts, took her everywhere, introduced her to all his friends, and thought only of winning her heart.

It was not the first time Bettelheim had been in love. In his autobiographical essay "How I Learned About Psychoanalysis" he refers to a girlfriend he saw on outings with the Jung Wandervogel.[2] As he would later confide to his friend Wanda (who was to marry his classmate Hans Willig), she was Lisl Lazarsfeld, whose elder brother Paul was at the time a rising star in the Social Democratic youth movement.[3] One Sunday toward the end of the war a former Wandervogel member named Otto Fenichel rejoined the group. Five years older than Bettelheim, he was on leave from the army in order

67

to complete his medical studies and was still wearing his uniform. Fenichel, who was to become a star of the psychoanalytic left, quickly attracted a circle of admirers within the Wandervogel group by reporting on Sigmund Freud's lectures, which he was attending at the university. One attraction was Fenichel's readiness to analyze his listeners' dreams.

Bettelheim was dismayed to see that Otto Fenichel appeared to hold a particular fascination for Lisl Lazarsfeld. At the same time, he could not help being intrigued by the dream interpretations the young man offered, which were mostly sexual. The subject made Bettelheim feel ill at ease. Yet the issue of sex education was central to the debate on education then going on in Vienna. "Only the transformation of sexuality can remedy our contemporary and crippled situation," Fenichel wrote around that time. "Affirmation of oneself means affir-mation of one's sexuality."[4] For Bettelheim and his friends, these prin-ciples remained somewhat abstract: although "committed to sexual freedom in theory," Bettelheim acknowledged, they practiced a good deal of self-repression, justifying it by "the principles of a superior morality." No doubt this was particularly true of a young adolescent convinced of his own ugliness.

That night Bettelheim went to bed deeply troubled, filled with jeal-ous hatred for his rival and contempt for psychoanalysis. The next day, however, he adopted a more positive attitude, he recalled. No sooner were his morning classes over than he rushed out into the maze of streets behind the Vienna Opera House to the Deuticke bookstore, which published the works of the Psychoanalytic Society. He emerged weighed down with as many of Freud's books as his pocket money would buy, notably *The Psychopathology of Everyday Life* and *Jokes and Their Relation to the Unconscious.* As he was interested in art, he also selected Freud's studies of Leonardo da Vinci and Michelangelo's *Moses.*

That first contact with psychoanalysis had a sinful feeling to it: "I soon realized that my Victorian family, although personally acquainted with members of the Freud family, would be utterly shocked to find me perusing such obscene literature. My solution was to hide it from them by taking it to school and reading it there surreptitiously while I was supposed to be attending to studies which, by comparison, were utterly boring."[5]

Within the week, Bettelheim writes, he had devoured the lot, and thus felt armed the following Sunday to face up to Fenichel for the attentions of his beloved Lisl—only to hear her brusquely declare that one weekend of psychoanalytic chat had been enough, and now she felt like talking about something else. Bettelheim does not tell us the rest of the story, simply noting, "The young lady and I lost our romantic interest in each other a while later, but remained good lifelong friends."

The purpose of this anecdote was not to illustrate Bettelheim's early love life but to explain how he first came to Freudian theory. "One week of complete concentration on psychoanalysis and I was hooked for life," he concluded. Regarding his emotional life, it should be noted that although he freely discussed sexuality, he rarely mentioned his own experiences. Such coyness was not restricted to his writings: his two daughters were only to learn in the late 1950s, when both were adolescents, that Gina Weinmann, the old family friend who was married to one of their father's colleagues and who regularly spent Christmas and Thanksgiving and on occasion even vacations with them, had been the first Mrs. Bettelheim, married to their father for ten years![6]

When the two met, Gina Altstadt was living on Burggasse, not far from the Ringstrasse and just behind the former imperial stables, with her mother and her brother, Leopold, who was three years her senior. Her father, a good-looking man who enjoyed life and doted on his daughter, had died only recently of tuberculosis. Gina had then been a little over fourteen.

The following summer, her mother had taken her on vacation to the Dolomite mountains. There she had met and fallen madly in love with a young would-be painter named Dolf. Art, breathtaking landscapes, long walks in the woods, and a first love affair: all the ingredients needed to help a sensitive young girl overcome the pain and anguish of losing her father. She spent hours lying in the grass, watching Dolf paint and dreaming of a world of beauty.

But the return to Vienna was to bring her down to earth with a bump. At the Fine Arts Academy, to which Dolf had just been admitted, his teachers recommended that he devote himself entirely to painting. At least that was the reason he gave her for his decision to break off the relationship. There could have been other considerations, such as social differences, or her Jewishness; Gina can't remember. Like many Viennese Jews, she does not much like to discuss such things. She remembers meeting Bettelheim shortly after the end of that unhappy love affair, which had come soon after her father's death. Gina was depressed; she was living in what she describes as "a fantasy world." She whiled away the hours daydreaming and embroidering out on the balcony, incapable of taking an interest in real life. But she had a true love of music. Her brother, whom she much admired ("he was very handsome, you know"), played the violin. So she was elated when the father of her friend Lotte, a child prodigy who had been giving piano recitals since the age of thirteen, offered to let her follow the same music lessons. Gina was only too happy to drop out of high school to pursue this new path. She had no thought for her future, or rather she had only dreams.

Life was anything but easy for the Altstadt family. Unlike the Bettelheims, who by this time had been settled in Vienna for two generations, they were relatively recent arrivals. Gina had been born on Christmas Eve 1905, in what was then known as Lemberg and is now Lvov, one of the principal cities in Ukraine. Lemberg was Austrian up until 1918, and as such was the capital of Galicia, a region in the farther reaches of the empire that the Austrians, Russians, and Poles had always fought over. Gina's parents were assimilated Jews, who spoke Polish and German.[7] She never heard them speak Yiddish, a tongue she viewed with some disdain as a corruption of German—"they didn't speak Jewish" is how she puts it. Later in Vienna, when she was to visit her grandparents in the Leopoldstadt neighborhood, she was to have the same irritated reaction on hearing her grandmother refer to non-Jews as "others" and even "enemies." "Some of my classmates weren't Jewish, but that didn't make them 'enemies,'" she remarks.

Max Altstadt, Gina's father, was the eldest brother in a large family. She was only two when he left for Vienna, at the request of his youngest brother, Moritz, who was considered the financial genius of the family. She recalls awaiting her father's return, all dressed up with a blue ribbon in her hair, in the courtyard of their home. She also remembers her mother's sadness. Mina Alstadt was a former seamstress, very pretty and sensitive but from a much poorer background than her husband and according to Gina, probably attributed his departure to her own lack of formal education. When Gina was five, her father sent for herself, her brother, and her mother to join him in Vienna. She was not to see much more of him than before, however, since Moritz, who had become a rich shoe manufacturer, had asked Max to go and manage a factory in Bohemia. This was around the beginning of World War I. Gina can recall marvelous moments spent with her father, but they were few and far between. Then one day Max Altstadt came home with a bad cough. The doctor diagnosed pleurisy, and Gina remembers the damp towels her mother applied to help him breathe. Later he was in the hospital, where she visited him. One day Max announced that to really get better, he would have to go to Italy. Shortly afterward her mother too left, to attend him on his deathbed, but Gina stayed behind in Vienna. She never saw her father again.

When Bruno Bettelheim met Gina, he was more worried than ever about the condition of his own father, though he hid his fears even from his closest friends. In September 1921 he had fulfilled his desire to become a university student. But only a few days after receiving his high school diploma, he had also enrolled in the Hochschule für Welthandel, or international trade school, to study management, for it was becoming more and more obvious that he would soon have to take Anton's place as the family breadwinner.

In a 1977 review of a book of photographs of Freud's home and offices, Bettelheim recounts a strange memory concerning Freud's apartment building on Berggasse,

> a dull and undistinguished street in a nondescript part of the ninth district of Vienna. And what goes for the street also holds true of number 19 . . . As a young man I used to walk by the building, more often than not choosing to use this hilly, unattractive street to where I was going only because Freud lived there. Upon looking up at his quarters, I always wondered why this great man chose to live there, when Vienna had so many other streets that were either more attractive in themselves, had more beautiful buildings, or at least offered charming or historically interesting vistas.[8]

Bettelheim goes on to explain how he eventually realized that the location of Freud's residence in a way reflected the latter's life story. It was halfway up Berggasse, a long street that runs from the banks of the Danube up to the university and some of the city's best neighborhoods, on the hill. The lower end, Bettelheim explains, started in a flea market area mainly inhabited by poor Jewish peddlers, not far from Leopoldstadt, where Freud's parents had lived. The top half, on the other hand, represented Freud's career: the university and the affluent homes of many of his patients.

A clever explanation, but what is particularly striking about the passage is the condescending tone Bettelheim uses when referring to Freud's residence. For although Berggasse 19 is indeed a clearly middle-class building[9]—a previous tenant of Freud's apartment had been the political leader Victor Adler—it does not seem much different in terms of social standing from the one the Bettelheim family then inhabited in the 8th district. On discovering that the Hochschule für Welthandel was situated almost directly across the street from Freud's home, I better understood the ambivalence of Bettelheim's tone. This probably had much less to do with Freud's social standing than with the frustration of a young man who, after nurturing great academic ambitions, found himself obliged to study accounting and management. And what Bettelheim presents as a voluntary detour was simply the route he had to take every day to get to his classes. But it must indeed have felt like a detour—one that he had been forced to take in his career due to his father's illness.

Bettelheim, however, would certainly never have admitted that. In his 1986 letter to Carl Frankenstein he writes: "You mention Kafka: his father probably was also a pretty good father but Kafka could afford not to see it. So he could be angry at him . . . " Note the envy. Young Bruno could not allow himself to harbor resentment against his father. Not only was Anton soon going to die, he was also worrying ceaselessly about his children's future. Having been painfully aware of his father's anxiety, Bruno Bettelheim later bitterly regretted that Anton had died too early to know of his son's successes. As for his mother, he sadly noted in the same letter that although she, having died in 1953, had seen his early breakthroughs, "her long life of sorrows did not permit her to really enjoy it."

Bettelheim was not afraid of hard work. He now resolved to reconcile the fulfilling of his own dreams with the rigors of the life that had been thrust upon him. He probably did so with a feeling of inner rage, as his later correspondence suggests. Without having any clues other than the character traits he was to display later on in life, one can imagine him being extremely intolerant of any interruption to his study time, and making heavy demands on those around him. "When I studied as a youngster, the door to my room had to be closed, and everything had to be quiet. Only then could I concentrate on myself and my work to the exclusion of everything else," he writes, in an article on the right to privacy.[10] This no doubt accounts at least in part for his habit of doing much of his work at night.

Faced with the obligation to take over from his father, Bettelheim thus began leading a double life. At the Hochschule he attended classes in international and commercial accounting, trade law, economics, what today would be called marketing, statistics, geography, foreign exchange dealings, letter writing in French, and even shorthand and typing. At the university, meanwhile, he continued to pursue a higher path of learning, which included five hours a week of Latin, a subject without which no young Viennese could consider himself truly cultured. This was to involve, in July 1923, an extra exam, since the subject had not been in the curriculum of the modern-minded Albertgasse *Gymnasium.* He also took three hours a week of seventeenth-century German literature, one of contemporary literature, one devoted to "readings of dramatic works," and a course on *Vor Sonnenaufgang* (Before Daybreak), a play of the Naturalist school by Gerhart Hauptmann.

In the essay "Essential Books of One's Life," Bettelheim states that he only became interested in art history at a later date.[11] Nevertheless, the courses he took as a freshman already show a clear penchant for the fine arts. He had a two-hour weekly course titled "Description of a Trip to Italy" with Julius von Schlosser, then the head of the sculpture department at the Kunsthistorisches Museum and a prominent specialist in the history of art literature, one hour of "Reflections on Art" with Josef Strzygowski, famed for being the first historian to have devoted a comprehensive work to the art of the period, and an hour on "Buddhist Art in Eastern Asia." Bettelheim also took a two-hour course on "Richard Wagner's Musical Dramaturgy." And he studied philosophy, with a weekly class on "Great Conceptions of the World," "History and Critique of Socialism," and "General Studies of Races."

By the start of the second semester, the young scholar had narrowed down his choices. His taste for theater, German literature, and the history of both art and ideas came through more clearly. In particular, he enrolled in a four-hour-per-week course on "The Religions of the Enlightenment," and a two-hour one on Indian philosophical systems. He attended some of the same classes as his cousin Edith Buxbaum, who had started her freshman year at the same time he did, but was less interested in art and more in history. At that time the two cousins were practically inseparable, and Bettelheim spent more time at her home than he did at his own. When she was not ill, his Aunt Jenny, Edith's mother, was a good pianist, and it was at her home that Bettelheim discovered music. It was also there that he met the brilliant and turbulent Wilhelm Reich, who was to be first the psychoanalyst and then the husband of Edith's best friend, Annie Pink.

With the exception of Edith and her friends, however, Bettelheim did not spend much time with his fellow-students. He was to be seen on occasion at the Landtmann, a famous café just opposite the university, which was co-owned by Walter Neurath's mother. But unlike most other students, who spent hours there reading newspapers, playing cards, or talking, Bettelheim was forever in a hurry, rushing from one place of learning to another. That first year at the university, Bettelheim's grades were uniformly excellent. At the Hochschule the only field in which his teachers considered him to have attained just the basic pass level was "accounting and practical office work"; in all the other subjects his grades were either "very good" or "excellent." At the end of the school year, by way of a reward, his parents paid for a trip to Italy. It was his first journey to the birthplace of the Renaissance, the cultural and artistic movement that was to occupy an important place in Bettelheim's life for the next ten years.

On returning from that vacation, in August 1922, he immediately started working at the Riunione Adriatica de Sicurta insurance company, where he was to spend a year as part of the requirements for his Hochschule diploma. At the end of the period, having gained the credentials that would allow him to run the family firm, he was able to resume, for a few months, the life of a college student. At the same time, though, his father was probably training him to take over the lumber business.

In his relations with Gina Altstadt, Bettelheim took care not to show just how tough his life was. She never knew, for example, about his courses at the Hochschule or his insurance job. On the contrary, he liked to act the gentleman of leisure. He may not have understood all her problems, but there was one, at least, that he could easily sympathize with: her feeling of impotence and guilt regarding her mother's deep sadness. But for a long time he told her nothing of his father's illness, or of his other worries, preferring to play a protective, Pygmalion role. No doubt he hoped that with time, he would be able to replace both the men she had just lost, not only her boyfriend Dolf but also her father.

Although head over heels in love, Bettelheim could not but realize that while Gina enjoyed being with him, she did not feel any real physical attraction to him. She did not admit this to herself at the time, but her strong need for beauty was frustrated by her suitor. She liked his personality, intellect, and even his moral qualities, but to really win her over he should also have been handsome like her brother, her father, or Dolf.

Far from discouraging him, the young lady's hesitations probably only served to strengthen Bettelheim's attraction. As he was to admit to his children toward the end of his life, he was very frightened of sex at that time. That had been the reason he had broken off with his second girlfriend, Lilly Krugh. He had still not been officially told that his father's illness was syphilis, but he sensed that sex had something to do with his parents' unhappiness and the depressive atmosphere in his household. Lilly had been a classmate of his cousin Edith, who had introduced her to Bruno when they were celebrating their *Matura*. They quickly became very close, and were to spend a lot of time together over the following two years. Lilly was a political revolutionary, however. She had discovered Communism with a previous boyfriend, a Trotskyite, but Bettelheim refused to be indoctrinated. Above all, she believed in sexual liberation, and could not understand why Bruno refused to plunge into such a fulfilling experience. Although he was fond of Lilly, his inhibitions proved too strong, as he would later admit. He therefore decided to introduce her to his friend Walter Neurath, whom he reckoned was readier for the experience. His hunch that the two would be a good match turned out to be right, and sixty years later he was still priding himself on their marriage.

Bruno had nothing of the sort to fear with Gina, whom he appears to have met shortly after the breakup with Lilly. His new girlfriend was no man-eating Amazon, just a very depressed young woman who put on a ladylike facade. He did everything he could to entertain her. They lived a few streets apart, and the walk between their respective houses on Burggasse and Neubaugasse provided the opportunity for endless discussions, in which he was able to deploy his knowledge of art, history, and literature. For her it was by no means the total communion she felt she had experienced with Dolf, but it was a door opened onto a world of culture and intellect. He took her to the movies, then a new form of entertainment, to concerts, which she adored, and to the theater, his favorite. Although they spent little time together with their respective families, Gina was well received at the Bettelheim home, where Anton was clearly responsive to her charm.

Bruno also provided Gina with an entrée to an idealistic new world, that of the Jung Wandervogel. Nearly seventy years later, Wanda Willig remembered the spotless white percale gloves Gina was wearing the evening he introduced them to each other. Gina herself needed no prompting to recall the event: "I was dressed to the nines, with an elegant outfit and, of course, white gloves." Then, laughing with retrospective embarrassment, she said: "They were in the Wandervogel. They would never have dressed that way!"[12]

Although not greatly interested in politics, Gina had a thirst for new ideas. She had already been wounded by life, having had to learn at an even earlier age than Bruno to grit her teeth and hide her pain so as not to deepen her mother's suffering. Both of them found solace in the contemplation of beauty and greatness, but while Bruno had gained an escape route from his inner conflicts via books and studying, she was still feeling her way. The art world attracted her, but being too much of a perfectionist, she could not believe there would ever be a place in it for her. The intellectual ferment of the Socialist youth group opened up new vistas. The world of yesterday was gone, its conventions and inequities dead, or so it appeared to these young people. They had nothing but contempt for the established order, which had led humanity through years of conformism to unprecedented butchery and ruin. They dreamed of a future based on justice and a deeper understanding of humanity. And it seemed that in front of their eyes a new world was indeed being born.

In Moscow, Budapest, and even in Munich, the Communists had seized power. In Vienna, the oversize capital of an empire that no longer existed, the upheavals of 1918 and 1919 had given birth to a compromise. The ruling Social Democrats, who favored a legalistic revolution, had combatted the workers' revolts that had broken out here and there in the aftermath of the war. They had managed to defuse the crisis without excessive repression, through an ambitious social reform program. They had since left the ruling coalition but still ran Vienna's City Hall, from which they continued to pursue their dream of creating a Socialist society by peaceful means. In the early

1920s the city was beginning to emerge from the worst of its suffering. Times were still hard, but every month brought a new round of social reforms, which earned the former imperial capital the nickname "Red Vienna."

The first-ever municipal low-cost housing projects were going up, and strict labor regulations—of the employment of women and children, night work, paid vacations—were being enacted. The city was beginning to live again, with outsiders attracted both by the social experiments of "Austro-Marxism," seen as an alternative to the Bolshevik Revolution, and by the work of Sigmund Freud, which was starting to gain worldwide attention. The young intellectuals of Bettelheim's generation were convinced they had the tools to create a new world, inhabited by a new type of human being. There was much debate as to whether the latter had to be created first, to then build the new world, or whether it was the other way around, but they had no doubt that they were on the way to something completely new, arising from the ashes of the old, unjust world that their parents had seen as unchangeable.

Bruno Bettelheim, however, was more skeptical than most of his friends as to the meaning of history in general, and of Socialist ideas in particular. One of the books in fashion at the time was Oswald Spengler's *Decline of the West* (1919–23), a vast, messianic history of civilization that Bettelheim was later to cite as one of the "essential books" of his life. Spengler's pessimistic vision was congruent with that of another of Bettelheim's favorite authors, the art historian Jakob Burckhardt. According to Spengler, the history of humanity has in itself no meaning and no final purpose. While he defined German culture as being socialistic by nature (in comparison, for example, with the individualistic British culture), he saw the rise and fall of civilizations as a cyclical, but not a continuous, process. Spengler posited a cycle of around a thousand years, and in a brilliant analysis which must have appealed to the young Bettelheim, he found points of comparison between different civilizations: parallels between Pythagoras and Descartes, Alexander the Great and Napoleon, and Greek art and contemporary Western painting and music, for example.

Spengler's analysis was based on a double opposition. First, he divided civilizations into those with an "Appollonian" or "antique," soul, characterized by an accent on the finite and the present (*hic* and *nunc*), and those with a "Western" or "Faustian" persona, which were dynamic and strove toward infinity. Second, he distinguished between the rise and fall of cultures: the creative buildup, which gave birth to great ideas, religions, and art, and the decadent decline, characterized by materialism and a stress on science and technique. The conclusion was all too clear: For Spengler, Germany (of which the "Republic of Austro-Germans" was but a part) was clearly in the decadent stage, characterized by morbid sterility masked by an external reliance on force. Its decline and fall, like that of the West as a whole, was ineluctable. But just as the decadent Roman Empire had followed the high point of Greek civilization, so the twilight of the West would be preceded by *imperium germanicum*.

In explaining his selection of the works he designated "essential" to his intellectual development, Bettelheim admitted: "I knew not all of them were great books while I was reading them, powerfully impressed by them as I was," but noted that in each case he had experienced a "shock of recognition."[13] They were books that "enlightened me about what were (at the time) my most pressing problems in finding my way in life." He went on to compare that shock of recognition to the experience he was to have later on a psychoanalyst's couch: " 'This is it!'—the 'it' being something with which I had been struggling, perhaps even to the point of obsession, without knowing that this was going on in my mind."

His mentioning Spengler, after Goethe and Freud, is therefore revealing. Although, like most of his contemporaries, he was deeply affected by the horrors of World War I and thus a confirmed pacifist, he appears to have been unable to follow his friends into the whirling torrent of hope that was to seize most of Vienna's intelligentsia for at least the next decade. At that time Walter Neurath and Lilly Krugh, along with two other couples, were founding one of a series of forward-looking communes based on equality and sexual freedom. Many of those closest to Bettelheim had answered the siren call of psychoanalysis, which was in the process of becoming a full-fledged movement and appeared to offer a path to a more just society by helping people rid themselves of their unconscious conflicts. Among them were Wanda Willig, who was studying medicine, and Edith Buxbaum, who remained deeply involved in left-wing politics (so much so that when the United States entered World War II, her name was on an FBI list of people considered a national security risk) while starting an analysis with Hermann Nunberg. Meanwhile, Edith's friend Annie Pink was about to marry her own analyst, Wilhelm Reich, who, along with Otto Fenichel and a few others, was trying to build bridges between psychoanalysis and Marxism. Gina too was attracted by psychoanalysis. While all this was going on, Bettelheim, according to his own account, was finding an answer to his deepest doubts and questions not in Freud or Marx but in the apocalyptic vision of Oswald Spengler. He could not but be aware of the social changes going on all around him: Just across the street from the offices and warehouses of the Bettelheim & Schnitzer company, the "Red" city council was erecting a huge low-cost housing project, dedicated to the principle that the poor too had the right to decent living conditions. Even Karl Kraus, another of Bettelheim's favorite writers, had temporarily curbed his acerbic wit enough to throw in his lot with the Socialists. Despite all this, something in Bettelheim clearly prevented him from becoming a true believer; behind the vision of a better world, he could not help foreseeing a catastrophic future.

By around 1925 Anton Bettelheim's condition had deteriorated so much that he had to be admitted to a clinic, at Tulln in the Vienna suburbs. Wanda Willig has no recollection of Anton's illness and death; although both she and her husband were very close to Bruno, he never once spoke to her of it. Wanda thinks Hans might have known about it, but if he did, he too did not betray the secret. As for Gina, she has but vague memories of a final painful decline that lasted only a few months. "It's true that Paula was very protective of her husband," she remarks. It is also possible that the demise of a man she liked, and who died away from home, reminded her of a past that she preferred to forget. Or perhaps, more simply, Bruno managed to protect her from the whole process. This would have been easy, since the two spent as little time as possible at their parents' homes. Edith Buxbaum was later to confess, somewhat remorsefully, that although she was vaguely aware of Anton's illness, she had pushed the thought into the back of her mind. The two cousins had been seeing much less of each other since Bruno had started dating Gina. They no longer moved in the same circles, or had exactly the same interests.

Much later, Bettelheim would admit to Edith that he had resented her absence from his life, which he saw as a betrayal. He had suffered greatly during his father's final illness, which lasted around two years. Bruno's sister, Margarethe, had left home early to study acting, notably in Germany, and even when she was in Vienna she went out a great deal, which meant Bruno was alone in the house with his mother much of the time. The drawn-out agony of a terminal syphilitic patient is a terrible experience for those around him. Witnessing the slow deterioration, both physical and mental, of his father was to mark Bettelheim for life.

Anton Bettelheim died on April 13, 1926; the family doctor had been only a few months wide of the mark.

On June 11, Bruno Bettelheim's name officially replaced that of his father in the statutes of the Bettelheim & Schnitzer company. That fall he re-enrolled at the university, but his new work schedule left him little spare time. The following spring, in early 1927, his name disappears from the university records. That February, Bruno's maternal grandfather, Adolf Seidler, also died, leaving him the only man in his mother's life.

Bruno Bettelheim, not yet twenty-four, was thus being called upon to make a great sacrifice. He had dreamed, as he often said, of a university career, but he was now convinced that it was out of his reach forever, just as, at age sixteen, his poor eyesight had forced him to drop his ambition to become an architect. He now had to face up to reality, shoulder responsibilities, and let his dreams take second place to his sense of duty. To be sure, there were some compensations. As Gina points out, he wanted very much to get married at that time, and to do so he needed money. Dropping out of school was thus also a way of asserting himself, of becoming independent of his family and carving out his own life. It is also true that a university career remained off-limits for Jews, especially in the fields that particularly interested him.[14] That was indeed the reason he would later give for dropping out of college.[15]

Nevertheless, the documents clearly show that Bettelheim's switch from student to lumber merchant took place only a few months after his father's death. It can be assumed that the influence of his partner, Hans Schnitzer, who had joined the firm seven years earlier at the age of twenty-one, had grown as Anton Bettelheim's condition had deteriorated; he was therefore probably not happy to see Bruno arrive, particularly as the latter was the majority shareholder and five years his junior. Bruno was certainly better educated than his partner, and furthermore had a business school diploma; it is probable that he did not show too much tact as he levered himself into his new job. In any case, there was no love lost between the two men. Right up until his departure from Vienna, Bettelheim consistently complained about his partner, whom he suspected of trying to cheat him.

In the meantime, the relationship with Gina was blossoming; the two had finally become lovers. But the young woman's feelings toward Bruno remained as ambivalent as ever. She got along well with him, and he was both generous and full of good advice whenever she was worried about her future. When she wanted to start psychoanalysis, for example, but did not dare mention it to her mother, he volunteered to pay the fees. A little later he gave her a beautiful leather-bound edition of Freud's complete works. But she would have preferred their relationship to have remained platonic. She enjoyed playing the emancipated young woman—indeed, she was proud to belong to a circle of intellectuals who thumbed their nose at bourgeois conventions—but she just could not find Bruno physically attractive. One of her ways of expressing it was to be forever chiding him for his poor posture. And their sexual relationship was not very satisfying, at least not for her. Both of them were novices.

Although Gina does not make any explicit connection between the couple's sexual problems and her desire to start a psychoanalysis, it is very likely that there was one. For although Freud's theories were beginning to be seen, particularly outside Austria, as a major discovery, at home they were still considered highly controversial and even scandalous, as is shown by Bettelheim's comments on his early reading. For most people, psychoanalysis remained synonymous with sex. Medical students pursuing the discipline, those who would become known as the second generation of analysts, had to run the gauntlet of daily leers and sneers. Foremost among the mockers was Wagner von Jauregg, head of Vienna University's Psychiatry Department, who was nonetheless on good terms with Freud himself.[16]

The group then known as the "young analysts," in which some observers would much later tend to situate Bruno Bettelheim, were markedly different from their pioneering predecessors. They were the first to have chosen psychoanalysis as a career, and the first to undergo real training at the Vienna Psychoanalytic Institute, which had been founded in 1925. Even more important, unlike their predecessors they had personal experience of a real analysis. On the couch, they had spent time exploring the intricacies of their own psyches, reaching beyond the mind games and the promptings of their conscious insights, sometimes against those very insights, to understand their previously inexplicable joys and fears and thus grasp the links that made up the geography of their unconscious. And because that process had not taken place only in their intellects, but through their relationship to their analyst, the experience had changed them deeply, which is why most of them were fired by a passionate desire to go even further, to improve psychoanalytic techniques and to expand the frontiers of their chosen science.

The slim volume that Richard Sterba, soon to be the analyst of Gina and then Bruno, published toward the end of his life is revealing of that generation's state of mind: "The tireless enthusiasm with which we devoted ourselves to the 'cause,' our shared pride at playing a role in propagating Freud's theories and discoveries, all gave us the exhilarating feeling that we were directly participating in Freud's monumental work. Even if we had only indirect contacts with him personally, we were close to his creative genius and his powerful mind." Of the 1924 International Psychoanalytical Congress in Salzburg he wrote: "The atmosphere of the congress made me feel I was witness to and participant in a cause that would be of tremendous consequences for the whole of mankind once it was generally recognized and became influential in all fields of human studies."[17]

Gina's first inquiry about treatment was to Grete Lehner Bibring, one of the first analysts to work at the Vienna psychoanalytic ambulatorium (or day clinic) run by Eduard Hitschmann. Bibring agreed to take the young woman on as a patient, but only if she broke off her relationship with Bettelheim for at least the time it took to see where the process would lead. In spite of her mixed feelings about her lover, Gina refused. It was then that she turned to Richard Sterba. Slightly older than Bettelheim, he was a medical doctor by training, and after his analysis with Hitschmann, he too had been awarded one of the clinic's first three salaried consultancy posts. Although he was close to Wilhelm Reich and shared some of his Socialist ideals, he was not involved in politics. As Gina remembers him, he had an engaging, charming personality and was all the more attractive to her in that he was also a good musician. She thus began visiting him on the Mariahilferstrasse five times a week, hoping to uncover the hidden wellsprings of her psyche.

Gina did not really know what to do with her life. She had stopped studying the piano, as she was convinced she would never be good enough to make a career of it. For a while she had taken dance classes with a student of Isadora Duncan's. She enjoyed that a great deal, as it went well beyond the basics of ballet; one summer the educator August Aichhorn came to lecture the dancers on psychoanalysis. But she finally dropped her dance classes too, once again convinced that others were much more gifted. Around the time she started her analysis, she decided to take a course in Montessori teaching methods. Among its many reforms, the Vienna city council was then promoting a wide variety of educational experiments. One of these was the much-talked-about Haus der Kinder (children's house), which had just opened on Rudolfplaz square. It had been designed and built in accordance with the principles of the Italian pediatrician and educator Maria Montessori, by then world famous. Her revolutionary teaching method relied not on getting the child to use his memory to imitate adults, as others did, but instead focused primarily on his feelings and his appetite for learning, leaving him to make discoveries for himself. Everything in the school was built to the scale of the children; the rigid classroom structure of blackboards, wooden benches, and desks had been replaced by a flexible, child-centered approach. Montessori teachers let their students express their creativity, make choices, and move around freely. They took games seriously, always making the child's way of approaching the world the starting point for their teaching.

Although Maria Montessori had not been directly influenced by psychoanalysis, her methods could not fail to interest Freud and his students. If, as many of them hoped, the unraveling of the secrets of the unconscious was to lead to the creation of a new type of human being, capable of changing the world more effectively than a whole army of Bolsheviks, then it was clear that education would have to be a top priority. Another reason for psychoanalysts to take an interest in the Montessori method was the light it shed on the development of children's minds. Although Freud himself was not much involved in that area of study, it attracted many of his younger students. The teacher-training seminars held at the Haus der Kinder drew a large audience and a wide variety of lecturers, including Anna Freud, who taught there once a week.[18]

If Bettelheim realized that Gina was less than wholehearted in her feelings for him, he succeeded in concealing the pain it caused him. More in love than ever, and eager to finally be his own man, he was determined to get married. He pressed her, and she continually found new excuses. The more she said no, the more insistent he became. She fell ill. So he visited with her daily, laden with flowers and gifts. Finally, she said yes.

Leopold Altstadt, who had for several years been working as an agent for his uncle's shoe business in New York, visited Vienna for a few weeks around the time of their engagement. Gina adored her brother, the one man in her life who had never failed her. He embodied everything that was important to her: music, beauty, and intelligence. During our interviews, the memories of that visit come back only with difficulty. She remembers one evening at her mother's house, looking up and seeing reflected in a mirror the elegant silhouette of her brother, talking to her fiancé. The contrast was devastating; how could she possibly spend her life with a man who was so gauche, so lacking in nature's graces? When Leopold was due to return to New York, Gina resolved to go with him. She too would find a life for herself in the New World, under the wing of her beloved brother.

Her dream was to fall apart in Paris. Gina has difficulty remembering the details; she starts out by citing Leopold's sudden death, getting her dates mixed up. Then, confronted with the contradictions in her first version, she slowly begins to get the story straight. She remembers sitting at a sidewalk café in Paris with a friend of Leopold's, an older man, who told her something about her brother—she can't recall what—that made her decide to return to Vienna and Bruno. Had the man told her her brother was a homosexual? No, says Gina. At least not in so many words. But the basic message was clear: After Dolf and her father, Leopold too was now abandoning her; he could not take care of his kid sister in New York. The only man she could count on to be faithful and reliable in spite of all his defects, was Bruno Bettelheim. Two years later Leopold Altstadt was to commit suicide in a New York hotel room. According to the *New York Times*, he had suffered from depression and had taken an overdose of morphine. Gina does not remember that. In the meantime, on March 30, 1930, she had become Mrs. Bruno Bettelheim. At the registrar's office, Hans and Wanda Willig, the two witnesses, had to lend their rings to the couple, as theirs were not yet ready.

Far from smoothing out the differences between Bruno and Gina, marriage increased them. In Taormina, Sicily, where they ended their long honeymoon, Gina fell ill again. They seemed to have different views on everything. She was attracted to mountains, he only liked the sea. She wanted to walk, climb, scramble up the rocks to discover

Mount Etna, he preferred to spend his time reading, or on occasion going swimming. And when they finally managed to agree on visiting the medieval castle or the Greek amphitheater together, she could not help teasing him about his need to plan his every move, and to take along his Baedeker guide wherever they went. She loved improvising, and trusted her own intuition.

In his essay about his favorite books, Bettelheim implicitly gave his own version of the same events: "At the end of my first year at the university, I traveled to Italy, motivated largely by my reading of Burckhardt's writings. His *Der Cicerone* was my vademecum; it is no exaggeration to say that for more than a decade it became my bible. I tried to make every year at least one and sometimes two prolonged trips to Italy, the *Cicerone* at all times in my hand."[19] It indeed appears that the two newlyweds had not gone to Sicily looking for the same things.

Other aspects of Bettelheim's personality began to grate on Gina once they started living together. Very demanding in all things intellectual, she was upset by what she saw as his casual attitude toward books. Earlier she had been impressed by his learning; now that she knew him better she realized that in many cases he only had to read the first and last fifteen pages or so of a book, plus a few pages in the middle, to talk about it as though he had read the whole thing. Rather than perceiving this as a useful gift, she saw it as intellectual dishonesty. Even the qualities they had in common, such as their intuition, could be a source of discord. One day Gina made a comment to Bruno about D. H. Lawrence's *Sons and Lovers*, which she had been reading with great pleasure. "You should write a book," he replied. Far from flattering her, the comment irritated her. "What arrogance," she thought, "to think that one can write a book simply because one has a good grasp of the characters in a novel!"

After their marriage, Gina and Bruno moved into a truly beautiful apartment. All their friends have retained vivid memories of its opulence and style. It was Gina who had found it on her return from Paris, on Glorietgasse, a pretty, tree-lined street in the 13th district's Hietzing neighborhood. Quiet and full of greenery, the area had been open country only half a century before, and it attracted the type of people who prided themselves on their good taste. Only a hundred yards or so from the Bettelheims' building were the ramparts of Schönbrunn Castle, the Hapsburg family's former summer residence, with its French-style formal gardens now open to the public. The cypress-lined alleyways were ideal for contemplative walks or long philosophical discussions. The gardens also contained a small zoo and a rococo but lovely little theater, where the Vienna Chamber Opera gave summer performances.

The inside of the Bettelheims' apartment was almost as grand as the neighborhood outside, albeit in more modern style. On Gina's prompting, Bruno had had its rooms completely remodeled during their six-week honeymoon. Out had gone all the wainscoting, friezes, and woodwork—everything that gave the place an old-fashioned, nineteenth-century bourgeois look. In had come oriental carpets and simple but elegant furniture, which Bettelheim had had designed and installed during their honeymoon. The fixtures included a gigantic set of bookshelves, of which he was especially proud. The two art lovers adorned the walls with a number of contemporary works, in particular lithographs by Käthe Kollwitz and Egon Schiele (who was a former Hietzing resident). Later they were also to acquire a painting by Schiele. Huge mirrors reflected the light throughout the large rooms from the garden outside. Whatever their political ideas, Gina and Bruno enjoyed the refined, upper-middle-class amenities of the period; they lived well. Indeed, Bettelheim was the first person in his circle to own a car, a gray Steyr Baby 50 convertible.[20] It was his pride and joy: cars at that time were still extremely rare, and thus a major status symbol. Although Bettelheim certainly still dreamed of academic glory and the life of the mind, he was clearly also more than happy with the things money could buy. And he knew how to use his wealth, showing both taste and generosity. Money was no object whenever he wanted to please his loved ones—or to impress the outside world.

The thing Gina Bettelheim disliked most about her husband, in fact, was his taste for ostentation. And she was not the only one to feel that way, as is shown by the following (no doubt apocryphal) anecdote. In a lighthearted little book of Viennese recollections written much later, on his return from exile in the United States, the Austrian writer Friedrich Torberg tells of a tea party that took place in the 1930s at which the essayist Egon Friedell was conversing with a certain "Dr. B, a soul doctor who was destined for great fame," on the subject of sexual symbols in everyday life. Dr. B pointed to a basket filled with small round Viennese buns, with their characteristic furrow across the middle, and declared with authority that they were female sexual symbols. To which Friedell shot back: "To he who is pure, everything is pure. To me, they look like babies' bottoms!"[21]

Torberg's description suggests that if he ever met Bettelheim it was not in Vienna but much later, and that the only authentic part of his story is the feelings it expresses on his part about "Dr. B." The latter is described as someone who, "having recently achieved analytical notoriety, was anxious to seize any opportunity to show off his knowledge." Throughout his life, Bruno Bettelheim indeed managed to exasperate certain people by his too-obvious desire to make an impression. Others, more aware of the fragility underlying this attitude, were able to get beyond the surface level to the real man, often using humor as the key. For many people, however, and notably for Gina, the effort required was just too great.

Bettelheim's own references to his first marriage are few and far between. In *Freud's Vienna and Other Essays*, he refers in passing to a "crisis in my married life" which finally pushed him to go into psychoanalysis. Elsewhere, he refers to a "bad marriage." People who knew them together usually remember them as a pleasant but not very easygoing couple. The impossibly high standards Gina set for herself became even more impossible when applied to Bruno. One witness notes that Bruno went to a great deal of trouble to please her, with the apartment, furniture, pictures, and so on, but nothing ever seemed to be good enough. It was as though he was not sufficiently handsome or noble to pass muster. And even if she never told him of them in so many words, he was clearly aware of his perceived shortcomings.

But an unhappy marriage is always two-sided, as Bettelheim himself was to point out in a letter to an old friend, written some fifteen years after his divorce: "My relationship with Gina, as you know, was very difficult, and we were both really to blame for that."[22] Although Bruno was starved of the admiring, positive feelings that would have brought out the best in him, he was also very demanding of his wife, while refusing to give her what she wanted most of all: a child. That issue was the cause of the only real quarrel between the two that Wanda Willig recalls witnessing. One day when the friends were traveling together, Wanda emerged from her room to enjoy the morning air and found Gina and Bruno in the middle of a blazing fight. Later, Gina told her about it. The argument put forward by Bruno for his refusal was rather strange: "You'll leave me if we have a child." Naturally Gina denied that this was the case, but she had already sufficiently lost interest in her husband to wonder about his real motives. On that question, it is again worth looking at what Bettelheim wrote about the Polish educator Janusz Korczak: "As far as we know, he never specifically said why he did not want to marry or have children, but it seems probable that he was afraid he might have inherited his father's tendency to insanity and feared to pass it on, or have a child suffer from such predicaments as he had experienced because of his father's mental instability."[23] The truth is that up until the 1940s, Bettelheim lived with the constant fear that he had inherited his father's illness. As Edith Buxbaum's memoirs confirmed: "Bruno told me he was afraid to be syphilis infected, not knowing whether he was conceived before or after the infection. What a punishment for forbidden wishes."

In the light of many years of hindsight, Bruno Bettelheim's first marriage thus appears to have been a mistake. He and Gina were clearly ill-suited to live together, with each partner's anxieties eliciting the behavior most likely to exacerbate the other's. Bettelheim later wrote, "I can hardly understand now why we were once so important for each other and even less why we made things so difficult for one another." It would nevertheless be going too far to call the marriage a total fiasco. Practically all I know about their relationship comes from Gina Weinmann, and she still shows herself to be a very demanding lady, who will not make do with second-best. But when, in speaking of Vienna, she chances on memories unrelated to her domestic woes, she on occasion shows that she shared many intellectual pleasures, and even friendship, with her first husband. And when this is pointed out to her, she ends up admitting, almost coyly, "It's true that we got on well together, that we had a lot of things in common, and that we had a good life in Vienna." With a charming smile she adds: "Sure. If it hadn't been for Hitler we would not have divorced."

Bruno Bettelheim later wondered exactly what role psychoanalysis had played in the breakup of his first marriage.[24] This is indeed a good question, although one that cannot be answered. When Grete Bibring asked Gina to suspend her relationship with Bruno during the time it would take to see where her analysis was headed, she was simply applying the golden rule laid down by Freud himself: There should be no major upheavals, no great commitments, in a patient's life during an analysis. Whatever happened on the analyst's couch, the experience had to remain a symbolic one, with no direct repercussions in real life. But there is often a large gap between theory and practice, a gap into which human emotions all too easily stream, especially when the powerful mechanisms of transference come into play, and before the patient has been able to identify them.

Whatever may have been the case, when Gina had returned from Paris to marry Bruno she had carried on as if nothing at all happened, with one difference: She had changed psychoanalysts.

4

❊

Patsy

Bruno Bettelheim was aware of the changes his wife was going through, but from a distance. It is a period about which he did not write, and from which few documents survive. Those that do indicate that he managed his business well. Under his direction the Bettelheim & Schnitzer company branched out, adding furniture-making to its lumber activities. Even though a business career had not been what Bettelheim had wanted, he clearly had a gift for running a company. Some members of the family may well have commented that he took after his grandfather Seidler, a comparison which would certainly not have been to his liking. Nevertheless he enjoyed bringing home comfortable amounts of money and used it to good effect, leading an active social life and often playing host in the couple's elegant apartment.

Bruno kept up with his two closest friends, Hans Willig and Walter Neurath, but with the exception of his mother he did not see much of his family any more. In particular, he lost touch with his cousin Edith Buxbaum. She did not much like Gina, and though she did not admit it to herself until later, she was jealous of her for having taken Bruno away.[1] He was also seeing much less of his friends from the Jung Wandervogel, both the politically committed ones and the students of psychoanalysis. His forced transformation into a businessman had not killed off all the idealistic impulses of his youth, and he continued to read a lot, but it had confirmed his basic pessimism as to the prospects of humanity's changing for the better.

Events in the wider world served only to confirm his pessimistic views. After an easier period in the mid-1920s, tensions were building in Austria under the Social Christian government, which was losing its grip. In 1927 the national guard had opened fire on a workers' protest held in the most famous of the housing complexes built in the days of "Red Vienna," setting off an unprecedented wave of rioting. Two years later, in the aftermath of the Wall Street crash, things got even worse. Although many Viennese continued to sympathize with the left, in the country as a whole more and more voices were clamoring for a strong leader who could turn back the clock to the stable days of the Hapsburg dynasty.

Farseeing though he may have been, Bettelheim was not endowed with powers of prophecy. Not even the election to the chancellorship in 1932 of Engelbert Dollfuss, who responded to the prevailing mood by setting up a clerical dictatorship, could give him an inkling of what was in store just a few years ahead. On occasion, he did toy with the idea of emigrating, particularly when he and Gina went to visit her uncle Moritz at his beautiful villa in their neighborhood on weekends. Then Bettelheim would talk of starting a new life in the United States, but as it became clear that Uncle Moritz had no intention of providing the required funds, nothing came of it. Bettelheim's private relationship with his wife, meanwhile, showed no signs of improving. They slept in separate bedrooms but they never had open fights, and had enough interests and tastes in common for their differences to remain hidden from the outside world.

One thing, at least, must have pleased Bruno: his wife's decision to change psychoanalysts, switching from Richard Sterba to his wife.[2] Editha Sterba, née von Radanowicz-Harttmann, was three years older than her husband. Gina thought her "a little masculine," but at the same time found her strong personality reassuring. Editha's father and grandfather were high-ranking military officers and she had traveled a lot during her childhood, but nevertheless got a solid education. At college, she studied musicology and psychology, and worked for a time as secretary to Otto Rank, then Freud's favorite student, later to be rejected by him. Editha Sterba began her own training in 1925; she was thirty-seven when Gina Bettelheim became her patient. With her, Gina played fewer games than with her husband, worked harder, and made more visible progress.

Gina Bettelheim continued to frequent the Montessori school after her training there was over, working for a time as an unpaid teacher and attending Anna Freud's seminars regularly. Thanks in part to what she was learning about child development, Gina was becoming more and more drawn to psychoanalysis. She loved her work, and was excited by the possibilities it was opening up for her. She also attended seminars at the Psychoanalytic Institute, where she met Fritz Redl, a young high school teacher who was equally fascinated by Freud's discovery, and who had also been a patient of Richard Sterba's. Redl was a flirt, and showed great interest in Gina. She found him charming, enjoying his intellectual company as well as his jolly disposition.

One day Annie Hatchek, a friend and fellow-teacher from one of the city's progressive training schools, suggested that she and Gina pool their experience to set up their own kindergarten. Vienna was then full of foreigners, many of them Americans who had come over to start a psychoanalysis, either for personal reasons or in order to learn the new discipline. A lot of them had brought their children, and there was thus a demand for educational facilities. Dorothy Burlingham, an American friend and supporter of Anna Freud, had just set up a primary school for such children, with the young psychoanalyst Peter Blos. Annie Hatchek's idea was to have the new kindergarten take in both the visiting American infants and Austrian children from poor backgrounds, with the former subsidizing the latter. It was to be a small institution, designed and run along Montessori lines. The aim was not only to stimulate the children's imagination and creativity, but also to promote social integration. Gina was enthusiastic about the project. Inspired by what psychoanalysts were discovering about children, she suggested also taking in a few disturbed children.

When asked to provide funds for the new venture, Bettelheim readily agreed. He was curious about the circles his wife was now moving in. In particular, he quickly became friends with Fritz Redl. Although the two men came from very different backgrounds, they had shared interests, and personalities that were complementary in many ways. Redl came from a Catholic family. His childhood had been even more tragic than Bettelheim's. At the age of five, he had seen his mother burn to death in a fire that also destroyed the family home. But he was no depressive; on the contrary, he was a great socializer, the life of the many parties he went to. He was a year older than Bettelheim and like him had studied philosophy. He had been a brilliant student, obtaining his PhD at the age of twenty-three on "The Epistemological Foundations of Kantian Ethics." Hans Vaihinger, the same philosopher whose writings had helped the young Bettelheim get out of his depression, had been so impressed by Redl that he had invited him to spend a vacation with him in Germany.

After his doctorate, Redl earned a secondary-school teaching degree and started work as a literature and philosophy teacher at the *Realgymnasium.* He had also written a few textbooks, including one on psychology. Redl later explained that he had been drawn to the study of the mind by observing the behavior of his students. He had undertaken a psychoanalysis at the same time he was attending the university courses of Professor Karl Bühler, who along with his wife Charlotte ran the Psychology Institute at Vienna University and was at the time considered the supreme authority on the subject. But Fritz Redl was interested in much more than pure theory. He had immediately applied his newfound knowledge to his students, and had gradually moved from simply observing them to proffering advice, devoting more and more time to adolescents with problems. This work had started to win him a reputation, and he was being consulted as an expert by several schools.

One summer, probably in 1932, Fritz Redl suggested to Gina Bettelheim and Annie Hatchek that the three of them jointly organize a summer camp for a group of difficult and deprived children. The two women liked the idea, but none of them had either funds or a place to take their charges. Once again, Bruno was asked to help, and once again he came up with a solution. Through business contacts, he obtained permission for the three to camp with the children in the disused imperial castle of Shalaburg. The place was falling apart, and they spent the month surrounded by piles of crumbling masonry, but it was nevertheless a magnificent setting. The experiment was a total success, as the abilities of the three adults complemented one another perfectly. Gina was very impressed by Redl's ability to handle group activities, while she got her best results in one-to-one relations with the children. While they were away, Bruno got his driver's license, and was thus able to surprise them one weekend by visiting in his flashy new convertible.

Gina was becoming thoroughly absorbed in her new pursuits when one day, probably in the fall of that same year (1932),[3] Editha Sterba told her about a little American patient for whom she was trying to find a school. Patsy was seven years old, but she behaved like a child two or three years younger. She was very introverted, and hardly spoke. Her mother, Agnes, came from the Piel family of Connecticut, second-generation German immigrants who had become a force in the brewing industry. Being very concerned about Patsy's development, Agnes had consulted a host of American specialists in vain, before bringing the child to Vienna, attracted by what she had heard about the Freuds, both father and daughter. But Anna Freud had found Patsy either too disturbed or too old for the preschool she was in the process of setting up, and she had referred her to Editha Sterba, who at the time was running the Psychoanalytic Society's clinic for children.

Gina immediately accepted Editha's suggestion that she admit Patsy to her school as a boarder. Some six decades later, she still has a vivid memory of her first meeting with the frail little girl, whose terrified eyes peered out from under brown hair cut short in a pageboy style. As the child sat twisting her fingers apparently without realizing it and wearing an absent look on her face, Gina felt deeply touched. Her mother, meanwhile, was explaining Patsy's symptoms, quoting the specialists she had consulted. But Gina was much more interested in the child than in the label. She gave Patsy some crayons and she drew animal pictures, in which Gina detected a clear artistic disposition. Then she held out her arms, and after a few moments' hesitation, Patsy let herself be hugged. Gina's instincts told her that a bath would reassure the child. Patsy did not resist, and Gina sat nearby, talking gently to her as she bathed.

Patsy was a very quiet child, probably too quiet. But apart from occasional jerky movements, and the absent expression she frequently wore, she showed few outward symptoms of being "disturbed." Gina decided to seek the opinion of August Aichhorn, whose skill with disturbed children was admired by all at the Psychoanalytic Institute. Aichhorn, then fifty-four, had trained as a schoolteacher, but his understanding of delinquents and other difficult children was such that the city authorities had put him in charge of two correctional facilities for minors. The results he achieved so impressed Anna Freud that she invited him to the Institute to discover psychoanalysis. It was ten years after that, when Aichhorn had just been put in charge of the Psychoanalytic Society's guidance clinic for adolescents, that Gina came to him for advice about Patsy. "When you cannot decide whether a child is disturbed or not, just turn to other children for an opinion," he told her. "They will know for sure." The test, applied to Patsy, was conclusive: Her peers treated her as someone apart. She kept to herself, and they quickly gave up trying to reach out to her.

Patsy's first week at the school went reasonably well. Over the weekend, however, she was clearly miserable at being left alone with so many other children she didn't know, in a totally foreign environment. Arriving at the school on Monday morning, Gina found the little girl in a state of complete distress. "We didn't have much money, and living conditions at the school were very primitive compared to what Patsy had been used to," she explains.

For that reason, or perhaps simply because she was becoming involved with the little American girl, Gina suggested to Agnes Piel that she let Patsy spend the following weekend at the Bettelheims' home. After a few such visits, it also became clear that the child hated spending even weeknights at the school, and soon she was living full time at no. 15 Glorietgasse. This was a great relief to Agnes Piel, who after several months in Vienna was becoming impatient to return to her home and friends in Greenwich Village.

Thus, not long after her attempt to leave for a completely new life, Gina had gotten herself the child her husband was refusing to give her. She became totally devoted to Patsy, caring for and playing with her as if she were her own daughter.[4] Everyone around her was amazed at the patience she displayed with the little girl. Gina, who could often be irritable and make provocative or biting comments, softened as if by magic whenever she was with her. This is not to say that Gina was indulgent. She insisted that the girl be obedient, that she behave well in public, and, like most Viennese mothers at that time, Gina would give her a slap on occasion. But her affection for Patsy was obvious to all. She spent countless hours trying to get through to the girl, to figure out what was terrorizing her.

After a year or so at the kindergarten, Patsy started attending classes at the Montessori primary school on Grünetorgasse, in the 9th district. A few months later, Gina even let her go alone on the bus. But it was a long ride, and fearing that the little girl, lost in her inner world, might miss her stop, Gina would for several weeks sit discreetly at the back, unbeknown to her charge, who never once noticed her presence. Over the years, Patsy learned to read and write, and to relate a little with other people.

Patsy herself has good memories of her stay in Vienna—with one big reservation: "I wanted to be with my mother. I never understood why she couldn't keep me with her," she says. It is a complaint that was to be echoed almost word-for-word by some of the children who, twenty or thirty years later, would attend the Orthogenic School in Chicago, and to hear that protest expressed so spontaneously about an experience sixty years in the past is troubling indeed.[5] It is difficult not to take it as a reflection on the concept of milieu therapy that Bruno Bettelheim was later to develop, even if one allows that it may simply reflect the difficulty a vulnerable child could have in admitting she had found happiness with someone other than her mother.

For Agnes Piel was not unlike many of the mothers who in the 1950s and '60s would bring their children to Bruno Bettelheim. Raised as the only girl among seven children, she was demanding and ambitious, dreaming of becoming a successful writer but managing only to publish a handful of articles, which failed to satisfy her desire for intellectual fame. Agnes was not the only eccentric in her family, but she was probably the one who best managed to live out her fantasies in her private life. She was restless, intellectual, emancipated, and sexually free, given to smoking, drinking, and partying. At that time, in the early 1930s, she was between her first and second marriages, and had come to view Patsy's erratic behavior, her refusal to utter more than a few sentences, as living proof of her own failings, perhaps even of her evil influence. Like many parents, Agnes Piel was prepared to do almost anything to assuage the feelings of guilt that her child's unorthodox behavior stirred in her. It is worth noting that Agnes's articles were usually on the subject of education.

In handing over her daughter to Gina, who was not only a schoolteacher versed in psychoanalysis but also an intelligent, sensitive, and elegant lady, Agnes must have felt a huge sense of relief. And the presence of Bruno at Gina's side must also have been reassuring, not only because it meant that Patsy would be living in material comfort, but also, and perhaps more important, that she would be growing up in a "normal" family, with a strong father figure. Agnes was probably not aware of the conflict between Bruno and Gina over having a child, and it is easy to imagine how the American woman, who had an eccentric love life, could have felt reassured by Bruno Bettelheim's obvious sense of responsibility.

It is also likely that Bruno Bettelheim was happy to turn on his intellectual charm for the unusual American woman who had showed up in his life, out of the blue. Agnes Piel, so different from any of the women he had known until then, probably inspired in him a measure of fascination. Her wealth and her authoritarian manner, contrasted with the obvious distress she was experiencing as a result of Patsy's problems, must have both confirmed and molded the image he had of America, the distant land to which he and so many of his friends dreamed of emigrating, and to which he had so nearly lost Gina. Such an opportunity to obtain insights into the United States and its people can only have aroused his interest.

What indeed was his idea of America at that time? He knew, of course, that it was rich and powerful, as it had saved many Viennese from dying of hunger during World War I and had finally tipped the balance of the conflict through its intervention. Other images had come from the first movie serials, such as the smash hit *The Perils of Pauline*, and the popular writings of German novelist Karl May, who dreamed up his Westerns long before he had even set foot in America, all of which must have added up to the cliché America of wide-open spaces, cowboys, and self-made men, a country that was rich and generous, but also brutal and uncouth. His grandfather Adolf Seidler must have told him about the fabulous fortune amassed by the sewing machine tycoon, Isaac Merritt Singer, of Austrian Jewish origin, and Bettelheim surely knew about the rags-to-riches stories of other European émigrés, such as Agnes Piel's grandfather, Godfried, who had left a small German village in 1883 and rapidly become one of the richest brewers in the United States.

But Agnes showed the Bettelheims another facet of American life: Greenwich Village chic, with its intellectual and artistic sophistication. Their fascination was, however, tempered by the customary condescension of educated Europeans toward Americans, whose naive aspirations to nobility and a sense of history were more often than not a source of mirth. Gina still remembers how much she and Bruno laughed at the Anglo-French film *The Ghost Goes West* (1936), which satirizes an American millionaire seeking to transport an entire castle, complete with its resident phantom, from Scotland to the United States.

During part of her sojourn in Vienna, Agnes Piel stayed at the Bettelheim apartment, Gina sleeping on the sofa and giving her her room. But Agnes too had started an analysis with Richard Sterba, and she socialized a lot, leaving the care of Patsy entirely in Gina's hands. When she was at the apartment she would talk to her hosts and their friends rather than attend to her daughter. These conversations took place in German, even though Bruno spoke a little English. Agnes liked Gina a great deal, and appeared impressed by the couple's standard of living. She would often complain about how difficult it was back home to find good servants, like the Bettelheims' Hedwig, who would still be up to serve them dinner when they returned from an evening at the theater. None of this deterred Agnes from returning to New York after a few months, however, once she felt confident that her daughter was being well cared for.

In June 1936, Gina took Patsy to the United States to visit her mother. For the first month of the stay, Agnes packed the two off to a summer camp run by one of her friends in Wellfleet, Cape Cod. Gina was given the status of camp counselor, but she took care only of Patsy. The young Viennese woman was avid to learn all about this strange new country. She remembers only one occasion on which she balked at the local customs. One Sunday, for reasons she cannot recall, her hosts wanted her to dress up in a strange green outfit with puffy pants and a sailor's collar to go to church. "Going to church in itself is not easy for me," she told them. "Don't ask me to also don a disguise!"

After the month at the camp, Gina and Patsy stayed in Connecticut with Agnes, who proved herself a marvelous hostess. Gina was enchanted by the New England landscape; she was reading Henry James's *What Maisie Knew*. But she also greatly appreciated a very different type of outing, with Agnes's younger brother Paul, a painter and the other eccentric of the family. He showed her the poor neighborhoods of Harlem and the Bronx, saying "You must get acquainted with all sides of America." The initiative infuriated Agnes, who was already making plans to have the Bettelheims come and settle in the United States. She spoke of buying a large house where they could all live together; Bruno would carry on his business affairs while Gina looked after Patsy. Gina was not interested, but her hostess persisted. "Be realistic," Agnes told her. "Look what's happening in Germany. How long do you think it will be before Hitler gets his hands on Austria?"

Gina stood firm, however, being unable to imagine ever living anywhere but Vienna, except maybe at a pinch in Paris. In October, therefore, she and Patsy took the boat back to Europe. On returning to Vienna, she felt that Bruno had changed, although she was unable to figure out exactly how. He seemed calmer, more at peace with himself.

One obvious change was that he had decided to re-enroll at the university, and had therefore handed over the day-to-day running of the company to Hans Schnitzer.

Before seeing what Bruno Bettelheim had been up to during the summer of 1936, let us for a moment examine his relationship with the little American girl who was to play a key role in his future life. For the story he tells differs significantly from the foregoing account, which is based mainly on Gina's recollections but also on those of half a dozen other people, including Patsy herself. What remains to be elucidated is the relationship between Bruno and Patsy during the six years that the two lived under the same roof. Here we are on much more slippery ground, as there are no completely reliable surviving witnesses.

Once he had emigrated to the United States, Bettelheim was gradually to appropriate the story of Patsy, as if the little girl had been put in his care, not his wife's. He was even at one point to paint a picture from which it could be inferred that he, and not Editha Sterba, was the little girl's psychoanalyst. Neither woman was ever to contradict his statements publicly. But while Dr. Sterba's reaction can only be surmised from a discreet footnote in her husband's brief autobiography, Gina was never able to forgive him.[6] She saw his appropriation of her story as not only a lie, but a total denial of herself. And the issue is all the more hurtful in that she never once dared to confront Bettelheim over it in the fifty or so remaining years of his life.

Gina states unequivocally: "Relations between Bruno and Patsy? They were practically nonexistent, like those of any European man with his children in those days. He saw her a little at the dinner table. The rest of the time, he was reading a lot and she didn't bother him. She was very quiet." Gina even denies that Bettelheim showed any particular interest in Patsy's strange behavior at a distance. In that, she is no doubt unfair. For if Bettelheim was able to spin such an elaborate yarn about what would soon be diagnosed as Patsy's autism, he must have at least observed her behavior while she was living in his home. It was a time when he was plagued by self-doubt, and he must have been intrigued by this child who differed from him in almost every way, but who had also deliberately "turned her back on humanity and society," as he himself had tried to do, intermittently, around twelve years earlier. The sight of this little girl who spent whole days lost in her own fantasy world must have reminded him of the hours he himself had spent lying in his darkened room, his mind a blank.

The tapestry Bettelheim wove around the story of Patsy became richer over time, almost as if the very silence of the people who could have torn it to shreds served as an encouragement. The most elaborate version of the story is to be found in his penultimate book, *A Good Enough Parent*, although Bettelheim was to add further touches during interviews after the book's publication.[7] Bettelheim loved telling stories, and was unable to resist the temptation whenever he had an appreciative audience.

Having described Patsy as "virtually mute" on her arrival in Vienna, Bettelheim writes: "It took more than a year during which we carefully respected her wish to be left alone, while still trying to take tender, loving care of her, before she moderated her total isolation and permitted occasional approaches, although she did not respond to these in any discernible way." Finally, Bettelheim writes, Patsy took to just one of the games her surrogate parents tried to engage her in, a variant of peek-a-boo. In the course of describing the game Bettelheim starts out in the first-person plural, but soon switches to the first-person singular. "Eventually she actually hid behind a curtain, even peeked out from behind it, mimicking what I had done innumerable times in my play of finding her." After that incident, Bettelheim writes, the little girl allowed him to cuddle her for the first time, spontaneously and without recoiling. Enchanted, he repeated the game on several subsequent days. It was during one such session, according to Bettelheim, that Patsy uttered the first complete sentence of her life—not only the first, but a sentence in perfect English, even though she was immersed in a German-speaking environment. This sentence, Bettelheim writes, was "Give me the skeleton of George Washington."[8]

Bettelheim is not the only writer to have noted that when autistic children emerge from their silence, it is often by uttering complete sentences, and that since such utterances usually relate to the central reason for their withdrawal from the world, they should be carefully analyzed. Happily, Bettelheim explains, he was able to comprehend the hidden meaning of Patsy's statement. "The tragedy of her life had originated in the fact that her father was completely unknown, not just to her but also to her mother, because of the strangest of circumstances." Although those circumstances are not spelled out in *A Good*

Enough Parent, Bettelheim later explained that Agnes had conceived Patsy with a stranger after a party where she had had too much to drink.[9] To avoid a scandal, her family had rushed her into a marriage, while she tried on several occasions to induce a miscarriage. When Patsy reached the age of five Agnes, racked with guilt at the idea that her daughter's problems must have resulted from her own desire to get rid of her, started looking for a therapist for the child. However, her mother's wish to be rid of her had not escaped the little girl, Bettelheim went on. The interpretation of Patsy's strange statement was thus that "what she needed was a father, and as an American girl with no known father she could think only of the father of her country as a solution to her problem. Since her unknown father was 'the skeleton in the closet' of her life, she asked for his skeleton."[10]

A fascinating story indeed, and one that is full of lessons for both the psychotherapist and the educator. The only problem is that it does not fit in with the recollections of a single other person interviewed. Everyone who knew the Bettelheims in Vienna confirms that Gina alone took care of Patsy. Patsy herself concurs: "All the nurturing and all the discipline were Gina's."[11] Gina goes even further: "When I was taking care of Patsy, Bruno took no interest at all in her psychological development. He didn't ask me any questions, and we hardly talked about it at all. It was my work, and he had his own business to take care of." As for the story about Patsy's purported "first words," it makes her burst out laughing. "I never saw Bruno play with Patsy. And Patsy was never mute. She would never have said anything like that." Indeed, according to other witnesses, when Patsy arrived in Vienna she spoke little, and poorly, but she did speak. In today's terms, her condition would probably not be diagnosed as autism. But it was, as the Piel family confirmed, the term used by Agnes herself, after having taken her daughter to see the most eminent psychiatrists of the age.[12]

As for the source of Patsy's problem, the facts, and the recollections of Agnes's cousins, appear to contradict Bettelheim's version of events. At the time of Patsy's birth, they say, Agnes was living with her first husband and, officially at least, the birth was perfectly legitimate. It is true, however, that Agnes could have confided things to Bettelheim that were not known to anyone else in her circle, and especially not to younger members of her own family. Certain chronological inconsistencies in official records do leave open the possibility that Patsy's paternity was not what it seemed. But if there was a secret, is it conceivable that Agnes would have mentioned it to Bruno and not to Gina, who was most directly concerned by Patsy's welfare?

Bettelheim's relationship with Patsy no doubt was a little more complex than it seemed to Gina. While not involved in the day-to-day care of the little girl, he may have had contacts with her that were all the more significant for being rare, as was indeed the case in many European families of that period. He gave her presents, and occasionally took her on an outing when Gina was busy. It is also established that Bettelheim attended a birthday party held for Patsy at her school. And the familiar way in which Patsy refers to "Bruno" to this day, not to mention the letters she occasionally sent him when he was living in Chicago,[13] imply that he was once very much part of her life.

That having been said, it is true that Patsy's stay in Vienna provided Bettelheim with his first "fine tale," all the easier to tell because, in accordance with Agnes's wishes, neither he nor Gina ever revealed the little girl's true identity.

Gina has no recollection of Patsy's first birthday party at the Montessori school, which probably took place in April 1936. She was no doubt otherwise occupied on that day, and Bruno stood in for her. The Montessori primary school was located on the first floor of a former boys' school on Grünetorgasse, and the premises, owned by the city, were small. There were only two classes, and at that time Patsy was in the senior one, taught by the school's principal, Emma ("Nuci") Plank, a pioneer of the movement. The other class, which also included one of Editha Sterba's severely disturbed young patients,[14] had been taught until the previous year by Emmi Vischer, a young Swiss woman. A trained teacher, Emmi Vischer had come to Vienna to find out more about psychoanalysis and to study the various educational experiments then under way in the city.

Her curiosity had first been aroused by the stories she had heard from Richard Sterba, when he had stayed at her family home in Switzerland. During the terrible Vienna famine, the young medical student had periodically found refuge in the Vischers' welcoming household. Not long after their marriage, Richard had taken Editha to meet his Swiss friends, and invited Emmi Vischer to come to Vienna whenever she wanted. She had done so in 1931, and before long the competent young woman had achieved everything she had set out to do in the city. As soon as she had completed her Montessori training, Nuci Plank put her in charge of the junior class at the school; meanwhile, Vischer had also been deepening her knowledge of psychoanalysis by attending Anna Freud's seminars at the Haus der Kinder and the Psychoanalytic Institute. There she had become acquainted with August Aichhorn, Fritz Redl, and Gina Bettelheim, among others.

Although shy, and by her own account very naive, Emmi Vischer was an attractive young woman. During a conference in Rome, where they had all met Maria Montessori in person and visited her Casa dei Bambini, Fritz Redl proposed to Emmi. But although she liked him, he was not her type, and in any case she had already met the man who was to become her husband: Editha Sterba's brother Hubert ("Bertel") von Radanowicz. In the spring of 1935, Emmi Vischer married him and left for Spain, where he was the Madrid representative of the German electrical company Siemens, handing over her class to Gertrude Weinfeld, the young woman who had been her deputy for the previous two years.

Trude Weinfeld, then age twenty-four, had been sad to see Emmi go. In the two years they had worked together the two women had become fast friends. From her contact with Emmi, Trude had not only gained a lot of insights into her work at the school, but she had also been introduced to psychoanalysis. On Emmi's recommendation, she too had become a patient of Editha Sterba's. The experience had spelled the end of her first love affair, since her boyfriend could not stand the idea of her discussing their relationship with a stranger. Trude, meanwhile, had gradually realized that she could not go on loving someone who did not see the point of exploring his own unconscious. For Trude, who had up until then suffered greatly from shyness, psychoanalysis had indeed been a revelation. But she had never told her family about it, knowing they would not have understood.

Trude's father was an accountant, and although the family had experienced financial problems during World War I and the Depression, she had had a relatively comfortable childhood in Vienna's 18th district. Her parents, who were liberal assimilated Jews, got along well. Even though her mother manifested a preference for Trude's younger brother, born during the war while the father was a prisoner in Siberia, Trude had not suffered too much from it, as she was otherwise well cared for. For example, when the generally well-behaved Trude was publicly humiliated and unjustly made to stand in the corner at her primary school for talking out of turn, her mother immediately found another school for her. Above all, Trude had a wonderful relationship with her father. He was always kindly and attentive, and she could not bear to disappoint him. She was generally successful in her studies, but her ambitions were more in the social than the purely intellectual field. After obtaining her *Matura*, she had attended a few classes at the university but then decided it was not the place for her. Inspired by her readings of Schiller and Goethe, she enrolled instead in the social work training school founded by Julius Tandler, the great reformer of Vienna's social services.

Trude had discovered the Montessori school during fieldwork for her studies. She was so fascinated that she decided to sign up for courses at the Haus der Kinder at the same time as she was completing her social work training. This turned out to have been a good move, since upon graduating in 1933 she was to realize how difficult it had become for a Jew to find work in Dollfuss's Austria. Thanks to the Montessori training, she was able to get a job at the Grünetorgasse school.

Exactly how Bruno Bettelheim and Trude Weinfeld met at Patsy's birthday party we shall never know. Maybe it was in the course of a conversation about Emmi, whom Bruno had met a few times with Gina and Fritz Redl. Much later, he would confess that he had been attracted to the young Swiss woman, without ever daring to tell her. Or perhaps they were introduced by Bruno's old girlfriend, Lilly Krugh, who also worked at the school. Whatever the case, Bettelheim drove Trude home that evening, and from then on he started going out with her occasionally, when Gina was otherwise engaged. On one such occasion, he invited Trude to go with him and Patsy to the Prater amusement park. During that outing, for the first time, Trude felt a real friendship being born, as she was to state not long before her death, in a brief account of her youth that she recorded on tape at her children's request.

What Bettelheim may have thought of the young woman, so very different from his wife, is difficult to surmise. It is certain, however, that he never for one moment envisaged that she could become his new life-companion. Divorce was simply not an option. Nevertheless, he was not happy. He was later to use an expression coined by Erik Erikson, "psycho-social moratorium," to describe this period of his life.[15] Of course, he led a comfortable existence but material advantages only served to underline how much in his life was unsatisfying and meretricious. What was the use of having a desirable wife if she did not desire you, or of having lots of money if you had had to sacrifice all your youthful ambitions to obtain it? The depth of Bettelheim's malaise can be gauged from the fact that he had slowly drifted away from most of his friends, particularly those who had continued to pursue their ideals, be it through psychoanalysis or politics.

The one exception was Hans Willig, who had also turned his passion—in his case, music—into a hobby in order to devote himself to the all-too-real world of business. He was practically the only old friend Bettelheim still had at the time he met Trude. And in 1935, Willig had left town, to move to Prague. All the intellectuals Bettelheim now mixed with were those introduced to him by his wife. Meanwhile, even though the couple never talked about it, the arrival of Patsy in the household had also modified somewhat the balance of power between them. From that point on, Gina was able to make a financial contribution, which boosted her self-confidence. Her nursery school had closed down after a few years, but she then started seeing patients at home, notably a deeply depressed Chinese woman with whom she spent several hours each afternoon. And then, having remained faithful to Bruno during the first years of their marriage, Gina started feeling more and more restless and flirtatious.

Trude Weinfeld was the opposite of Gina. She was tall, brown-haired, and sturdy, and concealed considerable shyness beneath a sporty, outgoing exterior. Although attractive, she was in no way coquettish; although intelligent, she had no great intellectual pretensions. She liked being able to help people, but her generosity often manifested itself as practical good sense and efficiency. And though her dynamic exterior could sometimes give way to an almost reserved mien, she had an iron will, and a certain type of self-assurance. People who knew her often refer to her upright posture, and some even admit to having been slightly intimidated by her.

What Bettelheim found first in Trude, I think, was a friend, with whom relations were reassuringly straightforward. She felt no rivalry with him, but simply listened to his thoughts and concerns. Thanks to her, psychoanalysis and the education of children were suddenly no longer Gina's private property, but fascinating subjects of conversation on which he too could make a contribution. Not only did Trude listen, she expressed admiration for what he had to say. Where Gina's critical and impatient ear detected only bluster and secondhand ideas, Trude saw new concepts being born. And because she was intelligent, she made him feel that his ideas were credible, thereby encouraging him to actually make them so. Indeed, it was she, during the summer Gina spent with Patsy in the United States, who persuaded Bruno to return to his studies and get his PhD.

Their relationship deepened gradually. After a few outings to concerts and the theater, they got into the habit of going swimming together. One day, Bruno took her out into the woods and let her drive his car, a memorable experience for a young woman who did not know anyone else who owned one. Little by little they grew very close. After Gina had returned from the United States, Trude would rush out from from work whenever she could to call him at his office. She felt guilty carrying on a relationship with a married man, but at the same time this made the affair even more exciting.

It was after a Shrove Tuesday ball that Trude realized just how much Bruno meant to her. She and Gina had dressed up as young maidens with long braids, and had helped each other with their makeup. During the evening, a dentist by the name of Peter Weinmann had shown great interest in Trude, who had a wonderful time. As it was too late for Trude to get back to her home on the other side of town, Gina offered to put her up in a spare room. There, she lay awake all night, unable to sleep from being so close to the man she loved.

Psychoanalysis, while having had a disastrous effect on Trude's first love affair, had freed her of a lot of sexual inhibitions. As she was to tell her children, self-mockingly, it was Editha Sterba who showed her the first pictures of naked bodies she had ever seen ("And I was over twenty-five!" she added). She was not, however, a virgin: Trude was very much in tune with the times, convinced of the need to break with Victorian traditions, and her relationship with her first boyfriend had been going on since their schooldays. But it was only around the time she met Bruno that she began to really understand and acknowledge her desires as an adult woman. I do not know at what point her relationship with Bruno Bettelheim ceased being a platonic one. However, if only because of the fear of syphilis that still haunted him, I suspect that it would have been she who made the decisive move.

The fact that the outwardly reserved Trude already had some sexual experience was probably reassuring for Bruno. On that level too, things were very different than with his wife. Although seemingly much more sophisticated and worldly than Trude, Gina had been as inexperienced as Bruno when they became lovers, and that no doubt had played a part in their failure to develop a good sexual relationship. In 1936, however, around the same time the affair between Bruno and Trude was becoming more serious, Gina was herself to meet the love of her life.

Patsy had a toothache, and on the Sterbas' recommendation Gina took her to see Peter Weinmann, the dentist who had paid so much attention to Trude at the ball. Although only forty, Weinmann already had quite a reputation in medical circles; he had just finished rebuilding Sigmund Freud's dental prosthesis, a very tricky job since cancer and several previous operations had destroyed half the jaw. He was also very charming. But above all Weinmann, for whom the University of Illinois would later create a chair of oral pathology, was a true man of science, more interested in research itself than in any honors it could bring. In Gina's eyes he was just the opposite of Bettelheim.

Gina and Peter Weinmann were immediately attracted to each other. But both were married, and the relationship developed slowly. Peter Weinmann and Richard Sterba were great friends, and as the rules of psychoanalytic etiquette, governing social mixing by doctors and patients, were not as strict as they are today, they often ended up having coffee together in the restaurant where the Weinmanns had their meals. And Gina has vivid memories of a trip to the south of France with the Weinmanns, some months before the arrival of the Nazis in Vienna, when she realized how deeply she loved Peter, who shared her passion for music, nature, and beauty, and preferred his own discoveries to those listed in guidebooks. Even at that point, however, neither of them envisaged divorce.

"Although some of my closest friends had become psychoanalysts, I had hesitated to follow their example, partly because I did not wish to be a copycat, and partly because I was not impressed by what becoming psychoanalysts had done for them personally . . . it was finally a crisis in my married life which convinced me to give psychoanalysis a try."[16] The Bruno Bettelheim who made an appointment to see Dr. Richard Sterba with a view to starting analysis was a grown man and a prosperous merchant, but one who did not like his career, and had problems with his wife. As these lines show, he went to that appointment with reservations, knowing that he was not committing himself to anything, and that he was free to change his mind at any point. Sterba was barely five years older than Bettelheim, but as the latter himself recounts, the young analyst soon got the measure of this patient to be.

Once they had discussed the practical details of fees and appointments, Bettelheim asked him whether he thought he needed analysis. Sterba replied that he did not have the faintest idea. It would take at least a year or even two to find out, by which time Bettelheim would know himself, he explained. The prospective patient's next question, according to Bettelheim's account, was "whether psychoanalysis could help me." The analyst's reply was equally neutral. Up to this point, the conversation had followed a classic pattern. Then Bettelheim thought of a new angle. "With some desperation, I finally asked him what reason there could be for me to go into psychoanalysis." Sterba said he had gathered that for many years Bettelheim had been interested in the subject. For that reason, "the only promise he felt able to give me was that I would find the experience very interesting because I would discover things about myself that I had not known before. This would permit me to understand myself better and would make many aspects of my life and my behavior more comprehensible to me."[17]

With this reply, Sterba clearly made an impression on Bettelheim, showing incidentally that he understood Gina's husband much better than he himself would have admitted. While apparently promising nothing, he was in fact offering Bettelheim the one thing he could not resist: the opportunity to extract meaning from apparent chaos. Deciding that Sterba was a man who could be trusted, Bettelheim resolved to "give it a try."

Precisely when this conversation took place and exactly how long Bettelheim spent in analysis afterward cannot be determined. In his own statements he was always vague, generally speaking of "several years." But this is one of the fields in which Bettelheim's assertions are not very reliable, in which he later tended to exaggerate to suit his professional requirements. Gina, on the other hand, tends to minimize things. "Less than a year, I'm sure," she says. But her statements cannot be considered fully reliable on this point either, although for different reasons. None of the other people who were in contact with Bettelheim at this stage of his life could provide an authoritative answer. A few of the surviving witnesses to Bettelheim's early life are also reluctant to contradict him on what they see as an essential point.

Wanda Willig, who seems to be the most reliable of those witnesses—because her affection for Bettelheim is so devoid of ambivalence that it would apparently not occur to her to protect him with a lie—cannot be of much help on this point. She knows that his psychoanalysis was not very long but she cannot not say anything about it because she and her husband had left Vienna in 1935. Which only tells us that Bruno Bettelheim had not yet started his analysis at that time.

When talking about it to his children, Bettelheim noted that it would have been "logical" for him to have started an analysis at about the same time as his cousin Edith Buxbaum and so many of his friends (around 1925), particularly given his already strong interest in Freudian ideas. He cited two basic reasons for not having done so: First, he feared reawakening the depression that he was just getting over at the time. And second, he saw little point in trying to analyze the events of his early life as long as he had not elucidated the dark secret that hung over his and his parents' lives. Conversely, Bettelheim gave two main motives in *Freud's Vienna* for undertaking an analysis: a "crisis" in his married life and dissatisfaction with his job. This suggests that his treatment started in late 1936 or early 1937. It was then that he must have begun to suspect that Gina was no longer simply flirting with some of her friends, but that she was beginning to fall in love with somebody else. Would he have known who? Gina feels certain that he did not. However, that trip to the south of France in 1937, when the Weinmanns and the Bettelheims traveled as two couples should have given Bruno, who was so good at tuning in to other people's feelings, an inkling of what was going on.

Another reason to believe that Bettelheim's psychoanalysis began in either late 1936 or early 1937 is Trude's influence. In the same way that she convinced him to return to university to get a PhD, it seems obvious that she would have wanted to share her enthusiasm for psychoanalysis with the man she loved and admired so much. In telling him of her own experience, she must not only have excited his curiosity but also soothed some of his fears about the analytical process. If I am right about the starting point of Bettelheim's analysis, it cannot have lasted for much more than a year, as it was to be abruptly ended by the German annexation of Austria in the spring of 1938. This would, however, have been a year of intensive Viennese-style analysis, five or six sessions a week. (Gina says five, Bettelheim said six.)

The second key question raised by Bettelheim's psychoanalysis is his choice of a doctor. "Being good friends with so many of the small group of younger Viennese analysts proved to be a problem, because

I had to find one with whom I was not well acquainted," Bettelheim wrote.[18] "But there was at least one among them—Dr. Richard Sterba—who was well recommended to me by an analyst friend whom I trusted. So with some hesitation I made an appointment with him to discuss matters." A strange statement indeed. Even if he was not personally acquainted with the analyst, Bettelheim surely knew that both his wife and Agnes Piel had been Sterba's patients and that, subsequently, Gina had turned to Richard's wife, Editha, for help, as had both Patsy and Trude.[19] The way Bettelheim tells it, one could be forgiven for thinking that at the end of the 1930s there were only a mere half-dozen analysts practicing in Vienna!

Richard Sterba's decision to accept this new patient was no less strange. Rules of professional ethics in psychoanalysis were still being developed; nevertheless, to take on a former patient's husband must have been a questionable practice even at that early date. While Bettelheim may have been seeking, perhaps unconsciously, to avoid washing his family's dirty linen in public by choosing a doctor who obviously knew of his marital problems, it is more difficult to understand how an analyst of Sterba's caliber did not regard this as suspicious, and therefore as fraught with risks for the would-be patient. Sterba could hardly have been unaware of Gina's ambivalent feelings toward Bruno, and he was best placed to appreciate the power of the transference that her analysis had initiated toward himself. Did Sterba not realize that Bettelheim may have seen him as a rival?[20]

One of Bettelheim's motives for choosing Sterba may have been the desire, conscious or otherwise, to find the magic spell that would rekindle his wife's affection for him. But even if that was the case initially, and whatever the exact duration of Bettelheim's analysis, there is no doubt that it helped him lay bare some of the hidden recesses of his psyche. Gina recalls noting quite a change in him during that period. And Bettelheim himself was later to write: "I can not blame my analysis for not having done a good enough job, because it made me ready for Trude, and she and our relation was my salvation."[21] He would also remark on many occasions, and particularly toward the end of his life, after Trude's death, that although his analysis had helped him to uncover the causes of his depression (which he usually described as "legitimate" ones), it had not given him the means to overcome it.

Bettelheim alluded to what he had discovered in his analysis with Sterba to his friend Carl Frankenstein, and also outlined it a little for his children. The experience, it seems, allowed him to uncover the role played by what he described as a "shameful secret" in his psyche. In his childhood, his father's hidden illness appears to have become mixed up in his unconscious with the mystery surrounding his grand-father Bettelheim's origins, fostering the idea of an indelible blemish on the paternal line. The burden was all the more difficult to bear in that during his boyhood an oppressive silence had prevented him from ever finding out exactly what was wrong with his family. Echo-ing this ignorance was the fact that he knew practically nothing about his Jewishness, except that it laid him open to humiliating remarks.

This is the only aspect of his psychoanalysis that Bettelheim alluded to. It is however worth noting that the young Bettelheim, who was continually being reminded by his mother that he would soon have to step into his father's shoes, singularly lacked positive mascu-line role models, at least if we follow his version of events, which from the psychoanalytic point of view is the only one that counts. The only male in his immediate family who had achieved real success without having had anything to hide was his maternal grandfather, Adolf Sei-dler. But he was a man who had ridden roughshod over everyone, both inside and outside his family. He had been a domestic tyrant who had literally turned his wife into a lifelong invalid, and who had so terrorized and castrated his sons that none of them had dared face up to him and pursue their own interests. His daughters, too, had been denied the right to choose their own destinies, as Bruno could see from his mother. Moreover, Adolf Seidler's success had been based on business methods that were shady, if not downright "fraudulent" (selling the same sewing machines as new several times over). The way Bettelheim talked about him provides ample evidence of his ambivalent feelings. While he was proud at having such a successful and clever grandfather, he obviously found the man's character and methods hateful and took pains to distance himself from them.

On his father's side of the family the picture was not much hap-pier, and from Bettelheim's point of view it was even harder to come to terms with. Jakob Morris Bettelheim's success had been achieved honorably. But as he had died by the time his grandson was born, taking the secret of his origins with him to the grave, Bruno inher-ited an image of him that was marred by resentment, and a feeling of injustice. Jakob Morris's having been abandoned as an infant instilled a deep-seated feeling that a wrong had to be righted, which may explain the considerable lengths to which his sons, Bruno's uncles, went in trying to establish their kinship with the influential Bettelheims of Pressburg. Whenever Bruno Bettelheim told that story, however, he never failed to point out that those efforts had been in vain. The wrong had never been righted.

As for Bruno's own father, far from removing the stain from his family's reputation, he appeared to have paid for it with his life. Although Anton Bettelheim was an honorable, caring man, concerned about his children's future, he emerges from his son's descriptions as above all a weak character, a victim. First of all he loses his wife's dowry in a foolhardy lumber deal, and is thus reduced to begging for further aid from the tyrannical Adolf Seidler. As a result he is forced into an unwanted partnership with his brother-in-law. Then he contracts a mysterious and shameful ailment that destroys him and plunges his family into misery and despair. Even Bruno Bettelheim's explanation to his own son, that Anton's illness had been contracted through treating some business acquaintances to an evening out at a brothel, only serves to reinforce the image of the father as a weak, luckless character, doomed to pay for the family curse with his life. To return to the classroom incident, does not Bettelheim's violent reaction to a "simpering eunuch" become clearer when set against the background of the deep doubts he probably entertained as to the virility of his own father? A man who had "not touched his wife for twenty years."[22]

It would be interesting to know exactly what happened during those sessions in Dr. Sterba's consulting room, especially given the complexity of Bettelheim's relationship to psychoanalysis as a discipline. Some clues about Sterba's technique can be gleaned from some of his other patients, and also from his slim volume of memoirs. Bettelheim's analyst was a strict Freudian in the sense that he intervened very little during sessions. Indeed, that was one of the complaints made about him by Gina, who found the long silences oppressive. But Sterba was also prepared to take liberties with orthodox procedures when he considered it necessary, such as when he allowed a young trainee psychoanalyst two sessions a day rather than one for a few months so that she could finish her training before emigrating to the United States. "It wouldn't have worked with everybody, but no doubt he knew that it would work with me," the former patient told me.[23] Later, when he too was in the United States, Richard Sterba had a problem with the Detroit Psychoanalytic Society concerning his fees. But overall nobody contests the fact that he was a very good analyst.

Similarly, one can only guess what type of patient Bruno Bettelheim was, by looking at later remarks he made on analysis. In a discussion of the defective development of the ego that characterizes an autistic child, for instance, he explains the "secret of psychoanalytic technique" as follows. In order to communicate his or her fantasies to the analyst in words, the analysand[24] is forced to sort through them and organize them into sentences. "Hence, as we tell our free associations they are no longer free, but ordered."[25] A little further on Bettelheim explains that only sentences constitute material for the analysis, as they reflect the way in which ideas follow on from one another.

Such a definition could be read as an indication that during his own analysis, Bettelheim did not get to the stage of letting his own fantasies express themselves freely. For while the words that an analysand utters on the couch do provide clues to his unconscious, the organization of those words into sentences already involves some control by the conscious mind, which is thereby acting as a screen. However this only becomes apparent to the patient once he has broken through the screen by letting himself listen to the words per se. And this would be particularly true in the case of a man who devoted so much of his mental energy to extracting meaning from (and thereby imposing order on) his life and surroundings.[26]

If we put together the various early memories cited by Bettelheim, it becomes obvious that although he was pampered in many ways, he was never allowed simply to be a child. At the age of four, fate in the form of his father's illness had already singled him out as the future mainstay of the family. But by that age, according to Freud, a boy is embroiled in the Oedipus complex, which leads him to fantasize about the death of his father. Little wonder that Bettelheim should thereafter have struggled to control his unconscious life by imposing order on things. When one has such dangerous fantasies (or rather, when life has played the dirty trick of making them come true), one can no longer afford to give them free rein. And when one has spent more than thirty years learning to live with them, it takes time, patience, and a great deal of trust in one's analyst to succeed in letting them come to the surface and facing up to them. However, time was one commodity that was fast running out for Bettelheim in Vienna. As for his trust in Richard Sterba, given the links between the two men, I find it difficult to believe that it could have been total.

And yet, *Freud and Man's Soul*, the long essay Bettelheim wrote toward the end of his life to denounce how the English translators of

Freud's works had emasculated their meaning, vibrates with passionate anger, and it shows an understanding of Freud which goes well
beyond what can be found in books alone. It reflects, more than just
an opinion about psychoanalysis, inside knowledge of the process
itself, knowledge of the type that arises from the phenomenon of
transference. But wherever Bettelheim acquired such understanding,
it seems unlikely that it was on Sterba's couch in 1937. On reflection,
the most remarkable aspect of his evolution is the way he seemed to
have rediscovered the "mystery" that lay at the heart of the analytical process, in spite of the shortness of his own classical cure, brutally
cut short by the arrival of the Nazis in Vienna.

On a less conjectural note, let us return to what Bettelheim himself
said about his analysis. Another thing he admitted to having discovered during his sessions was his fear of sex, made worse by all the
years he was kept in ignorance about the nature of his father's illness.[27] That was why Lilly Krugh's amorous advances had terrified
him so. This admission certainly sheds light on Bettelheim's remark
that his psychoanalysis allowed him to form a good relationship with
Trude. It is worth comparing it to his description of his first encounter
with Freud's writings, which he considered too obscene to be read in
the family home. He concludes that account by underlining the mixed
feelings of repulsion and fascination he then experienced. "Now I
believe that coming to psychoanalysis in such a personal way, becoming so deeply involved emotionally and yet so ambivalently, was a
most auspicious beginning."[28] A promising start, no doubt, but also a
remarkably "family-oriented," and even a somewhat incestuous one,
one is tempted to add.

5

❈

The Anschluss

When Bruno Bettelheim went to sign up for his second semester at Vienna University in the spring of 1937, he had to notice how much the political climate had changed. A new box had appeared on the enrollment form, beneath the one asking the prospective student to state his religion; now he also had to state the "people" he belonged to. Bettelheim thus had to enter not only "Mosaic," under religion, but also "Jewish." This was at a date when Nazism was still confined to Germany, and when Hitler had promised Austrians he would not seek fulfillment of the "most ardent and heartfelt wish" he had expressed in *Mein Kampf:* "the union of my beloved homeland with the common fatherland."[1]

Bettelheim had narrowed the focus of his studies considerably. Apart from two hours weekly devoted to art history (Renaissance painting in the first semester, the art of antiquity in the second), he was concentrating on only two disciplines, philosophy and psychology. All his courses were taught by Professors Reininger and Bühler, the two men who then headed the philosophy faculty. Both had taken part in the great teaching reform program of the 1920s.

Reininger, who oversaw Bettelheim's doctoral dissertation, was first and foremost a philosopher, although he had done some work at the Psychology Institute, run by Karl and Charlotte Bühler, on the social organization of school classes (at the time both sociology and psychology were merely branches of philosophy). Reininger's best-known work was a study of love, *The Problem of the Psycho-*

Physics, which placed him in the school of thought founded by the physicist-philosopher Ernst Mach with his *Analysis of Sensations*. During his first semester with Reininger (fall 1936), Bettelheim had studied Renaissance thought, rationalism, and the philosophy of Nietzsche. The following semester he focused on Aristotle and empiricism.

But Karl Bühler's teaching figured more prominently in the schedule of the returning student. Ten years earlier, Bettelheim had signed up for four hours a week of classes with Bühler. That coincided with his father's confinement in a clinic, however, and Bettelheim appears not to have attended very regularly, since in 1936 the university was willing to credit him with only four of the nine semesters he had supposedly completed during his first period as a student. This time Bettelheim signed up with Bühler for four hours a week of general psychology and two hours of language theory (*Sprachtheorie*) in the first semester, and for four hours of the theory of knowledge (logic and epistemology) in the second (spring 1937).

Bühler, whose work was to strongly influence Roman Jakobson and the other Prague School linguists, was a major figure at the university. Unlike the idealist German tradition, the Austrian strain of philosophy was analytical, owing more to Leibniz than to Kant.[2] It was a tradition that accorded considerable importance to experimental psychology. Bühler's *Sprachtheorie* was the core of his teaching. For him, all living creatures had to be seen from the point of view of the creativity principle, that is, their ability to perceive and create new forms. In that sense, he may be seen as one of the pioneers of Gestalt psychology, believing the perception of forms to be governed by precise laws.

Bühler was also the proponent of a biological view of the psyche that could not easily be reconciled with psychoanalysis. In spite of that fact, a large number of Freud's students frequented his institute and took his classes. In those days the distinction between psychology and psychoanalysis, both emerging fields of study, was much less clear-cut than it is today. Psychoanalysis was in fact a branch of psychology: a research orientation, and a somewhat offbeat one at that. In a society that remained in the grip of the Catholic church and bourgeois mores, the new discipline suffered from the stigma engendered by Freud's emphasis on sexuality as the primary source of human energy.

Psychoanalysis was thus regarded with considerable ambivalence in university circles. Although many of the best professors already suspected its potential, as guardians of academic orthodoxy they were often all too ready to encourage the popular view of it as somehow disreputable. This placed would-be students of psychoanalysis in a difficult position. It was easier for medical school students, as they could take psychoanalysis as a separate topic, either concurrently with their main studies or afterward. But the idea of lay analysis was also gaining favor; as Freud's work moved forward it was becoming less and less attached to its roots in medicine, and several of his most brilliant students were not doctors at all. Indeed, a glance at the minutes of the Psychoanalytic Society in the 1930s reveals that a solid grounding in the classics was much more relevant than medical training for those taking part in its discussions.

As psychoanalysis began to turn the spotlight on children and adolescents, many students, such as Bettelheim's cousin Edith Buxbaum and his friend Fritz Redl, followed the lead of Anna Freud and August Aichhorn and trained as primary- or secondary-school teachers. Others, more drawn to the theoretical side, opted to study psychology at the university. This led to a seeming paradox: In spite of the apparent incompatibility between the two views, Freudians flocked to Bühler's courses in such numbers that many joked about the door of the Psychology Institute opening directly into the Psychoanalytic Institute.

This does not necessarily imply that, foreseeing world events, Bettelheim had planned on becoming a psychoanalyst when he re-enrolled at the university at age thirty-three. But neither can such a possibility be completely ruled out. If it were to be the case, many of the later statements he made on the subject, seen today as lies, would turn out to have been merely half-truths, since Bettelheim would only have been prevented from changing his career orientation by the sudden arrival of Hitler. However, if he did not have some radical career change in mind, one is left to wonder why, when already a successful businessman, he should have returned to the university, and at a time when the prevailing anti-Semitism meant he could not possibly have hoped to ever teach in Austria. Bettelheim's immediate aim, however, was clear: to get his PhD. Eight months after his enrollment, on May 19, 1937, he registered his dissertation under the title *Das Problem des Naturschönen und die moderne Aesthetik* (The Problem of the Beautiful in Nature and Modern Aesthetics).

His central idea was that the aesthetic experience causes the boundaries between subject and object to dissolve, and that the viewing of real-life landscapes was the original form of that experience. Having examined from a historical standpoint how nature gradually became an object of aesthetic enjoyment, Bettelheim deplores the fact that idealism and formalism, the two main schools in aesthetics at the time, reduce it to second place. He analyzes how this happened, then seeks to show that the enjoyment of nature is an aesthetic experience in the full sense of the term, an authentic one—because unlike art, it is not mediated by a third party—and one that provides the subject with an opportunity to transcend the dualistic oppositions of rationalist thought, and to achieve a fusion with the world. Thus does the observer of a landscape become the artist, constructing a work of which he himself is a part.[3]

It was thus a rather academic piece of work, very much in keeping with the spirit of the times, in which Bettelheim demonstrated his familiarity with the main aesthetic theories then current as well as his knowledge of the history of art and the prevailing tendencies in the humanities, notably psychology. But it was also a well-written work, displaying intellectual agility and, already, a number of highly effective shortcuts. It showed no trace of any psychoanalytic influence, however, with the exception of one name in the bibliography: Ernst Kris, cited for his book *Die Legende vom Künstler*, published three years earlier. Bettelheim's dissertation was rewarded with a "very good" from Reininger and an "excellent" from Bühler and the other two examiners called upon to assess it.

Another reflection comes to mind, one that has no bearing on the strictly academic nature of the work. As anyone who knew Bettelheim can testify, he was fond of nature, but not excessively so. He enjoyed hiking a little, but was not the kind of person to spend hours gazing at a beautiful landscape—which suggests that Trude Weinfeld may have played some role in his thinking on the subject. She was less interested in art than he was, but she was fascinated by the natural world. Perhaps it was through observing her on the long forest walks they took in the summer of 1936, or listening to her hold forth on her love of nature, that Bettelheim decided on his subject. What is certain is that he did not discuss these ideas with Gina.

So this is another of those periods when Bruno Bettelheim managed to carry on two almost completely separate existences. Although he had plunged into his studies with determination, he continued to go to his office every day. He was no longer running Bettelheim & Schnitzer, but he was still doing the books, as the audit carried out by the Nazis a year later shows. Having set his heart on a goal, Bettelheim managed to make miraculously efficient use of his time. Alongside his work and studies, he was carrying on his psychoanalysis, leading a married life, and seeing Trude.

All in all, 1937 seems to have been a happy year for Bettelheim. The changes in him that Gina attributed to his analysis no doubt also had something to do with his growing involvement with a woman who believed in him—an affair of which, being too caught up in her own love life, Gina was unaware—plus an ambition he was determined to fulfill and a grinding daily schedule that left no time for doubts or depression. In February of that year he took out a life insurance policy, with the same Riunione company where he had once worked. It was a twenty-five-year contract with yearly premiums of 200 Austrian shillings, which was no mean sum. Bettelheim's future may have been uncertain, but he clearly felt that it was worth insuring.

He still had to take two oral examinations, in philosophy and art history. The former took place on July 17, 1937, the latter on January 16, 1938; his results in both were "excellent," and on February 2, 1938, he graduated *summa cum laude* as a doctor of philosophy. The diploma was grandly drawn up in Latin, to one *Brunonem Bettelheim.* On the cards he had printed up the very next day, however, Bettelheim dropped the accusative to announce the news to his friends and relations. Given the political situation in Vienna at the time, they probably had other things on their minds. But for the same reason, his diploma, among the very last to be granted to a Jew in Vienna before the war, was the passport that would get him out of collapsing Austria and into a new life elsewhere. Without it, wherever he ended up he would have been nothing more than a ruined lumber merchant. With it, he could use his past to create a future.

Six months previously his cousin Edith Buxbaum, faced with the threat of arrest for her political activities, had fled to the United States. In the space of a few months she had not only found a teaching job but was in the process of starting a psychoanalytic practice in New York, even though she was not a medical doctor. A few months before her, Fritz Redl had also left for the New World. He had not fled, he had simply been recruited by the Rockefeller Foundation, then actively seeking out European intellectuals. Neither he nor Edith would have gotten where they were without their academic credentials.

On Friday March 11, 1938, less than a month after Bettelheim finally obtained his PhD, Peter Weinmann and his wife came to the Glorietgasse apartment for a farewell dinner. With the Nazi invasion looming, the Weinmanns had decided to leave immediately for London, with a stop in Paris, where Emmi and Bertel von Radanowicz were then living. It was an icy cold evening, but the weather was not what they, or most other people in the city, were worrying about. Right up until the start of that fateful evening, the most optimistic Viennese had hoped that the last-ditch referendum on Austria's future, planned by Chancellor Kurt von Schuschnigg, Dollfuss's successor, would achieve its aim of heading off annexation by Germany. A massive yes vote would have undermined Hitler's stated pretext for unifying the two countries: the safety of Austrian Germans. And viewed from Vienna, at least, the yeses appeared set to carry the day by a huge majority.

What Hitler had in mind for the Viennese they all knew; in *Mein Kampf* he had described his own last days in the city, in 1913, as follows: "My inner aversion to the Hapsburg state was increasing daily . . . This motley of Czechs, Poles, Hungarians, Ruthenians, Serbs and Croats, and always the bacillus which is the solvent of human society, the Jew, here, there and everywhere—the whole spectacle was repugnant to me . . . The longer I lived in that city the stronger became my hatred for the promiscuous swarm of foreign peoples which had begun to batten on that old nursery ground of German culture."[4]

Precisely one month before that farewell dinner at the Bettelheim home, Schuschnigg had been summoned to Hitler's eyrie at Berchtesgaden to hear the dictator's conditions. After keeping the Austrian leader waiting for several hours, and then showering him with insults, Hitler had demanded that the Austrian head of the Nazi party, the Viennese lawyer Arthur Seyss-Inquart, be made interior minister with unlimited powers over the police, that all jailed Nazis be freed, including those who had assassinated Dollfuss, that the Nazi party be legalized, and that Austria enter into a customs union with Germany. Hitler stated that the demands were non-negotiable, and gave the hapless Schuschnigg three days in which to comply or face immediate annexation. Schuschnigg had complied.

Along with the jailed Nazis, however, the government had also freed the Social Democrats and the Communists. After seeking help in vain from other European governments, and after Mussolini had made it clear that he would not honor the Italian–Austrian defense treaty if Hitler made a move, Schuschnigg had turned in desperation to his former enemies, the very trade unionists and left-wing activists that his predecessor had outlawed in 1934, to try to create a broad Patriotic Front against the external threat. In exchange for the restitution of their civil rights, the Communists and Social Democrats had accepted the offer. Schuschnigg had then announced that a referendum on the future of Austria would be held the following Sunday.

For the past two days, therefore, anti-Nazis of all stripes had been rallying behind Schuschnigg in a motley alliance, and an atmosphere of sacred union was spreading throughout the country—or at least throughout Vienna, as described by the writer George Clare, then seventeen:

> On 10 March Vienna woke to a fever of patriotic fervour. The painting columns of the "Fatherland Front" had been at work all night stencilling Schuschnigg's portrait, huge "yesses," crutched crosses and slogans on walls and streets. Everything with a large enough surface had been covered with "Fatherland Front" symbols and with exhortations to vote for the Government. Aeroplanes showered leaflets over the city. Lorries draped in the national colours, packed with men and women yelling "Red-White-Red unto Death!" cruised through the streets distributing more leaflets . . . Vienna had last witnessed comparable scenes in August 1914, when its crowds acclaimed the outbreak of war.[5]

An idea of just how broad the coalition was can be gained from the fact that on the following day, Friday March 11, the leader of the Revolutionary Socialists, Karl Hans Sailer, was due to go on the radio to call for a yes vote.

Sailer never made his speech. From the middle of the afternoon, a rumor began to circulate that the referendum was being canceled. Early in the evening, it became official. The radio switched to playing nothing but slow and mournful music instead of the news bulletins and martial tunes that had made up its broadcasts for the past two days. In homes all over Austria, people kept their sets on.

At 8 P.M. Kurt von Schuschnigg went on the air. His voice breaking with emotion, he announced that Hitler had threatened to invade Austria if the post of chancellor was not immediately handed over to the man of his choice. Schuschnigg, who had again spent the afternoon in a fruitless quest for foreign help, informed his compatriots that he had decided to resign. It was a poignant speech, one that nobody who heard it was ever to forget. In it Schuschnigg also held the foreign governments responsible for refusing to come to his country's aid.[6] "President Miklas has asked me to tell the Austrian people that we have yielded to force, since we are not prepared even in this terrible hour to shed blood. We have decided to order the troops to offer no resistance."[7]

For the previous two hours, gangs of hoodlums wearing Nazi insignia, many of them drunk, had been marauding in the city center, insulting passersby. Their leaders were beginning to move into government offices, where they met no resistance. And as Schuschnigg spoke, Herman Göring in Berlin was on the telephone to Arthur Seyss-Inquart, giving him the go-ahead. Less than an hour after that call, Hitler signed the order for German troops to cross the border at dawn, officially "to help prevent bloodshed" in Austrian cities.[8]

Glorietgasse was some distance away from the main outbursts of hatred, but neither the Bettelheims nor their guests could have been unaware of what was going in the city center. They were no doubt still listening to the radio when Schuschnigg's speech was followed by the national anthem, and then by Seyss-Inquart announcing that he was taking over. The Nazi leader also stressed that the Austrian army would not resist the arrival of the German forces, thereby confirming that Hitler's ultimatum to Schuschnigg had been nothing more than a lie, and that the invasion had been intended all along, whatever the Austrian government did.

"Gina, why don't you and Patsy leave with the Weinmanns, in a couple of days?"

"No, I'll wait for you. I won't leave without you."

"That's impossible. I've still got lots of things to deal with, and I'll be able to cope much better on my own."

That is essentially how Gina remembers the exchange she had with her husband at that point. She comments: "Bruno would never have left Vienna leaving his mother behind." Trude's account of that evening was somewhat different, however. Some forty years later, she reported that "Although Bruno wanted to go with them [Gina and Patsy], I learned quite recently that his sister became hysterical when he tried to tell her and their mother what he was going to do. So he stayed behind . . . "[9]

Trude was not present that night, but her account is consistent with a remark made by Bettelheim to a counselor at the Orthogenic School in the mid-1970s: "My mother almost caused my death on two occasions. The first was the day after the Anschluss. I was all ready to leave with my wife and the little American girl we were looking after, when I made the mistake of calling her to say goodbye. After that, I no longer had the courage to leave."[10]

What documentary evidence exists, however, seems to back up Gina's version; she obtained her visa for the United States the next day, on March 12, 1938, whereas Bruno apparently did not apply for his until some weeks later. As for Patsy, over fifty years later she has only one memory of the evening in question: her mother's telephone call. Agnes Piel, having heard the news on the radio, was beside herself, and during her long conversation with Gina she on occasion shouted so loudly that everyone in the room could hear her. She did not want her daughter to stay a single day longer in Austria. Gina tried to reason with her, explaining how difficult it was to obtain the necessary papers, to get packed for such a major trip—to no avail. Agnes insisted that Patsy be brought home without further delay. And she pointedly reminded Gina of the warnings she had proffered during the summer of 1936: "If you'd listened to me, you'd have been in New York by now."

After dinner the Bettelheims accompanied the Weinmanns back to their home near the city center. The situation had already deteriorated considerably; no sooner had Schuschnigg finished speaking than trucks carrying SS and SA men converged on the Ring, with shouts of *"Heil Hitler,"* soon followed by *"Ju-da-ver-recke"* (Die, Jews!), filling the air. Among those chanting could be seen people who only that morning had been handing out leaflets calling for a "yes" vote in the expected referendum. Others had triumphantly pinned onto the front of their lapels the Nazi insignia that up until then they had kept hidden behind them.

Vienna had gone crazy. It seemed that even those who the previous day had been ready to line up behind Schuschnigg in favor of Austrian independence now had only one desire: to see Hitler arrive as soon as possible. The young George Clare observed the scene with his parents from the window of their 9th-district apartment, with the lights out so nobody could see them. He watched the neighborhood policeman, whose friendly "good morning" had for years reassured him every day on the way to school, furiously clubbing a man who had dared to complain about the marauding Nazi mobs.

Around 2 A.M., the Wehrmacht crossed Austria's southern border. In Vienna, persecution of the Jews started immediately. Shops were vandalized and passersby were seized by gangs of thugs and forced to kneel on the sidewalk, scrubbing off Patriotic Front slogans with a caustic solution that burned their hands.[11] "Work for the Jews! At last the Jews are working! We thank our Führer—he's created work for the Jews!" the gangs chanted, as Austrian policemen looked on, in some cases impassively and in others approvingly.

Of all the members of the Bettelheim circle, it appears that only Trude's mother was subjected to the humiliation of the scrub-brush treatment. But Bruno Bettelheim was soon to gain firsthand experience of the new methods, for on that very first day, the car he had been so proud of was confiscated—even before the German troops reached Vienna—by the no. III *Kreisleitung*, or local Nazi cell, in the 12th district, where his company was located. As the correspondent for the British *Daily Telegraph* reported, every single vehicle belonging to a Jew was expropriated on March 12, with the gangs often demanding money to buy gasoline as well.[12]

That Saturday morning the violence continued with increasing intensity throughout the city, while the sky was filled with the roar of the Wehrmacht's bombers, flying over at very low altitude to drop leaflets. The radio, meanwhile, brought more and more bad news. At dawn, SS chief Heinrich Himmler arrived in the city, with his deputy Reinhard Heydrich. Midday brought a message from Nazi propaganda chief Joseph Goebbels, announcing that a "real" referendum would be held, under the protection of the Nazi troops, which he said had been "called in" by the Austrian government to ensure the country's independence. Then at 7:30 P.M., Hitler himself arrived in the town of Linz, after a detour via his birthplace of Braunau. At his side, Goebbels launched the slogan that was to become the battle-cry of the Austrian Nazis: *"Ein Volk, ein Reich, ein Führer"* ("One people, one empire, one leader"). It was a motto that, beyond the lies of propaganda, perfectly summed up the situation: the remains of the once-proud Hapsburg empire had in fact become nothing more than an ordinary province of Germany.

During those hours Gina was furiously busy, getting ready to leave with Patsy for a period that seemed certain to be very long, if not indefinite. She gave final instructions to the faithful Hedwig, who had offered to watch over the Bettelheim's valuables and see whether they could be forwarded later, and she scrambled to assemble the required papers for her trip. At the U.S. embassy, which was besieged by a frantic crowd of would-be emigrants,[13] she appears to have been given priority treatment, for she got her visa on the same day. But the U.S. authorities were already becoming cautious about helping the fast growing number of people trying to escape Nazi persecution. In spite of the affidavit that Agnes Piel had given her, promising to support her until she found a job in the United States, Gina was granted only a tourist visa. This was to have unexpected consequences, but it nevertheless allowed her and Patsy to leave, either the next day or the following one, on the 9:45 P.M. express for Paris, passing through Innsbruck and Zurich.

In the pandemonium at the train station, Gina and Patsy said goodbye to Bruno and also to Richard Sterba, who had come to see the Weinmanns off on the same train. As the two parties were not in the same car, they resolved to meet up in Paris. But Gina was heavyhearted, knowing that the reprieve for her relationship with Peter Weinmann was to be a short one; he had decided to make his home in London. Patsy, convinced that Gina's sadness was due to her impending separation from Bruno, was even quieter than usual. She recalls that when some Nazi officers got onto the train, just before the Swiss border, Gina started to panic somewhat. Knowing that she was not allowed to carry a large sum of money out of the Reich, and preferring not to take any risks on her way to freedom, she threw an envelope full of dollar bills that Bruno had given her out of the train window, according to Patsy. Gina denies that any such incident ever took place.

It indeed seems that Bettelheim was not caught as unawares by the Anschluss as some other Viennese Jews were. According to a Nazi audit of his company carried out at the time of its "Aryanization," from 1937 a small number of transactions were no longer recorded in his ledgers. He had also mortgaged off his life insurance policy. Bettelheim himself claimed that he had been able to smuggle $10,000 out of Austria, with the help of an American journalist friend. Although the sum seems improbably large—worth over $200,000 today[14]—it is no doubt impossible to verify this, Gina having no recollection of any such transaction.

Nothing that had happened in Germany since Hitler had come to power could have prepared the Austrian Jews for the firestorm that was to descend on them the minute Germany annexed their country. The repression was so ferocious in the weeks after the Anschluss that it drew favorable comments in the SS newspaper *Schwarze Korps:* "The [Austrian Nazis] have done in one night what we haven't yet managed to do here in the heavy, slow-moving north. In Austria there was no need to organize a boycott of the Jews—the people themselves did the job, with honest joy."[15]

Some anti-Nazis had indeed started to send savings out of the country whenever they could, especially after the Austrian-German treaty of 1936. Richard Sterba, for example, although not Jewish, had had the foresight, three years earlier, to start asking the father of a young Canadian patient to send his fees to a Swiss bank account.[16] George Clare tells how his banker father had started preparing for exile long in advance.[17] However, many people did not have the means to take such precautions, or else did not see the point, believing that no harm would befall them as long as they did not stand out from the crowd. The Zionist historian and journalist Josef Katstein, in a famous article titled *"Was Nun?"* (What Now?), published in 1935 on his return to Vienna from Berlin, was quoted as saying that "once the Nazis got into power the worst that could happen to the Jews would be to be shut up in ghettos as they were in the Middle Ages, and obliged to wear a yellow star." However, he added, these passing problems would not be such as to warrant emigration, which was why Katstein recommended that only younger Jews go to settle in Palestine, while their elders waited for the storm to pass. That opinion had been very widely shared.[18]

Given the severity with which Bruno Bettelheim was later to judge the unpreparedness of many of the victims of Nazism, it is legitimate to ask just how far-seeing he proved to be as the Anschluss loomed. Disappointingly, the few scraps of information available do not provide a clear answer, especially since the statements Bettelheim himself made on the subject are often at odds with the recollections of other witnesses. For example, Bettelheim gave this account of the hours following the Anschluss announcement to the Nuremberg Tribunal convened in 1945:

> Immediately following the occupation of Austria on or about March 12, 1938, it became apparent to me that I would not be permitted to live in peace in Austria. Therefore I resolved to leave the country. My wife and I left Vienna on about 12 or 13 of March and were stopped at the

Czechoslovakian-Hungarian border that night. The next day we undertook to leave Vienna by train, and while my wife was permitted to proceed, I was detained by the police, ordered to remain in Vienna and my
passport was taken away from me.

Within the next day or two the police searched my home. I was exten-
sively questioned but not taken into custody, the police stating that it
did not appear that I had violated any of the laws of Austria. Three or
four weeks later I was taken into custody by the Austrian police and for
three days questioned about my political activities. At the conclusion of
the questioning the police officer who was in charge of the investigation
dictated a statement to the effect that there appeared to be no basis
whatever for any legal action against me. Thereupon I was released. Two
weeks later I was taken into custody and imprisoned. It was stated to me
that my confinement was the result of orders issued by the Gestapo in
Berlin. I spent three days in jail in Vienna after which I was transferred
to the concentration camp at Dachau.[19]

Gina however, was categorical when interviewed on the subject: At
no point did the couple attempt to cross into Czechoslovakia, either
by train or car. She no longer remembers whether she and Patsy had
left Vienna on the 13th or the 14th.[20] What is certain, however, is that
the pair were aboard the U.S. ship *President Roosevelt* when it
weighed anchor in the French port of Le Havre on March 17. They
had spent the night before with the Radanowiczes in Paris; there was
thus no room in Gina's and Patsy's tight travel schedule to have fitted
in a trip toward Bratislava.

The contradiction is all the more puzzling in that if Bettelheim
simply invented the Czechoslovakia story, it is difficult to understand
why. It would indeed be the only example I came across of a story
being made up by Bettelheim for which no obvious external motive—
be it the need to obtain a job, or the desire to pass himself off as being
cleverer or more important than he really was—could be found. For
although some Austrians did opt to flee toward the east, Czechoslovakia then being a democratic state with an apparently robust army,
they were of course soon to regret it. So that if he invented such a tale
for an American audience, Bettelheim would not even have been
likely to impress anyone with his foresight.

This is unfortunately another mystery that cannot be conclusively
resolved. As Vienna's police archives for 1938 remain to this day closed
to the public, it is impossible to check the facts, just as it is impossible
to determine in what circumstances Bettelheim was arrested and then

freed on two occasions before his final deportation, as he also told the U.S. prosecutor at Nuremberg.

What is indisputable, however, is that on May 28, acting on orders from Berlin, the Gestapo arrested Bruno Bettelheim at his home as part of the *Juden-Aktion*. This was a full-scale official pogrom carried out in the three months following the Anschluss and involving the arrests of some 70,000 Austrian Jews in all, most of them in Vienna.[21] Many were to be released after two or three days of detention and interrogation, but attacks and "home visits," during which neighbors and doorkeepers in apartment blocks often helped the Nazi gangs to single out Jews, continued, intensifying during the Passover period. In May the order had come from Berlin for the arrest of some 2,000 intellectuals whose names were on a list drawn up long in advance by the Austrian Nazis. Those arrests were to result in three trainloads of prisoners being sent to Dachau between May and June 1938; Bruno Bettelheim was in the one that left June 2. A previous deportation exercise on April 1, calculated to make a strong impression in the first days after the annexation, had taken all the leaders of Vienna's Jewish community, as well as a large number of leading political, media, and business figures, not all of them Jewish, to the same concentration camp. They were accused by the Nazis of having supported the ill-fated Patriotic Front.

Bettelheim was later to hint that he had aided the underground Social Democratic movement prior to his arrest, but I was unable to find confirmation of this involvement. Such political activity by definition does not often leave records. None of the witnesses who could have shed light on the subject were still alive, and Bettelheim's only documented political affiliation was his membership in the Patriotic Front. Since anti-Nazis of all tendencies had joined the Front en masse in the months prior to the Anschluss, that is not a particularly significant piece of evidence. To judge from his Red Cross certificate of incarceration, however, the truth appears both simpler and more tragic. Bruno Bettelheim, the refined intellectual who loved German literature and Expressionist painting, had been arrested solely because he was a Jew, and a prosperous businessman to boot.

The fate reserved for the Bettelheim & Schnitzer company only serves to confirm that impression. The firm was officially closed down on Thursday July 7, 1938, only to reopen a week later. The new owner was a certain Nikolaus Lackner, a Nazi activist of Croatian origin. At the time of the Anschluss he had been an accountant with the Frid &

Thiemann bank. This institution, specializing in finance for the lumber trade, was Bettelheim & Schnitzer's own bank. The takeover was carried out with rapid efficiency. Lackner appeared ideally suited to benefit from the company's "Aryanization," as the process was called. He had joined the Austrian Nazi Party in 1933, and as a letter of reference from the party dated September 1938 shows, he was considered a model activist, and authorized to carry a weapon. The purpose of the letter was to recommend that Lackner, who had been given a provisional lease on the Bettelheim & Schnitzer company in June, be allowed to purchase the firm outright. He was to get what he wanted, becoming the owner on September 22, 1938. He was even to go on running the company right up until December 1955!

The first contract with Nikolaus Lackner is dated June 9, 1938, which was less than a week after Bettelheim had been shipped off to Dachau. The documents for the so-called sale were drawn up by his partner Hans Schnitzer, who, being married to an Aryan, had not been arrested. They stated that the company employed four workers who were not Jews, and set its value at 28,055 Reichmarks, equivalent to around $250,000 today. Another document, dated 1942, records four payments made by Lackner over a period of just over two years for the total amount of RM 28,055. The payments were made into an account in the names of Bettelheim & Schnitzer, in the bank at which Lackner worked. But an accompanying letter stated that the two purported beneficiaries were forbidden from drawing on the account! Finally, a letter from the bank dated November 25, 1943, confirmed that the assets of Mr. Bettelheim and Mr. Schnitzer had been confiscated by the Moabit-West tax office in Berlin.

It was thus a classic case of "Aryanization," that is, outright theft dressed up to look like a legitimate sale thanks to an outwardly convincing mass of paperwork. Thousands of similar expropriations took place all over Austria at this time, once again bringing expressions of jealous admiration from the German Nazis.[22] It is generally reckoned that in the months following the Anschluss, seized Jewish assets were valued at around 50 percent of their true market value (later on, the percentage fell steadily), but in spite of the existence of a thorough audit of Bettelheim's company, it is impossible to assess the relative value of the sum decided upon. It is also difficult to determine what role Bruno Bettelheim himself played in the process. Once he had realized that the expropriation could not be prevented, it is likely that he opted to play the game in order to settle things as quickly as possible. After all, it had clearly become impossible for him to stay in Vienna. His wife was already settled in the United States, where he was lucky enough to have a few good friends and, thanks to Patsy, to be able to count on having a roof over his head. What clearly never occurred to him, however, as is shown by his letters from Dachau, was that he would not receive a single cent from the proceeds of the "sale."

Bettelheim was also trying to secure passage for his remaining loved ones out of the country. As a U.S. citizen could sign only a limited number of immigration affidavits, depending on his or her financial means, and as Prohibition had eaten into the Piel family fortune, Agnes was not in a position to provide such documents for all the people Bettelheim wanted to help. On May 5, Jenny Buxbaum, Paula Bettelheim's sister, managed to leave for New York, where her daughter Edith awaited her. That meant Paula would have a place to go if Bruno was unable to vouch for her upkeep in America. Meanwhile Bruno's sister, Margarethe, had contacts that could allow her to go to England. But there was also Gina's mother, Mina, to think of. And there was Trude. "It is almost impossible to describe the turmoil, fear and anxiety that permeated the lives of the Jews," she was later to tell her children, in the memoirs she recorded for them. She was also making plans to leave, of course, but was not sure where to go. On the day of the Anschluss, her father had been in Switzerland on business. On hearing the news, he wanted to return at once, but she persuaded him not to. She had a more difficult time convincing her mother to leave immediately and join him. But then she was subjected to the humiliating experience of scrubbing the sidewalk, which made her change her mind. Shortly afterward, Trude learned that one of her father's sisters had committed suicide. Trude knew nobody who could vouch for her in the United States. She had considered Switzerland, but as her parents were painfully finding out, that country had no intention of becoming a refuge for all the people made homeless by the Third Reich. (The Swiss Justice Minister in person had suggested to the Nazis that they mark Jews' passports with a large red 'J' to make them more easily recognizable.) And then Trude was in no hurry to leave Vienna as long as Bruno was still there.

She also had other worries. The Montessori school had immediately attracted the Nazis' attention as a hotbed of Jews and leftists. Although expelled from their Grünetorgasse premises, which belonged to the city, the teachers had managed to complete the school year. Nuci Plank had persuaded a Christian friend, a museum curator, to provide a cover for the school by becoming its official director. He was apparently a good-hearted and cultivated man, no doubt representative of that fraction of the non-Jewish Viennese population who were appalled at what was happening.

Amid the torment, Bruno Bettelheim had also lost his psychoanalyst. Richard Sterba had been present in November 1936 when the German analyst Felix Boehm came to Vienna to try to convince Sigmund Freud that psychoanalysis in Berlin had been saved by his agreeing to purge the Psychoanalytic Society of all its Jewish members. Sterba feared that the Nazis would force him to betray his Jewish colleagues in his turn, as he was then the only non-Jew on the board of the Psychoanalytic Society.[23] On March 16, Richard Sterba left Vienna for Switzerland, after informing his patients of his departure by telephone.

Bettelheim's application for a U.S. visa was held up by unexpected red tape. As soon as Gina and Patsy had arrived in the United States, on March 26, Agnes Piel (who in the meantime had become Mrs. Crane) had asked the U.S. Consul in Vienna to speed up proceedings for Bruno. She meant well, but would probably have done better to go straight to the State Department's visa division. Accusations of anti-Semitism have since been made against certain members of the U.S. mission in Vienna; whether they are true or not, it is clear that when faced with the sudden stampede of desperate people clamoring for visas, the first reaction of the diplomats in Vienna had been to say no. Although Bettelheim had all the required backing, and the profile of a "good" immigrant, his application was not treated any better than any of the others, at least not at first. Having acknowledged receipt, on April 8, of the affidavit that Agnes Crane had sent for Bruno, Consul General George Wiley appears to have mislaid the document. At least that was what Bettelheim was told when he responded to an invitation for an interview on April 20. A Mr. Medeley even told him not to return until the Labor Department in Washington had provided clarification of his wife's status.

Tipped off immediately by Bettelheim, Agnes Crane then launched into a furious exchange of letters with both Vienna and Washington. In early May she suggested that the affidavit she had originally signed for Gina be transferred to Bruno. But that was quite impossible, she was told, since the U.S. authorities could not give immigrant status to a man whose wife had entered the country as a simple tourist! Although Agnes Crane managed to keep the tone of all her letters within the bounds of courtesy, she was clearly boiling inside. It would appear, if my calculations are correct, that it was around the time this "technical hitch" came up that Bruno Bettelheim was arrested and held for three days.

Agnes stepped up her campaign, firing off letters and bombarding Washington with telephone calls. She pointed out that Gina had used a tourist visa only so that she could bring her daughter back home as quickly as possible. She rounded up all the help she could get, including the National Coordinating Committee for Aid to Refugees and Emigrants Coming from Germany and, through Edith Buxbaum, the New York Psychoanalytic Society. She even offered to pay for all the telegrams needed to settle the case, an offer that the State Department was only too happy to accept.

In spite of all her efforts, things had not moved much by May 28, when the police, acting on orders from Berlin, knocked on Bruno Bettelheim's door at no. 15, Glorietgasse. In the most recent of his letters on the matter, the head of the State Department visa division had courteously explained to Agnes Crane that for Bruno to be accepted as an immigrant, his wife would have to leave the United States and herself file a new application for an immigration visa from a foreign country. He helpfully pointed out that this did not have to be done from Vienna.

6

---❋---

Dachau:
The Making of a Survivor

"Now that all that has fortunately been behind me for fifteen years, I can admit it: the year I spent in concentration camps did me good," Bruno Bettelheim wrote to a friend in 1954. The ten months and eleven days he had spent at Dachau and Buchenwald had indeed played, and would continue to play, a key role in his life. Like all the survivors of the Nazi camps, he was marked for life by the experience. And the imprint stamped on his psyche may explain, for example, his obsessive desire to control his own death. But in his case there was an additional, more material effect. To put it crudely, as he expressed it himself on occasion, it also opened the door to the "second life" he was describing in that letter.

Long before the publication of *Love Is Not Enough*, *The Empty Fortress*, or any of his essays on psychotic children, and before he had even set foot in the Orthogenic School, Bettelheim had made a name for himself through his writings on the Nazi camps, and on the related subject of anti-Semitism. It was thanks to those essays that he achieved recognition in the United States as an expert on human behavior. His observations about the camps played a role in awakening Americans to the reality of Nazism, and they also gave a powerful illustration of the depth of Bettelheim's insights into the human soul. They invested him with moral authority. In other words, it was at Dachau and Buchenwald that the lumber merchant–cum–philosophy student, whose psychoanalysis had been so abruptly cut short by the Anschluss, gave birth, through a process of fear, pain, and permanent humiliation, to Bettelheim the psychoanalyst. It was there that his reading of Freud, his time on Richard Sterba's couch, his talks with Gina, and the experience of living with Patsy all came together to light the way ahead, both in the short and the long term.

Which is why I consider it essential to try and retrace, as faithfully and precisely as possible, the circumstances in which the experience took place. Fifty years on, this is no easy task. First for practical reasons: both documents and witnesses are rare, and although Bettelheim wrote a great deal about the camps, he went into very little detail regarding his daily life there, always preferring a more distant, analytical standpoint.

But another, more subtle, difficulty arises when trying to reconstitute the atmosphere of Dachau and Buchenwald in 1938–39. It results from the pictures etched on all our minds since Soviet troops entered Auschwitz in January 1945. As Bettelheim himself stressed, the logic of the death camps was different from that of the concentration camps. Even though, at least as far as the Jews were concerned, the former were but the diabolical extrapolation of the latter; even though Dachau served as the laboratory for Auschwitz.

Three types of sources were used in this research. First Bettelheim's own writings and statements, the testimony he gave in July 1945 to the Washington office of Judge Jackson, the U.S. Chief Counsel at the Nuremberg War Crimes Tribunal, the nineteen letters he sent to his mother while he was in the camps, and the few snippets of information he revealed later to those close to him. Second, books and other publicly available documents on the camps.[1] And finally, the testimony of two of Bettelheim's fellow inmates at Dachau and Buchenwald. One was Ernst Federn, the youngest son of one of Sigmund Freud's closest collaborators,[2] who was twenty-eight when he met Bettelheim at Buchenwald and remained an inmate right up until the liberation of the camp in 1945.[3] The other was Hans Bandler, an engineer ten years younger than Bettelheim, who arrived at Dachau in the same train as he did and was to go through more or less the same stages. Bandler, however, was released three months before Bettelheim.[4]

Three types of sources, providing data of three different types, which unfortunately do not always fit perfectly together. After several attempts to arrange them into some kind of hierarchy and thus create a seamless picture, I slowly came to the conclusion that they simply had to be allowed to coexist, without seeking at all cost to make them perfectly coherent. The reality of the camps is to be apprehended via these testimonies taken as a whole. Bettelheim's testimony, first of all, because even when it does not completely jibe with objectively known facts, it nevertheless reflects what went on in his head. And then the stories of his two companions in misfortune, men who were as different from him as they were from one another. From all of this there emerges a world, an experience, of which it is often more enlightening to feel before trying to analyze it.

Before many others, Bruno Bettelheim used the word *dreamlike* to describe life in the camps. *Dream* as in *nightmare*, of course, but above all as a world that was unreal, offering its inhabitants no way of linking their previous existences to the one they had been hurled into, a world from which, as the Austrian survivor Hermann Langbein put it, all the normal laws of human society had been banished.[5] It was a world in which everyday words such as *good, evil, work, honor, justice, merit, man,* or *Jew* did not have the same meanings, and in some cases had precisely the opposite meanings, as they did elsewhere—a world, therefore, that was quite literally unspeakable to all those who had not experienced it. Those who were never in the Nazi camps must resign themselves to the fact that whatever knowledge they can obtain about them will never be either completely real or totally rational (indeed, it is for that reason that some people can dare to claim that the genocide never occurred). The only objective truths that can be acquired about the camps are factual data such as the number of beds, the times of the trains, and even they are only partial. For the rest, for the essentials, we have only the testimony of men and women, the deportees and their warders, who were deliberately put in the situation of being unable to grasp objectively what was happening to them. And Bettelheim was indeed one of the first people to understand, or at least to explain, that crucial aspect of life in a concentration camp.

Before Bruno Bettelheim and his fellow-Viennese arrived at Dachau, the "model" camp on which all the later ones were to be based,[6] it was inhabited only by Germans. The Dachau *Konzentrationslager*, opened in 1933 in a former explosives plant a few miles from Munich in upper Bavaria, was originally designed to house 5,000 prisoners, mostly Communists. Soon, however, it was also taking in Social Democrats, and all those categories of the population that the regime defined as "asocial," such as the handicapped, priests, Jehovah's Witnesses, homosexuals, people labeled "work-shy," and criminals. At the beginning, however, there were not many Jews.

The Austrians who were shipped to Dachau from Vienna between April and June 1938, immediately after the Anschluss, were in fact the first major groups of Jews to be detained in concentration camps for no reason other than their Jewishness.[7] Bettelheim mentioned this fact in passing, but did not elaborate on it. Twenty years later, however, when he was to lash out at the "ghetto thinking" that he thought facilitated the extermination of many Jews by preventing them from fleeing,[8] those who accused him of arrogance and even of anti-Semitism, or who retorted with a "What about you, then?" tended to overlook the fact that, even if he had been able to get out of the camps relatively quickly, Bruno Bettelheim had been among the first to be detained as a result of the Nazis' *racial* policy.

Even though Germany's Jews had been subjected to persecution, insults, and plunder ever since Hitler had come to power in 1933, the only ones actually interned in concentration camps before the spring of 1938 were there either as a result of their activities, political or criminal, or because they had violated the Nuremberg Laws instituted in September 1935, which forbade sexual relations between Jews and non-Jews. And, although those laws did indeed single out Jews as such, there is a genuine difference in the way a man experiences ill-treatment resulting from a risk taken consciously through breaking a law, even an iniquitous one, and ill-treatment meted out solely on the basis of who he is.

The Viennese were also the first foreigners to be interned, even though their jailers refused to label them as such. The detainees were drawn from a wide variety of age groups, social classes, and professions—including politicians, shopkeepers, laborers, artists, and intellectuals—and yet they were all treated alike, which in itself was a shock for the Viennese, who had little experience of social mixing.

Bettelheim arrived at Dachau on Friday June 3, 1938,[9] and was registered as prisoner number 15029. In the signing-in book, he is recorded as "Sch. D. J." The "J" of course stands for *Jude* (Jew), and the "D" for *Deutsch* (German), a label which simply reflected the annexation of Austria.[10] The "Sch" is short for *Schutzhaft*, which literally means "protective detention." The term had been enshrined in law by the Nazi state in order to justify the indefinite detention of anyone who happened to get in its way—and thus to justify the existence of the new camps.[11] It was a catchall category that could include not only avowed anti-Nazi activists such as Ernst Federn, but also vague sympathizers, whose only crime may have been to have signed a petition or donated a bit of cash to movements supporting the underground struggle. According to Federn, Bettelheim fell into the latter category. And that is why his striped deportee's jacket, like those worn by Federn and Bandler, carried a two-colored Star of David: the upper triangle, in red, announced that he was a political prisoner, while the lower one, in yellow, symbolized his Jewishness.

As is well known, the Nazis were sticklers for administrative formalities. New arrivals had to wait for hours, watched over by SS guards and with their bundled possessions at their feet, to fill out the camp admission forms: surname, first name, religion, race, full address, name of closest relative, parents' address, membership in the Communist Party or other dissident groups, previous convictions. And anyone found guilty of "intellectual falsification of documents" could expect little mercy. Outside, the vast camp with its identical blocks lay spread out on each side of the *Lagerstrasse*, or central alley. On June 3, 1938, the weather was hot at Dachau. For the new arrivals the long wait, although frustrating, was a welcome respite after the harrowing twenty-hour journey they had just endured. In the words of David Rousset, another camp survivor, it was a period of "soothing indifference," before yet known tortures.[12]

Most of these men were educated, and many of them had already heard about the concentration camps. However, as Bettelheim himself later admitted,[13] they were at that point still at the stage of wondering whether the reports were really true. How many of them, for example, were taken in by the slogan displayed in wrought iron on the camp gate: *Arbeit Macht Frei* (Work Makes Men Free)? Heinrich Himmler, who as deputy police chief of Munich had insisted on being the one to announce the opening of the Dachau camp in March 1933, was to have the same slogan reproduced seven years later over the gates of Auschwitz.

In different circumstances, Bruno Bettelheim would probably have been the first one to point out the sick humor of the slogan. He would no doubt have found even more ironic the statement painted in huge white letters on the roof of the camp's administrative section. "There is a path to freedom," it read. "The stages along it are obedience, zeal, honesty, order, cleanliness, sobriety, sincerity, the spirit of self-sacrifice and love of the fatherland." At the time of his arrival, however, Bettelheim was in no state to appreciate such absurdities. In the train that had brought him from Vienna he had been brutally beaten about the head and even stabbed with a bayonet.

His practical initiation into Nazi dehumanization techniques had begun the previous evening at Vienna's principal train station, the Westbanhof, not far from the lumber company that was to go on bearing his name for a few days more. If Bettelheim's train had left just twenty hours later than it did, he might have crossed paths with Sigmund Freud, headed regretfully for exile along with his wife and daughter Anna.[14]

Up until that point the prisoners had certainly not been handled with kid gloves, but they had not been subjected to excessive cruelty. After their arrests they had been herded together in a school building and had suffered the anxiety of not knowing what was to become of them. But many of them, including Bettelheim, had been arrested previously, and they had usually been allowed to go home a few hours or days later. They had been ill treated, but they were still in their own city, close to friends and relatives. "I thought they'd send us home any time," Hans Bandler told me. "I had belonged to the Socialist youth group before Dollfuss. And when the Nazis marched in the streets, I looked out the window and I could see some of my former comrades from the Movement! The whole thing seemed absurd . . . I felt they were essentially kids claiming to be in command of things. I kept asking myself: 'When will they come to their senses?' "

The real nightmare had started in the late afternoon of June 2, when the Nazis had suddenly packed their charges into their notorious *Schwarze Marias* (black marias, or police vans), the windows blacked out to prevent the prisoners from seeing where they were being taken.

Bruno Bettelheim's account of his journey to Dachau, which took him across two-thirds of Austria and southern Germany, is relegated to a few lines of footnotes at the beginning of *Surviving*: "On the train ride from Vienna to Dachau, which had lasted a night and the better part of a day, all the prisoners were severely mistreated. Of the approximately 700 to 800 prisoners who were part of this particular transport, at least twenty were killed during the night. Hardly anybody escaped unharmed, and many were wounded severely."[15] That rather laconic statement was confirmed by everyone who survived the journey. There may have been discrepancies as to the figures, but all agreed that the SS guards were extremely brutal during the trip.[16] As the deportees were hustled into the cars amid shouts, insults, and barked orders, blows from rifle butts rained down on them. Whatever the age or status of the victims, the tone was always the same: "You, the Jew! Get a move on, get back, keep your eyes up," and so on.

Once on the train, the prisoners were ordered to sit down and keep their eyes fixed on the lights that hung from the ceilings of the rattling railroad cars. According to Bettelheim, the Nazis had deliberately put in more powerful bulbs, to make the lights more blinding. Machine guns were trained on the prisoners, and anyone who let himself slump down or appear to fall asleep was rewarded with a hail of blows. In some cases, this led to death. Hans Bandler, who was on the same train, could not tell me how many people died; as he kept his eyes glued to the ceiling during the whole trip he saw practically nothing. He did witness an execution, however: that of a young man who had tried to escape by jumping out a window during the night. The guards stopped the train and shot him dead. Some time later, Bandler discovered that the victim had been one of his classmates.

Bettelheim soon detected method in the apparent madness of the SS guards. The periods of physical torture alternated with psychological torture, which included obliging the prisoners to blaspheme their God or call their wives or mothers whores. On some occasions the guards also got the prisoners to fight among themselves. Bettelheim noted that the ill-treatment tended to decrease in intensity the longer it lasted, only to return to full strength each time the guards were rotated. He saw this as proof that the torture was part of a deliberate strategy. Around twelve hours into the journey, he heard an order being passed among the guards: "Stop mistreating the prisoners." The abuse stopped immediately, and did not resume until after their arrival at Dachau.[17]

It seemed to Bettelheim that the torture served two purposes: to break any resistance on the part of the prisoners, and to train the young SS guards, many of whom had been recruited only recently from rural regions. They obviously had to be taught that their charges, whose urban sophistication could all too easily have intimidated them, were in fact the inferior beings that the official ideology said they were.

Bettelheim's injuries were apparently inflicted at the beginning of the train ride. He does not describe the incident itself, but says he suspected the attack was inspired by his horn-rimmed glasses, which "marked me as an intellectual" and which, he writes, were shattered by the first blow. He lost a lot of blood, and became gradually weaker and groggier as the journey dragged on. He was also in a state of psychological shock; like Hans Bandler, he had simply not believed such things to be possible. But at the same time, he felt himself becoming curiously detached from what was going on, and began asking himself questions such as "whether man can endure so much without committing suicide or going insane."[18]

Although Bettelheim felt very much like fainting in order to escape the physical pain, he resisted the temptation, realizing, as apparently most other prisoners did, that to do so would be suicidal. "Anyone unable to follow orders was killed."[19] He also felt it was essential for him to observe what was going on. At the same time, he found himself fighting a growing sense of unreality, having to tell himself that no, it was not a nightmare, it was really happening. He wondered whether the guards were stupid, or simply sadistic. After a while, he even took grim comfort from their obvious lack of imagination. He almost smiled to himself on hearing them repeat how they preferred to beat the prisoners to death rather than shoot them, since a bullet cost six pfennigs, and they were not worth that much.

His overriding concern was "to safeguard his ego in such a way that, if by any good luck he should regain liberty, he would be approximately the same person he was when deprived of liberty."[20] That, at least, was the way he remembered it when he described the journey in his first article on the camps three years later. The passage was emphasized by italics. When he began "interviewing" his fellow-inmates, Bettelheim found that all the new arrivals expressed the same will to get through the nightmare so as to find both themselves and the outside world unchanged when they came out, to the extent that they sometimes went into a rage when they learned from a letter or other message that one of their possessions had been sold, even though the sale was often aimed at purchasing their freedom. Later, when Bettelheim tried to put his thoughts in order so as to write about the camps, he cited this desire to maintain both self and the outside world in the same state as one of the defining characteristics of what he called the "new prisoners," meaning those who had been inside for less than a year.

Once checked in to the camp, the new arrivals were taken to the clothing block, where each was issued underwear, a shirt, a pair of pants, a jacket, cap, and shoes, without the slightest attention being paid to sizes. They were then ordered to strip and were subjected to a humiliating body search. All the clothing they had arrived in, and all other possessions, had to be handed over to the inmates who were in charge of storage; all valuables such as watches and jewelry were put into a cloth bag with their name on it.[21] These formalities completed, the new prisoners were sent to their block.

Bettelheim had lost so much blood during the train ride that the morning after his arrival the prisoner in charge of block 22, to which he had been assigned, sent him, along with a few others, to the *Revier*, or camp infirmary. There, a doctor prescribed three days of complete rest, followed by three days of *Schonung*, or "preferred treatment." As Bettelheim later observed, this probably saved his life, giving him time to marshal his strength before plunging into the life of the camp. "What may have been more beneficial in the long run, it was also an opportunity to attempt taking stock of my experience, to sort out first impressions of what being in this horrible predicament was doing to my comrades and to me . . . Had I been projected immediately into the dreadfully destructive grind of deadly mistreatments and utterly exhausting labor, as were my comrades, I do not know whether I would have succeeded equally well in reestablishing some parts of my psychological protective system."[22]

The Dachau day started at 4 A.M., with the cleaning out of the blocks. The SS guards insisted that beds be made perfectly, which was no easy job, given that they consisted of shapeless straw mattresses laid two abreast on three-level bunks. It was "such a difficult task that prisoners sometimes preferred to sleep on the floor sooner than risk destroying their well-built beds."[23] The morning ablutions were performed in a rush; there were not enough washbasins to go around; screams, pushing, and constant anxiety were the norm. Then came two roll calls, the first just outside the block and the second, the main one, on the camp parade ground at 5:15. In theory, the work teams were formed at 6 A.M., but in practice the roll calls always went on later than that. The SS guards made so many mistakes in their count that the prisoners began to wonder whether they were not doing it on purpose. Each time a discrepancy was found, the whole process would begin again.

After the roll call, the prisoners were given their daily ration of around half a pound of bread. They then lined up, three abreast, to begin the long day's work. There was a one-hour break at lunchtime, during which they had to resist the temptation to wolf down all their bread in one gulp. Work would then continue until 6 P.M., when they returned to their blocks to await the evening roll call, an hour later. Dinner was a bowl of soup, which on good days might contain a scrap of sausage or whale meat. It was lights out at 9 P.M.

The Nazi regime was not yet concerned with getting as much free labor as possible out of its prisoners. Its aim was to break them, to strip them of all pride in themselves and their abilities, which is why plumbers found themselves pressed into activity as hairdressers (each prisoner's head was shaved on arrival) and tailors were made to do carpentry. As for the middle-class people and intellectuals rounded up in Vienna, they were forced, at least for a time, to spend the day carrying enormous rocks from one end of the camp to the other, only to carry them back again the next day.

Columns of men driven to their tasks like beasts of burden with mechanical movements and lowered eyes, always at the mercy of an accident, or worse still, of some whim on the part of an SS guard or a *Kapo* (a work team leader, chosen from among the prisoners). Men who appeared to be devoting all their remaining energy to merging into their surroundings, avoiding being noticed. "The most dangerous time was when you needed to go to the toilet—and, given what we ate, we often had diarrhea. You had to ask for permission. Then you never knew if a bullet wasn't going to hit you as you turned your back. 'Shot while trying to escape,' was the way they accounted for those deaths," Hans Bandler recalled.[24]

It was not yet Treblinka or Auschwitz, not yet systematic extermination, but death was nevertheless omnipresent. Death that could be caused just by some SS guard's need to let off steam, death from exhaustion, or the death that comes from simply giving up. Some prisoners, in a last desperate act of revolt, threw themselves onto the electrified barbed wire that surrounded the camp; others, a larger group, simply grew weary of fighting for survival. As Bettelheim immediately noticed, the first of many inversions that took place in the concentration camps, even at that early stage, was between life and death. In the world the prisoners had been removed from, life was the norm and death something accidental or unusual. Here in the camps, it was the other way around.

Survival could no longer be taken for granted; it required unremitting vigilance. Perhaps Bettelheim recalled, with bitter irony, the long drawn-out agony of his father, those two endless years during which he had had to watch helplessly as Anton, in spite of the terrible illness, the pain, the horrible deterioration of both his body and his mind, had clung on stubbornly to life. Perhaps it was that memory which gave Bruno Bettelheim the determination and strength to hold out against a despicable enemy, whether it be called syphilis or Nazism. Maybe he told himself, once again: "Not me! That won't happen to me."

One evening shortly after his arrival, while he was still recovering from his injuries, Bettelheim was staring at his soup, unable to touch it. A German Communist worker who had already been inside for four years told him: "Listen you, make up your mind: do you want to live or do you want to die? If you don't care, don't eat the stuff. But if you want to live, there's only one way: make up your mind to eat whenever and whatever you can, never mind how disgusting. Whenever you have a chance, defecate, so you'll be sure your body works. And whenever you have a minute, don't blabber, read by yourself, or flop down and sleep."[25] Bettelheim says he did not fully understand all the implications of that lesson in survival until several years later. But from that moment on, swallowing the awful soup became for him an act of freedom, simply because it was no longer something imposed on him by the Nazis, but the result of his conscious decision to remain alive.

Bettelheim's small stature, his extreme nearsightedness, and his frail constitution—in other words, all the characteristics that had made him vulnerable in the schoolyard—now became doubly dangerous. Furthermore, his quick temper and his physical clumsiness marked him from the start as a high-risk prisoner, the type who often did not make it through the first few weeks. The same inmate told him: "If you survive the first three months, you will survive the next three years."[26] Bettelheim immediately started calculating how he could avoid being assigned work that would rapidly prove too much for him. After spending several days pushing heavy wagons loaded with rocks alongside Bettelheim, Hans Bandler has a recollection of his friend being put at least for a while on latrine duty. The inmates who were given that foul-smelling job were derisively referred to as "Kolonne 4711," after a well-known brand of eau de Cologne. The task, which consisted of hauling buckets laden with excrement, had two genuine advantages, however. The nauseating odor kept the guards at a distance, and the workers were granted a warm shower every evening.[27] Although Bettelheim himself never explained what type of work he had done during his detention, Bandler's recollection is supported by the Austrian psychiatrist Eugen Kogon in his book on the camps.[28] Kogon states that although for a certain time latrine duty at Dachau was reserved for the Jews, the task was also at one point assigned to Max and Ernst Hohenburg, the two sons of Archduke Franz Ferdinand. This could explain why Bettelheim later wrote that he had rubbed shoulders with "two Austrian dukes, closely related to the former emperor."[29] In *The Informed Heart*, published much later, he was to describe an incident during which "a duke of Hohenburg, grandnephew of the Austrian Emperor, was cruelly mistreated and humiliated." The preceding sentence states that "at one time, I worked alongside of a count." The relative lack of surveillance of the latrine squad made it easier for the inmates to communicate with one another. Later, when analyzing the behavior of his fellow-inmates, Bettelheim would put the three members of the aristocracy he had met in the camps in a category all of their own, stressing how their innate feeling of superiority helped protect them against the general degradation, even though some SS guards singled them out for especially brutal treatment. Kogon also notes that the two Hohenburg dukes showed great courage during their incarceration.

"My year in the concentration camps . . . was to teach me much; so much, that I am not at all sure I have even now exhausted what was implied in that learning experience," Bettelheim wrote in 1960, as he sought to define the role played by the experience in his life as a whole.[30] The reaction is typical. While others simply suffered, Bettelheim felt from the outset the need to be in control of what was happening to him. And in the state of powerlessness that was the prisoner's lot, the only available option was to try to make mind rule over matter, to try to understand, and once again give meaning to, the events around him.

This defensive reaction had been triggered as soon as Bettelheim had been arrested. Even before he had fully realized what was in store for him, he had felt the need to observe, assess, and analyze the behavior of the men who had him in their grip. It was his way of holding his head up, of refusing to admit defeat. Although he credited his persecutors with both intelligence and power, as his writings clearly show, he quickly saw that they were already seriously affected by the very process of dehumanization to which they were subjecting their victims.

Very soon, however, Bettelheim's attention was drawn to something even more important to him than the Nazis' behavior: his own. "Almost from the moment I was imprisoned, and particularly during the transport to Dachau and my first days inside it, I was aware that I not only acted, but more important, often felt differently than I used to." Observing his own moods, scrutinizing his own behavior to check whether it was "normal" was an exercise Bettelheim was accustomed to. His long-running fight against depression had taught him to be on the alert for danger signs. "At first I made myself believe this was only on the surface, changes that did not touch my personality. But soon I realized that what had happened to me—for instance, the split within me into one who observed and one to whom things happened—was a typical schizophrenic phenomenon. So I began to ask myself, 'Am I going insane or am I already insane?' "[31]

When the Nazis had marched into Vienna, Bettelheim had been in the middle of a psychoanalysis. The analytic process does not end when the sessions do; the doors of the unconscious, which often require so much effort to push ajar, cannot be simply slammed shut again. The awareness that the analysand has sought to attain, over a period of months or years, of his or her most secret wounds, those that are the most painful and therefore the best-protected, cannot suddenly be made to go away. The habit of questioning every daily gesture, dream, or thought does not come to a halt simply because the treatment has. Why therefore should the process end any more easily after a shock like the one Bettelheim had experienced—the Anschluss, followed by separation, the expropriation of all his property, and internment in a concentration camp?

This concern about his mental health was what led Bettelheim to undertake the study that, several years later, would make his reputation in the United States. The idea occurred to him toward the end of his first month in Dachau: "Early one morning . . . I was deep in the middle of what was the favorite free-time activity: exchanging tales of woe and swapping rumors about changes in the camp conditions or possible liberation." Although they did not last very long, the conversations got the prisoners very worked up.

As before on such occasions, I went through many severe mood swings from fervent hope to deepest despair, with the result that I was emotionally drained before the day even began, a day of seventeen long hours that would take all my energy to survive it. While swapping tales that morning, it suddenly flashed through my mind, "this is driving me crazy," and I felt that if I were to go on that way, I would in fact end up "crazy." That was when I decided that rather than be taken in by such rumors I would try to understand what was psychologically behind them.[32]

At the same time, Bettelheim began to notice the strange behavior of many of his fellow-inmates. Even though nothing indicated that they had been anything but normal before their arrests, in Dachau Bettelheim saw them behave like pathological liars, incapable of controlling their emotions and having seemingly lost all ability to assess situations objectively. He wondered whether he was not headed down the same path. After all, perhaps what was happening to him was not the onset of insanity, but simply a process of adapting to the particular circumstances of camp life. But if that were so, another serious question arose: How could one protect oneself against such a process?[33]

When faced with his father's illness, the young Bruno Bettelheim had finally drawn on the strength of his own will to fight a totally unjust, oppressive, and deadly situation. Now, behind the Nazis' barbed wire, he found the same type of strength. He could count neither on his physical stamina nor on his charm, and he lacked any practical know-how. He had only his mental powers to rely on.

> All my thoughts, all my energies went into the desperate struggle to survive the day, to fight off depressive moods, to keep up the will to resist, to gain some small advantages that might make seemingly impossibly difficult efforts to survive just a bit more likely to succeed, and to frustrate as much as possible the SS's unrelenting efforts to break the spirit of the prisoners. When I was not too exhausted or downhearted to do so, I tried to understand what went on in me and in others because this was of interest to me.[34]

To turn what came naturally to him into a conscious project, he started talking to the prisoners around him whenever he got the chance. He would quiz them about their lives, their families, and their hopes. He would make them talk about their work. And then he would spend the long working hours trying to commit every detail to memory, since he did not have any way of keeping notes. Bettelheim soon realized that he had resolved another problem along the way: "By talking with my fellow prisoners with a particular purpose in mind, by pondering my findings for the hours without end during which I was forced to perform exhausting labor which did not ask for any mental concentration, I succeeded in killing the time in a way which seemed constructive."[35] On occasion, he even found himself forgetting that he was in a concentration camp. Even more important, Bettelheim realized a short time later that his undertaking had given him back his pride. After all, "it was one of the rare satisfactions that the SS could not deprive me of."[36] It was a purely private victory over the enemy, but it nevertheless pulled him out of a slide into depression that in those circumstances would almost certainly have proved fatal. He had found his own way of adapting to an environment that was, in the full meaning of the word, insane.

On Sundays, the prisoners did not work. They could talk to one another more or less freely, read some newspapers, and write to their families. They were allowed to send two letters a month. These had to be written on small sheets of ruled paper, twelve lines a page, with the camp regulations stamped on the first sheet. Bettelheim's letters to his mother were impeccable, his elongated hand usually filling all the available space on the authorized lines. The writing is quite legible (a requirement of the censor), and most of the time quite firm. Their tone is also firm; the letters discuss practical matters almost exclusively: forms to be filled out, debts to his tailor or shirtmaker to be paid off, and of course requests to be filed for the various documents needed for his release. Whether it was due to the censorship, or his desire to avoid worrying his family, Bettelheim made no mention whatsoever of what he was going through, either physically or emotionally. If it were not for their format, his letters could on a casual reading have been taken for those of an executive on a business trip, giving instructions to his secretary. A closer reading, however, yields hints of pain and anxiety. On July 3, for example, he wrote: "Don't worry about me; there's no point, as it would serve no purpose." On July 17: "Regarding myself, I haven't got very much to tell you. My life is filled with work, and the longing I feel for you . . . Think of yourselves, not of me, for over time that would be too heavy a burden." On July 31: "I am torn by feelings of longing . . . Tell Gina that all my hopes rest on the future she is building for us."

As one reads on, the image of the strong businessman in control of everything, displaying irritation when his orders are not carried out on the double, gradually gives way to a very different one: that of a man struggling desperately to remain in touch with the outside world, a man determined to repress the pain and yearning that threaten to overwhelm him, a man who has set himself a single goal: to make sure that no stone was left unturned in the effort to get him out, and should he be set free, that no red tape would prevent him from going abroad as soon as possible.

He had placed his business affairs in the hands of his cousin Norbert Bettelheim, a lawyer, to whom he had formally given power of attorney on the morning of his arrest. Norbert took care of the so-called sale of Bettelheim's company, made an official inventory of his assets, and oversaw the efforts of a variety of people to obtain his release. He was well connected, and as he was married to an Aryan and had converted to Protestantism, he appeared to have a good chance of being left alone by the Nazis, at least in the period immediately following the Anschluss. But as Bruno Bettelheim saw it, his cousin was not acting speedily enough. At the end of July, for example, he was expressing surprise that the business inventory had still not been completed, for he had sent Paula a second proxy statement, along with a list of all of his assets and liabilities, as soon as he had arrived at Dachau.[37] He was also bursting for news of his U.S. visa application, his receipt of taxes, and his *Ubedenklichkeitserklarüng*, the "certificate of innocence" without which nobody was allowed to leave Austria. Attending to every possible detail, he shot off a stream of instructions to his mother and sister. And in spite of what he was going through himself, he clearly did not imagine how appalling life had become for the Jews still in Vienna. Just as he did not mention his sufferings in his letters to Paula, she also refrained from mentioning her lot: how she had been obliged to seek refuge with her neighbors, and how she was surviving by selling off her jewelry, having not received a cent from the sale of his company.

At the same time, Bettelheim took an interest in the fate of all his near and dear, including Trude. Why had she not yet left Austria? And his aunt, Grete Bettelheim—if she had an opportunity to emigrate to Honduras, let her take it! What about Gina's mother, Mina? Was she being taken care of? In spite of his forced absence, he remained very much the paterfamilias, even down to remembering everyone's birthday. And above all, having quickly learned how to get his message across in spite of the camp censors, he succeeded in communicating the idea that henceforth, emigration was the only possible option for everyone.

On September 23, 1938, after the morning roll call, the inmates were told to get their possessions together. Then, in what Hans Bandler remembers as a bolt from the blue, the guards ordered them to pile into military trucks. *"Schnell, schnell!"* Each man was given a chunk of bread, a small piece of sausage, and a minute ration of margarine. Then, in great haste, all the camp's inmates were hauled off northward, with no idea of where they were being taken.

On the eve of his meeting at Munich with the French and British prime ministers, Daladier and Chamberlain, and with his invasion of Czechoslovakia already planned, Hitler had decided to empty the Bavarian concentration camp, considering it too exposed in the event of a Franco–British reaction. So the Dachau prisoners were being taken farther into the German heartland, to the Prussian camps of Sachsenhausen and, for the Jews, Buchenwald.

When Bettelheim arrived at Buchenwald, it was already known throughout the Reich as one of the toughest of the concentration camps.[38] Opened in 1937, it was in the process of being enlarged when the "Dachau Jews" arrived, and of course the job was being carried out by the inmates themselves. One day, Ernst Federn's labor team was ordered to form a human chain to supply bricklayers working on new blocks. The men were spaced just far enough apart so that they had to throw the bricks, rather than passing them from hand to hand. Federn quickly became irritated at his immediate neighbor, who managed to drop every single brick he threw to him. He didn't know the man, but did know that he was playing a dangerous game. He ran the risk of hurting his foot or, worse still, of getting himself noticed by a guard. Federn made a remark.

"Is that your brick?" came the reply. After a few similarly curt exchanges, Federn finally blurted out: "You nobody!" (*"Du niemand!"*)

"Who is a nobody for you? Are you an anybody? I am Bettelheim."

"And I am Federn."

"Are you a relative of Paul Federn?"

"I am his son."

Thereupon the two men "shook hands and remained friends from that hour. I think even friends of a very special kind, because as far as I can remember, Bettelheim has never raised his voice against me," Federn wrote.[39] The manner of their meeting was to set the tone for their whole relationship, a tone which, to judge from their correspondence, consisted of affectionate camaraderie spiced with a fair measure of rivalry.

There were considerable differences between Dachau and Buchenwald. The Prussian camp was much larger, the size of a small town.

Above all, it was filthy, the lack of paving, the endless rain, and the construction work having all conspired to turn it into a giant mud-bath. The sticky dirt was practically impossible to get rid of and made the inmates' lives a misery; in wintertime they were often up to their knees in the slimy mess. After a few days, some of them even ended up laughing at fellow-sufferers who collapsed into it, too weak to lift their legs out of the muck, which seemed like a metaphor for all their sufferings.[40] Inside the blocks, they were forced to spend their time sweeping, mopping, and boot-cleaning if they wanted to avoid yet more blows and insults from the SS and their surrogates. The latter were all the more fearsome in that it was the "Greens," or common-law prisoners, who were in charge of the camp at that time.[41]

The Nazis' system was based on having the concentration camps run by the inmates themselves, under a well-defined hierarchy that included the *Kapo* (work-team leader), the *Blockältester* (block leader), and so on, right up to the *Lagerältester*, who was a kind of shadow camp commander. (It was a hierarchy that resembled that of the SS itself.)[42] In exchange for material privileges (better food, more freedom of movement, including in some cases access to the camp brothel), certain of the inmates took on much of the SS's daily drudgery. Needless to say, these workers could be stripped of their role and privileges just as arbitrarily as they had been elevated to them in the first place. For the Germans, it was a system that shielded them from the everyday hatred of the inmates, but also no doubt from their own feelings of disgust.[43] Above all, it served to break the prisoners even more radically, by compromising them and undermining any trust between them.

But the effectiveness of the system depended on the type of men chosen to be so elevated above their fellows. On arriving at Buchen-wald, in the same convoy as Bettelheim, Benedikt Kautsky, another Viennese arrested after the Anschluss, immediately noticed the dif-ference between a camp run by political detainees, as Dachau had been, and one in the hands of common-law prisoners: being ruled by the Greens, he wrote, meant "corruption, torture, hunger, and ill-treatment inflicted on inmates by other inmates."[44]

Bruno Bettelheim did not write about his arrival at Buchenwald. Another firsthand account, however, that of the German journalist Walter Poller, is worth citing. A Socialist, Poller had been sentenced in 1934 to four years' imprisonment for his anti-Nazi activities, and after having served his term in various ordinary jails he was sent to

Buchenwald two months after the "Dachau Jews." His account of
arriving at the camp is very similar to that given by the Viennese
detainees of their first transfer: the terrible rush, being made to run
an SS gauntlet of gunshots and blows from rifle-butts along what was
known as the "Karacho way" (from a slang term meaning "at full
speed"), the long narrow alley that ran between the camp's administrative buildings. And woe betide anyone who stopped to worry about
those of his fellows who had not made it. Once at the other end, the
prisoners would be greeted with the phrase that was to become a leit-
motif of the concentration camps: "You are not in a sanatorium here!
Those of you who haven't yet realized that will be made to understand, you can count on that!"

On their arrival, the prisoners were given a long lecture detailing
the camp rules. Political discussion was forbidden, as were gatherings
of any kind. Anyone witnessing an act of disobedience was to report
it immediately. Any prisoner who failed to work to the limits of his
strength would be punished; the standard punishment was twenty-
five strokes of the whip, or blows from a club, delivered on the back
with the victim stretched out on the *Bock*, a crude wooden whipping-
block that stood in a corner of the huge parade ground. Those who
had money on arrival were allowed to keep ten marks; the rest had to
be handed over to the camp purser on pain of a beating. Inmates were
held at Buchenwald indefinitely, with release depending on their
behavior. They were allowed to write fifteen-line letters to their families, on condition that they contained no information on life in the
camp and no politics. The lecture concluded: "You are not convicts
here, you are only 'under detention,'[45] and what that means you will
soon learn, if you have not done so already! You are dishonorable and
defenseless! You are outlawed! Yours is a serf's lot! . . . That's all!"[46]

In addition to the down-to-earth details it provides, Poller's account
is interesting in that he viewed the Jewish blocks in Buchenwald from
the outside. As a non-Jewish German who, from his arrival in the
camp, had received discreet protection from a network of political
friends already there, Poller was somewhat privileged. In particular, he
was able to visit various sections of the camp. His account gives an
idea of the gulf between the living conditions of the "yellow triangles"
and those of the others. The "Dachau Jews" were not treated as hor-
rendously as the 10,000 "night of crystal" detainees, who had arrived
at Buchenwald six weeks later, in mid-November 1938.[47] However, as
Poller noted, their lives were in every respect more difficult than those

of the non-Jewish inmates. They had less food, even less space, and were subjected to extra deprivation on the slightest pretext. They were housed in wooden barracks in the center of the camp; Bruno Bettelheim and Hans Bandler were in block n° 17.

Even in *The Informed Heart*, by far the most detailed of his writings on the subject, Bettelheim sticks to relatively abstract terms when discussing the difference between Dachau and Buchenwald. He notes for instance, that at Buchenwald, which "reflected a later phase of National-Socialism,"[48] inmates were no longer treated as individuals. In particular, punishment was almost always collective, so that the group's resentment would be directed toward the person whose behavior had incurred it, and neither heroes nor martyrs could emerge. But Bettelheim never really discusses everyday life at Buchenwald in any detail; indeed he opens most of his texts by stressing that his aim is not to give yet another account of the horrors of the Nazi camps. And the rare personal anecdotes he indulges in are almost always relegated to the status of footnotes. Once again, he shows his determination to rise above the material, flesh-and-blood level of events.

Nevertheless, on reading the accounts of other inmates of Buchenwald—a camp on which both archives and personal accounts are more numerous and more comprehensive than those relating to any other—it is difficult to imagine how Bettelheim could so completely put to one side the purely material details of his life in such a place, where he spent more than six months without ever knowing whether he would come out of it alive. In his letters, which are shorter than those he sent from Dachau, his determination to go on settling his affairs with a view to a purely hypothetical release shines through, all the more so in that his handwriting has deteriorated. The reasoned content of the letters is belied by their spiky, frantic form, which suggests that the writer was, at the very least, physically exhausted.

Of course, Bettelheim the survivor had learned a lot during his four months of internment at Dachau. At Buchenwald, taking advantage of the extraordinary level of corruption presided over by *Lagerkommandant* Karl Koch,[49] he was able relatively quickly to maneuver himself into a somewhat "cushy" position. At least that was how Ernst Federn viewed Bettelheim's assignment to the camp's sock-darning workshop. The job allowed Bettelheim to work indoors during the bitter winter cold, and above all, it meant he was under the orders of a political rather than a common-law *Kapo*, and one who was relatively easygoing. As a result, he was spared the continual insults that were hurled at other camp inmates, at least during daytime. Bettelheim himself does not clearly state that he was assigned to the darning shop, but he does refer to conversations that took place in "very safe commands, such as that of the sock menders, where prisoners were seated rather comfortably at tables and worked quietly at a very easy task."[50]

Nevertheless, throughout the six months he was to spend at Buchenwald, Bettelheim shared his fellow-inmates' lot of overcrowded living-quarters, in which they had to stand even while they swallowed their evening soup. He had to sleep on the awful straw mattresses, on which the prisoners were so tightly packed together that if one turned over he awoke several others. He was forced to take part on occasion in the "sports sessions," during which the SS guards entertained themselves by forcing a few prisoners to exercise until they died of physical exhaustion. He also had to use the horrendous latrines, which consisted of huge pits over which were placed two parallel tree trunks. The prisoners, having quickly had to lose all sense of shame, sat crammed side by side, being pressured to hurry by those awaiting their turn and terrified of losing their balance or being pushed to a horrible death. That fear has continued to haunt Hans Bandler to this day. It also seems to have been one of the factors that triggered Bettelheim's long essay "Surviving," written after he had seen Lina Wertmuller's film *Seven Beauties*, in which such a scene is dealt with in a comical vein.[51]

During the winter he spent at the camp with the deceptively pretty name (Buchenwald means "beech forest"), located on Ettersberg, a hill best known up until then to music- and poetry-lovers as a place where Bach, Goethe, and Schiller all loved to stroll, Bettelheim also experienced the interminable roll calls in the freezing cold.[52] On at least two occasions that year, these ordeals, during which weaker prisoners would collapse and die under the eyes of comrades who could not do anything to help them without themselves risking death, lasted all night. Bettelheim must also have witnessed, equally powerless, a few suicides, and certainly saw some prisoners perish during punishment on the *Bock*. He saw others shot down like dogs, and he witnessed the disastrous effects of the typhus epidemic that broke out shortly after the arrival of the "November Jews."

That is not to mention the impact that the bloodbath staged by the SS guards to mark the latter's arrival must have had on the "Dachau

Jews," only recently transferred themselves. "How could anyone forget the sight of Captain Wolf, the Jewish officer who had commanded the World War I flotilla in which Göring had served, and who had thought he could invoke his Medal of Merit, the highest German distinction for acts of bravery, but who instead was rewarded by being crucified alive over the camp entrance, where he perished?"[53] The entrance over which was written "My Fatherland, Right or Wrong."

Bettelheim's remarkable detachment had at least two explanations: his determination to retain control by an effort of mind over matter during his incarceration, and the distance he very deliberately put between his personal experience and the account he wrote of it once he was in the United States.

But a third possible explanation is betrayed by a remark he made about his first hours as a prisoner. In *Surviving*, after describing that traumatic trip to Dachau, Bettelheim goes on to write, using the third person singular which is so disconcerting when discussing such personal experiences: "The author has no doubt that he was able to endure the transportation and all that followed because right from the beginning he became convinced that these horrible and degrading experiences were somehow not happening to 'him' as a subject, but only to 'him' as an object."[54]

One dimension that Bettelheim hardly touches on at all in his writing about the camps is the way the Nazis spoke to the Jews. In spite of the fact that he spent every minute of those endless days striving to memorize everything that had happened to him, for the want of pencil and paper with which to jot it all down, Bettelheim's writings contain no hint of the insults to which he was subjected day and night on account of his Jewishness. Those of us who are lucky enough to have grown up in societies where racist insults are considered impermissible therefore have to turn to other sources to get an inkling of what it was like. "Jewish swine," "hook-nose," "Jewish shit," "synagogue nag," "Jewish scum"—all of this from men who, although despicable, and amply despised by Bettelheim, nonetheless had considerable, indeed absolute, power over his body. "Get a move on, dirty yid!" "Get back!" "Run!" "Jump!" "Down on your knees, down on your belly, you son of a Jewish sow!"

What effect could such a continual outpouring of racist obscenities have on this assimilated Jew, who for all his life had felt much closer intellectually to the German poets than to the bearded talmudists from Leopoldstadt? In *Freud's Vienna*, Bettelheim writes that the positive sense of his Jewish identity he had found in Martin Buber's books became especially important to him, and even life-preserving, at Buchenwald. But that remark made at the beginning of *Surviving* may provide an additional answer to the question.

It is only a guess, but might it not be that the conviction he acquired from the very start that he was only the "object," and not the "subject," of his experiences under Nazi domination reflected in some way the feeling that "these horrible and degrading experiences were somehow not happening to 'him,'" to Bruno Bettelheim, but instead to that "other," a person similar to him yet not the same, whose reflection he kept seeing in the eyes of every SS soldier he encountered—to Bettelheim-the-Jew?

One of the most basic aims of that steely determination to observe, analyze, and understand may have been simply to escape from the bounds of identity within which his torturers sought to enclose him, to keep sight of the fact that even though his birth had made him Jewish, it was not his only destiny. Whence the need to rise above the merely physical, the flesh-and-blood level; to rise above a body enslaved by the enemy. A body upon which his Jewishness had been indelibly marked at birth, for better or worse and above all for worse, by the rabbi's scalpel.

7

---⁂---

Buchenwald:
The Price of Freedom

Aﬅer the evening roll call on December 14, 1938, the inmates waited in vain for the usual order to return to their quarters. In the early afternoon the SS guards had found out about an attempted escape by two Green prisoners, and had decided to inflict harsh punishment on the entire camp.[1] In the midst of a driving blizzard, without hats, coats, or gloves, and with empty stomachs after a twelve-hour work-day, the prisoners were kept standing at attention for nineteen hours under the camp spotlights.

One after another, the oldest and weakest collapsed; if any of their neighbors made a move to help them, the guards opened fire. After a day spent hunting for escapees, they were like mad dogs, beating and killing the inmates at the slightest excuse. Bettelheim noted that after a while, what was clearly an attempt to destroy all solidarity between the inmates began to have the opposite effect. Having seen around twenty of their fellows collapse and die of cold, the inmates began to feel supremely indifferent to their own fate. Once again, it was as if they had split into two parts, one of which was observing what was happening to the other. The guards' threats lost their potency; each individual's chance of survival was so slim that the fear of death receded, and he felt himself becoming more courageous, readier to help his fellows. Paradoxically, they were almost happy. When the order finally came for them to return to their blocks, the survivors were of course relieved. But at the same time, they felt the fear, which the overdose of torture had freed them from, surging up again, while the feeling of mutual support they had briefly experienced receded. The following day, the total number of deaths from the ordeal stood at eighty,[2] while several hundred other men had suffered such serious frostbite that they had to have limbs amputated.

A week later, Bettelheim wrote to his mother to ask her to have a new pair of glasses made for him, solid ones with a strong case. He did not explain how his existing pair had been broken. He still remembered to wish Paula a happy birthday, and sent Christmas greetings to everyone. He also asked for 30 marks.

On Christmas Eve the prisoners were to get a surprise. On marching onto the parade ground for the evening roll call, five abreast as usual, they saw that a gibbet had been erected, close to the *Bock* used for beatings. The SS commanding officer had decided to stage a hanging. Hans Bandler has vivid memories of the event; it was not the first of its kind and would not be the last, but it appears to have impressed the prisoners more than others. The entire SS hierarchy was present, including Koch and his wife. The victim was an officer who had escaped from the camp in May and fled to Czechoslovakia; he had been handed over to the Nazis after they invaded that country.

When there were no executions to stage, the SS diverted themselves by forcing a group of Jews to fight a group of Jehovah's Witnesses in front of the assembled prisoners. On other occasions, they would order the prisoners to form a circle, and then choose a few of them at random to inflict some form of cruelty on them, or even shoot them down like rabbits, depending on their mood. It was also at this time that the SS commander, Rödl, decided that Buchenwald should have its own anthem. On some evenings, the prisoners were kept behind for hours after the roll call in order to rehearse this ditty.[3] All the while, back in their living quarters, their thin soup of whale meat or "sausage," complete with fishbones, would be cooling down to room temperature, several degrees below zero.

Two weeks after Christmas, Bettelheim wrote to his mother to explain how to get his passport photographs certified, stressing every detail of the procedure. He gave instructions for the purchase of his transatlantic boat ticket, and asked Paula to mail 150 marks to a certain Frieda Goldstein in Berlin ("it is a debt of honor," he wrote, "and therefore very important"). He also asked for Gina's address in New York, and expressed concern for the fate of Trude, who had by then left Vienna. A week later he was able to send another letter, with even more demands, made in even more imperious tones. Among his new requests was one for an English phrasebook. It was as if the worse his living conditions became, the more he struggled to convince himself that he was mentally in control of things. Only his handwriting betrayed him: in spite of the new glasses he had received, it had become chaotic and straggly. He had a hard time staying on the lines, and the letters were ill-coordinated.

The mud which invaded every nook and cranny at Buchenwald constituted a major health hazard, as the slightest cut became infected. Given the extreme living conditions, this often led to gangrene, in effect a death warrant. Whence the anxiety that the Jewish prisoners felt when, after the *Kristallnacht* pogrom, they were abruptly forbidden to seek treatment at the *Revier* (infirmary) for anything other than injuries sustained during labor, as Bettelheim reported.[4]

With the onset of the harsh winter of 1938, almost all the inmates suffered from terrible frostbite, sustained while working without adequate protection in the stone quarries close to the camp, or during evening roll calls. If untreated, the ensuing inflammation could become infected, which is what happened to Bettelheim. In spite of the ban he decided to take his chance at the infirmary. He was by no means the only one; the line of prisoners outside the *Revier* was every bit as long as usual.

The decision on whether to admit a prisoner to the infirmary was made by an SS corporal posted at the entrance. As they shuffled and tried to keep warm in the long line stretching ahead of Bettelheim, the Jewish prisoners had only one subject of conversation: the careful stratagem each had worked out to get around the ban. Some planned to cite their service in the German army during World War I, mentioning medals won or injuries sustained. Others preferred simply to make something up—for example, to say that an SS officer had ordered them to report to the infirmary. When one of his neighbors asked him what his intentions were, Bettelheim said he didn't have a precise plan. He preferred to observe the guard's attitude toward those preceding him in line before making up his mind what to say. He added that in his opinion, as it was difficult to predict the reactions of a man one didn't know, it was not a good idea to have a cut-and-dried plan worked out in advance. This remark, according to Bettelheim, earned him jeering comments on the lines of "Gestapomen[5] are all the same." Other prisoners insulted him, accusing him of not wanting to share his plan with them, or even, of wanting to steal theirs.

In the line ahead of him, prisoners wearing the yellow triangle were being systematically denied access to the infirmary. Bettelheim noticed that the more strenuously an inmate tried to convince the guard, the more violent the guard became. The expressions of suffering appeared even to amuse him. When a prisoner tried to invoke his past military service in the German army, the guard became indignant, accusing the man of lying and saying proudly that he was not the kind of guy to be taken in by a Jew; the time when a Jew could get anything he wanted just by whining was over, and a good thing too. "When my turn came," Bettelheim wrote,

> the Gestapoman asked me whether I knew that work accidents were the only reason for admitting Jews to the clinic, and whether I came because of such an accident. I replied that I knew the rules, but that I could not work unless my hands were freed of the dead flesh. Since prisoners were not permitted to possess knives, I asked to have the dead flesh cut away. I made these statements in a matter-of-fact way, avoiding pleading, deference or arrogance.
>
> The Gestapoman replied: "if this is really all you want, I am going to tear the flesh off." He started to pull with force at the festering skin. Because it did not come off as easily as he might have expected, or for some other reason, the Gestapo soldier ordered me to enter the clinic.
>
> Once I was inside the clinic, he gave me a malevolent look and pushed me into the treatment room. There he told the orderly to attend to the wound. While this was being done, the Gestapoman again watched me closely. I succeeded in suppressing signs of pain. As soon as the cutting was accomplished, I started to leave. The Gestapoman seemed surprised and questioned me as to why I did not ask for further treatment. I replied that I had received the service which I had requested. At this he told the orderly to make an exception and to treat my hand. After I had left the room, the Gestapoman called me back and gave me a card entitling me to further treatment and to admittance to the clinic without inspection at its entrance.[6]

Before continuing our account, it is worth examining this anecdote, first published in April 1947. It was to spark controversy, with some critics saying that any exchange between a Jew and an SS man would have been impossible in the camps, some flatly accusing Bettelheim of lying and others reproaching him for failing to show support for his fellow-inmates. Bettelheim's aim in telling the story was to illustrate the idea that by reacting to the Nazis' ideological stereotyping of Jews with counter-stereotypes ("the Nazis are all the same, they are stupid brutes, they can be easily hoodwinked"), the victims in fact made their own situation worse, as they deprived themselves of the ability to react to real-life situations in which their lives were at stake. The article in which he outlined his thesis, brilliantly, was provocatively entitled "The Dynamism of Anti-Semitism in Gentile and Jew."

Ten months later Bettelheim published another piece on the same subject, in the Jewish monthly *Commentary*. This time he went straight to the point, as the title, "The Victim's Image of the Anti-Semite: The Danger of Stereotyping the Adversary," suggests. The article, aimed at a less specialized audience, is much shorter than the previous one. The writer's ideas have had time to mature; the style is even more effective, and details have been pared to the bone. He uses the same incident to support his argument, but devotes only half the space to it, and ends his account at the point where the SS guard reluctantly lets the prisoner into the infirmary. More surprisingly, the hero is this time presented as another person, identified only as "N . . . a trained psychologist, capable of observing the mental processes at work with substantial objectivity." Bettelheim was to rework the account a last time some twelve years later, for inclusion in *The Informed Heart*. There, he reverted to the initial version.

Is it absolutely essential to determine whether "N" and "BB" were one and the same person, whether the incident really happened to Bettelheim himself, whether it was told to him by a fellow-inmate, or whether he simply made the whole thing up? Essential, certainly not. Psychoanalysts who have worked with camp survivors are familiar with the process that sometimes leads them to confuse the stories of their fellow-sufferers with their own—not so much because they want to appropriate another person's experience as because, being but one of a mass of Jews deprived of any identity other than a number, a person can easily end up not being very clear about where his own suffering ends and that of his neighbor begins, and not even considering it important.

The ambiguity is interesting, however, because it touches on one of the most controversial aspects of Bettelheim's personality. Amid the storm of recrimination and accusations that broke out immediately after his death, one of the charges was that he had lied. And as there were indeed points on which he had touched up his biography, the accusation lent weight to other, less easily verifiable, charges. In my opinion, however, when he did lie, it was in a very specific context, over a short period of time and in relation to a very narrow set of facts.[7] Indeed Gina Weinmann, who is one of his sternest critics as regards his honesty, says that in Vienna, Bettelheim had not yet started lying.

That is why the Buchenwald infirmary anecdote stands out as one of the little white pebbles Bettelheim dropped along his path in the course of a life whose details he otherwise tried to obscure. Because his concentration camp experience was to play a crucial role both in the public figure he would become in the United States and in the way his thinking would develop. Because the closed, barbaric world of the camps was the ideal breeding ground for those larger-than-life stories that can help one stay alive. But also because all of Bruno Bettelheim's work on the camps consisted precisely of trying to retrieve the reality of this world which drove people mad.

Whether or not the story itself is authentic, Bettelheim's conclusion has the ring of truth. As is often the case with him, when one has finished reading through the argument (and even if along the way there were specific points one did not agree with), it all seems so crystal-clear that one emerges feeling somewhat disconcerted, wondering how one could not have worked out such an obvious chain of ideas for oneself. Skeptical readers nevertheless might point out that somebody assigned to the sock-mending shop would be less vulnerable to frostbite than most other prisoners. But it is also true that during the *Kristallnacht*, the roll call for Jews had lasted until dawn, and Bettelheim did not spend all his time at Buchenwald protected from the cold in the sock workshop.

Neither Ernst Federn nor Hans Bandler has any recollection of the frostbite episode. Bandler, however, finds it difficult to believe that an inmate could have carried on such a lengthy conversation with an SS guard. As he remembers it, communication with the guards was purely one-way, consisting of a series of barked insults and orders. But then again, what may have applied to the young Hans Bandler, an idealistic and somewhat naïve student, was not necessarily true of Bruno Bettelheim, a man in the prime of life, perceptive, cultivated, and used to holding his own in the world of business. It is clearly impossible to establish the truth with any certainty.

What is incontrovertible is that it was horribly cold at Buchenwald in November 1938, many of the inmates suffered from frostbite and some died as a result, and a ban on visits to the infirmary was a major source of anxiety to men who were famished and exhausted—and above all, that resorting to preconceived ideas is never the best way to get out of a dangerous situation. That is after all the only point that matters and it is also, I believe, the key to the problem. Bruno Bettelheim was a quick reader, of people as well as of books. He caught on fast, and although he let no details escape him, he was interested only in the essentials. In his constant search for meaning, he would consider an incident to be of relevance only if it helped him toward his goal of reaching a conclusion, or as some would put it, of identifying the moral of the story. To that end he was willing to ride roughshod over details if they did not fit in. This I believe was the basis of Bettelheim's overall attitude to truth, after his experiences in the camps.

The story of his broken glasses is another case in point. Contrary to what he was to write later, the letter to his mother at Christmastime seems to indicate that it was not during the train ride to Dachau that they were smashed, but six months later, at Buchenwald.[8] I was not able to ascertain in what circumstances, but what is certain is that the letter in which he asked his mother for new ones was sent a week after the December ordeal on the parade ground. Judging from his handwriting, that was clearly the worst period of his entire spell in the camps. Bettelheim had weighed 150 pounds when he arrived at Dachau; by April 1939 he weighed a mere 86. He had lost most of his hair (although as mirrors were not an everyday luxury in the camps, he was not aware of the fact), and his teeth were in a terrible state. He was also suffering from a stomach ulcer.

Two months prior to the letter mentioning his glasses, in mid-October, his mother had received a brief form letter bearing her son's signature. The printed message said: "I am currently subjected to a mail ban. I therefore cannot receive either letters or parcels. Representations to the camp commander are forbidden, and their only effect would be to cause the punishment to be extended." On November 22 he was allowed to send a short eight-line card, after which his letters resumed their normal twice-monthly flow. It was in the ensuing missives that his handwriting became the most erratic and disorderly. The terrible events in the camp following the *Kristallnacht* pogrom may be sufficient to explain that change, but the ban on Bettelheim's mail predates them by three weeks. Clearly, something had happened in the meantime. It could have been then that he had received the blows to the head which he said had smashed his glasses, which would imply that he had to wait two months before getting permission to write to his family for a replacement pair.

By the time he made that request, he writes, he knew that a prisoner should above all never complain of having been abused. When a guard asked about it, he said simply that his glasses had been broken. The SS man on duty then started beating him, shouting *"What* did you say happened?"* Realizing his mistake, Bettelheim explained that he had broken his glasses himself, by accident. The blows ceased, and, before sitting down to write out the permit, the SS man said: "Okay. Just remember that for the future." The change in the guard's attitude had been too sudden, Bettelheim concluded, to have been spontaneous. "No sadist bent on satisfying his desires will instantly stop mistreatment on getting a correct formula reply. Only a person simply after a specific goal will behave in that way."[9]

Bettelheim used the episode of the glasses to make three important observations about camp life. First, it was dangerous to attract attention to oneself. "Having learned my lesson, I requested—and a while later received—glasses of the simplest and cheapest kind. Even so, I found it best to hide my glasses and do without them whenever the SS went on a rampage; I was much safer that way. This was but one of the many precautions a prisoner had to take if he wanted to increase his chances for survival."[10]

Second, he realized that it was even more dangerous to see than to be seen. Indeed, in many situations "not to see or not to know was not enough; in order to survive one had to actively pretend not to observe, not to know what the SS required one not to know." And third, Bettelheim realized that the troops of the SS *Totenkopf* (death's-head) unit in charge of the camp were not simply cruel brutes: they were clearly obeying precise orders. The violence, torture, and insults they meted out were not in general the expression of ill-controlled tempers, but rather the application of a coldly thought-out plan.

Bettelheim thus used the glasses incident to illustrate the message that was hardest of all to get across to his American readers at the time he published it, two years before the discovery of the death camps: that the Nazis' behavior could not be simply dismissed as typical of all wars, part of the inevitable catalogue of atrocities and excesses, but that it was the specific product of a very specific system. Later, when the defeat of the Third Reich and the accounts of thousands of other camp survivors had corroborated Bettelheim's own writings, he was to present that system as the prototype of the modern mass state, which brings to bear the full panoply of science and technology in order to subjugate the individual.

"I saw prisoners come back to life on hearing Bruno tell stories about his own life," Hans Bandler told Trude Weinfeld when, a few months after his release on January 19, 1939, he met her in Australia. In light of that, who would dare blame Bettelheim for having on occasion embroidered the truth? Primo Levi, referring to his retrospective relief at having one day given a few words of advice to an eighteen-year-old Italian boy who had just arrived in Auschwitz, wrote: "I forget what I told him, certainly words of hope, perhaps a few lies, acceptable to a 'new arrival,' expressed with the authority of my twenty-five years and my three months of seniority; at any rate, I made him the gift of a momentary attention. But I also remember, with disquiet, that much more often I shrugged my shoulders impatiently at other requests." In the camp, Levi noted, "the demand for solidarity, for a human word, advice, even only a listening ear, was permanent and universal."[11] Of course, Buchenwald was not Auschwitz, and at the time Bettelheim was there, all the prisoners at least spoke the same language, which made communication easier. Even at that early stage, however, the golden rule of survival was to first and foremost take care of one's own needs. Bettelheim's willingness to simply listen to some of his companions in misfortune was therefore a priceless gift, even if, as he himself stressed, it was one given mostly out of a desire to preserve his own sanity.

"They can say what they like about Bruno, but I will always have the greatest admiration for him because, in the camps, he got us to talk about our previous lives," says Hans Bandler. "He was the only one to do that. And for me, being able to talk about things I knew, to see someone who was not at all involved taking an interest in my profession as an engineer, being able to teach him something, was an extraordinary aid to survival. It gave me back my self-esteem in a situation in which everything was designed to demean us, both in our own eyes and in those of others. For that, I will be eternally grateful to him."

Hans Bandler was clearly one of Bruno Bettelheim's "interviewees." Their conversations often took place after the evening roll call. Thanks to the Nazis' passion for alphabetical order, Bandler and Bettelheim were in the same block. Other conversations occurred when the two men found themselves side by side pushing heavy wagons full of stones at Dachau. Bandler recalled his engineering classes, and explained to Bettelheim how to build a bridge, what precautions to take to make sure it didn't collapse, and so on. Bettelheim listened, and asked questions. When it was his turn to talk, he discussed psychoanalysis, mentioning Freud, Wilhelm Reich, and others. Bandler, for whom the subject was completely new, was fascinated.

One of the first things Bettelheim noticed on questioning his fellow-inmates was that they preferred not to talk about everyday instances of abuse, insults, blows, kicks, and other humiliations, and would in some cases deny they even took place, as if they were ashamed of them. Whenever the ill-treatment went beyond the "normal" level, however, such as the December 14 roll call, they were ready to launch into detailed descriptions. And yet it was almost impossible to get them to discuss their feelings during such ordeals. The few who would do so spoke only in vague terms, as if trying to justify the fact that they had done nothing to defend themselves. In their accounts, Bettelheim detected the same feeling of unreality that had invaded him at such times, but he could not persuade them to discuss that either. He concluded that this was a natural defense mechanism, thrown up by the ego against unbearable assaults. He also noted that during the ordeals, which he was to call "extreme situations," many prisoners behaved as though their life bore no relation whatsoever to what it had been in the outside world; their way of viewing both themselves and others had changed. It was as if they were thinking: "What I am doing here, and what is happening to me, does not count. Here, anything is permissible inasmuch as it helps me to survive." Some inmates indeed asserted that this was the only way to behave.

Bettelheim also noticed a clear difference between the behavior of new prisoners and that of camp veterans. Recent arrivals would spend all their energy—and money—on trying to get in touch with their families and friends; all their thoughts were directed toward the outside world, whereas the old prisoners were concerned first and foremost with internal camp affairs. The appointment of a new *Kapo* was far more interesting to them than the results of the Munich conference. They appeared to have lost their ability to assess external events, as if the latter no longer concerned them. At Buchenwald such an introverted attitude was easier to maintain, as the prisoners were not allowed to receive newspapers. At Dachau, Bettelheim had at least been able to read, each Sunday, the daily newspaper to which Paula had got him a subscription,[12] and the *Frankfürter Zeitung*, which he had requested, obviously to keep abreast of what was happening in Germany. There was no such privilege at Buchenwald, where prisoners often spent at least half of each Sunday working. Bettelheim was by no means the only inmate to notice the contrast between new and old prisoners. Everyone was aware of it, so much so that some inmates decided to die before they turned into concentration camp types, as Eugen Kogon termed them. Bettelheim thus witnessed the suicide of a man who had resolved that six years was his limit. On the day, despite all attempts to dissuade him, he threw himself onto the electrified barbed wire fence surrounding the camp.

Old prisoners did not like to talk about either their previous lives or their families. When they did so, it was often with bitterness, accusing their relations of having abandoned or even betrayed them. Having made that observation, Bettelheim was shocked by his own reaction to a passage in a letter from his mother, in which she told "how one of my colleagues had presented a paper, using some of my ideas, and that it was very well received."[13] On one level, he explained, he knew perfectly well that Paula only wanted to please him. "Nevertheless, on a much more important level it sent me into a cold fury to think that my colleague was enjoying success with my ideas while I lived in such misery." The end result was that, rather than bolstering his courage, the letter filled him with anger, an emotion all the more destructive in that he could turn it only against himself (that is, by plunging into depression, as he had learned to do since his childhood—but he did not write that). This incident was to remain in Bettelheim's memory as the second occasion on which his mother had almost caused his death, the first being her exhortations for him to not leave Vienna at the time of the Anschluss.[14]

One thing surprised Bettelheim. Having often relived in dreams a car crash that had deeply shaken him a few years earlier, he had been expecting to suffer from recurring nightmares at the start of his imprisonment. Far from it; none of the incidents, not even the train ride to Dachau or other such trials, ever troubled his sleep. When he did dream about the camp, it was always to relive some minor incident, which generally provided an opportunity for vengeance against an SS guard. On questioning his fellow-inmates, he found they all had a similar story to tell.

For a long time Bettelheim kept his observations to himself. Then, at some point apparently at Buchenwald, he started trying to compare notes with other prisoners. "Unfortunately," he writes, "[the author] found only two others who were trained and interested enough to participate in his investigation. Although they seemed less interested in the problem than the author, these two each spoke to several hundred prisoners. Every day during the morning count of the prisoners, and while waiting for the assignment to labor groups, reports were exchanged and theories discussed. These discussions proved very helpful in clarifying mistakes that were due to taking a one-sided viewpoint."[15]

One of Bettelheim's two confidants was Ernst Federn. But in his first article on the camps, in October 1943, he refrained from citing his name, as Federn was then still in Buchenwald. Details on the second man, a certain Dr. Fischer, are hard to come by. Bettelheim wrote that in 1943 Fischer, a general practitioner, was working at a military hospital in England. According to the Buchenwald archives he was also a Viennese Jew, the same age as Bettelheim, and he was released from the camp on May 10, 1939.

Only two direct eyewitness accounts of this joint research project are therefore available: Bettelheim's and Federn's. When they met at Buchenwald, neither of them was as yet a psychoanalyst. But while Bettelheim had become gradually fascinated by the "new science" during his studies and the unfolding of his life in Vienna, Federn had been born into it. As a child, he had been bounced on Sigmund Freud's knee, and in 1936 he had become his father's secretary. Today, he still describes himself smilingly as "a psychoanalyst by birth." But the humor conceals a deeply committed stance; Ernst Federn takes his role as an intellectual heir very seriously, and has defended Paul Federn's work throughout his whole life. He is also an idealist, as is shown by the second paragraph of his memoir *Witnessing Psychoanalysis:* "From early youth—in fact, from the age of fourteen—I had decided to devote my life to the betterment of mankind, having taken this romantic idea from my father." Federn became politically active early on, his aim being to reconcile the ideas of Marx and Freud. He was fully engaged in the underground struggle against the Nazis when they invaded Austria, and he was among the first arrested in Vienna. As his father was Jewish, the Germans had also made him wear the yellow triangle, but to him it was clear that he was in Dachau because his side had lost. And as Bettelheim pointed out, "Those prisoners . . . who had expected to be imprisoned because of their political activities resented their fate, but somehow accepted it as something which happened in accordance with their expectations . . . [They] found support for their self-esteem in the fact that the Gestapo had singled them out as important enough to take revenge on."[16]

That was not Bettelheim's own situation. Whatever his ideas, his arrest could not be attributed to any political action on his part. Although he despised the Nazis every bit as much as Federn did, he had done nothing to outwardly express those feelings, beyond giving money and becoming a member of the Patriotic Front party. When he defines the category of political prisoner in his writings, however, he remains just vague enough to be able to count himself among their number. That is technically correct, as he wore the red political prisoner's triangle, and above all as he was clearly in the politically aware category. But when he writes of the stronger self-esteem that helped "Red" prisoners to endure the initial trauma of their arrest and imprisonment, he can only be referring to the politically active.

The two men were thus in very different situations when they met, even according to Bettelheim's own definition. With the exception of a certain sense of humor, they had mainly one thing in common, their interest in psychoanalysis. The fact that Federn was the son of the most loyal of Sigmund Freud's followers instantly attracted Bettelheim to him. For his part, Federn could not but be impressed by Bettelheim's astonishing intuitive power, and his determination to find meaning in everything going on around him.

No doubt the political activist in Federn was a little contemptuous of the accommodations his friend was prepared to make to the camp system, although he recognizes that without them, a man "so ill-prepared to face the practical aspects of life," as he describes Bettelheim in his memoirs, would probably not have survived the rigors of Buchenwald. That attitude can still be detected today in Federn's description of Bettelheim's labor detail in the sock-darning workshop, and the armband for the blind that Federn saw him wear on a few occasions at Buchenwald. "It cost him too much," is his comment.

That armband, of which Hans Bandler has no recollection, appears to have played a certain role in the Federn–Bettelheim relationship. I do not know at what point Bettelheim procured it, but it must have been when he was deprived of his glasses. There is no doubt at all that he would have paid to obtain it, as there was a price on everything in Buchenwald at that time. From the top echelons of the SS down to the lowly *Kapos*, the word was to "make the Jews cough up" for everything and anything. Indeed, in *The Informed Heart* Bettelheim makes no secret of the fact that he used his money to purchase a few advantages that helped him to survive, but he does not mention the armband. Without glasses, however, he was practically blind; his driver's license, issued in 1932, specifies that he could take the wheel only when wearing nine-diopter lenses on both eyes. Nevertheless, Bettelheim was ashamed of having worn that armband. He was to admit as much in a letter he wrote to Federn in 1969. Federn must have raised the issue, for Bettelheim says:

> Your point about hiding is well taken, but for me hiding was not the opposite of courage. It was a temporary defense, which often was absolutely indispensable, but, when it became habitual, it led to destruction. And I have seen that happen. Twice, during my time in the camps, I hid, which I could do very well, because I had the [armband] that declared me as blind . . . In both cases, after less than two weeks, I took it off and stopped hiding, because I found it too self-destructive, and had seen the destruction it wreaked in others. So much for that.[17]

Vintage Bettelheim, that willingness to confront an unpleasant memory, followed by a short, expeditious discussion of the subject. But those few words, repetitive and awkwardly put together, speak volumes about the struggle he must have waged at Buchenwald to avoid slipping into a state of mind he knew would have been fatal, to marshal the strength to go on living. As he would write later, he envied the Jehovah's Witnesses, whose unshakable faith allowed them to rise above the degradation of the camp in all circumstances. But his atheism was too deeply rooted; he could not bring himself to believe even to save his own life. In the absence of religious faith, he could have benefited from political convictions, which helped other of his fellow-inmates to remain themselves in this dangerous world. But there too, his skepticism was too strong.

What he means by *destruction*, a term to which he clearly attaches considerable weight, since he uses it and *destructive* three times in nine lines, is spelled out clearly in a section of *The Informed Heart* titled "The Last Human Freedom." After referring to the category of prisoners known as "moslems," those who gave up all hope and simply let themselves die, he writes:

> To survive as a man not a walking corpse, as a debased and degraded but still human being, one had first and foremost to remain informed and aware of what made up one's personal point of no return, the point beyond which one would never, under any circumstances, give in to the

oppressor, even if it meant risking and losing one's life. It meant being aware that if one survived at the price of overreaching this point one would be holding on to a life that had lost all its meaning. It would mean surviving—not with a lowered self respect, but without any.[18]

That point of no return, Bettelheim went on, varies from person to person, and with the different stages of incarceration. Over time, as material considerations gradually give way to interior demands and basic convictions, it shifts. The key thing is always to be aware of just where it is—to keep one's heart informed, as the title so aptly sums up the type of introspection involved.

This is central to the issue of the blind man's armband, and the relationship between Bettelheim and Federn. As the French Resistance fighter and former camp inmate Germaine Tillon has written, "One day, someone will bring together all the testimony about the concentration camps, and on that day it will have to be remembered that there were a thousand camps within each camp, and that for some people anything that was not of immediate concern to them did not exist."[19] Although they shared an interest when they were imprisoned together, it would be difficult to imagine two men more different from each other than Ernst Federn and Bruno Bettelheim. At Buchenwald, a place where one was constantly obliged to face up to one's own inner demons, their experiences were certainly very different.

Nothing better illustrates the gulf between them than the exchange of letters in which, thirty years after Bettelheim had left Buchenwald, that famous armband came up again. It was sparked by an article of his to which Federn had raised an objection: "The Ultimate Limit," which deals with the fate of survivors of Hiroshima.[20] In it, Bettelheim compared the effects of two extreme situations, the atom bomb and the Nazi camps. He also for the first time gave a theoretical definition of an "extreme situation," an expression he had coined more than twenty-five years earlier and used ever since. "We find ourselves in an extreme situation when we are suddenly catapulted into a set of conditions where our old adaptive mechanisms and values do not apply any more and when some of them may even endanger the life they were meant to protect."[21]

Bettelheim prefaced the article with a quotation from Horace, explaining his title: "Death is the ultimate limit of all things,"[22] and continued: "It is the certainty of death which gives human life its meaning."[23] Federn objected, saying that in his opinion it was love that gave life its meaning. "I fully agree with you," replied the author of *Love Is Not Enough.*[24] However, he went on, "I am equally convinced that without the awareness of death, what we call 'love' would be a very different thing. If there would be no end to it, and if there would be unlimited time for it, it might very well become so different that we would not recognize it."[25] The two men simply did not function on the same wavelength, and the subjects of their anxiety in Buchenwald were of a different nature. They were nevertheless friends, and in spite of the slight irritation that certain of Bettelheim's eccentricities inspired in him, Federn would be among those who were the most indignant at the scandal that blew up after his death.

The word *destruction* also recurs in "The Ultimate Limit." There, what is being destroyed is the ego, which disintegrates when a person is suddenly subjected to an "extreme" experience of death: for example, the prisoner who sees the bodies of his former companions piled ever higher, and wonders why his is not among them, or the Hiroshima survivor, who on looking about him discovers the potential deadliness of the very scientific progress with which modern men had replaced their religious faith as the key to salvation—a "defense against death anxiety," as Bettelheim puts it.

Bettelheim notes that the sight of a single corpse is in fact more shattering than the sight of thousands. If a person survives a gigantic massacre, he writes, "then the fact of survival is the problem—not the corpses piled all around one," and "the only way one could go about doing what was absolutely necessary for survival was not to be swallowed up by one's feelings," he added, referring here to Hiroshima. Thus it was with the camp inmate forced to carry corpses, to whom his burdens seemed like nothing more than logs. Bettelheim interprets this emotional numbing as a human being's reaction to the destruction of his ego. "One jettisons one's normal personality because its reactions now endanger one's life . . . the old ego, the old self which did respond, proved to be of no help in meeting the radically new experience." Faced with an extreme situation, Bettelheim goes on, "what is required is an equally radically new ego," even if it is only a temporary one.

In Bettelheim's thinking at that time, and in this essay,[26] the ego is akin to a conductor, in charge of managing the contradictory demands of the unconscious drives and the prohibitions and ambitions that result from the individual's upbringing. Sometimes the desires and fears generated by the unconscious gain the upper hand, and the individual's behavior appears irrational. At other times, the demands of his ideal are stronger, and he represses his drives, at the risk of drying up the very sources of life and creativity. Psychological health, or "integration of the ego," as Bettelheim calls it, lies somewhere between those two extremes, in a delicate and balanced regulation of the gates of the unconscious. In the concentration camps, there was no place for the prisoner's ego, or at least the Nazis did everything they could to ensure that that was the case. What indeed is an *Unterman* (subhuman, or under-man), as they called Jews, if not a person who has been stripped of his freedom to manage his passions according to what he believes to be right and wrong, a person reduced to being governed by his most basic instincts—to being *das Es*, an "it"?[27] It was hardly surprising that the people who stood up best to the experience were those whose ideals were the strongest, or even the most rigid, as Bettelheim noticed. And it did not matter whether the ideals in question were political, religious, or simply moral; they could even, in the case of aristocrats, consist of a grandiose idea of their own family heritage.

And it was also unsurprising that a man who was as hard on himself as Bettelheim was should have felt himself in mortal danger every time he reacted to the flagging of his hopes by donning the mask of somebody weaker than himself. Taking refuge behind the armband for the blind was certainly no crime. Considering the state of his eyesight, some people would simply have called it a measure of self-preservation, but for Bettelheim, whose lucidity had up until then served mainly to bolster a deep feeling of pessimism, it amounted to reducing even more the ego's room to maneuver. As he was to write later of his young patients, referring to the effect traumatic events in the outside world could have on them, "with each such experience the child becomes . . . more withdrawn from reality, more beholden to his unconscious alone, and consequently less master of it."[28] Instead of getting on with creating the "radically new ego" needed for survival, he thus gave free rein to his fear and shame, his eyes filled with a devalued image of himself, the very image to which the Nazis wanted to reduce him.

It was during free time on Sundays, and also in the evenings between soup and the lights-out siren that Bettelheim and Federn would try to analyze their experiences. Federn recalls, for example, how the two of them discussed an incident that seemed to them typical of the behavior of old prisoners. This is how Bettelheim later reported it:

Often an SS man would for a while enforce some nonsensical rule, orig-inating in a whim of the moment. Usually it was quickly forgotten, but there were always some old prisoners who continued to observe it and tried to enforce it on others long after the SS had lost interest. Once, for example, an SS man was inspecting the prisoners' apparel and found that some of their shoes were dirty on the inside. He ordered all prison-ers to wash their shoes inside and out with soap and water. Treated this way, the heavy shoes became hard as stone. The order was never repeated, and many prisoners did not even carry it out the first time, since the SS, as was often the case, gave the order, stood around for a few minutes, and then left. Until he was gone, every prisoner busied himself with carrying out the order, after which they promptly quit. Nevertheless there were some old prisoners who not only continued to wash the insides of their shoes every day but cursed all who failed to do so as being negligent and dirty.[29]

Bettelheim and Federn had seen the funny side of such behavior, as when certain other prisoners tried to obtain bits and pieces of old uniforms in order to ape their tormentors. At the same time, the two men tried to make sense of it. Today, Federn says casually: "Oh, I don't remember which of us first noticed how some prisoners tried to copy the behavior of the SS. In any case, it was nothing new; Anna Freud and Sandor Ferenczi had already mentioned it." In *The Ego and the Mechanisms of Defense*, published just two years before the two men's arrests, Anna Freud had indeed put forward the new the-ory of "identification with the aggressor."[30] She saw it as a stage in a child's normal development during which, having internalized the strictures of its parents and adopted their values, it begins to project the aggression that it nevertheless feels when reprimanded onto somebody else, such as a sibling, or a friend who is smaller or weaker.

More generally, Bettelheim and Federn had been struck by the process of infantilization that seemed to have set in for so many of their fellow-inmates—by the obsession with food and excretion to which camp life condemned them, and masturbation, which soon became the sole means (homosexual relations being relatively rare) for the prisoners to prove to themselves that, despite their state of deprivation, they had so far escaped the castration the guards were constantly threatening them with. The obligatory use of the familiar *du* form of address, the insults, the need to continually lie (as they could never do everything asked of them) and to hide (getting noticed was the surest way to earn an extra beating), the continual threats, the fear, and above all, the impotent, dangerous rage, which they could only either repress or turn against themselves or their fellow-inmates, were all conditions obviously calculated to make them regress to childhood. For the two apprentice psychoanalysts, measuring these symptoms against the arguments of Anna Freud was an exciting exercise. It not only allowed them to spend their time usefully, it helped make them aware of the camp's pitfalls, and provided the feeling of superiority that Bettelheim cites on several occasions as being essential for survival in such degrading conditions.

The two men promised each other that the first to be freed, should they be so lucky, would write down and publish their observations so that the whole world would know what was going on behind the barbed wire fences on the Ettersberg.

In mid-January 1939, Bettelheim's instructions to his mother became even more precise: He wanted Gina's address in New York and worried about his passport, emigration card, tax release, boat ticket. He wanted to be sure the debt to Frieda Goldstein had been paid, and asked that his sister go to Berlin "to wrap things up over there." He also asked for an English phrasebook. Concluding this catalogue of demands, he wrote: "Only when you have answered all these points, talk to me about other things." He expressed concern about the fate of Trude, who had by then left Vienna, and thanked his mother for his new glasses.

Recovering his sight appears to have provided a huge boost to his morale; he was determined to make it out of the camp. He knew that degradation threatened him. He was weak, not only physically but because of his own doubts about himself and about the meaning of life. In the camp, everything was calculated to reinforce such doubts. Rather than his father, who had died a complete physical and mental wreck, ought he not emulate his Grandfather Seidler, whose cunning had helped him make good even in the worst circumstances? And what about the political prisoners, those who had noble ideals to uphold; were they doing any better? Some of them were, indeed, but others were taking advantage of their power in the camp to obtain privileges for their friends, to the detriment of the weaker, the less organized, or the Jews. No, he could rely only on his own resources: He wanted to keep his self-respect, to still be able to look at himself in the mirror without shame, but he did not want to sink, he did not want to die.

As he needed an outlet for the mental self-lashing that he required to keep him going on some days, he used the only safe one available: his family, those who loved him—or at least those he knew would feel guilty if they failed to do all they could to save his life. "Follow my instructions to the letter," he wrote in one missive, one that contained not the slightest trace of either emotion or kindness. Poor Paula and Margarethe! Considering what living conditions were like for Jews in Vienna at that time, one can easily imagine the mixed feelings that such a letter must have inspired in them.

Bettelheim probably thought his mother and sister were unable to imagine just how far the Nazis' barbarity could extend, and that they also needed sharp prodding to take care of their own safety. When he asked German Jews upon their arrival in the camp why they had not left earlier, given that Hitler had been in power since 1933, so many of them had replied,[3] "How could I have left? I would have lost my house, my store . . . " that he felt it necessary to tell his mother over and over again that he didn't care about whether he got a few marks more or less from the sale of his company, and that his commercial affairs were secondary—what was important was the documents that would allow him to go. It did not even matter much where to: "If Grete has an opening for Colombia, she should grasp at it" (August 28); "Thank you for your efforts. Honduras will also do fine" (February 5). Also important were the debts to be repaid, a theme his letters constantly returned to.

On the latter question, I was not able to ascertain whether Frieda Goldstein was the wife of the German Communist whose advice was so invaluable in allowing him to organize for survival in the camp. He was later to refer to this all-important debt, which he had repaid before leaving. But if love is not enough, neither is money. After almost eleven months of concentration camp life, Bruno Bettelheim had run up another debt, a much heavier one than those 150 Reichmarks; it was a debt that he would devote the remainder of his life to paying off. On his arrival in Dachau he was already a deeply wounded man; on his emergence from Buchenwald he had become, in the full sense of the word, a survivor. That was a form of wealth, which he would now make it his duty to spread around.

———— ❂ ————

On Friday April 14, 1939, after the morning roll call, Bruno Bettelheim heard his number barked out from the loudspeaker; he was to report to the administration. As Walter Poller notes, such an order, which automatically implied contact with SS soldiers, was always cause for anxiety, even for a prisoner who had hopes of being released. Those summoned had to spend a considerable time waiting, in a state of excitement, only a few feet from the guards. An incident was always possible, especially at the last minute. Countless prisoners had already been shot dead just as they were about to be released.

Bettelheim, however, had reason to be optimistic. His hectoring letters, and his sister's trip to Berlin, had paid off. On January 26 he had finally been issued a passport, and on February 6 his mother had purchased his ticket for New York. As for his U.S. visa, it had been waiting for him at the consulate in Vienna for over six months. On hearing his number read out, however, Bettelheim balked. His hopes had already been raised too many times, only to be dashed. He did not want to go. At least that was how he remembered it when writing *The Informed Heart.* He had already been summoned for release twice before, and had each time handed in his prisoner's uniform in exchange for civilian clothes, to be told at the last moment that he was not being freed. On this third occasion, he had thus rebelled against a game he saw as being aimed at destroying him. This time, though, it was for real.[32]

As he survived to tell the tale, his demurral, which is not in itself totally inconceivable, must have remained discreet. It is indeed difficult to imagine the SS forcing a prisoner to leave Buchenwald against his will. As for the two false alarms he had endured, I was not able to learn anything more than what he wrote, as Federn has no memory of them. On the first occasion, almost all the prisoners summoned at the same time as Bettelheim were freed, but his release was postponed, "possibly . . . because I had provoked an SS official."[33] He gives no details of the purported incident, however, and the reader can be forgiven for being somewhat skeptical: Almost all the known incidents in which a prisoner was killed only minutes away from freedom were sparked by a remark that displeased the SS official in charge of the "political interview" that preceded all releases. The second false alarm was apparently due to the fact that there was not enough money in the camp safe to pay for train tickets for all the prisoners being freed that day; this seems a more plausible explanation.

Other former prisoners have described the Buchenwald departure ceremony. One was Rabbi Georg Wilde of Magdeburg, one of the

"November Jews," who was freed eleven days after his imprisonment, along with around two hundred others picked up during *Kristallnacht*. The prisoners were first given a lecture by a Gestapo officer, who said: "We are allowing you to go home to make arrangements for emigration. But if you say a single word about the concentration camp, we will come back to get you, and you will stay for good. And don't go thinking that you'll be able to say what you want from abroad. We have our agents everywhere, and they will make sure you are silenced forever." Next, the prisoners were examined by a doctor; Rabbi Wilde immediately realized this was to ensure that they did not bear any obvious marks of abuse. They were then made to sign a form certifying that they had been treated well, had no complaints to make, and would refrain from telling people outside about life in the camps. The group was then marched to the nearest village, where bread, cheese, mineral water, and coffee were provided in the local inn. The landlord appeared to know just what the new arrivals "from up on the hill" needed. "He was friendly and did not ask the least question," the rabbi wrote.[34]

Bettelheim also describes how the Gestapo had meanwhile kept Paula on tenterhooks regarding the date of his release. "My mother was several times given a date for my release, each one untrue. Once she was told I was probably home already, waiting for her, and to hurry home. Another time she was encouraged to travel from Vienna to Weimar . . . either to receive me on my release, or at least to have a visit with me. She presented herself in Weimar, where she was given a run-around for several days until in desperation she returned to Vienna."[35] Elsewhere, he mentions a Nazi lawyer his family had to pay to go to Weimar to meet him, once again to no avail. In early March, Paula or Margarethe had had the date of his departure for New York pushed back, from March 18 to April 29.

There is one other point which I was not able to elucidate: exactly why Bettelheim was freed. A week after him, some two thousand other Buchenwald prisoners were to be released, in a spectacular gesture to mark Adolf Hitler's fiftieth birthday. Federn remembers that event very well; the following Saturday, the prisoners had been exempted from work. Throughout the day the public address system barked out a series of prisoner numbers, keeping the entire population in a state of unbearable suspense. But by that day, April 22, Bettelheim was already far away. Why was he singled out a week early?

Many answers have been provided to that question. Bettelheim himself always remained evasive on the subject, stressing that at the time it was often easier for a Jew to get out of a concentration camp than for a non-Jew, on condition that he promise to emigrate from the Reich without delay and leave all his possessions behind. Non-Jews in Buchenwald even had a saying, Bettelheim writes: "There are only two ways to get out of here: feet first, or being a Jew."[36] But, there were no certainties. "The terror the concentration camps created was made even more effective by the utterly arbitrary manner in which the Gestapo imprisoned some people and set others free. There was no way to guess why one prisoner was let go after a few months, when another just like him was released only after several years, and yet again another was doomed to remain forever in the camps."[37]

From the available documents,[38] it is clear that Agnes Piel Crane kept the pressure on the State Department right up until Bettelheim arrived in the United States. Less than two weeks after his arrest and deportation, all the red tape holding up his visa application fell away as if by magic, which in itself shows that already in the summer of 1938, the name "Dachau" was enough to make an impression in Washington. At the end of July, Crane mounted a new attack with a letter to A. M. Warren, head of the State Department's visa division, thanking him for his help but also asking him to press the U.S. embassy in Berlin to seek information about her protégé. The answer was courteous but clear: As Bettelheim was not a U.S. citizen, no diplomatic representation could be made.

Agnes Crane was not to be put off so easily, however. As soon as Bettelheim was transferred to Buchenwald, she went on the offensive again. While Edith Buxbaum was persuading the American Psychoanalytic Association to intervene via its secretary, Lawrence Kubie, Crane was shooting off letters and phone calls to Washington. At the start of November, Warren relented, asking the Vienna mission to seek information on the prisoner, but stressing that this would be in a purely unofficial capacity. He nevertheless felt it necessary to justify the move by stating that the consulate had initially mislaid Bettelheim's visa application, thereby delaying his departure prior to his arrest. Two days later Paula and Margarethe Bettelheim were granted a meeting with the Vienna consul general, who told them that the transfer of the prisoners from Dachau to Buchenwald had been a purely general measure. The consul general nevertheless sent a cable to his counterpart in Berlin, seeking further information. At the end of November, in a telegram marked "This message must be closely paraphrased before being communicated to anyone," the Berlin consul general informed the State Department that he had "formally asked head of secret police to release [Bruno Bettelheim] here giving the assurance that his emigration has been arranged." The final sentence, however, was hardly promising: "Believe in view of arrest having taken place last May, release will be difficult." This obviously alarmed Agnes, who on receiving the message (not in paraphrased form, in fact), immediately demanded an explanation. The State Department dutifully passed the question on to Berlin: Why did the consul believe it would not be easy to obtain a release? The penultimate item in the file is a cryptic cable from Berlin to Washington, dated December 12 and stating simply: "Bruno Bettelheim referred to Vienna." The only other item in the State Department archives is a letter of thanks to Warren dated May 16, 1939, from Bettelheim himself, by then living in New York.

This evidence thus corroborates Bettelheim's 1945 affidavit for the Nuremberg Tribunal ("My release was effected through some influential friends of mine in America who were able to enlist the assistance of the State Department"), but it does not confirm the most famous of the rumors concerning his release, carried in many newspapers at the time of his death, that First Lady Eleanor Roosevelt had intervened on his behalf. A footnote in the opening pages of *Surviving*, while not confirming that story, at least gave it some credence. Bettelheim states: "It may have helped that one of the most prominent public figures intervened personally and also through the American legation on my behalf."[39]

Another famous name mentioned in connection with Bruno Bettelheim's release is that of Herbert Lehman, then governor of New York. Lehman, himself a Jew, was one of the very few U.S. politicians to take an active interest in the fate of the European Jews at that time. Again, however, the name Bettelheim is nowhere to be found in his correspondence.[40] One name that does appear, however, is that of Ernst Federn: In 1914, when Lehman was a young banker, handicapped by a serious stutter, Paul Federn had traveled to New York to spend several months as his psychoanalyst. So when he returned to the United States twenty-five years later, this time as an exile, he quite naturally turned to his former patient for help in securing Ernst's release.[41]

The possibility that Agnes Crane, weary of State Department vacillation, decided to seek support elsewhere, even if it was not from the First Lady, cannot, however, be completely ruled out. That would explain why the U.S. consul in Berlin intervened in person with the head of the Gestapo to seek the release of a man who, after all, was then officially a German national. In fact, Gina Weinmann remembers that Mr. Warren himself made a trip to Vienna to try to obtain freedom for several people, one of whom was her then-husband. What is certain is that Bettelheim's family and several of his friends had paid a lot of money to the Gestapo to secure his release, and that all the paperwork had been done to allow him to fulfill the second condition imposed by the Nazis: his departure from the Reich within two weeks, leaving all his possessions behind.

One last detail is worth noting. In *Surviving*, Bettelheim states that interventions coming from too high up sometimes achieved the opposite result to the one desired. He cites the case of one of his best friends, whose release had been requested on several occasions by "a member of a royal family," but who was in fact to remain at Buchenwald until the camp was liberated because the Nazis had realized that his connection made him valuable as a potential hostage.[42] With the exception of one or two details, this could in fact apply to Ernst Federn's story. After his release he learned of a letter in which Himmler himself had ordered that he be kept in the camp, because a man who appeared to mean so much to the Americans would make a good hostage.

By April 17, Bruno Bettelheim was back in Vienna, where he was to stay until the 27th: The two dates were recorded by Paula at city hall and, without slipping into excessive sentimentalism, one cannot help noticing in the ledger how triumphant and vengeful the words "New York" look in the space marked "destination." On the 18th, the U.S. consulate issued Bettelheim his immigration visa.

Ten days to obtain all the required papers, to locate all his loved ones and bid them farewell, to settle his accounts, and to get ready for a departure he knew would be definitive, a complete break with everything his life had been. But above all, ten days of living in fear that they would come to arrest him again. For although nothing is known about that short spell between Buchenwald and New York, Bettelheim cannot have enjoyed any feeling of newfound freedom in Vienna. Hans Bandler, released three months earlier, well remembers the raw fear that gripped him every time he had to go out to make the arrangements for his departure. In the street, former prisoners tried to blend in to the background, but their shaved heads made them instantly recognizable. And the fact that they did not have a swastika attached to their buttonhole singled them out automatically as Jews (to have worn one would have been even more risky).

Bandler also remembers his shock on first entering the apartment of his aunt, who had raised him: It was almost stripped bare, all the furniture and other objects of value having been sold to pay for his release. For Bettelheim the jolt must have been even worse: His mother's apartment had been requisitioned, and she had been forced to move in with neighbors. It was probably at that point that he learned he would not be getting a cent from the "sale" of his company. As several of his letters from Buchenwald suggest, he must also have spent part of his spell in Vienna trying to convince other members of his family to flee.

Paula, who was not to leave Europe until September 25,[43] told him of the circumstances of Trude's departure. Shortly after Bettelheim's arrest, the young schoolteacher had been summoned to Gestapo headquarters at the Metropole Hotel and kept there for a whole day. Between interrogation sessions, she was locked up in a hotel bathroom; she thought she was never going to get out alive. To her great surprise, however, she was released that evening, and a few days later the Gestapo even returned her passport. Apparently, they had been interested only in the Montessori school.

Until that incident, Trude had not exactly been hurrying to leave; she had made several attempts to obtain information about Bruno, or to get in touch with him. Knowing his aversion to any kind of manual labor and his lack of physical stamina, she was convinced he would not survive a spell of several months in a concentration camp. But she had come to the realization that, as she was not a relative, she could do nothing whatsoever to help him. After her arrest, Trude never slept in her own apartment again, and started actively preparing to flee. Some cousins gave her the name of a mountaineer who could help her get across the border into Switzerland. There she knew she could count on the help of the brother of her friend Emmi Vischer, who had traveled from Switzerland to Vienna shortly after the Anschluss to see what he could do to help. One fine day Trude therefore donned a knapsack and set out with her guide, whom she had been able to pay with a small sum donated by grateful parents of her Montessori pupils. Taking the train for the Tyrol, the two of them looked like any couple heading out for that favorite Austrian pastime, a mountain hike. But the trip over the border was not easy: they were detained by the border police, and Trude had to spend a night fending off the advances of her guide. She finally made it, however. Coming amid so much bad news, the knowledge that Trude had escaped must have been a great consolation to Bettelheim. His overriding concern at that time, however, was to get out of Europe as fast as possible, and without a backward glance, to join Gina and start a new life.

Almost all of Bruno Bettelheim's family was to perish at the hands of the Nazis, notably several uncles and cousins arrested in 1942. I do not know whether insufficient means or a lack of initiative prevented them from leaving the deathtrap that Vienna had become for Jews. What is certain, however, is that as soon as he arrived at Dachau, Bettelheim had started doing everything he could to persuade them to leave. His failure to do so must have been painful. Among the very few personal documents he kept to the end of his life was a long letter dated January 1941 sent to his mother and his Aunt Jenny from their elder brother, Alfred Seidler. It tells of an unsuccessful attempt by their younger brother Rudolf Seidler, the Wagner-loving uncle Bruno liked so much, and his wife, Grete, to get over the border. Writing from Vienna while awaiting Rudolf's return to the city, Alfred was clearly trying to keep his anxiety in check, and to while away the time. It is a superb letter, full of acceptance of his own terrible situation, which he barely alludes to, and tolerance for the foolhardiness of his brother, who had himself wrecked his attempt to escape by attracting attention from a Tyrolean wedding party. Alfred's generosity even extended to expressing sympathy for the problems of Paula and Jenny, by then set up in the United States. It is the letter of a man worlds apart from the terrible Adolf Seidler, and who had clearly not inherited his father's iron determination to defeat fate at whatever cost. A man who was never to return from the camp the Gestapo sent him to a year later.

On Saturday April 29, 1939, Bruno Bettelheim boarded the SS *Gerolstein*, a German ship flying the flag of the U.S. Red Star line, in the Dutch port of Flushing. He had his own cabin. His departure from the Reich had come none too soon: In August, the Nazi authorities stopped issuing exit visas to Jewish men aged between eighteen and forty-five.

8

✳

A Short-Lived Reunion

"No, Bruno, it's over. I don't want to live with you any more." With two short sentences, Gina had dashed her husband's hopes. Gaunt and sickly, but his eyes burning with the excitement of new-found freedom, he had just walked practically the full length of springtime Manhattan to her apartment. He poured out a torrent of words, pleading, coaxing, outlining his plans. He would enter politics, become a diplomat. He knew where he had gone wrong in the past; he had changed. Now he wanted children, lots of children. Gina, determined, just kept on saying "No," and he just as obstinately kept trying to make her change her mind. As she remembered it later, the discussion lasted for most of that day and a part of the evening.

That long and painful conversation is in fact the only memory that Gina can bring back of her reunion with Bruno. She has no recollection of having gone to meet him off the boat when he finally set foot on American soil. I wanted very much for her to recall those first moments, the first contact after a year of separation, the first glances exchanged since Bruno had emerged from hell. So I insisted . . .

The SS *Gerolstein* docked on the west side of the New York Port on May 11, 1939. On the page of the passenger manifest that listed Bruno Bettelheim's name, all but one are identified as both "Hebrew" and "German." This triggered my imagination; I could picture the ragged lines of refugees with the giant Statue of Liberty as a backdrop—a symbol which up until then had encapsulated their hope of deliverance, but which on arrival suddenly appeared so intimidating. Each person clutching in one hand the documents that he or she hoped—but how to be absolutely certain?—would open the door to this great New World, far from persecution; in the other, the suitcase containing whatever they had been allowed to take with them. And, somewhere in the line, perhaps standing slightly to one side, impatient but certainly careful not to let himself be jostled or even mingle with the crowd, Bruno Bettelheim. The man with whom she had spent the previous eight years of her life, a man who only three weeks earlier had still been in Buchenwald.

Gina rummages through her memories, but finds nothing. She can only dredge up some vague recollection of a dinner at his aunt Jenny Buxbaum's apartment, a few blocks away from her own. But that in fact took place some time later. Above all, obliterating all the rest, was the memory of that long afternoon spent saying, painfully but firmly: "It's over. I want a divorce." More than what she said, her inability to remember those first minutes with Bruno impressed me, suggesting how traumatic the event must have been for her too. Although she hardly acknowledges it, and that only when pressed, it was not easy to turn away this man she no longer wanted, whom she knew was not for her. She could have picked a more propitious moment, giving Bruno time to start rebuilding his life in the United States before rejecting him, but she would not. She no longer wanted to share his bed, his life, or his dreams. She probably sensed that her attitude would be judged sternly by others; one does not reject a just emerged survivor of the Nazi concentration camps. Paradoxically, she seems to have drawn the strength to break with Bruno from the uncertainty of her relationship with Peter Weinmann, who had by that time moved with his wife to Chicago and seemed unlikely to get divorced. Gina's gesture was that of a woman who wants to take control of her own life, without depending on a man for security. It was a difficult, cruel, but brave decision, and from her point of view the only dignified one, the only one possible.

Her first months in the United States had been tough, and at the start almost surreal. She and Patsy had arrived in New York on May 26, 1938. There she had immediately been taken in hand by Agnes and her new husband, Percy "Ed" Crane, an alcoholic whom she was rumored to have married primarily to provide Patsy with a father. The couple lived in a charming apartment in Greenwich, Connecticut. As it was far too small to accommodate two more people, Agnes had set Gina up in a luxury hotel nearby.

Although sick with worry about those she had left in Vienna, and completely unsure of her own future, Gina found herself dressing for dinner every evening in one of the elegant evening gowns Agnes had bought her at Lord & Taylor. After dinner in Agnes's tiny apartment, from which one could see the Long Island Sound, her hostess would play her Gilbert and Sullivan operettas until late into the night, while Ed nodded off. To Gina, it all seemed like a dream. Half-charmed by the relaxed, easy life of her rich American protectress, she had to keep a tight lid on her own contradictory emotions.

Almost every day, the mail brought new reports of the horrors going on in Vienna, along with requests for Gina to obtain yet another affidavit that would allow a relative or friend to leave for America. Although thanks to Agnes she was meeting quite a few people, she had soon realized that the situation in Germany was far from being the favorite topic of conversation for most Americans, who were only too happy to have emerged from the Depression and had no wish to be reminded of the imminence of another European war. This is not to say that Agnes or her friends had the slightest sympathy for Adolf Hitler. But discussing the political situation at cocktail parties was one thing; getting actively involved in events on the Continent, a vast ocean away, was quite another. Gina learned not to be too insistent, while taking advantage of the social events she attended to glean an affidavit here and there.

Almost immediately after her arrival, she had thought of getting a job, despite protests from Agnes, who was already looking for a large house where they could all live together—Patsy, of course, but also Gina, and Bruno, once he was free. Agnes's dream was of a kind of extended family, in which she could go on living as she pleased while Gina would take care of Patsy. Agnes had no inkling of her protégée's affair with Peter Weinmann; Gina had revealed the relationship to no one. She probably guessed that Agnes would never forgive her for shattering her well-laid plans. But although she was fond of Agnes, she had no desire to remain dependent on somebody so bossy and capricious; she was determined to start building a new life as soon as possible.

She knew only a handful of people in New York outside Agnes's circle of friends. Fritz Redl had been in the United States since 1935, but he lived in Chicago. Such was her desire for independence, however, that three months after her arrival Gina found a job through one of Agnes's friends. She was taken on as a social worker with the Jewish

Social Services, an agency where her knowledge of psychoanalysis and intuitive grasp of people brought her instant status among her colleagues. They were all eager to learn about the new science, so much so that it occasionally irritated her. "These people come here because they need a place to live, not to pour out the story of their childhoods," she would say to herself. Being thrown in at the deep end of the New York labor market was a fascinating but also a grueling experience. Her English was still poor, but because she was good at her job, she was often assigned the most difficult cases. She then had an extremely hard time drawing up her reports, which she was supposed to dictate into a tape recorder. Later on, Wanda Willig would help her, but at first she was very much alone. Luckily, the head of the agency, a Mrs. Kamschell, was well aware of the plight of German and Austrian Jews. She gave Gina plenty of spare time in which to seek affidavits, make contacts, and finalize all the formalities needed to help as many people as possible, including her husband.

For a while after starting her job, Gina commuted each evening to Greenwich, where she continued to care for Patsy. But she soon found this schedule exhausting. At the end of June 1938, Peter Weinmann had come from London, and Gina wanted some freedom to see him, if only briefly. When Agnes Crane heard of the affair, she was incensed. She had already shown some irritation during Gina's visit in 1936, when her brother Paul had taken her visitor under his wing. She had also been somewhat peeved when Fritz Redl had shown up and taken the young woman out. But learning that Gina was being unfaithful to Bruno, even as Agnes was laying siege to the State Department to get him released, was the last straw. A head-on clash between the two women had become inevitable; it was brief but violent.

"Gina gave me fifteen minutes to make up my mind: either to go with her or to stay with my mother," Patsy recalls angrily. At the time, she was a shy fifteen-year-old. She did not feel she had a choice: "I did what seemed the proper thing to do: I stayed with my mother." Half a century later, the hurt is obviously still there. Proper or not, for seven years Gina had in effect been her mother: it was Gina who had taught Patsy to laugh and to enjoy life, helping her make enormous progress. The two had been practically inseparable all that time. After that day, they never saw each other again.

In the fall of 1938, Peter Weinmann came to New York to teach at Columbia University for a semester. This was a happy time for Gina, after which he returned to Chicago, where his wife was obstinately refusing his requests for a divorce. For a few months after that, the lovers would spend an occasional weekend together, halfway between New York and Chicago. It was on the way back from one such meeting that Gina first came down with what she refers to as her "immigration disease," a stomach ulcer. She had lost so much blood by the time the train arrived in New York that she had to be taken to the hospital in an ambulance. As soon as Agnes got the news, she rushed over to give blood for Gina, but refused to see her. Finally, the same woman friend of Agnes's who had found Gina her job also provided her with an apartment, on the corner of Eighty-third Street and Lexington Avenue in uptown Manhattan. It was only one small room, originally intended for a domestic servant, but for the young refugee it was freedom itself.

It was there that Bettelheim came to see Gina the day of his arrival. He had not been allowed to take anything with him and he was incredulous to find himself in New York, a city he had seen in films and read about in books so often that he had the vague impression he already knew it. He was free, it was springtime, and he was on his way back to the woman he loved. All he had in his pocket was three dollars, but so what?[1] They were both young, intelligent, and hard workers, so they had every reason to have faith in the future. Gina already had a job, and he would easily find one. They were going to build a new and better life together in this country of the "self-made man," where dreams came true. His cousin Edith Buxbaum was already a practicing psychoanalyst; his friend Fritz Redl was achieving rapid success in the academic world. Fate had relieved Bettelheim of his lumber business, which he had never wanted in the first place. Now he could really do what he wanted. No more unwanted burdens, or debts to be paid off. When the immigration official had asked him his profession, he had shown all the required papers, but then he had insisted on also mentioning his PhD. It is scribbled in cramped longhand, squeezed in above the officially typed "merchant."

In later years Bettelheim talked little about his first days of freedom in America. On the few occasions that he mentioned Gina's rejection, he described the event with an almost detached air, explaining that he and his wife, after a long and calm discussion of their past marital problems, had decided to separate. As any former prisoner can testify, however, the prospect of being reunited with a loved one is the only thing that can make detention bearable. Bettelheim himself was to point this out: After a while, the prisoner starts to forget about any difficulties the couple might have had, gradually replacing the real memory of the relationship with an idealized one. This is illustrated by the letters he wrote to his mother from the camps. Although the first ones were mainly concerned with urgent business affairs, as time went by an increasing number of messages for his wife crept in. "Write to tell Gina that I'm very happy she's found a job, and that it reassures me as to her future. [Tell her] I think of her, as I do of you all, with the greatest love and the greatest longing," he wrote in July 1938. And although he added, "she, like you, must make her own plans without thinking of me, because my future is very uncertain," three weeks later, the emphasis had shifted again: "Tell Gina that all my hopes rest on the future she is building for us."

From that point on, every one of his letters to Paula contained a message for Gina—messages of love, messages to say "I miss you," but also messages of hope, reined in but nevertheless perceptible. Once Bettelheim had learned that a visa and a passport in his name were waiting for him, the tone became even more pressing. He asked for Gina's address so as to write to her directly, and wanted her to write to him. It clearly never once occurred to him that if he was lucky enough to be released, it would be to live without her. And although Trude's name also recurred, in affectionate terms, the way he sent her his best wishes for success and happiness clearly shows that he did not think of her as a possible future life-companion, if he had a future.

Much later, when he was about to lose Trude, who had given him the strength to go on living after the wound inflicted by Gina in New York, Bettelheim wrote:

> The strongest motive for staying alive is that one has something for which one is determined to remain alive at all costs, at all risks . . . The sheer will to live cannot take the place of the strength which one derives from support from the outside, real or imagined. One of the unexpected lessons of the camps was that, contrary to what I expected and what Darwinism taught, the will to live, the life drives, the *élan vital*, the libido, or whatever other name it may be given, provided little support unless it could attach itself to some loved person, some all-important idea, such as Zionism or Communism, or religious conviction. Compared to these, ideas of revenge, or the wish to bear witness, so often mentioned in the literature on surviving, carried little conviction.[2]

Gina's rejection of him played a major role in Bruno Bettelheim's later life, however much he may have tried to cover it up. Gina remembers that during that fateful discussion in New York, she was struck by what she calls his "grandiosity." "All of a sudden he wanted to go into politics. He even told me that, in this country, he could hope to be elected president." If she had not been so concerned with marshaling her strength to maintain her refusal of him, she would no doubt have seen the real distress that such bravado was meant to conceal. As usual with Bettelheim, the distress was mingled with arrogance. After all, if he had had the strength to get out of Buchenwald and make it to the Land of the Free, was he not entitled to the most extravagant dreams?

When Bettelheim realized that Gina was not going to change her mind, he left her apartment and walked the few blocks to his aunt Jenny Buxbaum's place. There he was reunited with his childhood bosom friend and cousin, Edith, who had also been putting in some efforts over the past few months to obtain his release. She welcomed him with open arms. Edith was pleased to get back the companion that another woman had taken away from her, as she acknowledges in her memoirs. He was emotionally distraught and physically debilitated; she took him under her wing.

Edith Buxbaum had by then been living in New York for almost two years, having fled Vienna at the end of August 1937, just as she was about to be arrested for her political activities. She came to New York in her capacity as a teacher, with the Cooperative School for Student Teachers, but like Bettelheim she had insisted that her PhD be clearly marked on her immigration papers. Edith had two ambitions: to establish a practice as a child psychoanalyst and, above all, to escape the emotional blackmail of her mother's continual illnesses, from which she had had but a short respite; Jenny came over to join her in May 1938. Toward her career goals, however, she had made rapid strides. Only a short time after setting foot in New York she had a sprinkling of patients, and had started consulting at social welfare agencies, notably the Community Service Society, one of the city's biggest. And in spite of the rule that excluded non-physicians from membership in most U.S. psychoanalytic societies, she was even teaching at the prestigious New York Psychoanalytic Institute, headed by Sandor Rado.[3] Thanks to these contacts, she was able, soon after

Bettelheim was arrested, to get the American Psychoanalytic Associa-tion to write to the State Department in support of Agnes Crane's efforts to win him a visa.

Bettelheim's first days in New York were spent simply recovering, seeing doctors and a dentist, but also walking around, enjoying free-dom, making new contacts, and getting in touch with friends and acquaintances who had also managed to escape across the Atlantic, such as Hans and Wanda Willig, who had arrived in New York two months before him after trying to settle in Sweden.

In July, Edith Buxbaum suggested to her cousin that they set out to discover the rest of America. He agreed; although he had been look-ing for work, there was really nothing to keep him in New York. Edith was later to acknowledge that, unconsciously at least, she had an ulte-rior motive. Seeing Bruno rejected by the woman who had taken him away from her, and being herself caught up in a complicated rela-tionship with a married man who did not appear to want to divorce his wife, she would not have been averse to an affair with her younger cousin.

So they lit out across America in Edith's old Cadillac convertible, much as years earlier they had wandered the Austrian woods together as "young migratory birds." She paid for everything, and as she did not have much money, they often camped out, occasionally checking in to a cheap motel. Their first major stop was Chicago, where Bet-telheim was reunited with his friend Fritz Redl and met a good num-ber of other fellow-Viennese who had been attracted to the city's highly rated university.

The atmosphere in the Windy City was a complete change from New York. Most of Bettelheim's friends and acquaintances lived in Hyde Park, the University of Chicago neighborhood on the city's South Side, a twenty-minute drive along Lake Michigan from down-town Chicago. Hyde Park was like a small middle-class village. With its parks, its tree-lined streets, and its individual houses with gardens in full bloom, it looked much more like an English town than Bettel-heim's idea of the capital of the American Midwest.

As he noted in *Freud's Vienna and Other Essays*, Bettelheim's image of Chicago had been derived from films and books: a mix of the clichés about meat-packing, money, and gangsters. And then he found himself plunged into a European-style cultural environment, a civilized neighborhood where people didn't even bother to lock their doors when they went out. Barely three months after leaving

Buchenwald, Bettelheim immersed himself in this welcoming and cultured atmosphere, enjoying swimming in the lake, picnics, and discussions with men and women whose interests and occupations were not far removed from those of the people he had been surrounded by only a few years earlier in Vienna. With one key difference, however: Far from existing on the brink of apocalypse, this was a country of boundless optimism and energy, one that was just beginning to emerge from the Depression and was ready to fund all kinds of research into what had gone wrong, and how to avoid it in the future.

Just as they had been in Vienna, Fritz Redl and his friends were swept up in great schemes for educational reform. And although the organizations providing the funding were less Socialist than they had been in Austria, they were almost as socially aware, the aim being to try to provide equal access to knowledge for all. The United States was in the throes of the New Deal, and for many of the young intellectuals in Chicago's very research-oriented university the key issue was to understand, and thus to find remedies for, the flaws of capitalism. One of Redl's friends who took a particular liking to Bettelheim was George Sheviakov. The son of the czar's last education minister, he had arrived in the United States a few years earlier after a series of extravagant adventures. He and Bettelheim not only shared the same biting sense of humor, they were also capable of distinguishing between truly progressive ideas and simple naïveté. Thanks to his intelligence and dynamism, Sheviakov was fast becoming one of the best teacher-training specialists in the country.

When Bettelheim and Edith Buxbaum visited Chicago, George Sheviakov was involved in a major project to reform high schools across the United States. "The Eight-Year Study" was a colossal enterprise, involving a whole team of researchers plus thirty schools scattered across eleven states, in which both teachers and students were to act as guinea pigs for a series of new curricula. The man in charge of the overall project, Ralph Tyler, had just been appointed head of the University of Chicago's Department of Education.

Bettelheim was attracted to Chicago immediately, and felt he could live well in the campus environment. Of course, New York was closer to his idea of what America was all about, and probably more exciting, but Chicago, or rather Hyde Park, offered the academic and cultural atmosphere he so craved, and was also friendlier and less threatening. Here, at least, nobody was rejecting him. And although he received no immediate job offer, everyone he met, notably Sheviakov, had promised to keep him in mind if something should come up.

After Chicago, Bruno and Edith headed west. She tried to entertain him, to shake him out of his gloom. But he was taciturn, and apparently unappreciative of her efforts. Edith encouraged him to discuss his camp experiences, thinking it would help him get them out of his system, but he stubbornly repelled all her advances. It was only much later, in 1979, after reading *Surviving*, the collection of essays that Bettelheim published on the subject, that Edith Buxbaum realized how clumsy her attempts to console him had been. She then wrote to tell him so, and in his reply Bettelheim admitted that his lack of communication during the trip had also been due to his guilt at being entirely dependent on her for money.

The purported aim of the trip, however, was to find him a job. From New York, Bettelheim had shot off letters to countless colleges and schools across the country, offering his services as a teacher. He was ready to teach almost anything: German, philosophy, psychology, and art history, among other subjects. The extravagant résumé he sent with his letters can be interpreted either as yet another sign of what Gina calls his "grandiosity," or as a simple indication of how dire were the straits he found himself in. Here he was, a man who for so long had been accustomed not only to earning a good living but also providing for other people, suddenly transformed into a penniless alien in a vast country he knew almost nothing about—a status made all the more obvious by his impossible accent.

Edith Buxbaum too found him both high-minded and obstinate. "He was not about to accept second-best. He had his heart set on Chicago, which he got," she recalled. Bettelheim himself had different memories of the period, however. As he told it, a little college in Redlands, California, had him come out for an interview and offered him a post for the following school year, with an assurance that his contract would be renewed for at least a second year. He accepted the offer immediately, even though it meant living far away from everyone he knew in America, and even farther from those, such as his mother, who had not yet escaped from Hitler's Europe. The only reason he did not start his American career in California, he said, was that in the meantime he received a better offer, to teach German at another college, in Oregon. Since the money for the Redlands job came from a fund for exiled Jews, he immediately resigned from it in order to allow another immigrant to take his place. At that juncture, however, Hitler intervened to change his life yet again. In September, just as he was about to leave New York for Oregon, he received a wire informing him that his position had been abolished because the war that had just broken out in Europe meant the number of students choosing to study German was not expected to be high enough to warrant a new teacher.

Thus on October 9, 1939, when Bruno Bettelheim filed his "Declaration of Intention" with the Southern District Court in New York City, the first step toward becoming a U.S. citizen, he was still unemployed, and being supported by his cousin because his wife had left him. To cap it all, his mother, who had gotten her visa on August 24, barely a week before the Nazi invasion of Poland sparked World War II, was about to arrive in New York, and would have to live with her sister Jenny because her son could not provide for her.

If Bettelheim's physical living conditions were tough, his psychological state was no better. Every night he was assailed by nightmares, in which he found himself back at Buchenwald with no hope of escape. What made things even worse was that he felt he had virtually nobody to talk to. Like Gina, he had quickly realized that most Americans were in no mood to hear about the horrors taking place in Europe. Although most of them were strongly opposed to Hitler, they found all the stories of anti-Jewish persecution somewhat difficult to believe. As for his fellow-immigrants, who did know what was going on, they were generally too wracked with anxiety about the loved ones they had left behind to be able to lend a sympathetic ear to another escapee. But most of all, Bettelheim himself found it difficult to talk about his experiences, even to those willing to listen, such as Edith or the Willigs. He had become irritable. "After the camps, his personality had changed. He had become very impatient, and of course he took it out on those closest to him," Wanda Willig remarks. Paradoxically, Bettelheim was not depressed. As he was to state later,[4] his spell in the concentration camps and the period immediately afterward were the only times in his life during which he did not once consider suicide. It was only later, after he had reestablished secure living conditions, that the idea began to haunt him once again.

Returning to New York after his cross-country trip with Edith had also meant seeing Gina again. They still lived only a few blocks apart, and administrative formalities brought them together on occasion. On September 8, Gina finally obtained her U.S. immigration papers by dint of making a trip to Havana in order to re-enter the country. After that, Bettelheim was able to set in motion his own naturalization process. When he did so, the address he gave was his wife's.

One of the first things Bettelheim had done on arriving in New York was to write to Trude Weinfeld. The two had never entirely lost contact: In almost all the letters he wrote to his mother from Buchenwald, Bettelheim had asked her to pass on affectionate wishes to Trude and, in the ones he sent from Dachau, he had even on occasion asked Paula to let the young schoolteacher take up a few of the lines permitted in her replies. His mother had scrupulously complied, keeping Trude informed of all news about him. Thus in April 1939 the young woman had received a telegram announcing her friend's imminent release. By that time she was in Australia, and although she rejoiced at the news, she did not for one minute imagine that the event could have any bearing on her own future.

Trude had traveled a long way since her extraordinary voyage across the Alps. Her arriving unannounced at the home of Emmi's brother had caused a sensation in his tiny village. Although he was a man of great generosity and more than happy to help refugees, he was also a bachelor living alone, and could not have offered shelter to a young woman without causing a scandal. So Trude spent the next three months in Basel at the home of one of Emmi's aunts. As she was later to tell her children, those few weeks of cosseting by a warm and generous family in a large, elegantly furnished house with a big garden did wonders for her, particularly since she was also able to go and see her parents, who had settled in the French town of Tours.

She was still hoping to secure a visa for the United States; indeed, Bettelheim had managed to get an affidavit in her name from Agnes Crane. But she got an even worse reception at the U.S. consulate in Zurich than she had in Vienna. When she handed over a letter of recommendation written for her by Anna Freud and Dorothy Burlingham, the consul simply tore it up in front of her, making it abundantly clear that if she persisted in trying to gain entry to the United States, she would have to wait a very long time indeed. So Trude, ever the pragmatist, decided instead to head for Australia, an underpopulated country that still welcomed immigrants, especially women, as long as they were white.

It was to be a long and eventful trip. In Naples, she boarded a ship that was packed with Australians going home from visits to England; from them she picked up a few addresses of people to contact in Sydney. She was also armed with the address of the only psychoanalyst in the whole country, given to her by the Sterbas, whom she had seen in Switzerland. Despite her fears for her own future and for that of her loved ones, she was bowled over by the succession of extraordinary landscapes along the way. The blazing heat of the Suez Canal was followed by a stop in Aden, the first oriental town she had ever seen, and then it was on to Ceylon, where she spent two days viewing elephants and shrines. Finally, after a full month at sea, she reached Perth, where she was amazed at the lushness of the southern Australian landscape.

Trude arrived in Sydney on December 14, 1938. After a number of disconcerting experiences, not the least of which was celebrating Christmas in torrid summer heat, she quickly found work. The Sterbas' psychoanalyst friend put her in touch with a liberal and progressive boarding school in Mona Vale, some twenty miles out of Sydney, where her Montessori training got her hired on the spot. Trude quickly felt at home with the staff. She was in charge of the youngest class, and she lived on the premises, so with her precious Montessori teaching materials, which she had brought from Vienna, she was well armed both to teach and to console those children who missed their parents. Despite her worries, she was happy there. Being a great nature-lover, she found plenty to keep her fascinated in the outback. Above all, she discovered the pleasure of living by the ocean, something she was to treasure the rest of her life.

Her brother and his wife soon came to settle in Australia as well. And then in the summer of 1939, she received a visit from another young Viennese: Hans Bandler, who had been released from Buchenwald three months before Bettelheim. From him, she learned all the things her friend had left out of his letters: the extent of the persecution, degradation, despair, hunger, and suffering of the camps. Bandler also told her of the comforting role Bettelheim had played for him and other inmates. This was no great surprise to Trude, who knew what he was capable of. She refrained from telling Hans about her own relationship with Bruno, however.

Rediscovering youthful pleasures, Trude Weinfeld and Hans Bandler set off whenever they could for long hikes in the bush and in the

Blue Mountains. Hans worked a lot, as he was both completing his engineering studies and teaching. He too had ended up in Australia somewhat by chance—it was the first country to offer him a visa. He was feeling a bit lost, so far away from his aunt and his half-brother, who were all that remained of his family, and running into Trude had made all the difference. She was warm and self-confident, and gave the impression of having already made a place for herself in this strange land, where the local accent made Hans wonder whether he had ever studied English at all. She impressed him with her apparent maturity; he liked her simple way of doing things, her intelligence, her unpretentious yet energetic personality, her habit of looking straight ahead and not getting sidetracked by nostalgia for a vanished past. It was not long before he was in love. They did not see each other as often as he would have liked, because the bus trip between Mona Vale and Sydney, where Hans had found a room, took three-quarters of an hour. Neither of them had much money, but they nevertheless managed to go regularly to the movies, and even on occasion to a concert.

But most of all, they talked. Like Gina and Bruno in the United States, Hans and Trude soon discovered that suffering was not a very exportable commodity, and that people who were far from a conflict had no desire to hear much about it. Like other former camp inmates, Hans quickly learned to keep quiet about the Buchenwald nightmares that haunted his sleep. Needless to say, having Trude to talk to was a godsend. They also quickly realized that it was not a good idea to speak German in public, and that although open anti-Semitism was rare, it was better not to advertise their Jewishness either. Australia, like other immigrant communities, was ready to accept them as long as they blended in. Trude had wasted no time in adjusting to her new environment. Even before war was declared, and thus before her nationality had her classified as an "enemy alien," she had followed the advice of friends who knew how strong anti-German sentiment was becoming in Australia and changed her name to Trude Field. For that reason, she almost failed to get the telegram announcing Bruno's release!

The love affair with Hans was a brief one. From the moment Trude received the letter from Bruno in New York, telling her that he and Gina had broken up, she could think only of going to join him. The letter had arrived while she was in the hospital, being treated for a gynecological ailment that had made her fear she would never be able to have children. In fact, she received two pieces of good news almost at the same time: that Bruno was now unattached, and that she had not lost her reproductive capability.

Having given up all hope of obtaining a U.S. visa, she now threw herself back into the fray, writing letters and seeking appointments. Unfortunately, she had to spend the three weeks after her operation convalescing in a sanatorium, during which time war broke out, making her Austrian passport worthless. As an enemy alien, she could henceforth leave the country only with the permission of the Australian armed forces. As soon as she was up and about, she went to their headquarters and asked to see the general in charge, who at first did not seem inclined to grant her request. Finally, after much pleading during which she mentioned her fiancé, just released from a Nazi concentration camp, and shed a tear or two, he agreed to let her go.

After another long sea voyage, Trude arrived in San Francisco on October 31, 1939. On the quayside, she was amazed to see Nuci Plank, the former head of the Grünetorgasse school, waiting to greet her, even though Trude had no recollection of having told her she was coming. The information must have traveled along the exile grapevine, which was of course buzzing at the time. Plank was working at a San Francisco school, and welcomed the arrival of a teacher with Trude's experience. She invited the young woman to stay with her, and as it was Halloween, Trude was just in time for a party, where she raised a few eyebrows among Nuci's guests with her uninhibited Australian patter.

Trude awoke very early the following morning. Able to think more clearly now, she realized that Nuci Plank wanted to keep her in San Francisco. She did not quite understand what was afoot; a little later she would also find out that the Sterbas, by then living in Detroit, had hoped she would settle in that city to set up a Montessori school, to which they could send their daughters. But Trude had only one destination in view: Chicago, where Bruno had just moved. At the crack of dawn, she went down to the port to get her bags and take them to the railroad station. She left San Francisco either that evening or the next.

Alighting in Chicago after three days and two nights of travel, she was to get another surprise: Bruno was nowhere to be seen. Instead, Trude was greeted by Maria Piers, whom she had known as a fellow–trainee teacher in Vienna, and her husband, Gerhardt, a psychoanalyst. She had last seen them in Basel, where they had spent several months awaiting their U.S. visas. But she had been so excited at the prospect of seeing Bruno again, she had a hard time concealing her disappointment. She probably did not know at that time that Gerhardt Piers had contributed money toward Bettelheim's release. While in Switzerland he had worked for a local psychiatrist, but his status as a foreigner meant he could not receive a salary, so he had asked his employer to give the money to a Nazi envoy to help free Bettelheim, "because he was the first one of our acquaintances to get caught by the Gestapo," as Maria Piers puts it.[5]

The Pierses set Trude up in a Hyde Park hotel, just a stone's throw from Fritz Redl's apartment. She settled down to wait for the return of her lover, who had gone to Ohio for a job interview. He was traveling by bus to save money, and this was the cause of yet another frustration: Knowing nothing of either Chicago or U.S. public transportation, Trude simply asked the hotel receptionist where the "bus stop" was. She was thus waiting at the local stop when Bruno's long-haul bus thundered past, headed for the main city terminal. When she finally made it there, she was reunited with a glowering Bruno, furious at having waited so long!

By this time Bettelheim was no longer exactly unemployed; he was working, but without pay. A month earlier in New York—Bettelheim recalls it was on the same day his mother arrived in the country, which was October 6—he had received a letter from George Sheviakov informing him that there was an empty desk at the offices of the Eight-Year Study team. Unfortunately, there were no funds to provide a salary. Nevertheless, this was clearly the ideal opportunity for Bettelheim to get a grounding in American work practices. It was also obvious that the job would put him in a good position to be awarded the next salaried post that opened up.

It had not taken Bettelheim long to make up his mind. In New York everything had gone wrong for him, whereas only a short stay in Chicago had sufficed to give him a glimpse of a life he had long thought beyond his reach: that of an academic. In New York, it had soon become obvious that he did not have anywhere near enough experience in psychoanalysis to be able to enter the profession without starting again from scratch. The rules had been tightened since Edith Buxbaum had arrived in 1937. American analysts were feeling threatened by the sudden influx of colleagues chased out of Europe, especially since so many of the exiles could claim to have worked either with Freud himself or with his key disciples. Most of the refugee psychoanalysts Bettelheim knew at that time were caught up in a frantic race to obtain American credentials, as their European diplomas were not fully recognized. Wanda Willig, for example, was doing a stint as an intern at a Virginia hospital while Hans Willig was trying to get set up in business in New York. A little later, with Gina's help, Wanda was to find a job as a doctor at a reform school in upstate New York, moving on to become a psychiatrist in a new service set up by the Salvation Army. For the time being, however, life was anything but easy for Bettelheim's friends.

Having greeted his mother and gotten her settled at his Aunt Jenny's place, Bettelheim had therefore set off for Chicago. Fritz Redl, who was teaching in Michigan and spending only two nights a week in Hyde Park, had suggested that they share his apartment there. Bettelheim had accepted gladly, and started work on the Eight-Year Study with such gusto that only a month later Ralph Tyler offered him a paid job on the team.

In spite of the nightmares that continued to haunt him, Bettelheim thus had every reason to be satisfied. Those dearest to him were now all safely out of Hitler's reach. And he had at last been offered an opportunity to make practical use of all those theories he and his friends had been mulling over since their Jung Wandervogel days. What was more, people were listening to what he had to say: all that youthful intellectual ferment, that hard-won experience, had not been in vain. Thanks to the gregarious George Sheviakov, Bettelheim also had a social life. He was beginning to feel comfortable with the Eight-Year Study team. As for its offices, a former Universalist Church building on Sixtieth Street on the southern border of the campus, although he did not know it then, he was to occupy them for a very long time.

Bettelheim was as yet unaware of the speculation swirling around the building next door, outwardly indistinguishable from many of the nearby houses occupied by Hyde Park professors. Purchased by the university in 1931 as part of the Rush Medical School, it had until recently housed a school for mentally retarded children. The university did not quite know what to do with an institution that was halfway between a school and an asylum, and that did not at first glance fit in with the university's lofty image of itself as a temple of graduate studies. The idea had emerged that alongside its purely therapeutic role, the school could serve as a laboratory in which to study child development. Thus it was assigned to the Department of Education, with the psychiatrist Mandel Sherman, a specialist in electroencephalography, as its director. The unusual institution had also been given an unusual name, perhaps to underline its new academic vocation. It was called the Orthogenic School, from the Greek *orthos*, straight, and *genos*, origin.

PART II

---⟡---

"Dr. B"

My life is split into two parts, and each one bears surprisingly little relation to the other . . . In Vienna it was difficult, complicated and in many ways unhappy; here it is fundamentally simple and happy.

— *Bruno Bettelheim, in a 1954 letter*

9

❈

From Chicago to Rockford,
and Back

Chicago is a beautiful city, but a very tough one. Bruno Bettelheim had discovered it in summertime, in all its flowery splendor. Now that he was settled there, with winter coming on, he was beginning to find out why it is called the Windy, and also the Gray, City. Sixtieth Street (also known as the Midway Plaisance since 1893, when it served as a Venetian canal at the center of the Columbian Exposition), which he had to cross every day on his way to work, is a huge divided thoroughfare with a median so wide that in summer children use it as a football ground. In wintertime, however, it turns into a conduit for the icy winds blowing off Lake Michigan, its central strip a perilous sea of mud or a skating rink. And Bruno Bettelheim, who had never been robust at the best of times, had still not recovered from the year of physical abuse he had suffered.

It had not taken him long to fit in to the Eight-Year Study team, however. There are differing versions as to how exactly he was finally hired. Ralph Tyler insists he found Bettelheim's name on a Rockefeller Foundation list of endangered European intellectuals.[1] If such a list ever existed, it is no longer in the Foundation's archives. Both Fritz Redl and George Sheviakov had indeed received grants from the Rockefeller Foundation, the former to help him emigrate and the latter to complete his training in the United States; it is likely that after Bettelheim's first trip to Chicago, they would have done everything in their power to ensure that he too could benefit from the institution's generosity, maybe even by adding his name to an existing list. Not only was he a friend, but as recent immigrants they had a good idea of what he had just gone through. Furthermore, Redl was well aware of the pain caused to Bruno by Gina's rejection.

In any case, Bettelheim had showed up at the right time. There was a vacancy on the team in charge of assessing the results of the new programs engendered by the Eight-Year Study, the one on which George Sheviakov worked. The vacancy was for a specialist in art teaching. Tests for all the other disciplines had been devised and were already being used in the thirty schools taking part in the study, but so far, no one had been able to come up with a working plan on how to assess the new art-teaching methods. The objective was not to ascertain students' knowledge of art history as such, but to measure their level of appreciation and understanding of the works them-selves, the aim of the new methods being precisely to make teaching less abstract, grounded more in the realities of modern life than the traditional curricula were. This was a difficult task, but one for which Bettelheim was uniquely well qualified. Not only had he studied aes-thetics and art history, his work under Karl Bühler had familiarized him with such projects. Charlotte Bühler, who ran the Vienna Psy-chology Institute along with her husband, was a specialist in children and adolescents, and she had spent time in the United States, return-ing with a passion for tests. Under her influence the Institute, which was partly funded by the city of Vienna, had designed several tests as part of the great school reform program set in motion by the left-wing post–World War I city council. Indeed, that program had been simi-lar in a number of ways to the one being carried out in New Deal America by the Progressive Education Association. Bettelheim had probably not paid a great deal of attention to Charlotte Bühler's work during his time at the Institute, as he was then busy with his disser-tation, but he cannot have been unaware of its existence.[2]

Having immediately grasped the type of tool required for Tyler's project, Bettelheim got down to work, with such gusto that when Lee Cronbach, a recent graduate, was put in charge of the test statistics in the fall of 1939, he did not even realize that Bettelheim had been on the job only a few weeks.[3] The atmosphere was just what Bettelheim needed, both friendly and stimulating. His fellow-researchers were always ready to get together for a cup of coffee to talk about their work. These informal discussions were remarkably fertile, often helping someone find the solution to an apparently intractable problem. Bettelheim spent more time listening than he did talking. Although he tried not to show it, he had everything to learn about the workings of the university in particular and American life in general. His English was still hesitant, and of course heavily accented, but according to the recollections of the people who knew him at the time, he had no problem making himself understood. With Redl or Sheviakov he was even capable, on occasion, of bursts of wit in English. But he always kept a certain distance. For the young Americans who worked alongside him, he was slightly intimidating, though always gentlemanly.

In November 1939 Ralph Tyler asked him to outline his progress for the rest of the team. Although the task he had been set was very difficult, the test he was creating was remarkable in its simplicity. One of the hallmarks of Bettelheim's later work, his ability to convey subtle ideas with such clarity that his listeners soon forgot that they had not thought of them themselves, was already apparent in this, his first professional assignment in the United States.

The aim was to measure children's sensitivity to and understanding of, verbal and nonverbal, a work of art. Several pitfalls had to be avoided: In particular, the results had to be independent of the children's ease of self-expression, and of their parents' tastes. This required an assessment tool that could allow the children to communicate their experiences without words or value judgments. It had become obvious early on that these conditions could not be fulfilled if the entire range of visual art forms was included. Bettelheim therefore limited his work to the field of painting. He toured the various schools involved in the project, discussing aims with the teachers and trying out his ideas on the children.

The result was a test that was truly innovative. The main tool was a three-foot-eight by two-foot board on which were laid out forty good postcard reproductions of paintings, ranging from the Italian and German Renaissances up to Picasso.[4] Some of the works were famous, others little known. The cards were arranged to give a harmonious overall impression, but in no apparent order, although an effort had been made to avoid having one painting interfere with the next one. Along with the picture board, the students were given a form to fill out. But before they began looking at the pictures, Bettelheim explained that there was no "good" or "bad" way of doing the test, since taste was a personal matter that varied from person to person and should not be made to fit preconceived notions. Having been thus reassured, the students were asked simply to form pairs of pictures, on the basis of shared characteristics. The form had room for thirty pairs in all, but the children were free to cite only a few, and could stop whenever they wanted. They did not have to give any explanation for the choices made; at the end of the test, they were asked to write down which picture they had liked best and which least, giving reasons.

With this simple exercise, more akin to a game than an examination, the children revealed not only their stage of development (by whether they chose to link two horses' heads, two El Grecos, or two chiaroscuros, for example) but also their sensitivity to color, atmosphere, and even the meaning of a work—all this without the need for structured discourse. By giving the test to pupils both at the start and at the end of the school year, the Eight-Year Study researchers could get quite a clear idea of the progress made by each child, in a field in which testing had never previously been carried out, at least not in the United States.

Ralph Tyler offered Bettelheim a salaried post in November 1939, on the very day that he was shown the outline of the test. Six months after having lost everything, Bettelheim had not only found himself a job but had also gained acceptance, on his first attempt, in the academic world to which he had always aspired.

Bettelheim's life was still by no means simple, however. Although he had been reunited with Trude, they were not really living together. Fritz Redl was still spending about two days a week in the Hyde Park apartment, and Bettelheim himself was often away. Trude had told him about her Australian affair with Hans Bandler. Hoping to soften the blow, she had explained that her attraction toward the young man had been mainly due to the fact that he had been sent to her by Bruno, but he had nevertheless found the news hard to take. The wound caused by Gina's rejection was still fresh. He managed to keep up appearances for the outside world, but in private he had a hard time controlling the waves of anxiety and anger that rolled over him. In addition, he was still having regular concentration-camp nightmares. All of which made him difficult to live with. As Trude later noted, it was a time when she wept a great deal.

Not long after Bruno got his job, she found one too, supervising the study hall in a Jewish orphanage in Hyde Park. The Montessori teacher in her hated the warden aspect of the job, particularly since she lived on the premises. Somewhat later she was employed by an Episcopalian institution, where she was much happier, in spite of the presence of nuns and the religious atmosphere, because she was working directly with the children. Finally, she became specialized in play therapy, working with groups set up by the Jewish social services in community centers throughout the city.

Trude was in a state of permanent anxiety about her parents. After France's defeat in June 1940, they were once again under threat from advancing Nazi troops. Continuing their exodus, they had left Tours and gone south to Limoges, where her father had been hospitalized due to an intestinal ailment. He could no longer work, and Trude regularly sent them money and food parcels (most of which never arrived), while seeking all possible means to bring them to the United States. Her father's health would not allow him to make such a long journey, however. He was to die in April 1941, before the Germans extended their occupation to all of France. After his death Trude's mother, Frederika Weinfeld, went to live in the small town of Puy-Lévêque in the southwestern region of Lot. She was to remain there until August 25, 1942, when she was arrested and interned in the French camp of Septfonds. The previous day, she had written a letter to her daughter to tell her how she had gone recently to the U.S. consulate in Marseilles to finally receive her U.S. visa, only to be told that France was no longer granting any exit visas. In the letter, she therefore asked Trude to sell the ticket she had purchased for her, and to send the money instead. She concluded by saying that she would commit suicide if ever they came to arrest her. Trude was only to receive the letter in 1946, from a neighbor to whom Mrs. Weinfeld had entrusted it at the moment of her arrest. The neighbor also gave her a few pieces of jewelry that her mother had left with her. Trude was never to know it, but her mother did not have the time to go through with her plan. Her name is on a list of a thousand non-French Jews who were taken by train from the Drancy camp, near Paris, toward Auschwitz on September 9, 1942.

At the start of 1940, however, Trude still had hopes of saving her parents. She was not the kind of woman to share her inner torment with strangers, however; she looked resolutely toward the future, quickly filing her naturalization papers, on January 23, and throwing all her energy into building a new life with the difficult but brilliant man she loved. They had friends, and they had jobs, even if hers was not satisfying. Above all, they were secure, in a country where the Nazis could never get at them.

It was a strange period in Bettelheim's life, at once very tough and anxiety-laden, and exciting. Professionally, things were going well for him, even though his job was by definition a short-term one. To set up his test, he had to travel to schools all over the Midwest and along the East Coast. He was chairing workshops on the teaching of art, and his English needed to be good enough for the delicate task of reassuring teachers, many of whom were reticent about having their methods put under the spotlight in a major national study project. Bettelheim only needed to look around him, at the accelerating flow of fellow refugees into the country, to realize how successful he had been, not only in gaining a toehold in American society, but in doing so exactly where he had wanted to.

But job insecurity was still just around the corner. Bettelheim was painfully aware that he would soon have to start looking for work again. He hated that prospect; he hated what he would later describe as "the imbalance between the newly-arrived in a country, and those who are well established there. One needs them because one has not built up a group of friends so much more than they do, who have become well-rooted in their life."[5] He noted that even in his work he had suffered from his status as a recent arrival: "I was much better at what I was doing than they who were old established. And they naturally resented it, grudgingly acknowledged the quality of my work, but made me pay for it every minute." Bettelheim, who wrote these words while spending some time in Chicago after his retirement, added that these recollections had come to him the previous day, when he had run into "a colleague from those early days, in every way far inferior to me, and much younger, [who] still continues to patronize me as a gifted but not knowledgeable newcomer, as it was true thirty-five years ago."

Although he kept it to himself, except for the odd burst of self-deprecating humor, he was very sensitive to what he perceived as a patronizing, even possibly anti-Semitic, attitude on the part of the university's establishment. This is shown in an anecdote he would later tell, concerning Robert Havighurst. The latter was a young professor who was in the process of setting up the Committee on Human Development, a unique cross-disciplinary department, taking in graduate students in psychology, sociology, and education. Havighurst also worked for the Rockefeller Foundation, and for the

Progressive Education Association, which was the driving force behind the Eight-Year Study. It was he who had discovered Fritz Redl, at a 1936 conference on childhood and adolescence in England, and brought him to the United States. But when Bettelheim asked Havighurst whether he could also help him find a job, the professor reportedly answered that before aspiring to a teaching post, he would do well to familiarize himself with life in America by taking up some more modest occupation. Why not become a shoeshine boy? he added, according to Bettelheim's account of the conversation. I was unable to obtain confirmation of this story and the last quote in particular sounds like a typical Bettelheim exaggeration. But he told the story enough times and to enough people to show just how susceptible he was at the time. Rather than simply dismissing his concern as paranoia, it is worth examining why he felt that way.

There were still few Jews at the University of Chicago, or so it seemed to Bettelheim. His best friends, Redl and Sheviakov, were not Jewish, and all the people on whom his future depended, such as Tyler, Havighurst, and Robert Maynard Hutchins, the youthful president of the university, who was determined to maintain its reputation as a top-flight institution, were all Gentiles, as were the leading figures at all the East Coast Ivy League colleges. The U of C was, however, particularly liberal and progressive in spite of its rather elitist atmosphere. Its tradition was that of the Rockefeller Foundation, a prime mover in the development of the university. To make culture available to the masses, to open up the roads to knowledge, to offer the opportunity of a great education to all those both willing and able were the avowed goals of many of the university's initiatives. First among them was Hutchins's famous Great Books program, which was then in full swing. To raise the issues of racism and anti-Semitism in this context thus seems almost a heresy, particularly given the number of Jewish academics who were to find refuge at the university after fleeing the Nazis. Critics will be gently reminded that the U of C's administrators, notably Hutchins, strove to make Hyde Park, located next to one of the biggest black ghettos in all of the United States, into one of the first racially integrated neighborhoods in the country.

However, it is fair to assume that the men on whom Bettelheim's future depended had much the same attitude toward Jews as that prevailing at the time among America's liberal elite. At bottom, it was a view not far removed from that expressed by Count Leinsdorf in *The Man Without Qualities:* admiration for the perceived intelligence, business acumen, and in some cases the artistic abilities of the Jews mixed with irritated condescension at what was seen as their social climbing. And Bettelheim had only recently discovered what consequences that image of Jews could lead to. It had been confirmed to him in the most heinous way that whatever he did, his Jewishness would always stick to him, a deadly and accursed label, impossible to scrub off. In Vienna, he had learned to live with that image, as had all the assimilated Jews in his circle. Now, he could no longer stand it. And he could smell it a mile off, long before people even expressed it, and while they themselves were in many cases totally unaware of it.

He generally kept such feelings to himself, talking about them only to Trude and a few close confidants. Many of his friends never saw that side of him. Others were occasionally surprised by an outburst, not knowing where it came from. One evening in 1960, Stuart Brent, a bibliophile and music lover who owned Chicago's first psychoanalytic bookstore, was given an unexpected glimpse of this dark, tormented side of Bettelheim's character. Brent had given a talk at the fashionable Drake Hotel on the lakefront, on *The Informed Heart*, which had just been published. Afterward, Bettelheim thanked the speaker profusely and then took his arm to walk with him the few hundred yards from the hotel to Brent's bookstore, on Michigan Avenue. "You know, Stuart, there's no need in talking, really. I'm an old Jew," Bettelheim declared sadly. He continued to ruminate on the same theme throughout the walk. What Brent found most striking was that this occurred at a time when Bettelheim was rising to fame, amid general admiration. His school was becoming well known, he was being invited to speak all over the country, and at the university, students were falling over one another to get into his classes.

The idea that Bettelheim needed to get to know the United States better was also put forward by Ralph Tyler when, as the Eight-Year Study work was concluding, he recommended a part-time teaching post at Rockford College, a small women's school some sixty miles northwest of Chicago. This was in the late summer of 1941. Bettelheim had finally married Trude Weinfeld on May 14, with the least possible ceremony, as she had just lost her father. The marriage took place nine days after a Cook County court granted Bettelheim a divorce from Gina, who was ruled to have deserted him. Trude and Bruno were at last living together, at 6033 Dorchester Avenue, near the former church building where the Eight-Year Study was then being wound up.

The opening was for an art history teacher. Bettelheim's name had been suggested to the president of Rockford, Mary Ashby Cheek, by Ulrich Middeldorf, head of the U of C Department of Art: "Though he was never affiliated with our department, we count him among our own people," he wrote. Ralph Tyler provided enthusiastic support, stating that Bettelheim not only had the required skills, including adequate English, but also that "he comes from a wealthy Viennese family who have had fine art collections of their own. Hence, his reaction to art is that of a connoisseur as well as of a student." That letter contained another inaccuracy concerning Bettelheim's résumé, one that would have implications for the future. Tyler stressed that Bettelheim was highly trained in both the arts and criticism, "although his Ph.D., I believe, is in the field of psychology."[6]

In early September, Miss Cheek asked Bettelheim to give two classes a week at Rockford. One, an introduction to art history, would be a yearlong course; the other would be devoted to the art of antiquity in the first semester and to Byzantine, early Christian, and Romanesque art in the second. He would receive a salary of $600 a year for two days' presence each week, during which he would be provided with bed and board in Rockford. Bettelheim accepted without hesitation.

Thus, on the morning of Monday September 22, 1941, he alighted from a train in the small town of Rockford, to be greeted by the college art studies director, a Mr. Paxson. Bettelheim probably did not realize it then, but this would be more than a small detour in his life. It was there in the heart of the American corn belt, near the point where Illinois, Wisconsin, and Iowa meet, that this city-dwelling Viennese immigrant was to learn how the New World into which he had been so brutally projected, and which was so different from anything he had ever known before, worked. It was also there—but how could he possibly have guessed it?—that his chrysalid-like transformation into a new Bruno Bettelheim would take place. Up to that point, the circles he had moved in—psychoanalysts in New York, academics in Chicago—had closely resembled those he had known in his youth, even if many of the people he was meeting were American-born. A few months later, the entry of the United States into the war would result in other European refugees arriving in Rockford, to replace teachers who had been drafted. But in September 1941, Bettelheim was still one of a kind at the small college nestled amid the cornfields and the trees.

Rockford College provided high-quality courses, as its links to the University of Chicago testified. The tuition fees were relatively high, and although most of its students had no intention of letting a career get in the way of their futures as mothers and housewives, they took their studies seriously. These young Midwestern women, for whom higher education was often an adventure in itself, had never met anyone quite like Bruno Bettelheim. There were occasions when his accent forced them to strain to understand a word, but that did not prevent them from appreciating the richness and depth of his teaching. He introduced them to art, philosophy, and psychology, without much regard for the traditional boundaries between those disciplines. Rather than giving them textbooks, he had them read the original texts, and whenever possible he sent them off to see the artworks discussed in class. They had never come across anyone so cultured. And once they had gotten used to his way of asking their permission before he took off his jacket, even in 90-degree heat, they began to see his manners as the very height of refinement.

Although he rarely brought the subject up himself, they had soon heard about what he had been through before leaving Europe. They discussed it among themselves, without really knowing what a concentration camp could be. But they noticed that he sat down most of the time. One of them, observing from a second-floor window as Bettelheim crossed the quadrangle, was so struck by the odd way he walked, holding his arms stiffly to his sides as if to protect himself from being beaten, that she wrote a poem on the subject for the college newspaper.

"It was a privilege to know such a man . . . " "He was such a remarkable, knowledgeable man . . . " "He was fascinating. Frightening too, but fascinating . . . " "His classes were very enlightening . . . But he wasn't easy." "I was intimidated, but I worked very well with him . . . " Such comments, gleaned fifty years later, reflect the deep impression Bettelheim made on his students.[7] "Socratic" is the word they use most to describe his teaching method. And many add: "He opened up a whole new world for me (us)." They still remember their surprise on discovering, with him, the hidden meaning of fairy tales. They remember the titles of some of the books he assigned them (notably Freud's *Psychopathology of Everyday Life*, and also works by Emile Durkheim and Erich Fromm), and some of the films he screened for them, in particular *Le jour se lève* (Daybreak) by Marcel Carné.

Within a year Bettelheim gained a whole slew of new assignments at Rockford. In the fall of 1942, Mary Ashby Cheek asked him to drop his art classes temporarily to stand in for the philosophy professor, who had gone off to the war. In that first semester, he therefore taught five classes in all: history of philosophy, history of ideas, general psychology, psychological theory, and German. The following semester it was Mr. Paxson's turn to be drafted, and Bettelheim reshuffled his schedule to stand in for him too. He also took over running the committee that selected movies to be shown on campus, a task he took very seriously. By this time Bettelheim was spending four days a week at Rockford, for an annual salary of around $2,000. He arrived on Monday evenings and left after his last class on Friday. He also participated fully in the little campus's social life. One of his students, who did some waitressing at meal times, remembers clearly the lively conversations he took part in at the teachers' table in the large dining room, where everyone ate. Another remembers the active support Bettelheim gave to the liberal Students' Forum action committee.

There was no shortage of inspiring causes to support and issues to debate, ranging from the effects of the Spanish Civil War to economic recovery and the labor situation. And of course, the World War, which the United States had finally decided to get involved in. At the start of the year, the students had taken a Victory Pledge and resolved to acquire professional skills that could be of help. They were learning clerical work in case the Army needed to call on them, training in emergency duties, and devoting some of their time to working at a local war plant. Although traditionally centered on the liberal arts, Rockford College had taken in engineering students and added classes in nutrition, first aid, and emergency child care to its course catalogue. Bettelheim was an energetic participant in all the debates, urging the students to think before acting, to always weigh the pros and cons, and to speak up whenever they had something on their mind. That was also something new for most of them. They had been taught to give unquestioning support to good causes—in other words, those defined as such by the majority. And now here was Professor Bettelheim, telling them that God, if he existed at all, could not be simply on one side.

But it was above all in his classes that he built up the extraordinary influence he came to hold over his flock. He would never sit at the teacher's desk. Instead he took one of the students' chairs with its attached writing tablet, turned it to face the class, and beckoned them to form a circle around him. Then, after a few introductory remarks, he would start shooting out questions. At first, many of the young women fell into the trap of viewing these sessions as a kind of quiz, in which the quicker-witted could show off their abilities. They soon learned otherwise. "At the beginning, he was very tough on me, because I was rather verbal and didn't give much thought to what I was saying," Ronnie Dryvage admits. "Then one day, when I left the room crying, he called me back and said 'Don't be sad. I know a thousand people who think that way.' So all my anxiety vanished and I thought to myself: 'This man really cares about me and I am going to learn something with him.'"

The components of what was to become the unique Bettelheim teaching system were already falling into place: encouraging open discussion, getting students to think for themselves and by themselves, and using sharp comments to chide those who were conformist, shallow, or pretentious. The two things Bettelheim hated more than anything else were stupidity and jargon, seeing the latter as a pedantic way of covering up the former. He was pitiless with students who failed to bring the same amount of intensity and seriousness to his classes as he did himself. And he would often use his exchanges with such students to demonstrate to their classmates—and to themselves, if they were strong enough to see beyond the immediate situation and understand what was going on—the very psychological mechanisms he was trying to explain in his courses. During such verbal duels, the classroom vibrated with tension. Some students found this method most enlightening, a few others did not understand what was going on and thought it a little hard to take. Strangely enough, though, few of the "victims" of such exercises felt that way.

Bettelheim already had favorites among the students. They included the brighter ones, those who were quickest at latching on to his train of thought or who dared stand up to him, but also the weaker ones, those most in need of help. With them, he was capable of infinite patience, being attentive not only to their problems but also to their needs. They would never be the ones singled out to have their psychological makeup dissected in front of the class. For another of Bettelheim's character traits, which is often cited by his former Rockford students, was his kindness. "He cared," they say. Each of them has some tale or other that shows how he devoted time to aid a student in distress or helped them find some needed piece of information such as an address or a book reference, even before they had thought to ask him.

An insight into the type of relationship Bettelheim developed with his psychology students can be gleaned from his essay "Self-Interpretation of Fantasy," in which he reports on an experiment carried out by an unnamed psychology instructor "in one of the smaller Midwestern women's colleges" in the spring of 1944.[8] As specified in the article's subtitle, it involved using the Thematic Apperception Test, or TAT, at the time the most commonly used measure of personality after the Rorschach test, as an educational and a therapeutic device. Bettelheim further noted that the students, whom he described as predominantly "middle class and rather conservative," were "in the throes of late adolescent development." They were past that stage chronologically, but not in emotional maturity. "Courses in psychology frequently attract students who are dimly aware of their own personality difficulties," and this class was no exception, he added.

It was not uncommon in psychology classes to submit students to the very tests they were studying, but it was much less usual for the teacher to take on a therapist's role so openly. This merging of the roles of teacher and healer that Bettelheim first tried out at Rockford College was to become his distinctive feature, the key to all his subsequent activity at the Orthogenic School. This is why the detailed account given in his article, which according to at least one of his former students is very accurate,[9] is particularly interesting.

The TAT uses a set of nineteen cards with black-and-white pictures that look like shots from realist films. On the first, a small boy is shown contemplating a violin that is lying on a table, another features a young woman carrying books while in the background a man works in the fields and an old woman, standing motionless, looks on; a third shows a distressed-looking young woman leaning against a doorpost, covering her eyes with one arm. A twentieth card is blank. The psychologist shows the cards to the subject one by one, asking him or her to tell the story behind each.[10] The basic assumption of the TAT is that "when interpreting a vague or ambiguous situation, [the subject] by so doing reveals significant aspects of his personality," Bettelheim explains. For example, the desires the subject attributes to the characters reveal those that worry him personally, while features he does not notice point to repressed material in his psyche. Nevertheless, as Bettelheim states from the outset, many other factors can influence

the content of the subject's stories, such as level of intellectual development, interests and recent experiences, and also the relationship
with the tester.

The aim of the article is to demonstrate that self-analysis by the
subject of his or her own made-up stories not only makes it possible
to avoid certain pitfalls (such as the examiner projecting his fantasies
onto the resulting material), but also has a number of advantages, for
the examiner, the educator, and the therapist. After listing all those
advantages, Bettelheim gives an overview of the content of the program up until the setting of the test. He explains that the exercise was
part of a course in dynamic psychology that deliberately used the students' personal experiences. Having studied several theories of personality, illustrated by case studies, the young women were asked to
write an autobiography. They were then "introduced to an understanding of some aspects of their own behavior."

When Bettelheim suggested that the students subject themselves to
the TAT, there was thus nothing to indicate that the experiment
would be any different from what had already gone on in the course.
Then, several weeks later, he sprang a surprise by handing the class
their own TAT results and asking them to analyze the psychological
content of each story, summing up what the whole exercise had
taught them. Once that task was completed, he asked them whether
they thought the test had given an accurate picture of their personality, and in particular whether certain aspects of it had remained
hidden. It was thus quite an experience. In his account, which he
illustrated with the analysis of three cases, Bettelheim makes no
bones about the fact that the results were influenced by the students'
relationship with "the instructor" (that is, him) and even uses the
term *transference* to describe that relationship, adding that without
that transference, the self-interpretation exercise would not have
given a student any more understanding than she had already gained
from the test itself.

Bettelheim had set limits to the exercise, however. He deviated
from the standard TAT procedure by not asking the students to ad
lib on the stories once they had completed each one. The creators of
the TAT intended such elaboration to allow the subjects to express
their fantasies, and thus bring up deeper layers of repressed material. Bettelheim explains that since the plan was to have the students subsequently analyze their stories themselves, he did not
want the initial versions to go too far. Citing Freud, he stresses that

the unconscious material that can generate the production of stories is relatively accessible and anxiety-free, since it has been organized into a presentable form by the ego—in contrast, for example, with the material expressed in dreams, which is much harder to interpret." Spontaneous improvisation, on the other hand, can be much more revealing. Despite such precautions, however, it is easy to understand the puzzlement of the young teacher who was to succeed him in his psychology class. She was later to tell a colleague: "I don't know who this Bruno Bettelheim is, but I can't do a thing with his students."[12]

If the Bettelheim teaching system was born at Rockford College, so too were the reactions that it was to provoke. Already, students were flocking to enroll in his classes, in such numbers that in September 1943 Mary Ashby Cheek asked him to take an overflow session on Saturday mornings. (He turned down the request because he was giving a course on art in Chicago on that day, but he adjusted his regular teaching hours so that all students who wanted to could attend.) And already, a number of students were dropping out only a few weeks into the class, either angry and indignant or simply unable to keep up. Some declared that Bettelheim was a sadist, and that they would under no circumstances be taken in a second time. Already, this strange Socrates-like figure was sparking admiration, fear, and jealousy among his colleagues. And already he was creating a circle of disciples, fired with enthusiasm for the perspectives he opened up. Intelligent, idealistic, curious, imaginative, and in some cases a trifle masochistic, many of them would find their vocation through his teaching.

In January 1942 it was Ralph Tyler's turn to ask Mary Ashby Cheek what she thought of Bruno Bettelheim. The Eight-Year Study had been completed, and the U of C Department of Art was considering offering him a part-time teaching job. The Rockford president's assessment was glowing indeed: "Everything points to the fact that he is an excellent and genuine teacher, as well as a scholar of parts." At the start of the following semester, Bettelheim thus found himself working part time for the University of Chicago. This time, his office was located in the basement of the former church building on Sixtieth Street. His job was to churn out exam subjects for a variety of teachers in art history, psychology, and German. His friend Fritz Redl was also working there occasionally. Bettelheim was to spend two years commuting weekly, four days at Rockford and three in Chicago. He and Trude lived simply, devoting part of their meager income to helping their relatives. Paula Bettelheim was by this time living in a Greenwich Village retirement home. Margarethe, who had just gotten married, was also living in New York after having spent some time in London.

Bruno and Trude lived well, however. They did not have a great deal of furniture but their apartment was tastefully arranged, and in spite of their heavy schedules they managed to spend a few evenings with friends, in particular at the Sheviakovs', where both wine and conviviality were in plentiful supply. Bruno was the one who did most of the socializing, for Trude had realized that if she wanted to find an interesting job she would have to go back to school, given that in the United States a social work diploma had to be gained at university. In the fall of 1940 she had enrolled at Northwestern University, taking classes while continuing to hold down a job.

The couple seemed happy together. Bruno was very attentive to Trude, and showed a great deal of respect for her energy and courage. "Bruno and Trude seemed to take good care of each other in those days," recalls Ruth Nedelsky, who attended one of Bettelheim's Eight-Year Study workshops. At the time, her husband Leo, one of George Sheviakov's best friends, was drafting physics exams in the same group as Bettelheim, and liked and admired him. The Nedelskys remember them as a courageous, hardworking couple, a little distant but sociable, amusing and interesting. "Bruno had the strongest Viennese accent I have ever heard. He had a lot of taste, and was a true art connoisseur; he didn't show the slightest interest in amateur painters like myself. He used to speak his mind, but never opened up about himself," Leo says.[3] In December 1942, Trude gave birth to the couple's first daughter, Ruth Colette.

Three months later, George Sheviakov decided to take a job in Vanport, Oregon, and Bettelheim suggested that he pass on his apartment to one of his old friends from Vienna, Peter Weinmann, who had finally married Gina a year earlier. Curiously, the Viennese circle had gradually come together again in Hyde Park. Indeed, when Paula went to Chicago to visit her son, she would often walk across the street to have tea with her former daughter-in-law, with whom she appears to have gotten along better than with Trude. In any case, the wounds left by Bruno and Gina's divorce were off limits for conversation. Thanks to traditional Viennese discretion or perhaps simply to the bonds created by exile, Trude, Gina, Bruno, and Peter were all the best of friends. As Gina's birthday fell on December 24, they got into the habit of celebrating Christmas at the Weinmanns' and Thanksgiving at the Bettelheims'. They spoke mostly English together, and often attended the same social events. Ruth Nedelsky, who was barely twenty at the time, has retained a strong impression of Gina's elegance and self-assurance. She had a hard time understanding how one man could have married two women as different from one another as were Gina and Trude. But that only added to the mysterious fascination exercised by these talented immigrants.

Most of his Chicago colleagues knew that Bettelheim had only recently spent a year in a concentration camp but, as Ruth Nedelsky recalls today with some embarrassment, the majority did not have any idea what that meant. He himself did not talk about it much. He was more forthcoming about his life in Vienna, relating anecdotes on art and psychoanalysis. And he talked about Patsy. Holding forth to an audience fascinated by education and psychology, he described the progress the American girl had made in the six years she spent in his household. He talked about her with the enthusiasm of a man who had followed the progress of his own child from day to day, and he made it sound as though it would have taken only a few more years for Patsy to have been completely cured.

He told the story in particular to one of his new friends, Benjamin Bloom, a doctoral student and assistant to Ralph Tyler. Bloom, who like Bettelheim was both Jewish and aware of being so, was more receptive than many to his tales of suffering. He got him to talk, and slowly but surely won Bettelheim's trust. As he too was very interested in the mechanisms of learning, he showed great interest in the story of Patsy. So one day when Ralph Tyler was complaining about the intractable problem of the Orthogenic School, Bloom suggested that he talk to Bettelheim. "He knows about disturbed children," Bloom said, "and has experience in the field."

The Orthogenic School was a real headache for the Department of Education and Tyler was at his wits' end. It was expensive to run, and although its fees were by no means low, they did not cover the full cost. Dr. Mandel Sherman, who was in charge of the place, had been continually asking for new funds ever since taking up the post. The premises were run-down and too small for the thirty or so children who lived there; the counselors were underpaid and poorly trained. The reason invariably cited by Sherman for seeking more money, however, was laboratory equipment, without which, he said, it was impossible to carry out serious research. As early as 1941, Tyler had told him that the solution lay not in squeezing more cash out of the university but in obtaining private funding. Tyler noted that some of the children who lived at the school had wealthy parents: why not get them to contribute?

Such suggestions fell on deaf ears. "Mandel Sherman was a very self-centered man, only interested in his own career," says Bernice Neugarten, who at the time was working toward her PhD and attending a seminar on child development given by Sherman.[14] She was particularly shocked one day when he asked her and around a dozen other students to visit the school to observe some cases. After the seminar students sat down, Sherman asked that a child be brought in. Then, without a single affectionate word or gesture, he had the child plunked down at one end of the room and said: "Now tell us what's wrong with you." Bernice Neugarten's initial impression was to be confirmed a little later, when she did summer replacement work for teachers at the Orthogenic School. Sherman "ran the place like a custodial institution." She was thus not overly surprised, one day in the summer of 1944, to see Ralph Tyler and Robert Havighurst showing a newcomer around the premises. It was a man she had never seen before, clearly of Germanic origin, with a very strong accent. Being busy with a group of children at the time, she did not have much chance to talk to him, but her first impression was a good one. "It was a real relief. The place needed taking over," she says.

The way he later told it, Bettelheim was practically trapped into taking on the job of director. At the end of 1941, with the institution under fire from all sides, Ralph Tyler had asked Robert Havighurst to head up a committee on the problem. The resulting report was not in itself unfavorable, but it stressed one of the Orthogenic School's basic contradictions. Since its brief was now to take in children who were emotionally disturbed but of normal intelligence, its aim should be to prepare them for a return to the mainstream educational system. But because it was so underequipped, and its teachers were so inadequately trained, the children were in fact falling even farther behind in the learning process. Havighurst's report therefore recommended that the institution be simply integrated into the Lab Schools system, which provided excellent primary and secondary education on the campus. But the idea had run into a wall of opposition from many of the professors whose children attended the Lab Schools.

In the fall of 1942, Mandel Sherman became embroiled in a legal dispute that proved embarrassing for the university. Bettelheim said it was around that time that Ralph Tyler asked him to draw up a report on the Orthogenic School with proposals on how it could be changed. He had been so shocked by what he had seen of the institution, and by the way the children were treated, that he had refrained from mentioning it again to Tyler, he said. The request came at a time when he already had an extremely heavy work schedule: Not only was he dividing his time between Rockford and his job as an examiner, he was in the middle of writing and rewriting an account of his concentration camp experiences. The publication of his article a year later in Harvard University's *Journal of Abnormal and Social Psychology* gave a boost to his standing at the University of Chicago.[15] Six months after that, the defeat of the Axis powers and the discovery of the first concentration camps would increase that authority even more.

Bettelheim's employment situation remained shaky, however. The end of the war brought the return of the Rockford staff members who had gone off to fight, and in particular the philosophy teacher. As for psychology, the Faculty Committee decided in the spring of 1944 that the teacher concerned needed to be present five days a week. Informing Bettelheim of the decision, Mary Ashby Cheek cited purely academic considerations, but there were probably other reasons. At least, that was how his students saw it. Several of them went to the dean of students to protest the decision, which probably only served to confirm just how much influence this unorthodox stand-in had gained in the institution. Bettelheim was obviously a remarkable teacher, but perhaps a bit *too* remarkable for a small Midwestern women's college.[16] Whatever the reasons, replying to Bettelheim's questions about his future on May 4, 1944, Cheek wrote that she was unable to offer him a contract for the following academic year that would justify his breaking his ties with the University of Chicago. She added that even if he were to work full time at Rockford College, his salary would hardly increase, and he would have to wait his turn, for many years, to get a professorship.

That letter, which meant the end of Bettelheim's career at Rockford, was probably crucial in persuading him to accept the Orthogenic School offer. For a few months after he commissioned Bettelheim's report, Ralph Tyler waited, then one day he called him into his office to ask him where it was. The two men had by then been working together for five years, and had gotten to know each other. Bettelheim felt free to speak his mind. As he later told the story, his advice was, "There's only one thing to be done with that school: burn it down," to which Tyler replied that he understood his reaction, but he was serious in wanting a detailed report on what was wrong with the Orthogenic School, and what should be done about it.

Bettelheim had no desire to take on the job of reorganizing the Orthogenic School, an institution that, as he had already seen, had brought nothing but problems for the man who was then running it. The career he envisioned for himself was that of a university professor, occasionally publishing lofty articles in prestigious reviews. He had had a taste of that life at Rockford, and wanted more. Ulrich Middeldorf had promised to take him on as a staff member in the U of C Department of Art at the first available opportunity. One thing, at least, was clear: He could not keep up the same punishing schedule much longer. At the start of the year he had been hospitalized with pneumonia, and overwork was no doubt a contributing factor.

Bettelheim was also reluctant to disappoint Ralph Tyler, the man who had provided him with every one of his jobs over the past five years. He therefore decided he had no choice but to accept the new assignment, while taking pains to stress that he would be acting only as a consultant. To help him assess the school, he called on Dr. Emmy Sylvester, one of the best child psychoanalysts around, and like Bettelheim a native of Vienna. Unfortunately, Bettelheim did not keep a copy of the note he drew up for Tyler, and the original is nowhere to be found in the available Orthogenic School archives at the university. According to his subsequent account, it was around two months after he had submitted it that Ralph Tyler invited him to lunch, and then without any warning took him into Robert Hutchins's office, where the president promptly offered him the job of running the school. Bettelheim, furious at being cornered, reportedly replied: "All right, but on condition that you triple the budget and don't ask me any questions for five years." To his great surprise, Hutchins agreed on the spot.

I was not able to ascertain how much exaggeration there is in the above account. It seems particularly unlikely, on the basis of the documents I found, that Ralph Tyler could have given Bettelheim a completely free rein over such a long period. Indeed, nine months after taking up the job, the latter submitted to Tyler a detailed report on the school's requirements.

What can be confirmed, however, is that in June 1944 there was a substantial increase in students' fees at the Orthogenic School, from $165 to $200 a month. And the following month, Philip Pekow, the father of one of the students, convened a meeting of rich potential donors. They concluded that the institution required at least $2 million a year to function correctly. But before launching a fund-raising drive, they wanted to know whether the university would be willing to provide matching funds.

In September 1944, Bettelheim asked several of his best former students at Rockford to come and work with him at the Orthogenic School. Three accepted enthusiastically; one who refused now says Bettelheim never forgave her for it. On October 1, he officially took up his new job. His salary was $1,900 a year, plus $1,700 for courses he was to teach in the Department of Education. The teaching job was no doubt used by Tyler, well aware of Bettelheim's academic ambitions, as bait to get him to accept the directorship of the school. A month and a half later, Bruno Bettelheim became a U.S. citizen.

10

❀

A New Man for the New World

Call me Ishmael.

—*Herman Melville*, Moby Dick

"**B**runo to head the Orthogenic School? Why not? Provided he does a new spell of analysis." Within the Chicago psychoanalytic community, Kurt Eissler was one of the few people not to criticize Bettelheim's appointment. Although very different, the two men, both Viennese, enjoyed each other's company in those days, and their wives were good friends.[1] Bettelheim had met Eissler's brother at Buchenwald and, before that, they had run into each other in the Jung Wandervogel. Kurt Eissler, a tall, proud, yet kindly person, had also met Fritz Redl in August Aichhorn's seminars, and although a medical doctor he had studied under Karl Bühler, but earlier than Bettelheim. In Chicago, however, what probably brought the two men together as much as anything was their views on all things American, and in particular on American psychoanalysis.

As events in Europe had accelerated, Chicago and its university had seen the arrival of an ever-swelling tide of refugees, most of them German speaking. They desired above all to blend in as quickly as possible with the host society, but their living conditions were often extremely difficult. For some, lawyers for example, exile meant going back to square one. Others, such as doctors or engineers, had to take a number of U.S. exams, wasting precious months at a time when they needed income as never before. Even traders had to learn to operate in new surroundings, with different rules. All the while, the new arrivals strove to conform to the "good immigrant" stereotype: putting a brave face on things, keeping up cheerful appearances while every day brought its load of awful news concerning loved ones and the world they had left behind.

Most of them, and notably the Bettelheims, made a point of speaking only English in public, even to one another. They had turned their backs on their old lives, and saw no point indulging in nostalgia. Nevertheless, these brand new Americans would get together from time to time for a European-style evening, to swap experiences, news, and gossip. There would be irritation at the Americans for their lack of refinement, tips on where to buy "real" coffee or bread, or how to adapt a cake mix to bake something that tasted of home. And, human nature being what it is, there would also be snide remarks about how this or that person was getting on in the race for assimilation.

Bruno Bettelheim was in a class of his own. Despite his persistent accent and a none-too-advantageous past, he had been one of the quickest to understand how this dynamic new society functioned. He was again working extremely hard, but now he was succeeding in everything he put his hand to. This New World, where he had fetched up empty-handed, appeared to be tailor-made for him. And though he found plenty to complain about in his new environment, American society's much-derided lack of refinement also made it all the easier for him to deploy his Old World charm—as when he amazed his Rockford students by asking their permission to take off his jacket, for instance.

Such a speedy adaptation was bound to spark jealousy and even resentment in those around him, particularly since his success appeared to be based not only on his talent and hard work but also on the revised version of his past that he had allowed to take root in the minds of his employers. The process had been facilitated by the silence of those who could have told the truth. Among the Viennese exiles, at least, even people who did not know Bettelheim personally had heard that his real past was different from what the Americans around him thought. If such talk went on behind his back, however, it remained within the community. One did not denounce a fellow-exile—"especially one who had just come out of Buchenwald," as someone who could have spoken up but didn't, and prefers now to remain anonymous, told me. What is more difficult to explain, however, is that nobody said anything to Bettelheim himself. Perhaps this was due to the desire to avoid a clash with a difficult man, and that very Viennese tendency to avert one's eyes when faced with an embarrassing sight. "After all, it was none of my business. And my life was quite difficult enough as it was. Nobody today realizes just how tough it was for us exiles," says Maria Piers, somewhat defensively. Meanwhile, Bettelheim donned more and more openly a persona that was not exactly his.

This was indeed the period when he reinvented his past. The actual untruths on which the process was based were few in number, but they were seminal. Whatever else he would achieve, he felt obliged to go on repeating them, and elaborating on them, throughout his whole life, and they were to pursue him up to the very end. I do not know exactly when his doctorate in aesthetics turned into a psychology degree,[2] when Patsy became his patient, or Eleanor Roosevelt the person who had saved him from the Nazis. But it was in the first half of the 1940s that these myths gradually took on the appearance of solid facts. It certainly did not happen all at once, and the process was helped by a few mistakes made by others (as in Ralph Tyler's letter of recommendation to the president of Rockford College, for example). But little by little, as the narrator of the fable realized that nobody was contradicting him, his tone became more and more self-assured.

The phenomenon in itself is not all that extraordinary; on close inspection many famous men turn out to have embellished their résumés. But with Bettelheim, the myth-making process is of particular interest because it would facilitate the opening-up of a gap between the real Orthogenic School and the way he portrayed it in his books. In other words, in a country like the United States, which prefers its heroes to be unblemished, the half-truths about his past ended up sowing doubts about all of Bettelheim's achievements, including those that were indisputable. The doubts troubled not only those who knew, but Bettelheim himself. The more famous he became, the more they seemed to echo in his mind with the "fraud" he associated with his grandfather Seidler, the forebear he was most afraid of resembling, yet the only one who had set him an example of success. Toward the end of his life, Bettelheim on occasion tried to duck questions about these fables, as if he had had enough of them, as if his accomplishments in the United States should have sufficed and he should no longer be called on to back them up with the legend of his Viennese past. But his interviewers would invariably return to the stories, and Bettelheim would end up telling them what they so obviously wanted to hear.[3]

Bettelheim made the cover of the Sunday *New York Times* magazine section for the first time in January 1970. Whereas he should have been delighted, his successor-in-training, Bert Cohler,[4] found him looking glum and asked him why. "There's a dark secret in my past which could destroy the school," Bettelheim replied. When Cohler first told me this story,[5] I must admit I was skeptical, believing it to be an exaggeration intended to impress me. Today, however, I feel sure it is true, if only because I have since heard the same expression, "dark secret," from Bettelheim's own mouth, referring to his childhood fears, the mystery surrounding his family's origins and his father's illness.[6] In four years of investigation I was able to find only one possible motivation for such a dramatic statement: that Bettelheim had not undergone a proper psychoanalytic training, and that the unidentified American child (Patsy) he refers to in all his books—and particularly in *The Empty Fortress*, the latest book he had published on the school at the time—had never in fact been his patient.

Before examining his relationship to psychoanalysis, therefore, it is worth reflecting on exactly why Bruno Bettelheim felt the need to rearrange his past. The explanation put forward by some critics, that he simply wanted to make a name for himself and therefore began telling tall stories, finally believing in them himself, does not seem convincing to me. Everything I have learned about Bettelheim indicates that he was not blessed with a self-serving memory, and that he knew a lie when he saw one. How, otherwise, could he have spent thirty years of his life helping children and adults alike to doggedly track down their own darkest and innermost secrets, often very successfully? Had he started believing in his own stories, he could not have understood as clearly as he did how certain memories can be deadly. And in his relationships with others, his insistence on saying things which would often have been better left unsaid made him enough enemies for us to conclude that his desire to get at the truth was strong.

"Dreams were given to prisoners so they could re-invent their past," the French writer Jean-Paul Kaufman has said.[7] The three and a half years that Kaufman spent as a hostage of the Hezbollah organization in Beirut can be compared with Bettelheim's period at Buchenwald on two counts only, but they are essential ones. Both men were held arbitrarily by people who hated them not for anything they had done but for who they were, and while neither knew up until the last minute whether he would be freed, both were aware from the out-set that they could be killed at any time. In such a situation, Kaufman explains, dreams and reality tend to balance each other, the prisoner drawing from one the strength he needs to face up to the other. It is only after release that nightmares come, an observation confirmed by Bet-telheim. "In the concentration camp, I rarely dreamed about imprison-ment or captivity. I dreamed of happy occasions."[8] As Kaufman writes: "At night, every prisoner in the world is out and on the run. Dreams pry open the most tightly locked door, and push aside the heaviest of iron bars." Thus does the unfortunate prisoner remind himself that life is worth living, and that he must hang on to it. Those few hours snatched from the all-powerful jailers are a time of "frozen happiness," of pure harmony that can never exist in real life.

And what can happen in the mind of the prisoner when he emerges to find a world that bears no relation to the one he knew before, when everything or almost everything in his life is new: country, wife, lan-guage, profession, environment, lifestyle? When what he had always dreamed of comes true, in a real world all the more credible because, unlike that of dreams, it is by no means a bed of roses? When at the same time the world of his past is vanishing, swallowed up in a night-mare of blood and fire?

On May 11, 1939, Bruno Bettelheim lost his marriage, and with it the life he had thought was to be his in America. On July 7, 1941, he was officially stripped of the citizenship of his birth, and, more impor-tant no doubt from a symbolic point of view, of his PhD from Vienna University.[9] As for the Bettelheim & Schnitzer company, it had been stolen from him long before. He had no past; he was dispossessed but free. He could at last throw away the key to all the dark closets con-taining the terrifying skeletons of his childhood. He was in a position, or even better he was forced, to create a whole new life for himself.

Which is what he proceeded to do. Those first few years in the United States brought such a change in him that by the end of the 1940s one can justifiably speak of a "new Bettelheim." New status, new profession, new family, and new past. New also because this man who had so long feared that he was a carrier of syphilis had fathered two children (his second daughter, Naomi, was born in November 1945). A new man, made to measure for the New World he now inhabited.

This new Bettelheim was forged from the shock of exile, coming hard on the heels of the trauma of the concentration camps and Gina's rejection. It probably came into being little by little, without him really being aware of it, with the protective complicity of Trude, who above all wanted to see her husband at last exploiting all the inner riches that she knew he possessed. But the metamorphosis could not but leave scars on a man who desired to be admirable and could not stand the idea that he was not. For even if the "fairy tales" he liked to tell about his past originated more from the basic human need to protect one's wounds than from professional ambition, he was certainly more aware than anyone else that they were fakes. And my impression is that the arrogance and aggressiveness for which he would later become notorious had a great deal to do with the guilt feelings associated with this awareness. As is generally the case, however, such behavior served only to spread doubts around him even more.

It was thus with his title of psychoanalyst, which was continually being challenged—in France, for example, when Daniel Karlin's television programs on the Orthogenic School were broadcast in 1974. Writing to a Parisian friend who had expressed concern at the accusations, Bettelheim suggested ignoring them. He nevertheless went on to write: "I have been elected a member of the Chicago Psychoanalytic Society. This is the only certification necessary to be officially an analyst." He also pointed out that, as had been the case earlier in Chicago, the Child Psychiatry Division of the Stanford Medical School had invited him to lecture in their discipline. All of which is true, but to paraphrase Shakespeare, the doctor appears to protest too much. As if to confirm that there is a problem, he ends his letter: "As if I cared whether or not I am a psychoanalyst, as if it would prove anything. We have helped children nobody else did, that's the only thing that counts, and we learned in the process. Who cares what it is called?"[10]

To understand Bettelheim's complex relations with the psychoanalytic establishment and with Freud's ideas a brief historical explanation is needed. In the United States of the early 1940s, the rule was in theory extremely simple: Contrary to the view that Freud himself had held, only qualified medical practitioners were allowed to set up as psychoanalysts. However child analysis was viewed as an exception, tolerated mainly because it had been invented by Anna Freud, who was not an MD. For the profession's official bodies it did not really count as psychoanalysis, since for obvious reasons it could not meet

the standard conditions defined by the International Psychoanalytic
Association: patient lying on a couch, analyst remaining silent while
the patient free-associated, sessions lasting fifty-five minutes, and so
on. This opened up a loophole, and one that was all the more significant because Nazism was sending waves of psychoanalysts fleeing
across the Atlantic, many of them very experienced but without medical degrees. By opting for child analysis, teachers like Edith Buxbaum
were able to get around the rule and open practices upon arrival. Even
some of those with medical qualifications chose this path in order to
avoid having to repeat their internships.

Bettelheim's case was different: he had not been trained as an analyst in Vienna. Which explains Kurt Eissler's remark, noted at the start
of this chapter. Had he undergone a new round of treatment in the
United States, this time a training analysis, it would have been enough
to qualify him to head the Orthogenic School, where he would be practicing analysis with children. Thanks to his studies with Karl Bühler,
his contacts in the Viennese analytic community, and his work as a
psychology teacher at Rockford, he was by no means lacking in credentials. For although psychoanalysts tended to look down their noses
at the kind of tests used by psychologists,[11] the borderline between the
two disciplines was sufficiently blurred for him to cross it without much
trouble. Indeed, the famed Berlin Psychoanalytic Institute, which had
been the model for the Chicago Institute, even demanded in the 1930s
that all its candidates undergo the Rorschach test, which Bettelheim
had introduced to his students at Rockford.

The situation of psychoanalysis in Chicago was an unusual one.
Elsewhere, and particularly in New York, conflicts between individuals and schools of thought generally ended in the creation of compet-
ing societies. Such conflicts were exacerbated by the wartime influx of
European refugees, who were also seen by their American colleagues
as potential rivals.[12] In Chicago, however, an unusual institutional feature prevented such splits: It was, and remains to this day, the only
city in the United States in which the body that trains psychoanalysts,
the Institute, is totally independent from the Psychoanalytic Society,
to which all practitioners belong. Separately, both bodies belong to
the American Psychoanalytic Association.

Chicago's psychoanalysts could roughly speaking be divided into
two groups. One was referred to as "the conservatives," because its
members defended strict Freudian orthodoxy; it was dominant in the
Society. The so-called "moderns," on the other hand, considered that

analytical techniques still needed to evolve, that Freud had only laid the foundations, and that his followers' task was to continue building the edifice while making allowances for their environment. Their leader was Franz Alexander, the founder and first director of the Institute (where only a few Society members were qualified as training analysts, with the right to supervise new practitioners). It was a harsh conflict, in which real theoretical differences were mixed up with vested interests and interpersonal rivalries.

Kurt Eissler, Emmy Sylvester, and most of the recent immigrants belonged to the first group, the one Bettelheim was closest to. Their figurehead was a flamboyant and highly eccentric American, Lionel Blitzsen, who had been trained as an analyst by none other than Franz Alexander. Alexander's strong personality was indeed an important factor. The son of a Hungarian academic, he had emigrated to the United States in 1930, at the age of thirty-nine, and had come not as a refugee but an adventurer in search of new challenges. Trained as a medical doctor, he had long hesitated before taking up psychoanalysis because of its bad reputation among scientists.[13] Once he had made up his mind, however, he turned out to be so brilliant that in the same year he became a member of the Berlin Psychoanalytic Institute, Sigmund Freud awarded him the prize for the best clinical essay of the year.[14]

The Berlin Institute, on which Alexander would model the Chicago one, had been the first of its kind. Set up in 1920, five years before the Vienna Institute, it was buzzing with new ideas on psychoanalytic techniques. Thanks to the breeze of freedom blowing through the Weimar Republic, and probably also because of the geographical distance separating them from Freud, the young analysts who had early on flocked to Berlin were ready to experiment. While Vienna was still struggling to emerge from the economic collapse that had followed World War I, the Prussian capital was a flurry of cultural and intellectual activity. When Alexander left the city for the United States, the Berlin Institute included Otto Fenichel, Erich Fromm, Georg Groddeck, Karen Horney, Melanie Klein, and Sandor Rado: most of the people who were to make a mark on psychoanalysis over the following three decades, leading it along divergent paths to create widely differing schools of thought. The route followed subsequently by psychoanalysis in the United States had its starting point not in Vienna but in Berlin.

That was no accident. The Berlin Institute was the first to insist

that all candidates follow a "training analysis" before setting up as
psychoanalysts. Consequently, these were the first practitioners to have
started out by testing Freud's discoveries on themselves with the help
of another analyst, which made them more concerned than their predecessors with the purely technical aspects, and the practical effectiveness, of the cure. Franz Alexander had thus called on a number of
original thinkers, women in particular, to seek ever more effective
therapeutic techniques. Then, as years went by, he drifted away from
Freudian orthodoxy. Having created the concept of short therapies and
having made many discoveries in psychosomatic medicine, Alexander
gradually moved toward the very medicalization of Freudian thought
that, along with Freud himself, he had contested in 1927 when he was
still in Berlin.[5]

When Alexander left Europe in 1930, Freud was indeed reported to
have commented: "I hope America will leave something intact of the
real Alexander." The statement reflected Freud's ambivalence regarding the future of psychoanalysis in the United States. Before seeing
what this was based on, however, it is necessary to clarify what we
mean by psychoanalysis, if only because Freud's ideas have led to
such divergent developments on either side of the Atlantic that the
same words can sometimes take on entirely different meanings, as
Bettelheim himself showed in his book *Freud and Man's Soul.* An
explanation is all the more in order since, although Bettelheim never
practiced standard psychoanalysis, all his clinical activity was based
on Freud's concept of the unconscious. It is indeed impossible to
understand what went on at the Orthogenic School without some
understanding of that concept.

This clarification is needed also because psychoanalysis is first and
foremost an experience, and only subsequently a theory. This statement does not turn analysis into an initiation rite, as its critics claim
("I don't *believe* in psychoanalysis," they say). It is a mere recognition
of the fact that the unconscious is precisely what we cannot bear to
face in ourselves. As discovered and defined by Freud, it is not simply
a lack of awareness but the result of an act of repression. The ego simply refuses to acknowledge as belonging to it a desire, a representation, or a voice that affects it, because that desire, representation, or
voice is incompatible with the image it has of itself; it endangers it.
But the repression of desires—that is, the refusal to acknowledge
them—cannot prevent them from seeking satisfaction. They therefore
look for undercover ways of doing so, via "symptoms" that disturb

the subject's everyday life. Psychoanalytic treatment consists of rein-
tegrating the repressed material by repeating it via the transference—
through the relationship between the patient and his or her analyst.[16]
If things go well, the analysand will then identify the repressed desires
and thus discover the origin of his symptoms.

To build on a metaphor used by the psychoanalyst Michèle Mon-
trelay in the powerful preface she wrote for the French edition of
Freud and Man's Soul,[17] the analysand is like a single-handed sailor
who sets out in foggy weather to discover the mysterious archipelago
of his unconscious. He will have to make landfalls hundreds or even
thousands of times before he finally realizes that he is continually setting foot on the same islets, although each time in a different place.
Only then will he be able to consider drawing a map. But the latter
will never be complete, since unlike a real-life archipelago the unconscious is in continual movement, doing everything it can to escape
detection. It is cunning and ruthless, and appropriates the surveyor's
discoveries even as he makes them, the better to confuse him.

By dint of patience, the sailor will finally learn how to get around,
or see through, such tricks. With perseverance and the help of a good
analyst, he will even catch a glimpse or two of that other himself hard
at work. At that point, having at last understood the shadow play that
is going on in his psyche, the lone sailor will be able to set foot on dry
land and take up his rightful place, no more but no less in the real
world. He will be ready to act rather than simply react, capable of
giving and taking according to his true needs and desires rather than
simply obeying phantoms from his personal prehistory.

And what part, one may ask, does the psychoanalyst play in this
odyssey? That of the wind, needed for the boat to fill its sails and
move forward. It is an elusive and mysterious wind in whose song
the spellbound sailor will soon hear ancient melodies that will send
him spinning in circles or heading straight for the rocks on which he
has already run aground thousands of times before. But, he will then
find out, it is a steady and reliable wind he can count on to help him
float off again until he is ready to spot through the fog the places
where underground currents he thought he knew so well collide,
producing the hidden whirlpools that swallow him every time. It is
a light, subtle wind that accompanies the sailor without directing
him, ever-present yet discreet, and as intangible as the unconscious
whose contours it occasionally helps to reveal, up until the point
when he feels strong enough to carry on the voyage on his own.

The idea is clearly far removed from any considerations of strictly therapeutic efficiency. Sigmund Freud was a humanist, believing that knowledge could of itself engender progress. It is in that sense that psychoanalysis is effective: Once recognized, the unconscious desires can find more acceptable, less debilitating, avenues of satisfaction, and the symptoms will disappear. At the end of his life, however, Freud was to admit: "We may say that analysis, in claiming to cure neuroses by ensuring control over instinct is always right in theory, but not always right in practice."[18] This expressed the realization that even when a psychological problem has been well analyzed, its strength and resilience can still be underestimated. Such an admission of relative helplessness in the face of an intractable unconscious was open to a variety of interpretations. Some people would see it simply as a noble stance, reflecting the integrity of the scholar and his determination to pursue his research ever further toward the attainment of his aims. But others, fascinated by the verb *to cure*, would view it as nothing more than an admission of failure, authorizing research into new types of therapy, away from the path carved out by the founder. By so doing, they would often throw overboard the essential tenets of his discovery.

Replying to an interviewer's question on the treatment of psychotics, also toward the end of his life, Bruno Bettelheim would say: "You can fix a broken arm, but you can never make it as if it had never been broken in the first place."[19] Different subject, similar idea: People's souls can be repaired, but there is no laser beam capable of totally erasing all traces of a problem. Scars will remain, sensitive and fragile, and there is never any guarantee that the analysis has gone far enough in exploring all the hidden corners of the psyche, or that one day the whole edifice will not collapse under the force of some new internal disturbance.

However respectable they may be, such reservations are not well received in the United States outside intellectual circles. And even there they are welcome only if they lead to some form of certainty, to what might be seen as a "happy ending." This country, built on the twin myths of an ever-expanding frontier and the self-made man, is interested above all in results, the more spectacular the better. Faced with new ideas, it shows much greater curiosity than the Old World. The outsider with an attractive project will initially be given his chance and provided with the resources needed to carry it out. But woe betide the newcomer who proves unworthy of such trust, or who takes too long to deliver. In the United States, even more than else-where, a loser is always in the wrong. Which explains the paradoxical reception given to psychoanalysis. Welcomed at the outset as a great discovery, even placed on a pedestal, it quickly invaded almost every aspect of life, as shown by Gina Bettelheim's experience with the Jew-ish Social Services in New York (see chapter 8). Almost as quickly, however, the new discipline was adulterated, falling under the com-peting influence of the very people Freud himself had identified as its two most dangerous enemies: doctors and preachers.[20] Maybe to save it from the latter, many of Freud's followers in America were the first to throw psychoanalysis into the arms of the doctors—from whose ranks many of them came, even though up until then the fact had often been of secondary importance to them. By so doing they not only gave support to the very medicalization of his theories that Freud opposed but became the theoreticians of that process.[21] This was why Freud could write that, in the United States, psychoanalysis had very quickly become "nothing else but one of the maidservants of psychi-atry."[22]

And yet Freud had been the first to be impressed by American enthusiasm for psychoanalysis. In 1909, on his first and only trip to the United States, he had been very surprised at the warm reception he got at Clark University in Worcester, Massachusetts. "My short visit to the new world encouraged my self-respect in every way," he was to write later. "In Europe I felt as though I were despised, but over there I found myself received by the foremost men as an equal. It seemed like the realization of some incredible day-dream . . . psy-choanalysis was no longer a product of delusion, it had become a valuable part of reality."[23]

When Freud made his trip, Europeans had no reason to believe that they might one day be forced to flee their homelands and start new lives in America. It is thus not difficult to imagine how excit-ing that same experience would seem three decades later to many of his followers, who after being dispossessed and humiliated found themselves offered choice posts in American hospitals, thanks to the very science which back home in Europe had brought them only distrust and condescension from the establishment. For, as Paul Roazen points out, the culture and theoretical abilities of the Euro-peans, plus "their special therapeutic experience, combined with their deep sense of dedication to a common cause, placed them in the forefront of American psychiatry."[24]

The price to be paid for this success would be a heavy one, as Freud himself had predicted as early as 1925. While the Americans manifested great enthusiasm for psychoanalysis, they tended to "water it down," he wrote, to use its name to cover "many abuses which have no relation to it" while creating "few opportunities for any thorough training in technique and theory." Moreover, in America, the new discipline would "come in conflict with Behaviorism, a theory which is naïve enough to boast that it has put the whole problem of psychology completely out of count."[25] In other words, Freud was aware that in gaining a foothold in the United States, psychoanalysis was in danger of losing both its depth and its subversive power. It was set to be co-opted, to become part of the established corpus of "useful" sciences, the results of which can be quantified.

The main direction that psychoanalysis was to take in the United States is entirely summed up in the above quotations from Freud. Starting out with the aim of "ensuring control over instinct" (the drives), a process that does not always succeed in "curing neuroses," it was to lead toward behaviorism, which in fact aims to eliminate psychology altogether. The drives are the basic sources of energy of the psyche, but they have an unfortunate tendency, as soon as one begins to identify their contradictions, to go and carry on the fight in some new and unexpected region of the unconscious. This is why Freud, after years of struggling as a clinician with the complexities of the human soul, became convinced that in order to cure neuroses, analysis had to be a long process. However, as Benjamin Franklin taught the world, in the United States "time is money," and the maxim applies to psychoanalysis no less than to any other field. Since what was required were results, and the quicker the better, many of Freud's American followers were to relegate the drives, unpredictable and rebellious by nature, to the status of outdated accessories. Instead they would devote most of their attention to the agent in charge, the captain of the ship: the ego.

The idea that there was a part of the ego that could be considered free of conflicts between drives, and therefore more reliable than the rest of the psyche, was thus to gain ground. This proposition drew its legitimacy from a number of texts approved by Freud himself, notably some by Paul Federn,[26] and Anna Freud's book *The Ego and the Mechanisms of Defense*. The conflict-free zone was said to be that of learning, and more generally adaptation. The analyst would therefore seek to strengthen it. Rather than accompanying the analysand on a deep-sea voyage into the unfathomable depths of his being to look for mechanisms that might turn out to be irreparable, he would act as a guide. He had a function; he was also to give himself a role (and one commensurate with his status in the New World). To return to the sailing metaphor, having deciphered the charts much faster than the voyager, the wind would no longer be a gentle breeze; it would become a steady torrent of air, and the disoriented sailor would feel a firm but heavy hand laying hold of the tiller to help him navigate.

The resulting voyage was a much shorter one, since the only job of the analysand would be to keep to the course mapped out by the analyst. More important, it was no longer the same voyage. The initial aim of discovery was replaced by that of efficiency. In many cases the patient would soon be surprised to find that the most troublesome of his behavioral problems, the ones that had most impeded his day-to-day effectiveness in society, were fading away or had disappeared altogether. The changes, however, would often remain superficial, easily reversed by the ups and downs of life. Having not mapped out the islands of his unconscious for himself, once on his own the lone sailor was likely to get lost again at the first sign of turbulence. But then of course he could always sign up for a new round of treatment!

This brief summary of the birth of ego psychology is of course very schematic, taking no account either of the time that the whole process took or of its intricacies. But it is enough to highlight the affinities between ego psychology and behaviorism, a doctrine that Bruno Bettelheim was to combat throughout his entire career. It also provides a background to some of the traits of analysis that have been frequently caricatured in the United States—for instance in Woody Allen's films, such as the endless series of cures, the analyst who speaks in ponderous sentences (as does Bettelheim himself, appearing in a brief scene in Allen's *Zelig*), or the much-ridiculed attitude of "Do as I say, not as I do" (illustrated, this time in *Crimes and Misdemeanors*, by a philosopher with a heavy Viennese accent, not unlike Bettelheim's, who after preaching survival ends up committing suicide).[27] One can also see how psychoanalysis, born from Freud's desire to understand the sufferings caused to his women patients by the stifling conformism of their bourgeois backgrounds, could turn into a technique for making people accept the established order, a function denounced by many leftists, notably in the 1960s. Finally, by seeing the gulf that has slowly been created between psychoanalysis as practiced in the

United States and the discipline as envisaged by Sigmund Freud, one can understand the relative decline in its influence over the past two decades, as patients have flocked to other, newer types of therapy, seen as still more "cost effective"—that is, shorter and more explicitly practical.

Bruno Bettelheim's place in all this is a paradoxical one. He successively pursued non-Freudian psychology in the Eight-Year Study, and dynamic psychology (a kind of passageway between psychology and psychoanalysis) at Rockford. In his book *Symbolic Wounds: Puberty Rites and the Envious Male* (1954), he flirted with the culturalist school of thought, fashionable in the United States just after the war.[28] The main criticism he makes of psychoanalysis in the opening pages of *The Informed Heart*—that it concerns itself only with the neurotic aspects of the individual and not enough with his or her strong points, and that it is therefore of little use to anyone in a life-and-death situation—is reminiscent of the arguments of Heinz Hartmann, generally considered the first theoretician of ego psychology. (Hartmann accused classical Freudian thought of putting too much stress on the pathological, to the detriment of normal behavior.[29]) Finally, in describing his work with the children of the Orthogenic School, Bettelheim used concepts drawn both from ego psychology and its offshoots, such as Heinz Kohut's self psychology, and from the works of Anna Freud and the British school of psychoanalysis, notably those of Donald Winnicott.

In all these cases, however, Bettelheim remained on the fringes of the schools of thought within which his work could have placed him; his habit of sniping from the sidelines had the effect of amplifying the controversy that many of his statements sparked. He has always been a choice target for the opponents of psychoanalysis; meanwhile, most orthodox Freudians have criticized him for focusing more on the manifest content of his patients' discourse than on what it revealed about their unconscious—and thus producing purely psychological rather than psychoanalytical interpretations. "Bettelheim?" such people generally say, in a tone that brooks no contradiction. "That's not psychoanalysis!"

Nevertheless, after a lifetime spent exploring the various paths taken by psychoanalysis outside Vienna, this self-taught Freud scholar was to rediscover near the end of his life the founder of the discipline—not the world-famous Sigmund Freud, but the young man who waged an almost single-handed battle against his own neuroses

Paula and Anton Bettelheim.

9/6 1915

Adolf Seidler and his wife.
Franziska.

Bruno Bettelheim as a child.

July 1921. *Matura.*
"What do you want to
do later?"
"Philosophy."

Bettelheim with Gina
Altstadt.

1932. Bettelheim's first
driver's license demands that
he wear 9-diopter glasses
before taking the wheel.

Bettelheim, Wanda Willig, and Gina Bettelheim. The photographer is Hans Willig.

Patsy and Editha Sterba spending the summer at Gmunden.

Bettelheim's PhD in philosophy.

COPIA.

NOS RECTOR UNIVERSITATIS LITTERARUM VINDOBONENSIS

ERNESTUS SPÄTH

PHILOSOPHIAE DOCTOR PROFESSOR CHEMIAE PUBLICUS ORDINARIUS

ALFREDUS HIMMELBAUER

PHILOSOPHIAE DOCTOR PROFESSOR MINERALOGIAE ET PETROGRAPHIAE PUBLICUS ORDINARIUS

ORDINIS PHILOSOPHORUM H. T. DECANUS

Guilelmus Havers

philosophiae doctor professor gramatice linguarum indogermanicarum publicus ordinarius

PROMOTOR RITE CONSTITUTUS

VIRUM CLARISSIMUM

Brunonem Bettelheim

Vindobonensem

POSTQUAM ET DISSERTATIONE CUI INSCRIBITUR *Das Problem des Naturschönen und die moderne Aesthetik*, *et examinibus legitimis, laudabilem in philosophia doctrinam probavit*

DOCTORIS PHILOSOPHIAE NOMEN ET HONORES IURA ET PRIVILEGIA
CONTULIMUS IN EIUSQUE REI FIDEM HASCE LITTERAS UNIVERSITATIS SIGILLO SANCIENDAS CURAVIMUS.

VINDOBONAE, DIE *II. mensis Februarii* MCMXXXVIII.

E. Späth mp.   *A. Himmelbauer mp.*   *G. Havers mp.*

L. S.

cum originali in charta signo publico instructo

ad verbum concordare fidem facit universitatis Vindobonensis cancellaria.

Vindobonae, die *II. Februarii* MCMXXXVIII.

Wagner

cancellariae universitatis director.

Summer camp in Shalaburg.
Annie Hatchek, Fritz Redl, and
Gina Bettelheim (seated left to
right).

Patsy.

Letters from Dachau
and Buchenwald.

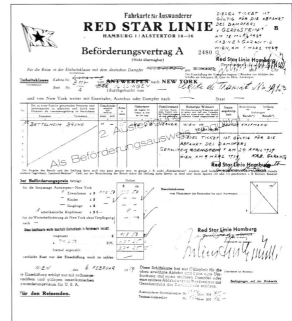

While Bettelheim was
still at Buchenwald, his
mother booked his
passage to the United
States and had the
date of the journey
moved back several
times.

October 9, 1939. Bettelheim's request for American naturalization.

April 1939. Bettelheim's last certificate of residence. In line with Nazi regulations, he has been given the middle name of Israel.

Gina Bettelheim in her Manhattan apartment.

May 11, 1939. Bettelheim arrives in New York with $3.00 in his pocket and a hand-scribbled PhD.

STATES IMMIGRANT INSPECTOR AT PORT OF ARRIVAL

FIRST-CABIN PASSENGERS ONLY

Arriving at Port of New York   May 11th , 1939   109

Edith Buxbaum.

HARVARD UNIVERSITY
DEPARTMENT OF PSYCHOLOGY

PSYCHOLOGICAL LABORATORY

Emerson Hall
Cambridge 38, Massachusetts

June 15, 1945

Dr. Bruno Bettelheim
Orothogenic School
University of Chicago
Chicago, Illinois

Dear Dr. Bettelheim:

You will be interested to know
that we received a cablegram signed by
Eisenhower asking for permission to translate and reprint your article on "Individual
and Mass Behavior in Extreme Situations."
The Headquarters had only the mimeographed
edition but we authorized the reprinting
and hope that your contribution will play
an active part in the education of occupation authorities. From returning army men
who have seen conditions first hand I judge
the psychological direction taken in your
article has been wholly validated.

Sincerely yours,

Gordon W. Allport
Gordon W. Allport

Eisenhower's request to
reprint Bettelheim's
work.

International Red Cross
Certificate of Incarceration.

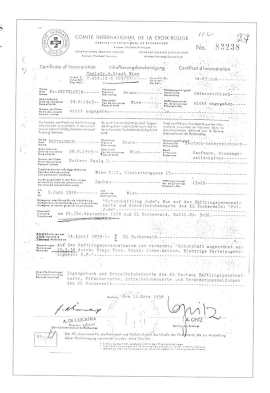

December 1945. Trude with her two daughters.

Christmas 1946 at the Orthogenic School. Gayle is the girl with a hand in front of her face. "Paul" is to her right. Bettelheim is seated at the right.

The famous "yellow door" of the Orthogenic School. (Copyright © Laurent Jurgensen.)

Early 1960s. Trude Bettelheim, Fritz Redl, and Bruno Bettelheim
with the daughter of Dr. Kavka, a consultant to the school.

1972. Leaving the Orthogenic School.

Old friends from Vienna in Portola Valley. Standing: Gina (left) and Trude (second from right) with Betty and Otto Modlei, who also attended the Albertgasse Gymnasium. Hans Willig is seated with Bettelheim.

1989. Bettelheim with Heda Bolgar: "He wasn't suicidal. He simply wanted to be sure . . ."

March 11, 1990. Bettelheim reads to his granddaughter on the day before his suicide.

to discover the existence of the unconscious. To that pioneer, Bettelheim would pay homage in *Freud and Man's Soul*, published in 1982.

That long essay shows in-depth understanding of Freudian thinking. Although written some four decades after Bettelheim's application to join the Chicago Psychoanalytic Society, it speaks directly to the problem that divided the body then, and one that had become progressively more acute, proving how fundamental the issue was. To label the orthodox Freudians as "conservatives" and those who were seeking to make therapy more cost-effective and efficient as "modernists" was indeed to negate the subversive, revolutionary nature of Freud's thought, and thus its very efficacy. What makes psychoanalysis different from other therapies is precisely its insistence on questioning absolutely everything, on refusing to take any kind of discourse, even that of the analyst himself, at face value. It is because no word or form of words is exempt from scrutiny that the process of exploring the darkest corridors of the unconscious can move ahead, slowly and sometimes painfully. Without such readiness to question anything at any point, it is no longer psychoanalysis. And Bettelheim tries to show how the process of curbing psychoanalysis's subversive power began, right at the beginning, with the translation of Freud's works into English.

Starting with a few simple but striking examples, Bettelheim stresses how the English translation stripped Freud's basic concepts of precisely what gave psychoanalysis its power: its closeness to everything human. Freud's "direct and always deeply personal appeals to our common humanity appear to readers of English as abstract, depersonalized, highly theoretical, erudite, and mechanized—in short, "scientific"—statements about the strange and very complex workings of our mind."[30] For these readers, psychoanalysis becomes nothing more than an intellectual construct, a system to be applied to the understanding of other people's behavior, and not an invitation to introspection, whereas in truth, the most precious contribution of psychoanalysis and the secret of its power, is that it was born from the struggle Freud carried on, throughout his life, with his own unconscious.

Being uniquely aware of what Bettelheim describes as man's "universal wish to remain unaware of his own unconscious,"[31] Freud, who was a brilliant writer in his native German, always expressed himself in the clearest, most direct and simple fashion, keeping as close as possible to his reader's experience in order to convey the complex

mechanisms he was trying to explain. However his English translators' desire for scientific respectability led them, for example, to use
Latin words for three of Freud's central concepts, which in the original German were *das Ich* ("the I"), *das Es* ("the it") and *das Über-
Ich*, a composite word that could be rendered as "the above-I" or "the
upper-I." The resulting terms of *ego*, *id*, and *superego* sound remote
and technical, Bettelheim points out, whereas the original terms *Ich*
and *Es* are two of the most common words in the German language.
Even more important, they are among the first a small child utters.
And although *Über-Ich* was of course created by Freud, it could have
been translated much better by retaining the "I."[32] Worse still was the
fate reserved for the word *Seele* in the English translation, Bettelheim
argues. This term, which would normally be translated as "soul," is
fundamental in Freud's writings as it refers to the very object which
psychoanalysis is supposed to investigate. It has nevertheless been
translated as the dry and cold "mind," stripping the original concept
of all its rich spiritual and emotional connotations. In such ways, Bettelheim writes, Freud's English translators completely distorted his
ideas, and thus misrepresented his discovery.

When asked for their opinion of the book, many psychoanalysts
tend to reply that its arguments are generally correct, but they are
nothing new, since "everyone knew that."[33] It is true that all German-
speakers who compare the translations to the originals are struck by
the discrepancies between the two. But Bettelheim was nevertheless
the first writer to offer a critique in simple, universally comprehensible terms, and in a publication that was accessible to educated lay
readers. He undertook the work late, forty years after he had abandoned German for English as a working language. He explains this
delay in his preface, noting that the first translations of Freud's work
had appeared during his lifetime, and later ones had been approved
by his daughter Anna, so that attacking them had seemed like "criticizing the venerated master himself." There is no doubt another reason for such a long silence on the subject. Psychoanalysis is a science
developed by a highly cultured man, working with men and women
who were also highly educated. As a verbal experience, it is above all
a science of the mind (the required route by which to reach the soul),
involving much use of symbols, word-play, and puns. For that reason,
practicing it with patients whose cultural and childhood references
one does not share intimately—even if one has managed to master
their language—cannot but alter its nature. But for men and women

whose very survival in the New World depended on their being able to make such a leap, it was obviously not easy to admit to that fact.

Bettelheim also wonders how Freud, who read English with ease, could have allowed the publication of a translation that so clearly robbed his work of most of its humanistic content. But he does not push that argument very far, suggesting that Freud's indifference could be explained by his animosity toward the United States. That is a little too facile. Although it is clear that Freud had a rather condescending view of the place he called "America" (that is how most Europeans then referred to the United States, which in itself is revealing; they saw it not as a country but as an entire continent, in other words as a remote, different, and somewhat uncivilized place, where a much higher price was placed on survival and expansion than on culture or the art of living), he was well aware, at least toward the end of his life, that it was there that the fate of his science would be determined. The survival of psychoanalysis was worth a few concessions.[34] In March 1939, Freud congratulated his friend Arnold Zweig for having preferred the United States to Britain as his exile home, writing that "America seems an anti-paradise to me, but it has so much space and so many possibilities and ultimately one does come to belong there."[35] Without having experienced it himself, the founder of psychoanalysis had thus grasped the basic parameters of exile in the New World.

The development of Bruno Bettelheim's thinking on Freudianism has been dismissed by some of his critics as opportunistic. Apart from the fact that the charge verges on absurdity, since Freud's popularity in the United States was in continual decline over the period in which Bettelheim was moving closer to his viewpoint, the criticism seems to me superficial. My hypothesis is that his process of introspection, begun in Dachau as a way of ensuring his survival, and carried on in one form or another throughout the rest of his life, gradually led Bettelheim to rediscover Freud on the latter's own turf.

Gina Weinmann often accuses Bettelheim of having taken himself for Freud toward the end of his life, when he was famous the world over and would proffer his opinion on any and all subjects in an overly abrupt tone. Hidden within this cruel insinuation there is a measure of truth. "That Freud, what a neurotic, and yet what a genius!" Bettelheim wrote in essence[36] to his friend Carl Frankenstein after rereading Freud's works in order to write his essay. This rediscovery of a

man who had spent his life struggling alone with his unconscious to
try and understand its workings had clearly brought a "shock of
recognition" for Bettelheim at that stage in his life.

Anyone pursuing a psychoanalysis beyond a certain point will
probably continue it as a process of introspection for the rest of his or
her life. And the fact that so many analysands suddenly discover a
vocation as psychoanalysts in the course of their treatment is symptomatic of their feeling of indebtedness, not only toward their analysts
but also toward Freud himself.[37] Bettelheim's seems to be a different
case, however. First, as we have seen, his analysis with Richard Sterba
was of short duration. But above all, by the time circumstances would
have allowed him to resume it, it was too late. Who among the members of the Chicago Psychoanalytic Society would have been in a position to help an analysand who had just returned from Buchenwald?

It was some time after World War II before it became apparent how
difficult it is for a former concentration camp inmate to gain relief
through psychoanalysis.[38] Bettelheim referred in passing to this problem in a letter written in 1980: "If the therapist has not himself undergone the same experience, the treatment will not work. But if he has
experience of concentration camps, the sessions will awaken too many
psychological problems in him."[39] As Freudian analysis concerns itself
only with the patient's fantasies, pursuing it becomes well-nigh
impossible when the real world has made such a traumatic and brutal mark on his or her life. This is why Bettelheim suggested that such
patients follow a particular form of group treatment, in which several
ex-inmates help one another to "analyze" themselves under the guidance of an experienced therapist.

He makes no secret of the fact that this idea is based on his own
experience. In his case, however, there was no collective therapy, but
rather a self-analysis, forced upon him by circumstances. As we have
seen, after his psychoanalysis was brutally cut short by his deportation, he resumed it in the camps in the form of introspection to keep
himself from going crazy. For the same reason, he began observing the
behavior of his fellow-inmates and discussing his observations with
Federn and Fischer. As he stresses on every possible occasion,[40] he
undertook this task first and foremost to save his own life, by allowing
him to defeat the Nazis' efforts at "disintegrating his personality."

And the effort had paid off. "The impact of the concentration camp
. . . within a few weeks, did for me what years of a useful and quite
successful analysis had not done," he wrote in *The Informed Heart*.[41]

What that meant is explained in the 1954 letter (see chapter 6) in which he recognized that his spell in the concentration camps "did me good": "Up until then, the circumstances of my life had never provided me with proof that I was able to stand up on my own two feet, even in very difficult conditions." Is that not precisely one of the main aims of a good psychoanalysis?

Although *The Informed Heart* is not exactly a song of praise to Freudian thinking, Richard Sterba's former patient does have some scruples about this passage, adding parenthetically, in a voluntarily lighthearted tone: "I realize that with this admission I lay myself, and my analyst, open to the criticism that my analysis provided me with insight, but did not lead to working through." This is a revealing aside. First, Bettelheim admits that his psychoanalysis in Vienna brought him only an intellectual understanding of his problems. At the same time, his remark shows that he clearly knows the way to a successful Freudian analysis: through the repetition of neurotic attitudes in the relationship with the analyst the gradual discovery by the analysand of the many effects his unconscious knots have on his life. Finally, with one of those intellectual flourishes that he often used to get rid of a bothersome subject, Bettelheim concludes by saying: "Perhaps it is to the credit of my analysis that the prospect does not trouble me."

These lines were written toward the end of the 1950s, when Bettelheim's career was really taking off. He was fully at ease in his new life as an American, the Orthogenic School was working well, and his family was not causing him any problems. His tone was one of self-confidence, that of a man who is succeeding in all his undertakings. A man surrounded by people who love and admire him, who does not yet know what it means to get old, and who chooses to believe that he has put the pain of his past life behind him once and for all.

How very different is the tone two decades later, when Bettelheim is writing the introduction to *Surviving*, a collection of essays of which the main entries had in fact already been published. The book opens with a long meditation on the purpose of life, suicide, Faust, man's destructive impulses, and death anxiety. It is as though Bettelheim, called on to select the essential writings of an entire lifetime for inclusion in the book, is once again struggling to avoid being submerged by the feeling that any attempt to leave a trace of one's existence is absurd, and that any progress man makes is doomed to turn against him to destroy him all the more effectively. Directly after these pages, and even before explaining why he agreed to produce *Surviving*, Bettelheim recalls the problems he faced in writing his first article on the concentration camps, "Individual and Mass Behavior in Extreme Situations." The juxtaposition of these two passages is no coincidence.

The importance of that 1943 article in Bruno Bettelheim's life can be gauged from the number of times he was to use it. After its initial appearance in the *Journal of Abnormal and Social Psychology* in October 1943, two abridged versions were to be published, one in the magazine *Politics* in August 1944 and the other in *Ten Eventful Years*, a four-volume supplement on the war produced by the Encyclopaedia Britannica in 1947. Bettelheim was to use the text yet again in July 1945, in his affidavit to the office of Judge Jackson, the U.S. prosecutor at the Nuremberg Tribunal,[42] and in a modified version in *The Informed Heart* in 1960, returning it to its original form for inclusion in *Surviving* in 1979.

The article is important also because it was to spread Bruno Bettelheim's reputation well beyond the confines of Chicago. In April 1945, U.S. troops liberated Buchenwald, and the photos they took in one of the blocks, into which detainees who had survived the Nazi evacuation of Auschwitz had been crammed, showed the world what had been going on in the camps. Two months later, on June 15, Gordon Allport, editor-in-chief of the *Journal of Abnormal and Social Psychology*, informed Bettelheim that General Eisenhower had asked for permission to reproduce his article for distribution to American officers in Europe. The U.S. troops had been completely unprepared for what they had found, and at the time Bettelheim's article was one of the only existing texts in English on what had happened in the concentration camps.[43] But the text is also crucial because a little later, when Bettelheim found himself caught up in a cruel confrontation with the death camp survivors (see chapter 13), some of his detractors would take it apart line by line in order to use it against him.

What Bettelheim's critics never did, however, was to view the article in its context. As the first analytical article on the Nazi camps, it took on instant authority, and almost everybody forgot that it was first and foremost a simple piece of testimony. What people focused on were the ideas it contained; nobody tried to figure out what state Bettelheim was in when he wrote it or what kind of theoretical material he had at his disposal both when he collected his observations inside the camps and when he committed them to paper a year later. As usual, readers let themselves be intimidated by the authoritative tone of his article, and thus failed to see the personal wounds that it concealed. Yet that article was not only the first major nonacademic text Bettelheim had ever produced, but it was written at a particularly crucial juncture in his life, after the trauma of the camps and the shock of his rejection by Gina, at a time when exile, at once harsh and generous, offered him a chance to start anew. He could undergo, as it were, a "second birth"—a concept he would place at the heart of his work at the Orthogenic School.

Any examination of the circumstances in which Bettelheim wrote that first article also needs to take account of studies into the workings of the memory, since, as I was to verify on several occasions during the research for this book, mental recall is never completely reliable, even in people motivated by a strong desire to tell the truth. No reconstruction of the past is ever free of interference from the present.[44] And the recall of traumatic memories is always affected by the mind's efforts to make them less painful. Among luckier victims this leads simply to forgetting; among others it often results in rationalization and anger.

Bettelheim states that he began jotting down his recollections almost as soon as he was released, but that he waited until he had been able to distance himself somewhat from his emotions before actually writing his essay. He had, he wrote, "hesitated for nearly three years to interpret [his experiences] because he felt that his anger about the treatment he had received might endanger his objectivity."[45]

What he does not say is that the first draft of his essay was completed shortly afterwards. That initial version had nothing impersonal about it; it was the raw and painful account of a just-released prisoner.[46] None of the psychoanalytic journals he submitted it to wanted to publish it, however. "My story was met with utter disbelief," he noted later.[47] Some potential publishers accused him of getting carried away by his hatred of the Nazis into painting them blacker than they really were, while others felt that, on the contrary, he was overestimating their intelligence and the scope of their program. Some even criticized Bettelheim for not having taken notes, "implicitly revealing that they had not believed a word of what I had written about conditions in the camps." The frankest among the editors to whom he submitted the article simply admitted that they considered its contents "unacceptable" for their readers.

It was certainly not the best of times to try to get an article published on the concentration camps. Not only did the vast majority of

Americans have no idea what these were, but even those willing to listen had a hard time believing what they heard. Two 1940 movies had alluded to the camps: Frank Borzage's *Mortal Storm* and Charlie Chaplin's *The Great Dictator*. Although attacked by the isolationist lobby, the latter film had finally enjoyed widespread success, thanks both to Chaplin's talent and the fact that it was a comedy. The Borzage movie, however, had been a total flop and was panned as being both partisan and slanderous. Three senators even asked the White House to ban it on the grounds that it was offensive to Germany![48] In fact, the concentration camp shown in this well put-together but not particularly subtle film about the tearing apart of a family under Nazism was far less harsh than the real thing.

In truth, Bettelheim was completely alone in trying to deal with his memories, which were much too vivid at nighttime and seemed all the more unreal during the day in that he could not communicate them to anyone else. On this particular issue, having Trude by his side did nothing to ease the pain. The state of anxiety she was in over the fate of her parents could only sharpen his determination to make his voice heard. Similarly, every rejection slip, and every passing month, must have increased his feeling of guilt at not having yet kept the promise that he and Federn had made to each other one Sunday in Buchenwald. Federn had still not been freed.

The awful roll call which had lasted all night on the *Appelplatz*, the all pervading cold, the dirt, the smashed glasses, the screams of prisoners being flogged, the sudden silence of those who collapsed. It is not difficult to imagine how Bettelheim must have struggled with such images, which probably invaded his mind at times when he was least expecting them. Perhaps when he was watching the Illinois countryside slip by as he rode the train to Rockford, or when walking along the muddy central strip of the Midway. They were images which he must have had a hard time getting across in English, a language he had still only partially mastered. As nobody was interested in his suffering, he resorted to the one quality he could be absolutely sure of, and which nobody had ever questioned: his intelligence. Once again, he needed to give things a meaning. He read a lot at this time, searching for theoretical tools to help him make his experiences more presentable and comprehensible. It was a fruitless quest, however, as "at the time psychological thought had not yet developed the conceptual framework necessary for dealing adequately with these problems, so I was forced to struggle with it myself."

His article was finally published in October 1943. Bruno Bettelheim had thus spent over two years being gnawed by doubts, wondering how to organize the observations he had so painstakingly collected in the camps in a presentable fashion, and seeing in every rejection slip a confirmation of his inability to do so. It should also be noted that in the mass of unruly facts with which he was grappling there were a few memories that were even more painful than the rest but which he had no intention of including in his article, such as the armband for blind prisoners, for example. All of which added up to an ordeal. He slept badly, and in daytime, while keeping up appearances in the outside world, he was irritable and difficult to live with, as is shown by Trude's memoirs. He was angry at others for displaying such indifference to what was going on, but he judged himself more harshly for not succeeding in carrying out his mission, in spite of, or perhaps even because of, his rapid professional success. But while he could vent his indignation, his shame remained hidden and thus all the more painful. It is therefore no surprise to read, in the opening pages of *Surviving:* "My desire to make people understand received much impetus from my need to comprehend better what had happened to me while in the camps, so I could gain intellectual mastery over the experience." In other words, to give an account of the exercise he had undertaken in Dachau, he had to continue it.

Bettelheim starts his essay by filing, classifying, counting, and generally marshalling his data. He lists the four key objectives of the concentration camp system, distinguishes between three types of behavior, and outlines four stages in the development of detainees' behavior. In passing, he notes that his study, which he undertook not in a spirit of scientific inquiry but as a means of survival, is the only example of private behavior he can discuss. Thus does the subject, identified as "the author," become the object of the analysis, and his work "a particular type of defense developed . . . to protect this individual against a disintegration of his personality."[49]

Next, Bettelheim gives his observations on each of the stages enumerated (see chapters 6 and 7 of this book) and then comments on them. For example, he classifies the types of reactions prisoners had during the first phase of detention according to their socio-economic background, noting that the people who came off worst were the apolitical and law-abiding "middle-class" prisoners. Unlike criminals and political activists, for whom arrest had always been on the cards, they were wounded in their dignity and self-esteem by what had happened to them. They clung to the idea that it must be the result of an error, and although ridiculed and insulted for this by both their captors and fellow inmates, it took a long time for them to realize that there had been no mistake.[50] Then they generally went to pieces; Bettelheim notes that it was in this category that most of the suicides occurred during the early stage of detention, and that the most flagrant examples of antisocial behavior (theft, denunciations of fellow inmates, and so on) were observed later on.

Leaving aside the overall scope of such a remark, two features stand out for anyone who is aware of Bettelheim's own life prior to his arrest: the severity of his judgments and the fact that they are delivered against precisely the category of prisoners he himself belonged to.

When he comes to discuss the differences of behavior between "new" and "old" prisoners, and explains how the latter adapted to life in the camp, his tone becomes even more critical. Whereas the "new prisoners" were above all concerned by the world they had left behind, spending all their money on keeping in touch with their families and obtaining information about the political situation outside, he writes, the "old" ones were interested only in improving their lot within the camp.

As we have seen, Bettelheim's own behavior was somewhere between the two: while keeping in touch with his mother, and striving through that contact to remain present in the lives of friends and relatives, his everyday efforts in the camp were directed toward avoiding conditions in which he would not have survived. This does not invalidate his observation; many subsequent writers have confirmed the hardening of camp detainees as they adapted to their new environment.[51] But his own example does show that the process was a gradual one, that it started earlier than he stated, and that for a long time the prisoners were neither completely "new" nor definitively "old." Above all, Bettelheim's description expresses his inability to accept his own weaknesses. In judging other people's behavior so harshly, he is indeed judging himself.

Clearly Bettelheim was not one of those happy mortals who, on reviewing the events of their lives, invariably cast themselves as the good guy. These two examples give the measure of the battle he must have waged against himself in order to write his article, at a time when he could still hope to save lives by alerting the American public to what was going on in the Nazi camps. If the burden of responsibility had been less heavy, or the struggle less arduous—if, for example, Bettelheim had been able to enlist the aid of an analyst to unearth the origins of the "debts" that he was also seeking to pay off by writing it—then perhaps the essay that was to make him famous around the world would not have returned to haunt him until his dying day. It would have taken its rightful place in the history of concentration camp literature, and only the remarkable accuracy of most of his observations would have remained in people's minds. Instead, his article, the record of the painful self-analysis that he was obliged to resume after his release, is now usually quoted mainly for the extreme severity of some of its judgments.

Most of the criticism leveled at Bettelheim for his article centers on his use of the concept of "identification with the aggressor" to describe the behavior of some of his fellow detainees, and his remarks on their "regression" and "infantilization." These terms shocked people: What right did this man, who had had the luck and the wherewithal to get out of the camps, have to take such a patronizing view of others? To this question, which was asked of Bettelheim in many ways and on many occasions, sometimes in the most insulting manner, one can reply with another: How can people who profess their devotion to the memory of the camp victims be so lacking in understanding for the struggle that one of those victims had to wage in order to bear witness? After all, the Nazis took their prey as they found them, neuroses, physical handicaps, warts, and all. And when some of their victims miraculously escaped their clutches, they had to contend with those same handicaps and neuroses in trying to deal with the experience.

This brings us back to Bettelheim's relationship to psychoanalysis, which his use of the concept of "identification with the aggressor" throws a certain amount of light on. At the time of his deportation, that relationship was in its early stages, made up of a combination of book-learning and a brief analysis undertaken in somewhat peculiar circumstances. In the second stage, at Buchenwald (probably much more than at Dachau, as he met Ernst Federn in the second camp), he found himself in a position strangely akin to that of an analyst in training. On the one hand he had his "patients," Hans Bandler and the other people he interviewed, and on the other his "supervisors," Dr. Fischer and the psychoanalytically oriented Federn. To try and interpret their observations, the two men used the theoretical concepts at their disposal, in particular those of "regression" and "identification with the aggressor," which they had found in Anna Freud's book on the development of the child's psyche, *The Ego and the Mechanisms of Defense.*

The fascination the Nazis inspired in many of their victims is as undeniable as the repulsion they simultaneously stirred in them. Expressed in its most simple form, the least affected by shame, it resulted in reactions like that of the seventeen-year-old George Clare, a Jew and a Socialist, on observing the arrival in Vienna of the Wehrmacht on March 13, 1938. "The exhibition of perfect discipline and splendid equipment made a great impression on me. The men were mostly, or so it seemed to me, tall, young, handsome, elegant and well turned out, and incredible as it may seem, I suddenly realized, that I admired these soldiers and was even proud of them."[52] Clare was shocked to find himself experiencing such feelings, and immediately sought to justify them by telling himself that the real enemies were the SA and the SS, not the regular army. He was only half-convinced by this argument at the time, however, and when he came to tell the story a few years later he had seen through it completely.

At Buchenwald, of course, things were more complicated. There was no way of dissociating the handsome soldier that one admired in spite of oneself and the feelings of horror and terror he inspired. The SS troops of the Totenkopf unit were the very incarnation of evil; as if to underline the point they had a death's head symbol on their caps. Without trying to analyze the unconscious mechanisms through which Bettelheim may at some point have identified with the Nazis who were torturing him, or how he may have felt himself slowly regressing to infantile forms of behavior when subjected to their ill-treatment, one can draw up a list of clues and put forward hypothetical interpretations. Bruno Bettelheim was a middle-class intellectual who disliked any form of disorder, albeit idealistic and revolutionary, an assimilated Jew who had a hard time accepting that he belonged to the same category as the religious, sidelock-wearing *Ostjuden*, whose bigotry he condemned as obscurantist. He was also a frail man, very conscious of his lack of physical courage ("a cowardly lion" is how he would describe himself later[53]). It would seem logical that he initially perceived in himself the mechanisms that he was to describe in such detail in other people.

If one does consider that hypothesis, it is easy to imagine the anxiety that such a discovery would have sparked in him, to picture how his need to always find the meaning of things would once again have served only to feed anger directed against himself. The opening pages of *Surviving* then take on an extra dimension, and one can better understand why, after describing the intellectual difficulties he had in finding a framework for his article, he writes: "Even harder was trying to deal with the anxiety-provoking and otherwise deeply upsetting memories which constantly intruded . . . Trying to be objective became my intellectual defense against being overwhelmed by these perturbing feelings."[54]

In a way, it was a good thing for Bettelheim that people did not believe him when he told them about the camps. In his case, indignation was a good coach, allowing his anger and aggressive feelings to be directed outward. It gave force to his writing. Once the article had been published, he could at last relax, freed of his feelings of guilt. His efforts had finally proved useful, and it was the man whose very name symbolized victory, "Ike" himself, who had declared Bettelheim right against the skeptics. That was something he would remain proud of for the rest of his life.[55] He had fulfilled his mission; he had transformed his sufferings into a useful message. He could thus get on with his new life.

But Bettelheim's self-analysis had not completely routed the old enemy within; it had remained on the lookout for any opportunity to come welling back up again. Perhaps his storytelling provided such an opportunity, or simply his growing renown, since the feeling of being a fraud seems to always have been at its strongest when he scored some new success. Or perhaps it occurred when the first heaps of corpses were found in the camp that he had been able to get out of six years earlier.[56] Whatever the reason, the feeling is clearly apparent in the first letter Bettelheim sent to Ernst Federn when the latter was released from Buchenwald. He wrote it in Chicago on July 11, 1945, the day after he had gone to Washington at the invitation of the War Department to record his affidavit on the camps for the Nuremberg Tribunal. That visit is the first thing he mentions, informing his former fellow-inmate that he is to be "one of their main witnesses." Interestingly, the letter is written in English. Even if, as Federn puts it, this was a way for Bettelheim to signify he no longer wanted to have anything to do with the country that had persecuted him, I cannot but see it also as an affirmation of his new status as an American, vis-à-vis a man who had just spent seven years in the camp about which Bettelheim was now being viewed as an expert by the U.S. government, even though he had been there only a few months.

Only in the second paragraph does Bettelheim seek to make real contact with his former camp companion. "I do not know whether you still remember me. We spent some time together in Buchenwald. I was much more fortunate than you by being able to leave the camp." The arrogance of the first paragraph is thus offset by the modesty of the second, into which one could even read an implicit acknowledgment that Federn would probably have been better placed to testify than he was.[57] "*It so happened* that I published an analysis of the concentration camp as a social institution, a study which received quite some attention (I think *undeservedly*) by such persons as, for example, Victor Serge, to mention only one name with which you still might be familiar," the letter goes on (my italics).

Undeservedly: Here it is, the ugly whiff of fraud. As we have seen, the success of Bettelheim's article was anything but undeserved; not only did it display remarkable intelligence, it was no doubt the most difficult piece of writing he had ever done, the one that had caused him the most painful soul searching. But none of that effort and suffering had any intrinsic value for him, as the more important fact was his inner feeling that he had in some way cheated to gain the mantle of expert. Whence the extraordinary understatement: "It so happened that . . ."

Bruno Bettelheim had two ways of reacting to the nagging feeling that he was enjoying undeserved privileges. One was arrogance, which required him to continually seek further successes, distinctions, and important names to drop. And the other, at the opposite extreme, was an excessive modesty, which those close to him sometimes found difficult to bear. With Federn, who was more experienced than Bettelheim in political action and camp life, but who was eleven years his junior, he would constantly switch from one to the other. In the letter, having both staked out his territory and acknowledged what could be seen as his "fraud," he adopts a fatherly tone, stressing how pleased he is at his correspondent's release. He takes care to add that he went to see Federn's father (a celebrity, at least in psychoanalytic circles) as soon as he set foot in New York to make a few suggestions on how his son's release could be obtained. He also offers his services, mentioning in passing that he has given Ernst Federn's name to the Nuremberg prosecutor's assistant as that of "a reliable witness," and then tells him that he is now in charge of a school for disturbed children. In backing up this second "admission" (subtext: "Now I'm a psychoanalyst"), as with the first, he goes on to list his distinctions (U of C faculty member, head of the Orthogenic School), while sliding over what makes it really important for him in just a few words: "a job which interests me very much."

Like Bettelheim's fellow-Viennese exiles, Ernst Federn was never to betray his friend's little secrets. Being more tolerant of Bettelheim's failings than he was himself, Federn would simply note on occasion that their views did not always coincide. As for the increasingly war-like tone that Bettelheim would adopt as the controversy over the camps intensified, Federn simply smiled, being better placed than anyone else to know that his former companion in misfortune would himself have been incapable of putting up a real fight. This was no doubt an amicable and understanding attitude, but one that left his friend alone, once again, to face his inner demons.

Much later, in his last book on the Orthogenic School, Bettelheim would write that the therapist for psychotic children is someone who can "bridge the gap" between reason and the chaotic world of insanity. "The difference between the patient and the therapist is that the therapist can at will walk back and forth across that bridge."[58] By then he had indeed spent three decades working tirelessly to cultivate that ability in the school's counselors—in his own way, with obstinacy, severity, and even brutality, but always attentively, encouraging the reticent and holding back the foolhardy, and above all, profoundly reassuring in his role of "bridge-keeper." Nobody else would be capable of crossing that bridge as spontaneously as he was, however, even though he had never benefited from anyone else's guidance. During the process through which he "trained" himself, those around him had remained silent; just as, in his childhood, his well-meaning father had never reprimanded him. I believe that training process took place during those two years in which he wrestled with himself in order to get across a message that nobody wanted to hear. If the research he undertook while in Dachau as a means of survival was a way of car-rying on the work he had begun on Richard Sterba's couch, its working through was impossible while he was still in the camp. That process took place, through much suffering, when Bettelheim was obliged to analyze his experience in order to communicate it to other people. Little by little, and through much struggling with self-doubt, he was able to locate his own inner "bridge" between madness and sanity, and thus the vantage point from which he could address others. Thus did he in effect bring about his own rebirth, through self-analysis. The new Bettelheim was indeed a psychoanalyst.

In fact, the idea of self-analysis was not as far removed from established psychoanalytic thinking then as it is today. There was much discussion of its pros and cons, with those in favor often drawing their arguments from one of Freud's last essays, "Analysis, Terminable and Interminable," which advised the young analyst, once he had completed his training, to continue to keep up with his own unconscious. *Self-Analysis*, by Karen Horney,[59] was published just at the time Bettelheim was writing his article. Horney, a Berlin-trained German analyst, had played a role in setting up the Chicago Psychoanalytic Institute along with Franz Alexander.[60] While stressing its pitfalls and difficulties, she believed that self-analysis could be very fruitful, especially when carried out as a follow-up to a classic psychoanalysis.

Unlike most other critics of *The Informed Heart*, Franz Alexander acknowledged Bettelheim's self-analytical approach. "This is a dignified book, convincing because it is not derived from textbook knowledge, but from insights gained in the laboratory of the author's own life," he wrote in an article that also noted the writer's unusual detachment from his subject and saluted his "fine introspection."[61]

Bettelheim's approach to psychoanalysis was thus not entirely iconoclastic. What was rather special, however, was the way that approach meshed with his concentration camp experience. This "marriage," brought about in the extreme conditions of the camp, was to last throughout his life. It would color Bettelheim's therapeutic work at the Orthogenic School, and as we shall see, it also opened the way to his progressive rapprochement with Freudian thinking.

On November 27, 1946, the Chicago Psychoanalytic Society informed Bettelheim that he had been admitted as a non-clinical member. This meant that the Society authorized him to apply his psychoanalytic knowledge in the field or fields of his choice, with the exception of conventional treatment itself. His admission had been approved unanimously, on the basis of his presentation of his work on the concentration camps.

Bettelheim's relations with the official institutions of psychoanalysis were to quickly become tangled, however. A few months after his admission, the Society's Commission on Membership and Education —set up in September 1946 in a bid to end the ascendancy of the "moderns" on the training of new analysts and thus settle the main conflict between the two arms of the Chicago establishment—moved that he be admitted to the Institute. But Franz Alexander was against this, and Bettelheim never became either a training analyst or a member of the Institute. From 1951 to 1955 he was nevertheless allowed to hold a training seminar for child analysts there. Very much later, in November 1973, six months after Bettelheim had retired and moved to California, he was made a life member of the Chicago Psychoanalytic Society thanks to Dr. Charles Kligerman, its president that year. To have the decision adopted, however, Kligerman had to get around the violent hostility of many of his colleagues towards Bettelheim. As if to underline the ambivalence of the decision, the letter informing him of it was mailed to the Chicago address he had been living at in 1946!

11

---❁---

Orthogenic School:
The Magical Years

... So there you have the story of my life, and also the
explanation why I could devote it so single-mindedly to
work strenuously to help children overcome the damages
their childhood experiences did to them.
  —*Bruno Bettelheim, letter to
  Carl Frankenstein, November 19, 1986*

Meeting the former inhabitants of Bruno Bettelheim's school is
rather like visiting with the members of a once-large family that
is in the process of dying out, or encountering an indigenous tribe in
the final stages of assimilation. There are memories that the inter-
viewee at first hesitates to dig up, fearful that they will not be understood, and that surge back after a while, surprisingly intense and
emotionally charged. Former loves and moments of tenderness, jealousies and other scars that have lost little of their edge—in some cases
even hatreds. Full of shared references, jokes, and a common language. "That day, I was behaving very orthogenic." The sentence just
slips out in the middle of the story; no need to translate. After four
and a half years of investigation, the writer has indeed become used
to the lingo. *Orthogenic*, that ugly word Bettelheim inherited but
never liked, had over the years taken on for his charges (he rarely
used the word *patient*, preferring *kid* or *student*)[1] a meaning somewhat

removed from its etymological one. "Orthogenic behavior" was that of people who took life seriously, who were, as we would say today, "in touch with their feelings," and who never did anything without thinking about why they had done it—an idea too redolent of virtuous effort, of playing the good student, to be very much fun. The kind of idea you laugh at, while suspecting that it might be good for you. For some people, of course, it smacks of the straitjacket. They are among the younger ones. For the others, who are more numerous, recalling it sparks the amused, slightly self-mocking reactions that often accompany a childhood memory.

What is most striking when one meets a large number of former "O.S." people is that whatever their position, for or against Bettelheim, they are all thinking men and women, who seek to understand and go beyond surface appearances. Some will on occasion use flatfooted arguments against Bettelheim: "Do you realize that we weren't allowed to play baseball?"; some in the opposing camp are a little too quick to reel off quotations from his books to be entirely sincere. But such facile weapons are merely polemical. What all these people have in common is a readiness to question received wisdoms, and to never take things at face value. I did not meet a single one who could remotely be described as either a fool or a timeserver. Bruno Bettelheim did not believe happiness could be achieved by simply closing one's eyes to reality; for him there was no such thing as a happy moron.[2] And the people who surrounded him for some thirty years certainly prove his point.

Like other tribes, the Bettelheim community has its clans and its outcasts. The former tend to be defined chronologically; as the timespan stretches from 1944 to 1973, the first recruits were long gone when the last generation entered the school. Some, however, kept in touch, returning to visit from time to time. They were held up as examples for the younger generation, rather like older brothers or sisters. Others would never ever go back, preferring to cross the street rather than risk bumping into anyone who might remind them of their time in that most unusual school. And yet others never got to make such a choice; they had left the school one day for a psychiatric hospital, after which the tribe had lost track of them. This did not mean they had been erased from people's memories. Some former students still cite the names of those lost sheep with great anger, seeing their fates as incontrovertible proof of their arguments. Others recall them with sadness, occasionally blended with fatalism and always with a dose of guilt. Again, what is striking is the existence of a link between all these people. Those who became outcasts, either voluntarily or involuntarily, have remained present in the collective memory, but more like ghosts than some kind of dark secret. For although Bettelheim did seek to minimize the number of failures at the Orthogenic School, he never concealed the fact that such failures existed.

Now definitely grown up—the oldest among the "ex-kids" are going on sixty—the school's former students and counselors are scattered all over the United States, and in some cases abroad (in France, Switzerland and Italy, for example). It is a rather quirky tribe, the members of which are not always easy to approach. The men tend to be abrupt, highly logical, and somewhat aggressive, at least on first contact. The women are more varied. Some are down-to-earth and "up front"—warm, reassuring, and practical. But although they are generally forthcoming about their experiences, unlike the men they are rarely categoric in their judgments. Other women are more reserved, waiting for the interviewer to bring up a subject before discussing it. But all have interesting things to say, and often raise questions that are difficult to answer.

It will not be possible to write the full history of Bruno Bettelheim's Orthogenic School before legal restrictions protecting the privacy of its former students expire. Until then, except for a handful of administrative papers released under the University of Chicago's thirty-year rule, individual accounts are all the researcher has to go on. In most cases this means trying to choose between the statements of people who have at some point in their lives been declared "mad," or at least "disturbed," and those of people whose entire careers were often founded on their experiences alongside Bettelheim. With both types of witness, the interviewer finds it at first nearly impossible to give an impartial hearing, fully respecting what the person has to say. With former students, she finds herself veering between sympathy and a kind of unhealthy curiosity. ("If he was really crazy when he entered the place, what amazing progress he must have made there! But then was he really crazy at all?") And the second category of witness tends to inspire suspicion. ("Even if there were abuses, he [she] wouldn't tell me about them, of course, to avoid sullying his [her] reputation.")

The purpose of this book is to tell Bettelheim's life story, not that of his school. However interesting the stories of his individual patients may be, they have no place in it. And indeed, to talk about them they would have to be handled as "cases," which would mean hiding them under false names,[3] and that would be contrary to this writer's approach. Having ploughed through countless case studies, I can see all too well how the use of an alias allows one to take liberties with the truth and overlook awkward details. Bettelheim himself pointed this out in his second book on the school.[4] This may be of little significance for the specialist, whose only concern is with clinical technique. But for the man whose history I am trying to trace, the "cases" he was surrounded by day in, day out, were real live people, each with their own face, way of talking and moving, smiling or crying. Their movements were often disorderly, they shouted or screamed, made unreasonable demands or suffered from irrational fears: in short their actions triggered off strong reactions in him. They were human beings, children; anything but "cases." Which is why, rather than adopting a pseudo-scientific stand to discuss them and their problems, I think it better to enter the world that was Bettelheim's during a good third of his life as a voyager free of preconceived dogmas but with ears, eyes, and a heart wide open to the discovery.

A number of impressions quickly harden into certainties—for example, that the tribe's patriarch was feared by all its members. He was always there, omnipotent and ubiquitous. Some worshiped him; a few hated him. But was that quite as true at the time? It is interesting to discover, for example, that at least two of his most virulent detractors suffered when they were students from not being among his favorites. (The researcher seeking to understand what went on in the school is continually being faced with such dilemmas.) Before setting out to explore the strange universe of the Orthogenic School, those whose image of it has been shaped solely by reading *The Empty Fortress* and the three other books Bettelheim devoted to it will need to jettison a few received ideas.

First and foremost is this one: Bettelheim did not love children—he understood them. And he used all the means at his disposal to try to unlock the mental universe that not only prevented them from leading normal lives, but also caused them great suffering, as he was one of the first writers to point out. He did, however, love *some* children. At the school, as in his classes, he always had his favorites. Those were more often girls than boys, but not always, and they could generally twist him around their little fingers. On one occasion, for example, he spent hours feeding an anorexic girl who had arrived at the school on a stretcher. By patiently getting her to swallow one raisin at a time, he literally saved her life.

But the fact that Bettelheim laid great stress on listening to and understanding the children in his care does not imply that he was brimming over with love for all of them. Nothing could be further from the truth; indeed, the mawkish image of Bettelheim projected by many of his admirers does a terrible disservice to all concerned. First, it is damaging to some of the former students he tried to help because it presents them with a distorted picture of that essential experience in their lives, and thus affects to this day the very relationship to reality that Bettelheim tried to foster in them. Second, because it is simply untrue, the fairy-tale image tends to obscure the true value of Bettelheim's contribution. When passing through the famous yellow door that leads into the Orthogenic School, at 1365 East Sixtieth Street on Chicago's South Side, this is one preconception that the reader must leave behind.

In its place, let us pick up the large white pebble that forms the title of Bettelheim's first book: *Love Is Not Enough.* In other words, "What I give these children is something else." Implied meaning: "You, with all your love, have often done them more harm than good." In an article published in 1949, he put it in a nutshell: "With the exception of love at first sight, an adult's immediate love for a child can only be due to emotional starvation and keeps the child from one of the most maturing experiences—that of a slowly developing, mutually satisfying personal relationship."[5]

Another certainty the researcher acquires on speaking to people who worked with Bettelheim throughout his life—not only the counselors, but also the mothers he brought together on Wednesday nights to advise them on bringing up their children, and the young psychologists and psychiatrists he helped, first in Chicago and then later in Stanford, to understand how to treat their patients—concerns his power of insight. Bettelheim had the rare gift of being able at a glance to see through someone's behavior, and even more to grasp the internal workings of a relationship between two people. He could feel instantly where the pain was. He was sometimes wrong, but rarely. It was this intuition that allowed him, for thirty years, to do everything in his power, everything he believed appropriate, to help the children in his care become independent and responsible individuals. Here again, the word *everything* has implications that sit uneasily with the kindly and rather harmless image his books may give of him. Curing his charges was, and remained to the end, his number-one priority. This led him on occasion to use controversial methods and to systematically exploit his counselors. Most of them have no regrets on that score: they see it as the price to be paid for a unique formative experience which, they all agree, they have used ever since. It is nevertheless essential to point out that Bettelheim, while being capable of great compassion, was not Mr. Nice Guy. He was a man with a mission, a survivor who had made a choice and stuck to it.

One last observation: The Orthogenic School was a living organism, in continual motion and development throughout the thirty years Bettelheim spent as its head. That period can, broadly speaking, be broken into three stages, each lasting about a decade. They are the years of discovery, the years of fame, and the run-up to Bettelheim's succession. The evolution obviously corresponds to developments in his own life, but it also reflects deep social changes in the world outside, in people's hopes, and in the moral climate. Such changes could not but affect the tiny world of the school, which for a time was to be at the forefront of the age: a model and a unique experiment.

The early years were an extraordinary, almost magical time. In spite of his reluctance to take over the school, Bettelheim was quick to grasp its potential. Although a heavy responsibility, it did provide an opportunity to try out all those ideas he and his friends had been discussing over the previous twenty years—and of course an opportunity for him to show his true mettle, to put his past far behind him. Trude's influence had been decisive in persuading him to accept the job. Not only had she, as usual, reassured him that he could do it, she had been able to contribute her years of experience as a Montessori teacher. Bettelheim also turned for advice to his faithful friend Fritz Redl, whose reputation in the treatment of disturbed adolescents was by now well established in the States—a collaboration Bettelheim duly acknowledged in his first book: "My long and close friendship with Fritz Redl has helped me immensely in developing the School's working philosophy and in setting it into practice. Our many conversations and our constant exchange of ideas have now created a situation in which I no longer know exactly where his ideas end and mine begin."[6]

For practical help, Bettelheim called on Emmy Sylvester, already acknowledged as a brilliant child psychoanalyst, whom he soon had appointed psychiatric consultant at the school. In her, Bettelheim had found an interlocutor on a par with himself. Although seven years his junior, she possessed the very academic qualifications he lacked. A medical doctor, she had also earned a PhD in child psychology at Vienna University in 1932, while working both as an assistant to Charlotte Bühler at the Psychology Institute and at the university's pedriatric clinic. She had been in analysis with Editha Sterba and attended seminars at the Vienna Psychoanalytic Institute, taking on her first patients under the supervision of Richard Sterba and a member of Freud's circle, Jeanne Lampl-de Groot. After leaving Vienna at the time of the Anschluss, Sylvester had continued her psychoanalytic training at the Chicago Institute, supervised by Franz Alexander, while doing an internship in psychiatry at Michael Reese Hospital.

Although Emmy Sylvester's qualifications and experience were no doubt reassuring for Bettelheim, the key to their close working relationship lay elsewhere. They had the same type of intuitive intelligence, the same need to go straight to the point, the same Viennese charm and arrogance, and even the same way of being aggressive. In the early days of her work at Michael Reese Hospital, for instance, Sylvester had been introduced to a patient who was distractedly wandering the corridors, repeating: "Oh, I feel guilty, I feel so guilty." The man had been interned after murdering his father. She took one look at him and shot back: "And you're damned right, because you *are* guilty." Her colleagues, who had always used the opposite tactics to try to pacify this violent patient, were stunned. Telling the story later to a few friends, Sylvester confessed, a little sheepishly, that her reaction had been completely spontaneous. But she added that, far from disturbing the patient, it had calmed him down instantly.

Working with Emmy Sylvester, Bettelheim was to lay the theoretical foundations of the Orthogenic School. Drawing on the way August Aichhorn had used psychoanalysis to treat juvenile delinquents in Vienna, they would carry out the first real-life experiment in total "milieu therapy"—the creation of a living environment in which every single detail of everyday life was designed with a view to the treatment of its occupants.[7] The students' needs, as well as the therapeutic methods, were conceived entirely on the basis of Freud's teachings. As Bettelheim and Sylvester would write later, once practical results had started to confirm their theory, "Milieu therapy is not new as a psychotherapeutic technique. It is no more than the application of psychoanalytical concepts to the specific task of creating a setting for emotionally disturbed children who are in need of residential treatment."[8] The Orthogenic School was therefore designed as a place where "psychoanalytic concepts [were put] in action." It offered its residents what they could not get from individual psychotherapy sessions: a life in which their psychological development was catered to twenty-four hours a day, seven days a week. That idea was the cornerstone of the whole edifice.

"Don't forget, at that time mad children were seen as bad children," says Patty Pickett McKnight, who worked as a counselor at the school from the fall of 1946 to the summer of 1952.[9] To write psychoanalytic theory into the constitution of a facility for severely disturbed children was indeed a revolutionary act. It was to state that people labeled as insane were not in fact fundamentally different from the rest of us, that their difficulties in life were due to damage sustained during their emotional development rather than to some original sin in their or their parents' past. The mentally ill were no longer monsters but simply sick people. Their condition resulted from neither a curse nor divine punishment; it was simply a type of malfunction and could thus be repaired.

The idea was simple enough, but its implications for everyday life at the school were not. If the mad were not evil, just sick, then they should no longer be punished or locked up, but treated. This involved trying at every point to alleviate their suffering and to determine the inner reasons for their strange behavior—accepting that when a child attacked another, bit his counselor, beat his head against a wall, ran away, screamed without apparent reason, wet his bed, excreted into his bathwater, threw furniture out the window or into the stairway, he was not doing this to annoy other people, but simply because he was suffering—and that this behavior was the most effective way he had found to alleviate his inner torment. This was the reasoning behind the two golden rules of the school, which applied to everyone from the director down to the maintenance staff: to make life as easy and pleasant as possible for the children and to try to understand what lay behind their "crazy" behavior, rather than seeking simply to make it go away. Even though such ideas were implicit in Freud's thinking, they had never before been implemented in a residential institution for the mentally ill.[10]

"There was an atmosphere. You could feel it: 'Something is working here.' It was like a great big stew, with the emotions and everything, and something was holding it together—his conviction, the dedication of the staff." Patty Pickett was twenty-one, with two years

in college behind her, when she knocked on the door of the Orthogenic School looking for a job to help her pay her way through her
studies at the Committee for Human Development. Having grown up
in the conventional setting of small-town Illinois, and being unaccus-
tomed to hearing people raise their voices, she was amazed at the way
the children were allowed to behave at this very strange school. "We
didn't judge them, we tried to understand them, to create an environment in which they could feel accepted. Dr. B was always telling us:
'These kids have a right to be here. They have a right to their behavior, given the way they've been treated.' And after a while, because we
were kind to them, because we accepted them, you could see it: the
kids were getting better."

In order to get to that point, however, Bettelheim first had had to
move mountains. But he had to use tact and be careful not to scare
anyone—least of all the children, but also the university and the handful of rich donors who supported the school. The latter, although
shocked by the parlous physical state of the institution, were not ready
to fund a revolution. At that time, the school was home to around
thirty full-time students, all boys, plus a handful of day pupils. For a
full decade already it had stopped taking in mentally retarded children, accepting only those with psychological problems. But most of
them did not correspond to the type of child Bettelheim and Sylvester
wanted to carry out the experiment with. They were either too deeply
disturbed or had already spent too much time in institutions for there
to be any reasonable hope of curing them before they reached the age
limit for the school, which at the time was fourteen.

In spite of his lack of experience, or perhaps because of it, curing
his charges was Bettelheim's only objective. He had no intention of
presiding over a holding center for incurably sick children. He could
not simply eject in one day all those children or staff members who
did not fit in with his project, however. In fact, he spent a lot of time
finding adequate placement in other institutions for the former. The
departure of the adults, too, was gradual. Finally only one teacher,
Miss Lukes, stayed on.

In recruiting his counselors, Bettelheim was able to harness the university's aims for the school—to be a training center as much as a
therapeutic one—to his own ends.[11] Rather than taking on counselors
who were already set in their ways and working methods, he preferred
training the people he would work with himself. His three years of
teaching at Rockford College had shown how good he was at getting

through to, and stimulating the enthusiasm of, young women students eager to serve a worthy cause. And that was the kind of help he needed for this adventurous undertaking. Financial considerations no doubt also played a role in his decision, for the school was poor and what Bettelheim had in mind for it required money.

Bettylou Pingree Rellahan and Marjorie Jewell, two of the three psychology students who had accepted Bettelheim's job offer, arrived at the school in early September 1944. Inexperienced, but eager to please the man they referred to since Rockford only as "Dr. B," they immediately took a group of boys out to play football on the Midway. With the best of intentions, they plunged into the game, kicking at the ball with as much energy as their charges. In the space of a few minutes, the boys had become angry and totally unruly—one of them had even torn a sleeve off Bettylou's blouse. When the two young women finally managed to return to the school with all the boys, Bettelheim was waiting for them in the hall. The two were completely shattered. Weighing the situation at a glance, Dr. B got a nurse from the previous team to look after the children, while Bettylou and Marjorie retired to their room in tears. They felt humiliated by their failure. Later that evening, Bettelheim took them to his apartment, around the corner from the school. There, they sat with Trude, and he explained where they had gone wrong. By behaving in the same way as the children, Bettylou and Marje had triggered their anxiety; by becoming like them, they had given up their control of the play, and with it their ability to protect the boys. This was why, he explained, the children had become enraged at them. "Day one, lesson one," concluded Bettylou Pingree, recalling the incident forty-two years later.[12]

The first change Bettelheim ordered was that even regular bedwetters were not to be woken up during the night. In the morning, he wanted their sheets changed without any fuss or any remark likely to make them feel guilty. One day, in one of the children's bathrooms, he noticed a chart on the wall. "What's this?" he asked. Bettylou explained that the night nurse wanted the children's bowel movements recorded daily, in order to determine their laxative doses. Bettelheim snatched the chart off the wall, and "that was the end of that," Pingree says. Then he had the locks of the various doors changed so that one key could open them all and the counselors stopped looking like prison wardens with bunches of keys dangling from their belts.

During the first month, Mandel Sherman and his graduate students continued to come and go, while the new team gradually eased in to the driving seat. In the basement of the building was a large laboratory full of forbidding-looking machines that intrigued the newcomers. The day the surgical bed and the EEG and other electrical gear were moved out, Bettelheim had the black drapes covering the windows ripped down and replaced with patterned linen curtains. He then had a ping-pong table installed in the place, which was designated the game room.

Ronnie Dryvage, the third Rockford student to respond to Bettelheim's invitation, arrived at the school soon afterward. One of the first tasks she undertook was to similarly spruce up the children's dormitories. But it was no doubt the hiring of the fourth counselor, Gayle Shulenberger, a few weeks later that best sums up the way the school operated during that transitional period. Gayle had come to Chicago with her depressive sister-in-law and the latter's baby, while her brother was away fighting in Europe; she did not dare abandon the two of them. She was looking for an office job, preferably "somewhere with children." The university had thus put her in touch with the Orthogenic School, where the secretary asked about her experience. As she had practically none, Gayle mentioned that in high school she had occasionally been sent to watch over some younger children when one of the teachers was absent. The secretary dutifully noted "a little teaching." The only job available was a fill-in for the night nurse, who was leaving for two weeks' vacation.

So I met this woman, who looked like the Wicked Witch of the West in her uniform. And I thought this was the craziest place I'd ever seen in my life. There were children with epileptic seizures, there was a mixture of all kinds of kids. It didn't make any sense. But I was fascinated. So I slept there and my only job was, if a kid came and knocked on my door at night, I'd jump up . . . There was one very disturbed boy who looked like he belonged in a mental hospital and who had been there forever. They were trying to find a placement for him. He had a complete set of keys that he had had made and the nurse told me disapprovingly that the director didn't want them taken away from him. Knowing nothing, I thought, "Good for the director."

That night, everybody was asleep, except this kid who was walking around the hall. I followed him around and he locked himself inside the broom closet. So I sat outside the closet, and I heard him say: "Don't take away my beautiful keys, my beautiful keys, my beautiful keys . . . Don't take away . . . " I didn't have anything to do, so I counted how many times he said it and it came to about seventy some times. Then there was a pause and he started again: "Don't take away . . . " So I said: "I won't take away your beautiful keys." This went on for a long, long time. But each time he said it, he said it less. I asked: "Are you hungry? I'll get you some food." I don't think he talked to me. I went down and got him some food, left it outside the closet, and went away. And when I came back he'd eaten the food and left me the plate. Then, later, I would go and check that he was asleep.[13]

The same scenario was played out every night of the two weeks. When the night nurse returned, Gayle was offered a job as an assistant counselor, a non-residential position, which involved looking after the handful of children who opted to stay behind at the school when the others went on an outing. She had met Bettelheim only once, on the first evening. He had asked her where she was from, and she had told him a little about her childhood on a farm in South Dakota, amid a flock of cousins. In his strange accent, he had remarked that she was the first native of that state he had met, and that had been the end of the conversation. But Gayle continued exploring her new world. Among the children she occasionally cared for in the afternoon was a certain Nicky, who had been described to her as mentally retarded. Without telling a soul, she started observing him; he played the piano a little and also spoke on occasion. She became so sure he was not retarded that on returning home each day she made notes about his behavior. Later, when she had gotten to know Bettelheim better, she raised the subject with him. He burst out laughing: "Of course he isn't retarded. Why do you ask?" When she told him that she had filled up several notebooks on him, he chided her for not having brought them straight to him. At the time, though, Gayle would not have dared.

It was when she sat in on her first staff meeting that something finally clicked. "We were all in the living room and this man comes in and he starts talking about everything that's wrong in this place and how he's changing it. And I thought 'My God, he knows it!' and I remember walking home that night: I was walking on air. Because that was the most exciting time in my life."

This account not only tells a lot about the empirical way staff were recruited in the early days of the school, it also gives an insight into what was to make those first years such a magical time: Bruno Bettelheim's charisma, and the way he could, with only a few words, make each person who worked with him feel like a true pioneer. "We were convinced that we were doing something very revolutionary, something that had never been done before," Gayle recalls. "I wouldn't have changed places with anyone, even if I had had to work twenty-four hours a day." Forty years later, all the first counselors have retained similar impressions.

Gayle's recollections also give an idea of the personalities of many of the young women Bettelheim was to rely on to help him build his school. Although many were shy and naive, they were sharp-witted and not about to swallow just anything they were told about their charges. It was not in their nature to throw in the towel when faced with a case they had been told was incurable; instead, they would draw on all the resources of their imagination to detect the chink in the child's armor and thus make contact. These young women had grown up during the Great Depression, and many of them came from families that had known bad times. They were hard workers and wanted to feel that their labor was doing some good. Nicky and the "key boy" did not stay at the school; they had already spent too much time in institutions, burdened with an "incurable" label. But with the help of two welfare agencies whose officials had soon been impressed by his eloquence, and probably also by his camp experience, Bettelheim went about choosing new students, as he found placements for the ones he had inherited. It was a slow process. According to his book *Truants from Life*, which was published in 1955, it was only in the fall of 1947, three years after his appointment, that the Orthogenic School was running in full accord with his ideas.

If the counselors were at first recruited more or less by chance among young people at the university who were not sufficiently well off to pay for both the tuition and their living expenses, the children were carefully selected. The diagnosis was not the most important factor. Psychoanalysis, psychology, and psychiatry were all in fashion, and words like *schizophrenic*, *schizoid*, and *disturbed* were bandied about somewhat loosely. The psychiatrist Leo Kanner had recently provided a clinical definition of autism, but in those first years the school was not yet taking in such severe cases. Regarding the criteria for selection, Bettelheim himself spoke of "primary behavior disorders." Whether they were delinquents or runaways, hyperactive, suicidal, sufferers from hospitalism[4] or afflicted with truly schizophrenic traits, however, the first students generally had two things in common: intelligence that was at least normal and in many cases above average, and behavioral problems affecting their lives in several areas. "If they'd simply had problems at school, they could have been treated in connection with their families. If their problem had been at home, another type of therapy would have been possible. We took them only when they didn't succeed anywhere," says Gayle. They were basically "problem children," either rejected by, or incapable of living with, their parents, and who, if admitted to an orphanage or other residential center, quickly found themselves in trouble because of their uncontrollable violence or their inability to form normal relationships—in other words, children unwanted by the rest of the world, and who had no place to go.

In each case, nevertheless, somebody somewhere, be it a social worker, psychiatrist, psychologist, physician, or a teacher, had decided that the child could be cured if provided with appropriate treatment, and that he had a fighting chance of one day becoming an autonomous adult. These children would be referred, generally by either the Jewish Children's Bureau or the Illinois Child Services, to the Orthogenic School. There was a trial period of a few weeks. After meeting the child, the staff and Bettelheim would decide which group to put him in, while leaving open the possibility for him to change to another one if he felt more comfortable with it. The aim was to see whether at least one adult was able to establish contact with the newcomer. That was the basic condition for admission. "We wanted kids that we could help," says Gayle. In fact, rejection at this stage was rare, and would generally be viewed by the counselors as a failure on their part. "On paper, they always looked sicker than in real life," says Gayle, true to form.

The aim was indeed to achieve a complete cure. "We expected the kids to make it . . . It was going to be hard. It's never easy to give up an old way, and all growth is painful, as he said lots of times. But I was absolutely convinced that he knew what he was talking about," Patty Pickett says of Bettelheim. "And when we started to see results, we were hardly surprised at all." That was what made the school magical: these inexperienced, but intelligent and courageous, young women pouring all their energy and imagination into serving a challenging idea that was given shining clarity by the way Bruno Bettelheim and Emmy Sylvester developed it. What was meant by "cure" was understood by all to be the ability to take control of one's own life, to behave as a responsible, independent adult. "To stand up on one's own two feet," as Bettelheim had learned to do in the camps.

The method was to be created empirically, step by step over time, with each staff member making his or her own contribution. The team Bettelheim built did not simply apply his instructions; they played a role in developing and elaborating on them. It was a process of mutual exchange that went on twenty-four hours a day, seven days a week. And Bettelheim gave credit where credit was due, warmly paying homage to his collaborators in all his books on the school. He and Emmy Sylvester were the theoreticians and the guides, but the counselors were the ones in constant contact with the kids. So Bettelheim asked them to record their observations about their charges—not their ideas or analyses, but simply what they had seen and heard, leaving nothing out, as even the smallest detail could be significant. He wanted this done every day if possible, while the impressions were still fresh.

> What the children actually do and say, the very words and intonation they use, their facial and bodily expressions, are easily forgotten or distorted unless they are quickly written down . . . Dictation that is separated by a week or longer from the observations reported tends to be stale and of much less value in helping us understand the child's and our own behavior . . . Instead of reflecting the impact of a symphony of feelings, interactions and experiences, played, so to speak, by full orchestra, a stale report recalls to mind only selected motifs played by but a few instruments.[5]

He would then read everything, and if he did not feel he was getting the full picture, he would make it known, as when he showed up at a staff meeting and said: "I have read all your dictations with great attention, and I have some important news for you . . . " With all eyes fixed on him, he concluded: "None of our children has been to the toilet for the last two weeks!"

Some counselors had a real gift for drawing up their reports. Gayle, for example, clearly had an eye for detail, and jotted down her impressions in a spontaneous, lively, and often amusing style. Others found this part of their duties an ordeal, and their daily reports were much less detailed. But the mere fact that they had to pay attention to every detail made them much more conscious of the children's behavior, deepening their understanding. At the same time, their observations provided grist for the theoretical mills of Bruno Bettelheim and Emmy Sylvester.

Sylvester came to the school every Friday and saw two or three children individually, after which a meeting about those children would be held with their respective counselors. All the former staff members I was able to interview recalled those meetings as a revelation; for many of them Emmy Sylvester became a role model. The effect of her remarkable intelligence, extensive culture, and cutting wit was certainly enhanced by the fact that she was both beautiful and an elegant dresser; Bettelheim himself was always very attentive to her. But she impressed them most of all with her ability, whatever the subject under discussion, to turn things around so as to see them from the child's viewpoint. Bettelheim would engage her in discussion, and their young American listeners would be fascinated by a dialogue that blended intuition, wit, concern for the children, and scholarliness. Little by little, even the most obscure of vistas would become clearer, and explanations would emerge for the strangest types of behavior. Listening to the two Viennese, the counselors felt they were discovering, week after week, the essential meaning of what they had just lived through, but which had not struck them at the time as significant. Yet Sylvester continually underscored the key role being played by the counselors. "She made us feel like queens," Gayle Shulenberger says. "She was always telling us that what we were doing with the kids was marvelous. Nobody else ever showed so much respect for our work. Listening to her, you'd think it was us who were the real therapists."

So it appears that Emmy Sylvester played a leading role in getting Bruno Bettelheim to develop, or at least to make use of, what was to become his most distinctive quality, the one that would impress all the young therapists who were to work with him, and that could still be detected in the seminars he was giving shortly before his death:[10] his ability to surmise instantaneously where a child's suffering was coming from—the famous empathy that he would make the cornerstone of his therapeutic method. Sylvester would kick off the conversation and Bettelheim would listen, respectful both of what she had to say and of the relationship she had with the counselors. Then he would take up where she left off, pushing the analysis a little further, bringing in a new piece of interpretation. Their relationship appeared to be based on mutual respect and involvement, and devoid of any trace of the rivalry that some of the same young observers could often detect in conversations between Bettelheim and Fritz Redl, who was another frequent visitor to the school during the early years.

Nevertheless, at the start of the 1950s Emmy Sylvester was to abruptly break off all contact with Bettelheim, accusing him (not publicly, however) of having appropriated all the credit for what had been their joint undertaking, which he was in the process of turning into a famous institution. "He's a monster," she is even rumored to have said within the small circle of Bettelheim's early collaborators.[17] Nobody, however, was able to tell me exactly which incident, if any, sparked her decision to up and leave for California. Among other differences of opinion, one concerned authorship: She apparently wanted to restrict their publications to academic journals, while he was already eager to reach out to the widest possible audience. In all, they were to co-sign six articles, all of which appeared in psychoanalytic reviews.[18] Indeed, their articles are, of all Bettelheim's writings, the most classically psychoanalytical. The split did occur when he was bringing out *Love Is Not Enough*, a work intended to reach beyond specialist circles to everyone interested in children's problems. That being said, it is also noteworthy that, although Emmy Sylvester was undoubtedly both brilliant and creative, she in fact published very little in her own name. So, obviously, Bettelheim too brought something to their relationship.

As for the Orthogenic School itself, the question is no simpler. This was another of those situations in which Bettelheim, while having a pressing need to feel reassured as to his ability (or maybe his moral right) to carry out a task, at the same time possessed all the abilities needed to do so. For although Emmy Sylvester may well have shown him how to use his intuitive understanding of other people in order to help his young patients, that faculty clearly had to be there in the first place. No doubt having her at his side in 1947 when they first presented their work to the American Orthopsychiatric Association's annual meeting helped give him self-assurance. But once he had received confirmation that he had the right to do what he was doing, his innate therapeutic gifts were there to let him advance under his own steam. Indeed, although Bettelheim and Sylvester were very similar in their way of looking at problems, their practical approaches were markedly different. Ronnie Dryvage, who had great admiration for Emmy Sylvester, nevertheless says: "She was very intuitive and very learned—more intellectual than he was. But I never felt warmth emanating from her, whereas Dr. B was real, warm, and very concerned." This opinion was shared by two of Sylvester's former patients. "She didn't have the same empathy as Dr. B. She was very sharp and knew all the theory. She was a very good teacher. But she asked intrusive questions and didn't give me the feeling that she wanted me to get better the way he did. In fact, I hated my sessions with her," says Bert Cohler, for example.[19]

As Patty Pickett McKnight points out, there was much more to the school than therapy sessions and meetings: there was everyday life, with upward of thirty very difficult children. And once Emmy Sylvester, Fritz Redl, or any other outside consultant had left the premises, it was Bettelheim who stayed behind, in charge and always available, ready to seek the most "orthogenic" solution to the problems that never failed to arise. For behind the lofty principles of the school, the actual nitty-gritty of putting the children first, even the least attractive among them, was a tough discipline, forcing one to continually question one's reactions, however spontaneous. Patty once complained to Dr. B about a new child who had been assigned to the older boys' dorm, of which she was in charge. As usual, outings for the group had been suspended until the newcomer could feel sufficiently at ease with the others to be able to take a bus or a train without anxiety, or without behaving in too disorderly a way. But the new boy continued to be very aggressive, and Pickett found the situation unfair. Not only were the other boys, who had learned so well how to behave in public, being deprived of their regular outings to the Museum of Science and Industry, the planetarium, or the movies, they were also having to put up with continual attacks from the newcomer, who had been picking fights in the dormitory every night since his arrival. Patty was expecting a little sympathy from Dr. B., or at least some advice, but certainly not the response she got. "And what have you done for him recently?" he asked. Being a good counselor, she got the message immediately: Her complaint proved that she was more worried about the overall functioning of the group than the needs of the new boy. And the latter's aggressiveness was probably caused, at least partly, by what he saw as her rejection. Indeed, after a few weeks of attention from her, the boy had calmed down enough for the group to be able to resume its outings.

Letting children's symptoms express themselves freely, day after day, was by no means easy. Gayle, for example, had in her group the seven-year-old boy Bettelheim referred to as "Harry" in *Truants from Life*, whose particular problem was running away. This meant that for six weeks she spent every evening ("except two," she specifies, discussing the affair as if it had all happened only yesterday) waiting up for him to come back, which would usually be between midnight and one in the morning. Then she would feed him, give him his bath, and put him to bed—until the day when Harry suddenly showed up at 3 o'clock in the afternoon, just as Gayle was starting her afternoon shift!

Another of her charges, identified in *Truants from Life* as "Paul," recalls the atmosphere in the school dining room. "A lot of antics went on during the meals. Everybody was together in a room, eating, and there were different tables and there were lots of distractions. Some kid would pick up his dish and throw it on the floor and that would upset the next table, and they would spill their milk and some kid would go into his shell and crawl underneath the table sucking his thumb, and it was a kind of an abominable thing. He [Bettelheim] would say 'What's going on here? Get up, sit down!'—just like any parent at the end of his tether. And things would calm down."[20]

At all times the children had to be reassured that they were safe, shown that they were accepted as they were and that nobody at the school saw them as monsters, even when they screamed, bit, kicked, soiled or wet themselves day and night, flooded the bathrooms or the stairway, or even if they stole. (Bettelheim was merciless with any adult who had money stolen, accusing them of having exposed the children to temptation by leaving it lying around.) At the same time, the children had to be shown that although their behavior was being accepted because it was a comfort to them, it was not the best way for them to escape from their suffering and solitude. Little by little, they had to be convinced to give up their defensive behavior, so inadequate for living in society.

All the adults at the school were steeped in this philosophy, which was at the time even more revolutionary than now. That meant all the staff, including the cook and the maintenance man (who, for example, had to repair all the toilets in the building several times a day for several weeks because one newly arrived boy could overcome his terror of losing part of his body only by stuffing various objects down them), the secretaries, the cleaning women, and the switchboard operator. "Very few people said 'I' at the school: it was 'we.' We were all working together toward that very important goal, each one in our own way," says Mary Ellen Cowan, who headed Bettelheim's secretarial staff, acted as his administrative liaison with the university, and supervised the kitchen and the maintenance staff for six years. She never hired anyone without first making sure he or she could put up with such conditions. "Anybody self-centered or who thought they knew it all, I turned down immediately. I made it clear to them that the school was run for the children, but I added that if they stayed the course they would find a lot for themselves too," says Cowan, who also did the first screening of prospective counselors. "I knew the type of people Dr. Bettelheim was looking for. It is not easy to verbalize. There was a feeling about them, a dedication, a caring, a desire to be part of it . . . Sincerity was paramount, more so than experience, because he had an innate ability to see in each of us what we could do, far beyond what we had achieved before or thought we could achieve. Dr. B also had the reputation for liking pretty girls, and he did. But that was never enough."[21]

Up until 1952, the school was a single building, a good-size house but one that had to accommodate both the children and their counselors (the teachers in general did not live in). There were thirty-two full-time boarders and three day pupils. Groups of six (and later eight) children were formed on the basis of dormitories.

Besides considering the child's own choices, and his relationship with at least one counselor, the team was also attentive to the influence the children had on one another. It had taken only a short time for them to realize how important that influence was. One day, as Harry was coming back from yet another escapade, one of his dorm mates, himself a former runaway, whispered to the others: "Remember, guys, 'thin air!' " Gayle, who overheard the exchange, was baffled. When Harry entered the room, instead of listening to the fantastic adventures he claimed to have had during his outing, the seven boys simply kept on talking among themselves, ignoring Harry as if he were indeed thin air. This went on for the whole evening, and happened a second time, after which Harry finally got the message. "They talked through him . . . And he was so furious. I had nothing to do with it," says Gayle. "But they were mad at him for behaving so stupidly. In my view, that was the most amazing thing; the tremendous investment the children had in each other. It was as though the progress made by one child showed the way to the others. And they weren't about to let it go to waste."

In the evening, when the children were at last in bed, the adults would get together downstairs, in the kitchen. However late it was by the time the last counselor had tucked in the last of her children, Bettelheim would always be there to greet her with a cup of tea. They would go over the events of the day, and if it was not too late, someone would often ask: "Dr. B, tell us about Vienna." And Bettelheim would always have some interesting story to relate about Anna Freud,

Wilhelm Reich, and so on. Then he would go back to his office; it was the only time of day when he could write. He would often not get home until 4 A.M.

He was nevertheless back at the school every morning around 10:30 (and earlier still, in the first months). His smallish office, located next to the secretaries' on the first floor, was open to all, children and adults. To prove it, the door stayed ajar, except when he had visitors. There was a small bench nearby for people who wanted to wait, or simply to cool down before going in to see him. On his desk, which was always tidy and almost empty, was a pink pig-shaped cookie jar, from which each child who came to see him was invited to help himself. This benevolent gesture did not in any way prevent Bettelheim from giving the visiting child a good talking-to immediately afterward if he deemed it necessary—that is, if he thought it would be reassuring for him to have clear limits laid down. "Bruno was a wonderful actor. He could put on an act of being terribly angry, while at the same time giving a wink to whatever adult was present in the room," recalls Gayle, echoed by both Patty Pickett and Bert Cohler. Cohler adds: "In my opinion, even in later years, he never got carried away with a child. He always knew exactly what he was doing." Not everyone agrees on that last point, however.

But Bettelheim was certainly the ultimate source of discipline in the school. "I am the Big Bad Wolf here," he used to say. And indeed there was a need for one. In order for the counselors to devote all their efforts to being caring mothers, there had to be someone they could rely on to let out a growl or two when things got out of hand. The very early counselors are unanimous in saying that they never saw him actually hit a child. But even at that time, his comments could be extremely harsh. Patty remembers a child who was about to leave, having reached the age limit of fourteen. One day he went wild, shouting "I'm going to my father's! I'm going to my father's!" She tried to calm him down, but nothing would do it. He was brandishing a suitcase when Bettelheim walked into the dormitory. "And just when did you last see your father?" he asked him coldly. That stopped the boy in his tracks: he had not heard from his father for several years. The incident left Patty almost in tears. On reflection, however, she now believes that the reason Bettelheim appeared so cruel was that the boy was about to find himself confronted with the real world, where he would not be able to survive if he kept on deluding himself. She is convinced he would not have spoken to the boy the same way two years earlier.

Most of the time, however, Dr. B did not even need to raise his voice; his very presence was enough to restore calm. Gayle recalls that on certain occasions one or another of the boys would go up to his office, not to talk to him, but just to check that he was there. The children were in awe of him, but they were not scared of him. On the contrary, his presence was reassuring for them. At mealtimes, it was common for a child to go over to the staff table to chat with Dr. B. Some of them even made a point of doing so, as the act gave them status with those who were less daring. Bettelheim would answer all questions and respond to all expressions of anxiety, often with a story. And when he made his evening rounds in the dorms, he would willingly play a game of checkers or chess if a child should ask him to.

Alongside his role as the Big Bad Wolf, Dr. B was also Santa Claus. His generosity is legendary among those who worked with him. He never forgot a birthday, and would always have a carefully chosen gift, often brought back from his travels. They were beautiful gifts, which always had a meaning for their recipients, and which he took the time to wrap himself. Whenever he was away, he would send postcards to the children, as well as to the counselors. The message was often a short one, but always meaningful. Everyone interviewed marveled at his ability to remember all those dates and to find the time to seek out each gift and write each message. Bettelheim did not much like receiving gifts, however. Lou Harper, who holds the record for length of service at the school—a total of twenty-two years, as a counselor briefly, then as a teacher, and even at one time as the school's principal—still squirms at the memory of when the staff decided to offer Dr. B an electric drill, the year he moved to a new home. "I don't want you to spend money on me. It's for me to give you presents, not the other way around." Bettelheim's expression was even more eloquent than his words, Harper recalls. Nevertheless, the young man later undertook to build Bettelheim a table—but never got around to finishing it.

During those first years, the atmosphere at the school was still quite relaxed, and even if everyone worked very hard there was plenty of laughter. Bettelheim's heavy accent and his linguistic idiosyncrasies, such as when he would gravely announce that "something's perspiring in the playground," were a regular source of jokes among the staff. But his charisma was such that on occasion some counselors were unsure whether to laugh or not—for instance, when he mixed up the metaphors he was so fond of using, saying "Hook, line, and barrel," or "Lock, stock, and sinker." Gayle was so fascinated by Bettelheim's ability to bring out the hidden meaning in things that she sometimes found herself seriously wondering what these strange-sounding expressions could refer to.

Others, however, were able to take a more distanced view. Bettylou Pingree, perhaps because she had known him when he was a beginner at Rockford, was much more aware than Gayle of how much insecurity still lurked behind Bettelheim's apparent self-confidence. She has even kept documentary evidence, in the form of an invitation to a party at his home that he pinned up at the school in the fall of 1945: "My dear friends: You have suffered during this last year, and the gods know, so have I. Don't you think it is time that we all get together for one big lament, so that we can get the horror and sorrow of this first year of suffering out of our system and get ready for the horrors and sorrows of the second year?" He had obviously typed the invitation himself as it was dotted with typos and much too long: ". . . There won't be enough chairs, or things to eat and drink, but I assure you there will be enough people who will join you in swearing at me. This is an occasion (namely to be able to swear at me) which no self-respecting staff member of this institution can afford to miss . . . Don't you worry, I'll get even with you during the rest of the year."

The later workings of the Orthogenic School, those of its legend, have been described fully enough by Bettelheim and others to require no detailed account here. There was the candy closet where the children were allowed, at almost any time, to stock up on M&Ms, KitKats, Hershey bars, Reese's Peanut Butter Cups, Chuckles gumdrops, Kraft cheese paste, salted peanuts, Hollywood chewing gum; the doors that freely opened out only, so that the kids knew they could leave if they wanted to but at the same time felt protected against intruders; the cuddly toy that each child was given on arrival and then on each anniversary of that event; the special relationship that grew up between each child and one adult (counselor, teacher, or social worker) in particular; the way children of different ages and with different problems were mixed together in each dormitory and classroom; the freedom each one had to take part or not in group activities; the beautiful tiles and painted wallpaper decorating staircases and corridors to alleviate the anxiety brought about by transitional periods.

In his first book on the school, *Love Is Not Enough* (1950), Bettelheim explained his philosophy, illustrating it with concrete examples taken from the children's daily life, ranging from the bathrooms, toilets, and bedrooms to the classrooms and dining room. Five years later, *Truants from Life* outlined more detailed case studies of four children (including information about what had become of them after they had left the school). A third volume, *A Home for the Heart*, completed the series in 1974. In the meantime, Bettelheim had written *The Empty Fortress*, his bestseller on autism, which, although not dealing directly with the Orthogenic School, made it famous the world over. In spite of this prolific output, and notwithstanding the two hundred pages devoted to the staff in *A Home for the Heart*, there is one fundamental aspect of life at the Orthogenic School that Bettelheim never dealt with directly in his books, even though it was often raised implicitly: his relationship with the young people, predominantly young women, who were in day-to-day charge of the children. And yet all the people who worked with Bettelheim at the school freely admit that it was precisely this relationship that made the experience so different from any other they have known. Bettelheim's enemies fully agree with this, since they depict him as a guru and his institution as a cult. Most of all, those who continue to this day to draw on the inner riches they developed at the school through all their activities, be it teaching, therapy, or simply living, stress that they gained that knowledge not so much in his books as in their everyday exchanges with Bettelheim. For his therapeutic work translates poorly into theory. As is so often the case, his talent as a clinician sprang from his personality, his history, and his wounds. It was not best expressed in words, or at least not in the kind of words that one can commit to paper.

Contrary to what one might expect in an institution run by such an autocratic man, the counselors enjoyed considerable freedom in the way they carried out their duties. Bettelheim rarely intervened between them and their charges. They alone decided what activities their group would take part in, and how to manage their relationships with the children. When it came to deciding whether or not a child should be allowed to go home during a vacation, it was the counselor's opinion that carried the most weight. Insurance against errors and abuses came from the watchfulness of others, both counselors and children—a well-adapted student would not hesitate for one moment to criticize a counselor whose behavior was not "orthogenic"—and above all, from the regular exchanges with Bettelheim. But to grasp how the system worked, it is necessary to understand first what the counselors' daily life was like. And as their working conditions were particularly tough, it is also important to understand what made them stay.

A key document for this exploration is by Jules Henry, a social anthropologist who had specialized in the study of hospital structures and who spent almost a year at the Orthogenic School as an observer in the mid-1950s. In 1957, comparing the workings of the school with those of other psychiatric institutions, Henry gave a detailed account of a counselor's daily life.[22] It is written in the third-person feminine, because during his time at the school all but two of the counselors were women.

> At seven-thirty in the morning she goes to the dormitory to get the children up and ready for school. Once there she dresses or helps dress the children who cannot do this themselves, she comes to grips with the emotional problems of children who are not able to get out of bed, she helps wash children who are not able to do it themselves; she sees to the toileting of children who are in a similar situation. She breakfasts with the children, continuing the process of guidance as necessary. Shortly before nine o'clock she goes with the children across the play yard to school. At every point the counselor brings the insight, empathy and understanding she has acquired to the resolution of the emotional problems at issue.

Then it is back to the dormitory, where there are always toys to put away, clothes to leave out for the laundry, wet sheets or pajamas to take to be washed.

> At about ten o'clock, the counselor begins to see her children in therapy sessions. Experienced counselors see from one to four children for one hour several times a week. If a counselor is not otherwise occupied, she may take one of her children out for a walk during school recess. It may now be time for one of the regular staff meetings, in which the children are discussed by the assembled counselors in consultation with one of the two visiting psychoanalysts and the Director.

Then comes lunch, which is in principle a free period for the counselors, as the children eat with their teachers. But as meals make up a part of their salary, and as the food is excellent (Bettelheim insists strongly on that point), they often prefer to eat at the staff table, in the same dining room as the children, instead of going out. Three days each week the staff meeting resumes after lunch, for discussion of the counselors' own problems and general issues affecting the school.

If it is a Monday or a Friday, the counselor has about an hour between the end of the staff meeting and the time she goes on duty, and this may be taken up with any of the following: dictating records, writing to parents, making a quick trip to a store to buy something for a child or for the dormitory, or looking after her own personal affairs. Shortly before three the counselor is in the staff room, ready with her after-school snacks for the children, and making arrangements with the counselors of other dormitories for use of the play facilities at the School [such as the swimming pool, gymnasium, and sandpit].

. . . At three o'clock sharp the counselors are in their dormitories awaiting the return of their children from school. The return of the children, bearing their schoolroom tensions or pleasures with them, at once presents the counselor with therapeutic problems that may be handled on the spot. Then plans for the day's activities are discussed among children and counselor, with the occurrence of behaviors one might expect in a group of psychotic children. This again is an opportunity for therapeutic management. The afternoon ends at a quarter to six when children and counselor enter the dining room of the school and sit down together at supper, each dormitory at its own table . . .

After supper is activity time, until about eight-thirty, when the children get ready for bed, lights go out and the counselor reads the evening story by flashlight. At this time anxieties often well to the surface, and the counselor spends much time in the darkness by the children's bedsides giving help, although avoiding "deep" explorations. She may remain until ten or after; when a child is overwhelmed by anxiety she may stay in the dormitory far into the night. While long night vigils are relatively infrequent, some counselors, especially when a seriously disturbed child is newly admitted to the dormitory, may undergo a long and wearing stage until the child grows calmer. There is no sedation, no packing, no mechanical constraint and no isolation.

Although laborious and detailed, this description omits the entire housework dimension of the counselors' job, which in spite of the fact that the school employed well-qualified domestic staff was considerable, since Bettelheim could not stand seeing a broken toy lying around. Whatever the time of day, the children were expected to be able to find their dormitory neat and pleasant, in a state that testified to their counselor's concern for their well-being. Apart from her regular duties, one of the counselors was responsible for the menus: every month, she went around to all the dorms, asking for each child's preferences and then carefully planning the month's meals with the cook. Another was in charge of the candy closet; she had to make sure it was at all times stocked with everyone's favorite snacks. It was the counselors who organized all school parties, of which there were many, since celebrations played a key role in Bettelheim's therapeutic environment. In addition to the standard civic holidays, and some of the Christian ones, notably Christmas, each child had two birthdays: his real one and the anniversary of the day he had entered the school, which was seen as his "second birth." On such days leave was canceled for the staff members in charge of the child's group; one counselor would devote herself entirely to the birthday child, while the other would take care of the other kids. Furthermore, every party would be accompanied by a large number and variety of gifts, all of which had been carefully selected and wrapped.

The two counselors assigned to each group had to divide up their working time, including weekends, when each had a twenty-four-hour shift. Scheduling systems changed over the years, but during the entire period of Bettelheim's stewardship working hours were extremely long, the more so because it was during their "free" time that counselors found it easiest to develop the close relationships with their children the school's therapeutic methods demanded. At other times, when they were in charge of the whole group, it was difficult. The one exception was bathtime, which was seen as an important moment in the children's day, since most of them suffered from an inability to come to terms with their own bodies. Every Wednesday evening there was a general staff meeting at 10; to attend it, the counselors were often obliged to speed up the bedtime routine. Although they received room and board plus laundry services, the counselors were paid a mere pittance in terms of salary. In 1950, the last full year she worked at the school (she had by then become an assistant to the director), Gayle Shulenberger earned just $1,600. In 1970, when Geneviève Jurgensen was hired as a counselor, Bert Cohler, who was then in the process of taking over Bettelheim's job, proudly told her that given her four years of experience as a speech therapist in her native France, he could offer her $3,000 a year—$500 more than the regular starting salary.[23]

It is clearly worth asking just what, in that age of full employment and rapid economic growth, could incite young people to accept such sacrifices of both money and time. Gayle says laughingly: "I often told myself that if I'd been Catholic, I could just as well have been a nun! It was practically the same—I was there twenty-four hours a day."

Jules Henry answers the question in the same impersonal, matter-of-fact style he uses to describe the counselors' working day. Their workload was so heavy, he writes, that a process of self-selection took place in the first months, with people staying at the school only if they had "rather special inner needs."

> Rather than impose upon the counselors a transparent mask of adjustment, routine and frozen professional competence, as often occurs in American institutions, the School recognizes the existence of powerful inner needs and uses the resultant energy in a training and guidance program which takes these problems into consideration and works to resolve them. But note that the process is circular. Only those who perceive that the resolution of their problems lies in this direction, who need possession of and can help young children in this way, are motivated to remain.

To back up this statement, Henry notes that the school's director was giving psychotherapy to several of his counselors.

Henry's analysis points to the conclusion that the Orthogenic School was vastly superior to the other structures that generally take in psychotics, but one can easily see how critics could discern a very different pattern: that of an institution where a counselor needed to be afflicted by serious personal problems in order to treat the children's disorders, and of working conditions that were not much better than slavery.

That is indeed the way Bill Blau, one of Bettelheim's most implacable detractors, portrays the school. This avowed enemy of psychoanalysis spent almost a year as a counselor at the institution in the late 1940s, and the experience left him with a burning hatred for Bettelheim. Blau considers it his duty even now to denounce him at every opportunity, and he devoted considerable time to doing so on the occasion of Bettelheim's death. Blau's testimony is interesting for several reasons; first, because he is perfectly sincere in his crusade against Bettelheim. He tells no lies, and does not try to selectively edit his memories to make them fit his story. He acknowledges, for example, that he never saw Bettelheim actually hit a child—or rather, he corrects himself, that he does not remember seeing him do so. When the interviewer points out that if he had, it would therefore not have shocked him particularly, he ends up by admitting it. His testimony is also interesting because it helps to highlight the origins of the misunderstanding that sprang up around Bettelheim's method, particularly since Blau's experience at the school dates from that early, enchanted period.

In essence, Bill Blau accuses Bettelheim of having been an impostor, and of having done a great deal of harm, particularly to parents of autistic children. Interestingly, Blau claims to have seen through what he believes to be a "fraud" not at the school itself, but during Bettelheim's classes. After military service in World War II, he had enrolled for psychology courses at the University of Chicago and ended up working at the Orthogenic School to complement his GI Bill scholarship. He had been working there for several months, in charge of a group of young boys, when Bettelheim invited him to attend one of his lectures. There, the young man was shocked at the way Bettelheim treated his students. "He was really a brute with them. He'd pile on the readings, of Freud and others, with no concern for how long it takes to read. Later, his technique was to call on a student and ask all these questions about the Freudian texts and then to ridicule him with his answers. He'd savage them."[24]

The moment of truth for Blau came when he himself had to answer a question. Far from ridiculing him, Bettelheim congratulated him for his answer—and that made Blau furious. "I didn't know any more than the others—in fact, much less, because I didn't have much time to read. But because I worked for him, I had to be right, in order to prove what a good teacher he was!" Unfortunately, Blau has now forgotten both the question Bettelheim asked and his answer to it, so it is impossible to find out why his reply might have been worthy of the teacher's praise. Perhaps it was because, unlike those of the other students, it was based on experience, and did not seek to conceal woolly thinking behind a wall of jargon. But even if one were to attempt such an explanation, Blau would probably not accept it.

From that day on, Bill Blau began feeling suspicious of everything Bettelheim did. He saw the staff meetings as unjustified exercises in tyranny; he felt that some of the young women looked on Dr. B as a kind of god, that they told him only what he wanted to hear, and furthermore that they were being disloyal to the children by squealing on them to the director. He started to see Bettelheim as such despot that he even suspected him of abusing his position to obtain sexual favors from some of the young women. Blau also believes that the children who attended the school were no sicker than many of the kids he had rubbed shoulders with when, at the age of twelve or thirteen, during the Depression years, he had been sent to an orphanage by his mother after his father committed suicide. He sees Bettelheim as a coward: "He had little experience of life. We had just returned from the war; we were tougher, meaner, than him. He was very intelligent, but he was sick, and more interested in his own image than in the truth." Listening to Blau, one cannot help wondering what he was looking for when he joined an institution whose principles were so diametrically opposed to everything he believed in. He replies that at the time, psychoanalysis was all the rage at the University of Chicago, the subject on everyone's lips, and that Bruno Bettelheim and the Orthogenic School were considered the ultimate experience in the field.

Here, then, is a witness who casts a different light on the picture painted by Jules Henry. For if it is true, as Henry argues, that "inner needs" were essential to the makeup of a successful counselor, Bill Blau clearly had just as many needs as those for whom the Bettelheim method worked wonders. But for reasons of his own, he reacted with repulsion to what others found invaluable. It is true that Bettelheim usually felt more comfortable with women than with men, but that did not prevent the school from having some very good male counselors on its staff. It is also true that at the time Blau was there, even more so than today, taking care of children was considered a woman's job. As the school's students still numbered four groups of boys and only one of girls, finding more male counselors was indeed one of Bettelheim's major concerns. But that is not the crux of the matter.

The expert on the question of what motivated the counselors who stayed the course is Ben Wright, professor of statistics in the University of Chicago's Department of Education. After working as a counselor himself for several years, he not only devoted his doctoral thesis to the subject but wrote the first drafts of two articles on it that he was to co-author with Bettelheim. He is also responsible for all the data and some of the writing in the section of *A Home for the Heart* devoted to staff training, although the commentary is Bettelheim's. Like Jules Henry, Wright stresses the heaviness of the counselors' workload. They had to act both as parents and therapists for the children in their charge; they started to see an individual child in one-hour sessions two or three times weekly after about a year of working at the school. The sole function of the consulting psychoanalysts who succeeded Emmy Sylvester, visiting the school once a week, was to guide the counselors in their work, and not to treat the children themselves.

Wright (with the blessing of his co-author, Bettelheim) explains this system by citing the seriousness of the children's condition.

> Being repeatedly bitten, kicked, defecated upon or otherwise abused results in defensive or punitive actions, cold indifference, emotional distance or superior looking down on such "animal-like" behavior. Though these may be rationalized as necessary interference, as the setting of healthy or socially required limitations, such attitudes interfere with rehabilitation. They can be avoided only if staff members know it is their responsibility, and only theirs, to help these children, if they receive all the narcissistic and interpersonal rewards that derive from being the children's main therapists.[25]

Wright then points to an important characteristic of staff members: Due to their youth and lack of experience, they had a different type of relationship with the children than the other adults at the school did. "Still basically in opposition to (what to them appear to be) the oppressive mores of adult society, the young staff members, far from experiencing the children's anti-social behavior as a threat, tend to enjoy it," he and Bettelheim wrote.

Bettelheim had noticed early on how some counselors clearly got a thrill out of seeing children cursing and swearing, breaking toys or crockery, in a way they themselves had never dared to do. He observed the fascination, concerned that it should not reach the point when a child might be tempted to exaggerate his symptoms to please his counselor. But he noted, "Such common feelings, unspoken and not acted upon by the workers but acted out by the children, permit the severely disturbed child to feel understood and appreciated in his rejection of the world."[26]

Just like the children in their care, the counselors were still seeking their way in life, and as they were young, they believed that anything was possible. It was a hope that bore in it the seeds of healing, and the young counselors were better placed than anyone else to transmit it to their charges, since they had so far led normal lives and been successful in their studies. (Very quickly, the criteria for recruiting counselors had become stricter, with Bettelheim demanding that they have a college degree.)

This parallel between the students and their counselors illustrates the basic tenet of the Bettelheim approach: the difference between crazy and sane people is one of degree only. The validity of this affirmation was being demonstrated every day at the school. Gayle clearly recalls the day when this dawned on her. "I remember walking into his office. He was writing, so I waited. But I was boiling inside. Then, finally, he looked up and I said: 'Dr. B, everybody is crazy, is that it?' and he said: 'Did you just discover that, my girl?' For me, it was a revelation."

Reaching that moment of understanding was no doubt the decisive event in the training of a good O.S. counselor. As long as the recruit had not arrived at that point, taking care of the children was just another job, and a grueling, poorly paid one at that. Until counselors realized that by working with the children they would learn as much about themselves as about their charges, as long as they had not accepted with humility that they had to sort out a few things in their own heads, and that they could get the help they needed from the very children they were trying to assist, they would not be good counselors in Bettelheim's eyes.

And to help them get there was Bettelheim's most essential role at the school. It is true that he also acted as a father and a reassuring symbol of authority to the students, making his rounds twice a day, once in the daytime and again in the dormitories just before lights-out, ever ready to respond with a story, a kind word, or an angry one to the continual requests for help he received from both children and adults. But he could have fulfilled those functions in another setting. What was unique about the Orthogenic School was the way he gradually got its counselors and teachers to become aware of their own problems, their own quest in life, thereby making therapists of them too—how he taught them to "walk back and forth across that bridge."

Bettelheim carried out this work on two levels simultaneously: individually, during the one-to-one talks he had regularly with all his counselors, and collectively in the daily staff meetings. The memories of those assemblies are among the former staff members' most vivid. Their tone could vary from the warm, family-like atmosphere of the early days to what some witnesses refer to as public torture sessions. There are as many different recollections as there are people, but all are intense.

The system evolved gradually over the years. In the early days, any time a counselor had a problem, or simply an idea that seemed important, he or she would drop by Bettelheim's office. As Gayle Shulenberger says, "Everything was a bit mixed up. I would go to see him about a kid, and I would end up talking about myself." And it had not taken long for Bettelheim to realize that the only really intractable problems that arise in an adult's day-to-day relationship with a child, whether disturbed or not, are those that touch on some painful memory from the adult's own childhood. They are memories of which the adult is often unaware, but they offer her the opportunity to either punish the child she once was, or give him what she had been deprived of, by force if necessary, for she is then convinced that she knows better than the child himself what he needs. This is the blind spot in the relationship, when the adult ceases to see the child as a separate person.

Thus when a counselor came to him to discuss a problem, Bettelheim would ask a few questions, and would soon get around to: "How do you feel when . . . ?" For example, " . . . when he starts screaming and biting?" In most cases, the answer to that question contained the solution to the conflict with the child. A typical reply might be: "I don't really know—it scares me. It shocks me. I know I should stop him, that he's bothering the other children, but I feel he needs to do it, after all those years spent at the orphanage, where he wasn't allowed to do anything at all, where he was nothing but a retarded child. He needs to scream out that he exists, make others acknowledge him, even if it disturbs them . . . As a kid, I never screamed, because I lived with my aunt, and she was so good to me that I never felt I had the right to . . . " With the brightest or the best trained among his counselors, Bettelheim would often not need to push the conversation much further. They would immediately detect the repetition in their mental images, see what was getting in the way of their relationship with the child in question. With others, Bettelheim would have to be more forceful, probing them with questions, and reassuring them as well, until the light finally dawned and the counselor understood why that one child struck more of a chord in her than the others did, or why she was unable to establish contact.

But it was in the staff meetings that the technique took on its full force. A recent recruit would explain in detail how she had been unable to handle a child's erratic behavior, expecting a few words of advice. Instead, with the others looking on, Bettelheim would say: "Imagine what could make you act that way." Surprised, the new counselor would often mumble, searching desperately for the "right" answer, and then come out with something like, "Oh, I understand. If I were in his shoes . . . " She had fallen into the trap. The aim of the exercise was not to put oneself in the child's place but to dig down into one's own emotions to find what could bring about such behavior in oneself. As Karen Zelan, one of Bettelheim's all-time favorites among the counselors, says, this is almost the opposite of putting oneself in the other person's shoes. For unlike compassion, which involves a movement of one person toward another, empathy, which is what Bettelheim sought to foster, is an encounter with the other person inside oneself—first, in order to accept him, and then to hold out a hand to help him cross the bridge toward reality; a firm hand, that no fear, no repulsion, can push away.

It was a tough training. Trying to identify within yourself the defiant child who, after defecating on the floor, is in the process of methodically smearing your blouse with excrement, or, even more terrifying, the enraged child struggling with his desire to kill someone, either you or himself, is by no means easy. It took time, and gritty determination, to graduate. Indeed, many people never did so; they left the school after a few weeks or months.

In May 1986, when the University of Chicago organized a small conference in honor of Bettelheim, Josette Dermody Wingo gave a lively account of her first months as a counselor at the school forty years earlier. Speaking in the presence of her former boss, she explained how she never knew exactly what he expected of her, and thus was continually nervous about making a mistake, and saying or doing something that would thwart a child's progress toward recovery. "Since most of the time I was flying blind, I never knew when I would be blindsided," said Wingo, who had joined the school in 1946, after leaving military service. She went on to describe the continual fatigue, and her struggles to dictate her reports on the children in her care: "Anxiety over owed tapes hung like a guilty albatross around my neck all the time . . . The requirements were for a flat narrative style with no interpretations but with an emphasis on what children and counselors said and did."[27] Josette then quoted an extract from one of her dictations:

Pete walked into the dormitory and threw his model airplane onto the floor. I said: "If you don't like it anymore, Pete, I'll be glad to keep it for you." He kicked the pieces to flinders.

Daniel said, "He's always breaking things. He's just trying to UPROAR you, Josette." The other kids gathered around the table for their snacks. "Want a piece of chocolate cake, Pete?"

"You know I hate cake. You know I hate chocolate. It's shitty. You're shitty, shitty, shitty, shitty!"

I shrugged my shoulders.

Next, Wingo reported on the subsequent staff meeting:

Dr. B: "Why did you shrug your shoulders?"

Stupefied silence. I thought I had been doing well just to have Pete not get to me.

Dr. B: "He was being hostile to you. Why?"

Resisting an impulse to shrug my shoulders and riposte with something clever like "Beats the hell out of me," I bit my lip. There was more to come—there usually was.

Dr. B: "I saw Pete yesterday, wearing that ridiculous, poisonous-green hat. He looks like Happy Hooligan. Even our most neurotic parents would never let a child looking like Happy Hooligan out of the funny papers."

By this time, Dr. B was mad and it was perfectly clear to me that it was up to me to "Do Something" about Pete's hat, but whether the sound psychological reasons were Pete's self-image or Dr. B's dislike of arsenical yellow-green plaid wool hats with ear flaps were beyond the scope of the discussion. Lots of things were. When to shut up, when to speak up, when to put up: I spat on my finger and held it up to the wind, trying to decide whether to tack or to jibe, but mostly staying the course.

Bruno Bettelheim was never an easy man to get along with. The originality of his technique and ideas only seemed to compound the idiosyncrasies of his character, including an innate irascibility which was to increase over the years, giving him a reputation for being completely unpredictable. Some people saw this as nothing more than fickleness and a lack of self-control; for others it was yet another proof of his remarkable talent—psychoanalytic wisdom residing precisely in the capacity to acknowledge that no two people are ever alike, and that, in dealing with human beings, everything must remain flexible, for it is the overly rigid rule that negates the individual. For Josette Dermody Wingo, as for all those who both gave and received a great deal during their time at the school, the two images of Bettelheim, the ill-tempered man and the talented one, corresponded to successive stages in her perception of him, as she gained a better understanding of her own role without one ever completely blotting out the other. "Technique, if that was what it was, became almost second nature by the beginning of the third year. No longer did fear hobble me at work . . . the lessening of fear freed the intuition. Like Gayle, Joan, Patti, Ping, and Florence White,[28] I became a living feedback loop for what was going on with the children."

While many things changed at the Orthogenic School during the thirty years of Bettelheim's stewardship, the training of counselors remained the same throughout. Geneviève Jurgensen, joining the staff a quarter of a century after Josette Wingo, gives a vivid account of the hell she went through in her first two months in charge of a group of adolescent girls. As she was about to start her shift, she often fantasized about slipping on the steps, which would give her an excuse to go home. (She was married and therefore didn't live at the school.) Each time, however, she kept at it. The same feelings of discouragement and revolt can be found in the unpublished memoirs of Candace Hilldrup, who started at the school in 1969.[29] But there is also the same determination to overcome her powerlessness, to get in control—in a word, to understand.

Another thing Dr. B was well aware of, probably because he had experienced it himself during his cohabitation with Patsy in Vienna, was just how much anxiety disturbed children can generate in the adults who live with them: anxiety about not being able to help them, or fear of being similar to them. Dr. Ugo Formigoni, who today heads a psychiatric hospital for children in the Chicago suburbs, has vivid memories of the first staff meeting he attended at the Orthogenic School, in 1960. Aged twenty-nine at the time, Formigoni had come from his native Italy to complete his medical degree with some experience of U.S. hospitals. He was then a psychiatric intern in Oklahoma and somewhat disillusioned at what he saw as the depersonalized treatment in the two institutions where he had worked since his arrival. Having read *Love Is Not Enough*, he wanted to spend some time at the Orthogenic School. Bettelheim did not welcome live-in observers, but he had finally agreed to Formigoni spending a month there as a counselor. At that first staff meeting, Dr. B had spoken at some length about the difficulties counselors experienced when a child made them lose their tempers. The problem, he explained, had to do with their self-image. "We like to see ourselves as Saint Georges helping children to get well. To be confronted with the negative feelings those kids can evoke in us, and especially anger, is totally unacceptable to us."

As Dr. Formigoni was reporting on the meeting, I could not resist interrupting him: "But don't you think Dr. B was really talking about himself?" And this competent sixty-year-old man, who has spent over thirty years treating people with mental problems, paused in the middle of a sentence, reflecting. Then he said: "You're right, I can see it now. He must have been talking about himself . . . But it did not even cross my mind at the time. To me then, he was talking about me, about us. About feelings that we were struggling with, feelings that we were trying very hard to repress."[30] Such was Bruno Bettelheim's impact as a therapist, and such was the influence he wielded over those who worked with him. That meeting made such a deep impression on Dr. Formigoni that when Bettelheim suggested he continue to work at the school, not as a psychiatrist but as a simple counselor, "to learn," hinting that there could be better prospects in the future, he accepted almost immediately.

However one wishes to label it, as therapy, psychoanalysis, or (more appropriately) as "supervision," this was the core of Bettelheim's work at the Orthogenic School. It was the same task that he was to carry out, in a more classical fashion, with a group of young lay analysts who started attending seminars with him in 1959. On Tuesday evenings, they would come to the school to discuss their most difficult cases. The sessions were taped, and the unedited transcripts make fascinating reading.[31] Each case unfolds somewhat like a detective story (Bettelheim liked to compare the role of the therapist to that of a lawyer).[32] A particular case would be outlined, with Bettelheim interrupting from time to time to ask for more details. Then there would be a period of discussion between him and the analyst presenting the case. The transcripts make it clear why some people who attended his courses (where he used the same technique as with his students) use the word *sadistic* to describe them. Bettelheim's questions would of course probe the most sensitive area of the psychoanalyst's relationship with his or her patient. If the analyst then stiffened, failed to give a direct answer, or tried to hide behind a ready-made theoretical one, the dialogue could become painful. Bettelheim would keep up the pressure, finding different ways to ask the same question. Other participants would join in, and their contributions often seemed to convince their unfortunate colleague that he was the only member of the group who had failed to see what was so glaringly obvious for everyone else. In each case, however, the discussion has a constructive ending, generally with the laying bare of some hidden wound in the analyst's own makeup, which could well be the cause of his problem with his patient.

The whole process is almost too perfect. When one reads several such accounts in succession, one is forced to conclude that Bettelheim could not possibly have gotten it right every time. And indeed, he did not really claim that he had. He offered hypotheses and opened doors, but rarely put forward his interpretations as the only possible ones; the recipient was free to do what he or she wanted with them. When his interlocutor was clearly very ill at ease, Bettelheim would on occasion extend a helping hand to get around an obstacle. But his tone could also be very harsh, and the authority he wielded over the group was indisputable. "With his glasses that made his eyes enormous, he could look very intimidating. I felt I was face-to-face with Erich von Stroheim!" Ugo Formigoni admits.

Socratic is the term most often used by Bettelheim's former students to describe his courses and supervisory sessions. For throughout his whole career, from Rockford to Stanford, via the Orthogenic School and the University of Chicago's lecture halls, his working method never varied. A glimpse of it is revealed in *The Art of the Obvious*, a work compiled by Alvin Rosenfeld from seminars he and Bettelheim ran jointly in California in the 1980s. An even better illustration is to be found in *Dialogues with Mothers*. At first glance, this little book reads like just another child care manual. But it is not. The actual content of the book is of little importance; what is significant is the exchange itself, the path taken by Bettelheim to get the mothers (and sometimes fathers) to become aware of what they are actually saying. When read from that standpoint, the book not only illustrates its author's method, it also reveals what was remarkable about his way of looking at children.

The dialogues started at the end of the war. To cater to the huge influx of newly discharged GIs who wanted either to start or complete studies in Chicago with their grants, the university had a prefabricated village built at the end of the Midway, a few hundred yards from the Orthogenic School. Many of the couples who moved in had their first children there, and so many of Bettelheim's students asked him questions about child rearing during his regular classes that he ended up organizing informal meetings with them or their spouses every other Wednesday. For, as he states in *Dialogues with Mothers*, which was compiled from the tape recordings he made of the sessions, "the most appropriate advice, the most carefully explained theory, is of little use when it comes to handling specific everyday events with a child."[33] In only a few months the experiment had proved so successful that he made the meetings weekly. The sessions ran from 1948 until 1952, when Bettelheim gave them up for lack of time. He was to resume them on a less regular basis later on, and he would use them to feed a monthly column that ran from 1965 to 1975 in the *Ladies' Home Journal.*

An example of the "detective work" side of his technique was filmed by Daniel Karlin during one such session in April 1973. The scene opens with a mother telling how her daughter, almost five, is incapable of persevering in any difficult task, becoming discouraged and giving up at the very first hurdle. What should the mother do— keep on encouraging her to try harder, or ignore her, leaving her to manage on her own? Bettelheim asks for an example, and she tells how her daughter gave up trying to learn "Mary Had a Little Lamb" on the piano, becoming irritated and lapsing into thumbsucking. "Try again! You know very well that, in order to learn something, you have to work at it," the young mother had told her child. Bettelheim interrupts her: "Suppose you were crying and upset; what would someone have to say to make you feel better?"

The mother replies, "Something like: 'Try again, it'll be better next time.'"

Dr. B: "I'm trying to find something in your own experience . . . Suppose that your husband had tried in vain to climb a mountain, and then gave up, saying: 'It's too hard, I'll never make it.' What would you say to him?"

"'Sure, you can make it!'"

"I wouldn't like to be married to you, my dear lady. I would never have succeeded in life if my wife had reacted like that. Do you know what she has always said to me about the school?"

Several other mothers volunteer answers:

"That it wouldn't work?"

"That your ideas are excellent, and that . . . ?"

"That it's a tough job, but she's there to help you?"

At each reply, Dr. B waxes ironic, with comments such as: "Between you and me, all your husbands should be filing for divorce! You are quite unbearable." Then he finally gives the answer, pausing for dramatic effect to emphasize his punch line. "For twenty-four years she has been telling me to . . . give the whole thing up!"

The mothers express surprise. "You think that's so marvelous?" To which Bettelheim replies: "Yes, because she doesn't want me to tire myself out!" At that point he becomes gentler and tries to explain to them, in a few sentences, the difference between encouragement and pressure, between things that one is forced to do, such as take a med-icine, and things one chooses to do (play the piano). Another mother suddenly points out that maybe the little girl is only playing the instrument because it is important *for her mother.* "Exactly," says Bettelheim. "She doesn't really know what importance it could have for her . . . But when you tell her to try again, you show her clearly that you want her to make the effort. But why?"

"Because I want her to be successful!"

"Precisely. That's exactly the point! . . . Your child's frustration and anxiety are caused by your insistence that she has to *succeed.*"

From this point on, the whole plot unravels. "It's even worse than that," the mother starts. Now feeling guilty, she blurts out the "truth," which is that she is trying to keep her daughter a baby because she fears the day when her children will no longer need her. She doesn't know why, but she has never allowed herself to be successful in life. Bettelheim interrupts her again.

"What did you study in college?"

"English literature."

"And what did you want to do with it?"

"I didn't have the faintest idea. It seemed the best thing to do, given my abilities. I was interested in other things, but I wasn't gifted for them . . . "

"Which things?"

"Music."

"Ahah—interesting!" This last remark brings a burst of general laughter.

If this dialogue were not there on film, it would seem too good to be true. And in a way, it is. The exchange is typical of the way Bettelheim operated toward the end of his career in Chicago.[34] The technique was more abrupt and less analytical than in the earlier dialogues, with Bettelheim using a heavier hand to steer the conversation the way he wanted. Cathy Kaiser, one of the first mothers to take part in the Wednesday meetings, remembers him as much more considerate and kinder than the person who emerges from the above exchange— more concerned about his listeners and probably also more optimistic as to the progress the discussion could yield.

She remembers the sessions clearly; the war had just ended, and Dr. Benjamin Spock had revolutionized the field of pediatrics with his *Baby and Child Care.* This was supposed to be a reassuring book, since its basic message was that mothers should not worry, that they in fact knew their children better than did any of the books they con-sulted. However, as it also went against the precepts of strictness that had dominated child rearing up until then, its initial effect was in fact to throw its readers into a state of anxiety. Young mothers were sud-denly being told that all those key decisions on feeding, weaning, toi-let training, which the new psychology manuals described as being of crucial importance, were in fact up to them. As a result, they were continually worrying whether they had done the right thing. Their husbands had just returned from saving Europe (Cathy Kaiser's had been involved in air operations over Germany); they did not have the right to mess up their sons' upbringing. "What I got out of those meetings was not recipes, but a way to be with my children. Thanks to Dr. B, I was no longer afraid to make mistakes," says Cathy.[35] The mother of the young pianist, however, may feel differently. Yet, the latter discussion does have one advantage: it points very clearly to the enemy that Bettelheim continually had in his sights.

The pain that a mother, however loving and devoted, can inflict on her child with her own unfulfilled desires, how she can become blind to what he really is, negate him without even realizing it, by project-ing images from her own past onto him, was indeed one childhood misfortune Bettelheim knew firsthand. After all, was the empathy that he tried to foster in his counselors any different from that which little Bruno had been craving when he insisted on doing his homework next to his mother at the dining room table, at the end of a day when he had been made fun of in the schoolyard or beaten up on the way to school? Was it not the understanding that he never got from her? For as far back as he could remember, Paula had burdened him not only by handing him the role of the father, who had been found wanting, but also by asking him to open the doors that had remained closed to her. He had to become a real man and a breadwinner, to take the place of the inadequate Anton. He also had to become rich and influ-ential, like Grandfather Seidler, and like the businesswoman she had not been allowed to be. Who he, Bruno, really was, with his own ambitions, pleasures, and fears, she did not see. Would she otherwise have made such a noisy entrance when he was giving one of his first lectures in English? (See chapter 2.)

The worst of it was that he could be in no doubt that she loved him. Her devotion to her children, and especially to her son, was the object of universal admiration. Did he have any right to blame her for the suffering that, unknowingly, she caused him? And if he felt that he did not measure up to what she wanted, whose fault was it? Certainly not hers. "My parents . . . tried their very best to be very good parents . . . So we could not blame them, and if we occasionally questioned their depressive way of life, we had to feel guilty," he was to write later. And about his own "relative success," he said that although his mother had lived long enough to see the start of it, "her long life of sorrows did not permit her to really enjoy it."[36] Upon reflection, if those early dialogues with mothers were kinder and more optimistic in tone, it might also be because Paula Bettelheim was still alive at the time, and her son had not given up all hope of changing the way she too saw her child.

Bettelheim was said to be merciless with mothers. And, on occasion, he was. But all he was ever trying to do was to give back children their identities in their mother's eyes. "I don't remember ever being afraid of him," says Cathy Kaiser. She was fascinated by the way he managed to get even the shyest young women to speak, always with delicacy, and can remember only one situation where he would really become harsh with a mother. That was "when it became obvious that she didn't really want to help her child." It was the same at the school. If Bettelheim demanded of his counselors that they be at all times attentive to what the children actually said and did, it was because the children had to learn how to become themselves, rather than the model child, or more commonly the monstrous child their mothers saw in them—to help them break out of the mold they had always been trying to conform to, at the cost of forgetting to live for themselves, which resulted in self-hatred and self-destruction.

With the young mothers whose children were growing up normally, and whose desire to get it right was manifest, Bettelheim was engaging in preventive work. He would remind them of a few obvious truths. "Never again in your life will you be so important to a human being. And if you don't enjoy that, you're sunk," he tells a mother who has been complaining that her four-year-old son tyrannizes her. She nevertheless insists: " 'But before Christmas he would play around the house and he could entertain himself for hours. He was very quiet and very happy.' "

Dr. B: "Who told you he was happy?"

"Well, he seemed to be. He wasn't demanding; he wasn't crying."

Dr. B: "That's right. The mother is ignored and that's identical with the child being happy. Isn't that a funny kind of attitude?"[37]

Bettelheim was not unaware that a young mother's life is often difficult. During the discussions, he notes in the introduction to *Dialogues with Mothers*, "they began to see and hear for themselves how others felt and—encouraged by me, whom they considered an authority—they could admit to themselves that caring for a small child is not always wholly blissful and entails genuine hardship. It was a relief for them to learn that all mothers are sometimes exhausted from the labor of caring for babies, the home, and a husband distracted by the desire for professional advancement and the need for making ends meet." Yet while reassuring these young mothers, he also tries to get them to glimpse what they were keeping silent: the hidden side of their maternal love, the repressed desires that they imposed on their children, and also the aggressiveness, anger, and even hatred their children could trigger in them at times. He never tells them, "You should do this," but always asks, "What do you expect from your child? What sort of child do you want?" In other words, he seeks to pin down their unconscious, in the hope that once they have been confronted with the ambivalence of some of their desires, they will stop making their children pay for conflicts that they themselves have not been able to resolve. His aim is not that they change, but that they accept themselves as they are.

Over the years, however, the tone of the dialogues was to evolve, as did Bruno Bettelheim's relationship with the Orthogenic School counselors. The magic of those early years was that of jointly made discoveries, the excitement of the first results, the joy felt by pioneers who had set out on the right track. Then the first counselors began to leave: Marjorie Jewell first, followed by Bettylou Pingree and Ronnie Dryvage in 1947. Gayle Shulenberger, who had become Dr. B's assistant, stayed until 1951, but even she finally moved on. During 1946, Bettelheim had struck up a friendship with Morris Janowitz, a young sociologist from New York who had spent the war in London analyzing the content of the German radio broadcasts in the Psychological Warfare Division of Supreme Allied Headquarters. Deeply affected by the war, Janowitz had come to Chicago on the GI Bill to pursue his doctorate. Soon thereafter, he had started work on a book with Bettelheim, and he had become a frequent visitor to the school.[38] Encouraged by Dr. B, Gayle started dating him. When they got engaged, Bettelheim was very proud, even though the prospect of Gayle's departure filled him with anguish. He was best man at their wedding, along with Jeremiah Kaplan, his (and Janowitz's) publisher.

Josette Dermody's wedding had taken place at the school in September 1949. There had been a lot of discussion about whether to include the children in the ceremony, the idea being to introduce them to a "normal" progression into adulthood. Finally, Bettelheim decided that the school "family" could act like a regular one and the boys in Josette's group were allowed to express their anger at seeing her taken away by another male, by furiously bombarding the couple with grains of rice as they stepped out of the building. After her marriage, Josette returned for a while to work at the school during the day. But it was no longer the same.

12

❊

Dr. B the Enchanter

The publication in 1950 of *Love Is Not Enough* was rapidly to make Bruno Bettelheim well known across the United States. The years of discovery thus gave way to years of success. He had been accepted as a member of the American Psychology Association. He was now a full-fledged university professor of psychology and education. He had achieved his ambition, and, as he was to tell Bert Cohler twenty years later, he was starting to be bored.

The world around him had meanwhile changed. The victory over Nazism had been seen as confirmation of the superiority of the American system, in terms of both justice and strength. American children also had to be the best. Mental illness, which had never been well accepted in the United States in the best of times, had to be defeated at all costs. Some people even blamed all the horrors of the just-ended war on the madness of a single man, Adolf Hitler. If mad people could not be cured, then they needed to be gotten rid of; there was no place for them in American society. This was the time when some states had laws on their books providing for the locking up, or in some cases the lobotomization, of people who did not fulfill the basic conditions required of a good citizen. Meanwhile, the Department of Health and private foundations had started funding innumerable psychiatric research projects. In 1952, a federal law banned from U.S. territory aliens suffering from psychotic symptoms.

The mood of rabid anti-Communism that set in within months of the end of the war could only increase the pressure for conformity.

Stalin's mind, like that of Hitler, was analyzed for signs of madness. For many people it seemed clear that if humanity could rid itself of mental illness, there would be no more wars, atrocities, or totalitarianism.[1] Needless to say, by no means everyone in psychological and psychoanalytic circles shared these simplistic views. But intellectuals were the prime targets for the McCarthyists, and the European immigrants in particular were not about to risk their newfound security by defending progressive ideas against the "Reds-under-the-bed" consensus. Even committed Marxists like the analyst Otto Fenichel gave up discussing social or political issues in public.[2] Ego psychology, with its individualistic and reassuring message, was in its heyday.

Anti-Communism was not a problem for Bruno Bettelheim, who had become aware of it well before the rise of Senator Joseph McCarthy. In September 1945, in a letter to Ernst Federn, he apologized for not being able to send any of the documents on Marx or Freud his friend had asked him for. The reason was simple, Bettelheim wrote—such literature simply did not exist. He went on:

> Wilhelm Reich is living and working in Brooklyn, New York. He is the only one who is really concerned with Marxism, but he is by now so confused that nothing comes from it. The only somewhat more interesting contributions were made by some of the sociologists, but they again don't understand Freud. You will have to learn that in this great country there is not a single real Marx scholar, and probably with the exception of your father and a very few old analysts no Freud scholar either. They publish all right, but it does not amount to anything.[3]

While the view that mentally ill people had no place in American society was diametrically opposed to everything Bettelheim believed in, the two philosophies did have one idea in common: the possibility of a cure. And on reading *Love Is Not Enough*, it was easy to become convinced that Bettelheim had indeed created a method that could cure mentally ill children. Even better, it was a humane, kindly method—just the ticket for the liberal philanthropists who were eager to devote a little of their wealth to the betterment of their community by fighting mental illness. And Bettelheim was to benefit greatly from the largesse thus made available to those in the front lines of that war. From day one of his tenure at the Orthogenic School, the quest for funds was a major part of his job. He had first met, and won over, Philip Pekow, a rich industrialist who was the father of a former student and who chaired a Concerned Parents Committee. In July 1944,

Pekow had offered to raise the money needed to repair the school's crumbling infrastructure. Having lost confidence in Mandel Sherman, Pekow said he could find $2 million for the construction of a new building, on the condition that the university appoint a new director and match what he raised. Ralph Tyler still remembers the first meeting of the fund-raising foundation, which was to be named after its most generous donor, Sonia Shankman. He jokingly refers to the event, in January 1945, as "the extortion meeting."[4] The man who conducted the bidding had also clearly been won over by Bruno Bettelheim's charm. "Come on, you can do better than that," he told the assembled donors. "You can give more, I know. Remember: I'm also *your* lawyer!"

Despite the relatively high fees, which were paid either by the parents themselves, or in the case of orphans or children from poor families by sponsoring charities, the school was chronically short of funds. All the university contributed was the upkeep of the building, maintenance, and the director's salary.[5] All other expenses had to be covered by the school itself. Personnel costs were high because the institution employed a lot of people, and the only ones who were underpaid in relation to the amount of work they put in were the counselors. Last but not least, Bettelheim needed to hire students to carry out the research that was also part of the school's charter.

And he was a very good fund-raiser. The wives of several members of the Sonia Shankman Foundation set up an auxiliary branch, running a thrift shop to raise money. Bettelheim kept them under his spell, dropping in to see them from time to time with one or two of the children, and occasionally inviting them to visit the school. These women provided day-to-day help; it was they, for example, who bought the school its first station wagon, used for picnics and other outings. Bettelheim's skill in raising funds, from private individuals but also from government agencies and major foundations, earned him the admiration of the university authorities, as the letters from the university president's office stored in the Regenstein Library show.[6] With the exception of one or two missives referring to his books, all the congratulations to Bettelheim relate to donations of $10,000, $20,000, or more to the Orthogenic School.

As the university's aim was to spend as little as possible on the school, Ralph Tyler was delighted at the successes being chalked up by his protégé, and gave him strong backing. For example, at a Sonia Shankman Foundation fund-raising dinner in November 1947, held to try to raise $1 million for the construction of a new building, he gave a glowing speech in which he rated Bettelheim's work just after that of Enrico Fermi, the physicist who five years earlier had achieved the first controlled nuclear reaction in an underground lab only a short distance from the school. Tyler also told the assembled donors that, in recognition of their efforts, the school would henceforth bear the name of their foundation.

Bettelheim had quickly grasped the workings of the U.S. system, and understood how to use it to the school's advantage. But in exchange, he was forced to bow to the system's demands. The constant search for funds took up a huge amount of his time, which gave him the impression, when he was feeling depressed, that when Tyler and Hutchins had chosen him to run the school it had been above all for his skills as a businessman. That at least is how I interpret the disillusioned comments he would mutter on occasion to Ben Wright, Stuart Brent, and a few others. These ruminations were unfair, but behind them lurked a misunderstanding that was to poison Bettelheim's existence: it concerned the meaning of the word *cure.* For the successful industrialists and businessmen who bankrolled him, men who were lords of all they surveyed, from Third World dictatorships to the workers in their plants, the word could have only one simple meaning. But it was not the same meaning as for the therapist, faced every day with the suffering of children, and for whom each new word spoken, each gesture achieved, was a victory in itself. Because Bettelheim belonged to both those worlds at the same time, he was aware of that difference. He played on it for the benefit of his school, but the price to be paid would be a high one.

This misunderstanding was to affect the way he presented his work, or at least the results of that work. For the books he was to write about the school were all reports on the use of the grants he had obtained. Their real value, of course, lies elsewhere, but the financial dimension was not negligible, and Bettelheim took care, in each volume, to thank his sponsors. On reading his correspondence, one sometimes gets the impression that almost up until the end of his tenure he was always late with some report or other. *Love Is Not Enough* and *Truants from Life* resulted from a grant provided by the National Institute for Mental Health, a newly created branch of the U.S. Department of Health, for a study of "the institutional treatment of emotionally disturbed children." *The Empty Fortress,* published in 1967, was the final report on a research project into infantile schizophrenia, sponsored by the Ford Foundation in 1956.

The latter grant, for $342,500 was to have a considerable influence on the development of the school. The results of the five-year study it was initially intended to finance would forever link in the public's mind the name of Bettelheim with the psychological condition that at the time was seen as the ultimate form of schizophrenia in the child: autism. And because it amounted to a huge sum of money, the Ford Foundation grant would place a huge burden on its recipient's shoulders. An outsize grant called for outsize results, Bettelheim apparently concluded. Why else would he have felt obliged to assert, in *The Empty Fortress*, that with the children involved in the study, he had achieved 42 percent of "good" results, 37 percent of "average" ones, and only 20 percent of failures, thus shattering all known records in the treatment of autism up until (and indeed since) then?

This huge exaggeration, which would prove detrimental both to the school and to Bettelheim himself, was simply the logical conclusion of a process that had started much earlier. For although *The Empty Fortress* is the most striking example, it was not the first book in which Bettelheim had given an idealized image of the school.

"Your book's great, Bruno," Fritz Redl said during a visit to the school in 1950, just after *Love Is Not Enough* had come out. "But why did you turn it into a fairy story?" Redl was lunching at the staff table. Having thus gotten everyone's attention, he went on: "Why didn't you talk about the most difficult? Why didn't you address the issue of discipline?" Ben Wright, who told me of the exchange, does not remember exactly what Bettelheim said in reply, but he believes it was something along the lines of: "Because people wouldn't understand what I was trying to say. Because they would use it as an excuse to mistreat their own children." Whatever his exact response, Wright adds, Bettelheim looked very irritated, and nobody else at the table said a word.

Before examining the issue of discipline (see chapter 14), the above exchange is worth considering, for it sheds light on at least one aspect of the Orthogenic School's development. I have found no one else who recalls that dining room conversation, but it is perfectly believable, as other examples of such behavior by Bettelheim can be cited. For him, certain things were better left unsaid. And contrary to what his enemies say, this was not just for the wrong reasons. The most explicit example I found does not directly concern the school. It occurred in July 1981, when Macmillan, Bettelheim's former publisher, was about to bring out *Mother Love: Myth and Reality*, by the French writer Elisabeth Badinter.[7] As its title suggests, the book examines what is generally known as the "maternal instinct," and concludes that it does not in fact exist. Bettelheim had been asked to write a preface for the U.S. edition, but he refused, explaining his decision by letter in the following terms:

> All my life I have been working with children whose lives have been destroyed because their mothers hated them . . . The demonstration that there is no mothering instinct—of course there is none, otherwise there would not have been the many children who needed my professional services—and that so many mothers reject their own children will remove these guilt feelings which were the only brake which saved at least some children from destruction, suicide, anorexia, you name it. So I can not lend my name to remove this last barrier which offered many unfortunate children a chance against being destroyed.

Shortly afterward, he was furious to learn that his letter had been published in the French daily newspaper *Le Matin de Paris*.[8] Badinter, amazed by his reaction, had decided to make the debate public. While paying tribute to Bettelheim's work, and acknowledging that his position was consistent with the therapeutic rescue mission he had been running for the previous three decades, she described his letter as "an appalling admission of failure." It was absolutely essential to tell the truth, Badinter wrote. This was "perhaps the only way to ensure that psychiatrists, historians, thinkers and moral philosophers are forced to think in new ways about the mother–child relationship." In a subsequent unpublicized letter, to another French writer, Bettelheim dismissed Badinter's riposte as "an intellectual reaction."[9] In his view, the idealism of her position on truth-telling was simply irresponsible, and was above all self-serving.

It is difficult to take sides in such a debate. On the one hand, it is normal and right for a young woman, whose life has so far spared her any extreme experiences, to believe in facing up to the deepest recesses of human nature. On the other, one cannot deny an old man who has spent his life fighting the demons hidden in those recesses the right to have given up hope of winning the battle by fair means. Nor the right to state that, given the tenacity of the enemy, all possible subterfuges may be used in order to defeat it. The debate between these two viewpoints has been going on ever since human beings started living in society.

When the debate is moved from the theoretical level of whether the maternal instinct exists or not to that of the need for discipline in the day-to-day running of an institution housing some forty seriously disturbed children, however, then without talking about "truth," the need for simple frankness becomes obvious. For by too often demanding that others should "do as I say, not as I do," Bettelheim not only gave his enemies a stick with which to beat him, he also disarmed his friends.

"He was so goddam moral!" says Gayle Shulenberger Janowitz, as if still amazed at the fact. Diana Grossman Kahn, who arrived at the school fifteen years later, puts it another way. "He had such a strong sense of duty." The disquiet that the accusations of brutality made against Bettelheim after his death inspired in the early counselors illustrates the impact that the books had on the development of the school. Gayle never saw Bettelheim strike a child. Look angry, shout, yes, but strike, no. Or at least, she has no memory of that. It is true that at that time the occasional slap, or a smack on the rear, was nothing exceptional; perhaps it happened, when the situation required it, and she simply didn't notice. She finds the doubt infuriating. She knows that the school changed after she left it, and she strives to get a clearer, more accurate idea of what it really became.

But she also knows that the picture of the school given in the books even in which she features prominently, was a bit too glossy. "The books were the ideal—the ideal we were all aiming for," she says, a view expressed by all the early counselors interviewed. *Love Is Not Enough*, in which Gayle features prominently and which is packed with photos, unlike later books, described events that they had lived through perhaps a little differently from the way they had experienced them, but as usual, what counted in their eyes was the meaning Bettelheim was able to draw from those events, this time for public consumption. In its essentials, the picture was true, and the school of the books was the one they had lived in. If Bettelheim had omitted certain aspects of its workings, it was because he was only describing what was new, and important. And it is undeniable that his books changed the way people viewed disturbed children. Countless institutions, all over the world, were inspired by them, and notably by *The Empty Fortress*, to at long last pay attention to such children's suffering.

However, Bettelheim never saw anything wrong with being economical with the truth in order to promote a good cause. In 1947, for example, when staff members at the school became worried that children could jump out the windows of the dormitories, on the second floor of the building, Bettelheim had bars put up. But as this was clearly contrary to his "open door" policy, he immediately assembled children in the living room and told them that the reason for the barriers was that the neighborhood was changing (which was true), and he wanted to make sure nobody could climb *in* through the windows. Bettelheim believed it was less disturbing for the children to think that the threat he was protecting them from came from outside, rather than from themselves.[10]

The counselors were well aware of Bettelheim's taste for neatly packaged parables. Former counselor Josette Wingo remembers them fondly:

> Dr. B's teaching stories were special. They usually involved a friend who had had a similar problem and had reached such and such conclusion or resolution. Dr. B was never at a loss for an appropriate anecdote, which usually had the satisfactory feeling of reducing anxiety, freeing energy to live through it, if not to resolve it, perhaps to become a protagonist in another story told to some other suffering soul someday . . . It took a while to tumble to Dr. B's stories, as his masterful technique—some of the stories may even have been true—was crafted to fit the current situation. They were certainly psychologically true.

When the scandal broke after Bettelheim's death, Gayle and her former colleagues found it impossible to square what they were hearing with a certain number of facts, of which they were completely sure. They knew, for example, that the counselors were not allowed to strike the children—because that was unusual—and that some newcomers had been immediately dismissed for doing so. The rule was so well established that the children would sometimes use it to tease a recently arrived counselor who had still not gotten her or his bearings. ("You're going to get fired, you know, when Dr. B hears that you hit him!")[11]

The case of Gayle Janowitz is significant, as she is a solid, no-nonsense person who, after serving as Bettelheim's assistant at the school and marrying one of his friends, never lost touch with him. She knew who he was, both his good and bad sides. But the gap he helped create between the reality of the school and its public image has made it difficult for her to defend him against accusations concerning events that occurred after she had left. It is the same for the others: All the former counselors and teachers I was able to speak to expressed, in their own different ways, the difficulty that Bettelheim's writings created for them in their attempts to defend the school from its detractors. Those who do not say so outright express their unease in their way of talking about the school, or in the way they brush off certain objections ("I didn't read that one. You know, I didn't get time to read . . . ") Each person has their own way of seeing things and their own opinion; some are harsher than others. Some are aggressive, others philosophical. Many feel that each time they tried to explain what they had lived through at the school, and what Dr. B had taught them, their statements were distorted, somewhat as if, by playing games with the school's image, Bettelheim had prevented them from ever being able to pin it down. One of the few among them to have tried to was Bettelheim's successor as director, Jacquelyn Sanders, who described an Orthogenic School that had very little in common with Bettelheim's, except for the physical setting.[12]

The gap between the reality of the school and what Bettelheim wrote about it, even in the early days, also made it more difficult for the children themselves to accept what he said about them. Several years after *Truants from Life* was published, one former student whose case was described in the book ("Paul") paid a visit to the school. When Bettelheim asked him what he had thought of the book, he replied, "I didn't know I was so bad." Dr. B first sought to reassure him: "No one is bad." He then asked Paul to explain, and the young man told him that when he had arrived at the school his only problem had been that he felt the orphanage where he had been living was not the right place for him. "Precisely," Bettelheim said. He went on to remind Paul of the antisocial behavior he had used to express that feeling, and explained that in order to be understood by his readers, he was obliged to stick labels on that behavior. This cleared up the problem for Paul, but he points out that some of his former schoolmates never came to accept the way Bettelheim portrayed them in his books.[13]

Writing about the school nevertheless involved a real difficulty: that of describing unconscious phenomena in a way that was at once comprehensible for lay readers and convincing for specialists. Bettelheim's texts were packed with examples, and they did indeed, on occasion, use psychiatric concepts. Inside the school, however, Bettelheim had from the start made it clear that there should be no diagnoses. Of course, the children arrived with medical records, which their counselors and teachers could consult if they wished. But during the everyday life of the school, labels were never used. Staff members would refer to Richard's running away, Sandy's bouts of rage, or Linda's refusal to eat, but such behavior was never given a clinical name, at least not during the early years; the school thus felt hardly at all like a psychiatric hospital, and as much as possible like a home. But the intentional, therapeutically determined vagueness that surrounded goings-on at the school made them difficult to describe. To understand this, one need only dip into the books Fritz Redl wrote about his own work with problem adolescents.[14] While he, unlike Bettelheim, devotes much space to the question of discipline, for example, he does so in an abstract, theoretical way, with a dryness of tone that does not do justice to his remarkable talents as an educator and therapist. In both cases, the picture is incomplete, but Bettelheim's books at least have the advantage of reaching a broader public, and not just the specialists, who are usually suspicious of new ideas, particularly when they are put forward by someone from outside their circle.

To help him get his ideas across, Bettelheim had found a talented assistant. Ruth Soffer (later Marquis), the daughter of Jewish immigrants from Russia, was an editor in the Chicago offices of Encyclopedia Britannica. In August 1944 she was working on a four-volume history of World War II, to be published three years later. A subscriber to *Politics*, a left-wing weekly, she was deeply impressed on reading Bettelheim's concentration camp article when it was reprinted there. She immediately suggested that he be asked to write the entry on concentration camps for Britannica. Ruth lived in Hyde Park, and had on occasion run into Bettelheim socially. "I have no time. But if you can get something out of this, go ahead," he told her, offering her the original version of his article, much longer than what had appeared in *Politics*. Seeing the young woman's worried expression, he added, "Don't worry—I'll read over what you do." When he did, he was so pleased with it that soon afterward he asked Ruth to become his personal editor. She accepted without hesitation. At first, she restricted herself to correcting the mistakes in his English. Then, as she gained self-assurance, she started cutting passages she thought redundant or complicated, resolving contradictions, and generally transforming the rather repetitive and imperious prose of the German-speaking intellectual, a little too eager to convince his readers, into something more accessible to a broad English-speaking public. Of course, Bettelheim always had the last word, but he had great faith in her judgment, and agreed readily to cuts that made his writing better and more effective.

Ruth Marquis shared the first counselors' enthusiasm for Bettelheim's ideas and approach. Pretty, intelligent, and hardworking, she enjoyed a relationship with Bettelheim that many at the school envied. When she was there, the two of them would shut themselves away in his office to work. Although she admired Bettelheim greatly, she would not hesitate to voice any disagreements she had with him. They talked a great deal; he opened up new worlds for her, introducing her to books such as Freud's *Civilization and Its Discontents* and *The Psychopathology of Everyday Life.* She would drop by the school in the morning to pick up what he had written the previous evening, and after her day's work at Britannica she would come back around II P.M. with her corrections. Today, Ruth Marquis still wonders whether it is possible to convey the magnetism, vitality, and energy that Bettelheim then radiated.

Bettelheim's first books owe a great deal to their work together. Although she would not say so herself, his exchanges with Ruth Marquis were undoubtedly decisive in molding his special style, and her admiration freed him from a tendency to labor his points and assert his credibility, letting him exploit his true talent as a storyteller to describe phenomena that are not easily explained. Writing about the unconscious is indeed a thankless task. Many have tried, without much success. The reason is always the same, circular one: If something could be said easily, then it would not be unconscious, and if it is unconscious, that is because it is crude, basic, and not very pretty. Freud was the first to acknowledge that the best way to describe unconscious phenomena was through fiction. Like him, Bettelheim frequently expressed regret that he lacked novel-writing skills. And if both of them nevertheless succeeded at least partly in their attempts, it was because they both knew how to spin a good yarn. By stimulating their readers' imaginations they helped them to feel, through what was being said, the depth of what was not being said.

In 1948, Bettelheim met Jeremiah Kaplan, who had just founded the Free Press, a small company producing academic works in the social sciences. Bettelheim promised to write him a monograph on the school. Almost two years later, when Bettelheim handed over the manuscript of *Love Is Not Enough*, Kaplan was dumbfounded. Although the two men, who both lived in Hyde Park, had met often in the meantime, Bettelheim had not told him that he was working on a real book, rich, exciting, and easy to read. As he would with all the books Ruth Marquis helped him with, he presented the publisher with a polished manuscript, ready to go to the printer. Kaplan tore up the initial contract, not very favorable to the author, and replaced it with a regular one.[15] *Love Is Not Enough* was to launch the Free Press into the wider world, beyond strictly academic publishing.

Some of Bettelheim's detractors have accused him of not having written his books himself. Later, he would even be accused of plagiarism. The accusations generally come from former O.S. students, Bettelheim's colleagues, and journalists, but not from people who worked directly with him in his capacity as a writer. The latter generally say: "There's no doubt about it. He wrote his books himself. Even though . . ." The qualifier is an allusion to the fact that most of his books were stitched together from pre-existing parts, such as essays, articles, case studies, and conference addresses (of which he produced a considerable quantity). Using these as building blocks, Bettelheim would play the architect. With the search for meaning as a plumb line, he designed the overall structure, stood back and took a look, then produced the cement and the missing parts. He left to his editor, at least during Ruth Marquis's tenure, the task of fixing the details. Once that had been done, he would revise the whole thing, switching a few pieces around or adding new ones.

That was particularly true of his books about the school. For raw material, Bettelheim used the dictated reports of the counselors and teachers, transcripts of staff meetings, and any other document he considered useful.[16] It was all the easier for him to do in that he had already put his name to the monthly reports that counselors and teachers had to write as well as their daily dictations. Those reports often constituted the only news about their children parents would get. Each month, and for each of the students, Bettelheim would edit one of the reports, adding his own comments and signing them. He did this to prevent any direct contact between parents and counselors, be it only through a name. The counselors belonged entirely to the children's world and he did not want parents to use the reports during vacations to undermine the relationships their children were developing in that world. This tradition, which was the rule during Bettelheim's entire tenure at the school, was well understood in the early years. Some of the later counselors, however, did not find it so easy to accept.

As for his other books, there is no doubt that the material is his own. (This does not mean that every one was composed only of new material written expressly for the book, for Bettelheim, as noted, was an expert recycler.) As the editors who succeeded Ruth Marquis appear to have been less bold about making changes than she was, one can get a pretty good idea of how Bettelheim really wrote from his later works. *The Uses of Enchantment* (1977), the first of his books produced without Marquis's help, and subsequent works have one thing in common: They are repetitive, even the very brief *Freud and Man's Soul*. The structure is in places more tangled, and less direct, than in the earlier books—but only in places, for it is clear that when Bettelheim was gripped by the force of his argument, his ideas flowed onto the paper without one word too many. One day, he admitted to Ruth Marquis that he would have liked to have written novels like those of Trollope or Austen, but added that he was unable to because the desire to write came over him only when he was carried away, either by anger or the desire to outwit a rival. (This latter aspect is nowhere more apparent than in his book reviews, of which he produced many. Most of them were ferocious.)

The 1950s was a fertile period for Bettelheim the writer. Two of his books appeared in 1950: *Love Is Not Enough* and *Dynamics of Prejudice*, the one he wrote with Morris Janowitz. His second book on the school, *Truants from Life*, appeared in 1955, a year after *Symbolic Wounds*. He was also starting to be in demand from periodicals, such as *Parents* magazine, the *University of Chicago Magazine*, and *Elementary School Journal*, for contributions on child rearing. *Scientific American*[7] published a few of his case studies, while the Jewish press wanted him to write on children's reactions to anti-Semitism. And weightier publications, such as the *American Journal of Sociology*, printed his book reviews.

Although Bettelheim's contribution to the ideas and analyses of *Dynamics of Prejudice: A Psychological and Sociological Study of Veterans* is undeniable, the book owes too much to Morris Janowitz to be a good example of Bettelheim as a writer. An analysis of racial prejudices among a group of newly returned Chicago servicemen, it was published as one of the five parts of a project on the roots of anti-Semitism commissioned just after the war by the American Jewish Committee.[18] The aim of the huge study was to determine what kind of society could give rise to Nazi-type persecution, and to see whether any of those social features were in evidence in the United States. In 1944 the Frankfurt philosopher Max Horkheimer, then living in exile in New York, and who headed the Committee's Department of Scientific Research, asked Bettelheim to take charge of one of the projects. Several ideas had been put forward, including a study comparing racial prejudice among a group of psychotics to that among a control group. Bettelheim, who was then just getting started in his project as head of the Orthogenic School, did not want to undertake such a project on his own. He therefore asked the sociologist Edward Shils, whom he had met when he worked as an examiner, to help him. Having agreed in principle, Shils was then posted in London by the military and had to stay there longer than planned. He sent Morris Janowitz to help Bettelheim out, and the two of them went ahead with the book. Having participated in the initial discussions and sent several long essays from London, Shils was taken aback when the book came out without his contributions, even though the authors paid tribute to his efforts in their introduction.[19] He remained somewhat bitter about that, although he never said so publicly.

The meeting of Bruno Bettelheim and Morris Janowitz, who had spent the previous two years monitoring and analyzing Wehrmacht radio transmissions for the OSS (U.S. secret service), was to be the start of a real friendship. The young man was already specializing in the sociology of the military, a field in which he was to be a pioneer.[20]

Bettelheim helped him deepen his understanding of, if not actually discover, psychoanalysis. The data they used for *Dynamics of Prejudice* was Janowitz's, gathered for (and used in) his PhD dissertation.[21] Bettelheim's influence could be felt in the use of Freudian concepts (inspired by Anna Freud as well as by her father) to analyze the data. That influence consisted in "reminding the reader that an individual's childhood experiences have an effect on the way he confronts the ups and downs of his existence, for example during military service," and that "the more self-assured the ego is, the less the individual needs to bolster his own sense of self by hatred that identifies another ethnic group as evil."[22] The study's conclusions are indeed quite close to those Bettelheim had reached about the anti-Semitism of the SS in the concentration camps.

With *Symbolic Wounds: Puberty Rites and the Envious Male* (1954) in contrast, Bruno Bettelheim wanted to make his mark in the realm of ideas. It was the first time he had set out to write a full-fledged book from scratch, and it was one of the works he felt the most committed to intellectually. The Orthogenic School was running the way he wanted it to, and his ability to get results was beginning to be generally acknowledged. With the excitement of the early breakthroughs having somewhat subsided, Bettelheim was in need of new challenges. He felt the time had come for him to produce an original work, for despite his new role in the world of therapy, this had remained his prime ambition. Many of those who, like him, had fled Europe, such as Heinz Hartmann, Erich Fromm, and Otto Fenichel, were hard at work creating a sequel to the history of psychoanalysis. So was Erik Erikson, whom Bettelheim had known in Vienna at a time when he was a penniless artist.[23] After a brief psychoanalysis with Anna Freud, but without any academic training, Erikson had launched a brilliant career in the United States. His *Childhood and Society*, published in 1950, was already seen as a landmark in the developing relationship between psychoanalysis and the social sciences. The time had come for Bettelheim, in his turn, to make a contribution to the growing edifice. He was to do it with an idea that had been in his mind for a long time, but that he had not been able to formulate clearly until his observations at the school confirmed it.

It was one of the children in Gayle Shulenberger Janowitz's charge who first aroused his curiosity. "Harry," as Bettelheim was to call him in *Truants from Life*, had arrived at the school at age seven. He was a perpetual runaway, and his behavior was provocative in every other way, particularly on the sexual level. He was continually showing off his erect penis, chanting, "Look at my beautiful . . . " He also had an obvious fear of castration; on one occasion he threatened to emasculate a superb snowman he had built, because, he said, it had run away. On another, sitting in his bath, he held his penis with one hand and pretended to saw it off with the other, asking Gayle: "Do you think any mother would do this to her little boy?" Speaking of his mother, Harry also used to say, "She has no tits. She's a man." In his most agitated moments, he often asked his (female) counselors to show him their penises. What struck Bettelheim most was the pleasure Harry derived, a little later and when circumstances such as Halloween allowed him to do so without being ridiculed, from dressing up as a girl. At first glance, this might be seen as resulting from his mother's treatment of him ever since his birth as a "mean boy," with all the ambiguity the idea contained, while showing loving and maternal behavior toward his sisters, who were born after him. But Bettelheim suspected something else was at work. A little later, his attention was drawn to a kind of initiation rite invented by a group of four adolescents at the school. When two of the girls began to menstruate, the boys took to cutting their own fingers every month, with the intention of mingling their blood with that of the girls.

In 1949 Bettelheim published a long case study on Harry, by then well on the way to recovery, in an academic journal.[24] Presenting it to fellow-analysts, he produced a number of hypotheses suggested to him by the behavior of his young charges. Stressing that within the safe boundaries of the school children often allowed themselves to express crude feelings that are generally repressed in society, he said he had observed expressions of a desire to belong to the opposite sex in all preadolescent children, in one form or another. He suggested that Sigmund Freud had not paid sufficient attention to this factor in his theory of the Oedipus complex. Reactions to his talk had been so aggressive and patronizing—or so, at least, he felt—that Bettelheim immediately set out to prove he was right. It was a time when many social anthropologists were flirting with psychoanalysis. Having explained his idea to Ruth Marquis, he asked her to sift through the rich ethnographic literature of the period to find data that would complement—and confirm—his observations from the school.

Symbolic Wounds is a treatise on puberty rites, particularly those centering on circumcision. Having noted that it is a universal rite, found in one form or another on all continents and at all periods of history, Bettelheim refused to see in it only the symbolic castration of sons by fathers that Freud had portrayed in his *Moses and Monotheism.* In line with the positive approach of ego psychology, Bettelheim criticized the Freudian interpretation for putting too much emphasis on the aggressive, negative aspect of the rite. In order for it to have survived everywhere, circumcision also had to have a positive function, he wrote. According to Freud, its purpose was to ensure observance of the incest taboo by generating castration anxiety. Bettelheim wondered whether it was not, on the contrary, a relatively effective way of mastering the fear that arises in a young boy's mind when he discovers that only women can bear children.

His survey of primitive societies provided him with evidence of that fear from all over the world, and of the rites aimed at surmounting it

when boys reach the age at which society expects them to fulfill their
sexual role. As the goal of such rites (to provide men with mastery
over reproduction) could never be achieved in reality, however, they
were always surrounded with a dense aura of mystery designed to
cover up that failure. That was what Bettelheim called "the secret of
men." The most astonishing example he quoted was "stopping up the
rectum," performed at puberty by the Chaga of Africa, as described
by O. F. Raum.[25] Shortly after being circumcised, a young boy was
dressed up in women's clothes, and then led into the "Men's House,"
where his true initiation would take place. This was not a physical
act, but only the simulation of one, a secret he learned only at that
moment of becoming a man. From that time on, he was supposed to
stop defecating. This was seen as a proof of his virility, just, Bettelheim stresses, as the halt of menstruation at the start of a pregnancy
was seen as a proof of womanhood. Nobody of course really believed
the men's story; the older men would give the initiate tips on how to
relieve himself without being seen, while the women would joke
among themselves about the men's secret, all the while pretending to
believe in it in their presence. But the fiction created an illusory par-
allelism between the sexes—just as the act of circumcision provided
the young boy with both the appearance of a vaginal opening, and, by
exposing the head of the penis, a permanent affirmation of his virility, thereby helping him overcome his fear about not mastering the act
of procreation.[26] Here once again is the Bettelheim for whom every
symptom, even the most apparently incomprehensible, has a meaning, and is the most appropriate way the subject has found to fight his
or her anxiety.

The tone of the book, however, is not peremptory. It is that of a
prudent seeker of truth, carefully opening up avenues of research but
refusing to close any off. The work is solidly documented, but Bettelheim is careful to emphasize his lack of credentials in anthropology.
As for his dialogue with Freudian ideas, it is more subtle than one
might expect. He does not see "vagina envy" as excluding castration
anxiety, but simply as the other side of the same coin. However, he
writes, "It seems that in any society, envy of the dominant sex is the
more easily observed."[27] And though the book's central thesis may
seem incompatible with that of *Moses and Monotheism*, Bettelheim
nevertheless bases himself on Freud's ideas to demonstrate it, as he
stresses in his dedication: "To the memory of Sigmund Freud, whose

theories on sex and the unconscious permit a fuller understanding of the mind of man."[28]

Such precautions were to no avail. Although *Symbolic Wounds* attracted a handful of enthusiastic reviews, and even today retains a small number of unconditional supporters who consider it unjustly neglected, the overall reaction to it was rather negative. The anthropologists accused Bettelheim of paternalism and ethnocentrism, since he appeared to be lumping together the rites of primitive societies and the outlandish behavior of the schizophrenics in his school. The psychoanalysts, meanwhile, were hardly less critical of Bettelheim's book, which they saw as promoting "vaginocentrism."[29]

Bettelheim may have been prepared for the criticism, but he was nevertheless hurt by the book's failure to convince his peers. He attempted to reply to the anthropologists' arguments in a second edition, revised to take certain objections into account.[30] He stressed, for example, that his use of the word *primitive* to describe desires was in no way pejorative, as he was referring to the original desires of human beings, whoever they may be. And that if he lumped together children, schizophrenics, and "primitive" peoples, it was simply because those desires were more visible in such people than in "normal" adults in Western societies. This did not convince the critics, however.[31]

But the book deserves better than the disdain most experts have continued to show it. Some observers still see it as being ahead of its time. Whatever the case, it at least had the merit of asking an original question, from an unusual viewpoint, in a field in which research and theory had always been, with a few notable exceptions, dominated by the masculine viewpoint. *Symbolic Wounds* marked an important stage in Bettelheim's life. As Ruth Marquis notes, it summed up "all he thought about men and women." Ben Wright confirms that Bettelheim was "not angry, but hurt" by the incomprehension that greeted it. This time, he had tried to state the whole unvarnished truth as he really saw it. He had indeed tried to do away with fraud, since he had gone so far as to reveal "the secret of men"—that phallic superiority is a myth, one that can only be perpetuated with at least the tacit acquiescence of women. And his conclusion was above all an appeal for tolerance, because the acceptance by our societies of the individual's polyvalent tendencies "would go a long way to lessen the negative effects of the antithesis between the sexes." He adds: "If we could give greater recognition to boys' desire to bear children, to the desire of male adolescents and adult men for the more passive and leisurely enjoyment of life, instead of having always to 'fight and to strut,' our boys and men might feel less envy and anxious hostility toward girls and women." They would then also have less need to "assert power through destructive inventions," Bettelheim concluded.[32]

For anyone interested in Bettelheim's life, and not just his ideas, these words take on a somewhat tragic dimension. This appeal for society to recognize, behind the deceptive image of the all-powerful phallus, the right of men also to be fragile, can indeed be heard as a cry from the too-powerful and too-responsible director of the Orthogenic School, seeking to make people realize that he was only human under the magician's costume that he could don to such convincing effect.

"If I had to sum up in one word what I learned from him, I would say: autonomy," says Ruth Marquis. That indeed was Bettelheim's aim, to turn the children in his charge, his college students, and the young people who worked for him into autonomous, responsible, self-respecting adults, capable of running their own lives, fully aware of the choices facing them, and in full possession of their faculties. Capable of loving and working, as Freud said when summing up the aims of psychoanalysis. Throughout his life, Bettelheim would respect people who could stand up to him and maintain their integrity, whatever treatment he meted out to them. He did not much like resistance, but if that resistance sprang from real feelings, he respected it. What he really hated was what he called "passive aggressivity": hostility that dared not speak its name.

Being able to stand up to him, or at least resist being overwhelmed by him, was a matter of temperament, not age. Adrian Kuypers, who was a student at the school for a long time before returning as a teacher, adored Bettelheim, and the feeling was mutual. But even as a child, she never let him affect her to the point where she lost sight of her own identity. "Dr. B thought I was anorexic. I didn't think that was true. But I didn't say anything, because he seemed to like the idea." And indeed, in a photo published in *Love Is Not Enough* where the eight-year-old Adrian is seen reading a book, her arms are far from skinny. But the exact diagnosis was not very important.[33] What counted was that, while acknowledging that Bettelheim was doing a great deal for her and that she was afraid of him ("he could see right away what you were thinking and all the terrible things you had done"), she was aware that "there was always that softness inside of him," and never believed him to be infallible.

That was by no means the case for everyone. The spreading fame of Bettelheim's books had started to affect the people around him. Now the mothers who brought him their children were expecting miracles; they had read *Love Is Not Enough*. And as the years of Depression and war had given way to a new affluence, the profile of the students who applied to work at the school had also changed. No longer were most of them tough, hardworking young women who saw Bettelheim as an immigrant who had lost everything and wanted to help him in doing something useful before having children of their own. Those who came knocking on his door now had grown up in better times, and had more college degrees, as over the years Bettelheim had become more demanding on that score. But they were also more malleable and more fragile. And for some of them the fact that women's roles were now less clearly defined than before, which meant their stint at the school could be seen as the start of a career, only added to their anxiety. Psychoanalytic jargon now permeated the media, and the once-poor immigrant had become a renowned public figure. The desire to do good was still there, but applicants for counselors' jobs now no longer came to help Dr. B as much as to seek help—and answers—from him.

Just when did Bettelheim first encourage one of his counselors to lie down on the couch in his office for a session? It is difficult to say with any precision since, as Gayle Janowitz points out, the distinctions were blurred from the outset. Those one-on-one discussions in the director's office could be seen as debriefing sessions on the counselor's work, supervisory activity, personal talks, or all of the above. Some of the counselors who had regular appointments with Bettelheim would see them simply as an opportunity to deepen their professional understanding. As Diana Grossman Kahn, a counselor from 1961 to 1969, puts it: "It was the one occasion when an incident could be analyzed, not in terms of the child's welfare, but of mine."[34] It is true she had been in analysis before arriving at the school, and was thus able to tell the difference. Others, however, were certainly convinced that the regular meetings they had with Bettelheim in the privacy of his office amounted to an analysis, or in any case to psychotherapy.

During the first years of his directorship, Bettelheim encouraged his staff to seek therapy outside the establishment. And right up until the end of his tenure, he would hand out the names of analysts to anyone who asked for them. But quite early on, it seems, he stopped broaching the subject. In fact, practical considerations—the low pay and long working hours—ruled out outside therapy for all but the most determined staff members. In the unlikely event that the counselor could set aside the money to pay for it, he or she would have to find the time for the sixty-minute roundtrip commute downtown, where most analysts had their offices, plus the time for the treatment, several times weekly. A few brave souls tried it, but gave up after a few months. As Dr. B was right there, and as the young people had the opportunity to witness his astonishing gifts of understanding daily, it was difficult to resist his helping hand, whenever he honored them by offering it.

Bettelheim did not in fact call it analysis, or even therapy, but rather "dynamic supervision," which was how he explained this aspect of his work to Bert Cohler when the latter was about to succeed him as director (see chapter 16). He liked to say that psychoanalysis was "the icing on the cake," implying that he and his staff at the school were still at the stage of making the cake itself. Bettelheim also explained that although milieu therapy was everyday life organized according to Freudian principles, it was not psychoanalysis. For his staff, however, a regular appointment with him became a status symbol. Strong rivalry existed between the counselors, and those who were "in therapy with Dr. B" most certainly earned extra points with their colleagues. He knew this, and at times he used it. On a few occasions he even offered sessions to a counselor who was about to leave the school. Some of those who accepted were glad they did so; others now regret that they did not go through with their initial decision to leave. Still others simply said no.

George Kaiser, who worked at the school from 1948 to 1952, was one of the latter. It is a subject he still finds embarrassing, as he has retained not only a lot of affection but also a profound admiration for Bettelheim. Having instinctively perceived the incident as manipulative when it occurred, he finds it difficult to talk about. And yet Bettelheim's relationships with men were simpler than those with women. What had first impressed Dr. B about Kaiser, a twenty-seven-year-old Jewish American, was the fact that he had served in the U.S. Air Force during the war. When taking visitors through Kaiser's class, he would always introduce him with the words: "This is George Kaiser, who dropped bombs over Germany." Kaiser had been attracted to the school by the stories his wife, Cathy, brought back from the mothers' Wednesday meetings. He had quickly realized, however, that although one could learn a lot at the school, it was very clear who was boss. He went to offer his services as a teacher, but Bettelheim insisted that he first take charge of a group as a counselor for six months, "so you can see what the school is all about."

One day during his first week, George picked up his group after class. "What are we doing this afternoon?" the children shouted, jumping all around him in the hallway. "Let's go into the dorm and talk about it" was his reply. But Bettelheim, who was observing the scene, interrupted him. "You tell them now, George," he said sternly. A few minutes later, softening his tone, he added: "You see, Tom and Bobby can wait till they get to the dorm. But Billy can't. That's why you've got to tell him now." Like other counselors, George Kaiser was faced with the sudden realization that he had a lot to learn before he could respond spontaneously to these children's needs. But he also could not forget that the incident had taken place in public.

Later on, Bettelheim gave him the impression that he would like to groom him to be his successor. In June 1952, he made Kaiser his deputy director. He was thus in charge of receiving the parents and chairing staff meetings during Dr. B's absences, in particular his August vacation. George found the position uncomfortable, however. As the staff meetings were always tape-recorded, Bettelheim made a few critical remarks on his return. Even in the subsidiary tasks he was given, Kaiser felt he did not have any real scope for initiative. For while Dr. B allowed his counselors plenty of leeway in dealing with the children, he could exercise his prerogative on any detail, however minor, from the color of the curtains to the contents of the candy closet. Kaiser therefore decided to take a job at the Lab School, on the other side of the Midway. It was then that Bettelheim made the offer of therapy sessions, which Kaiser turned down.

Here again, it is easy to rush to judgment and condemn Bettelheim over appearances, but much harder to reach a truly informed opinion. From a formal point of view, things are relatively clear: An arrangement in which one person acts as both the school's director and the staff's psychotherapist is subject to criticism. Fantasies are one thing, reality another, and to mix them up is to open the door to all sorts of manipulative behavior. In practice, however, things are more complicated. Bettelheim was certainly neither the first nor the only head of a psychiatric institution to wear both hats at once. And the way he worked with, or rather through, his counselors did indeed create a relationship of transference, not unlike the one an analysand develops with his or her analyst. The fact that in some cases he considered it useful, either for the counselor herself or for the children in her group, to analyze that relationship during one-on-one sessions is not in itself shocking. It is certainly not very orthodox, but then was it not the function of the Orthogenic School to seek new solutions? Furthermore, the authority Bettelheim wielded over most of his counselors was such that it would have necessarily interfered with any transferential relationship they developed with an outside analyst.

Conversely, if a counselor had developed a strong therapeutic relationship outside the school, it would probably have interfered with Bettelheim's power; it should not be forgotten that the counselors themselves saw the children in one-on-one sessions, and it was essential that Bettelheim retain his ability to supervise those relationships. After all, the children had been put in his care. Being in a good position to appreciate the power that the process of transference gives to the analyst, he knew that if his counselors were to undergo analyses outside, "his" children would in effect be falling under the authority of other analysts. Could he, who continually criticized his fellow-practitioners, accusing them of being mainly interested in money, allow that to happen?

The school's therapeutic system had two tiers: children–counselors, and counselors–Dr. B, and one could not work without the other. Although some counselors labored under an illusion, their function as Bettelheim saw it was not really to act as therapists. If he asked them to see two or three children for regular one-on-one sessions, the aim was for them to deepen their relationship, to give the students an opportunity for individual contact, not to engage in analysis. That was his job (which he carried out both via the reports of the counselors, and through his relationship with them) and, secondarily, that of the consultant psychiatrist. The former counselor Leslie Cleaver, who is herself an experienced psychotherapist, explains the difference well: "We didn't analyze the transference as you would in a regular session because we also had a parental function with the kids. The point in milieu therapy is that you deal with what actually happens and how the kid feels about it at the time. So that the kid can get organized around you, the other kids in the dormitory, and Dr B, and that they become aware of how they feel. But you don't deal with it as if it was from the past. You deal with it in the present."[35] Bettelheim provided implicit confirmation of this in 1971, when, after leaving the school in the hands of Bert Cohler, he returned nine months later to resume control. In his absence the psychoanalyst Al Flarsheim, a consultant at the school, had started giving the counselors a little training in therapy, explaining certain mechanisms of the unconscious and how to deal with them. Although Bettelheim was fond of Flarsheim, a young analyst who had attended his seminars and was also in frequent contact with Donald Winnicott in London, he immediately wanted to put a stop to the courses. He was prevented from doing so by strong opposition from a handful of counselors (see chapter 16). But that only went to show that the school had already started slipping out of his hands.

That then was the Bettelheim system. The specialists will no doubt hand down their verdicts, if they can. One can simply hope that their judgments will be based not on preconceived ideas, but by comparing the principles with the practical results, and without forgetting the conditions under which the system operated. Besides, Bettelheim's therapeutic practices were not a secret in any real sense; it was not because he had asked them to keep quiet that the counselors did not talk much about them to people outside. From the early 1960s, the fact that he played therapist with his (mainly female) counselors was an open secret in Chicago's psychoanalytic and psychiatric community. It was the object of much whispering, generally with suggestive overtones. Ugo Formigoni's wife, Maurie, experienced this after leaving the school. "So you worked at the Orthogenic School? And were you in therapy with Bettelheim? On the couch?" She got tired of hearing such remarks from colleagues of Ugo, whom she had married after he left the school. As she found them both unpleasant and unfair, she would refuse to reply, a fact that probably only gave more currency to the rumors.

Depending on whom one speaks to, the end of the "magical" period at the school can be situated between 1951 and 1956. In a letter congratulating Gayle on her marriage in 1951, Bettelheim already expresses nostalgia for the old days. Then he backtracks: "They weren't [better]. We have now a better school," adding: "But I was younger and had more idealism." A turning point certainly seems to have been reached in 1952. That year, Bettelheim had a son, and he also achieved tenure as a professor in the Department of Education. Meanwhile, the extension and renovation of the school was completed. With an extra building and new play areas, the environment had changed completely, and the number of groups rose from four to six.

Soon the rule that required students to leave the school at age four-teen was dropped. Early experience had shown that results could only be obtained over time, and it was often just when a child was begin-ning to improve that he had to leave. Although Dr. B had devoted a lot of energy to finding suitable foster families to take care of such children, many would stop improving, or even regress, on leaving the school. Some asked to return; others experienced their departure as a rejection, and suffered from it. Meanwhile, the break between the children and their parents became more pronounced. Now when a child was admitted, Bettelheim demanded that he not see his family at all for at least the first nine months, whereas in the early years, the students had often spent all their vacations with their parents, except in severe cases.[36] But they would frequently return disturbed and filled with anxiety once again, as if months of effort had been wasted. Of course, the children were allowed to receive mail, but for the same reason this was read by the counselors before being given to them. In the mid-1950s the idea that parents alone were responsible for the psychological problems of their children was widespread in profes-sional circles; Bettelheim was simply putting it into practice.

The six-week trial period, during which the counselors tried to see whether they could get through to a child, was also dropped. It no longer had much meaning, because the school was now beginning to take in children who were more and more seriously disturbed. On a visit a few years after her departure, Bettylou Pingree told Gayle Janowitz that the school looked much more like a psychiatric ward than it had in their time. Thanks to the influx of donations and grants, however, the surroundings had been greatly improved. From the start, Bettelheim had done everything he could to ensure that the children had pleasant living conditions; now he wanted them to be luxurious. The old flower-patterned sofas were replaced by velvet-upholstered items, and the plastic crockery by fine china. Bettelheim even brought in red crystal drinking glasses. The theory was that surrounding the children with beautiful objects was a way of show-ing them that they were accepted, and that their well-being was the number-one priority for both himself and the staff. Both Gayle Janowitz and Bert Cohler think he went too far, however. "It was more to please himself than the kids. Besides, the old furniture was much more comfortable," says Cohler, who after being a student at the school until 1956 went back to work there in 1969.

At the university, Bettelheim's reputation was by now well established. His aggressiveness toward his students was legendary, but far from driving away recruits, it tended to attract them. Bernice Neugarten, who ran the Committee on Human Development, recalls that two or three times as many students would be enrolled for Bettelheim's courses at the start of the year as for any other teacher's. This did not worry her much, however; she knew that after a couple of weeks, many of them would be asking to switch.

He was respected for his results, but was also in conflict with many of his peers who questioned his ideas and methods. He was an indefatigable worker, who seemed to be everywhere at once, forever churning out courses, lectures, and articles, while still managing to read hundreds of pages of reports and dictations every month in his capacity as director-cum-therapist. But the latter task provided him with the opportunity to know every last detail of what was going on, and thus the temptation to exercise universal control. And although he had demonstrated the necessary limits to such omnipotence in *Symbolic Wounds*, the tendency increased over the years. After the lukewarm response to that book, in which he had sought to state his own personal truth, but one that hardly anyone had wanted to hear, Bettelheim returned to writing about the school.

Ruth Marquis had left Chicago, but she and Bettelheim stayed in touch. At her request, she assembled *Dialogues with Mothers* because Bettelheim did not really believe in the project. She worked from the transcribed recordings of the meetings, which she had attended before becoming a mother herself. She also played an important part in putting together *The Informed Heart*, insisting that Bettelheim include more of his own feelings in the work and interviewing him to help him recall the inner tumult he had experienced at Buchenwald.

Once a manuscript was complete, she would shut herself away at home for a few days and dip into her favorite writings, in particular the poems of William Blake. Then she would draw up a list of twenty or so possible titles, from which Bettelheim would make his choice. Sometimes she would use an expression drawn from the text itself, such as "empty fortress," which had been used by one of the teachers at the school, Luitgard Wundheiler, in a report on an autistic boy in her class. Ruth Marquis provided Bettelheim with the titles for all his books, with the exception of *Symbolic Wounds*. They were such good titles, showing such a subtle understanding of the text, that they became common property around Bettelheim.[37] A former student related a conversation he had with Bettelheim as he was about to leave the school at age fourteen. He was discussing his mother and said: "Oh, you know, everything she did to me, she did out of love." Then, after pausing for a few seconds, he blurted out: "But love is not enough." The incident no doubt occurred—after the book's publication. But such is the power of words, when they suddenly take on their full meaning, that the former student is convinced that he gave the phrase to Dr. B.

Ruth Marquis's role in helping Bettelheim shape his ideas was so important to him that he not only provided the standard acknowledgments in each of his books that she worked on, but also dedicated one of them to her. That was *The Empty Fortress*, which came out in 1967. It was one of the last books she was to be involved with, for toward the end of the 1960s she no longer agreed with all of Bettelheim's ideas. The divergence was initially political: their opinions on issues such as the Vietnam War and the student revolt were at odds. Then, more subtly, she began to observe that sometimes the effect of her friend's books was the exact opposite of what he had been aiming at. One day, she found one of her neighbors in tears. "I did it all wrong," the woman wailed, having just read a few pages of *Love Is Not Enough*. Ruth had tried to calm her down, explaining that Bettelheim did not provide recipes to be applied word for word, but that his aim, on the contrary, was to encourage young mothers to be freer and more spontaneous in their relationships with their children. At the same time, she felt somehow responsible for her neighbor's distress. So in the early 1970s, when she learned of his latest manuscript, she blurted out: "Oh no! We're not now going to start telling mothers how and when to read fairy tales to their children!" Bettelheim did everything he could to get her to change her mind, but to no avail. While declining to work on the book, she nevertheless gave him a title for it: *The Uses of Enchantment*.

•

13

❋

The Ultimate Limit

My task which I am trying to achieve is, by power of the written word to make you hear, to make you feel—it is, before all, to make you *see*. That—and no more, and it is everything. If I succeed, you shall find there according to your deserts: encouragement, consolation, fear . . . and, perhaps, also that glimpse of truth for which you have forgotten to ask.

> *Joseph Conrad*, The Nigger of the Narcissus, *quoted by Bettelheim as the last lines of* Surviving

"My life is my work, Trude and the children. And, if I am completely honest, in that order," Bruno Bettelheim wrote to a friend in September 1954.[1] The director of the Orthogenic School had indeed little time to devote to his family. When he woke up, around 9:30, his wife and children had already left. On weekdays, he would return home between 6:30 and 7. After freshening up, he would join the family for the evening meal. Dinnertime was sacred in the Bettelheim household. It was a European affair with a tablecloth and napkins, a formal style that used to grate somewhat on Bettelheim's daughters. They were forbidden to leave the table before the meal was over, a rule that was relaxed somewhat in the 1960s, when it was their brother Eric's turn to fidget with impatience while waiting to go outside and play.

After dinner, Bettelheim would relax for a while. He would sometimes play cards or another game with the children, especially when
Fritz Redl was there. While Trude was busy bathing Eric, or tidying
up the kitchen, he would also help the girls with their homework
when needed. Or else he read the counselors' dictations while drinking his coffee. Then, around 9:30, he would return to the school. This
was the routine six days a week. On Sundays he would get up a little
later than usual, and the family would enjoy a leisurely brunch. But
in the afternoon Bettelheim would be off again to the school.

People who dined informally at the Bettelheims' home, such as
Gina Weinmann, her daughter Catherine, or Ruth Marquis, all recall
that the conversation was lively, and that one had to fight to get a
word in. Bruno and Trude would discuss world affairs, or their
respective jobs, which both were totally caught up in. And their elder
daughter, Ruth, would try very hard to catch their, or rather her
father's, attention. Her younger sister, Naomi, was the only member
of the family to remain aloof, lost in daydreams and playing little
part in dinner-table conversations. "She was like Cinderella," says
one eyewitness. It might be more accurate to describe her as a wild
flower, growing free without needing to be tended. "I have two
daughters," Bettelheim liked to say. "One of them had to be continuously pampered throughout her childhood, the other one would
have been top of her class, no matter what."[2] And when a psychoanalyst friend of his once asked him why he was "so hard on Naomi
and so lenient on Ruth," he did not feel guilty at all—or so he would
write later.[3] Of his three children, Naomi was the one who most
resembled him, both physically and intellectually. Lively and intelligent, she had the same biting sense of humor as her father, and her
little face was often screwed up into a frown. Some observers even
thought they could detect some rivalry in Bettelheim's attitude
toward his younger daughter.

Caught between an elder sister who did everything she could to
monopolize their father during the rare moments he spent with them,
and a kid brother who was their mother's pride and joy, Naomi had
decided early on that she had better make her own life for herself,
independent of the family dramas. She had her own interests, her
girlfriends, her books, and her school life. She was not quite eight
years old in 1953 when the Bettelheims moved into a townhouse at
5725 Kenwood Avenue, but when asked which bedroom she wanted
for herself, she had no hesitation in picking the only one on the top

floor. In early childhood, her best friend had been Catherine Weinmann, who was born a month after her. And when Gina and her family moved from Hyde Park to faraway Highland Park, one of the affluent suburbs north of Chicago, Naomi would often go and stay with the Weinmanns during weekends and school vacations.

Bettelheim's relationship with his elder daughter was more complicated.[4] Later he would attribute his problems with Ruth to the fact that she had been born when he and Trude were still recently arrived immigrants, struggling to make their way and living in precarious conditions. To make up for the time he was unable to spend with her, he was continually buying her gifts. This was why, he would explain, she had turned into "a grabby little girl."[5] Although this explanation sounds a little self-serving, there is ample evidence that Ruth was indeed what is called a spoiled child, moody and difficult. She needed to be loved and admired, and to be constantly reassured that she was. For example, she hated having to wear the clothes her mother picked for her. Pragmatic above all, and conditioned by her Montessori training, Trude did not share the enthusiasm of many American mothers for ribbons and frills. When she found comfortable and sensible garments at the school's yearly rummage sale, she had no qualms about buying them. As Trude worked a great deal, Ruth also had to learn to dress herself very early on. One day her nursery school teacher made a disparaging comment on her report card about the way she was dressed, which left Ruth with a deep feeling of injustice.

Ruth was nevertheless the eldest child, adored by both her parents and particularly by her father. In her early years, she was often a source of worry, due to a series of minor problems. According to an unconfirmed story Bettelheim told some friends, he took her to the hospital one day to see whether she was suffering from a urinary ailment, as she had suddenly started wetting her bed again. Such was the vogue at the time for psychological explanations of everything that the doctor burst into laughter: "What, even you, Dr. Bettelheim!" But, Bettelheim concluded triumphantly, Ruth did indeed have a urinary ailment.[6] When Ruth was eight, her father wrote an article titled "How to Arm Our Children Against Anti-Semitism" in which he recounted how his daughter had at a very early age wondered aloud why a friend had called her a "Shoe" and, a little later, how she had been very upset by more explicit racist comments (and how he had managed to defend her).[7] Later on, he became worried that she did not have any friends; both Trude and he devoted much energy to remedying that situation. Later still, he worried about the company she was keeping, particularly during her hippie phase. He introduced her to other young people, and at one point he reportedly even tried to convince an already married Ben Wright to spend more time with Ruth. And in 1968, when his younger daughter, then living in Mexico, announced her engagement, he said to Gayle Janowitz: "Naomi should have waited for her elder sister to marry first!" However advanced his ideas may have been in his work, at home Bruno Bettelheim was quite simply a father like other fathers, and a rather old-fashioned one to boot.

One weekend in 1947, the Bettelheims were visiting the Sheviakovs in Oregon when somebody suggested going for a walk. Everyone was in favor except Bettelheim, and as two-year-old Naomi was likely to slow the party down, it was decided that she should stay behind with her father. He immediately dropped into a rocking chair and started reading; the little girl soon became bored and started playing with her diaper. When the group returned, some two hours later, they found Naomi busily smearing excrement over the living room walls, while her father was rocking furiously back and forth. The story unfortunately does not tell at exactly what point Bettelheim looked up from his book and discovered what was going on. Too late, no doubt, for him to imagine that he could actually do something about it!

"At home, he was a different man," Ruth Marquis recalls. "He was always apologetic. For being late, for not being able to start the car, for not having done this or that." She remembers Trude speaking sharply to her husband on occasion, sometimes with a measure of irritation. Marquis's description seems at odds with those of other observers, who paint an almost contrary picture with Bettelheim often being rather offhanded with his wife. This may be simply due to the fact that Marquis left Chicago in the early fifties, but it could also have to do with her being one of the very few people who saw Bettelheim at close range in both his worlds; the Big Bad Wolf usually shed his coat on leaving the school for home. It is true, however, that the relationship between Bruno and Trude Bettelheim seems to have undergone quite a change after he started running the Orthogenic School. The first counselors remember a day when Trude arrived at the school in tears and closeted herself with Bettelheim in his office. It was not in keeping with her character, and the onlookers assumed that she was at the end of her rope, having to wait endless hours for her husband. The cause of her distress may well have been something else entirely, but that was the explanation that seemed obvious.

Bettelheim ended up behaving somewhat like a guest in his own home, leaving the running of the house entirely to Trude. She took care of everything: the children, the housekeeping, his clothes, the car, even the family dog and the gardening (at which she became very proficient). The only practical aspect of the family home that Bettelheim took an interest in was the decoration and furnishings. With the exception of the children's bedrooms, which were left up to them, he made all the decisions in that area, and even built the family's bookshelves himself.

In the mid-1960s, Bettelheim was to spend some seven weeks at an Israeli kibbutz, researching what would become *The Children of the Dream* (see chapter 15). After his departure, on entering the little apartment in which he had stayed, the woman who had made sure that he received a change of sheets every week was shocked on discovering the six pairs, untouched, piled up on a chair! In Chicago, however, Bettelheim's dislike for any type of housework was well known, and he made no excuses for it. "Most of us are quite happy to master one of two environments (professional and domestic) and let the other marital partner take care of the other," he would say.[8]

That statement, of course, did not apply to Trude. She had her own professional life to deal with, along with her domestic functions. Now a trained pediatric social worker, she worked full time for the Chicago Child Care agency. Although her specialty was play therapy, she was in charge of adoptions. She found adoptive families, carried out checks on them, and monitored the children once placed. It was work she loved, and she did it with total dedication. To help her with the housework, she had hired Lillian, a black woman from the South. Intelligent, skilled and devoted, Lillian quickly became an indispensable member of the Bettelheim household, acting as a stand-in mother for the children during the day. She was to stay with the family until Eric left home to go to college, toward the end of the 1960s. Later, when Lillian fell ill, Naomi made sure, from faraway Vienna where she was then living, that she was well taken care of until her death.

Trude's heavy workload probably grew heavier with the realization, increasing day by day, of just how much her husband was getting drawn into his work, in a frenzy of activity that excluded practically everything else. If that was the case, however, she never said so publicly, and even in private, it is doubtful she ever expressed it fully either, for she knew how much his work meant to him. But the situation no doubt left its mark on her. Some people now tended to interpret her natural reserve as a sign of coldness.

Others, on the contrary, had enormous admiration for her courage, intelligence, boundless energy, and the great compassion she brought to her work. But Trude Bettelheim was so good at hiding her feelings that nobody was able to give me the slightest idea of what it must have meant to her to see her husband spending so much time surrounded by young women, many of them attractive, over whom he had almost absolute power and most of whom idolized him. If she did feel jealous, she must have had extraordinary strength of character, for nobody I interviewed would even venture a hypothesis on the subject. But quite early on, Trude stopped visiting the Orthogenic School, except to admire some new fixture or extension at the invitation of her husband.

At first, the barrier between the two halves of Bettelheim's world was not absolute. Many of the first counselors even did some babysitting at his home on occasion. Their relations with Trude were straightforward and friendly; only Paula Bettelheim, on her occasional visits to her son, intimidated them. After the first two or three years, however, the director of the Orthogenic School stopped inviting his colleagues to his home, except for the party he threw each New Year for the school staff.

Shortly after Naomi's birth, in 1945, the Bettelheims moved into a larger apartment. The best bedroom was assigned to the girls and the smallest was Bruno's, which was separate from Trude's. To anyone who dared ask him why, he would explain that in his view a man should enter his wife's room only when she invited him to do so. Later, his teenage daughters would often joke about the subject, expressing amazement that they had even been conceived, and wondering at what time of night such an event could have taken place. Bettelheim's lair was tiny, and crammed with books, statuettes, and other items purchased on his various travels. The children would go there in the summer to play Monopoly, as it was the only air-conditioned room in the apartment. Bettelheim was meticulous in his personal habits, and Naomi liked to observe him as he groomed himself, clipping his fingernails or wielding a small circular mirror and a pair of tweezers to pluck out stubble that had escaped his razor.

It would be mistaken to conclude—as some visitors, mainly male, did—that Trude no longer counted for much in Bettelheim's life after he took over the Orthogenic School. As he himself said in the letter quoted at the start of this chapter, and as he would repeat countless times in the five and a half years between his wife's death and the day he killed himself, his relationship with Trude was the most important thing in his life, apart from his work. In that same letter, in which he summed up the preceding two decades of his life, he also wrote: "My first years in America were not easy, but they were nevertheless much better—not materially, but emotionally—than what I had before [in Vienna]." And as his correspondent knew Trude well, he added: "I am convinced that our marriage is the best one possible, the best I could ever have had."

The statement is interesting, for although the first impression it may give is of lukewarm feelings, what it does express is the poor image Bettelheim continued to have of himself, in spite of all his success, and the arrogance he could display in public. The letter is that of a man who knows how to count his lucky stars, a man who truly appreciates what life has given him. "Back there, I rarely admitted it to myself, but in fact I always wanted to be a university professor . . . It can therefore be said that I have fulfilled my childhood dream. I still have a hard time believing that all these good things have really happened to me: Trude, the children, my job. And I am happy that I am not so arrogant as to believe that all this was my due. I have been incredibly lucky."

This was a far cry indeed from the public image of Dr. B, the rising star of child psychology and a man renowned for his stinging remarks and short temper. And it was a far cry even from the warmer image the school's counselors had of him, of a man of such towering authority that it left no room for any kind of doubt. Very few people ever met that serene Bettelheim, a man at peace with himself, no longer haunted by feelings of illegitimacy. And it is on that level I believe that Trude's influence was essential in his life. As if to prove it, she indeed comes first in the above quotation.

From the young women he worked with, Bettelheim gained reassurance on two important points: the value of his work and his power of seduction. But deeper still there remained a gnawing doubt that only Trude seems to have been capable of silencing, concerning his very right to exist. And indeed, every evening before going back to the school, Bettelheim spent some time alone with Trude, usually in his room. What he saw reflected in the admiring eyes of his counselors was an image of the larger-than-life person he wanted to be. But he needed Trude, who really knew him as he was, warts and all, and who saw beyond all his clever stories, to help him truly accept himself. On his own, he was incapable of finding such reassurance. In the last years of his life, the flattering image reflected back at him by his entourage, far from satisfying him, only served to strengthen his own lack of self-respect. The more he appeared great and beautiful, the more he felt small and ugly inside.

During a conference on the student revolt of the late 1960s, Bettelheim was to give a very simple explanation of what he saw as the role of the family: "We all need a place where we can let our hair down, where we can expect understanding, generous acceptance of us as we are, including our failings. Our perfections everybody will appreciate. For them we do not need a family. What makes a family is the readiness with which it accepts our failures and shortcomings."[9] As usual, Bettelheim drew from his own life a lesson filled with humanity and wisdom. But as was often the case, the ideal he put forward was in fact unattainable. Parents capable of accepting everything without passing judgment was the role he had conferred on the counselors of the Orthogenic School, and no doubt the role Trude played in his life. But once again it was a role that he, as a father, had a difficult time fulfilling.

Bettelheim's relationship with his own children is often questioned by his critics: "He was so hard on other parents," they say in essence, "but what kind of a father could he himself have been, spending all his time with the school kids?" The question may also be asked at a less strictly material level. For the outside world, Bettelheim was a magician and a leader, a creator of rules and a wielder of authority. At home, the presence of Trude allowed him to be simply a fallible human being, with weaknesses that could be accepted. And indeed this setup did not leave much room for his own children. The way he himself saw it can be found in a letter written to Ruth Marquis in 1973: "Many things I did wrong, as does any parent, but I never felt guilty . . . I was always convinced that we as parents had to live our own lives, were doing the best we knew by our children, convinced that this would be enough."[10] The family spent a month of vacation together each year, generally in the Rocky Mountains or on the New England coast in the early years; later, it would often be in California and occasionally Europe. What is certain is that Bettelheim did not behave toward his children in the same way he behaved with the students at his school. He was at once more absentminded and more indulgent—perhaps as Anton had been with him. Later, after Trude's death, he was to maintain something of a buddy relationship with his son, to the extent that some observers occasionally wondered which one was the father.

But although Bettelheim's children can justifiably accuse him of having always given a higher priority to his work than to them while they were growing up, those critics who describe him as an absentee father are mistaken. Family was extremely important to him, as his correspondence throughout his life shows. His children were part of his life, even though he did not look after them very much. He talked to them when he was at home, took an interest in what they had to say, and although each of them at one time or another felt anger toward him, none of them appears to have at any time doubted the strength of the bonds between them." Once again, the point is not to pass judgment on whether or not Bettelheim was a "bad father" (each person is free to draw their own conclusions on that), but to try to understand what made this complex man tick. His absences did show that he had more exciting things to do with his time than to spend it with his children, but not that they were not important to him. He knew they were in good hands, with Trude and Lillian to look after them. He may even have feared, consciously or not, reproducing with them the errors that had overshadowed his own childhood. On Trude's side, there was no family curse to worry about. Her childhood had been a happy one, in spite of her mother's preference for her brother. She at least had enjoyed a rich and strong relationship with her father.

Bettelheim had lost his mother. Paula died in 1953; Bettelheim had her ashes sent back to Austria, to be buried alongside those of her husband.

"My life is my work, Trude and the children . . . " When he drew up that list, in September 1954, Bettelheim omitted another important aspect of his "second life," and one that, as he stressed a little earlier in the same letter, bore "surprisingly little relation" to the previous one. This was the inner work he was pursuing about the key experience that had catapulted him into his American life: his period at Dachau and Buchenwald. Gayle, however, remembers clearly. "He read everything that was published on the concentration camps. His desk was stacked with books." For alongside his professional work, Bettelheim continued all through his life with a process of self-analysis to develop his thinking on these subjects, which, given the circumstances, had triggered in him a highly personal struggle.

The first long article he wrote on his own after his arrival in the United States was devoted to his camp experience, and the final chapters of his last book, *Freud's Vienna*, published nearly half a century later, were to be on the same subject. The very construction of *Surviving*, which came out around eleven years before his death and can be viewed as his testament on the subject, confirms that Bettelheim continually reworked and thought about the camps and the Nazi genocide throughout his American life. For this collection of essays, assembled thirty-some years after that first article on the camps, he included a longer version of that article, stripping it of the personal anecdotes he had added for *The Informed Heart* and returning it to its impersonal third-person form. One wonders about this to-ing and fro-ing between the *I* and the *he*, of which another example is the article about the frostbite incident (see chapter 7). Why was it always when he was writing about the concentration camps that this practice occurred? What were the memories he was wrestling with, what fear was he trying to conquer, what was the dark secret he wanted to free himself of?

In order to unravel this painful inner process, which had indisputable repercussions for his work as a therapist, we need to temporarily step outside the chronology of his life to follow the thread of his thinking. An examination of the main texts he wrote on the subject, in the order in which he wrote them, reveals three main periods.

Following the publication of his first article on the camps, Bettelheim's views had become the benchmark for a handful of progressive newspapers on issues relating to the Nazis' persecution of the Jews. His articles were appreciated because they were different from others, they always provided food for thought, questioning received wisdom and raising new questions. For example, when in 1945 the American occupation forces obliged groups of Germans to visit the concentration camp sites with a view to educating them, Bettelheim did not join in the general applause, but instead pointed out the dangers the approach entailed. To blame an entire people for a crime was undemocratic, he explained; it would be better to identify those responsible and publicly punish them. Showing piles of dead bodies to Germans selected at random might have no other effect than to convince them that they had been right all along not to try to oppose the Nazis![12]

Writing before the start of the Nuremberg trials, he tried to show his American readers how the German people must have felt, exhausted by the war, weary of politics, and suspicious of their victors. For the trials to make an impression on them, he pointed out, the notion of individual responsibility (a concept they had become unfamiliar with over the twelve years of Hitler's rule) was not enough: they would have to be made conscious of their own involvement in the Nazi machine, for example by the indictment of organizations that one or more members of every German family had joined. At the same time, it was important that Nuremberg not appear to be the trial of a whole nation, which could only unite all Germans against the prosecutor. Mission impossible, Bettelheim concluded.[13]

Then, as his first writings on the Orthogenic School were appearing in print, Bettelheim published his two articles on frostbite and the incident at the Buchenwald infirmary.[14] To illustrate the dangers of stereotyping one's enemy, he was, as we have seen, harsh in his judgment of his fellow-prisoners. In 1948, he was to focus his anger on the American Jews, accusing them of irresponsibility for supporting the ill-fated voyage of the *Exodus*, a vessel packed with Jewish war refugees from central Europe, some of them former concentration camp inmates, which in July 1947 was turned back by the British authorities when it tried to dock without permission in Palestine. After much suffering among its passengers, the ship eventually headed to France, from where the refugees were sent back to Germany. "I doubt that many American Jews who insist on the Jews' *right* to Palestine would be willing to give America back to the Indians," he wrote.[15] Rather than inciting the Nazis' victims to break British laws, and in the process to endure more suffering, Bettelheim went on, American Jews would do better to spend their money on bringing them to the United States, "the land where they would be safe from persecution, and where history has shown they can be integrated into an existing community of power and culture." He added: "I cannot help feeling that this anger against the British was a projection of the anger of American Jews against themselves for not doing their duty towards the Jews in Europe."

It can be seen that Bettelheim had hit his stride as a writer during those first years of exile. His tone of intelligent remonstrance, based on acute observations and the constant questioning of what others took for granted, grew firmer and more self-assured with each article. There was always a strong moral undertone, and he was generally more concerned to attack the complacency of his friends—or those who saw themselves as such—than the crimes of his enemies, which were frequently disposed of with a few words such as: "It is not the intention of this paper to recount once more the horror story of the German concentration camp."[16]

But in 1947, noting that the Germans had definitively lost the war, Bettelheim wrote that the time had come to speak out frankly about what had gone on in the camps. Reviewing books about Buchenwald by the Austrians Benedikt Kautsky and Eugen Kogon, he focused on the class structure in the camps, the power relationships between inmates. He stressed in particular the cynicism of the Communist prisoners, who had been all too ready to sacrifice the lives of innocents to save their own. And while acknowledging the merits of Kogon's book, he accused the author, who had acted as a medical secretary at the camp, of having been one of the "elite prisoners," and of taking in his book a patronizing and contemptuous view of the lower-class inmates. Indeed, Bettelheim went on, "almost all those who survived the camps and could therefore report on their experiences had in one way or another been beneficiaries of a class system whose lowest strata rarely survived."[17] He even acknowledged that at Buchenwald, an inmate's awareness of his superiority over other prisoners was an important psychological defense mechanism against his own fear of falling to the lowest level, even though this class system could only serve the interests of the SS. Here again is a subtle and clear-sighted analysis, focused not on the flaws of the oppressors but on those of their victims. It is a convincing, intelligent, and uncompromising piece of writing. Yet a great deal of its strength and appeal is due to the fact that its author himself belonged to the very category of inmates whose behavior he takes apart so vigorously. For the reader, the harsh, peremptory tone is at least partially canceled out by the implicit *we* that lurks behind the *they* in every paragraph.

This was the first stage of Bettelheim's post–concentration camp thinking, the positive phase, during which he strove, and successfully so, to derive lessons from his experience. It was the phase during which Bettelheim wrote that his year of detention "did me good." It ends in 1956, with the publication of the first article in which he drew a parallel between the hell experienced by the children in his charge and the hell he had been through in Buchenwald.[18] At the school, meanwhile, he was continually urging the counselors to learn and progress from their worst experiences. "When something bad happens to you, turn it around and use it," he would say. "Make a project out of it."

At the same time, Bettelheim was involved in the debate over the reconstruction of Germany, which exposed divisions among American intellectuals over the analysis of Nazism, the denunciation of Stalinism, the Marshall Plan, and so on. Are there ways of preventing any relapse into barbarity? Are certain peoples antidemocratic by nature? The debate had engaged many people who in the past had been interested in Marxism, and in particular the members of the Frankfurt Institute for Social Research (better known as the Frankfurt School), many of whom had found refuge at Columbia University. By then, however, the label "neo-Hegelian" had replaced all intellectual traces of the now-infamous epithet "Marxist."

At the University of Chicago, the discussions took place at the Chaos Club, so called because it kept no roster of its membership. One evening Max Horkheimer, the president of the Institute, who along with Theodor Adorno had chosen to return to Frankfurt almost as soon as the war was over, had just concluded a talk in which he argued that Germany was a profoundly democratic country, as shown by developments there at that time, the early 1950s. A graduate student in sociology, Albert Reiss, Jr. (who was then sharing an apartment with Morris Janowitz), spoke up: "But how can you say that after the death camps?" David Riesman, who was chairing the debate, icily tried to put him in his place. "That statement is unworthy of the brilliant speech that we have just heard," he said in essence. At which point Bettelheim stood up and shouted: "You'd do better to listen to him. He's the one who is right."

Bettelheim was never one to be swayed by ideas just because they were in fashion. Toward the end of the 1950s Luitgard Wundheiler, a young German woman who taught mathematics to Naomi's Lab School class, offered to work at the Orthogenic School. She had just lost her husband, a Polish Jew whose brother had died in the Warsaw Ghetto, and she could not get over her feelings of guilt at having grown up in Nazi Germany. Bettelheim's reaction astounded her: "You shouldn't feel guilty for being German. If you blame all Germans, you're like the Nazis: you're condemning human beings on the basis of what they are as a group, not of what they do as individuals."

As early as 1954 Bettelheim agreed to return to Germany, to spend three months in Frankfurt running a teacher-training seminar on the subject of democracy. Trude was firmly against the idea. "I don't know how you can go back to Germany," she told him. And indeed, the experience was a difficult one, as he confessed to the Janowitzes, who were also in Frankfurt at the time. Morris had received a Fulbright Fellowship to spend the academic year at the Institute for Social Research, and Bettelheim was very thankful for the occasional dinner at the home of these close American friends. He found himself again dreaming in German about the concentration camps. He was deeply upset to see how limited the process of denazification had been, but was at the same time struck by the well-meaning attitudes of the young teachers who attended his seminars. Even they, however, had the utmost difficulty understanding that one simply cannot use authoritarian methods to teach democracy, he noted.[19] Nothing seemed to have changed in Germany's educational methods, and not even those who most sincerely wanted to believe in democracy could rid themselves of the notion, which Bettelheim detected in most of the people he met, that it had been the Weimar Republic, and later on the Allied democracies, that had plunged Germany into the state of chaos it was then struggling to emerge from. Bettelheim also met young Germans from the Soviet-occupied zone, and although he was shocked by their political indoctrination, he was also struck by the breadth of their philosophical, aesthetic, and sociological interests, compared to the materialism of their Western counterparts.

One day he returned to Dachau, alone. The visit was to result in one of the most serene of all his articles on the subject.[20] It focused on memory and the impossibility of keeping the traces of such a tragedy alive. It was a highly personal, simple, and descriptive piece, in which Bettelheim did not seek to lecture anyone, but just related his impressions during the visit, as they evolved from cold anger at the indifference of the local populace, to a final feeling of inner calm that came with the realization of the heavy burden the Germans had to bear in order simply to go on living there, next to what had once been a concentration camp. Whatever he had suffered, he did not envy them their situation.

In the same year, with the help of his cousin Norbert Bettelheim, who had returned to Vienna from exile in France after the war, Bruno Bettelheim undertook to obtain reparations for the loss of his business and his deportation. He spent two years fighting doggedly for this, going so far as to file a lawsuit against the Austrian administration, which had pointed to the highly restrictive time limit it had set on requests for compensation by the victims of Nazism.[21] Finally, the Austrian administration gave him partial satisfaction, and he dropped his suit. He was given a deportee's pension and, later on, compensation for "interruption of professional activity." However, in spite of unceasing efforts, carried on with the help of both his cousin and his cousin's son, up until 1969, Bettelheim never received any reparation for the loss of his company.[22] (There is a repetition here that may be of interest to a psychoanalyst: Anton had fought in vain to gain compensation for the stocks of wood he had lost during World War I, and a little later his brothers had striven, also to no avail, to prove the existence of blood ties between their father and the Bettelheims of Pressburg).

At the same time, Bettelheim was honing his ideas on the issue of totalitarianism, in a direction not unlike that taken by the Frankfurt School.[23] Like them, he attached particular importance to the notion of individual autonomy. In October 1952 the *American Journal of Economics and Sociology* published his "Remarks on the Psychological Appeal of Totalitarianism," a brief article about the psychological conflict the modern totalitarian state imposes on all those who defy it. For him, the specificity of twentieth-century totalitarianism lies in the way it bases its power on the disintegration of the independent ego in all its citizens, by penetrating every nook and cranny of their lives, including the most private ones.

He uses as an example the Nazi salute, an everyday gesture that was required of all citizens. Several times a day, the anti-Nazi was thus confronted with an inner conflict, the outcome of which could only weaken his ego. Either he refused to give the salute, thereby following his conscience (the superego) but risking his life (and as Bettelheim points out, the conservation of life is the most basic of all the ego's functions),[24] or he went through the motions, while telling himself that the gesture was of no importance, thereby demeaning himself in his own eyes by failing to live up to his own moral precepts. "Thus, the opponent of the totalitarian regime, who must have a strong ego in order to survive in an inimical society, found himself, because of the very nature of this society, continuously in a situation that forced him to work on his ego's own destruction." Bettelheim went on to note that for most human beings, the desire for conformity was a very strong one. To resolve a conflict between their ideals and their survival, little by little, they would quite naturally adjust their ideals. "In the final analysis then, the ego can protect the individual in a totalitarian society only by accepting the system as it is."

Three years later, Bettelheim's thinking on totalitarianism had evolved further. As if his stay in Europe had opened his eyes to the

shortcomings of his adopted country, he published in 1955 a hard-
hitting critique of American society. In this long essay, large extracts
from which are reprinted in *The Informed Heart*, he used the concept
of individual autonomy to draw correlations between the totalitarian
state and mass society.[25] Expressing for the first time a lot of ideas
which a few years later would achieve such widespread currency that
they would become clichés, he demonstrated how the individual
gradually became alienated in the modern world, in which an apparent plethora of choice in fact only served to conceal the limited scope
left to each individual's responsibility. Practically the only areas in
which modern man still enjoyed some freedom to define and claim
his own identity were the most private ones. There were people to tell
him what to drink, what to eat, which car to buy, how to furnish his
home. He was even advised on how to spend his leisure time by those
who stood to make money thereby. He appeared to enjoy freedom of
choice, but in fact he listened to the same radio station and read the
same books as his neighbor. "Thus, in exchanging opinions, they
enjoy the comfort of conformity until they suddenly realize the
emptiness of a life which offers no experiences particular to themselves."

Like the Nazi state, mass society thus presupposed the weakness of
its subjects' personalities. ("When life activities are not selected on the
basis of internalization of the values of cherished persons, but solely
on the basis of the wish or need to earn a livelihood in a convenient
fashion, doubts, insecurity and inability to integrate are the consequence.") Perversely, it nevertheless maintained the illusion of great
freedom, thereby reinforcing the feeling of failure in the person who
did not succeed in fulfilling his or her desires. Being unable to truly
exercise his personal choices, he invests more and more in the power
of the mass, in the society he is a part of, just as the Germans were
led, by the Nazi regime, to place more and more faith in the reputedly
magical powers of their leader.

Bettelheim was no revolutionary, however. He was not against the
American system, he simply sought to underline its inherent dangers,
to point out that too great an imbalance between society's ability to
control and each individual's internal autonomy was a source of emotional disturbance. He cited the Nazi state and its concentration camps
as the ultimate form of a process at work in all mass societies that
based themselves on technological progress but failed to measure all
the implications of that progress. The instruments science made avail-

able to the managers of society were never neutral, he wrote. One should never "neglect the powerful modifying forces which flow from any external control of man and [deny] the individual responsibility in which man's dignity resides."

The second period in Bettelheim's writings on the camps began at the end of the 1950s, when, after discussing Buchenwald, he started to write about Auschwitz, and in the same lecturing tone. In May 1960 he agreed—not without much hesitation, he stressed—to write a foreword for the memoirs of Miklos Nyiszli, a Hungarian doctor who had survived the extermination camp only by agreeing to collaborate in the sinister "medical research" carried out there by Josef Mengele.[26] The importance of accounts of the death camps lay "not in their all too familiar story but in something far more unusual and horrifying," Bettelheim wrote on page one. "The unique feature of the extermination camps is not that the Germans exterminated millions of people— that this is possible has been accepted in our picture of man, though not for centuries has it happened on that scale, and perhaps never with such callousness. What was new, unique, terrifying, was that millions, like lemmings, marched themselves to their own death."

He was not the only Jew to be putting forward that argument. Raul Hilberg's minutely detailed analysis of the Nazi killing machine, which the historian had been working on for over ten years, was published the following year. The conclusion of *The Destruction of the European Jews* was that the Nazis' Jewish victims, prisoners of their history, had precipitated themselves into catastrophe. The philosopher Hannah Arendt, in her writings on totalitarianism and anti-Semitism, also pointed the finger, although a little less harshly, at the role played by Jewish traditions in determining the scope of the Holocaust. In their different ways, each writer—Bettelheim, Hilberg, and Arendt—was holding the disaster out at arm's length in order to understand it, thereby trying, as Bettelheim repeatedly stressed, to prevent any repetition.

One evening Naomi, then almost fourteen, came home from school with Anne Frank's *Diary of a Young Girl*, which she was studying in class. Surprised, Bettelheim read the book overnight. It filled him with indignation, and in November 1960 *Harper's* published his fulminations under the title "The Ignored Lesson of Anne Frank."[27] In Bettelheim's view the acclaim that had greeted the writings of the little

Dutch Jewish girl—worldwide, but especially in Germany—proved only one thing: the tendency we all have to deny the reality of Auschwitz and the existence of the gas chambers. He agreed that Anne's account of her two years in hiding with her family in Amsterdam, before she was sent to Bergen-Belsen where she died, was touching, and he was aware of the risks he was running in taking on such an emotional symbol. However, the real reason for the success of Anne Frank's diary, he went on, was to be found in her insistence, right up to the end, that human beings were basically good—that is, in her denial of the reality of Nazism.

Instead of taking measures that could have saved them, Bettelheim wrote, the Frank family had opted for the most dangerous plan possible: hiding all together in a closed space with only one exit, from which they could not escape even if alerted of danger. In other words, they had put their desire to remain together—to carry on "life as usual"—above what they should have known to be going on in the real world.[28] This refusal to believe in the Nazis' barbarity, to believe that human beings could be so inhuman, was why the public liked the family so much, even though, with the exception of the father, they had all perished in the camps.

This article perfectly sums up Bettelheim's ideas on survival, and also sheds light on the title of the book in which it first appeared. *The Informed Heart.* In all circumstances, and particularly in extreme situations, survival is a question of balancing the yearnings of the heart against the strictures of reason. By giving priority to the latter, and using his professional pride as a doctor to avoid seeing what he was doing, Miklos Nyiszli had ended up taking part in experiments that were so appalling Bettelheim asks: "How could he do it and live with himself?" At the opposite extreme, Anne Frank's father, by choosing to listen only to his heart, had led his family into the arms of their executioners. Clinging to one's previous life or—in the case of those Polish Jews whom Bettelheim also accused of having carried on with business as usual even though they had been informed of the advancing German troops—to one's house and other possessions was like believing that one had only to close one's eyes for the danger to disappear.

Although his argument was built on convincing foundations, in backing it up Bettelheim went too far. He was particularly unjust with Otto Frank, a German-born Jew who had in fact left Frankfurt with little Anne and the rest of his family just six months after Hitler came to power, to seek refuge in the Netherlands, a country that had remained neutral in World War I. Overlooking the fact that Mr. Frank's minutely prepared plan had come within months of succeeding (the family was only arrested by the SS on August 4, 1944), Bettelheim blithely asserted that if Mr. Frank had acted otherwise, as "thousands of other Jews in Holland (as elsewhere in Europe)" had done, he probably could have saved his family. Adding insult to injury, Bettelheim went on: "There is little doubt that the Franks, who were able to provide themselves with so much while arranging for going into hiding . . . could have provided themselves with some weapons had they wished." As they were going to die anyway, they could at least have killed one or two of the SS men who came to arrest them; they would thus have "sold their lives for a high price instead of walking to their death."

A little over a year after the Anne Frank article, Bettelheim published an even more provocative essay under the title "Freedom from Ghetto Thinking."[29] This came at the height of publicity over the war-crimes trial of Nazi leader Adolf Eichmann, precisely when many Jews felt it was time for their people to close ranks. The man who was seen as one of the key orchestrators of Hitler's "final solution" had been abducted by Israeli agents in Buenos Aires in May 1960; the story of his capture and subsequent trial in Jerusalem between April and December 1961 had been followed in its every detail by the thousands of Nazi victims then living in the United States. Up to that point, few of them had spoken out, and their feelings about the case were fairly straightforward. Having been disappointed by the Allies' refusal to deal separately with anti-Jewish persecution at the Nuremberg trials of Nazi leaders, they found in the Eichmann trial the opportunity to have their sufferings at least recognized, if not avenged. The fact that it had been the fledgling Israeli state which had undertaken to hunt down Eichmann, thumbing its nose at international law in the process, served only to amplify their feelings, which were played up in their most simplistic form by the media. For most of them, it was a contest of Good versus Evil, with the Jewish people once again alone in defending its victims.

Eichmann's death sentence had been handed down and the Israeli Supreme Court was due to hear his appeal when Bettelheim's piece appeared in *Midstream*, a Zionist magazine. The article opened with a discussion of the phrase "innocent victim," which had been heard countless times from witnesses during the trial. Why was it, Bettelheim asked, that this label was invariably applied to Jews murdered by the Nazis, but never to the German Gypsies, who had been wiped out in toto, even if they were less often talked about? He then launched into a long analysis of how centuries of living in ghettos, bowing down before oppressors and pretending not to notice, carrying on with "business as usual" as if nothing was wrong, waiting for the storm to pass, had led to some Jews' opting to "remain 'innocent' in the jaws of disaster" when Hitler came to power.

Those not affected by "ghetto thinking," Bettelheim contended, had believed the dictator when he announced there would not be a single Jew left in Europe by the end of the war; they had escaped in time. Most of the others had perished. But "ghetto thinking" was not to be found solely among inhabitants of the shtetls; Bettelheim also detected it in the United States—for instance, among the Jewish friends who refused to believe him when he told them that most of his fellow-inmates at Dachau and Buchenwald had in fact not been Jews at all. "Only what happened to Jews counted: they were not aware of what happened to others. Lacking interest, they could not learn from others' experiences." The ghetto Jew, Bettelheim went on, was typically an exiled Jew. And the main reason he indulged in "ghetto thinking" was to avoid having to act. "It is a type of deadening of the senses and emotions, so that one can bow down to the mujik who pulls one's beard, laugh with the baron at his anti-Semitic stories, degrade oneself so that one will be permitted to survive." In other words, "to believe that one can ingratiate oneself with a mortal enemy by denying that his lashes sting, to deny one's own degradation in return for a moment's respite."

Bettelheim had never gone this far before. Once again, several of the points he discussed raised real issues, but once again it was his tone that for many people verged on the unacceptable. It was a blend of arrogance—people have to fight, like the Israelis today, or the Warsaw Ghetto Jews yesterday—and condescension toward what he called "ghetto thinking." Even Hannah Arendt, whom Bettelheim was clearly seeking to get on his side (his article praised the way she had escaped from the French camp of Gurs, where she had been interned as a foreign Jew after the defeat of France in 1940), felt it necessary to distance herself from his remarks, which she considered anti-Semitic. In a letter published in the following issue of *Midstream* she acknowledged that she too had found the huge success of Anne Frank's diary to be suspect, particularly in Germany, but added: "There is such a thing as an inverted chauvinism, and when discussing the wrongs of the Jewish people one should be careful not to fall into that trap." This from an assimilated Prussian-born former student of Karl Jaspers, Edmund Husserl, and Martin Heidegger, who since those years had never ceased to question what it meant to be Jewish, and had placed the Holocaust at the heart of her philosophical thinking.

Due to that concern, Arendt had offered to travel to Jerusalem to report on the Eichmann trial for the *New Yorker*. Whatever her personal views of Bettelheim may have been, the resulting articles, published in February and March 1963, were to get both of them lumped together by many critics in the category of anti-Semitic Jews. On attending the trial, Arendt had been astounded to discover that far from being a monster, Eichmann was no more than a petty, vain civil servant who spoke only in clichés. While seemingly ready to cooperate with the court, he could clearly remember the acts that had sent millions of people to their deaths only inasmuch as they had coincided with key points in his career. He seemed to be merely a small-minded bureaucrat, who looked sincere when he claimed that he had never killed anyone other than by passing along orders. The way Arendt portrayed him, the fact that she challenged the judicial validity of the trial, and above all that she raised questions about the role played by the Jewish councils in the occupied countries in helping with the deportation programs, brought a storm of protest from all over the world. The controversy rose to new heights a few months later, when Arendt published an edited version of her articles in book form. The title, which her adversaries considered scandalous in itself, was *Eichmann in Jerusalem: A Report on the Banality of Evil.*

When the *New Republic* magazine asked Bettelheim to review Arendt's book, the resulting article only added fuel to the flames.[30] He who was so adept at demolishing the credibility of a book in a few lines, and who did so more often than not, had almost nothing but praise for Arendt's work. He started out by trying to show that the trial had in fact been a misunderstanding, because it was not Eichmann as an individual who was being put in the dock, but anti-Semitism through the ages. This explained why it had been necessary to portray the man as a monster, Bettelheim wrote. What should have been on trial was the totalitarian state, rather than a man who had been only one of its cogs, and not a very interesting one at that. To show what he meant, he quoted an expression Eichmann frequently used to justify his acts: *Kadavergehorsam*, which he translated as "the obedience of a corpse." Although inherited from Prussian army traditions, the term took on its full meaning only in Hitler's Germany, Bettelheim noted. "The obedient servant of Hitler and the prisoner who walked to the gas chamber became alike as true symbols of the total state. The rewarded servant and the prisoner to be murdered, each had lost his free will, his ability to act out of personal conviction."

Following Arendt, Bettelheim stressed how much the Jewish organizations in the Nazi-ruled countries had facilitated the extermination program, even if their actions had only been aimed at easing conditions. "Arendt's point—and it is well taken—is that any organization within a totalitarian society that compromised with the system became immediately ineffectual in opposing it and ended up helping it," he wrote, bolstering his own argument with that of the book he was reviewing. Only active resistance to the oppressor, either open or underground, could possibly have changed the course of events, he went on, if only because it would have made it more difficult for the rest of the world to act as if nothing was happening. Bettelheim illustrated this argument with an example that his readers were then seeing every night on their TV screens: "Many of us were impressed by the way Negroes in Birmingham marched, singing and upright, to jail. But much deeper feelings were aroused in us when we saw pictures of a solitary Negro being dragged down by policemen because he refused to march to jail on his own." This was certainly a telling point for the liberal readership of the *New Republic*, but although the great majority of U.S. Jews were at that time supportive of the civil rights movement and Martin Luther King, not all of them identified the fate of their people with that of American blacks. A few lines further on, Bettelheim denied that Eichmann's trial had been the trial of the century, which it should logically have been since it dealt with the crime of the century. Instead, he preferred to retain the title for a cause célèbre of the 1920s, the trial of Nathan Leopold and Richard Loeb, two University of Chicago students who had murdered a younger boy in a completely gratuitous act, "to see how it felt," as one of them said. Theirs had been a crime committed "because of the most inhumane principles and to assert their superiority," Bettelheim wrote. But their trial in 1924 had been historic because, thanks to defense attorney Clarence Darrow, "the incredible inhumanity of their deed was put within the broad context of human nature. The result was that . . . enough empathy was aroused with these errant human beings so that the trial . . . aroused in us the determination to create a better society, one that could not and would not produce another Leopold and Loeb." This argument was not likely to endear Bettelheim to those who had accused him of anti-Semitism: Leopold and Leob were Jews.

This time, for those who demanded total respect for the victims of Nazism, Bettelheim had really gone over the edge. "From the comfort of Chicago, Bettelheim presumes to award patents of heroism and/or cowardice to Hitler's martyrs," wrote Alexander Donat, a former Maidenek inmate. Noting that Bettelheim had chosen "to start a war against Anne Frank" and her family for hiding in a place with no exit, he continued: "Doesn't the man know that hundreds of thousands of Jews perished because they had *no* place to hide, with or without an outlet?" But it was the condemnation of Otto Frank's failure to get himself a weapon that most enraged Donat, who had taken part in the Warsaw Ghetto uprising. He recalled that the Jewish Fighters' Organization, set up in July 1942 to organize the revolt, had been able, in six months of existence, to obtain only fifty revolvers from the Polish underground. "In Bialystok and Vilna, the Jewish fighters received nothing."[31]

For the death camp survivors, and even more for the relatives of those who had perished, Bettelheim's statements were intolerable. Simply to tell of their experiences was difficult enough, but to find their story being hijacked by a group of German Jews who had been lucky enough to sit out the war in the United States, and who dared to blame them for their own sufferings, was too much to bear. It was made even worse by the fact that, while Bettelheim and his fellow detainees at Dachau and Buchenwald had mostly been German, the majority of those gassed at Auschwitz, Treblinka, and Sobibor had been *Ost juden*, the eastern Jews who from time immemorial had had to contend with the arrogance of their assimilated brethren in Vienna, Berlin, and Frankfurt. For them, Bettelheim's credentials as a deportee did not carry the same weight as they did for his other readers. "He forgets that by comparison to the later camps, the camps in 1938 were like summer resorts," Alexander Donat wrote.[32]

Initially confined to the letters columns of Jewish journals and a few New York papers, the controversy now widened, affecting Bettelheim even in his professional life. In 1964 a debate on Hannah Arendt's book was held at the University of Chicago branch of the Hillel Foundation, a Jewish cultural organization. It was chaired by Hans Morganthau, himself a former concentration camp inmate and a friend of both Arendt and Bettelheim. When the latter stood up to speak, the hissing, shouting, and heckling were so loud that he had to sit down again without saying a word. Although his stormy temperament was already well known on campus, and the subject was emotionally charged, several of Bettelheim's friends and colleagues were shocked to see so much hatred directed at him in an academic debate. A professor from a neighboring university even waved his bare arm, tattooed with an Auschwitz number, in Bettelheim's face, while another shouted: "We knew about you in the camps; we knew you had a visa in your pocket."

Bettelheim did not even try to answer the accusations but "poohpoohed them off," as one witness recalls.[33] Indeed, he generally feigned indifference to such displays. He could afford to: *The Informed Heart* had won him support from thousands of readers, who admired his lucidity and viewed any attack on him as but further proof of the correctness of his ideas. And to brush off most of the objections, all he had to do was to return to his central argument. Alexander Donat, for example, was the first to admit that, right up to the end, nobody in the Polish or Ukrainian ghettos had been able to imagine just how far the Nazis' murderous folly had taken such a civilized people as the Germans.

Privately, however, it is hard to believe that Bruno Bettelheim could have taken this controversy lightly. The mid-1960s was precisely when, at the Orthogenic School, he was forced to acknowledge that despite all his efforts, the results he was achieving with autistic children were not as conclusive as he had hoped. It was also when he chose to go to Israel to study kibbutz children, a trip that stirred intense and contradictory feelings in him (see chapter 15). Bettelheim had by this time achieved celebrity status. He was writing on almost any subject: education and children, of course, but also the role of women, violence, jealousy, sexuality, racism, John F. Kennedy's assassin. He had just embarked on a new, highly ambitious expansion program for the Orthogenic School, which involved a lot more fund-raising, as well as accounting for funds already received. He was autocratic, irritable, and liable to take offense at anything and nothing. For example, when the American Orthopsychiatric Association failed to publish his contribution to its twice-yearly conference in a year when his friend Fritz Redl was its president, Bettelheim decided to stay away from its next meeting.

Why should this man, who was otherwise so busy, have plunged into these concentration camp quarrels, which, after all, related to a previous chapter of his life? To answer that question, one has to consider the major development that had occurred since he had written his first article on the camps: the return of death camp survivors. During an initial period, they had remained silent, or at least nobody had listened to them. Then, toward the end of the 1950s, their accounts had started to appear in print, and the story they told was worlds apart from what Bettelheim had described. He himself stressed that difference in *The Informed Heart*, which was published in 1960, noting that in the death camps "no effort was made to modify personality since their only purpose was to exterminate prisoners as efficiently as possible."[34] The distinction was of prime importance, since his entire study was concerned precisely with changes in prisoners' behavior during their internment. It also made it clear that, however hellish Buchenwald had been, Bettelheim had not experienced the most extreme of situations. Nevertheless, the remark was consigned to a footnote.

When he wrote *The Informed Heart*, Bettelheim had thus not yet realized, or else refused to see, that the conclusions he had drawn from his stay at Buchenwald were not applicable to the people who had returned from the death camps, that he no longer had the right to use the first person plural to speak in the name of all the survivors of the Nazi camps. And what had he in fact learned at Buchenwald? Quite simply that life meant a lot to him, which is how I interpret his decision to turn down the opportunity to wear that destructive armband. And that when his enemy was clearly identifiable, when he could hate him without feeling guilty, or without having to punish himself for doing so, he was no longer depressed. As he was to tell the French journalist Daniel Karlin, the period he spent in the camps was the only time in his life when he never had thoughts of suicide.[35]

Hardly had Bettelheim been released when he found himself faced with a conflict between his now explicit desire to live, and to live well, and the old burden of responsibilities and unpaid debts, made even heavier by the memory of those he had left behind in the camps. They, who were neither any better nor any worse than he was, had not been lucky enough to get out. *Lucky?* That was a dangerous word, evocative of the accidents of birth, sex, physique, race, or family—a taboo word for a man who felt responsible for his own fate, the heir to a family tradition in which everything had to be earned, either through work or fraud, because it was never free. A man who had never been granted the right to be unlucky, to be simply a victim. No, luck had no place in this process. As he was to endlessly repeat at the Orthogenic School, there is no such thing as an accident.

The work of interpretation that Bettelheim carried out to write his first article on the camps therefore consisted of uncovering the hidden necessity behind the chance events of deportation and internment. This was his way of shouldering his share of the responsibility for those who had stayed behind at Buchenwald. No wonder he was so hard on them, since he was deriving his understanding from what he discovered in himself. To do this he was forced to wrestle not only with his memories, but also with the ever-present pessimistic, nihilistic streak in him, that old enemy Freud had called the "death instinct" but that Bettelheim, who knew it well, then referred to as inertia. It was the force that whispered in his ear that nothing was worthwhile, that was bolstered by his reading of Oswald Spengler, the drive he had always combated by trying to draw meaning out of every event, and finding a "happy ending" to even the most awful among them, so that they could serve some useful purpose.

The trouble is that in seeking at all costs to give a meaning to events, some of which are literally beyond human understanding, one may find oneself asserting as truth anything one is not in a position to prove, and on occasion rearranging the facts a little. Such as when Bettelheim switched the time of his story about the broken glasses, or attributed to himself a role he had not in fact played, so as to lend more weight to his story. As long as the ultimate goal is just, though, what does it matter? If the end is to be a happy one, it must surely justify the means—the story—used to arrive at it. But when one has been haunted from childhood by a feeling of fraud, the storytelling exercise is fraught with risks. All it takes is to have the legitimacy of the ending suddenly called into question for the whole edifice to collapse, leaving behind it nothing but guilt and shame. If this happens, what started out as mere inexactitudes and omissions can, over time, turn into unatonable crimes.

However strong his convictions, and whatever the validity of his arguments—and it is clearly essential on this point to distinguish between the content of his statements and their tone—it is inconceivable that being plunged into such a furious and even hateful confrontation with the death camp survivors could not have affected him personally. After having spent over two years in the early 1940s locked in struggle with himself because he felt it his duty to alert the world to what was going on at Buchenwald, how could he have faced the reproaches of the Auschwitz survivors without shame?

A hint of the inner turmoil Bettelheim must have gone through at that time can be found in his review of Jean-François Steiner's book *Treblinka*, his first piece on the camps in four years.[30] One might have expected him to like this book, which tells the story of the uprising by the last thousand prisoners in Treblinka, a camp built for the sole purpose of exterminating Jews. Before that, it briefly relates the arrival of the Nazis in the Lithuanian capital of Vilnius, and the first mass executions in the nearby woods, showing how the Vilnius Jews refused until the last minute to believe the people who tried to warn them of the impending disaster. The book is written like a novel, based whenever possible on the firsthand accounts of survivors, and this triggered Bettelheim's first objection. "Steiner turns the story of this deepest of horrors into a gripping escape fiction," he wrote. In a further criticism of the form of the book, he accused the writer of failing to make a choice between fiction and the telling of history, thereby creating inauthentic-sounding dialogues. For example, commenting on the prisoners' discussion of the need to survive in order to tell the world what they had seen, Bettelheim wrote:

> The truth is that to tell about the horrors of the camp was a very strong motive. Certainly it was for me, for my friends at some moments. But our goal was revenge; to bring the world down on the SS, not to warn people against "making decisions lightly without knowing where they will lead them" . . . [That] came typically as an afterthought . . . the prisoner wanted to scream out against an abomination so that the world would take action against the Nazis . . . He did not care about any lessons to be learned from the camp. In fact they took years for me to learn.

What is striking about this article is the way Bettelheim's thinking on the subject has deepened. He has clearly read all the testimonies published about the camps, and reflected on the difference between his own experiences and those of the death camp inmates. At several points he is careful to underline that difference. Meanwhile, he also uses the article on Steiner to distance himself from Raul Hilberg's position: It is not Jewish traditions per se that are to blame for the Jews' passivity toward the Nazis, he stresses, but specifically ghetto-related traditions. The reason for this was that since Napoleonic times all Jews who had a spark of rebelliousness in them had left the shtetls.

The lack of initiative was not due to some atavism but to the impoverishment of certain characteristics in a historically defined group.[37] Bettelheim does not believe in innate racial or national characteristics. For him a human being, be he Jewish or German, is above all an individual, and reacts as such to his surroundings. But, he writes, in order for Martin Buber, Marc Chagall, or Isaac Bashevis Singer to create such touching portrayals of the shtetl, they first had to leave it. Despite the phrase that traditionally marked the end of anti-Jewish pogroms, "The Jewish people lives," Bettelheim went on, Hitler had succeeded in wiping out the shtetl, with its very specific customs and culture. The state of Israel, whose mentality Bettelheim saw as diametrically opposed to that of the ghetto, existed only because a totally assimilated Viennese Jew, Theodor Herzl, had launched a movement that had been taken up by the most active elements in the Jewish community. "It is precisely the absence of this activist element, and the many hundreds of years of 'compliance' that explains ghetto mentality, and not any racial inheritance of the Jews."

In the space of four years, the tone has become firmer and the ideas clearer and better laid out. In this article Bettelheim seems more concerned to explain, and less aggressive, his severity toward Steiner's book is even tempered by the recognition that its author, whose father died in the camps, had been driven to write to fulfill a sacred duty. He nevertheless criticizes Steiner for wanting to save everyone: both those who, like his father, fought, and those who submitted to their fates in the name of what the author presents as their philosophy. In passing, Bettelheim gets in a dig at the French philosopher Simone de Beauvoir, for writing in her preface on things she knew nothing about, and at General De Gaulle, for having misunderstood the book's message. But his aim there was probably to stress that the book was a French one, and that its success among non-Jews could not be seen as a vindication of the ideas it expressed.

More important for our purposes, this is the first piece of writing in which Bettelheim places insistent emphasis on the guilt of the survivors. He criticizes Steiner for concentrating his narrative on the inmates who plotted and carried out the uprising, thereby allowing the reader to forget that in the same period some 700,000 people had let themselves be gassed. In order to turn the few into heroes, Steiner had drawn a distorted picture of them, pushing into the background the fact that if they were in a position to revolt, and that only at the last minute, when their own lives were threatened, it was because up until that point they had agreed to be collaborators in the extermination program. And although nobody who has not experienced death camps has the right to condemn them for having sought to survive, even for a few days, and having thus accepted the horrendous tasks they were given (even before the death camps, "prisoners in the concentration camps were often in situations where their survival may have cost the lives of others," Bettelheim notes), they were not heroes, but rather "desperately ashamed men."

Further in the same article, Bettelheim comments on the relative lack of success of accounts written by death camp survivors, compared to the acclaim that greeted Steiner's book, suggesting that this was because survivors' accounts had been written by "people who were broken by the knowledge of how they had let themselves be degraded, broken by the knowledge that they had taken part in destroying their brothers in order to live another day of such a life." Clearly Bettelheim had finally understood that no survivor from Auschwitz, Treblinka, or Sobibor could ever have written, as he had, that "the impact of the concentration camp . . . within a few weeks, did for me what years of a useful and quite successful analysis had not done."[38] From that point on, everything he would write about the camps would include in some form or other the ideas of shame and guilt. It was almost as if, having come to such a painful realization of the gulf that separated his experience from that of the death camp survivors, this was the only bridge he had found between himself and them, or even better, as if their testimony had finally helped him to confront what had been haunting him since his own release, and which was the source of so much of his aggressiveness.

The guilt feelings, which run like a continuous thread through *Surviving*, are indeed a distinctive feature of accounts by death camp survivors. But they do not permeate in the same way the testimonies of former concentration camp inmates. Ernst Federn, for example, does not recognize any such feelings, and they cannot be detected in the accounts of Eugen Kogon or Walter Poller, who were also at Buchenwald at the same time as Bettelheim. Guilt feelings do not obsess Hans Bandler, either. The experiences of all these men left them with feelings of rage, of enormous pity for the weaker inmates who did not survive, and sometimes, as Bettelheim reports, of shame at having been reduced to such a state of powerlessness and degradation. On occasion they also express feelings of injustice because they survived while others did not. But such feelings do not color all their memories,

as they do, for example, in the accounts of Primo Levi,[39] or in those
of Bettelheim toward the end of his life. "Being one of the very few
who were saved when millions like oneself perished seems to entail a
special obligation to justify one's luck and very existence," Bettelheim
wrote in *Surviving*. This was a problem "which one cannot solve, but
with which one must live."[40]

And yet, from all we know about the conditions of Bettelheim's
incarceration, it is hard to discern why he should have reacted differently to the experience. As we have seen, the "sins" he committed while
in the camps (wearing a blind man's armband which he was almost,
but not quite, entitled to, and using his money to purchase a few
advantages without which he would probably not have survived)
could not be viewed as having been detrimental to other detainees,
except in the general sense, stressed by Bettelheim, in which a privilege accorded to one inmate was thus not available to another. But,
precisely, it was at Auschwitz that that kind of privilege became automatically deadly, when simply staying alive meant that other people
died. At Buchenwald, when Bettelheim was there, conditions were
horribly harsh, degrading, and extremely dangerous, but the logic
was not that of extermination. It was easy to die there, as could be
seen from the regular passage of coffin bearers, but one could also
survive, if one had strength, the clear will to live—and luck.

The unease that Bettelheim no doubt felt about his minor compromises with the camp system must have been aggravated by the
contradiction between his own past behavior and the lessons in survival he had retrospectively handed down to Anne Frank's father
and other victims. Although he never admitted it publicly, he could
certainly not have forgotten that he himself had not been much
more prescient than the people he was criticizing. Once arrested, he
had indeed thrown all his energy into being able to leave. Before
that, however, he had, like many others, sought to put his affairs in
order before fleeing, without realizing what the resulting delay
would cost him. Why therefore did he so obstinately refuse to
acknowledge that human beings, however well informed, simply
could not imagine the death camps until they had seen them? Why
did he have to point the finger at the victims—he who, at the same
time as he was embroiled in this controversy, was every day demon-
strating his extraordinary ability to understand the sufferings of the
children in his care?

But that is exactly the point. If, as I believe, it was at Buchenwald that this chronic depressive discovered the strength of his own will to live, if he owed his survival to that discovery, and if it was what led him to devote himself to helping others, then his first encounter with the death camp survivors must have been quite simply unbearable. For their experiences meant the negation of all the positive conclusions he had drawn from his Buchenwald sojourn, and thus the negation, at a critical juncture, of his life's work, notably at the school. At Auschwitz he would never even have had the choice of whether or not to wear an armband, for there blind people were immediately gassed. Before his self-analysis had allowed him to absorb this new reality with all its implications, he had reacted precisely in the way he himself so often denounced in others—with denial. In somewhat the same way as he would, thirty years later, angrily suggest that AIDS sufferers ought simply to refrain from sex, this miraculously healthy child of a syphilitic father had lambasted the Auschwitz survivors for their "ghetto thinking." Why couldn't they have fought? By shifting the blame for the main part of their suffering onto the victims themselves, Bettelheim had rid himself of a dangerous threat to his own hard-won equilibrium.

But, to go a little further, is this not precisely what made Bettelheim's message about the genocide so appealing to a segment of the younger generation, who, while not wishing to deny the past, wanted above all to look toward the future? In the mid- and late 1960s these young people were faced with much more immediate dangers than those that obsessed their parents: the Kennedy assassinations, that of Martin Luther King, the Vietnam War, a changing society. For many of them the appeal of Bettelheim's message was, no doubt, that his status as a former camp inmate gave him the right to say what they, who had never known Nazism, did not even dare to think: that, horrendous as it was, it was not their problem, and that no, they were not responsible for Hitler's crimes. It was indeed tragic, but it was too much so for them to be able to do anything about it. The only thing they could do, apart from feeling compassion for the victims, was to try and make sure that it never happened again. Which is exactly what Bettelheim was continually saying—a preoccupation that he pithily summed up in the opening sentence one of his very last essays on the subject: "My business is not with the dead, but with the living."

This essay, one of the most forceful he wrote on the subject, is titled "The Holocaust: Some Reflections, a Generation Later."[41] It is essentially a long meditation on the death instinct. For the first time, Bettelheim stressed that the denial of such a monstrous crime could only have been unconscious. This time, however, the bulk of his criticism was not aimed at the victims. Instead, he concentrated on how, since the war, everything possible had been done, particularly in the United States, to avoid facing up to the reality of Hitler's crime. Denial, he wrote, begins with words. The Nazis were the first to try to disguise what they were doing, by calling it the *Endlösung*, or "final solution." But as early as 1944 the Allies had also contributed to the process by choosing the neologism *genocide*, half-Greek, half-Latin, to designate what was in fact the mass murder of Jews. A similar motivation inspired the Americans, who opted for the word *Holocaust*, borrowed from the liturgical vocabulary and referring to sacrifice by fire, Bettelheim pointed out. While it was true that Hitler's victims had ended up as ashes in the camps' crematoria, the religious reference was "a sacrilege, a profanation of God and man," because it robs the victims of this abominable mass murder of the only thing left to them: their uniqueness."

So after all those years, Bettelheim's inner travails had finally brought him back to the only position he could occupy without betraying himself in his own eyes: that of authentic defender of the memory of the victims. Authentic because the defense was based not on sentimentalism, which he considered to be blind and therefore guilty, but on extreme clear-sightedness—on a lucidity that pierced the depths of the soul, to the point where it hurt the most, to dig out what had been denied, what could not be expressed. To reach that point, however, he first had to express the rejection that the victims inspired in him, too. "My business is not with the dead, but with the living."

But how could a man whose own father had been reduced (through his own "fault") to spending two years hidden away in a Viennese clinic, like one of the living dead, consciously entertain such a thought? From that instinctive rejection, Bettelheim had thus arrived at guilt—not the superficial emotion of social convention, but remorse that cut into the soul like a scalpel. In 1968, he had pointed out that, in extreme situations, the guilt of the survivor was not the noble sentiment it was sometimes made out to be. "I believe, on the basis of my experience, that this guilt is not for the death of the other but for how one felt about it."[42] That feeling was not just one of relief at still being alive when others were dead, it was "the morally unacceptable feeling of happiness" that wells up uncontrollably when one discovers that it is the next man who has drawn the unlucky number.

Facing up to such feelings had not been easy. But he had to go through it in order to overcome the terrible conflict between his desire to live—a powerful drive but one that he had difficulty accepting unless he could justify it by passing on to others what he had learned in the camps—and what he could read in the eyes of the men and women who had found themselves locked in a confrontation with death from which no one could emerge a winner. These were people for whom surviving was not, and could not be, a victory, for whom no "happy ending" was possible.

The last phase of Bettelheim's thinking about his concentration camp experience, which was to lead him to undertake the essay "Surviving" at a time when he thought he was through with the subject, was certainly the most disturbing for him. It started with the shock he experienced on seeing the film *Seven Beauties*, by the Italian director Lina Wertmüller. In the article he wrote about his reaction, Bettelheim's indignation is also directed at a book called *The Survivor*, published around the same time. The criticism of the two works is so tightly intertwined, however, that the reader has a hard time realizing that they in fact have nothing to do with each other—an intellectually questionable procedure, as the author of the book, Terrence Des Pres, was to point out.[43]

In the United States, Lina Wertmüller had shot from obscurity to quite extraordinary popularity in just two years, and when *Seven Beauties* opened in January 1976 it was greeted with widespread critical acclaim as her masterpiece. This tragicomic, baroque, and expressionist film starts in Fascist Italy. The central character is the seductive but totally amoral Pasqualino, a young Neapolitan thug, who rapes, robs, and murders his way through life until he finds himself thrown into a concentration camp. There, in the hope of winning his release, he decides to seduce the camp commander, a massive German woman. Pasqualino's plan works, but not exactly as he had intended: The commander, who is no fool, offers him a good meal and a good night's sleep to recover, at the end of which if he fails to get an erection with her he will be killed. He accepts the bargain. There follows what is obviously meant to be the high point of the film: a burlesque scene in which the frail and sickly youth struggles to fulfill his part of the bargain—finally with success. "Your thirst for life disgusts me, you shitty little Neapolitan," the woman spits out, sadly ruminating that for that very reason her "master race" will probably not survive the war. All the idealists in the film end up dead: The one who dreamed of a new man in a better world commits suicide by throwing himself into the open latrine pit; Pasqualino, promoted to the rank of *Kapo* after his sexual performance, shoots his friend, a Socialist and man of principle. The film ends in Naples after its liberation by U.S. troops, where the wretched hero, now free, is reunited with his girlfriend. She has in the meantime become a prostitute, and will remain one. Pasqualino tells her that he wants to have lots and lots of children.

Even leaving aside those details that must have particularly affected Bettelheim by evoking painful memories, it is easy to see why he found the work so disturbing. Whatever else he thought of her film, he had to acknowledge that Wertmüller, a former assistant to Federico Fellini, had talent. She had also done her homework (the film portrays many of the known features of Buchenwald, such as the *Bock*, the hanging of inmates by the arms, and the majestic surrounding forest). The central character is also remarkably acted, by Giancarlo Giannini, who often manages to win the audience's sympathy for the contemptible Pasqualino. The shots of the camp even feature the bluish fog often mentioned by survivors; by contrast, Naples is shown as a riot of color.

After attending a private showing of *Seven Beauties*, Bettelheim immediately informed the *New York Times* that he would not be able to comply with their request for a review. Still upset about the film two weeks later, he agreed, however, to see it again. On that second viewing he found it even more disturbing, but better understood why, as he recounts in the introduction to "Surviving." This resulted in the article that three years later would form the title piece of the collection of essays.

Bettelheim had in fact been expecting to see another of a spate of films, like *The Night Porter*, that exploited Nazism for erotic purposes. That would have been easy for him to deal with. To gain pleasure from hurting others, or from pain inflicted on oneself, was clearly not "decent," to use a word Bettelheim was fond of employing to assess human behavior. But Wertmüller's film was not erotic, it was philosophical; it glorified sadism not as a means to pleasure, but simply as an essential component of the survival instinct. That is precisely what makes it so disturbing. It shows a crude, grotesque, and despicable lust for life that carries all before it, triumphing in particular over all forms of ideal. The film portrays the life instinct as essentially obscene, grasping, sadistic, and above all power-hungry. Message: Forget all the rest; this is what really makes the world go round. It was the absolute negation, in other words, of everything Bruno Bettelheim had been teaching for thirty-six years. He had spent his entire life struggling against just those unacceptable elements in his own life instinct (and those of the children in his care), trying to channel them (or, as a psychoanalyst would put it, sublimate them) into the most productive, the highest life-enhancing actions. Wertmüller's film did not just negate such efforts, it actively ridiculed them by emptying them of meaning.

In his article, Bettelheim accuses Wertmüller of being confused. He does not doubt that, consciously, she is against Fascism and the concentration camps, but at the same time she is fascinated by their brutality and power, their "rape of man." All the noble characters are shown to be losers; good is feeble and only evil triumphs. Unconsciously, she is seeking to justify the world that has spawned the camps, Bettelheim writes. "Pasqualino is not a person whose experiences have added to his depth; understanding, compassion, the ability to feel guilty, all of which were lacking in him before, continue to be lacking in him, despite world-shaking experiences that one feels should have changed him completely. It is this depiction of the survivor that robs survivorship of all meaning. It makes seeing the film an experience that degrades."

But the worst aspect of all for Bettelheim was the acclaim that greeted the film in American intellectual circles—the same circles where many of his own admirers were to be found. One cannot help but feel that this success appeared to him as a betrayal, as evidence that his efforts had been in vain; that almost a half-century of trying to point out the road away from barbarity had failed, that absurdity had won out over meaning, ugliness over beauty. This impression is strengthened by what he then goes on to write about *The Survivor*: "By quite different routes Professor Des Pres . . . and Wertmüller . . . arrive at parallel conclusions about what is required for survival in a world dominated by the concentration camp or standing under its specter . . . The main lesson of survivorship is: all that matters, the only thing that is really important, is life in its crudest, merely biological form."

There is no need to delve too deeply into the debate between Bettelheim and Des Pres (carried on solely through their writings; they never
actually met) to see that its significance, for Bettelheim at least, had
little to do with details of camp life provided on each side. Indeed,
other writers have already pointed out that their descriptions do not in
fact differ very much.[44] What is important in the confrontation is that
Bettelheim appears to have reacted to it with total bad faith, thereby
showing just how deeply this new controversy had affected him.

For *The Survivor* bears little relation to Bettelheim's description of
it. Terrence Des Pres in fact shows that in order to survive in the
camps, inmates could not afford to consider their own individual
needs alone. If they did not help one another, they were lost. And
although he does defend a viewpoint that could be described as "biol-
ogist," it has nothing to do with the cynical "thirst for life" of Wertmüller's antihero. For Des Pres, the lesson to be drawn from the concentration camps is that what keeps people alive is not great ideas,
but their awareness of their condition. "The survivor is evidence that
men and women are now strong enough, mature enough, awake
enough, to face death without mediation, and therefore to embrace
life without reserve," he writes.[45] The message is that one should
beware of all ideologies, religions, and other beliefs (among which he
includes psychoanalysis), because while claiming to save humanity
they often end up annihilating it.

It was a message that was in tune with the times. In the mid-1970s,
idealism was on the wane, with Watergate and the Vietnam War forcing the United States to reassess its world role. Rather than the victory over the self proposed by Bettelheim, Des Pres preached observance of Voltaire's famous dictum "We must cultivate our garden."
This was not a new debate, and it could have remained a simple difference between two humanist views of man, explicable in part by the
difference in age between its protagonists (Des Pres was thirty-seven,
Bettelheim seventy-three). Furthermore, Bettelheim would probably
not have found it very hard to counter Des Pres's arguments, and
point up the misunderstandings in his book, which was indeed not a
work of history: Des Pres was a professor of English at Colgate University in New York State, and his work had grown out of a research
project on the theme of the survivor in literature, a figure he viewed
as the epitome of the antihero. In it, however, he lumped victims of
the Soviet gulag together with those of the Nazi genocide, and he
failed to emphasize the all-important distinction between concentra-

tion camps and death camps. Above all, Des Pres's research was purely literary, and his analysis of what constituted a survivor was therefore strictly intellectual. The work is nonetheless moving in places, and frequently brilliant and insightful, being well documented and built around a clear idea. But although it remains nothing more than a textual analysis, it takes upon itself to decide which of the survivors' accounts are right and which are wrong.

Among the former inmates whose accounts Terrence Des Pres dismisses are most of those who sought to analyze camp behavior from a psychological standpoint, first and foremost Bruno Bettelheim, whom Des Pres criticizes for using the concepts of infantilization and identification with the aggressor, which he sees as meaningless within the framework of a camp. He also condemns Bettelheim for imposing his own interpretations on the behavior of his fellow-inmates, in particular that of Eugen Kogon, without seeming to realize that that is precisely what he, Des Pres, is doing to Bettelheim—with a key difference, however: Bettelheim had actually been at Buchenwald, while Des Pres, who had not, considered himself entitled to play the testimony of one inmate off that of another. More generally, Des Pres accuses Bettelheim of always portraying his own actions in a favorable light, and attacks his position as an uncontested authority, going so far as to write that Bettelheim's "first analysis of the camp experience— 'Individual and Mass Behavior in Extreme Situations'—appeared in 1943, adding the weight of precedence to a position which has never been challenged and which has influenced all subsequent study."[46] It does not appear to have occurred to him that its precedence was precisely what gave it authority.

According to some of his friends, Des Pres had in fact been an admirer of Bettelheim's, until his reading of other survivors' accounts led him to question his writings.[47] He thus veered from admiration to hostility, as did many of Bettelheim's detractors. Des Pres ended up in effect denying Bettelheim his validity as a witness, without any regard for a man who, whatever his position, was but a human being and therefore fallible. All of which, coming from the author of the above-mentioned lines, was paradoxical to say the least!

That Bettelheim should have been angry, not to say furious, at being so criticized by a disillusioned young man who felt himself entitled to judge him without taking into account the fact that before becoming an authority on the Nazis Bettelheim had been one of their victims is easy to understand. He was an irritable man who, while preaching autonomy, did not much like to be challenged. But that fact alone does not explain the way he couched his article, shooting down Des Pres with images from Wertmüller's film, and without ever informing the readers of the *New Yorker* that Des Pres had attacked *him* in his book. Bettelheim was very protective of his reputation in academic circles. This was not the first time he had been criticized. He could very well have answered Des Pres by pointing out the omissions and contradictions in his book, not to mention its literary effects, which on this issue could be seen as a little out of place. He could also have decided to ignore the attack altogether. So why did he choose a path that, if Des Pres had decided to reply in a mass-circulation paper, could have led to his being publicly accused of intellectual dishonesty?

In a letter to his friend Carl Frankenstein, Bettelheim admitted that he had had a lot of trouble composing his article, but that he had felt it to be his duty. "Although in opposite ways—Des Pres attacked me personally, but this is beside the point—the film and the book, in my opinion subtly, in camouflaged ways, preach fascism, glorify, as Des Pres calls it, 'living by the crude demands of the body, beyond the compulsions of culture.' "[48]

So Bettelheim's attack on Des Pres was not in fact merely for revenge, as Des Pres himself, and a few others after him, believed.[49] Bettelheim was sincere; he was even shocked that others had not seen the same hidden danger he had detected ("Even Jewish magazines reprinted Des Pres, so much were they taken by his thesis," he wrote to Frankenstein). In his view, all of this was to be lumped together with the popularity at the time of the memoirs of Albert Speer, one of Hitler's former ministers, and other books on Nazism. Not long afterward, while browsing in an antiques store in California, he would get a similar shock, as he told his friend in another letter. On examining a medal bearing Goethe's head, which he thought would make a good gift, he suddenly noticed a Nazi symbol on the back. The object was extremely expensive. Repressing a desire to hurl the medal in the dealer's face, he simply stated that he would not want it even if it was free. Surprised, the man replied: "But the Nazi sign is precisely what makes it valuable!" Bettelheim commented sadly to his friend: "So the catastrophes in our lives have acquired rarity value, so far has this time removed itself from them."[50]

Here we see an aging, weary Bettelheim (he had recently had a mild heart attack and was suffering from arthrosis, among other ailments), waging one last fight against what he saw as the creeping revisionism of the period. But that is not all. His reaction to the book and to the film seems too passionate, too based on gut feeling, to have been entirely rational.

It could be that the source of his discomfort is to be found in the lyrical closing words of *The Survivor*, where Terrence Des Pres appeals to his readers to be content with being simply human, rather than supermen: "A biological wisdom exists, prompting us to know that in life's own needs the spirit can find a home. Not noble or god-approved, not especially dramatic or sublime as in the old days, but rooted in the plain happiness of work and communion with others, and in the small shared universe of physical joy which is our due as creatures of flesh."[51] In both his article and his letter to Frankenstein, Bettelheim singles out that last expression as evidence that Des Pres is "glorifying living by the crude demands of the body." Such emphasis on a few fleeting words of conclusion is worth a second look; it seems to indicate that Bettelheim is reading more into them than they seem to deserve. Perhaps they reminded him of "the crude demands of the body" which, seventy years earlier, had deprived him of a father he could respect, a moral authority he could lean on, leaving him all alone, and much too young, to face up to his own actions, at one and the same time an inflexible judge and an eternally guilty party.

In addition to the reminder of Anton, or rather of Anton's weakness, that it may have stirred, this reference to "physical joy" in the conclusion of a book that deals with Auschwitz survivors is indeed somewhat shocking. On that point Des Pres does have something in common with Wertmüller. Indeed, unless someone has been impelled by circumstances, and thus by a feeling of duty, to spend a large part of his or her life studying the Nazis' cruelty, there is always something a little suspicious about such an exercise, something that has to do with the sadistic dimension of the life drives. For man's aggressive instincts are indeed on the side of life, which is what all survivors, in one way or another, discover—precisely in the horrible jubilation one feels, in spite of oneself, when it is the other guy who draws the short straw, a jubilation that is immediately tempered by a strong sense of guilt, except perhaps in people for whom "in life's own needs the spirit can find a home." But one must have lived through such an ordeal to truly understand. And the writer who does not realize this can do no more than string out empty statements, serving only to camouflage the reality of man.

What Bettelheim had been trying to get across for the previous forty years was that in the extreme situation of the camp, the continual struggle that Freud described between the life drives (including sadism) and the death instinct (which aspires not to victory but to the simple ending of the battle, to nothingness), was liable at any moment to reach the "ultimate limit," the point beyond which there is no turning back—the point at which the aggressive instincts line up their forces on the side of death. In the early writings those were not the words he used, but the idea was already there. He explored every possible avenue to try and get it across. Over the years, as he carried on the inner struggle to understand these things, to put an end to the pain they caused him, the idea became clearer in its outlines. In his last essays on the subject, written to tie together the articles published in *Surviving*, it came into sharp focus.

As he had already noted in his foreword to Nyiszli's book, the specificity of the Nazi genocide had less to do with the murderous wish expressed by Hitler himself than with the echo it found in the minds of so many of his victims. This did not mean that those victims had consented to their fate. Once again, Bettelheim was talking about the unconscious (but in such a peremptory, and often such a convincing, fashion that his readers did not realize it). What he was trying to say, because he had felt it in himself, was that the real danger point is reached when the deadly desire of the killer touches on the hidden feeling that lurks in every human being, the feeling of having no right to be alive. It is a feeling that is stronger in some people than in others; there are even people who deny its existence. Bettelheim, for his part, had known it only too well since childhood, when he would shut himself away in his room, not exactly unhappy but convinced that his life was not worth living. He had heard that same feeling echoed in every anti-Semitic remark—for what a racist is in fact saying is that the other person does not have as much right to be here as he has. And Bettelheim may also have detected it in some rather obsequious attitudes displayed by one or the other of his parents.[52] This would explain his anger at "ghetto thinking," and also his fascination with the state of Israel. One day in Jerusalem, Bettelheim asked Carl Frankenstein why he had chosen to live there rather than in the United States, where his life would have been so much more comfortable. His friend smiled at him, and replied: "Because here, I'm not a Jew."

To glorify the life instinct, whether it be with intentional vulgarity like Wertmüller, or by dressing it up in natural lyricism like Des Pres, while ignoring the constant struggle that it has to wage against its toughest enemy, the death instinct, in the murderous environment of the camp—that was the true obscenity. And that, for Bettelheim, was real negationism, the denial of the camps' reality. What right did these two goyim have to preach to him about survival? What did they know about the camps? Did they not realize that, for someone who has spent time in the hands of the Nazis, nothing can ever be the same again? He had indeed experienced sadism in its most naked forms; other people's sadism, but above all his own, without which he would have died. For precisely that reason he had devoted his life to telling people how to make good use of that sadistic component of their life instinct—by turning it not against themselves or their own kind, but against the enemy. Was that not the purpose of all his writings? Was it not precisely because "it is the certainty of death that gives human life its meaning"[53] that he sought always to give his stories the happiest possible endings?

But already the public appeal of those stories appeared to be waning, or at least was no longer strong enough to satisfy his need to feel useful. Since the Chicago campus revolt of 1969, Bettelheim had appeared to many students as no more than an ill-tempered and reactionary old man. At Stanford, where he was by then teaching a few courses, many viewed his ideas as old-fashioned. The California campus was the temple of behaviorism, and psychoanalysis was not in favor. Bettelheim's teachings no longer appealed to most students, and neither did his style. And when he went back to Chicago, for three months of classes in the spring, he was brought face to face with the loss of the Orthogenic School. True, the rest of his life was still going well, and his book *The Uses of Enchantment*, published in 1976, was a bestseller. But not even that could make up for what he perceived more and more as rejection by his young audience, the prime targets for his message. As he wrote shortly before this period, "I always felt that teaching students, although at times trying, is so very important because the personal contact is something no written word can replace."[54]

Bettelheim wrote in *Surviving* that when the title article of that book was first published in the *New Yorker* in August 1976, it resulted in a large number of grateful letters. He cited only one, from a German woman who had been saved by a Dutch clergyman during the war, and who asked him to write more about the guilt felt by survivors, a feeling that had dogged her ever since. The space Bettelheim devoted to the letter, which he quoted practically in full, suggests that it had had on him the effect of a badly needed antidote to the poison of *Seven Beauties* and the Des Pres book. Someone still needed him, and what she wanted to hear about was guilt, the psychological mechanism he understood best of all, the instrument that had served, throughout his whole life, to give a meaning to his existence.

Six months after that article appeared, Bettelheim took part in the San Jose Holocaust Conference, to which he submitted his beautiful piece on the death instinct, "The Holocaust—One Generation Later." In it, he stressed the importance to prisoners of feeling they were being heard, and the role the silence of the outside world had played in the Holocaust:

> Murderers can only kill; they do not have the power to rob us of the wish to live nor of the ability to fight for life. Degradation, exhaustion, and utter debilitation through starvation, sickness, and mistreatment—all these seriously weaken our will to live, undermine our life drives, and with this open the way for the death drive. But when such conditions— in which the Jews found themselves because of Nazi persecution and degradation—are worsened by the feeling that the rest of the world has forsaken us, then we are totally deprived of the strength needed to fight off the murderer, to refuse to dig our own grave.[55]

To illustrate this state of despair, Bettelheim quoted lines by the poet Paul Celan, a Rumanian Jew whose parents died in the death camps, and who was himself a camp survivor:

> *There was earth in them, and*
> *they dug.*
> *They dug and dug, and thus*
> *their day wore on, and their night . . .*

He stressed the final lines of the poem:

> *Oh someone, oh none, oh no one, oh you:*
> *Where did it go, if nowhere it went.*
> *Oh you dig and I dig, and I dig myself towards you,*
> *and on our finger the ring awakes us.*[56]

Bettelheim added: "The Nazis murdered the Jews of Europe. That nobody but the Jews cared, that the world, the United States, did not care, was why Jewish life drives lost the battle against death tendencies. This was why the camp inmates had already relinquished life as they dug their own graves, and why, as the poet put it, 'there was earth in them.'" Then, finally acknowledging that his place at that point had been in the outside world, he noted: "We ought to have been their someone, but we were their no one. This is our burden. Just because we cannot atone for it, it is wrong to deny or obfuscate it."[57]

This time, Bettelheim was fully accepting his position in relation to the camp victims, no more and no less. No longer needing to fight against himself, he had stopped pointing the finger at them. A little later, on the publication of Miep Gies's book *Anne Frank Remembered*, he even implicitly made peace with the young Jewish girl's father, through his tribute to the woman who had helped hide the family and had saved Anne's diary. "It was Miep's courage that made her ignore the risk to herself and her husband, and her wish to protect Anne's privacy that alone preserved Anne's diary . . . Her courage, her humanity, and her decency give us hope for humanity," Bettelheim concluded.[58]

It had been a long and painful voyage, as he acknowledged when putting together *Surviving:* "The basic motive for both writing these essays and assembling them now has been at work in me for some forty years, dominating my private thoughts and feelings during all that time."[59] Indeed, the compilation of *Surviving*, which he initially thought would require around six months, since it was mainly a question of selecting essays and writing a few connecting pieces, in fact took him two years.[60]

In one of the last pieces he was to write on Nazism, one of the three linking chapters he composed for *Surviving*, Bettelheim again quotes Paul Celan:

> *Black milk of dawn we drink it at dusk*
> *we drink it at noon and at daybreak we drink it at night*
> *we drink and we drink . . .*

These are the opening lines of *"Todesfuge"* (Death Fugue), the poem that made Celan famous in Germany. After pointing to the small word that is changed in the final stanza:

> *Black milk of dawn we drink* you *at dusk,*

Bettelheim then makes a terrible confession: "When one is forced to drink black milk from dawn to dusk, whether in the death camps of Nazi Germany, or while lying in a possibly luxurious crib, but there subjected to the unconscious death wishes of what overtly may be a conscientious mother—in either situation, a living soul has death for a master."[61]

Two years after *Surviving*, Bettelheim was to write a postscript for a French book based on accounts of Jews who as children had been taken in and protected from the Nazis by Christian families, *Je ne lui ai pas dit au revoir*.[62] He found here an opportunity to write about the terrible silence of those whose parents had disappeared at the hands of the Nazis. In their deepest recesses, he said, these people "realize, or at least think, that others wish that they could make their peace with what had happened to them; and this, they know, is impossible," because "in order to be able to continue to live, to do well in school, to pass exams," and later to hold down a job and build a family, "the victims hid their true feeling so deeply, in the innermost layers of their very being, that they can hardly reach it themselves . . . all they know is that life is extremely difficult for them, and that in the deepest sense it is empty."[63] In a letter to the writer Madeleine Chapsal, he added that the accounts of the deportees' children tell us "once more how the sins of the generation of the parents destroy the lives of their children." This was why, he added, "I devoted all my life's work to helping children, because this chain of one generation destroying the next must be broken, or one must at least try to do whatever one can to break it."[64]

14

---❋---

The Big Bad Wolf

All my life, I did what came simplest to me; and what is praiseworthy about that? It is true, what to me seems obvious does not seem so to many other people.

Bruno Bettelheim, letter to
Madeleine Chapsal, June 24, 1977

"Joey" arrived at the Orthogenic School in early 1952. He was nine years old and fragile-looking, with something imperious in the expression that played around his large eyes. "Something a little sadistic, like a two-month old sitting on the throne," his counselor recalls. He spoke little, stammering heavily when he did, and balked at uttering certain words, such as sugar. He did not pronounce any names, particularly not his own. Joey could spend hours sitting silently in a corner, rigid and immobile. From time to time he would explode, running around in all directions screaming "Crash!" and smashing the light bulbs and vacuum tubes that he always managed to hoard in large quantities; then he would revert to his apathetic, switched-off robot mode. Before eating, playing, or going to bed, he would unroll imaginary cables connected to a large electric motor that he carried with him everywhere, plugging them into equally illusory wall sockets. In the early days, he could do nothing without his motor. When "switched on," however, his gestures were so precise and convincing that, in the dining room, it was not uncommon for counselors or children to carefully step over his connections, as if they were really there.

His bed was festooned with electrical circuits and dials, and if he should happen to knock one of them over in his sleep, somebody would always be sure to put it back in place, so that Joey did not switch off upon awakening.

Joey held a special fascination for the staff and was well accepted by the other boys in his dorm. His elaborate rituals could get on their nerves at times, notably when they held up the start of some group activity or outing, but his companions were also impressed by his extraordinary grasp of all things electrical—at least, "when we had time to think about it," as one fellow-student says, adding that most of the time they were too wrapped up in their own problems to take much interest in the other boys. Joey's periodic panics could be extremely violent, but the rest of the time he was a shy, retiring child who caused no trouble at all, a fascinating blend of emotional distress and almost superhuman technical skill; a crazed scientific genius locked up in the body of a terrified child. For Bruno Bettelheim, Joey was a living metaphor for the profound imbalance he found in the technological society around him.

One Memorial Day, four years after entering the school, Joey made a banner for the parade. It read: "Feelings are more important than anything under the sun." He still had a long way to go, but he was clearly on the road to recovery. Today he lives like millions of other people. He still stammers a little, but he has a regular job—in electronics, of course. He is single, but he has friends and manages his life himself. The first article Bettelheim published about his case upset Joey: he thought the description of his symptoms was exaggerated, and was shocked by the portrayal of his mother.[1] He nevertheless paid regular visits to Dr. B after leaving the school, and was saddened on hearing of his death.

On the phone, in 1994, the slightly hesistant voice that politely declines to answer my questions is indeed that of a man responsible for his own life, who knows what is best for him: "I am sorry, but I have had some bad experiences. I would rather not take part in your project . . . I'm sorry you're calling from so far away." (I was calling from France.)[2]

"Joey the Mechanical Boy" was to become the most famous of Bettelheim's patients. He emerged as a touching little victim of the technological age who, deprived of human love, could trust only machines and barricaded his own emptiness behind a fortress of electrical wires—"the most telling case of autism in all the literature," as the writer Geneviève Jurgensen put it. It should, however, be pointed out that Joey's problem would probably not be diagnosed as autism today. He had arrived at the Orthogenic School with that label, but it seems likely that even by the time Bettelheim was writing his case study for *The Empty Fortress*, in the mid-1960s, he no longer considered him autistic. As early as 1956, Bettelheim described an unidentified child with symptoms very like those of Joey, but categorized him as "delusional with autistic features" rather than autistic.[3]

Why then did Bettelheim decide to use Joey as one of the three cases of autism described in *The Empty Fortress* (1967)? The simplest answer to that question is probably the right one. Not only did Joey's symptoms offer great material for analysis, but Bettelheim needed a success story to validate the treatment methods outlined in the book. And Joey indeed represented a true success for the school, and for the Bettelheim method. This could not be said of "Laurie" and "Marcia," the two other cases described in *The Empty Fortress*, both of whom were undoubtedly autistic, even under the stricter definition prevailing today.

Laurie, as Bettelheim himself reports, was removed from the school by her family too early, before the astonishing progress she had started to make could lead to a durable improvement in her condition. The case of Marcia is more complex, and may illustrate insurmountable barriers to the treatment of autism, as well as the school's own limitations. At first, the young girl made spectacular progress, as evidenced by the miles of film of her, shot month after month at Bettelheim's request.[4] After four years of constant care and attention, Marcia could perform simple household tasks and take care of herself; most notably, she had started to communicate with other people. Unfortunately, by the time she emerged from her isolation, she had already reached fourteen, and she was intelligent enough to understand just how much of a gulf separated her from other girls her age. Realizing that she would never catch up with them, she became discouraged, and her rate of progress slowed considerably. Three years later, she stopped making any progress at all, after Karen Zelan, her counselor, left the school. Marcia then went back to her family, immensely better than she had been on arrival, but still incapable of looking after herself alone. "We did everything we could for her; we helped her to go half the way," Bettelheim told Ruth Marquis one day.

Much later, at Stanford, Bettelheim would admit to the young therapists attending his seminar that "nobody knows how to treat these
children." And when one of them reacted with surprise, saying, "But
you yourself have treated some autistic children rather successfully," he
replied honestly: "We did the best we could . . . Unfortunately, in quite
a few cases, our success was limited."[5] That was not, however, how he
described things in *The Empty Fortress*, his seminal work on autism.
And in an interview in 1973, he asserted that the school "cured eighty-
five percent" of all autistic children admitted before the ages of seven
or eight![6]

Of all Bettelheim's exaggerations, this is clearly the most serious.
Not only did it offer false hope to families already suffering greatly
from their child's handicap, it deflected attention from the school's
genuine achievements, notably those with autistic children. Furthermore, in the minds of those who knew that the claim was false—and
there were quite a few—it sowed a seed of doubt about *The Empty
Fortress*, a book whose remarkable insights and observations should
have earned it an unquestioned place among the standard references
in child psychology. Here again, Bettelheim's need to be the best, and
to have the last word, succeeded in tainting his work with a suspicion
of fraud, thus confirming the deepest fears of this man who could not
bring himself to believe in his own legitimacy.

It should, however, be noted that in the early 1950s, when the Orth-
ogenics began taking in "the non-talking kids," as the other children
called them (even though some were not completely mute), the accepted
definitions of schizophrenia and autism were vaguer than they are
today. The first such children admitted were simply stranger, and more
difficult to get through to, than the others. It was somewhat later that
the school started to deliberately take in autistic children, around 1956
and the obtainment of the Ford Foundation grant.

At that time, the term *autism* was applied to the most severe forms
of infantile psychoses, which were then referred to as schizophrenias.[7]
In the first publication to distinguish between autistic and mentally
retarded children, the psychiatrist Leo Kanner had, in 1943, drawn up
a list of symptoms that gained general acceptance.[8] In the early fifties
the psychoanalyst Margaret Mahler further distinguished autism from
another form of extreme mental disturbance in children, "symbiotic
psychosis." She described the autistic child as one who, in spite of an
intelligent and even thoughtful facial expression, never looks anyone
else directly in the eyes. He is often believed to be deaf, since he

behaves as if he cannot hear anything. Typically, he is mute; if he does speak, the words are unintelligible. Unlike other psychotic patients, he only appears content when left completely to himself. In his relations with the outside world, he often acts as though he were a magician, signaling in a robotlike fashion to others to do things that he cannot do himself. His only emotional attachments are, in some cases, to a single object, or to some stereotyped gestures, which he repeats indefinitely. He is totally intolerant of any changes in his environment, apparently impervious to pain, and subject to crises of extreme violence. Rather than auto-eroticism, he often engages in self-mutilation—such as bashing his head against a wall, or biting himself and drawing blood.[9]

According to Fae Lohn Tyroler, who was both Joey's counselor and Bettelheim's assistant at the time he decided to take in a number of autistic children, he had long hesitated over the move. Emmy Sylvester, with whom he had discussed the issue before she left Chicago, had been against it. From his first experiences with very sick children, Bettelheim knew that it would profoundly change his school, which up to then had been doing very well. But his wariness had finally been overridden by his need to continually expand the limits of what he could achieve, combined with his intellectual curiosity and his unending quest for funds. These kids were said to be incurable, and yet he knew he could help them: they were no different from the ones he had helped up until then, just a little sicker. He felt certain that with dedication, hard work, intelligence, and adequate funding, he and the staff could meet the challenge. Bettelheim thus decided that the Orthogenic School would become the laboratory in which one of the great psychological riddles of the age would be solved, and that he would devote most of his own time to it. The message was implicit in his "Application for a grant permitting a research program in therapy of infantile autism and dynamics of early ego development," submitted to the Ford Foundation in 1955.[10]

The new challenge had immediately stimulated Bettelheim's creative intuition, as is obvious from both his grant submission and the first of his annual reports. Autistic children often look both beautiful and intelligent (Kanner thought them of above-average intelligence), which may explain the fascination they generally hold for those who work with them. Despite their inability to communicate with others, their appearance creates the illusion that it would not take much to reach them—that if only one could break through the shell, one would find an intact human being beneath it. The impression is so strong that it is not unusual, even today, to find traces of it among people looking after autistic children, who should know better than anyone else just how unrealistic it is."

In that pioneering age of the 1950s, the autistic child also seemed to hold out the hope that psychologists and other specialists could one day understand just how the personality is formed. Those who did not see autism simply as resulting from an organic, genetic, or chemical defect, but rather as an accident in a child's emotional development, thought that studying it could reveal the stages in the formation of the ego. As Bettelheim stressed in his application to the Ford Foundation, most of the theoretical models of personality development up until then had been inferred from memory traces elicited during therapy on adults. If, however, one was able to observe autistic children twenty-four hours a day, as they emerged from their isolation, one would in fact be witnessing the process by which the ego becomes integrated in the first years of life under ordinary circumstances. He therefore proposed to study six boys and six girls in the six-to-eleven age group. "Since these children are old enough to talk," he wrote, "and begin to talk as they acquire an ego, they can convey much more to us about this process than the observation of infants only" (the latter method being the one adopted by some psychoanalysts, notably in Great Britain, to try to answer the same question).

The arrival at the school of these deeply disturbed children immediately led Bettelheim to exciting discoveries. As early as July 17, 1958, in his second report to the Ford Foundation, he noted that, rather than suffering from arrested development, as many experts thought at the time, autistic children seemed to have acquired "isolated islands" of specific experience, both sensory and motor, but these islands "do not merge to permit formation of a continuous internal structure." It was as if these children had been able to acquire a few of the bricks needed to create a normal ego, without being able to start building one.

Treatment and observation of the children selected for the study was only one part of the program. Bettelheim also asked George Perkins, the school's consultant psychiatrist, to work with the mothers of three of them, while supervising the corresponding children's therapy. Jules Henry, the social anthropologist, was to observe a number of families in their home life, while Ben Wright would pay particular attention to the counselors' interactions with the most disturbed children. The school's psychiatric social worker, Florence White, also worked for the Ford Foundation project. And the new funds allowed Bettelheim to hire a few psychologists and psychiatrists on a part-time basis to help with the research. His reports to the foundation, which he would later use in the opening chapters of *The Empty Fortress*, were therefore packed with notes on the children's families and hypotheses about the causes of autism. But what made them truly remarkable was the way they portrayed the children.

To this day, it is not uncommon in psychiatric manuals to find "autists" classified under the heading of "mentally retarded" and described solely in terms of their deficiencies. In Bettelheim's reports, however, those same children appeared as living human beings, acting and even reacting to their environment. They were individuals who, although they had problems, were described in terms of what they actually did rather than what they could not do. This above all is why *The Empty Fortress* was to be a revolutionary book that would have an impact on how psychotics were viewed and handled the world over. Once again, for Bettelheim "mad" did not mean "deficient," but simply "ill." As he did with his other patients, he gave autistic children "the benefit of the doubt,"[12] working from the assumption that, however disturbing or obnoxious, their behavior had meaning for them, that it was the best way they could find to express their pain and maybe alleviate it. As he says in *The Art of the Obvious*: "Freud taught the rest of us to suspend our disbelief—our refusal to believe—that patients, whether neurotic, psychotic, or autistic, act with intelligence or good purpose. I think we ought always to proceed on the assumption that the other person's thoughts and actions are worthy of being considered in the most positive way possible."[13]

The word "positive" may be interpreted as moralistic, but it is clear that Bettelheim is not referring here to the purity of the child's intentions, but simply to the intelligence of his actions. Good and evil are not part of the equation when a psychoanalyst is seeking to decipher a patient's behavior. And it is precisely because unconscious motives are never pure that people have so much trouble accepting them. The therapist's role is not to pass judgment, but to discover exactly what the patient is trying to achieve, and the fears that prevent him or her from doing so. This is why Bettelheim never used drugs, even with the most disturbed children. "Maybe it would help to add what medication means to the child," he once suggested to a former counselor writing about her work at the school. "To some it means that they are being poisoned. But all know that through medication one wants to force them, or their bodies, not to do what they otherwise would do (not to be too active, and so on.) That is, if one gives them medication, they can't believe that one wishes them to be as they feel like being. In this way their bodies are manipulated. How can they believe that one does not also wish to manipulate their minds?"[14]

Between what he believed to be a meaningful intent and the crazy behavior it resulted in, Bettelheim detected a blind terror he thought he recognized. What triggered the connection in his mind, he explains in *The Empty Fortress*, was the arrival at the Orthogenic School of "Anna." By the age of ten, the little girl had already tried to kill her younger brother several times, and no psychiatric hospital would keep her for more than a few hours. She resembled the popular image of the feral child: she would suddenly scream, run, and jump around in all directions, rip off her clothes, and attack both children and adults, often biting them until they bled.[15] The rest of the time she would crouch in a corner, totally withdrawn from her surroundings.

Although she had not been in a concentration camp, Anna was also a victim of Nazism. Born to Jewish parents in occupied Poland, she had spent her infancy hiding with her parents in a windowless basement owned by a farmer, for whom her father had to work all day as a weaver in exchange for protection. Her parents did not get along with each other, and her mother was extremely depressed after Anna was born. Even worse, as soon as the baby gave signs of starting to cry, one of her parents would rush to gag her with a hand, for the slightest noise could have cost the family their lives. "Through her, the phenomenon of the camps which had long occupied much of my personal and theoretical interest became somehow linked with my daily work, the treatment of severely disturbed children," Bettelheim wrote.[16]

Observing the little girl with her crises of rage and despair, he concluded: "Some victims of the concentration camps had lost their humanity in response to extreme situations. Autistic children withdraw from the world before their humanity ever really develops."[17] He too had once been in a situation of total powerlessness, in the grip of a world uniformly hostile and unpredictable. That is when he realized that the expression he had used to describe the most terrible experiences of his spell in the camps was also applicable to these children. And he defined it for the first time in *The Empty Fortress*: "This, psychologically, is what constitutes an extreme situation: when we ourselves respond to an external danger—real or imagined—with inner maneuvers that actually debilitate us further."[18]

Two pages earlier, Bettelheim had engaged in an extraordinary exercise: that of describing madness *as seen from the inside*. He did not distinguish between the various types of mental disturbances, but only between their levels of intensity, so that each pathology corresponded to a different stage in the patient's alienation from the outside world. The picture Bettelheim thus builds up ranges from the kind of temporary withdrawal from reality that most of his readers may have experienced at one time or another, to the permanent and dramatic isolation of the autistic child. And what does he find *inside* the deranged mind? The "overwhelming anxiety" of someone who feels completely powerless to defend himself in the face of a world seeking to destroy him.

But one does not have to fall into the hands of the Nazis to experience such a situation: "inner hostility, for example, can arouse tremendous anxiety if we are convinced that giving vent to it will cause our destruction." There is a difference, however: "As long as the person views his anxiety as caused by something on the outside, he remains in some distorted contact with reality." Panic-inducing anxiety, in which the subject's links to the outside world truly break down, occurs when he no longer experiences his own aggressiveness as coming from within. As a result, he feels totally unable to exercise any control over the dangers that his very anxiety generates. The world then ceases to have any meaning at all, and reality becomes utterly terrifying. "Living in such an unreasonable, unpredictable world, the best thing, the only protection, lies in doing nothing." A strictly unvarying environment, and zero feelings, thus become the subject's most urgent needs. "This is autism as seen from inside the person," Bettelheim concluded.[19]

Bettelheim first drew a comparison between his concentration camp experience and the condition of the children in his care during a symposium on infantile schizophrenia in 1955, some ten years before he wrote *The Empty Fortress*.[20] What struck his audience above all were his conclusions, which could be summed up as follows: If an unrelievedly harmful environment can push a hitherto normal subject into schizophrenia, a uniformly beneficial environment may offer a schizophrenic the opportunity to be "reborn" out of his madness and eventually take his place in society.

This exciting idea made a strong impression, but it also aroused some skepticism. Ernst Federn, for example, saw it as no more than an effective literary flourish that had come to Bettelheim through hindsight. However, examination of his work at the school, based on the testimony of former counselors and students, and even including the criticism that followed his death, demonstrates that the connection was real in his mind. But here too, Bettelheim's desire to put a gloss on his work, to round off its awkward angles and retain only the "happy ending," did him a disservice. Its effect on the world outside the school—but not, however, on most of the people who actually worked with him—was to attract a following of uncritical admirers. And when they finally found out that the reality had not been quite as smooth as Bettelheim's picture of it, they were the first to put him in the dock.

Bettelheim's concentration camp experience truly was at the heart of his work as a therapist, and probably even before he himself realized it. This was inevitable, given how intimately the course of his self-analysis had been bound up with it. If he could show so much intuition into the problems that tortured sick children, it was because they found an echo within him. However, playing to his well-meaning, liberal audience, he kept certain things quiet. He dropped hints, particularly toward the end of his life, but he never clearly stated what he had discovered at Buchenwald: that nothing is more effective in defeating self-destructive anxieties than a high-profile, visible enemy, someone one can hate without reservation. And that although a closetful of candy can help convince a child that life is worth living, it will not suffice to strike down the monsters that haunt his psyche. As he muttered to Fritz Redl that day in the school dining room: "People would misunderstand what I was trying to say."[21]

This is indeed where the issue of violence at the school comes in, but not in a scandalous or simplistic way. Bruno Bettelheim was not a hypocrite, preaching one doctrine and practicing another. One can disagree with his way of thinking, but it was consistant. And if nobody took him up on the reply he gave to his friend, it was because it made sense to the people who worked with him.

That Fritz Redl raised the question was no accident. He himself had invented a system of physical restraint, using force but no violence, in his summer camps for problem adolescents, and he had written a great deal on the subject. He and Bettelheim must have discussed the issue at length, and they agreed to make a clear distinction between punishment and discipline. Both of them were against the former, which they saw as being aimed mainly at calming the adult who administered it. "The child nearly always knows that he has done wrong," Bettelheim wrote, "Isn't guilt—the pangs of conscience—a much better and more lasting deterrent than the fear of punishment?"[22]

Bettelheim was opposed to corporal punishment, not because he believed it was too tough on the children, but because he thought it only resulted in Pavlovian-type reactions. And as there are situations in which such conditioned reflexes can be necessary, he made exceptions to the rule. Cathy Kaiser recalls one of them from the early meetings with mothers: "If a child starts to run across the street without paying any attention to cars, a smack on the behind, saying 'Don't you ever do that again!' is protective of the child. But don't overdo it—do it for emphasis," Bettelheim used to say.

Discipline, on the other hand, was something Bettelheim valued. He saw it as indispensable in giving life meaning, in shaping an autonomous adult. He liked to point out that the word is derived from *disciple.* In the 1960s, nothing irritated him more than seeing his name linked to the permissive mores of the time. "What was wrong . . . with old-fashioned, authoritarian education was not that it rested on fear. On the contrary, that is what was right with it. What was wrong was that it disregarded the need to modify the fear in a continuous process so that irrational anxiety would steadily give way to more rational motivation," he wrote in 1969, about the student leaders of that time.[23]

The Orthogenic School's special kind of permissiveness had strictly therapeutic goals. Depressed, self-destructive, or suicidal children had to develop the taste for life which they had never acquired, or had lost, in their infancy. For that to happen, they had to feel accepted, along with their symptoms, and be allowed to regress to the point at which the derailment in their development as healthy human beings had occurred. This implied specific living conditions, which had nothing to do with unbridled permissiveness. Bettelheim explained it this way: "To put our philosophy in practice we had to create a very specific environment . . . This particular society has developed mores of its own . . . For example, tolerance and even temporary encouragement of asocial or regressive tendencies often takes preference over the encouragement of academic progress. In respect to sex behavior, verbal expressions, orderliness and cleanliness, polite conventions yield to emotional honesty. Protection of property takes second place to emotional needs."[24]

But in this uniformly well-meaning universe, among these "good mothers" who, unlike real-life ones, were not likely to abandon their children or project unbearable feelings onto them (Bettelheim made sure of that), there was also a need for a fighter. Someone invested with force, capable of guaranteeing the children's safety, not only against external threats, or against one another,[25] but also and above all against their own internal demons. That fairy tale world needed its Big Bad Wolf to confront the monsters that lurked in the children's heads, and had brought them there in the first place—a "reassuring enemy," as former counselor Leslie Cleaver puts it.

In defining his role at the school, Bettelheim would occasionally replace the Big Bad Wolf image with a more Freudian one: "Here," he would say to the counselors, "the children are the id, you are the ego, and I'm the superego." For anyone accepting his stated intention to put psychoanalytical concepts into action at the school, the statement is very clear. For the superego in each of us is indeed the "Big Bad Wolf," the part of us that adopts the values of our parents and thus "identifies with the aggressor" to become our internal law-and-order agent.

Bettelheim's concentration camp experience had clearly taught him that his worst suffering came not from the outside world, but from his own inner forces, from the ferocity with which his superego judged his own acts rather than from the pain his enemies inflicted on him. Indeed, when his torturers appeared explicitly as such, in the uniform befitting their role (during the terrible Buchenwald roll call, for instance), it was a relief. To allow his charges to get better, Bettelheim had to free them, for the time it took them to sort out their own desires from those of their parents, from the merciless judge who prevented them from living. And to facilitate this type of "rebirth," he had to adopt the appearance of the aggressor who was torturing them from the inside. Punishment was not the object.

"Dr. B knew," says Tom Lyons. He is talking about the occasions— "approximately two or three times a year," he says—when Bettelheim slapped him.[26] One was soon after he came to the school, at around the age of eight. He had let the bathtub overflow, and he even recalls that this caused some damage to the wall in the stairway. "I was old enough to run a bath. I had done it many times at home. But I figured that since my counselor had turned it on, she might as well turn it off," he says. He was always very concerned about his rights and thought this was only fair. When the accident was discovered, the counselor indeed took full responsibility for it. But Bettelheim knew that young Tom had purposely kept quiet about the overflow, and that this had little to do with fairness: "I don't want you to take revenge on your counselor," he said after giving him several slaps.

Discussing the incident some forty years later, Tom Lyons remembers perfectly well how enraged he was that his counselor insisted on always taking his hand when they were outside. He was not treated that way at home.

Similarly, Bert Cohler clearly remembers the slaps he got from Dr. B one day when he returned from class with an excellent grade for a German essay. I had heard the anecdote mentioned in a radio program as an example of Bettelheim's sadism, shortly after his death, by one of Cohler's former dorm-mates. The story sounded so unbelievable that I felt certain there had to be some mistake, some malice or some distorted memory somewhere. But when I asked him about it, Bert Cohler burst out laughing. "Dr. B knew exactly what he was doing: In my essay I attacked Arthur Schnitzler. And I knew Schnitzler was one of his favorite authors."

So the story was true! It took me a long time to understand it, to overcome my initial shock. After a very serious trauma suffered in early childhood, Cohler had lived, until his arrival at the Orthogenic School, in constant terror of expressing even the slightest amount of anger, for he had been led to believe that if he dared to show the aggressiveness he felt toward one of his relatives, he would be killed.[27] Being highly intelligent, he had opted to escape into a dream world, where he settled his conflicts in thought only, or in puppet shows, which he was very good at. Attacking Bettelheim via Arthur Schnitzler was more sophisticated indeed, but it was a repetition of the same dynamic. And since the incident occurred just as the young man was preparing to leave the Orthogenic School, Bettelheim no doubt considered it useful to show him what he was doing. By acknowledging the aggression implicit in Cohler's act (the essay), by showing that he knew it was aimed at him, and by responding with overt violence, Dr. B was playing his role as a lightning rod, ensuring that the dangerous charge was mortal neither for its originator nor for its recipient.

Whatever one may think of the method, Tom Lyons's and Bert Cohler's reactions, and the fact that both spontaneously remember, forty years later, the hidden motives that had inspired Bettelheim to slap them, at least show that Dr. B had been right on target—that his action had allowed them to face up to their own aggressiveness rather than feeling guilty, unworthy, and therefore bad, about their deviousness. In the case of Bert Cohler, whose affection for Dr. B is very deep, it is easy to imagine how, if Bettelheim had merely congratulated him for his essay, the young man would soon have felt ashamed of his underhanded attack, particularly since he had received an A for it. He may then have concluded that the praise was undeserved, and instead of gaining satisfaction and encouragement from it, he may even have become convinced that he was nothing but a fraud.

"Murderer," "obscene," "monster": such words may seem excessive when applied to overflowing bathtubs or essays with hidden agendas. Viewed by outsiders, they are indeed disproportionate. Which is just why writing about the unconscious is near impossible. For the unconscious does not work with kid gloves, and it does not reason. It expresses and represses, desires and punishes, without nuance. And it always takes its wishes for reality. At the unconscious level, when we hold a grudge against someone, we do not retaliate proportionately; we kill him.[28] Or at least we believe we have killed him. The task of adapting outrageous desires to the real world is that of the ego (and therefore no longer totally unconscious). The captain of the ship decides what is possible and what is not—and occasionally makes mistakes in doing so. It is the ego that decides in what more-or-less presentable form an unacceptable hatred can be expressed, such as letting a bathtub overflow (which does not prevent Tom's "id," forty years later, from boasting about the damage done to the stairway!).

This crudeness of the unconscious desires has a great deal to do with the misunderstandings surrounding Bettelheim's works. Commentators generally present Bettelheim as the number-one accuser of the mothers of autistic children. And yet if one places *The Empty Fortress* in the context of its time, one finds he was, on the contrary, the first author to stress the mutual nature of the mother-child relationship, pointing out that there is no such thing as a perfect mother (which is fortunate, since otherwise children would never need to learn the ways of the world), and stating clearly that the problems of the autistic child cannot be blamed on an external cause (such as the mother's behavior). "I would stress that the figure of the destructive mother (the devouring witch) is the creation of the child's imagination, though an imagining that has its source in reality, namely the destructive intents of the mothering person," Bettelheim writes in *The*

Empty Fortress.[29] Indeed, in that book he constantly refers to the (unconscious) death-wish that a mother can feel for her child. Like Freud, he believes that all mothers (and fathers) from time to time feel an unconscious desire to see their offspring disappear. He therefore stresses that it is not the mother's attitude that produces autism, but the child's spontaneous reaction to it.[30] He does not claim to know why one child should be more receptive than another to the unconscious wishes of his mother, and even leaves open the possibility that such hypersensitivity could have organic causes. Yet the idea that a mother can desire her child's death, even unconsciously, is so difficult to accept that it is this image which has stuck in most of his readers' minds.

Similarly, Bettelheim often mentions murderous instincts that can be so powerful in certain children that they could kill others, or more commonly, themselves. That idea too is hard for people to accept. It is easier to talk about madness than to recognize, within ourselves, such terrifying vestiges of infancy. And yet there was a time when each of us experienced the raw and irrepressible desire to eradicate someone else, be it a parent or a sibling, because he or she had denied us what we wanted, or reprimanded us, or usurped our place. In growing up, most of us have learned how to transform such primary instincts into more acceptable traits, such as a competitive spirit, a love of hunting, or even creativity. But it does not prevent them from occasionally flaring up, almost as violently as before, and stirring painful guilt feelings. Indeed these instincts were so familiar to many readers of Tom Lyons's novel *The Pelican and After* that they wondered why its protagonist had to live in a school for emotionally disturbed children!

Tom Lyons, who had himself spent almost twelve years at the Orthogenic School, had put the problem up front, with the subtitle *A Novel about Emotional Disturbance* featuring prominently on the dustjacket of his book.[31] For *The Pelican and After* is a perfect illustration of the inner violence with which most of the young pupils at the school were struggling. Indeed, the unconscious is never more unbridled, or more ferocious, than when one is young. Before he arrived on Bettelheim's doorstep, the author, a hyperactive boy of eight, had been diagnosed as incurably "schizophrenic," and even the Menninger Foundation's Southard School had declined to admit him, suggesting to his mother that he be institutionalized for life. Droll, well-written, and somewhat reminiscent of J. D. Salinger's *Catcher in the Rye, The Pelican and After* is, to date, the only book published by a former Orthogenic School student about his or her experience. The central character is a fourteen-year-old boy named Tony who lives in a Chicago school for disturbed children run by the fearsome "Dr. V," whose thick Austrian accent is rendered in graphic detail. The book is a mine of information on the Bettelheim method from one of the people that method helped to become an autonomous adult.

It is all there. The struggles with inner and outer violence, of course, because they were at the heart of Tom Lyons's problems, but also the warmth, the devotion of the counselors and teachers and their ways—for instance around Christmas, "a time when the staff was always on the lookout for feelings"; the moments of great emotion and the crises, such as the removal to a psychiatric hospital of Mark, a very disturbed boy Tony had spent time trying to play with. Tom Lyons gives us the whole story, because he is trying to see it clearly himself (thus giving us a good idea of what an "orthogenic" attitude may be). There too is his youthful desire to be a grown man, a tough one, who commands respect from women—such as when he meets a little girl who closely resembles the terrible Anna of *The Empty Fortress*, and finds himself secretly hoping that she will attack him in order to check whether he can overpower her this time. Tony also wants to get out of this godamm school, in which he feels treated like a baby and robbed of his privacy. Deep down, though, he knows that he is not quite ready to leave. He has a strange feeling of pride whenever he can help a fellow student more unlucky than himself, such as little Freddy, who is making progress, or even Mark, who used to spit out everything he was given to eat. Tony is provocative, sarcastic, and aggressive; he flies into rages. One day, while in the shower, he has a flash of insight: "Hate is a killer of fear." Whenever he does something really stupid, he regrets it immediately, but more often than not his efforts to make amends only make things worse. He knows that he is at the school to break out of his isolation, and he is becoming aware of the barriers that he keeps erecting between himself and others, but he is not yet able to rid himself of them.

But the book is also about the complexities of love: the ambivalent feelings of its youthful hero for his grandmother, whom he adores, but about whom he once fantasized that he had killed her, by leaving her out in a rainstorm in her wheelchair. When the grandmother is really dying, she gives Tony the blue porcelain fox that her own mother had given her before dying. They had often played with it when Tony was small, and he knows how much it means to her. Once back at the house, Tony picks up the little fox, which he had not touched for years, and is once again struck by the loving expression on the animal's face. Then his hands slip, and the little fox smashes into myriad pieces at the very moment when Tony's mother calls from the hospital to tell him his grandmother is dead. The boy collapses among the shards of blue porcelain. "Oh Granny! No! I love you! . . . I didn't mean to hurt poor Fox!'" But then another, familiar, inner voice cuts in: "'What do you mean, you bastard. You know you don't love anyone but yourself.'"

Unfortunately, that passage went unnoticed by most critics when the book came out. What attracted all the attention were the events depicted inside Tony's school. For example, during a game of dodgeball, Ronny, one of Tony's dorm-mates, and Ted, an older boy, are the only two left in the circle. When Ted is eliminated, Ronny mockingly congratulates him, shaking his hand with exaggerated emphasis. Then, as he jumps one last time to dodge the ball, his elbow hits a girl standing behind him in the eye. In short, a typical accident. This brings the game to an immediate halt. The counselors utter suitably "orthogenic" instructions as they gather the children. Tony's group returns to its dormitory in an atmosphere of tense expectation. In the courtyard, Tony "walks" his hand along the low wall between the two buildings. "He pretended his fingers were the legs of a man being walked to execution deep in the recesses of a large prison somewhere in a small alien country. Surrounding this country there was another country to which the man belonged, but from which he was now totally isolated." Suddenly, he finds himself thinking about the Midway, only a few yards from the building, where there were "people who knew nothing about Dr. V's anger, who had never heard about hidden feelings and accidents that weren't accidents. Tony envied these people, but he also felt that they missed out on something basic to life although he was unable to say just what."[32]

Then comes the anxious wait in the dormitory. As the young counselor continues to talk to Ronny ('Have you tried to think about why you did that?' 'Yes,' he answered. 'I jumped up and my elbow went out. I didn't *see* her'), the five other boys busy themselves in their own areas. An unusual calm reigns in the room. Igor, sitting on his bed, is making himself as unobtrusive as possible. He turns a knob attached to a piece of cardboard, one of the innumerable "electrical" contraptions affixed to the wall by his bed (this is indeed Joey, who was one of Tom Lyons's dorm-mates). When Tony, who chooses to go to the bathroom before the storm, passes by his bed, Igor whispers to him, indicating his electrical setup. "Do you know what it's for?" "No," Tony replies softly.

> Igor becomes a bit more bold. "Th-this switch is to turn down the voltage power in that robot so that when he comes in here, Ronny won't get into too much trouble."
>
> "Look, Igor," Tony says sympathetically, "if he were really a robot, you would have turned him off long ago."
>
> "No, y-you can't do that," Igor smiles. "That would ruin his batteries and we don't want to kill him."

Dr. V then arrives in the dorm. After slapping Ronny copiously, he suddenly stretches out his arms in front of him, palms upward, shrilling in mock imitation of the boy: "I didn't mean to! It vas an accident!" Then, resuming his normal voice, Dr. V asks: "Does zat make it feel any better?" Ronny shakes his head. "All right, zhen, remember zat ven you have accidents, I vill have zem also. Is zat clear?"

Once things have calmed down, Dr. V points out that the act of congratulating a companion who has just lost a game can be very aggressive, and suggests a connection between this and the incident with the girl. Tony wants to say that the congratulations and other forms of foolery are due to the "electric mix of boys and girls," but he does not say anything; he is afraid of Dr. V. The latter meanwhile alludes to the resentment older boys may feel at having to play with younger children, especially girls, and he invites the other boys to join in the discussion. Behind the caricature—for the reader should keep in mind that the whole episode is being seen through the eyes of a kid who is crazy about violent movies—the young Tony never forgets that things are not as simple as they seem.

Very few former Orthogenic School staff members admit to having read *The Pelican and After*, and among those who do, few liked it. The reasons given for this lack of interest range from "It's a not a good book"; "I couldn't get hold of it"; "After leaving the school, I didn't want to read anything about it"; "Oh, I know what Tom thinks, I don't need to read his book"; to the extreme "He wrote it to get back at Dr. B." And, strangely enough, such reactions appear to verify Bettelheim's prediction that "People would misunderstand what I was trying to say."

For Tom Lyons's book is in fact a striking tribute to the Orthogenic

School in general, and to Bruno Bettelheim in particular. It is telling that Fae Tyroler, who spent five years as counselor to Tom and Joey's group, the "Pandas" (later renamed the "Panthers"),[33] did read the book, and that she liked it. Not only does *The Pelican and After* prove that Tom Lyons was able to master his inner demons, but behind the verbal aggressiveness it is also full of feeling and hope. The book demonstrates a great deal of self-knowledge, and the biting humor that runs through it is indeed the expression of a violence that has been conquered and channeled into constructive activity. Even the caricatural Dr. V character clearly testifies to the lightning-rod function fulfilled by the real-life Dr. B, as viewed from the other side, from that of the child. Tom had clearly understood the system so well that he felt he could tell all.

When his book came out in 1983, far from using the resulting interviews to settle scores, Tom Lyons persistently stressed just how special a place the Orthogenic School was, even talking about "the magic" of the experience. Asked about autism, he replied that he heard the word only after leaving the school. For him, the children thus referred to were simply some of his childhood companions, only "more unlucky" than he. And when radio host Studs Terkel asked him, "When did you feel that you were cured?" he spontaneously replied, in vintage Bettelheim style: "Well, let's take you for an example. You'll agree with me that you are more mature now than when you were three years old. But you didn't wake up one fine morning and realize 'I'm big.' You were always the same person. Well, the process at the school was as gradual as growth itself."

All my own discussions with Tom Lyons indeed show that he has remained the same, even though he has learned to live with himself. The ambivalence of his feelings for Bettelheim ("Did he save my life, or did he ruin my childhood?") come out in practically every conversation. As does his "ferocious superego," which, although it no longer prevents him from leading a normal life, still makes it difficult for him simply to enjoy things as they come. The day I met him, he told me: "I think that one of the deepest hurts at the school was the constant belief that [Dr. B's] brutality was therapy . . . because then, the kid was in limbo." Three years later, when listening again to the tape, I finally understood the full meaning of that statement, and congratulated him for it during our next phone conversation. He expressed shock. "Brutality? No, I didn't use that word, it's too strong . . . You've got it on tape, really? I meant his violence. No, *brutality* is too

strong a word. Dr. B wasn't brutal . . . Look, I really don't want to
interfere with what you write, I'm a firm believer in freedom of
expression. But, in this particular case, maybe, you should let me
check my quotes." Similarly, Tom is clearly uneasy at the way Bettelheim portrayed his friend Joey in his book. He knows that it caused
hurt in Joey's family. Careful not to breach his former schoolmate's
privacy, he tells me nothing at all about him, but encourages me to
speak with him directly (while at the same time refusing to give me
his phone number), and with his mother. Then, the day after he has
criticized *The Empty Fortress*, Tom sends me a fax: "I stand by my
reservations. But recently it occurred to me that there is a real difference between BB's case histories and those of Freud. BB's are almost
like love stories in which it is very easy to care about the central character . . . Is BB the first to [have] put 'soul' into his cases?"[34]

The circumstances surrounding the publication of Tom Lyons's
book served only to exacerbate the ambivalence of his feelings toward
Bruno Bettelheim. For he suspects, without being sure, that Bettelheim had something to do with the decision by Macmillan, which was
also Bettelheim's publisher at the time, to turn down his novel, after
initially accepting it.[35] Having studied the voluminous file gathered by
Tom Lyons, and discussed it with some of the protagonists, I am
inclined to think that the publisher simply decided to play safe by
avoiding a book he thought might be offensive to one of his star
authors. Whatever the case, the affair seems to indicate that, once
again, Bettelheim was pretty close to the mark when, on the publication of Lyons's novel twelve years later, he answered a journalist who
asked him whether he had ever hit his charges: "That's between me
and the children."[36] He and Tom Lyons were practically alone in having truly understood what *The Pelican and After* was about. As soon
as he had read the manuscript, in April 1971, Bettelheim wrote to Tom,
saluting his "very considerable talent as a writer," and adding: "I am
sure it is a true picture of how you saw things when you were fourteen."[37] When the book finally came out in 1983, the two of them had
lunch in California. The atmosphere was relaxed and the conversation
lively. That was the last one-to-one meeting Tom Lyons was to have
with Bettelheim. Some time later he heard of a lecture during which
Dr. B had predicted that a lot of his former students would publish
books accusing him of the most terrible things, but he was never able
to confirm the information. And he still has a hard time accepting that
Bettelheim could at once be truly proud that Tom had been able to

write his book, fearful of the damage it was likely to cause him, and hurt by the caricatured image it gave of him.

"I much prefer that he should hate me than himself," or "I can never hurt him as much as he hurts himself," Bettelheim would say to the counselors who showed surprise at seeing him slap a child. And when, thanks to a timely smack, a child stopped banging his head against the wall or biting himself, the argument carried weight. In other cases, the effects, though less immediately obvious, would be noticeable over the longer term. But as Bettelheim never publicly admitted to the use he made of violence at the school, even those who were convinced by his arguments have a hard time facing up to the problem.

Exactly when the Big Bad Wolf went beyond simply baring his teeth at the children is unclear. The number of incidents requiring his intervention appears to have increased substantially after more seriously disturbed children started entering the school. The change in staff also played a role, for it was almost always at the request of a counselor who could not cope that Dr. B used force. Some people, such as Ugo Formigoni, made it a point of honor never to call him. But as situations could degenerate very rapidly, few counselors could do without Dr. B's occasional help. Whenever an incident occurred, a great deal of discussion among the staff and the children ensued. Generally, the counselor who had called on Dr. B considered this to be an admission of failure, and felt guilty about it. During staff meetings, Bettelheim and the counselors would try to figure out what had sparked the crisis, probing the anxieties of both the child and the adult involved.

In this area, however, even the most sincere testimonies can be deceptive. Often, such incidents are mentioned to the interviewer by third parties. At first this seems a good thing; the accounts are therefore likely to be more objective. But after a while, one begins to realize that things are not that simple—that, for instance, when X mentions slaps administered to Y, the situation described has in fact more to do with X's own feelings about the event (pity, guilt, unavowed satisfaction at seeing a fellow-student punished) than with what really happened. In most cases, the onlooker had in fact no idea of what was going on between Y and Dr. B (as with Bert Cohler's dorm-mate reporting the incident involving the German essay). This is particularly true when X considered Y to be weaker or "less lucky" than himself. For example "Paul," a sturdy, muscular man, told me that he felt

Dr. B was harder on the girls than on the boys. This turns out to be inaccurate; there is no doubt that Bettelheim resorted to force more often with boys. Similarly, a few former students said that he was harder on the autistic kids, but this was denied by many, and particularly by the counselors who had some of them in their groups. What is undeniable, however, is that those impenetrable children, given to extraordinarily stressful forms of behavior, could arouse in those looking after them a cocktail of feelings, exasperation mixed with pity and guilt, that were often difficult to control, and even to express.[38]

Problems involving the autistic children were indeed the ones that upset people the most. The incident that led teacher Nina Helstein to leave the Orthogenic School occurred in 1971, on a day when an older boy had had to be sent off to a mental hospital. The atmosphere was gloomy, with everyone wondering what could have been done to avoid such a failure. In her class, Nina had a seven-year-old autistic girl who was beginning to break out of her isolation. On that day, however, "Erin" was clearly upset: she had spent the whole morning lost in her own world, rocking back and forth and muttering the name of the departed boy. Nina had tried to reassure her, but to no avail. During lunch, when Dr. B came up to her table, she told him about it. He thereupon turned to the little girl and gave her a series of slaps, repeating, "That's enough. Stop that right now!" Erin did not say another word, but Nina Helstein was shocked. Later that night, during the staff meeting, Bettelheim questioned her: "Why did you think Erin was upset?" "She wanted to be told that she wasn't going to be sent away too," the teacher answered. "That's right. So why did you have me hit her?" Nina looked him straight in the eye. "Dr. B, you don't hit children because I tell you to: you did that." The meeting was coming to a close, and he did not reply. Shortly thereafter, Nina Helstein discovered that she had mononucleosis. After two months of sick leave, she decided not to return to the school. Today, while affirming that what she learned with Bettelheim is unique and has enlightened her entire working life as a therapist and consultant to social work agencies, Nina Helstein remains convinced that during his last years at the school he on occasion lost his self-control. She believes that, on that day, he was very disturbed by the boy's departure and, later, feeling somewhat ashamed at having struck Erin, he was seeking to shift the blame for his action onto her.[39]

That is not the way the incident is viewed by some other counselors from that period with whom I discussed it. They stress that because of her background (her father was a prominent labor union leader, her family belonged to the long assimilated liberal Jewish middle class, and she had also been a classmate of Bettelheim's daughter Ruth), Nina Helstein had an unusual relationship with Dr. B, seeming constantly to question his power—something she does not deny. They wonder why Nina felt the need to call on Dr. B. Implicit in their comment is the idea that Nina, troubled by Erin's behavior, had not done enough to reassure the little girl. Nina's answer is that, as she did not live at the school, she did not feel in a position to guarantee to Erin that she would not be sent away; only Dr. B had the authority to do so. As can be seen, the arguments are not on the same plane. But this does not rule out the possibility that Bettelheim was indeed upset by the day's events, or that he had simply misunderstood Nina's remark to him, accustomed as he was for counselors to call on him only when they needed help with a hopeless or potentially dangerous situation. He may have thought that Erin had spent the whole morning shrieking, since that was one of her symptoms. This is lent credence by what he said to her; for "his slaps were always accompanied by a clear message," stresses former counselor Diana Grossman Kahn. Whatever the case, this disturbing incident seems characteristic of his final years at the school, when the ground rules were less clearly delineated.

The message to Erin, however, seems clear to all the former staff members I interviewed: "Since I am disciplining you, that means I intend to keep you. Now it's up to you to get a grip on yourself, to stop behaving like a mad girl, if you don't want to be treated like one." Kathy Lubin, one of Bettelheim's favorite counselors, had already left the school when the incident with Erin occurred; when asked about it, she replied instead with another recollection.

One day, a woman was murdered only a few yards from the school. At 3 P.M., when the children were due to return from the classrooms, the body was still lying where it had fallen, visible from all the windows at the rear of the building. The counselors did not know what to do. Should they bring the subject up, or should they try to make sure the children did not see the body? Informed of the situation, Bettelheim told them to do nothing. He then went around to all the dormitories and talked to the children about the crime, addressing more specifically those who had strong homicidal tendencies. He told them that what had happened to the woman could one day happen to them if they did not make any progress. Kathy Lubin was dumbfounded. "His speech was completely on target. For each one, he picked up what would concern her the most. Whereas we were terrified by that corpse, he had brought it inside the school and was using it with remarkable efficiency."[40]

That was indeed where Bettelheim's real violence lay: in his ability to look straight at the darkest recesses in the psyches of those around him. And much more than his slaps, that was what scared them. For the violent incidents were not very frequent. Bettelheim did not in general need to resort to force to inspire fear in his charges; so explicit was his function that his simple presence was enough. Only one of the counselors has tried to explain that function publicly. Like Fae Tyroler, Leslie Cleaver had been in charge of a boys' group, and she had therefore been confronted with the issue of violence quite directly. In 1986, during a conference in honor of Bruno Bettelheim, she described him as "a worthy enemy— unflinching, highly visible, ultimately absolutely responsible and reliably indestructible." She took a dig in passing at his accent ("Vell, how are sings?") and verbal tics ("Oh, it vas an accident? I can't control my hand," and the more serious "Permit me to disabuse you of zat notion"). To illustrate the general feeling at the school that Dr. B saw and heard everything, she cited two counselors vacationing in a remote part of Ireland. Passing a local movie theater, they saw that a film called *The Most Dangerous Man Alive* was playing. "He's here! He's found us," one of them shrieked. And, concerning the children, Leslie referred to "the high jinks that went no further because there was someone in Hyde Park besides Muhammad Ali who could glide like a butterfly and sting like a *B*."

Far from being offended by Leslie's speech, Bettelheim thanked her for it. His relations with her had never been very close. Arriving at the school in 1969, a difficult year for Bettelheim, she had immediately seen through "the goofy stuff," as she calls the rivalry that his attitude generated among the counselors, and had remained outside the charmed circle of his favorites. Unlike her friend Nina Helstein, however, Leslie Cleaver had played the game of the school fully. Although she was not in therapy with Dr. B, she had been willing to "face the mirror," as she put it, in search of the "monsters" within her that could help her understand the children in her care. She simply made sure not to let her work drag her into a relationship of complete dependence on Dr. B. And that is why, on that day when the University of Chicago was paying homage to a figure whom Bettelheim knew not to be totally himself, the testimony of this young woman was a precious gift. For Leslie Cleaver's candid and realistic words were clearly addressed not to the Dr. B of legend but to the real flesh-and-blood man. She went beyond describing Bettelheim's role as the school's bogeyman; she also tried to explain it. "I want to stress that many potentially 'dangerous' feelings and 'dangerous' actions were able to be experienced in their full vigor, as high-spiritedness, fun-loving, loving and hating, because Dr. B was willing and able to fulfill his enemy function." She also explained how Dr. B was always on hand, ready to deal with everyone's slightest fears and needs, and above all to stand protectively beside a counselor when the mirror revealed that the monsters lurking in a child's unconscious were also present in the recesses of her own mind. She described his unique way of passing on his experience: never through ideas, always through lived feelings. She cited his "strong sense of original sin," but also his "almost religious faith" in human beings' adaptive capacity. And in comparing her experience at the school with those she had had at other institutions, she did not balk at using the word "perfection."

This testimony on Bettelheim's later years at the Orthogenic School, coming from someone who was never one of his uncritical fans, confirms that even in that most difficult period, when his behavior could be incomprehensible and apparently lacking in self-control, and when most of the incidents occurred that were to be held against him after his death, the essential kernel of his teaching and his method was still intact. This conclusion is supported by other testimonies, but they come from people who were too close to Bettelheim for their statements to carry as much weight.

The third and final period of Bettelheim's stewardship at the Orthogenic School started around the middle of the 1960s, when he began to realize that, in spite of his and the staff's best efforts, the progress being made by the autistic children was not up to his expectations—nor to his promises, since in his 1956 article he had put down Margaret Mahler's pessimism about their chances of recovery to the fact that she saw her patients only in consultation, rather than in residential care.

The biggest change at the school since the arrival of the first autistic children had indeed been the slow erosion of the staff's faith in
their capacity to cure their charges fully. The gritty determination of
the first counselors ("We're going to pull them out of this") had gradually given way to a more realistic view, at least for those in direct
contact with the most disturbed children. Karen Zelan, who started at
the school in 1956, just when Bettelheim received the Ford grant, took
care of "Marcia" and two other autistic girls during the eight years
she spent there. And she had hopes of completely curing at least one,
the little girl she was to call "Vivienne" in her master's dissertation.
On her arrival at the school, Vivienne was an extremely violent five-
year-old.[41] She spoke only rarely, inverting her pronouns when she
did, and manifested all the other symptoms then associated with
autism. After a year in the school, however, Vivienne was behaving
more or less like a normal child of four.

It was a little later that the intractable stubbornness of autism
started to become apparent to those who were grappling with it, when
Bettelheim was forced to admit that what he had termed "isolated
islands of experience" could in most cases not merge to form a whole.
It appeared clearly in 1964, when Karen Zelan left the Orthogenic
School: in spite of the progress they had made, none of the three
autistic girls who had been in her care continued getting better afterward, mainly because they were not able to strike up the same kind
of relationship with another counselor. Marcia returned to her family
a few months later; Vivienne stayed at the school until 1970, but
regressed seriously. As for the third girl, she suddenly had a psychotic
breakdown around a year after Zelan's departure, forgetting even her
own name, and had to be hospitalized shortly afterward. The same
type of problem is being encountered today, over forty years after the
first autistic children arrived at the Orthogenic School. Through constant care, a single individual can pry open a crack in the shell-like
defenses of the autistic child, but that does not often have much effect
on the child's relationship with other people; there is no real opening-
up to the rest of the outside world. When there is, specialists now tend
to conclude that the case was therefore not one of genuine autism.

That type of circular argument makes Karen Zelan see red. Having continued her career as a psychotherapist treating young psychotics, she has read all the literature, and points to the continuing
discrepancies between the various definitions of autism. Even Joey
could still be categorized as autistic today by some authors, she

stresses. Rather than get involved in a specialist debate, let us simply examine the influence this issue had on Bruno Bettelheim's life. It is clear that although his first results were very encouraging (according to Zelan, they were in some cases better than those achieved today, if rated in terms of overall progress rather than simply in modified behavior patterns), he gradually abandoned the hope of any complete recovery. The school's ascendant phase, the period in which even the most extraordinary dreams seemed within reach, was over.

Bettelheim's experience with very disturbed children seems also to have reinforced his belief that healing is achieved not by ideas, but by harnessing one's own psychological problems to the task. With autistic children, even more than with others, the gains made depended on the personality of those who took care of them. It had hardly anything to do with the counselor's intelligence, knowledge, or even depth of devotion; it was a matter of intuition or, as Bettelheim put it, of communication between two unconsciouses. For he had noticed that, whatever overt attitudes staff members took to them, the most seriously disturbed children were above all sensitive to their unconscious motives. And, as was shown by the story of Karen Zelan, widely acknowledged to have a special gift for communicating with the most impenetrable of children, such intuition often goes with somewhat whimsical temperaments.

Karen was twenty-one when she arrived at the Orthogenic School. Originally set to be a pianist, she dropped her music studies for psychology after an attack of stage fright prevented her from playing in her senior recital at Oberlin College. Reading *Love Is Not Enough* had sparked a strong desire to work with Bettelheim, but lacking self-confidence, she had called at the school to offer her services as a secretary. Dr. B himself had greeted her at the door. After a few questions about her life, he asked: "Well, do you want to be a secretary or a counselor?" She was amazed. "You mean I could start working with children right away, without training?" she asked. Her first month as a full-fledged counselor was very tough. The girls in her group gave her a hard time, while Dr. B kept her under pressure. She was constantly feeling inadequate. And then she received her first newcomer, a deeply disturbed little girl who quickly became very attached to her. This gave Karen the opportunity to show off her psychological finesse and intuition. Her skills were partly founded in experience: Zelan's sister, nine years her junior, had serious emotional problems, and a few years earlier Zelan had spent a lot of time teaching her to read. After three years at the school, Zelan's talent as a therapist was so widely accepted that she dared on occasion to challenge some of Bettelheim's diagnoses. He would accept this, because he recognized that her objections were based on a genuine understanding of the children, and in the early 1960s he would write nothing about autism without first discussing the issues with her. Karen Zelan had become for him the epitome of a good counselor for very disturbed children.

Although Bruno Bettelheim's results were not the triumph that he claimed, they were not so far removed from those obtained today, thirty years later, by those therapists who seek to do more than simply train such children to eat properly, wash, or take a bus. As the novelist-cum-therapist Howard Buten, who has worked with autistic children in the United States and France for over twenty years, says: "With a real autistic kid, there's only one alternative: Either you train him like an animal, and some are very good at it, going so far as to use electroshock treatment, or you can try and make the child suffer less."[42] At the Orthogenic School, some autistic children made great progress, others did not; but all lived better there than elsewhere in that they were treated as human beings whose sufferings, rather than deficiencies, were the object of everyone's attention. That is in itself no mean achievement. It was not enough, however, to satisfy Bruno Bettelheim.

It was around 1963 or 1964 that some of Bettelheim's co-workers, such as Diana Grossman Kahn, began to detect a subtle change in him, something that looked like discouragement, with perhaps a hint of depression. It is difficult to be more precise than this, since very few of Bettelheim's colleagues could stand back far enough to view him as a simple, vulnerable mortal. And his fame was then at its height, making him more flamboyant and autocratic than ever. The Orthogenic School was now serving some fifty children, and parents were prepared to wait years to have their offspring admitted. Mass-circulation newspapers were vying with one another to carry his words of wisdom. He was also starting to appear regularly on television. "Now I've seen the canonization of a saint," quipped John Fink of the *Chicago Tribune* Sunday magazine, emerging from a press luncheon with Bettelheim in February 1963.

A close examination of the chronology reveals a different story, however. In 1964, Karen Zelan had informed Bettelheim of her intention to follow her husband to Boston. Three years earlier, the school had lost another of its key staff members. Inge Fleischmann had not only been Karen's co-counselor but also a remarkable group therapist, adored by the children, and a woman of powerful organizational skills, whom Bettelheim could rely on to run the school when he was away. Perhaps even more important on a personal level was the fact that the Ford Foundation grant had expired in 1963, and Bettelheim had still not written the book he was announcing back in 1960, when he had asked for an extension of the deadline.[43] He was caught. Having arrogantly promised so much, what definitive answers could he now provide to the puzzle of autism; what happy ending could he find to a heartbreaking story, whose victims failed to respond to his best efforts to understand and heal them? And at the very moment Bettelheim was faced with that dilemma, Auschwitz survivors were clamoring to tell him that the vital lessons he had drawn from his camp experience were worthless—that he had in fact understood nothing. It was then that he decided to go to Israel.

15

❋

Israel: Understanding Is Not Enough

The relationship between Bruno Bettelheim and Israel resembles one of those exasperating love affairs, dogged by endless misunderstandings and missed appointments. They seemed to have been made for each other, but in fact they were forever squabbling, until it was too late, Bettelheim was too old and Israel seemed like a faraway friend, or rather like a grown-up son, whose father can only follow his development from afar, worried and nostalgic but powerless to influence events. Bettelheim's *The Children of the Dream* (1969), a book that, although it makes some criticisms, is largely a defense of the kibbutz system of education, was received in Israel like a slap in the face. No publisher would bring it out in Hebrew.

Bettelheim arrived in Tel Aviv early in March 1964. The aim of his visit was to study the psychological effects of the communal upbringing of children in kibbutzes, and to see how the example could be adapted to underprivileged urban American children. His destination was Ramat Yohanan, one of the oldest of the collective farms Israel was then famous for; in *The Children of the Dream* he was to call it Atid, the Hebrew word for "future."

The first incident occurred right at the airport; it was of no real consequence but it gives the flavor of the whole visit. Bettelheim had brought with him three large boxes of toys for the children of Ramat Yohanan, and he simply could not understand why the Israeli customs officials insisted on inspecting them. His hosts, meanwhile, did not see why he should be so upset by what they saw as a necessary, if tiresome, formality in a country that had lived under the threat of terrorism ever since its creation.

Bettelheim's decision to make the visit had come all at once, but the idea was not a new one. Since the end of the 1940s many Western psychologists and educators had been taking an interest in the kibbutz children. The oldest of these children had reached adulthood by then, and they provided a unique sample for a generation of researchers haunted by the question of whether individuals mold society or are molded by it. The kibbutz children had been raised from infancy in homes specially designed for them, in a system where everything—housing, resources, tools—was collective, yet in a society that was open and democratic. Bettelheim's curiosity was aroused; the question *he* was interested in, which he discussed often with his friends and colleagues, in particular with David Rapaport, a Chicago psychoanalyst who knew Israel well, was: What happens when a child grows up outside the triangular nuclear family—Dad, Mom, baby—of Freud's theories?

Bettelheim had another, more practical concern. Since November 1963, he had been chairing a weekly seminar for a group of Chicago teachers on the problems of children from poor urban backgrounds.[1] It appeared that drug use and delinquency were practically unknown among kibbutz children. Was the reason to be found in the social model that was handed down to them by their parents, as Rapaport appeared to think, or was it perhaps, as Bettelheim hypothesized, that their development had not been based on the oedipal conflict?

Ramat Yohanan had been founded by immigrants from Central Europe in 1932. Located in Galilee, Israel's most fertile region, it was one of the richest kibbutzes in the country. At the time Bettelheim visited it, the population consisted of around 300 adults and 170 children. They were all living in permanent housing, rather than the large tents and huts that took in new arrivals and visitors in other kibbutzes. Having by then abandoned the Marxist credo of Hashomer Hatzair (the young guard), the Zionist youth movement that had founded it, Ramat Yohanan was politically on the right of the kibbutz movement.

The first settlers of Hashomer Hatzair, who arrived in Palestine in the 1920s, brought with them two books, Marx's *Capital* and Freud's *The Interpretation of Dreams*, and they designed their collective farms to be the realization of those two sets of ideas.[2] Their Zionism aside, their concerns were much the same as those of the German youth movements, notably of the Jung Wandervogel to which Bettelheim had belonged. They sought to create a new, egalitarian, and just society by freeing the individual from the oppressive weight of tradition in the areas of education and sexuality, by sharing work and resources, and by going back to nature.[3] Whether he admitted it to himself or not, Bettelheim was also revisiting his own youth at a particularly troubled period of his life, by going to Israel.[4]

The country he was arriving in was one where men and women he could have met in Vienna, inspired by the determination to set up a Jewish state, which they saw as the only adequate response to anti-Semitism, and faced by geographical conditions forcing them to start from scratch, had tried to build the ideal society they had all discussed passionately as students, often seated around a campfire—the same type of campfire that was generally used to illustrate life in the kibbutz. Yet by 1964 Israel had already evolved away from the project of those young idealists. While 7.3 percent of the population had lived in kibbutzes at the end of World War II, now less than 4 percent did so. The Labor Party was still in power, but it had become clear that Israeli society had opted for the Western democratic model, that of capitalism. While young sabras (native-born Israelis) continued to claim to share the spirit of the pioneers, more and more of them aspired to the comforts of middle-class life. Born in the Middle East and raised under the Mediterranean sun, in often harsh conditions, they were already very different from their parents—less idealistic, probably, but also less ambivalent about their own Jewishness. On that score, at least, Zionism had succeeded perfectly. For an Israeli, being a Jew had little in common with what it meant to a Jung Wandervogel member in Vienna, or an inhabitant of a shtetl. And that difference would be a source of incomprehension between Bettelheim and many of the Israelis he would meet.

In opting for Ramat Yohanan, he had chosen one of the kibbutzes where the flame of the pioneers still burned strongest. But his own contradictions would make communication difficult with its inhabitants, men and women shaped by thirty years of simple and hard communitarian life. Intellectually, he may have admired the ideal of the kibbutz, in which everything belonged to everyone and nothing to anyone in particular, where nobody was at anyone else's service and the common good was more important than individual needs. But it was not his way of life, and he had a hard time accepting it during the weeks he spent in Galilee. A few months before his arrival, during a major conference on the aims and practice of rearing children in kibbutzes, his friend Fritz Redl had described in his characteristically frank manner the ambivalence of his own feelings about the first kibbutzniks he had met.[5] His initial feeling, he said, had been one of "admiration for such selfless people, living with so much restraint, as far as egotistic demands for privacy, etc." were concerned. But quite rapidly, he added, he had begun to feel a measure of anger at such saintliness. "There must be something wrong," he thought to himself. Redl also underlined the kibbutzniks' defensive attitude, stemming from a deep-seated impression that outsiders could not possibly help them. At the same conference, Yehuda Messinger, the director of a kibbutz teacher-training center and a member of Ramat Yohanan, had expressed the fear felt by the pioneers of the early farming communities about the way Israeli society was developing around them.

Bettelheim knew Yehuda Messinger, who had spent a sabbatical year at the University of Chicago in 1957–58 and assiduously attended one of Bettelheim's classes. During his stay in the kibbutz Bettelheim would frequently visit with his former student in the evenings. They talked of education, of course, but for Bettelheim the visits were above all an escape from what he felt as the stifling atmosphere of the kibbutz into a less foreign environment. Messinger, twelve years his junior, was from Saarbrücken, in Germany, where he had headed the Zionist youth movement. He had emigrated to Palestine in 1936, after his mother had bought his freedom from a Nazi jail.

The first real sabra Bettelheim got to know well was also from Ramat Yohanan. Nechama Edelman was the principal of the kibbutz's primary school; it was she who organized his stay, neglecting husband and children to be his interpreter, driver, and general guide for a little over six weeks. Although in her fifties, she had at least as much right to the title of sabra as did the children of the pioneers, if not more: her mother's great-grandfather had left Lithuania for Palestine back in the eighteenth century! She was born in Jerusalem in 1908 and, unlike most of her fellow-Israelis, she grew up speaking Hebrew as her native tongue. For her, exile, diaspora, and assimilation are abstract notions, and the Bible is not a religious text but a history book. "I was born with the sky over my head and the ground under my feet," she says simply, a statement that neatly sums up the complexity of her relations with Bettelheim.[6]

In 1956 Edelman had written to ask him whether everything she had read in *Love Is Not Enough* was true. This was not impertinence, but a genuine question. She had delicate psychological problems to tackle in her own fifty pupils, ages nine to eleven and coming from eighteen different countries, with as many languages. All were separated from their parents. Some had survived Nazism in Europe; others came from Arab countries, where Israeli agents had spirited them away to protect them from the reprisals that Jews had suffered since the creation of the Jewish state. If what Nechama Edelman had read in *Love Is Not Enough* was indeed true, she had a lot to learn from Bettelheim.

"Come and see for yourself," Bettelheim had written in reply to her letter. A year later she got the opportunity, when Eleanor Roosevelt visited Israel and was so impressed by Nechama Edelman's work that she gave her a grant to spend a year at Columbia University. From there, Nechama wrote to Bettelheim to ask whether she could visit the Orthogenic School during her vacation. When she arrived in Chicago, Fae Lohn Tyroler met her at the airport and there was a room waiting for her at International House, a student residence just opposite the school. At dawn the following day, Nechama rang the bell on the yellow door, and was shown into the staff room. There she sat down to wait. And wait. People came and went, and nobody seemed to notice her. She watched, but said nothing—not out of shyness, but because she was simply satisfied to be there. "I know that great men have great *meshugass*," she says, using the Yiddish word for "eccentricities." "But it doesn't worry me: I also know what I can learn from them." In the afternoon she quietly left. The next day she came back, and sat in the same place. A man brought her a bundle of reports to read; she found them fascinating. "The more I read, the more I was impressed. Everything was so serious; so much thinking went into it," she says. She did not feel that she was wasting her time; she was ready to wait for as long as it took.

Whatever the reason for Nechama Edelman's long wait—Bettelheim could have been away, or there could have been a crisis, or perhaps simply a difference between her schedule and the school's (in a kibbutz, work starts very early, so that labor in the fields is over by the time the sun is at its hottest)—the way she reacted to it is symptomatic of her personality. She is calm, determined, knows what she wants, and is not easily deflected from it.

Finally, on the third day, Bettelheim met with her, and asked her what she was interested in. "Whatever I can learn from you will be a benefit," she told him. He looked at her, and then asked Margaret Carey, one of the school's two psychiatric social workers, to show her around. Nechama was struck both by the seriousness of the condition of many of the children and by the fact that the school felt like a real home, even in the classrooms. She was deeply impressed. The next day, without further ado, Bettelheim asked her whether she would like to take charge of a group. Thus the principal of the Ramat Yohanan primary school had worked, for two months in the summer of 1957, as a counselor at the Orthogenic School. The experience taught her a great deal. Her relations with Bettelheim were direct and straightforward; he never gave her a hard time in the staff meetings. One day he even asked her to talk about the school to members of the Sonia Shankman Foundation. When she left, she invited him to visit Ramat Yohanan. But for the following six years she had no news of him.

As early as 1959, however, Bettelheim had joined in the debate about communal child rearing, with a critique of the book *Children of the Kibbutz*, written by Melford E. Spiro after he had spent a year at Bet Alpha, Hashomer Hatzair's first kibbutz.[7] While praising Spiro's observations, Bettelheim found his conclusions ethnocentric, betraying an unconscious bias in favor of the middle-class-American child-rearing model. Three years later he wrote another review, of the by-then abundant literature on the subject, in which he notably criticized the British psychoanalyst John Bowlby for writing that it was "essential for mental health . . . that the infant and young child should experience a warm, intimate, and continuous relationship with his mother." Bettelheim contrasted the slipshod care of an anxiety-stricken mother, who spends all her time with her child but is often too distracted by household tasks, too demanding, or simply exasperated, with the continuous and attentive care provided by a maternal substitute, whose only task is to look after the child's well-being.[8] In other words, before he actually set foot in a kibbutz, Bettelheim's image of it was a blend of his youthful ideals and what he himself was trying to accomplish at the Orthogenic School. As he notes in *The Children of the Dream*, however, the more he thought about the issue, the more he felt the need to go and see for himself.

He therefore wrote to Nechama Edelman. He proposed to do his research at Ramat Yohanan because he knew people there, and also because Ron Polani, who had set up Bet Alpha's educational system, lived there.[9] In *The Children of the Dream* he adds that as all previous studies had focused on the more radical kibbutzes, those in which the split between parents and children was the most complete, he thought it would be interesting to see how things worked in the others, particularly since the trend within the movement was then toward greater flexibility in family relations.

As soon as she received his letter, Nechama Edelman got the kibbutz leadership to organize a welcome befitting Bettelheim's reputation. He was assigned a small apartment comprising a bedroom, living room, kitchen, and shower, of the type normally reserved for a couple. The kibbutz would cover all his expenses, and he was invited to stay as long as he wished, with everything possible being done to facilitate his research. Nechama was to place herself at his disposal.

Their day started at 6 A.M. It included visits to nurseries and day-care facilities, observation of infants' behavior, interviews with *metapelets* (the women in charge of the children's quarters), interviews with parents, exchanges with children of various ages, seminars at the Oranim teacher-training center, visits to two other kibbutzes, plus group discussions and communal meals in Ramat Yohanan's huge dining room. Thanks to Nechama's energy, and Bettelheim's appetite for work, the project moved along at a furious pace. In principle it was he who decided on each day's schedule. But there were so many things to discuss with this "Jewish genius," as Nechama puts it, so many things to show him . . .

"They are very nice to me, but actually make it impossible for me to do what I set out to do. My entire day is so regulated by them that I have no time to take notes. I must do this and that, and most of all I must not have time to think on my own. Either one gives in to them and then one cannot do what one wants, or it is impossibly oppressive. In short, it is a totalitarian society populated by basically lovely people, but totalitarian nevertheless," an exhausted Bettelheim wrote to Ruth Marquis just over a week after his arrival. A few days later, when he had settled in a little, his tone would soften somewhat. For although Bettelheim always loved to travel, he in fact found it difficult to live away from home for any length of time, and the beginning of every new trip would always find him looking on the dark side.

The kibbutz leadership had high hopes for Bettelheim's visit. Nechama Edelman and Yehuda Messinger were influential members of the community, and their reports about him, his books, and his reputation had combined to give him an exceptional aura. He was mostly spared the instinctive suspicion of outsiders mentioned by Fritz Redl, and even the slight bitterness Israelis usually feel toward Jews who have resisted the call of Zionism. When his visit was announced, there had been a few protests from former camp inmates living in the kibbutz, angered by his recent writings on "ghetto thinking" and Anne Frank's father. But their complaints had had little effect. Nechama and most of the kibbutz leadership were convinced that Bettelheim's study would be useful to them.

There was nothing manipulative in that view; they were proud of what they had achieved and wanted to show it off in the hope that Bettelheim's advice would help them make improvements. The kibbutz had always made the education of its children a top priority, and as Rahel Messinger, Yehuda Messinger's widow, confirms, Bettelheim's visit had sparked an intense process of brainstorming among the teaching staff. "On the way to school, we would talk about what we were about to do with the children. On the way home, we talked about what we had done, and in the evenings we would take part in discussions with Bettelheim. We had never asked ourselves so many questions."[10] She was a nursery school teacher at the time, and she recalls with a smile the day when she asked him whether having two strong feminine influences in their lives—that of the *metapelet* and that of their mother—could be damaging to infants. "Who said that to be loved by two people is bad for you?" Bettelheim shot back.

So much enthusiasm and goodwill left Bettelheim trapped in his own contradictions. For he was very disappointed. He liked and even admired the people, but the defects of their society were obvious to him. "I feel like a traitor because I will have to come out with critical evaluations, but I can't help it," he wrote to Ruth Marquis. "I do not want to hurt them or their cause. Maybe I'll write only a report for the Foundation and never publish anything.[11] And maybe I'll even write a book on it. I just don't know. I must give myself time to digest it all from far away."

He was not impervious to the charm of kibbutz life. In his letters, he even admitted he found it "tempting" in its simplicity, in spite of its harshness. But he was simply allergic to the conformism imposed by the group. "What would you like to see changed in the kibbutz?" he asked a group of seventeen-year-olds one day. "To have two movies a week instead of one," one replied. Surprised by the stony silence of his friends, he quickly added: "Oh, it was only a joke." Bettelheim remarked that even jokes have reasons, but everyone in the group, including the teacher and the boy who had spoken, emphatically disagreed. The worst of it was, Bettelheim stressed in a letter to Marquis, that nobody saw any reason why the kibbutz should not show two films a week. But it did not, so one had to be enough. As for the conclusions of his study, he felt he could sum them up in one sentence: "The educational system works simply because the children grow up in a closed society that feels itself, as [do] all utopian societies, vastly superior to the rest of the world. This solves a great many questions with which our children have to struggle."

Bettelheim had soon noticed that there were people who flourished in the egalitarian kibbutz environment, clearly fitting in and full of enthusiasm for their chickens or carp, the latest crop or some new factory being built. But there were others. "The kibbutz is full of people who are sullen, talk to nobody, do their work and don't want to be bothered. They would be driftwood in the big cities, if not worse. Here, they are useful members of their community. But short of that they are as persons as unhappy as they would be anywhere else," he wrote.[12]

In spite of the language barrier, Bettelheim was, as usual, keenly aware of the psychological tensions between people, and maybe even more aware of their efforts to deny those tensions. "Since they have voted to abolish jealousy they really believe it no longer exists among them. The result is that the kibbutz is fine for the very strong who run and dominate it, and for the weak, who in all ways are protected and taken care of by the community. But it is very tough for the large middle group who have to stay and can't help themselves, and they pay for it with a depletion of their personalities, a self-destruction imposed by the fact that they have to repress so much."[13]

He did not doubt the sincerity of the kibbutzniks, but he could not accept their determined efforts to convince him of the superiority and justice of their form of society. He even began to doubt the accuracy of Nechama's interpreting (needed mainly with the children, as most of the adults could converse with him in German, English, French, or even Yiddish, which he understood a little). Assailed by contradictory feelings, Bettelheim, true to form, took refuge in hard work. The light often burned in his room until 1 or 2 A.M., to the admiration of his hosts, and particularly of Nechama Edelman, who on several occasions found him up and at work before 6 in the morning.

Relations between them were not what they had been in Chicago. Nechama found Bettelheim moody, disagreeable, and subject to childish tantrums when he did not immediately get what he wanted. As a convinced kibbutznik, she could not grasp the doubts he had about the system. And, being determined to show him everything, she underestimated the degree to which he needed to be alone from time to time.[14] She did not understand the distance he always placed between himself and others, nor his abrupt way of refusing whatever was offered him. "He didn't even say 'No thank you,' but simply 'No, I don't need it,'" she notes. One Friday evening, his tape recorder broke down, and he asked her to accompany him to Haifa to get it fixed. "But Dr. B, it's Sabbath—everything is closed," she protested. To no avail; he insisted on leaving right away. In the town, they drove around until they found a shop that looked open. He got out of the taxi without a word, and waited for three hours while the device was being repaired, as Nechama paced up and down outside. When he finally emerged, still without a word, he hailed a taxi and they returned. "I don't think he even thanked me," she says.

"If I hadn't been convinced that his research would be beneficial to us, I would not have let him treat me like that," she adds. Recalling how, after Bettelheim's departure, she had found six weeks of bed linen untouched and neatly piled up on a chair, Nechama mutters, "I wasn't going to make his bed for him as well, was I?" She speaks without bitterness, an emotion that is clearly foreign to her, but she was obviously hurt by Bettelheim's attitude—and also intrigued. Although it is not her style to indulge in speculative interpretations, after six weeks of being subjected to his moods and tyranny her guess was that, as a child, he must have been not spoiled, as so many people believed, but mistreated, and deprived of a real childhood.

Bettelheim did have an "official" reason to be disappointed. Only days after his arrival, he realized that he had been mistaken as to what he would find at Ramat Yohanan. Although they did not sleep in the same houses as their parents, the children enjoyed a very strong relationship with them, which was contrary to the model he had set out to study. This was a genuine reason for concern, and one his hosts could understand. Rahel Messinger recalls how, at the start of his stay, Bettelheim would often come to see her husband and lament: "This is terrible—I'm going to have to return the grant. The example of the kibbutz just isn't applicable to American ghettos." In his letters, he went further. Writing to Ruth Marquis, he explained how a communal upbringing did not protect children from the "pathogenic impact" the parental relationship could have on them, it simply prevented their neuroses from breaking out into the open: "The neuroses do not become fulminant, because for that you have to be an individual and not all your life part of a group . . . they feel very secure within their group, there is much less tension, anxiety."

Bettelheim chose his editor to vent his disappointment on because she had been closely involved in planning his trip. Ruth Marquis was then an academic adviser to the psychiatric department of Michigan State University, where Albert Rabin, the author of a major study on kibbutz children, taught. The two men knew each other. Having edited *Dialogues with Mothers,* and being a mother herself, Marquis was personally curious about the outcome of an upbringing in which the maternal influence would not predominate. She had encouraged Bettelheim to go to Israel, and he could count on her not to let anyone know how disappointed he was. His doubts could be summed up as an opposition between individual and security: The strength of the kibbutz was that it offered its members total safety; its weakness was that it prevented them from developing fully as individuals. Except, that is, for the élites, i.e., those who regularly left the kibbutz to go to work or to travel—the very people with whom Bettelheim was in contact.

Things began to improve a couple of weeks into his stay with the arrival of the filmmaker Charles Sharp, who was to shoot a documentary on Bettelheim's research.[5] "A fellow American is a blessing," Bettelheim wrote to Marquis. "I received him as a saving angel—a person with whom one could say whatever one wanted, and who also would not stand to have his own life in all minutiae run for him. Since I can unloose my frustrations with him, it's OK." Not long after Sharp's arrival, Bettelheim went to spend a week in Jerusalem, and his mood improved even more: "I am glad now about the experience: even though sixty, I could still learn and change opinions."

Simply being able to get away from the closed world of the kibbutz and return to the more familiar environment of a university did him good and allowed him to sum up his impressions. "My research, for all practical purposes, could be finished now," he wrote. "[The kibbutz] is very much a class society, like all others. Only they share property and that's fine . . . As I see it, the kibbutz is a most noble experiment—it had its great moments, but now it's an anachronism." About his hosts, he added: "Still they are very fine people and I love them as soon as we meet outside the confinement of the kibbutz, and that tells the story, theirs and mine."

It was during those few days in Jerusalem that Bettelheim first met Carl Frankenstein, who was then dean of education at Hebrew University. The two had previously exchanged a dozen or so letters on their respective writings, and Frankenstein had published one of Bettelheim's articles on the Orthogenic School in his review, *Megamot.*[16] As a PhD in philosophy, a psychoanalyst, and an educator concerned with the problems of children from underprivileged backgrounds, Frankenstein had a lot in common with Bettelheim. He had been born in Berlin into a highly assimilated Jewish family, just over a year after his friend. The two spoke the same language and had the same cultural references. They had both experienced the arrival of Nazism as an unforgivable betrayal by a culture they had always considered their own, and therefore as a deeply personal wound. And although Frankenstein had emigrated to Palestine in 1935, he liked to tell people that he was not a Zionist, but had simply gone where he could be useful. In spite of their academic qualifications, both men were intellectual mavericks, despising pretense and pedantry. Both were suspicious of religion and all forms of orthodoxy. One of their common references was Vaihinger's philosophy of "as if" (see chapter 2), and it would recur frequently in their later correspondence, as they vented their disappointment at either the political situation or the prevailing thinking of the time. Carl Frankenstein, however, would never become as conservative as Bettelheim.

In spite of their shared interests, the two men were in fact very different. Frankenstein had lost his father at an early age, and had spent his youth defending what he saw as just causes, such as fund-raising for young artists who had come to Berlin to study, while his mother, although protesting such idealistic dilettantism, continued to pay for his upkeep. After the war, he had never returned to Germany, and never claimed the damages that were his due. He was the kind of man who gives up a post just before retirement, simply because he has found something better to do: at age sixty-five, he stepped down from his job at Hebrew University to found a school for culturally deprived children. As his widow, Ljuba, puts it, "He had a very peculiar sense of money. Like Bettelheim, only the other way around."[17]

Frankenstein was tall and handsome (his female students used to refer to him as "Prince Charming"), a lively, witty character, clearly in love with life. His wife, also very attractive, was a nurse with psychoanalytic training. Like Gina, she hailed from one of the eastern provinces of the Austro-Hungarian empire, in her case Bukovina.

Between her and her husband, however, these differences of origin, and the prejudices they generally give rise to, were treated as jokes. They never had children, and carried on a close, often playful, relationship right up until his death. On viewing photos of the couple together, hearing anecdotes of their encounters with the Bettelheims, and reading the correspondence between the two men, one begins to realize that beyond the strong intellectual bond and the mutual admiration, Frankenstein was probably the man Bettelheim wanted to be, rather like a brother who had chosen happiness. This aspect of their relationship would gradually become more apparent as time passed, until Frankenstein, who had never been a father, took on more and more of that role with his friend, who had never been allowed to be a child, trying to revive Bettelheim's fading taste for life.

Meeting Frankenstein probably contributed to Bettelheim's regaining some inner peace during his visit to Jerusalem, in particular by helping him to decipher some of his complex feelings about Jewishness, his own and that of others. Everyone who met him during the Israel trip was indeed struck by those feelings, which some people rather hastily interpreted as a rejection of his origins.

On the first night of Passover, Bettelheim announced to Nechama Edelman that he did not want to attend the traditional dinner, or seder. She was amazed. He must really hate his Jewishness, she thought, to refuse to share the joy of the festival commemorating his people's exodus from Egypt and the end of their slavery. Furthermore, at Ramat Yohanan, Passover also marked the beginning of the early spring harvest. Having finally convinced him that his absence would truly offend his hosts, she was surprised to note that during the ceremony he was murmuring the prayers, although he continued to look furious. When I suggested that Bettelheim, as an atheist who had been forced in his youth to learn prayers that meant nothing either to himself or to his parents, probably had a hard time sitting through any religious event, Nechama exclaimed: "But Passover isn't a religious festival! It's like the Fourth of July in America; it's our Independence Day." For Nechama, born and bred in Palestine and a Hebrew speaker from birth, "Jewish self-hatred" is an alien concept. The only oppression she has experienced is that of colonization, the same as that suffered by her neighbors, Christians and Moslems, a type of oppression one faces with both feet firmly on the earth one knows to be one's own, against people who have come from elsewhere. How could she understand the inner conflicts of a man who had grown up in Vienna, a city that, while offering some of its Jews prominent positions, had continually undermined their self-image, turning them against one another and then exterminating them?

An early incident had left her perplexed. Before his arrival, Bettelheim had asked her to set up only one appointment for him, with the philosopher Gershom Scholem. But when Edelman, who had been one of Scholem's favorite students, contacted him, he replied in no uncertain terms: "Nechama, if you go around with that man, we will no longer be friends." Bettelheim should have known better. He should have guessed that his articles on Eichmann and "ghetto thinking" would not be to the liking of Scholem, a Berlin-born historian of Jewish mysticism, who had always seen assimilation as the worst of all pitfalls. He seems, on the contrary, not to have understood it. For him, Israel was the country of Jewish warriors, the ones who had opted to get out of the shtetl. It was a clear-cut opposition in his mind: submission on the one hand, combat on the other.

Bettelheim's image of Zionism had been forged in Vienna. It no doubt closely resembled that of his compatriot and near-contemporary, George Clare, who wrote that, above all, "it held out the promise of the rise of a new and different type of Jew, different from the insecure assimilants and different from the ghetto-created perversions of Jewry. The Jews who killed themselves rather than surrender at Massada, the warrior-Jews described by Flavius Josephus . . . were proud men and women, different from the downtrodden, cringing, ghetto-Jews. The return of a whole people to its true nature, that was the ultimate aim of Herzl's Zionism, that was and is the greatness of his vision."[18] Being forced to compare that vision to the real world of Ramat Yohanan reignited in Bettelheim both the dreams and the doubts he had felt deep within himself ever since childhood.

The cypress grove that graced one's first view of the kibbutz, the sight of muscular Jews, tanned from working in the fields, Jews proud of what their labor had drawn from the soil and ready to die for it, all these scenes must have deeply affected the Viennese-born visitor, whose mind had been filled with images from the age-old canon of anti-Semitism. The myth of the rootless, landless Jew had indeed been laid to rest by the kibbutz. Yet this closed world, made up of ordinary people with ordinary feelings, in which their common good demanded a kind of conformity troubling to Bettelheim, also evoked old images in him: those of the shtetl. As he was to write in *The Children of the Dream:* "What I did not find stressed in the literature was how their poor preparation as colonizers forced kibbutzniks to repeat, though in a deeply different way, the close unity that had characterized the ghetto, and for similar reasons: because it helped them survive in a basically hostile environment."[19]

Real memories also interfered with his view of this world that was strange to him. They were brought home to him one day when he and Haim Hadoumi, a regional educational official, were on a visit to a school outside the kibbutz. "Mister, what difference is there between a kibbutz and a concentration camp, if there too the clothes belonged to everybody?" a child asked him. Hadoumi's wife, Leah, recalls that Bettelheim came back to that question with her husband continually during the following days.[20] In Jerusalem, Bettelheim had visited Yad Vashem, the great Holocaust memorial, and Nechama Edelman was struck by how overwhelmed he looked on his return. At the same time, in his letters, he often spoke of the low value put on life in a country living in a permanent state of siege.

Two weeks after Passover, one or two days before he was due to leave, Bettelheim once again tried to duck out of a holiday banquet, wanting Nechama to go with him for one last interview instead. But once again, he had to give in. On this occasion, however, the festival was not a religious one. It was the annual Day of Remembrance, when Israelis honor the victims of the Nazi genocide. Nechama was not the only person present to notice his expression during the ceremony: it was not the same as at Passover, that of the obstinate child dragged into something against his will, it was a look of profound suffering.

As is shown by the correspondence he carried on with Frankenstein to the end of his life, Bettelheim never quite managed to see either Israel or the Israelis in realistic terms. Despite his ever-strengthening attachment to the country, and all his efforts to understand it, he never completely accepted that having "the ground under one's feet," as Nechama puts it, had turned Israelis into a new type of Jew, different not only from himself but from the "dream" referred to in the title of his book. When France's Pompidou Center asked him to write about the city of his birth for the 1986 "Paris–Vienne" art exhibition, he made the following remark in a letter to Frankenstein: "In rethinking those years, some before my birth, others I lived through, I realized how hopeless the situation of Vienna-Austria really was, and how this led to an internalization, introspection if you want, in thinking (Weininger), writing (Schnitzler), music (Mahler, Schoenberg, etc.), in painting (Klimt and Schiele) and, of course, Freud. I saw these connections better than ever before. So my question: Why does not a parallel situation in Israel lead to a parallel introspection? This would seem particularly appropriate to the Jewish temper."[21] A year later, he remarked sadly: "Israel just went the way of all nations. It was silly of us to hope for anything better."[22]

After shortening his stay by a few days and spending a week in Paris on his way home, Bettelheim arrived back in Chicago at the end of April 1964. *The Children of the Dream* was to come out five years later. His Israeli friends, who did not know he would write a book about his visit, had expected Bettelheim to get back in touch with them. During all those years, he did not. Once away from the object of his study, he mulled over his ambivalent feelings. The rise of youth protest and the anti–Vietnam War movement made him more aware of the advantages of a kibbutz education. Haim Hadoumi was Israel's cultural attaché in Detroit for a time, and he occasionally discussed the issues with him. Then the Six-Day War helped Bettelheim overcome his doubts. Between his trip to Israel and the publication of his book, he had completed *The Empty Fortress* and published numerous articles, but up until July 1967 and his critique of *Treblinka*, he had not written anything else on the concentration camps, Jews, or Nazism.

How his trip to Israel had brought back images from his youth is made clear in *The Children of the Dream*, in particular in a long introduction analyzing how all relations within the kibbutz, notably child rearing, had been molded by the founders' determination to free themselves of ghetto ways and thinking. The migrating bird (*Wandervogel*) is by definition one which flies away, and the desire to flee the cloying atmosphere and authoritarianism of the family unit was indeed one of the main motivations of the youth movements. According to Bettelheim, the pioneer women, even more than the men, were determined to sweep away the old structures. Having come to Palestine to be free, they demanded absolute equality, particularly in work, and had no time for the role of mother that tradition assigned to them. But Bettelheim went deeper. After pointing out the profoundly misogynist nature of Judaism,[23] he cited an unresolvable contradiction that could explain the first female pioneers' desire not to raise their own children: "Deep in the Jewish girl's unconscious, from earliest childhood, the idea was embedded that the good daughter is the one who grows up to be a good mother. She is the daughter who repays the mother's outpouring of love by giving her a grandchild. And at this the daughters rebelled." And yet, "Much as they were ready to cast off their mothers' role in practice, psychologically they remained beholden to an image of their mothers who had instilled in them the unconscious feeling that only giving all is enough."[24]

While other authors before him had presented the kibbutz as the antithesis of the shtetl, Bettelheim was the first to highlight the survival of unconscious patterns of thought. His insistence on this point was to anger both his Israeli hosts and, even more, the leadership of the kibbutz movement, notably that of Hashomer Hatzair. "His book shows, I think, that blending Marx and Freud is an impossibility. His idea that one could not simply change people's personalities made them mad; the book was seen as an attack on the 'new Jew,'" says Moshe Kerem, who was the principal of Western Galilee high schools for kibbutzes at the time of Bettelheim's visit.[25]

For, although *The Children of the Dream* was never published in Israel, the English-language edition was read all over the country as soon as it came out. It sparked expressions of anger that were out of proportion to the book's actual contents, which are in general favorable to the kibbutz upbringing. But Bettelheim's tone was considered too dogmatic, and his attitude condescending. He was accused of not knowing his subject matter: "How can one write such a definitive work after only a few weeks of research?" many critics asked. Others accused him of relying too much on psychoanalytic explanations. Those who had been against his visit from the start felt vindicated. At Ramat Yohanan itself the reactions were a little less harsh, but the disappointment was greater. As Bettelheim had read everything he could find about the kibbutzes while working on his book, his arguments at times seemed more applicable to the more radical ones, which had been subject to greater study. And yet the incidents he cited were those he had gleaned at Ramat Yohanan. Many people there felt somewhat betrayed, even among those who, like Yehuda Messinger, considered *The Children of the Dream* to be an important work containing many useful ideas.

The critics focused mainly on what Bettelheim had to say about adolescents. He found no fault with the education provided for small children. The burden of conformism and its effects had become apparent to him on listening to the older children. And he gives a very convincing portrayal of the malaise felt by the kibbutz's young people. His book, which has the advantage of highlighting the mythology, ethics, and historical role of the kibbutzes before discussing his findings, makes a clear distinction between generations, and subtly brings to light the gulf that had grown up between them. It shows in particular how the children of the pioneers were weighed down by the ideals of their parents. As the founders of a new world, the first kibbutzniks did not realize how heavy a burden they were placing on the shoulders of their offspring. For them, every new skyscraper or factory built in Israel was a reason for pride, a proof that they had won their battle. For their children, however, every such development was but another threat to the survival of the world they had grown up in, the only world they knew, that of the kibbutz—a world from which they could not dream of escaping, since "the fast growing new nation around them with all its turmoil, competition, expansion [had] been depicted to them as one of injustice, inequity, sometimes pure evil," Bettelheim wrote.[26]

Nechama Edelman was first in line for the protests, for "Bettelheim was Nechama's project," as another kibbutznik said. And yet, she is convinced that Bettelheim genuinely tapped into, and correctly interpreted, the deepest feelings of the young people. When, at the end of the five years, she received a copy of the book, she read it attentively. And what did she feel? "Jealousy! How had he managed, in such a short time, to see so clearly what had escaped me during forty years of experience?" the former school principal admits frankly. "He was right, even though many of us didn't want to admit it."

What is most striking is indeed that twenty-five years later, even those who had criticized *The Children of the Dream* most strongly on its publication now acknowledge that many of its observations were well founded. Rahel Messinger, for example, had been all the more upset by some of Bettelheim's assertions in that her husband had played a decisive role in the warm welcome he was given in the kibbutz; today, however, she admits that *The Children of the Dream* allowed her to understand at least one important thing about her own children: the very specific relationship that develops in a communal nursery between a baby and his crib-mate—the child in the next crib, the first person he sees on opening his eyes and who, unlike the mother or the *metapelet* coming and going, is always there.

One of Bettelheim's remarks about the kibbutz adolescents was particularly offensive to Israelis. In outlining the pragmatic, down-to-earth attitudes of the second generation, which he contrasted with the idealism of the pioneers, he described the younger kibbutzniks as more shallow and "emotionally flat" than their contemporaries reared in families. That remark is but the logical result of the book's opening analysis of the origin of the kibbutz: Feeling unable to give enough to their children, Bettelheim wrote, the pioneer women had created a system in which mothers would get less in return. And indeed, once in adolescence, their children no longer showed the same kind of attachment to be found in a traditional family. But along with the neurotic aspects of such a relationship, the dynamic aspects had also disappeared.

In his introduction, Bettelheim stresses the exemplary role played by kibbutzniks during the Six-Day War. Not only were many of them among the officers, they had been predominantly in the front lines. Twenty-five percent of the 800 Israelis killed during the conflict came from the kibbutzes, although they provided only 4 percent of all troops. "This was the true measure of their heroism, courage and devotion to duty," Bettelheim wrote. "Once more, as in the settling of the land and in the war of liberation, the kibbutz ethos gives special meaning to the lives of Israelis today."[27] In his book, he did not discuss the issue any further. But privately, he had more to say. Moshe Kerem has a vivid memory of a discussion on the issue among Bettelheim and three army officers that took place at a Tel Aviv sidewalk café in 1972. "Don't be so proud of them," Bettelheim said. "This may have been simply a consequence of their inability to take the last-minute decision that could have saved their lives"—a reference to the kibbutzniks' habit of making group, rather than individual, decisions. Needless to say, the remark had made Bettelheim's companions very angry. As soon as they got back to their offices, though, they commissioned a study to find out whether there was any truth in his statement!

Although a member of the kibbutz "establishment," Moshe Kerem is convinced of the value of Bettelheim's book, and has used it in his classes at Haifa University. He also believes that *The Children of the Dream* was the determining factor in changes that were subsequently made to the kibbutz system of child rearing. Today, children live with their parents. Kerem thinks the hostility that Israelis expressed toward the book arose mainly because of its patronizing tone. Bettelheim seemed to feel he had put himself out to serve the cause of the kibbutzes. Kerem was also able to see just how much Bettelheim had been hurt by their negative reactions to his book, rather like a father who has given his son a gift, only to find it spurned because he accompanied it with a few pieces of advice.

That wound was to remain hidden, however. Bettelheim would never express it to the people who had caused it. When he returned to Israel it was not to the kibbutz, but to Jerusalem, where he ended up feeling almost at home, with Carl Frankenstein and Seymour Fox, a former student who invited him to run seminars at the Milton Center for Education, which he had set up at Hebrew University. When the leaders of the kibbutz movement invited Bettelheim to debate with them after his book came out, he did not go. But three years later he willingly took part in a discussion at the teacher-training center where Rahel Messinger worked. She heard him speak once again in 1987, during an international congress on early childhood education held in the suburbs of Tel Aviv. And she was astonished by the very pro-kibbutz tone of his address, on "The Effects of Industrialization and Technology on the Family." As for Nechama Edelman, on the occasion of a visit to the United States in 1973, she decided to end the silence that had set in between herself and Bettelheim since his visit. Bruno and Trude received her with great kindness, showed her around Chicago, and showered her with gifts (for her grandchildren, since she herself insisted that there was nothing she needed).

16

❋

The Bad Guy

There'll be courses, even in your own field, that will bore
you. Don't try to make A's in them just because it'll look
good on your record . . . Concentrate instead, and give
your very best to those courses that excite you . . . Play
with knowledge . . . Most of all, don't forever be preparing for something else. Today counts too . . . When Ein-
stein and Freud entered college they started out with no
more than what each of you can bring to your college
career: all they had to go on was the conviction that the
creative mind of one single person can revolutionize the
field he makes his own, and because of that, the whole
world.

—Bruno Bettelheim, graduation speech,
Wayland Academy, May 30, 1973

In 1966, Anna Freud came to Chicago at the invitation of Heinz
Kohut, then director of the Psychoanalytic Institute. During her
stay, she paid a visit to the Orthogenic School, and Bettelheim granted
her the rare privilege of taking part in the 3 o'clock meeting with the
children. This meeting, in which all children, counselors, and teachers participated, was created in the early 1960s as a transition
between classes and other activities; Bettelheim attended it when he
was free. Seated on the floor as usual, the students felt intimidated
while waiting for the old lady whose visit was visibly important for
Dr. B. They knew she was the daughter of the man he admired the

most, and that she had come all the way from England to visit them. But as soon as she arrived, Anna Freud, with characteristic kindliness, put them at ease. As someone was getting her a chair, she pointed to the large wooden rocking horse in a corner of the room. "That's what I'd really like to sit on. But it wouldn't be sensible. I'm too old for that."

At the end of the meeting, she spoke a little about her father, saying in essence: "As you know, my father only treated adults, but he thought his teaching could be extended to children. I hope you will honor his teaching." Diana Grossman Kahn, as a typical Bettelheim-trained counselor, was outraged. "What right does she have to use the children like that?" she recalls saying to herself. "They are at the school to get better, not to honor her father!" But counselor Kathy Lubin was deeply moved by the whole event, in particular by the fact that each time the old lady said "my father," she was referring to Sigmund Freud himself. She above all recalls Anna Freud's closing remarks: "His dream was for psychoanalysis to be used to cure children. And today I see that his dream has come true."

Only one sour note marred the brief but memorable visit. When Bettelheim took his guest on a tour of the school and they arrived at the famous candy closet, it was, for the first time in two decades, locked! Once she had departed, he flew into a rage. The incident, due no doubt to the desire of a counselor or a housekeeper to ensure that the school's most famous closet was impeccable for the much-awaited visitor, sums up pretty well the atmosphere at the school during the later years of Bettelheim's tenure. It was a situation characterized by excessiveness of all kinds, suggesting that Bettelheim was weary of it all, and no longer completely in control of either his desires or his impatience. On the material level, the end of the 1960s was the Orthogenic School's age of splendor. A reflecting pool with contemporary sculptures had been installed, beautiful to look at but definitely not intended for the children to wade in, as Diana Grossman Kahn was to learn to her dismay one very hot day. There were fine china, cut-glass decanters, and contemporary furniture; the children's surroundings had become truly luxurious.[1]

In October 1966, Bettelheim organized a lavish reception for the inauguration of the Adolescent Unit. Meant for children who were getting ready to leave the school, this wing had been designed to serve as a halfway house between the overprotected atmosphere of the dormitories and the harshness of the "out there," as Bettelheim generally called the world beyond the school. (It was an expression he used with increasingly menacing emphasis as the years went by.) The Adolescent Unit had been five years in the making, and as planning progressed it had become ever more ambitious. It was separated from the rest of the school by a long corridor, complete with statues and an artful lighting system. The one-person bedrooms looked like monastery cells; the overall impression was one of cold elegance. "Bruno has built his mausoleum!" Morris Janowitz commented to his wife Gayle on the inaugural evening. A little later, Bettelheim was himself to adopt the expression, self-mockingly. For this costly architectural venture turned out to be a fiasco; the wing was inconvenient and generated much anxiety in its occupants. It was not long before the walls between the bedrooms were being knocked down to create new dormitories.

Bettelheim was becoming more and more touchy, unpredictable, and irascible. His classroom style was also growing much more rigid, as Ruth Nedelsky noted when she returned to Chicago in 1965 and enrolled once again for the class in psychoanalytic theory she had so loved in the 1950s. She was astounded to find a completely different Bettelheim. "I was so disappointed. He was tired. He no longer invested anything of himself in the class." His habit of holding up one student's errors as an example from which the whole class could learn, which had earlier been luminous, had become frankly unpleasant. "Can't he see that he's defeating his own purpose?" Ruth Nedelsky thought. The Bettelheim who had been so good at laying bare the mechanisms of interpersonal power was now clearly wedded to his own. Nedelsky was also troubled by the curt way he now spoke to Trude. She had a hard time accepting that anyone could change so much.

Her testimony is significant, for few people were thus able to compare Bettelheim's teaching over a twenty-year gap. One should add, however, that among those who discovered Bettelheim's classes only during the later period, many still found him to be an exceptional, if difficult, teacher. Geneviève Jurgensen, who besides being an Orthogenic School counselor was also his student between 1970 and 1972, is one of these. "I find it difficult to talk about this teaching, which made such a strong impression on me," she writes in her book on the school.

That was probably because the teacher did not use anything that could really be described as a method. Depending on the day of the week, his mood, the students and the atmosphere in the lecture hall, he would deal with one subject rather than another. It would be too easy for me to draw up a list of his witticisms, or to count the points he scored at our expense. To show how he emerged the victor from each and every debate . . . in a word, to concentrate on his style. But that would not be serious, and his courses were nothing if not serious. They may often have taken the form of a duel between the teacher and one of his students, yet they were as fundamentally interesting as life itself. And indeed life was always what they were about.[2]

Inside the Orthogenic School, Bettelheim tended to play more and more with the boundaries, as in 1965 when he admitted as a student the grandson of his earliest and most faithful sponsor, Philip Pekow, after whom, a year later, he would name the new Adolescent Unit.[3] That was a dangerous mixing of roles, for whatever the reasons may have been for Charles Pekow's admission to the school, he always felt he was there more as his grandfather's descendant than as a patient of Bettelheim. Convinced he had no valid reason for being there, Charles resented Bettelheim's authority all the more in that he was sure if he tried to tell his family about some of the things going on at the school, they would not believe him. It is certainly no coincidence that the young Pekow, although a somewhat puny boy, remains in many of his fellow-students' memories as the one who dared to punch Dr. B back.

It happened one Monday in 1968, during lunch. Charles Pekow was then fourteen and his counselor had become worried about his sudden loss of some fifteen pounds—due, Pekow claims, to his becoming tired of "institutional food." Those were days of intense political unrest in the world outside the school, with the recent political assassinations of Martin Luther King and Robert Kennedy, and the young boy felt very concerned about it all. His sympathies were with the left and the Palestinians, and he resented his political views not being taken seriously. When Bettelheim went over to his table and instructed him to eat, after explaining to his teacher that he was losing weight because he was jealous of a couple of anorexic girls, Pekow protested vehemently. According to him, this is when Dr. B slapped him (he adds that he had seldom been hit before then). Pekow whirled around and pasted Bettelheim on the jaw. Visibly surprised, Dr. B grabbed Pekow's hair with one hand and continued to slap him with the other until the boy got hold of Bettelheim's arms, while kicking him in the leg and in the groin, causing him to scream in pain. Pekow says he repeatedly offered to stop fighting if Bettelheim agreed to stop too. In return, Bettelheim told him to let go of his arms. When Pekow complied, the fight ended. Later, someone asked Bettelheim why he had not done anything about Charles Pekow after that incident. He replied that he had been too angry.

In spite of all Bettelheim's agonizing, his trip to Israel had given him a boost. But before deciding what to do with his kibbutz findings, he had to put the final touches to *The Empty Fortress*, a project he had been working on for years. The manuscript was practically finished, yet he was not satisfied. He was unable to complete the job. In his everyday practice, he had come more or less to accept that autism was not as easily curable as he had earlier hoped; the rate at which autistic children were being admitted to the school had slowed. In the writing of the book, however, he appears to have had a much harder time coming to terms with his relative powerlessness. His public statements on autism were no doubt triumphalist, but his critics were saying things he considered dangerous and despicable. Asserting that the condition resulted either from a genetic abnormality or a defect in brain development, they recommended forms of treatment that amounted to nothing more than conditioning, treating human beings as if they were animals to be tamed—with drugs, punishment–reward therapies, and so on. Bettelheim's experience, however, proved that a genuine therapist was dealing not just with mental or behavioral disturbances but with children in difficulty. That was the message he had to get across, above all else. The trouble was that his results in themselves were not conclusive enough to counter the arguments of his enemies. He needed incontrovertible evidence. Bettelheim was dissatisfied with himself, furious at his inability to land the knockout punch that would force the whole world to finally show respect for autistic children—and to acknowledge that he was right.

What appear to be details of the cases quoted in the book are contained in a small index file, which gives a good idea of how Bettelheim must have had to grapple with the feeling of fraud as he was writing it.[4] The cards correspond to forty-six children, as stated in *The Empty Fortress*, and the percentages relating to the number of successes and to the intellectual level of the children's parents are the same as those given in the book. But in order to achieve the success rate announced, he had boosted his sample with the cases of some children who had never been autistic.

In March 1965, one of his main critics wrote Bettelheim to ask him for his results to quote in his own book. Bernard Rimland was the father of an autistic child, and a vigorous campaigner against all psychological explanations of the condition. Bettelheim replied curtly that he refused to have anything to do with a work that was "ill-conceived and based on erroneous and biased judgements," and referred Rimland to the book he was about to publish. A year later, *The Empty Fortress* had still not appeared, and Rimland repeated his request. He felt so confident about his own conclusions that he offered to give Bettelheim five pages at the end of his book in which to contradict him, on condition that he, Rimland, could do the same in *The Empty Fortress*. Manifestly pleased with this suggestion, Rimland went on to express regret that Karl Marx had not thought of doing the same thing. Anyone else might have been touched by such naïveté. Not Bettelheim. He once again turned Rimland down flat, adding haughtily that the proposal only showed just how little its originator understood of human emotions. On the latter point he was probably right, but the tone of his reply betrayed how embarrassed he was by the request itself.[5]

These were but surface conflicts, however. On a deeper level, on the fundamental issues, Bettelheim did not cheat. Although unable to provide anything like a recipe for curing autism, he needed to give an account of his method in order to demonstrate why those advocated by Rimland and his ilk were mistaken. "Much of modern psychology seeks to know about others; too much of it, in my opinion, without an equal commitment to knowing about the self. But I believe that knowing the other—which is different from knowing about the other—can only be a function of knowing oneself," he wrote.[6]

To discover meaning in the children's crazy actions, and thus find the responses capable of calming them without shutting them up, the therapist has no need for batteries of tests and assessment charts. He can count only on his own self-knowledge, on condition that he has pushed that self-knowledge down to the deepest and most archaic mechanisms of the unconscious, those that appear only when defenses and rationalizations have collapsed, when all adaptive attempts have failed. Bettelheim had gone through that painful exploration in two ways, in his analysis and in the concentration camps. The analysis had helped him perceive the fortress that, in protecting him from his childhood fears, was keeping him from self-fulfillment and love. And then, just when he was beginning to emerge, the Nazis had hurled him back, with the greatest possible violence, into a world of death and hatred. They had even sold him the miserable armband, which by providing a few pathetic improvements to his daily lot could only push him toward abandonment. That was how he had been able to understand and describe "autism as seen from inside the person."[7] With an upsurge of determination, he had refused the illusory protection and carried on the fight to survive, while remaining himself. Autistic children were just like those inmates that other camp prisoners referred to as "moslems": those in whom the crucial upsurge simply did not take place. Neither drugs nor carrot-and-stick forms of treatment could pull them back. However, someone who had experienced both states, who had crossed the bridge in both directions, could perhaps, by dint of perseverance, find the way to spark the required jolt of energy.

The Empty Fortress gives a detailed description of the emerging to the world, to others, of an autonomous human being. Of central importance in that process is the infant's gradually acquired feeling that his actions can affect his surroundings, as he forms a couple with his mother, who plays a significant role in fostering, or failing to foster, in her child the conviction that life is something of value. It goes on to outline the stages and critical points in that development; the possible deviations and their consequences, such as turning in on oneself, or the decline of the self.[8] The opening pages of *The Empty Fortress* are so rich, so packed with crucial observations and original remarks, that they inspired the following slightly irritated comment from the British psychoanalyst Donald Winnicott: "I find [Bettelheim] difficult to read simply because he says everything and there is nothing to be said that one could be certain has not been said by him. But one must read him because he can be exactly right, or more nearly right than other writers. This applies especially to his opening chapters of *The Empty Fortress*."[9]

Next, Bettelheim illustrated his method with the case histories of "Laurie," "Marcia," and "Joey," at once exciting and moving, showing how even the worst clinical situation could be modified or amended. These were stories capable of inspiring new hope in even the most despairing parent or practitioner. Nevertheless, on his return from Israel, Bettelheim was still not satisfied. Once again, he plunged frenetically into the literature on his subject. With the aid of Ruth Marquis, he had read all the material on the infantile psyche and on autism, from Piaget to the most recent studies. He had also entered into correspondence with some of the researchers across the world who were studying children. He explored every possible direction in search of the conclusive and incontrovertible answer that his clinical research had failed to provide. And then one day, he suddenly called a halt to the research (which makes up the third part of his book). His editor had dug out some lines from William Blake, which summed up his beliefs in a nutshell:

> *Thought is life*
> *And strength and breath*
> *And the want of thought*
> *Is death.*

He made them the final words of his book.

The mid-1960s saw major changes in the staff lineup at the school. One after another, the counselors of the "second generation," those who had arrived when the school was in full growth, had left. The team was now made up of young men and women born after the war, at the time when Dr. Spock's influence was spreading. Only the really good counselors stayed on; anyone who did not fit in soon found themselves being shown the door. Bettelheim had his favorites, such as Kathy Lubin, and those he knew he could count on, such as Diana Grossman Kahn, who had taken over the managerial responsibilities previously assigned to Inge Fleischmann and Jacquelyn Sanders. Such counselors were by now the only ones to have individual sessions with him. Some critics accused him of having created a caste system within the staff, of having built himself a pretorian guard.

Bettelheim had turned sixty. He was now extremely famous, and in the habit of handing out advice in the form of aphorisms. "I know only three things . . ." was his usual opener. There were many more, of course. Some of them never varied, such as "The end is in the beginning," his favorite one and a key concept in his thinking. It had a double meaning. It was an obvious reminder that people's psychological makeup is shaped in the early years of life. But it above all meant that even if it took years to bring it out, the very first contact between a therapist and his patient contained within it the outcome of the treatment. On the basis of that observation, reached through years of experience, Bettelheim advised the psychologists who attended his seminars, and the counselors at his school, to consult a patient's file only after they had met him or her at least once.[16] As for the other maxims, each counselor has retained memories of specific ones. For example, "If a person does something it's because they have a need to do it" was recalled by Karen Zelan; "Better a wrong decision than to remain hung up in ambivalence" (Maurie Formigoni). In Zelan's recollection, the latter maxim becomes: "Don't be afraid of making mistakes." Bettelheim also liked to paraphrase Aristotle: "Do everything in moderation." The one Diana Kahn recalls is "The patient is always right." With some counselors, the promised third aphorism never came. Dr. B would tell them: "You'll learn it when you've spent enough time at the school."

The departure of a counselor, especially a good one, was always a difficult process—for the children, of course, but also for the rest of the team, which had to find a new balance, and for Bettelheim himself, who found it less and less easy to accept the loss of those he could count on, and who counted for him. There was no satisfactory solution to the problem, only palliatives. Departures were never announced more than a month in advance, to avoid creating unnecessary anxiety. But, as Bettelheim said, children could always feel whatever adults tried to hide from them. And the children at the school were particularly observant and sensitive.

The slightest incident could set off a crisis. Karen Zelan had been gone for two weeks when one of her former charges, "Vivienne," then age ten, broke into uncontrollable screams one evening, hitting her head against the wall. Maurie Formigoni, who had built up a good relationship with the little girl, was unable to do a thing. She sent for Dr. B, who calmed the child down, and then asked Maurie what had happened. The counselor had not the slightest idea; she had been reading a bedtime story to the children, and everything had been going fine until the screaming started. "What story?" Bettelheim asked. Nothing terrifying, said Maurie, simply an Arabian tale, set in the Persian Gulf, on an island. The name of the island? "Karan." The sound of her former counselor's name had been enough to send the little girl into a frenzy.

Over the years, a tradition had gradually set in: The person who was leaving became identified as the "bad guy," thus providing a kind of scapegoat onto whom the children, and to a lesser extent even the counselors, could project their aggressiveness whenever things went wrong. Here again, the idea was to prevent the children from turning the pain of the departure against themselves ("It's my fault if she's leaving," or, more crudely, "If she's not here any more, that means I killed her"). Bettelheim's overriding concern remained to relieve the children of their self-directed destructiveness. On occasion, he would back up this concern by quoting Freud, who indeed saw the origin of melancholy—deep, deadly depression—in the turning against oneself of the aggressivity one cannot direct against its true target, the lost love object. "Our job is to help our patients to feel angry," Bettelheim would tell the students in his Stanford seminar.

The "bad guy" did not have an easy time. Bettelheim would be the first to make her or him feel the odd one out, notably at staff meetings. Everything the future departee said might suddenly be judged either stupid or uninteresting. The treatment was all the more striking in that Bettelheim's favorites were usually the target. And it was very cruel, given that, after devoting several years of their lives to the school, the good counselors generally had a very hard time making the decision to leave. Abandoning children who had such a great need for them, and to whom they had given so much, was always a painful and guilt-ridden process. Some of the counselors accepted the rite of passage as inevitable. Others, such as Karen Zelan, refused it. After witnessing the change in Bettelheim's attitude to another of his favorites, she went to seek him out. He was alone in the basement, wrestling with the editing of the film about Marcia, and apparently having a hard time of it. Feigning to ignore the funny side of the situation (he was tangled up in strips of film, moaning "I can't! I can't!"), she barked angrily: "You're not going to do it to me too, I hope." Putting on his "doctor" voice, Bettelheim replied: "tell me what you're feeling." "You know perfectly well what I'm talking about," Zelan shouted before calming down and finally helping him untangle the film. Later, when her time came to leave the school, Bettelheim made no attempts to turn her into the bad guy.

Strangely enough, although many people offered vivid memories of this departure rite from the last years of Bettelheim's tenure at school, a few counselors from the period energetically deny it existed. Kathy Lubin and Diana Grossman Kahn, for example, both say they were not subjected to it when they left, nor did they ever witness it being inflicted on others. It could have been that they found leaving the school such a difficult process in itself that they did not notice that particular aspect of it. But if the reason for this discrepancy between different people's reports remains a mystery, the fact that it exists highlights the ambiguity of the practice. For all those who have recollections of the rite of departure are torn between an understanding of its aim and resentment at the cruelty it involved. This touches on the central contradiction in Bettelheim's behavior in the period leading up to his retirement: It looks as though he was less and less able to clearly distinguish in those last years between the children's good—which he had made into the school's raison d'être—and his own. It was as if, through years of understanding the children from within, he had somewhat lost the ability to hold in check the child inside himself. He knew he should not be trying to prevent his counselors from going, but he could not resist doing so. He respected those who stuck to their decision, but made them pay for it. This was indeed because he was aware of the children's needs, but not only. And he used all his powers of seduction to dissuade those he wanted to keep from leaving.

Nonnie never managed to leave. By the spring of 1969, she had spent thirteen years working at the school. She was a strange girl, very bright and sensitive, with a somewhat ethereal manner. With her tall, slim figure and her blonde looks she could have been very beautiful if she hadn't always seemed to be apologizing for being there. She stooped continually, and paid no attention to her appearance, with the result that she looked twice her age. Nonnie's relations with Dr. B were very particular. He was not charmed by her, but deeply moved by her obvious distress, and her fierce desire to ease the sufferings of the children in her charge. Later, Bettelheim would say that of all the people he had known, Nonnie was "the one who came closest to being a saint." That was not exactly a compliment; it was a reference to Nonnie's self-sacrificing tendency. For a long time, the young woman had refused payment, considering that the personal progress she was making at the school was ample compensation for her work. When Bettelheim finally did persuade her to put the checks in the bank, she promptly donated the money to charity.

Nonnie and Bettelheim had enough in common—a painful childhood, a desire to make amends for some perceived sin, physical self-loathing, great sensitivity and intelligence—for him to have seen something of himself in her. More important, Nonnie's own condition when she arrived at the school was such that she could in fact have been admitted as a patient, and hers seems to have been the first case where Bettelheim thought he could actually heal a counselor at the same time she was healing children. This was not always to the liking of the other counselors. Karen Zelan, for example, recalls a time when Nonnie was off sick. Not only did the others have to take turns looking after her group, but Dr. B also asked them to sit at her bedside. When Zelan went to him in exasperation and told him she had had enough of listening to Nonnie talking about the wonderful vacation she would take once she was better, Bettelheim shot back: "If the school can't take care of a Nonnie, then I wonder what the point of it is? Don't you know that that's the way one gets better, by fantasizing about better times?"

At the same time, Bettelheim was by no means easy on Nonnie. She was in therapy with him, but he never let her off lightly, and she came in for more than her share of singling-out at staff meetings. Over the years, she had become a very good counselor, showing particular skill with the more severely disturbed children. One of her dreams was to open a school for autistic children only—an idea Bettelheim disliked because he felt that being surrounded by less troubled children helped bring autistic children out of their isolation. In the summer of 1969, Nonnie went off on vacation with her boyfriend, another counselor. Bettelheim disapproved of the relationship, considering the young man to be not good enough for her (he often reacted that way when one of his favorite female counselors took an interest in another member of the team). Then, on their way home, they had a car crash. The young man, who was driving, survived, but Nonnie died.

Sorrow, guilt, or anger: it was difficult to tell which of these three emotions was uppermost in Bettelheim's mind. His first reaction was to call Nonnie's boyfriend and tell him never to set foot in the school again. "The children might kill you," he told him. Geneviève Jurgensen, who arrived at the school the following year, adds: "And not only the children." In fact, that crash marked a turning point in Bettelheim's life. Needless to say, he could never accept that it had been simply an accident. Even in front of the children, he hinted that Nonnie's boyfriend had deliberately killed her. A short time afterward, during a TV interview, he also complained about the indifference shown by the other members of the staff to the young woman's death, asserting that in a kibbutz, the whole community would have gone into mourning. Much later, in California, he told Karen Zelan that he had been trying out a new method with Nonnie, which gave Zelan an insight into why her death had plunged him into such a crisis.

Nonnie's death came at a time of great agitation in Bettelheim's life. Ever since his sixtieth birthday, three years earlier, he had been worried about who would succeed him as director of the school. And while he had always been given to hypochondria, he was now beginning to have some serious health problems, notably circulatory difficulties in his legs. In 1966, he had cataract surgery. Just before the operation, he had taken aside, one at a time, some of the most experienced counselors and told them that if he came out blind, which was possible, he intended to commit suicide. He asked them whether he could count on them to see the school through the transitional period should that occur.

Politics was another source of worry. In the Middle East, Israel's lightning victory in the Six-Day War had indeed given the lie to the image of the helpless Jew, but had also increased the country's isolation.[11] In the United States, the protest movement was building up steam and, the previous year, the Democratic National Convention had attracted to Chicago its entire spectrum: anti–Vietnam War activists, Black Panthers, hippies. The violence of the clashes with the police had shocked America.

The University of Chicago was a world apart from the city center, where the convention was held, and for five months after the event it seemed the campus would remain untouched by the fires of protest sweeping the rest of the nation. But at the end of January 1969, the flames reached the sociology department, now chaired by Morris Janowitz. The spark that ignited them was the university's refusal to renew the contract of a young lecturer. She was one of two women in the department, and she was also a radical.[12] The decision triggered a sit-in by a group of students. Janowitz, caught off guard, spent a whole night negotiating with them, but to no avail. It was not long before the protesters were also occupying the administration building. It was two weeks before the crisis was finally resolved; a number of students were expelled, but Edward Levy, the university's president, refrained from calling in the police. That fact is still a point of pride for many a faculty member.

Bruno Bettelheim was not directly affected by these events, either at the Orthogenic School or in his classes. He nevertheless jumped into the arena on day one. At a press conference, he described the protesting students as paranoid, and went so far as to compare them to the members of the Hitler Youth who stormed the faculties of Germany when he was in Vienna. From then on, Bettelheim became a prime target for the protesters.

The reasons for Bettelheim's placing himself in the forefront of the opposition to a handful of students, whose demands hardly went beyond the framework of campus affairs, were no doubt many. There was the fact that his friend Morris Janowitz was in the students' line of fire. And there were his memories. The University of Chicago and, beyond, the United States had saved his life and allowed him to fulfill his childhood dreams. He could not stand by while they were attacked. It is also possible that he was genuinely afraid. A few months later, on a visit to a former student then living in Cambridge, Massachusetts, Bettelheim suddenly let drop: "All of this will be bad for the Jews."[13] He was not the only Holocaust survivor to have this gut reaction to the events of 1968–69. Others, in Chicago and elsewhere, reacted instinctively and irrationally to the wave of unrest that suddenly seemed to threaten all the major democracies. But Bettelheim's reaction to the Chicago campus occupation seems above all to be symptomatic of his state of mind in the last years of his tenure at the Orthogenic School. It was a disproportionate, passionate reaction that revealed first and foremost his level of anxiety. It is worth noting, however, that once he succeeded in channeling it, that anxiety encompassed most of the themes he was to work on after leaving the school, and which would figure in *A Good Enough Parent.*

Once calm had returned to the campus, Bettelheim outlined his viewpoint in an interview with the *Chicago Sun-Times.*[14] The protesters' anger resulted from their own self-hatred, he said. "They are so unable to make a go in this world that they feel the only way they can is by destroying it—so the chaos in the external world will be comparable to the chaos in the internal world."[15] Their behavior was thus "an extreme defensive maneuver to avoid a total, a complete break with reality." These shocking assertions were just for starters. What made Bettelheim really angry was what he saw as the failure of the young people's parents. They had brought up their offspring both spoiled and unloved, and had thus failed to play their required roles. It was in such terms, going far beyond the events of Chicago, that Bettelheim was to discuss the youth protest movement over the following three or four years. He would repeat his views in the newspapers, on TV, in lectures, and also in testimony to the many committees that would be set up to study the problem in both houses of Congress.

If the leaders of the Movement reminded him of the fascist students he had known in his youth, he explained, it was because he was struck by their blanket condemnations of the "Establishment," just as the German youth had lashed out at *"Das System."* He was also shocked to hear of books being burned once again in Berlin, thirty-five years after the Nazis. He saw other parallels between the 1960s student leaders and those of his youth: their anti-intellectualism and their "moral absolutism," the unshakable conviction that they held the high ground. Even though the aims of the two groups were very different, he saw both as "true believers," rather than adults who had made a reasoned, thought-out choice. "Revolution without a definite picture of what the future would be like when the revolution is over, can only contribute to the creation of a well-founded anxiety," he wrote.[16]

Bettelheim believed the young people were rebelling because they felt the new technological society had no need for them. "It is unnatural to keep a young person for some 20 years in dependency," he said in the *Chicago Sun-Times* interview. "I think this may be a way of life for a small elite which always in the past went to universities . . . In the past, the vast majority of young people, when they were at the height of their physical strength—which is around 20—were active meeting life outside, proving themselves as men or women . . . Now we pay them all to go to school. Which makes them dependent when they should be, psychologically speaking, independent. And this is a very hard thing to take." The postwar generation of young people was generally believed to have been brought up according to liberal and permissive principles, but that was in fact an illusion, he went on. In reality, their parents only "indulged them when it was convenient." And there had been a price to pay, because the parents were in effect saying to their children: " 'I indulge you now. But for that you have to be the brightest kid in school. Haven't I let you have the bottle? Now you go and be a whiz in school.' "[17] What Bettelheim found particularly striking among the student leaders was the discrepancy between their overdeveloped intellects and their lack of emotional maturity. Many of them were still at the stage of temper tantrums, Bettelheim said. He saw such immaturity and unease with society as resulting from repressed desires, the absence of strong role models (fathers working far away, spending what little time they had at home hiding behind a newspaper or watching TV), and a failure on the part of authority figures to fully accept their authority. On the grounds that children should not be repressed, modern parents had failed to teach them to deal with either their desires or their aggressiveness. And to avoid incurring their offspring's displeasure, they had not been strict enough when giving orders. Victorian-style education had at least had the merit of being coherent, whereas its modern counterpart was shot through with contradictions. Even worse, what repression there was was carried out not in the interests of the children, but in that of their parents.

Politically, this period saw Bettelheim lining up once and for all with the conservative camp. He defended the U.S. involvement in Vietnam, was outraged by the exposure of the Watergate affair and the threatened impeachment of Richard Nixon, and was later to become an active Ronald Reagan supporter. On all major political issues, he thus found himself in the opposite camp from many of the people who were most attracted to his theories about mental illness; the contrast is striking. Yet Bettelheim's political views point to a central tenet of his thought. Having spent a quarter-century trying to heal those left behind by the liberal methods of upbringing, which had evolved from the half-digested Freudian notions then in vogue among the middle classes in the United States, Bettelheim was convinced of one fundamental thing: A good parent is one who fully accepts and plays out the role of an adult in relation to his or her child. This may sound obvious, but it is not. A good parent, according to Bettelheim, is someone who lets the child be a child by not forcing him to think when he should be playing, or to grapple with the problems of the adult world before he is mature enough to do so. A child should not have to share his parents' problems, or try to console them, Bettelheim believed. The child's role is to take advantage of his childhood to learn about life, and become a strong individual. The parents' role is to create an environment that encourages that process to take place, to set limits to that environment by exercising authority, and also, at every opportunity, to seek out the "happy ending" to each problem, which will foster the child's desire to live and to grow.

This idea, so apparently simple but so difficult to apply in practice, sums up the whole of Bettelheim's theory of child rearing. The role he thus assigned to parents was a tough one, as he deprived them of the right to act like children themselves—that is, to demand understanding and indulgence from their offspring. To play such a role unfailingly at all times is impossible. Parents are also human beings, liable to be overcome by their emotions and behave in ways detrimental to their children. To pretend otherwise was to to put forward valuable advice in too harsh a tone, as Bettelheim was to do in *A Good Enough Parent* (1987). But that exasperated, peremptory tone was probably the expression of an inner vicious circle: That impossible adult role was the one his family had assigned to him from the earliest age. It was the only role Bettelheim knew how to play spontaneously—and the one he had once again felt compelled to adopt when faced with the student revolt, at a time when many of his colleagues preferred to line up without a murmur alongside those who were attacking them. He was incapable of abandoning it with anyone but Trude. With other people he never allowed expression to the child within, except by moaning about his health problems. And now, at the end of the 1960s, when he was weighed down with both responsibilities and honors—celebrations of the twenty-fifth anniversary of his arrival at the school, various distinctions and titles—it was as though the balance between the responsible adult and the inner child had finally collapsed and that, having been too long repressed, the child in Bettelheim would on occasion take over, making him demanding, grandiose, provocative, and determined to ignore all boundaries.

The day Bettelheim learned of Nonnie's death, the Orthogenic School was practically empty. Kathy Lubin, who had married and moved out of the school but continued to work there, had invited most of the counselors to a bridal shower for Diana Grossman. As the event was mostly for Diana's friends, she had not invited the newest member of the staff, who had been there only a few days. Her name was Candace Hilldrup and she was an unusual young woman. Pretty and very intelligent, she hid a secret personality behind an outgoing exterior. She was petite, and her long red hair stretched down below the waist. She would pin it up when with the children, but at other times she let it loose. Coupled with her bouncy way of walking, this gave her something of a wild-animal look.

Candy, as she was known, had abandoned a budding career as a modern dancer to work at the school. Her real age was twenty-one, though within herself she felt no more than fifteen (her first impression on meeting Dr. B was that he looked like Mr. Magoo; but, "as soon as he came in, his presence filled the living room," she adds).[18] She had been born into a modest family in rural Virginia and felt very naive and very lonely in trying to cope with growing up. Besides dance, Candy had been studying psychology at the University of Virginia when one of her teachers had brought to her attention a job offer from the Orthogenic School. Neither dancing nor her classes had succeeded in helping her sort out the violent and conflicting emotions that her mother's recent death, after a long and harrowing illness, had triggered in her. Then she read *Love Is Not Enough* and two other books by Bettelheim and felt that a door had suddenly opened, and a void been filled. In the short life history she had to send with her application to the school, she chose to be totally candid about the conflicting feelings that made life so hard for her to face.

Perhaps it was the fact that Candy Hilldrup happened to be around when Bettelheim received the news about Nonnie's death that made her so special in his eyes, as Kathy Lubin seems to think. Or perhaps it was her undeniable physical resemblance, in spite of differences in age and complexion, to his first wife, Gina. It could have been that she also had something of Karen Zelan, or the fact that she was a dancer, just as Karen was a pianist. Or it was her straightforwardness in asking questions about the things that worried her, or her obvious intuition. Or it may have been the combination of all of the above in one young woman who was very ill at ease with herself and yet proud, lively, and amusing. What is certain is that the complicity that developed between Candy Hilldrup and Bruno Bettelheim was special. It was clear that she needed him: "I should not have come here as a counselor," she kept thinking, "but as a child." As he had done with Nonnie, he would care for her, teaching her to respect herself, while she was caring for the children. But with Candy, he would succeed, because with her, things were different: She could make him laugh, she moved him—in short, he loved her.

Candy Hilldrup thus became his baby, his favorite child. She was good at impersonations, and she would amuse him by mimicking the voices or gestures of those around them. They shared a passion for the Middle Ages, and would tell each other marvelous stories about knights, princesses, and dragons. They would leave one another little messages, and spring surprises on each other. Some people suggested that maybe other things went on as well when, after the evening staff meeting, Candy would go into Dr. B's office for her daily session, occasionally dressed in the cotton jumpsuit that served as her pajamas, and obviously impervious to the black looks she got from the other counselors in therapy, who had only weekly appointments with him.

Such suggestions, however, show a total misunderstanding of the nature of Candy's relationship to Bettelheim, or rather, they project onto the relationship fantasies that were alien to it. Bettelheim felt that Candy needed to regress to get at the source of her problems, and she was totally, avidly ready to do so. She had blind faith in the man she still refers to as her "Poppa." He, while remaining in control of the exercise, found in it the opportunity he badly needed to indulge the child in himself. Having since become a psychoanalyst herself, Candace Hilldrup sums up the situation as follows: "The relationship between us was pure affect, a meeting of spirits. There was no intellectualization, and therefore no resistance. Dr. B had that type of relation with some children, girls in particular, the ones he could feed by hand, hold, rock, and so on."

For all that, Bettelheim had not lost sight of his role as head of the Orthogenic School, and the good of the children. Candy was totally devoted to her charges. At the time, her life had but one focus, Bettelheim, and two fields of expression: the children and her therapy with him. As had Karen Zelan and Geneviève Jurgensen, among others, she found the first few days at the school very tough. "The children were getting so much emotional attention there, people were so involved with them, that they treated newcomers with arrogance, almost with scorn, and they verbalized it. They didn't need you, and you had to prove that you had something to offer before they came to you. It took months." Very soon, however, she had created a strong relationship with a group of girls. It was not the group that Bettelheim had chosen for her at first, but the dormitory next door. After a couple of weeks, therefore, an exception was made and she was allowed to switch groups. This was not the first time Bettelheim bent the rules of the school for her. He had already done so by allowing her to keep her nickname, Candy, which otherwise she would have had to drop, as it carried too much of a symbolic charge. But Candy had not wanted to change it, and Dr. B had yielded.

Food in fact played an important role in their relationship. At the end of Candy's second day at the school, Bettelheim asked her for her impression. "It's the eatingest place I've seen," she commented. That was the first thing she could think of: Since the morning she had three full meals with the children plus three snacks and a late-evening drink with her fellow-counselors. At lunch, she had been seated next to an anorexic, and had watched another girl vomiting into her plate and then eating her own vomit. Candy, who was herself prone to anorexic attacks, had found that pretty hard to take. She had never-theless resolved to continue with her meal, being determined not to buckle—and also being greatly impressed by the quality of the food. She not only finished the piece of German chocolate cake she had been eating, but helped herself to another one. "If they don't keep me on, at least I won't have missed out on that," she told herself, between mouthfuls.

Bettelheim was clearly delighted at her "eatingest" neologism. "That's a good sign," he told her. He himself was fond of his food, although he kept an eye on his waistline. In particular, he had a pro-nounced sweet tooth ("When I was a baby, my nurse used to put a piece of chocolate under my tongue to help me go to sleep," he once told Candy). He was interested in "oral" problems, and was particu-larly skillful at treating anorexics. Their manifest will to achieve total control over their bodies struck a chord in him, and he was often the only person capable of finding the word or gesture that could per-suade them to give up their life-threatening abstinence.

Candy had several anorexic girls in her group, and she too knew how to get through to them (as did Karen Zelan and several of Bettelheim's other favorites). In fact, she had the type of intuition Bettelheim valued most: the kind that short-circuits the mind's reasoning system to act directly through gestures and affect, from unconscious to unconscious, as he used to say. Shortly before her arrival, the school had admitted "Erin," and Candy soon became the only person capable of calming her down when she started shrieking, attacking others, and biting herself. Step by step, the little autistic girl began to take an interest in the out-side world, and would learn to read and write.

Bettelheim was convinced that Candy had the potential to be a truly great counselor. His affection for her probably blinded him to the unhealthy atmosphere their highly exclusive relationship created around them. But he would never have devoted so much time to the young woman if he had not been convinced that her influence on the children was beneficial. A few years earlier, he had brought to the school an Israeli poetess to whom he was clearly quite attached. But she had not survived more than a couple of weeks, as it soon became clear that her overexcited behavior was detrimental to the children. His powerful sense of duty had come into play and he had not hesi-tated to ask her to leave.

Candy was unstinting in her devotion to her girls. After a year, she was seeing three of them, including Erin, for individual sessions. A few other girls were drawn to her, and she found time for them too. Bettelheim had also asked her to give the children dance classes. Some of the boys, notably Charles Pekow and Ronald Angres, found this humiliating. But Candy threw herself wholeheartedly into the task, fascinated by the new possibilities Dr. B's teaching opened up for her even in that field. The two of them also loved parties and holidays, especially Christmas, which was Dr. B's favorite, and a major event at the school, because it celebrates a birth—that of the child in each of us, as he put it.

One Monday evening, a few weeks after her arrival, Candy was suddenly gripped by severe anxiety for no apparent reason. Bettelheim was not at the school, and she found herself unable to calm down, to shake off the feeling that something terrible was happening. Finally, she went into his empty office and left a little note on his desk, saying "I'm very frightened. Please, don't die." The following morning, during the staff meeting, Bettelheim suddenly announced: "Do you know we have a psychic person among us?" He went on to explain how, the previous evening, a group of angry students had knocked on his door at home. When he opened it, he had found himself face to face with a gun! "At the very same time, that person felt that my life was threatened," he concluded, enigmatically. The following summer, while on vacation in Europe, Candy sent him a postcard of *Eva*, a painting by Ernst Fuchs; on her return she found that Bettelheim, who had also been on vacation, had sent her the very same card!

A few of the other women counselors liked Candy, but others detested her, many of them out of jealousy, as Bettelheim's attachment to her was so obvious. ("Don't talk to me about Candy. To this day, I can't think of her objectively," one counselor admitted. She had been at the school for four years when Candy arrived, and had up until then been one of Bettelheim's inner circle.) But others disliked her because, while acknowledging her qualities, they thought her too unstable and too much in need of help herself to sustain wholly beneficial relations with the children. What is sure is that Candy was a walking, talking provocation. She appeared unaware of other people, and was both excessive and exclusive. Seeing herself as a fifteen-year-old, she wore schoolgirl-style skirts. To others, however, she was a young woman in miniskirts so skimpy as to border on indecency. And Dr. B, who was generally so prudish on such issues, said nothing. One year, Candy went to the Bettelheims' regular New Year's party decked out in an extraordinary medieval princess's dress, with long skirts and a Tyrolean-style bodice covered with hearts. She had chosen it for Dr. B, of course, but the other guests found it shocking. Being ill at ease with idle chatter, Candy vanished in the course of the evening with Eric, Bettelheim's son, providing yet more grist for the rumor mill. In fact, the two were upstairs thumbing through family pictures and, later, jumping up and down on Trude and Bruno's bed having a pillow fight!

Leslie Cleaver arrived at the school a month after Candy Hilldrup, at the same time as two other new counselors. She does not harbor animosity toward Candy, but nevertheless considers her presence at the school to have been disturbing and detrimental for the children. She cites Bettelheim's "megalomania" at that time, which led him to believe he could handle everything at once: taking care of Candy and the children, while also ensuring respect for the very limits he himself was flouting. As for what this end-of-an-era atmosphere may have revealed about Bettelheim's own anxieties and psychological needs, although she acknowledges them today, Cleaver feels that such considerations had no place at the school. Dr. B's role did not include sharing his own problems with the staff.

In August 1963, Ruth Marquis visited Bettelheim at the school on his sixtieth birthday. Entering his office, she was thunderstruck at the sight of his desk: there was not a single scrap of paper in sight. "I have to settle all my affairs. Now that I'm old, I must retire," her friend told her, in a lugubrious tone of voice.

Six years later, however, the issue was still pending. Over the years, Bettelheim had hinted to several of the men who had worked with him, notably George Kaiser and a few of the psychoanalysts who had served as consultants, that they could become his successor at the school. In 1964, when Ugo Formigoni, tired of changing sheets and putting children to bed, decided to leave and seek a position more in line with his qualifications, Bettelheim had told him as he passed the door: "When I think that I wanted to make you my successor!" He was very fond of the charming Italian, and angry about his departure. In 1962, he had devoted much effort to getting him a permanent residency permit, citing his exceptional and irreplaceable activities at the school. And Formigoni had the added advantage of being an MD. After leaving the school, he headed a psychiatric service for which

Bettelheim worked as a consultant, and the resulting reversal of their roles did not help matters. Formigoni was no doubt hoping that Bettelheim would call, but he did not.

Another candidate was Lou Harper, head of the teaching team, who had been at the school for twenty years. Bettelheim trusted him totally. He was everything Bettelheim was not: tall, fair-haired, and calm. With Harper, most problems got solved via peaceable means. "That's the way it is: I'm slow at getting angry," he says, matter-of-factly.[19] All the children loved him and found him a reassuring figure. But Lou had never taken the time to get a PhD.

When the time came, it was U of C education professor Ben Wright Bettelheim wanted to succeed him. He fitted the bill perfectly: He had the required degrees, was at ease with the university hierarchy, knew the school very well, and was loyal to it. Bettelheim did everything in his power to persuade him to accept the job, telling him that the school's future depended on it. But Wright knew what the task involved. He did not feel capable of taking on Bettelheim's mantle, and was in any case not prepared to make the required sacrifices in his private life. He stood firm in his refusal.

In the meantime, Bert Cohler, one of the school's great success stories, had obtained his PhD in clinical psychology from Harvard, something Bettelheim knew about from Cohler's regular visits. In April 1969, Yale University had just offered him a lectureship when Bettelheim came to Boston for a conference. Afterward, as Cohler was driving him to the airport, Bettelheim, looking gloomy, suddenly told him that the school was going to have to close unless he agreed to step into his shoes. Cohler, then just twenty-nine, barely hesitated. Although he knew full well that a teacher's life at Yale would be far easier and more pleasant, his devotion to Dr. B and the Orthogenic School won out. His wife agreed with the choice.

The Cohlers thus returned to Chicago in the fall of 1969. At first, Bert Cohler's position was a strange one. In the university directory and on his pay slips, he was identified as the school's deputy director, but Bettelheim had not breathed a word about that to the counselors. He took Cohler with him everywhere he went, introducing him to the managerial sides of the job, but clearly Bettelheim wanted Cohler to establish his authority on his own. Or perhaps he was simply testing him. In the end, it was Cohler himself who informed the staff of his status. Little by little, Bettelheim began to bow out, leaving Cohler to make the major decisions on his own, even if he laid the groundwork for them. In December 1970, for instance, it was Cohler who officially hired Geneviève Jurgensen, but it had been Bettelheim who had spotted her at the university and asked her whether she would like to come and work at the school.

In the event of disagreements, however, Bettelheim now let Cohler have the last word. The director-to-be thus admitted, against Bettelheim's advice, a severely autistic girl. As Bettelheim stated in a staff meeting, he considered that to begin with, Bert should concentrate on less serious cases, so as to start out with a few successes and thereby gain self-assurance. But of course Bert wanted to measure up to his mentor, by undertaking the same impossible tasks he had, and without delay. Had not Bettelheim called him in an emergency, giving him the impression that the school's survival depended on him?

Even before Bettelheim left for Palo Alto, California, where the Center for Advanced Study in the Behavioral Sciences had invited him to spend a sabbatical, the trap that was to doom the Cohler directorship had already been sprung. Unlike some of his critics, however, I do not think that Bettelheim had created it intentionally; he had become very manipulative over the years but he was never Machiavellian, and although he had a hard time handing over the reins of what he often called, in letters from this period, his "life's work," he had no desire to see his school disappear. Far from it: At a time when his authority was being noisily challenged by people who, a few years earlier, would no doubt have been the first to be enthused by his ideas, and when psychoanalysis was beginning to lose ground in the United States, he ardently desired to see the school accepted once and for all as a respectable and unchallengeable institution.

It was shortly after Cohler's return to Chicago that Bettelheim made his comment about the "dark secret" in his life. It came around Christmas, after Bettelheim had just seen an advance copy of the cover story that the *New York Times Magazine* would devote to him and the school in early January. He had been very agitated, asserting that he risked being ejected from the university, or even from the United States altogether. In Cohler's recollection the incident has certainly been overdramatized, since it disturbed him considerably. But considering this anecdote in light of others that betrayed Bettelheim's inner turmoil at that time, it seems likely that he was once again grappling with his fear of being a fraud. In fact the article, in which he was presented as "Doctor No, the anti–Doctor Spock," contained only the usual exaggerations (about his psychoanalytic training, Patsy,

Eleanor Roosevelt). However, seeing them put together in a newspaper that was read all around the world must suddenly have given
Bettelheim a terrible mirror-image of himself, at the very time he was
preparing to leave forever the sanctuary he had spent twenty-six years
of his life creating, a sanctuary for troubled children, but also for himself; a sanctuary (the term is also used by the *Times* magazine writer)
he could hand over only to someone who knew it from the inside, as
it also contained a few secrets.

Bert Cohler had the required credentials, awarded by the most
prestigious university in the country, to put the school firmly on the
academic map, and he had undergone a regular psychoanalysis. This
is why, contrary to what Cohler himself appears to believe, Bettelheim
probably never saw him as a second-best choice to succeed him. Nor
was he used as a sacrificial lamb, sent to the slaughter for the sole
purpose of proving that Dr. B was irreplaceable. The daring idea of
handing over the school to one of its former students was an extraordinarily ambitious one; had it worked out, it would have proved not
only that Bettelheim was a remarkable therapist, but that his analysis of psychological ailments was exactly right. The wheel would have
turned full circle, and his mission would have been accomplished
beyond his wildest dreams: the perfect "happy ending." In his correspondence at the time, he referred to Cohler's appointment to run the
school as the fulfillment of a dream, and expressed genuine joy at the
young man's decision to accept the proposal.[20]

But Bettelheim must have realized that Bert Cohler was too young
for the job. He must have known that Cohler would not be able to
keep the counselors in line as he had done, possessing neither his
authority nor his experience, being fresh out of college. But Cohler's
progress since his departure from the school, not only in his studies
but also in his private life, had impressed Bettelheim. Cohler was
uniquely qualified to take over. He was intelligent, loyal, and good.
Having grown up there, he knew the school's philosophy almost as
well as Bettelheim did himself: the constant attention to the children's well-being, the need to make them feel that their actions had
an impact on the outside world, the use of empathy—it was all
totally familiar. Bettelheim could count on him. Sure, he was young,
but that could prove to be an advantage in giving the school a more
up-to-date image. Over time, he would find his own style and assert
his authority.

Of course, these thoughts (reconstructed from confidences Bettelheim made to various people around him) did not prevent him from being very disturbed about having to abandon his school to another man. But his ambivalence expressed itself more through his relations with his chosen successor than through his acts. Regarding introductions and handing over responsibilities, he did what was necessary for Bert Cohler, much more than he would do for Jacquelyn Sanders later on. But when he had been a student, Bert had had to come to terms with the fact that, even though Dr. B liked him well enough, he would never be one of his favorites. He wasn't charming enough, or sick enough. In his group, Dr. B's favorite had been Sandy Lewis, who was tall, fair-haired, and arrogant. Cohler had learned to live with the disappointment, but, twenty years later, by making him feel he was only his second choice at precisely the time he was asking him to assert himself, Bettelheim could only undermine him.

With Bert Cohler easing himself in to the job, Bettelheim was undertaking ever more lectures and trips. He was interviewed about the student revolt and *The Children of the Dream*, which had just come out. *The Empty Fortress* had been published in France, where it had achieved enormous success. He was being showered with honors and appointments, and invited to speak all over the country. But he was still not freed from his obligations, conflicts, and other problems. This was the time when he learned of the existence of Tom Lyons's manuscript, and also the time of the slapping incident with little Erin. When he was in Chicago, Bettelheim was still very much the director, while he was also giving his classes and even seeing a group of mothers every three weeks.

Bert Cohler began changing the rules somewhat, to adapt them to his own management style. In early 1970, he informed the staff that there was to be no more hitting the children: "Control must remain verbal." Shortly after that, still in Bettelheim's absence, he announced that tears were to be proscribed during staff meetings. "That type of exhibition is unnecessary between responsible adults," he stated. In July 1970, Bettelheim formally handed over the reins of power. A year later, on June 27, 1971, after a few moving yet discreet farewell dinners, he left the school in the evening, as usual, but did not return the next morning.

Just over a week later, Candy Hilldrup got a postcard showing the "Lady and the Unicorn" tapestry from Paris's Cluny Museum. "In a fashion the only way I can put my second life behind me is to return to the first one, in Europe, only I am no longer at home there either," Bettelheim wrote from that city. Although he tried to hide it, he was very frightened by the reality of retirement. No more children to worry about or counselors to train, no more of the responsibilities that had weighed him down. The only remaining one was to enjoy life. Having Trude at his side, quiet in public but dynamic in private, was a great help. After the trip to France, they visited Central Europe, then spent a few days in Vienna at a psychoanalytic congress. ("Life here is so much more relaxed than in the States, but unfortunately it is a dying city, living on the glories of its past . . . To be and feel a stranger in the place where one has spent more than half one's life, I find this time particularly difficult as I am surrounded by American analysts who rave about the city that so utterly expelled and robbed me," he wrote.[21]) Then on to Salzburg for the festival, a visit to Emmi and Hubert (Bertel) von Radanowicz in Switzerland, and a two-week safari in Kenya, the latter requested by Trude but enjoyed by Bruno more than he had expected. It was the longest vacation the Bettelheims had ever taken together.

Arriving in Palo Alto in early September, Bettelheim was clearly in a better mood. He was rested, and generally pleased with the house the couple had rented on the Stanford campus, even though he remained harsh in his criticism of American ways. "In Europe, even poor people manage to make their home very comfortable. In the house we rented, there isn't a comfortable chair, and the light is so miserable that one hardly sees what one eats, not to speak about reading. The only two places with good lighting—and that is neon which I hate—is the kitchen and the study. Obviously where one works (the wife in the kitchen, the prof in the study) one can have some semblance of adequate equipment, but where the family supposedly lives, no."[22] Delighted with the garden, Trude had immediately dismissed the Japanese gardener who tended it, and busied herself once again with hoes and rakes.

Being located just far enough from San Francisco to avoid the ever-present fogs of that city, and even farther from the heat and smog of Los Angeles, Palo Alto has offered many a stressed-out academic the ideal venue for a sabbatical. Not even Bettelheim was entirely immune to its villagey charm. The climate was easier on his aches and pains than that of Chicago, and he already knew some of his neighbors when he arrived. Several of his former colleagues and students were teaching at Stanford University, and others, such as Fritz Redl and Morris Janowitz, had preceded him as fellows at the Center for Advanced Study in the Behavioral Sciences. The Center had been founded by Ralph Tyler in 1954 with a Ford Foundation grant that was part of the same program that had funded Bettelheim's study of autism. The premises of this high-level think tank were located slightly away from the Stanford campus, on a small wooded hill overlooking it. Each year it took in around fifty fellows, selected on the basis of their potential complementarity, in the hope that their interdisciplinary contacts would advance the cause of knowledge. In addition to their stipends they were provided with typists and researchers, leaving them completely free from material considerations, with nothing to do but think. As if to underline the fact, their small studies were not even equipped with telephones, something Bettelheim frequently complained about in his letters. The only formal obligation for fellows was to produce a report on their stay, but Ralph Tyler took great pride in the large number of books they wrote, or started to write, while they were his guests.

"Being out here with no other purpose but to write, I find writing nearly impossible and I realize how closely all my writing was really connected with the daily clinical experience. Suddenly nothing comes to mind," Bettelheim wrote to Ruth Marquis. A week after his arrival at the Center, the fact that he was now in retirement, far from his school, was finally brought home to him. He had initially planned to devote the year to writing the last volume of his trilogy on the school, the one that was to focus on the counselors, explaining how their understanding of their own problems helped them to better care for their charges. Before leaving Chicago, he had gathered all his notes and writings on the subject and ordered them sent to him by registered mail. But his orders had not been followed and the package had gotten lost.

Fortunately, Bettelheim was by then interested in another project. "What I would really like to do here," he wrote to Ruth Marquis on his arrival,

> is the book on children and how to raise them. More and more I feel a need for it, and particularly of a book that sees the kid in contact (or, if you want, emotional back and forth) with the parent. That is, I would like to write something that is impossibly difficult to bring off, though it makes such good sense to me in theory: We know perfectly

well what makes the child tick. We know preciously little of what it does to the parent, though this is what has the greatest impact on the child. Analysts seem to have studied adults only as children, and never as parents, or if so, only in respect to their own childhood residues. But there is in addition a great chunk of reality in a parent's attitude to the child, and today more so than ever because parents are so dumbfounded by their kids though they understand them so much better than other generations. So there is a problem: We know so much better what makes them tick, and are so much less able to live with them.

So the book that was eventually to appear as *A Good Enough Parent* in 1987 could just as well have been called *What Makes a Parent?*—indeed a question that is rarely asked. As he is writing here to his old friend and former editor, with whom he had already discussed the issue, Bettelheim's wording is too concise for us to see exactly where he is heading. We can nevertheless surmise that he is touching on one of psychoanalysis's gray areas. Alongside the image created in the child's mind, who exactly is the parent? How does he or she function as such (and not simply as former child) when communicating, consciously or unconsciously, with the child? Was Bettelheim inspired by the proximity of the Palo Alto Mental Research Institute, the cradle of "family therapy"? Or was it that, deprived of his school, he had begun thinking about his relationships with his own children? The book, which was to be over twelve years in the writing, does not provide explicit answers to the questions raised in that letter. But once again Bettelheim's vigorous drive to ceaselessly further his quest for understanding human relations, as disrespectful of labels as he was of the boundaries between disciplines, is worth noting.

Almost as soon as they had moved in to their new home, the Bettelheims began visiting the many friends, both working and retired, they had in the Bay Area. Three weeks later, Bruno was writing to Ruth Marquis about another idea. He had recently seen two friends who were no longer able to write due to strokes, and as he was still suffering from writer's block, he had been moved to "put my literary house in order" by compiling a collection of essays. "I haven't put much thought into the selection, but here are some articles I liked when I wrote them . . . Maybe I'm looking for an easy way out. If so, what's wrong with that?" he asked, as if trying to convince himself. The selection he went on to make was highly eclectic and lacked a common thread, but it contained many of the essays that would eventually make up *Surviving*. It would be another six years before he actually assembled that work, however, which highlights the fact that for Bettelheim, the longest and most difficult part of any book was always the ordering of ideas, the drawing out of meaning.

Finally, he chose to work on his initial project during his stay in Palo Alto: the third part of his trilogy about the school, to be titled *A Home for the Heart* (thanks again to Ruth Marquis, who vetoed his idea of calling it *The Secular Cathedral*!). Enlarging on his original plan, he began to review his work as a teacher and therapist as a whole. Perhaps this was another way of giving form to the idea he had outlined to Marquis, or perhaps he was simply trying to understand his role as "parent" to the school, to students and counselors alike. Whatever the case, his approach betrayed a concern for coherence and order reminiscent of his first article on the Nazi camps. In his introduction, he reviewed all his writings, with *The Informed Heart* and *The Empty Fortress* interspersed between the books focusing on the school and seen as necessary stages in the deepening of his understanding of mental illness, based on his own experience. Until, that is, he cut out part of the manuscript. The book also provides an explanation for his torments while writing *The Empty Fortress*. As autism was the most serious form of mental ailment caused by nonphysiological factors, he wrote, "success in helping autistic children would, more than anything else, establish the merit of the school's philosophy and of its methods."[23]

But Bettelheim did not enjoy the peace of mind needed to carry out such a project, which implied not only reflection but also a process of mourning over the loss of the school. At the end of September he returned to Chicago, for a visit that set off deep anxiety, and even paranoia. Candy Hilldrup was by then desperate, convinced that Bert Cohler was destroying her "Poppa" 's school and that the children and she were no longer safe. With Bettelheim gone, some of her female colleagues seemed to be taking their revenge on her for past jealousies, and Candy's distress was contagious. That was enough to bring to the fore Bettelheim's ambivalence toward his successor. Once back in California, he kept in almost daily telephone contact with Candy, and a few others among his favorite counselors. The situation rapidly got out of hand, with him wanting to know everything and countermanding Bert Cohler's decisions from afar. By December 1971 Cohler could not take it any longer; he went to the university authorities and asked them to choose: Bettelheim or him. When they hemmed and hawed, clearly embarrassed, he tendered his resignation, agreeing nevertheless to stay on until the end of the academic year.

Bettelheim had in fact tried to fight the temptation to interfere in the school's affairs, as is confirmed by his letters to Candy Hilldrup: "I think that much that happened to and around you has to do with the feeling that I am not really gone and may return any day. But after a while it will sink in that the days of my running the school are over, and what they now fight against will become the memories of the good old days."[24] Being aware of her self-destructive anxiety, and no doubt feeling guilty at having abandoned her too early, he sought to calm her fears, telling her he was sure that Bert would finally get it right.

In January 1972, when the University of Chicago persuaded him to return for at least a year, the time needed for another successor to be found, he sent Candy a lengthy and beautiful letter to warn her that he would definitely not be staying any longer than that. He talked about himself for once, explaining how the preceding six months had changed him. "For a quarter of a century I lived only for the school, which meant in practice a group of people, children, staff—not everybody, some very much more than others, such as you—but I did not live, not a life of my own. Suddenly, I discovered that I do have such a life, that I want it, and equally important, that unless I do, I won't live one, as I was damn close to it last winter."[25] It was as though he had suddenly woken up an old man. He still had things to do, useful and even important things, but he had realized he could no longer work with the same intensity. He had started taking an afternoon nap. He regretted not having attended to his health earlier on, and acknowledged that when he had left the school he had been in an alarmingly run-down state, physically and also mentally. He had no intention of going through all that again. "I do care very much about the school, but I care differently. It was 'I have to do it, even if I die.' Now I want to live a little longer, and do a few things in life. I no longer want to die for the school to keep it going, because as the example shows, sooner or later it will have to go without me, or become something very different."

Which is precisely what happened. On his return to the school in July 1972, Bettelheim announced that Jacquelyn Sanders would become director at the start of the following academic year. Having failed in his quixotic attempt to have the school run by one of its former children, he had turned to the woman he knew he could count on to play the role of the mother. He had first made another effort to persuade Ben Wright to take the job, but when that failed he contacted Sanders in California, where she was then raising her son alone after a brief marriage. It was not an exciting choice, but it appeared to be a safe one.

Jacquelyn Seevak Sanders had started working as a counselor at the school in 1952, and had spent almost fourteen years there. She was the youngest child of a large family of Russian immigrants, and had attended Radcliffe on a scholarship. In terms of qualifications and breeding, right down to her Boston accent, she was impeccable. During their first meeting, Bettelheim had criticized her for speaking too softly, and had remarked that the photograph she had sent with her application did not look like her. He had, however, approved of one thing: She did not wear red nail polish. That at least was Sanders's recollection of their first meeting, as she was to describe it at a funeral service held for Bettelheim at the University of Chicago's Rockefeller Chapel. She also recalled that he had asked her to dress more simply when she returned the next day, and she of course obeyed. She always obeyed, and she knew how to get obedience from others.[26] Gradually, she was thus able to carve out quite a special place alongside Bettelheim.

She was in charge of a boys' group, and she took care of several autistic children. Her devotion to her charges was acknowledged by all: Karen Zelan recalls how, during her training period, she despaired of ever being capable of spending three or four hours silent and motionless while waiting for a child to get to sleep, "the way Jacqui did." Within a few months, however, it was Jacquelyn's turn to envy Karen, for in spite of being less rigorous and more temperamental, she was getting better results with her autistic children. It was also clear that Bettelheim was responsive to Karen's charm. Unable to be the favorite, Jacquelyn Sanders had chosen to make herself indispensable. Little by little, she had become the "enforcer" whenever Dr. B was away. When he was there, she was the faithful assistant, totally devoted to him and always putting his every wish ahead of her own needs and those of others. Although a few of her colleagues called her "the snitch" behind her back, she got along well with most of them, but with the exception of Inge Fleischmann she had no close friend at the school. Her desire for power was already manifest, but she had placed herself entirely at Bettelheim's disposal, going so far as to make the sandwich he often called for around 11 at night. Jacquelyn Sanders was intelligent, a hard worker, and a good manager. As a potential director, she thus had all the qualities needed to reassure Bettelheim as to the smooth running of the school.

As for the rest, it is more difficult to reach an opinion. Having spent four and a half years questioning people who knew her at the school, both during and after Bettelheim's tenure, and having met her on two occasions, I find that Jacquelyn Sanders remains one of the institution's great enigmas. From our very first encounter, everything about her seemed to me to be at odds with what I had found important in Bettelheim's books.

In November 1990, having arrived in Chicago in the midst of the scandal surrounding the accusations of abuse that emerged after Bettelheim's death and spoken to several of his critics, I was forced to realize that my image of him was idealized, but just how much I did not know, since I had barely started my research. In other words, I was hoping to get from his successor a more balanced, objective view of the work he had accomplished. After giving me a whirlwind tour of the school, Jacquelyn Sanders took me into her office for a brief discussion. She had made it clear that she was seeing me only reluctantly. A few days previously, in Washington, D.C., I had met Ronald Angres, the author of one of the most strongly critical articles on Bettelheim, and he had shown me the dissertation that Jacquelyn Sanders had written about his case after being his counselor for over seven years. I therefore asked her: "Would you still maintain today that Ronald was autistic?"

"Of course not," she replied spontaneously. Then, with a start, she stated: "I shouldn't have told you that."

Surprised, I asked her why not.

"I had warned you that I wouldn't discuss the children."

"Don't worry. It was Ronald himself who gave me your paper to read. He certainly wouldn't be offended at your talking to me about it."

She thought for a moment, and then said, with due concentration: "If Ronald asks me—but only if he *does* ask me—I shall authorize you to go public with this." While listening to her, everything I had read about the Orthogenic School, about the use of empathy and the creation of a very special relationship between each child and a particular adult, was racing through my mind. Unable to keep quiet any longer, I blurted out: "Are you telling me that you, who were his main counselor for seven years, could doubt for one minute that Ronald would like to have that awful label, which he has had to live with for the past thirty years, removed from him?" I remembered the tall man I had met in Washington, so intelligent and yet so obviously ill at ease with himself; the way he had uttered that terrible word *autistic*, both indignant and shameful, drowning the hurt in a torrent of brilliant rationalizations. Struck by my reaction, Jacquelyn Sanders gazed intently at me for several seconds, then, in the voice of a little girl who has just been caught doing something naughty, said: "Oh, anyone can make a mistake!" and I was unable to tell whether she was referring to the original diagnosis, or to what she had just said. Very shortly afterward, she terminated our discussion.

The handover of the school to Jacquelyn Sanders did not take long; she did not require any training. On arriving from California in July, Bettelheim had reassumed his powers abruptly, immediately canceling most of Cohler's reforms, in particular the newly created wage differentials among the staff. He had also vetoed the fund set up by Cohler to allow counselors to undergo therapies outside the school. "If you need a boyfriend, an analyst, and an apartment, you don't belong at the school," he had told Leslie Cleaver, when he discovered how independent she had become. Then he informed her that he intended to put an end to Dr. Al Flarsheim's "teaching the counselors how to be therapists." Shattered, Leslie had immediately written to Flarsheim to try and persuade Bettelheim to relent. The young psychoanalyst had raised the question with Bettelheim, saying that some counselors had contacted him, but without naming them. At the next staff meeting, Bettelheim was in a state of great agitation. "There are traitors among us, people who are trying to destroy the school," he said. "Dr. Flarsheim has received an anonymous letter . . ." He went on to say that he would seek out "the culprits" and throw them out of the school. Leslie Cleaver called Flarsheim and asked him to do something.

The next day a delivery boy arrived from Marshall Field's, the big Chicago department store, with a large package addressed to the staff. It contained a superb assortment of candies and other delicacies, along with a note from Flarsheim thanking the counselors—without naming anyone—for their letter, and telling them that he would raise the issue with Dr. B. This clever move had the required effect of calming people down, notably Bettelheim himself, who never mentioned the question again.

A few weeks after Jacquelyn Sanders's arrival, in September 1972, Bettelheim had started withdrawing from the day-to-day running of the school. He gave his classes, worked in his office, but left her, his deputy, to keep things ticking. Many of the counselors had resented his imperious and erratic comeback and had taken to avoiding him. That hurt him; he felt alone and rejected. Part of him was already no longer there. He knew that this time he would finally have to let go, that he could not make a second false exit. As if to make the break more definitive, he was working intensively on his book about the school. In December, with the first draft completed, he wanted Ruth Marquis, who was visiting him in Chicago, to take the manuscript. He had the feeling he had written it all too fast, "more to free myself and not enough to communicate with others."[27] He expressed regret that her successor as his editor did not have her capacity for dissent. "I need somebody who can really question my ideas," he stressed. But Ruth Marquis had agreed only to look for a title for him. Shortly afterward, he sent her the contents page, plus, "since the end is in the beginning and the end is the end,"[28] the first and the last two pages.

In early January 1973, Bettelheim returned to Israel, this time with Trude. One of his former students, Seymour Fox, was in the process of setting up the Milton Center for Education at Jerusalem's Hebrew University, and he had asked Bettelheim to lead a three-month seminar on the training of teachers. Once again, Israel had an invigorating effect on Bettelheim: "Israel is [as] exciting, tense, upsetting and all-consuming as the first time. Much has changed, and not all for the better, though people are much better off than before. I visited Ramat Yohanan, so far only for a day, and still feel the kibbutz is the most exciting thing in Israel."[29]

Despite the controversy sparked by *The Children of the Dream*, he received a warm welcome, and also had the pleasure of being reunited with Carl Frankenstein, who was taking part in Fox's project. The five months Bettelheim had just spent in Chicago had left him exhausted; after his arrival in Jerusalem he was sleeping fourteen hours a night. A couple of weeks later, however, he was taking an active interest in Frankenstein's problems in the school for culturally deprived children (mainly from Arab countries) that he had set up. The two friends were comparing its pupils with the children of American ghettos and discussing the best ways to harness psychoanalysis to the learning process. A whirl of debates and conferences, interspersed with tourism, helped Bettelheim feel he was once again being useful, which was all he needed to get him back on track. When the French film-maker Daniel Karlin, who had just read *The Empty Fortress*, called him in Jerusalem to request a long interview, he immediately agreed, and set an appointment for April. Karlin, who also wanted to film inside the Orthogenic School, offered to send Bettelheim a copy of one of his TV programs so he could get an idea of his work. The answer surprised him: "No need, I know you're a good one."[30]

Back at the Orthogenic School, Jacquelyn Sanders was consolidating her power. Having tried to get Candy on her side, and having briefly thought she had succeeded, she abruptly decided at the end of February to fire her. She had learned from Bert Cohler's experience; neither was able to keep the young woman in line. The new director probably also resented Candy's implicit judgment of the way she was running the school. In the space of twenty-four hours Candy had to pack her bags and say goodbye to her children. She found refuge at the home of Adrian Kuypers, one of the school's teachers, for a few days. She was shattered; it felt as if her entire life had been taken away from her. From Jerusalem, Bettelheim could not do much, except worry himself sick. He tried to calm her down, by both phone and mail, reminding her that she had plenty of resources to fall back on, pointing out how her too-high expectations of others always ended up pushing them away from her, and telling her how much she meant to him. But as he would explain to Geneviève Jurgensen a few months later, he had already real-ized that with him gone, Candy could probably never have been happy at the school.

On returning to Chicago at the end of March, Bettelheim had a new problem on his hands: the imminent arrival of Daniel Karlin and his film crew. At the school, the announcement was seen as Bet-telheim's latest extravagance. Never before had he allowed a film intended for public viewing to be shot at the school. Jacquelyn Sanders and most of the counselors were opposed to the project, fearing the negative impact the intrusion would have on the chil-dren in that troubled period. Right up to the last moment, Karlin was not sure he would be allowed to film the children. In the end, Jacquelyn Sanders, realizing how important it was for Bettelheim to have his life's work immortalized at the moment of his departure, relented. She set very strict limits, however: The shooting would be of short duration, people would take part only if they agreed to do so (children needed written approval from their parents), and Karlin would undertake both to conceal their identities and to ensure that the film was never screened in either the United States or Canada. The French crew had three weeks in which to get to know the premises and their occupants, and one in which to shoot. Their presence set off a storm of controversy, but even the loudest critics now acknowledge that the disturbance had no lasting effect on the children. In fact, the person most deeply torn by the event was probably Bettelheim himself. Coming on the heels of so many other upheavals, the project was indeed at odds with the philosophy he had tried to instill in everyone he had worked with. He felt guilty about it, but the filming provided a welcome distraction at a very difficult juncture for him. In the preface he was to write for Karlin's subsequent book, he would claim that if the filmmaker had contacted him in Chicago, rather than in Jerusalem, he never would have accepted. Being in Israel, he said, had reminded him how completely the Nazis had eradicated the first half of his life. "That someone should offer to prevent a repetition of that annihilation by making a visual record of my work, produced by a person who seemed to me to be as sincere as possible in his approach—that was a prospect that suddenly seemed very attractive to me," he wrote.[31]

That statement seems to be sincere, yet deceptive, in that it glosses over more complex feelings. It is sincere because the meeting of minds between Bruno Bettelheim and Daniel Karlin, who is both Jewish and the grandson of a concentration camp inmate, was as much about Nazism as about the Orthogenic School. But there was more. Bettelheim had just completed *A Home for the Heart*, an overview of his life's work he had hoped would be definitive but that he was only half satisfied with, when Karlin appeared on the scene. The journalist was intelligent, and he seemed to have read Bettelheim so well that he might be able to translate his ideas to film. He came from France, a country whose culture Bettelheim admired, and where *The Empty Fortress* was being hailed as a seminal work. Moreover, Karlin was unaware of all the controversies that had been dogging Bettelheim for about a decade. He could listen to him with an open mind, and hear only what was essential.

Contrary to what Karlin seems to believe, Bettelheim never lost sight of the fact that Karlin was a Marxist, as his correspondence shows. He also sensed that the young Frenchman was in the midst of a personal crisis—that is how he interpreted the intensity of the relationship that Karlin immediately established with him. But he too was undergoing a crisis (Karlin reports Bettelheim stating sadly, in French, "The King is dying,"[32] to explain the limits to his power within the school). In fact the arrival of the long-haired leftist filmmaker, who was at once close to and different from the protest movement leaders whose psychology he had been dissecting from afar over the preceding five years, provided an aging Bettelheim with a unique opportunity to sort out his thoughts as he was about to leave the Orthogenic School. He was aware of the influence he had over Karlin, and he knew what he was doing in granting him a right he had always denied to other television journalists. However conservative he had become, the ideals of the young Frenchman remained familiar to him. And while he was lashing out at the liberals and leftists who at the time were besieging the Nixon administration, Bettelheim also knew that his theories about mental illness were generally better understood and accepted by those who questioned the existing social order.

A year later, after attending a preview of Karlin's films, Bettelheim would write: "There is no doubt that no American TV man would have been able to produce anything approaching it. He has put a lot of himself into it, and it shows . . . [But] it is amazing how much he saw, filmed and understood in these few days."[33]

I have often wondered what it is about Karlin's films that gives them their magic quality, so different from other documents. For once, Bettelheim appears at peace with himself, neither overly dogmatic nor aggressive. He even looks happy, unusually so for him. And today I can find only one explanation for that: This dialogue with the grandson of a former death camp inmate, who like him was looking for a meaning to life, is the very image of Healing. Illustrated by images of real flesh-and-blood children who are in the process of returning to the world, and say so on camera, it is tangible proof that man's humanity has survived Nazism and that we have the right to go on living and hoping. It was indeed a testament.

In looking at the broader picture when Bettelheim's life was about to take him away from the Orthogenic School, the same question keeps recurring. Why is it that this psychoanalyst, who spoke in rather stern terms, disliked small talk, and decried fads, became such a unique reference for so many people—and that instead of being sent to purgatory after his death like most famous writers, he was instantly forked into hell? Why did Bruno Bettelheim inscribe himself in the imagination of so many people in so many different countries, as some sort of a secular saint, untouchable and unquestionable?

Critics may answer that if he had not painted such an idealized picture of his school, he would never have achieved such celebrity. But that is precisely where the Bettelheim mystery lies. If good self-promotion was enough to gain the respect, even the love, of the multitude, the list of idols would be long indeed. Kurt Eissler once told me: "Bettelheim had all the trappings of a genius, without being one."[34] Although judicious, the remark still does not explain the man's worldwide fame. Many may call themselves magicians, but few are recognized as such. Here was a man with no particular psychiatric qualifications other than his birth in the same city as Sigmund Freud who, without medical degree or support from the psychoanalytic establishment, said: "I am going to cure people who have been identified as incurable. And I shall do it without drugs, straitjackets, or electric shocks; I will do it by simply listening to them, and showing them that I love them." Why was he believed?

Paradoxically, Bettelheim's attitude toward the student protesters of the late 1960s helped me to answer that question. Having been one of those protesters, I felt personally concerned by it: How could this man whose ideas about mental illness—but also about ghetto thinking and personal autonomy—were so attractive to us, so in line with what we were demanding, have totally rejected our revolt? Was he hypocritical, neurotic, or simply inconsistent, to the point that he no longer knew what he had said twenty years before? Then Marc Lubin mentioned the "This will be bad for the Jews" comment, so typical of the shtetl, and which had so surprised him in Bettelheim's mouth. I realized that there was something else, and that it had to do with the question "What is a Jew?"—a question that had run through Bettelheim's whole life like a continuous thread, one for which he had been robbed, humiliated, and almost killed, and to which he had tried to provide an answer in each stage of that life.

For anyone born and bred in Europe, as Bettelheim was, there are two types of Jew. One sees himself as one, based on his beliefs, culture, or lifestyle; the other, as was shown by Jean-Paul Sartre, is identified as a Jew by the anti-Semite.[35] Whatever the latter does, or does not do (respect the Sabbath, circumcise his sons, eat kosher, attend synagogue), he will be stuck with a yellow star from generation to generation. Even if he converts, or if he and his sons marry non-Jews, his grandchildren will always run the risk of hearing (or, perhaps even worse, of not hearing) themselves insulted as "yids," suspected of avarice or social climbing, and so on. And, to add insult to injury, they will be labeled as ashamed of their Jewishness. Thus humiliated, they will be called upon to defend themselves (if only in their own eyes), even if, knowing nothing of Judaism, they have not the slightest idea what they are supposed to be ashamed of (or proud of—but it comes down to the same thing). Even in South Africa under apartheid, it was easier for a colored person to cross the racial Rubicon and be reclassified as "white," on condition that he or she had a pale enough skin, straight enough hair, and passed a number of other legally defined tests. In our democratic societies, however, the descendent of a converted Jew remains one forever.[36]

As numerous writers have pointed out, that type of Jew, the one who never sets foot in a synagogue, inspires the most virulent hatred, precisely because he is so like those around him.[37] He is perceived as the "enemy within the walls," generating all kinds of fantasies—in the anti-Semite first, and soon in all those who hear him rave. He becomes the object onto which they can project everything they hate, or are frightened of, in themselves. Bettelheim was not the first writer to point this out, although the particular case he discusses (the Jew as perceived by the Nazi guard, inside the concentration camp) is strikingly unique, because it is located in the very place where anti-Semitism reaches its ultimate limit, where the fantasy became reality.

After the war, or more specifically after the discovery of the "final solution," it was possible for a while to believe that a page had been turned, that, having witnessed the ultimate in inhumanity, "informed" people had learned to recognize the limits beyond which they could not go. There was thus a naive belief that phantasmagorical anti-Semitism was dead, and that the Jews could finally take their place among other minorities, henceforth suffering only from "ordinary" racism.

And indeed the Holocaust engendered a taboo. For years, certain epithets and ideas were no longer heard in public. The first postwar generations thus enjoyed "protected" childhoods. Coincidence or not, it was precisely those generations that in the late 1960s were to take to the streets all over the globe chanting "We want the world, and we want it now!" The demand of course was expressed differently in different countries (in Paris, a former center of collaboration with the Nazi regime, it became at one point: "We are all German Jews!").[38] Nevertheless, in Chicago as in Berlin, Milan, and even Prague, the thirst for social justice and authenticity was the same. And everywhere, the voices of Jews, half-Jews, and "Jew-lovers" of all types were preponderant.

This was just the time when Bruno Bettelheim chose to reveal his deep pessimism. Turning his back on Herbert Marcuse, Jean-Paul Sartre, and many others among his fellow-academics, he attacked the leaders of the revolt head-on. And what exactly did he call them? "Spoiled children!" The lover of Goethe and German Expressionism, who was forced one day to consider himself privileged to be allowed to haul pails full of excrement to fertilize SS officers' gardens, had immediately sensed that such an appetite for freedom, equality, and truth could only be "bad for the Jews!" For if these young people had been "spoiled," it was above all because they had grown up in a world in which the anti-Semites had been silenced. As a result, they knew the truth without knowing it, without understanding what had really happened. And they wanted to be told everything, secure in the illusory belief that national or international laws and courts were there to protect them against any repetition of a past which they viewed as dead and buried.

Bettelheim appealed to these "spoiled children" of anti-Semitism, those whom the Holocaust had paradoxically protected against the traumas of hatred—and, when they were Jewish, against self-hatred; they liked to hear a Jew speak out proudly to say that everyone has a duty to protect his own life and that of his family. Whether he actually had the courage of his convictions was beside the point; what mattered was his tone. It was the tone of a man who was not waiting for God to determine his destiny.

And they also liked his way of handling what others called madness. There appeared to be parallels between Bettelheim's ideas about mental health and those of the 1968 protest movement about politics. In both cases, a simple desire to repair the world's unfairness, provided the desire was sincere, seemed to be all that was needed to change it. To chant "Make love, not war," "*Sous les pavés, la plage,*"[39] "Do it!" or "Workers and students, unite!" seemed to make it all come true. It was an idea that the French writer Marguerite Duras summed up neatly with the slogan: "Be realistic; demand the impossible."

In fact, there was a misunderstanding: Bettelheim, who was speaking as a psychoanalyst, was not saying that madness does not exist, but simply that it is alien to nobody, that the ossified categories of classical psychiatry, like the institutions they had engendered, are prisons, within which human beings whose only crime is to suffer are trapped. To translate his ideas into the social or political realms was already to distort them. Yet those who did so had an excuse: the place from which Bettelheim had chosen to speak out. It was a place so real that it transcended psychoanalysis: the concentration camp. Once Bettelheim had drawn a parallel between his experience in the camps and his work at the Orthogenic School, that parallel had come to life in his readers' minds, endowing him with a role that went well beyond the field of psychoanalysis.

Having experienced the worst that human nature can devise, Bettelheim appeared to have the right to demand, and therefore to promise others, the best that humanity can give. He would wipe away the injustice he had suffered by requisitioning the enemy's weapons to destroy another menace, every bit as arbitrary as the one that had struck him: mental illness in children. It was a just aim, and a good one. After the return to peace, and its unavoidable compromises, its omissions ("Life must go on"), and its pettinesses, Bettelheim the magician offered a hope as daring, as immense, as Nazism had been monstrous. If out of the horrors of the Holocaust could come a way to save insane children, then God had not died at Auschwitz. That was the message everyone had heard, the one that had set Bettelheim apart. The young protesters, just because they were "spoiled," were simply demanding from the adult world what everyone was expecting of him, overlooking that he was simply another fallible human being, and more severely wounded than many.

After his death, people started calling him to account—as if, in the field of mental health, results could be summed up in figures. The impossibility of obtaining documentary evidence of his therapeutic effectiveness fed suspicions. Yet, in psychology, what answers can material data provide? With the right type of tests, one can claim to measure scholastic aptitude (but not really the qualitative factor in teaching), and one can evaluate a person's effectiveness in certain types of behavior (personal hygiene, eating, mobility). But only the patient himself can provide the overall picture, and answer the only truly interesting question: "Am I happier than before? In other words, can I make more effective use of my energy to become the person I would like to be, and achieve my aims?"

Only the testimony of those who attended the Orthogenic School can thus provide a valid reply about what Bettelheim accomplished there. Of the fifty some individuals I talked to, two-thirds were there as adults, either counselors or teachers. For it requires a great deal of courage—or a lot of pain—for someone who has since created a whole new life, perhaps with family and children, to stand up and say: "I was once a student at the Orthogenic School." The interviews took place between November 1990 and December 1994. In many cases, I spoke several times to the same person, and sometimes noted changes in his or her feelings over time. Of the former staff members, only one was totally hostile to Bettelheim. Two others, while acknowledging the value of his teaching, believe that during the final years he was so distracted that he on occasion acted in ways that hurt the children. All the others, without exception, are convinced that the mistakes he may have made with them were negligible, weighed against the good he did. Most of them also think that, even today, there are very few places in the world where disturbed children have as good a chance of recovery as at the Orthogenic School under Bettelheim.

In interviews with former students, bittersweet memories often surface, even as someone is recounting a breakthrough. Five of those I spoke to expressed anger toward Bettelheim, in two cases even hatred. Those who acknowledge their need to have gone to the school say in general that they learned to overcome several of their handicaps while there. Some even say they were happy there. Many speak of Bettelheim with true affection, others do not. With a single exception, all those who vehemently denounce him were still at the school when he left, at least the first time. One is reminded of the "bad guy" departure ritual, while being aware that it is only part of the story.

Such testimonies must indeed be taken "as is," without looking for hidden meanings or omissions in each person's story. Nobody is deliberately lying and, overall, nobody challenges the truth of the events related. It is simply that the same incident recounted by two different people sounds so different as to be unrecognizable. The story of Alida Jatitch in the shower, for example, was told to me by a half-dozen different witnesses, including two of her dorm-mates, and it thereby lost a lot of its power to shock, and all of its indecency. Nobody is right. In matters psychological—for that is indeed what is at stake here—there are no bad marks to be handed out. Just feelings to be recovered.

The fifty-six-year-old man who says, with a lump in his throat, "Dr. B saved my life; without him, I would never have made it into adulthood" certainly knows what he is talking about better than the former counselor who, filled with hatred for Bettelheim, shrugs his shoulders and says: "That kid was simply a little difficult. He was no crazier than you or me." The life of which the former student speaks is precisely what other people do not have access to, other than occasionally, by intuition or empathy. It is the realm of his personal phantoms, of his closets full of skeletons, and also of his dreams, acceptable or not. It is the life that Sigmund Freud gave back to us, the life of the mind or, as Bettelheim might have called it, the inner life. It is the life behavioral therapies seek to smother with conditioned reflexes.

Hence most of the misunderstandings and doubts about Bettelheim's work. His aim was not to adapt the unhappy children in his care to their parents' social mores. It was not to make them "well behaved." His aim was not even to make them happy, but to get them gradually to understand, because that discovery had once saved his life, that even the most miserable of lives ("even the life of a Jew in the hands of the Nazis," he used to say) is valuable as soon as one succeeds in giving it meaning. This is what recovering, or being cured, meant for him: finally to acknowledge the value of one's own life. And to get there, he always worked with the inner lives of those around him. For, in spite of appearances, that is the only life that matters to individuals, because it is the only one that produces meaning.

"He saved my life." This is the statement that occurred most often in the testimonies of the former students and counselors I spoke to. It takes time to understand what it means; time to recognize the existence of that inner life, which is not parallel to the other, but woven into it, giving it texture; time to become aware of it in oneself—the time it takes for a good analysis—and also time to learn to respect it in other people. When I heard those first "He saved my life" statements, armed with my microphone and the certainties of one who knows all about the "real world," I interpreted them as expressing the total loyalty of cult members. But I heard it too often, from too many different people, and, every time, in a tone that commanded respect. The people who used the expression knew what they were saying. However their behavior appeared to an outsider, the phantoms they had had to struggle with in their minds were indeed killers. And it was

Bettelheim who had helped them to put those killers out of action, that is to say, return them to their rightful places in the past, so that, ceasing to be phantoms, they became memories, and stopped cannibalizing the present.

"Everything is perfect in your films, except that awful character—the old director," Bettelheim said in late March 1974, when David Karlin showed him his work at Francis Ford Coppola's studios, in San Francisco.[40] He was not just being coy. By now retired and age seventy, he had a harsher self-image than ever. Six months after moving to California, this time for good, he was making great efforts to free himself from his lost school. In a letter written to Candy Hilldrup nine months earlier, on the very day he was saying goodbye to the children, he had these comforting words for her: "That it now all seems unreal to you is how it has to be—it's too painful to accept that it was real and now is no longer . . . This is part of the process of separation, when it all has to become shadowy so that one can take it."[41] The advice was drawn from Freud, but it was aimed as much at himself as at her. Karlin had come back too soon. To see the children looking so very alive on film, with the school and himself in the middle, had been a painful experience indeed.

A few days after the screening, Bettelheim was due to travel back to Chicago to give two months of classes, under the contract that still tied him to the university. He was filled with apprehension at the idea of returning, and once there, he was overwhelmed by feelings of loss and abandonment. There was no longer a place for him at the school. When he visited, he felt many people were avoiding him. He understood their need to push ahead, without him, but he suffered from it. He nevertheless enjoyed seeing former colleagues and some former Orthogenic School students on campus, in that other world to which he now belonged, and he also enjoyed the teaching. The following year, he no longer really felt like going at all. Although he had had a tough time settling in, he had gotten used to a life of active retirement in the California sun. He had just finished *The Uses of Enchantment*, and had no desire to take another trip into his Chicago past. And in 1976, the last year he made the teaching trip, the whole exercise had become a burden, shouldered solely for financial reasons. He hated staying in a hotel in the city where he had been a resident for so long. He found the climate, which was exceptionally hot and humid that spring, particularly disagreeable. Six months earlier he had suffered a mild heart attack during a trip to France. It had taken him a while to recover, and his overriding desire was to turn the page on what had once been his work. Candy Hilldrup, by now living in Paris, had sent him a manuscript of some seven hundred pages about her experiences at the school. After reading it attentively he sent her seven pages of comments and suggestions. In the accompanying letter, he wrote: "I was glad to read what you wrote because reading it was kind of a communication with you. For the rest my desire is not to hear another word about the school. It is all over for me. I did it, we did it, it is no longer mine—may the others have it, but please they should not bother me with it when it is not mine."[42]

That last wish was to be granted him beyond all his expectations. After his departure, his relations with Jacquelyn Sanders had remained cordial, even though it was clear that her way of running the school did not have much in common with his. When people criticized her, he would express faith in her, and say it was normal that she should adapt the institution to what she herself was able to do with it. "Without Jacqui," he once told Candy Hilldrup, "the school would already have fallen in the hands of the behaviorists."

During the first year of his retirement, Bettelheim continued to rely a great deal on the school for material support in his own work. He had one of the secretaries type out his texts, while Sanders took care of procuring books he required. Up until 1975, she continued to seek his advice regularly on new admissions. But their relations gradually soured. Finally, in April 1982, as Bettelheim was about to pay a flying visit to Chicago, he received a note from Jacquelyn Sanders telling him she no longer wished to see him. With that, he felt the door of the Orthogenic School was closed to him once and for all. Although hurt, he had not taken it too badly at the time, as he was too busy tending to Trude's illness. Over the years, however, the loss of the school would rankle more and more, combining with his other troubles to cast a painful shadow over his final years.

Neither Bettelheim nor Jacquelyn Sanders herself had fully realized just how much bitterness lay behind the new director's devotion. She indeed acknowledges the fact. After Bettelheim's departure, she chose for an analyst the man against whom he had warned her. Little by little, the reasons for her resentment started to come out. She was angry about the power he had wielded over her in his role as director-cum-therapist; she later told him this, in a letter. As she freely recognizes,

she was also bitter that he had not helped her in her career. She
became particularly aware of this on seeing Daniel Karlin's film.[43] She
felt insulted by the short passage in which Bettelheim refers to her.
Karlin asks him whether "out of all the counselors you have trained,
there is a single one of whom you can say: 'I have managed to make
him or her capable of replacing me.'"

"Yes, a few," Bettelheim answers. "But they have chosen less difficult jobs. One of my best staff members is now one of my colleagues
at the university, where he teaches. I had wanted him to succeed me,
but he refused. Those long hours, every night . . . He could have done
it, even though he chose not to do it. I think Dr. Sanders, who has succeeded me, will manage very well. But of course, it's always a personal
creation."[44]

Jacquelyn Sanders did what she thought best. She very carefully
preserved the school's overall framework, and even wrote a book, *A
Greenhouse for the Mind*, in which she explained the need for it.[45]
She stopped admitting autistic children, banned all forms of physical violence, and ended in-house therapies for counselors. In other
words, Sanders knocked off the rough edges and made the school
presentable. She also got it in tune with the times, introducing co-
ed groups and allowing teenagers to go downtown alone for medical
and dental appointments. But in this new irreproachable institution,
what had happened to psychoanalysis, to empathy, to the fantasies
and phantoms that made living so unbearable for the children? To
all those awkward, not-so-presentable feelings? One asks such
questions in vain. Once Bettelheim had left, the Orthogenic School
stopped seeking out and confronting hidden "killers." Instead, it
tried to lull them to sleep.

As this is a biography of Bruno Bettelheim, and not a history of the
Orthogenic School, we will leave the matter there. It is nevertheless
worth noting how conformism, the desire to be presentable, and an
apparent concern for justice can camouflage feelings and deeds that
are anything but nice, how the suppression of all physical—that is,
visible—violence can be used to ends that are no less violent, while
remaining hidden. It is one thing that Jacquelyn Sanders decided to
place in the publicly available Bettelheim archives, without any
explanation, a copy of the letter in which she informed him that the
children at the Orthogenic School were no longer being hit, and that
she had put a stop to in-house therapies.[46] It was not exactly a delicate move, but it remained within the bounds of their professional

relations. It was a response to the secrecy Bettelheim had maintained about his therapeutic methods: He had never clearly faced up to his use of violence, and she was thus refusing that part of his heritage.

The role Sanders played in the "Bettelheim affair" is quite another thing, however. Several of the former students who publicly attacked Bettelheim after his death contacted her before doing so. "I didn't want to prevent them from expressing their reality," she told me, clearly convinced that she had done the right thing. From the outside world, it sounded convincing: Did these "former children" not have the right to shout from the rooftops that their lives at the school had been very different from what Bettelheim had described in his books? However, having spent fourteen years working alongside Dr. B, how could Jacquelyn Sanders not have known how difficult it would be for these former patients to handle the public expression of their hatred for him, now that he was dead? Was this not jeopardizing everything he had always tried to do to calm their inner conflicts? How could she have let these former students, toward whom she professes such devotion, face alone a public baying for sensational revelations, and lay into the corpse of the man who had for such a long time served as a lightning rod for their own internal storms? All of this knowing that he could no longer stand up to prove to them, even by growling at them, that they were not murderers, that they had not killed him, that they were not responsible for his suicide?

It is difficult to answer such questions for I have no doubt as to Jacquelyn Sanders's good intentions. Yet nothing helped me to understand Bettelheim's therapeutic method better than the scandal that broke out after his death. Shortly thereafter, I spoke to several of the people who had publicly attacked him; I was to see a few of them two years later, and speak to others again on the phone. Over time, the vigor, often mingled with jubilation, of their recriminations had dissolved. All that remained, obsessive, obsessing, and disturbing, was the complaint: words, lots of words, and bitter trains of thought that kept chasing their own tails. But the Big Bad Wolf was indeed no more. The words, echoing in the void, fell, vengeful, hurtful, painful, and sterile, back onto those who had uttered them.

And yet even the scandal could serve a purpose. Like the body of the murdered woman lying near the school. Like the revolting soup at Buchenwald. It was "Paul" of *Truants from Life* who showed me how: "On reflection, I think the scandal helped me to overcome the anger I felt when I heard of his suicide. I had never felt so let down in my life.

I was so angry at him. Then those nasty letters began to appear and I started to think back on all the things he had done for me. So my anger fell," he said.

In May 1986, the University of Chicago decided to stage a conference in honor of Bruno Bettelheim. Putting her feelings to one side, Jacquelyn Sanders undertook to organize it. Although she was on sabbatical, she did her duty. The program was laid out like clockwork, with only one afternoon out of the two days devoted to the workings of the Orthogenic School; six former counselors were invited to speak.[47] It was mainly to Bettelheim the writer, thinker, and academic that homage was being paid. Besides Bert Cohler, the only former student invited to speak was at the time a high-ranking academic at another university. But feelings disrupted the carefully planned event. Former staff and students flocked from all over the country, and even from abroad (Geneviève Jurgensen, for example, traveled from Paris). The atmosphere that was lacking on the podium was spontaneously created on the floor, with former students gravitating naturally toward their former counselors. The ambivalence of people's feelings was also in evidence, and at least one person who was to attack Bettelheim violently after his death attended. To sum up, it was warm, occasionally difficult, but always moving and enriching, bringing a bit of life into the existence of a depressed old man who had just lost his wife. A gift from some of the people whom he had earlier helped to recover their own love of life.

On this occasion, former counselor Leslie Cleaver found simple words with which to bring back to life, beyond people's fantasies, something of what Bettelheim's Orthogenic School had once been. "When I started to write this paper, I wrote down a number of anecdotes in apparently random order," she said.

> The last one was an exchange between a twelve-year-old boy who had been at the school for two years and me, who had been there six years, about an autistic boy of five, who was then just, joyously and very movingly, learning to talk. Billy, the older boy, was very jealous of the fragile and desperately ill younger child to whom he behaved in a very tender and protective way. Quite properly (a range of feelings, not a range of actings out), he directed his angry and jealous feelings towards me . . . Then he said: "The thing I'm most jealous of is . . . I wish I had learned to talk at the school like Jonny. I wish I learned to talk to express

myself, instead of to protect myself. My life would have been so different." To know that, to be able to say that, to be able to say how things really are, didn't make all the difference, but it made enough difference that for Billy, for me, and for that, there aren't enough words to say "Thank you, Dr. B."

Epilogue

Modern technology has produced lack of respect for the unknown and unknowability. The terrible arrogance of the technicians, the mathematicians, the measurers, the consumption addicts, the status-seekers, all these dervishes of the rationality and consciousness cult. They have superbly succeeded in turning the external aspects of life into the sole contents of man's mind. And what makes this perversion even more painful is the fact that the one revolution that could have brought about a real change, depth psychology, has helped distort human truth into the falsity of denying unknowability. They have misinterpreted Freud, who knew the malaise of civilization. But Freud is not free from guilt for his sons and daughters, his disciples. At least he did not do enough to counteract this dangerous superstition of seeing the unconscious in terms of potential consciousness.

Carl Frankenstein, letter to Bruno
Bettelheim, August 31, 1975

Trude and the Children

It took us a long time, Trude and I, to get ourselves free of
Vienna, and in spite of that we haven't become Americans. In a way, we are between the two, perhaps a little
more over here than over there; at least that's the feeling
I have.

Bruno Bettelheim, letter to ER,
September 10, 1954

"Which Dr. Bettelheim do you wish to speak to?" The question,
and even more the hard tone in which it was asked, took
Geneviève Jurgensen aback, leaving her ill at ease. It was early spring
in 1988, and Jurgensen was calling from Paris to ask her former teacher
for an interview, on the occasion of the publication in French of *A Good
Enough Parent.* Since leaving the Orthogenic School she had seen
Bruno Bettelheim only twice: at the Chicago conference two years earlier, and in the fall of 1975, when he had dined at her home in Paris.

But they had kept in touch by mail, and this had always meant a
lot to Jurgensen. Her life as a writer and journalist in France was
worlds away from the one she had led in Chicago, and over the years
their correspondence had become that of old friends, discussing
everyday life with no didactic or philosophical pretensions. But
when the going got rough, Jurgensen had always found in Bettelheim that same combination of clear-sightedness and compassion
that had earlier helped her to become an adult.

In 1980, when a reckless driver killed both her young daughters, Bruno Bettelheim had been the only professional to approve of Jurgensen's seemingly crazy desire to become a mother again as soon as possible. Doctors, psychoanalysts, and others had all told her to wait a while, until she had finished mourning her lost children. Otherwise, they said, she would not be able to love the newborn for himself; she would burden him with a load of suffering too heavy to bear. Only the author of *The Empty Fortress*, the man who had so often been accused of unfairness to mothers, had fully understood her instinctive need to create a new life immediately. Only he had trusted her ability to love and give anew. And fifteen years later, Jurgensen can still quote from his letters almost word for word: "So, what I trembled for during the 30 years I ran the School has happened to you . . . "[1] And then the sentence that "cut through all the complications," as she puts it today: "Of course you will raise your children with great anxiety. It is perfectly natural, and it cannot be avoided."

Having made an appointment with Bettelheim, Geneviève Jurgensen arrived in Los Angeles in April 1988. He was then living in a beautiful hacienda-style house on Adelaide Place, a tiny and exclusive street running up a hill near the ocean, in Santa Monica. He greeted her in what appeared to be his study, adjacent to the front door. She was struck by how old and frail he looked. He had always dressed with care; now he had stains on his lapels. He had lost a lot of weight and walked with difficulty. Most notable was how he seemed constantly afraid of making too much noise, of causing a disturbance. He looked somehow diminished, humiliated, and she got a feeling of satisfaction from seeing how her visit quickly gave him back some of his old bearing.

Jurgensen had no way of knowing it, but she had arrived in Los Angeles at a tragic juncture in Bettelheim's life. He was just recovering from a pancreatic infection and, now unable to ingest any solid food, was in a state of near starvation. But most of all, he was in a deep depression. After a year and a half of cohabitation, the old man and his daughter Ruth—the other "Dr. Bettelheim"—were past the breaking point. Ruth had just bought a new house, a few streets away from Adelaide Place, and she had not given her father either the address or the phone number. He was himself looking for an apartment. The atmosphere in the house had become unbearable; the two were no longer on speaking terms and Bettelheim was convinced that his daughter wanted him dead. He felt horribly alone, abandoned and hated, as he confided in letters and verbally to a few close friends.

His distress even showed through in the interview he gave Jurgensen.[2] It was a bitter irony for the old man to have to defend *A Good Enough Parent*, a book that often adopts a peremptory tone to discuss the raising of children, at a time when his own relationship with his eldest child had fallen apart and he could not but be aware of all the mistakes he himself had made as a father. In reply to Jurgensen's opening remark—"The thing that strikes one most on reading your book is that bringing up children today is not exactly simple"—he mentioned the owner of a hardware store in Harlem, who ran his business with the help of his seventeen-year-old son in perfect harmony. "That has become extremely rare," Bettelheim commented. He went on,

> It has always impressed me very much that of the Ten Commandments only one, the fifth, refers specifically to parents and children. And it does not say "Love thy father and mother," which would be in line with the expectations of modern parents. It says "Honor thy father and thy mother." To honor one's parents is very easy if one works with them, alongside of them. It doesn't take any commandment to tell a blacksmith's son to honor his father when he sees him pulling the iron out of the fire and beating it into shape! Seeing how skilled the father is automatically inspires admiration, and the father feels great gratitude to the child for providing him with such narcissistic satisfaction.

Although Geneviève Jurgensen could feel the bitterness in those remarks, she could not imagine how deep it ran. She did not know it was that of a man who had been forced to succeed his own father in a trade he didn't like and thus to give up, or so he believed at the time, all hope of ever occupying the noble position he aspired to— and that because of his father's "sin." Neither could Jurgensen know how painful was the wound resulting from the break with Ruth, the only one of his three children to have chosen the same career as himself.

This latest drama in Bettelheim's life, from which he would not recover, indeed appeared to be a replay of all the preceding ones. As in a nightmare, it showed traces of all the worst fears and crises of his life: the fear of being a fraud, with his book on child rearing coming out just when his own life was revealing his failures as a parent; the issue of paternal impotence, as he had proved unable to give his elder daughter the support she expected when she had found herself

alone with two children. But it also involved a replay of his grandfather Seidler's despotism and his illnesses, as Bettelheim's last years
were punctuated by emergency hospitalizations, heart attacks, strokes,
and other ailments. And lastly, there was the feeling of being despoiled,
first of his school, which, like his former company, had been taken
away from him—or so he felt—but also of his money, as he now had
the impression that Ruth wanted more than her share. The family
curse had indeed returned. Only this time Trude was not there to help
him rout the ghosts that haunted him. To help him live.

The Bettelheims' final move to California in 1973 had been anything
but easy. From an Austrian engineer they had bought a house poised
spectacularly on a hilltop in Portola Valley, a few miles west of the
Stanford campus. Access was by Sierra Lane, a winding road that led
to a short track with only one other house. Theirs, no. 1, was at the
top. It was like another world: lush vegetation all around, near total
solitude, and the ocean in the distance. A little too wild, perhaps, as
if man did not really belong there. The wilderness even got the better
of Trude's passion for gardening. "The deer come every night and eat
all her flowers, and what the deer don't do, the rabbits, gophers, rac-
coons and what not finish off. All which they don't touch—like
cacti—we don't like," Bettelheim wrote.[3] There nevertheless remained
a few laurels, oleanders, and rhododendrons scattered among the
pines, cacti, and orange trees that surrounded the house.

"City-dwellers just shouldn't suddenly try to live out in the country, least of all in California, which is less a state of the Union and
much more a state of mind, and not our type of mind," an exasperated Bettelheim wrote to Ruth Marquis on his arrival. The slightest
shopping trip was a major expedition. He appeared to doubt whether
he would be able to stand living in such an out-of-the-way place for
long, and he raged against his and Trude's willingness to be won over
by their stay in Palo Alto. "The difference between the year at the
Center which seduced us to move out here is fantastic, exactly the difference between a lovely vacation and settling down in a vacation
place to live and work. It was a crazy idea. We should have known
better," he added.[4]

In spite of such recriminations, Bettelheim gradually got used to his
California retirement, as he would realize on his first trip back to
Chicago. Although he missed the city atmosphere, the balmy climate

plus, once they were settled, the comfort and convenience of their new life had their charms. Stanford was a campus free of noise, traffic jams, and dirt, yet prestigious enough to attract a good number of interesting visitors each year. Although he would admit to it only when he felt uncomfortable somewhere else, he had become used to California.

Their house was far enough from Palo Alto to protect them from the crowd, yet they had enough friends in the area to provide a pleasant social life. There were musical evenings and pleasant dinners, at other people's places and at theirs. Since his leg operation, Bettelheim was supposed to walk as much as possible. He and Trude took a daily one-hour stroll in the big natural parks that dotted the region. Trude had also joined the Sierra Club, played tennis regularly, and even began riding a bicycle that Naomi had given her. Bruno was still very active with work, although it did not feel like much compared to his schedule in Chicago. He taught a few hours of classes each week at Stanford and held regular meetings with a group of local psychiatrists and psychologists, plus an occasional meeting with mothers. Soon he was giving a seminar in the Child Psychiatry Division at Stanford University Medical School. And of course there were lectures and conferences, both across the United States and abroad. The couple traveled a lot, now most of the time together.

Above all, Bettelheim wrote. Long before retiring, he had already started worrying about how inactivity would affect him. As he told Carl Frankenstein, "I know I had to give it [my work] up, but I also know what is right for others was the wrong thing for me to do. As long as I was busy all day running a clinic I did not have time for thoughts which are only depressing. In one's work one has to be optimistic or it won't work. Now nothing forces me to be optimistic, and that makes things much more difficult."[5]

Before leaving Chicago, Bettelheim had made plans for work he would do in Portola Valley. He was thinking about his planned book on child rearing, a project he mentioned in most of his letters to Ruth Marquis. But at the same time, he had been awarded a $123,000 grant from the Spencer Foundation for a study on the role of the unconscious in school learning. The program, for which he planned to carry out fieldwork, was due to take three years. He wanted to find out how psychoanalysis could contribute to teaching, or "what little kids think when they sit in classes and are being taught . . . How does their preconscious support or interfere with what goes on in class, and how should they be taught, so that their preconscious will support the learning?"[6] Bettelheim had long denounced the inanity of American schoolbooks. Seminars he had given for elementary school teachers in Chicago had only confirmed what he had known all along: that children growing up in neighborhoods racked by drugs, violence, and poverty, often in single-parent families, would not learn to read, even at the age when the appetite for knowledge is the strongest, so long as their textbooks contained only bland, noncontroversial stories about well-behaved children living in middle-class suburbia; that a child's appetite for reading stems from his desire to understand what is happening to and around him.

Bettelheim therefore started arranging visits to local schools, and he asked Jacquelyn Sanders to send him all available U.S. readers, and also French, British, and German ones for comparative purposes. Meanwhile, being especially interested in the child's initial contacts with the written word, he began rereading the first texts most children encounter: fairy tales. He starts mentioning this work in his correspondence in October 1973. The subject enchanted him immediately. All the feelings and emotions he found lacking in the modern textbooks—anger, jealousy, curiosity—were there in the fairy stories, in all their raw intensity. Like the unconscious itself, the characters in *Grimms' Fairy Tales* do not bother with nuances. Evil parents or hated rivals are killed, often with great cruelty. Love expresses itself orally most of the time. Good mothers often vanish, to be replaced by evil stepmothers, while brothers or sisters are invariably wrong. Things are simple: If one is not good, one is bad. And when one is bad, if one fails to repent, one is doomed. All of which is perfectly clear to a child, while a happy ending generally shows him the way to resolve his conflicts.

His correspondence suggests that the two years Bettelheim devoted to writing *The Uses of Enchantment* were the happiest in the later part of his life. Deciphering the meaning of the stories was a source of delight to him, and he even wondered aloud to some friends, almost embarrassed, whether he was going through "a second childhood." It was a huge relief for him not to be writing about either autism or the concentration camps any longer. It felt like being reborn. He thought of his mother, and regretted not having told his own children any fairy tales, "because, in our then rationalistic period, we thought that they were bad for them. What fools men be."[7]

Bettelheim's interpretations have become well known. There was

Hansel and Gretel, the story featuring a gingerbread house and a little boy whom the witch fattens up in order to eat him, teaching very small children how to get past the oral phase of development. *The Three Little Pigs* illustrates the three stages in a child's development. *Jack and the Beanstalk* shows young boys how to grow out of their oedipal conflicts, while *Little Red Riding-Hood* warns pre-pubescent girls not to play seductive games they are not old enough to handle, and *Goldilocks* tells of a little girl's search for identity. There is the dormant period of adolescence, during which *Sleeping Beauty* is getting ready for marriage. *Cinderella*, a more complex tale, touches on sibling rivalry, ambivalence, and the castration complex.

The Uses of Enchantment is Bettelheim's most famous book, the one that reached the largest number of people throughout the world. It also drew some critical fire. Apart from those who challenged the psychoanalytical approach per se, some found it too long and poorly structured. Bettelheim was also chided for leaving out Hans Christian Andersen and modern children's stories, and, almost immediately, a few writers accused him, if not of plagiarism, of having failed to cite his sources correctly.[8]

The accusation is partially justified. In this, the first book he wrote without the scrupulous and demanding assistance of Ruth Marquis, Bettelheim failed to observe all the rules of academic writing.[9] He cited all the authors he had consulted, but not always at the right place, and sometimes even with errors in his references. It is also true, as a scholarly article pointed out in 1991,[10] that his text contains around half a dozen sentences that are very similar, both in form and content, to those of Julius Heuscher.[11] The latter's book is indeed cited, but only in order to position it halfway between the Freudian and Jungian standpoints. All of which creates an unpleasant impression of negligence.

But nothing more. "All of this is not to say that Bettelheim's book is not infinitely superior to Heuscher's," Alan Dundes, the author of the 1991 article, acknowledges. Bettelheim indeed took the analysis of fairy tales much further than those he is accused of having plagiarized. As Alison Lurie points out, Erich Fromm was the first writer to note that the color of Little Red Riding-Hood's clothes is that of menstrual blood,[12] but his analysis is sketchy and does not explore the whole range of the child's unconscious desires, or the ambivalence of her feelings, as Bettelheim's does. It is difficult to tell whether Bettelheim's borrowing of some of

Heuscher's expressions was due to sloppy note-taking, or whether, like Jacques Lacan before him, he "took his assets where he found them," considering that what mattered was not so much where he picked up an idea but what he did with it (in my view, the erroneous references, Bettelheim's pride, and the stupidity of such a "theft" lend credence to the first hypothesis). What is clearly established from his correspondence, however, is that the book is indeed the result of original thinking that he had pursued passionately for over two years.

The Uses of Enchantment seems in fact to have sparked the train of thought that would lead Bettelheim, five years later, to write *Freud and Man's Soul*. After expressing regrets for not having introduced his children to fairy tales, he wrote to Frankenstein:

> The interesting thing is that in rejecting them I followed the psycho-analysts, who should have recognized how deep these tales really are. But in a strange way, Freud and his followers are really afraid of the unconscious. They say it contains the mainsprings of our strength, but somehow they all shied away from it, even Freud. Before him we did not know what it was . . . so we did not defend ourselves against it. Freud taught us what it is all about, and I guess instead of teaching us how to use it, he taught [us] how to live without it. As any other prophet, his teaching bore its own defeat within it. What a topic this would be for a book on psychoanalysis. But I am too old for it.[13]

Around the same time, Bettelheim wrote to Candy Hilldrup, who had asked his advice: "About reading: I have to include in their reading lists things so that the students feel that they know the field. For yourself, read only old man Freud, you'll spend your time much better with him than [with] anybody else."[14] That summer of 1975 he read Paul Roazen's book *Freud and His Followers*, recalling with nostalgia and just a hint of bitterness "all the struggle and all the excitement of the early days of psychoanalysis and how we hoped that it would be another important step toward freeing man and making this a better world."[15]

His correspondence with Carl Frankenstein was becoming more regular, and also more intimate and varied, ranging from psycho-analysis to politics, from Vaihinger to the Yom Kippur War to Watergate to French intellectuals.[16] The two friends understood each other; they shared the same references, the same past, and the same Spenglerian pessimism as to the way the world was going. But above all, what they had in common was, as Frankenstein put it in reply to Bettelheim's observations on fairy tales:

> I feel I always have understood where your love for children and where the tenacity of your refusal to take a "No" (or a seeming "No") for an answer comes from, when it comes to helping a badly mishandled youngster. Your anger at "growing up at any price," that seldom if ever leaves some remains of sincerity and humanity intact in us, has always been mine . . . We belong, I feel, to the same company of fools who have managed to remain children, to some extent at least. Imagination is still a value for us. And we are angry with "them," as only children can be angry with "omniscient" adults.[17]

And among those whom Frankenstein referred to as "the dervishes of the rationality cult," one of the two friends' favorite targets was the psychoanalytic establishment, which they found guilty of having fallen into "this dangerous superstition of seeing the unconscious in terms of potential consciousness."[18]

Bettelheim found regular confirmation of that at Stanford. What the young psychiatrists and psychologists who attended his seminars were looking for, even those most interested in psychoanalysis, was technique, and not his "philosophy," as one of them, albeit well disposed toward Bettelheim, calls it.[19] They were seeking practical advice drawn from his experience as director of the Orthogenic School, not outdated reflections on man's soul, as most of them perceived them; they had no desire to go through the inner work that was at the core of his teaching. With these students, in fact, Bettelheim did not go in for much Socratism; he simply gave them what they wanted.[20] At Stanford, he noted, "all is drug-related research and treatment and nothing longer than the ninety days the insurance pays for."[21] At this time, his letters to Frankenstein were becoming more and more pessimistic. He was not yet mentioning suicide, but his reflections on the impotence that comes with old age and the vanity of even the noblest human undertakings, were those of a man who is continually asking himself "What's the point?" It was around this time that the controversy with Terrence Des Pres and Lina Wertmüller's film moved Bettelheim to resume his writing on the concentration camps, to produce *Surviving*.

✳

Each year, the Bettelheims made at least one trip to Europe. They had in fact briefly considered retiring to Switzerland, where their old friends Emmi Vischer-Radanowicz and her husband, Bertel, lived. The couple had had an eventful time since leaving Vienna in 1935. After the Anschluss, they had chosen not to emigrate to the United States so as to leave open two more places for Austrian Jews in the strict U.S. quota system. But when the Siemens company invited Bertel to run its Tehran office, just before World War II broke out, they gladly seized the opportunity to get out of Paris. In Iran, apart from some friction with the German embassy, which did not understand why the local representative of such a major company was not a Nazi Party member, and the sad news they received from their friends, they led a relatively peaceful existence, until the Anglo-Soviet offensive against Iran that was sparked by Hitler's decision to attack the Soviet Union in June 1941. The Soviets too felt that the head of the Siemens office had to be a card-carrying Nazi, and they immediately arrested Radanowicz as a German spy; he was thrown into the Lubianka prison, in Moscow, tortured, then shipped off to Siberia. Emmi and their three young children took refuge with her family in Basel, and she spent the next fourteen years not knowing what had become of her husband, nor whether he was still alive. Once the war was over, Trude Bettelheim made contact with her again, and helped as best she could. Emmi's situation was made more difficult by her refusal to declare her husband dead, which would have allowed her to regain her Swiss nationality, and many material advantages along with it. "I don't know that he's dead," she kept answering to civil servants bemused by such lack of practical sense. And then, one day, her many efforts paid off: Bertel came back, emaciated and in terrible shape, but alive.

Bettelheim, who had been very attracted to Emmi in Vienna, even though he had kept it to himself, was now also deeply impressed by her and Bertel's courage. Over the years their friendship had played an increasingly important role in his life. And now that he was retired, he rarely visited Europe without stopping off in Basel. Bettelheim also had some acquaintances in Vienna, at least one school friend who had never left the city and a few, like Ernst Federn, who had returned after exile. But each time he went back it was with mixed feelings of nostalgia and resentment. He now knew a lot of people in Germany, France, and Israel. He was often invited to lecture, and each time, he was clearly delighted to find abroad some of the respect for his ideas that he felt his new home environment was denying him, turned as it was toward the Pacific and fascinated by technology. He had a good life there, but felt more than ever like an exile. "What will we all do, when other forms, such as retrieval systems and computers will have taken the place of books?" the old man wondered, perched in his aerie just a few miles from what was soon to become Silicon Valley.[22]

An even greater dose of culture shock was in store. In September 1976, just after his article "Surviving" had appeared, and he had begun compiling the book of the same name, Bettelheim received an invitation to spend a year as a guest professor at a Japanese university from the education minister, Michio Nagai. After a great deal of hesitation, he agreed to teach for three months, provided it was at Kyoto University. So in September 1977, Trude and Bruno Bettelheim flew to Japan. The experience shattered him: "After the concentration camps these were for me personally the most difficult times in my life, as far as external conditions were concerned," he wrote on his return.[23] During the first weeks, he had dreams of dying every night. The couple were then staying with a Japanese family; after a few weeks they moved into a hotel, and his letters became calmer. He expressed amazement at a people he found incomprehensible: "I soon . . . realized that all that we had been told about [the Japanese] and read was simply nothing but the fantastic wishful projections of Westerners, who project so well."[24] He was nevertheless quite receptive to the charm of the old imperial city, its decorative screens, gardens, and traditions, whereas he found Tokyo uninteresting, if easier to handle.

He was particularly baffled by the impossibility of entering into a real dialogue with his hosts. He wrote to a friend:

Despite their superficial attempts to resemble the Western world, everything here is different in the deepest sense. The structure of the language and, with it, the thinking are fundamentally different. The ego, which to us is the center of all human experiences, is almost forbidden here. One doesn't say "I" even though the word does exist. Verbs don't have past or future tenses . . . One word is used to designate both the singular and the plural . . . This is to show how timeless events are. Every word has several meanings, so one is never sure of what [someone] means exactly but mustn't show it. For example, I had to analyze the behavior of a little boy. The main word that he said was KAMI, which among other things means "army," "the spirit of a dead person," or else "paper." The therapist thought that the child meant "army," but other elements clearly indicated that he meant "the spirit of a dead person." It was however impossible to check with the child, since one mustn't ask questions. And, like everyone else, he mustn't say "No." The closest thing he may say is: "It would be difficult."

To show what he meant, Bettelheim drew the ideogram for "a man," which consists of two lines, one leaning on the other. "Beautiful, isn't it? It means that one does not exist without the other. And that is why there is no ego," he noted.[25]

By the end of February 1978 Bettelheim had completed *Surviving*. Exhausted and feeling completely empty, he doubted he would ever be able to write another book. The perpetually sunny California weather only added to his gloom. "If the climate is harsh, one's energy goes in fighting it and in surviving. When the weather is always pleasant, no energy is eaten up by surviving, and one is robbed of the feeling that one accomplished something by sheer staying alive."[26] He envied Carl Frankenstein, who was still teaching and working with children. Bettelheim's nostalgia for the Orthogenic School had been reawakened during the Christmas period, and he had dreamed about it several times. He felt himself getting older, and remarked sadly, "If one stops being a therapist, this leaves an emptiness one must fill out some other way."[27] His health problems were becoming more numerous: a cataract operation, a minor heart attack during a trip to France, trouble with a hip joint and his neck (for which his doctor prescribed an hour of swimming each day), then dental problems, new heart problems, an intestinal infection, and so on. None of them were very serious, but he tended to dramatize them. This made him very demanding with his family (his daughter Naomi still remembers the panicky tone in which he asked for her help when he was stricken by a raging toothache while in Japan). In his letters he often referred to his age, although in generally calm terms, and more and more often he mentioned his no longer distant death.

At the beginning of June 1979, Trude discovered that she had breast cancer. That his wife, who was eight years his junior, might die before him was something Bettelheim had never envisaged. It was a local tumor, and Trude did not want to die. She would fight. Stanford was at the forefront of research into radiation therapy, and the head of the department was one of the Bettelheims' friends. Although mastectomy was the usual method of treatment in the United States, Trude decided not to have it. She underwent three operations, fought an infection, and had to put up with a long series of radiation sessions, but four months after the initial diagnosis, Bettelheim was able to write: "I am happy to report that thanks to this complicated treatment my good wife is completely cured."[28] Trude was very tired, however, and so was Bruno, after a summer filled with anxiety and hospital visits. But as the therapy had had no side effects, they both reckoned the scare to be over.

As his correspondence shows, this is the time when Bettelheim started to realize just how much he depended on his wife. He still had a need to charm women, be it only via letters. But the only one with whom he could live—and who could live with him—the only one who understood and accepted him as he really was, was Trude. "From time to time, I feel very tired of life and I would not mind if it came to an end. Without Trude, I could not and would not go on. But I would not like to abandon her either, so I go on," he wrote in the fall of 1979.[29] They argued at times, and when no stranger was around, Trude was not the self-effacing wife many of his friends remember. She indeed put up with a lot, but she occasionally let him know how she felt about it.

Although always polite with her in public, Bruno could be less than tactful. Karen Zelan, who was living in Berkeley at the time, remembers a concert in San Francisco when Bettelheim abandoned his wife at intermission to go and sit with Gina. For the Viennese threesome had been reunited in Northern California. Twenty years earlier in Chicago, when Peter Weinmann had died, the Bettelheims had helped Bruno's first wife, even offering to have her and her daughter move in with them. They had later met up again in San Francisco, where Gina had made her home and was working as a psychotherapist. They saw one another on occasion, and Trude sometimes joined Gina for outings with her experienced hikers' group. When Bruno gave a lecture, Trude was often the first to stand up and reply to his critics, in lively and incisive terms—and it was not unusual to see Gina figuring prominently in the ranks of those critics.

Ever positive, Trude quickly returned to her normal pace, and wanted to hear no talk of her recent illness. Freed from his anxiety over her health, and having overcome the empty feeling that had invaded him on finishing *Surviving*, Bettelheim once again plunged into work with his usual ardor. On his seventy-sixth birthday, in August 1979, Bettelheim seemed surprised to find that in spite of his many ailments and a sickly childhood, he had lived longer than both his parents and any of his aunts and uncles. He noted the effects of aging with some detachment: "Without knowing it or without wanting it, one starts to withdraw from life, so that it is not too hard to leave it. But, please, do not be mistaken: I say all this without sadness. I am quite happy with my life, particularly now that Trude is again in good health."[30]

In the space of two years Bettelheim was to write *Freud and Man's Soul* and finally complete the project on learning to read, with Karen Zelan. When he was beginning to work on *The Uses of Enchantment*, she had mentioned to him that she wanted to write a paper on the psychological meaning of children's misreading and he had asked, "Why not do it together?" Flattered, she had agreed immediately and, while he finished his book on fairy tales, she collected most of the observations they were going to use. At first, she mostly analyzed and wrote up the data. As he liked what she was writing, he asked her to do some editing of his texts and, in the last year, urged her to contribute some discursive writing of her own to the project.[31] They ended up co-authors of the book—with Bettelheim specifying in the preface which chapters were his, at his agent's suggestion.

Despite statements to the contrary in his letters, he was still taking a lively interest in world affairs, particularly in events in the Middle East. He hated the Carter administration, and blamed his liberal Jewish friends for having voted it into office after celebrating the fall of Nixon, a friend of Israel. "*Judische Selbsthass à la Lessing, wie immer*" ("Jewish self-hatred à la Lessing, as usual") he noted in a letter to Frankenstein.[32] He nevertheless detested the very term "Jewish lobby": "The self-importance of Jews combined with the paranoia of the anti-Semite had created the image of this lobby. Actually the Jews here are exactly as powerless as they were in Weimar. But the gloating of the populace that the Jewish lobby was defeated is worthy of a Goebbels, whose diaries are now the hot issue in the liberal literary magazines," he wrote.[33] Not even the signing of the Camp David agreement calmed him down. He saw the fall of the Shah of Iran and the advent of an Islamic republic in Tehran, to applause from the same liberals, as yet another terrifying result of the West's, and especially America's, self-destructive tendencies.

> It is sad to see a great power tottering into impotency because nobody is willing to make any sacrifice. I guess nobody ever does . . . For a few

more fat years we gamble away the freedom of man. Well, what is this, the freedom of man? To live free to think, to express ideas, or whatever we value? Or is it to live in as much comfort as one can, the devil may take the hindmost? . . . Carter wants to be reelected for four more years, and if he can get that, the world may fall apart after it. And the American people want to drive their cars for a few more years, if this means to sell out to the Arabs, who cares?[34]

It is clear that such letters, often written under the influence of raw emotion late at night,[35] do not express thought-out ideas, intended for public consumption. Indeed, their tone varies considerably from one recipient to another. When writing to Candy Hilldrup, for example, Bettelheim remained very much the therapist, the provider of friendly advice. The tone was paternal and attentive, and the letters centered almost exclusively on her problems. With other friends, when he complained about his health and age, it was in an almost philosophical mode, most often with a tinge of hopefulness. When writing to women his tone was always chivalrous, sometimes even flirtatious. Carl Frankenstein was possibly the only correspondent with whom he thus gave free rein to his profound pessimism. In a way, Bettelheim's letters to his Israeli friend were a perfect illustration of the process of turning in on oneself, which he described in them as being ineluctable in old age. More and more frequently, ruminations on anti-Semitism and the futility of life suddenly came in between often highly interesting observations on psychoanalysis or education. The old wounds and obsessions had never healed, despite a lifetime spent trying to help others.

The letters also show Bettelheim's children occupying a growing place among his concerns. Ruth had been living in the Los Angeles area since the mid-1960s. After taking a long trip to the Far East and then earning a PhD in early childhood education at UCLA, she had established a practice as a child therapist. In 1974 she had married a city planner. He was a Mennonite and very good-looking. Although Bettelheim disapproved of his elder daughter's choice of husband, he had financed a lavish wedding ceremony, celebrated in a church. Ever since, he had provided generously for the young couple and their two children. Naomi was more independent of her father. After graduating from college she had lived in New York for a time and then spent a year in London, where she had worked for Thames & Hudson, the art books publishing house founded by Bettelheim's old friend Walter Neurath. In 1968 she had married a Mexican, but the relationship did not work out. After barely a year, to Bettelheim's great relief, she had left Mexico City to enroll in a master's program in city planning at the University of North Carolina. In 1981, after spending a year in Palo Alto, she got married again, this time to an observant Jew who had formerly taught at Berkeley and now worked for the government. After a honeymoon trip to Israel, the couple moved to England, where her husband had been posted. As for Eric, after graduating in law studies at Oxford in 1975, he had, at his father's urging, obtained an equivalent degree from the University of Chicago the following year. He preferred life in England, but Bettelheim had persuaded him to ensure that he could also practice in the United States. He had just joined a San Francisco law firm.

Bettelheim was seeing his children quite often. Regardless of where they all might be living, the family would come together at Christmas, and sometimes also at Thanksgiving. Relations between them were fairly easy, even though Bettelheim could on occasion be quite tactless with his children. Naomi remembers one Christmas, for example, when he informed them that, the night before their arrival, he had dreamed the Nazis were coming! But even when he disapproved of their choices, be it of spouses or of studies, he tried to persuade them, not to impose his will. Meanwhile, their reactions and beliefs loomed ever larger in his thinking. During the summer of 1979, when Trude was undergoing radiation treatment, he wrote the preface for *Je ne lui ai pas dit au revoir*, Claudine Vegh's book about Jewish children who were hidden in Christian families while their parents were taken to concentration camps. That made him wonder at the very different attitudes his two daughters had adopted toward their Jewishness. He saw Ruth's marriage as quite simply a rejection of it, and was intrigued that an atheist like Naomi had ended up choosing a husband with such firm beliefs. He was not displeased at his second daughter's choice, and always had a good word to say for that son-in-law. He rarely mentioned the other one. But of his three children, Eric was the one whose whereabouts seemed to interest him most. Ten years younger than his eldest sister and very much Trude's boy, Eric had had little to do with his father when he was a child. Now, he had become a subject of wonderment for Bettelheim, who often mentioned Eric's witticisms and his pranks in his letters to friends, and gently poked fun at his certainties. After visiting him in England Bettleheim reported, with more than a touch of pride, that "Eric is playing the gentleman scholar in Oxford."[36] Another time, he was struck by the young man's attributing his bouts of anxiety to the fact that his parents had been persecuted by the Nazis.

During all those years of semi-retirement, Bettelheim had continued to think about his planned book on child rearing. He had come to see it as a summing-up of all his experience, so it weighed heavily on him, and he would put it aside each time another project turned up. Yet he was constantly ruminating about what it took to be a good parent. The development of his two daughters took him back to his reflections on the role of women, and of mothers. Ruth Marquis once commented that psychoanalysts exacerbated parents' guilt feelings about their children, and he replied vehemently:

> I cannot accept that psychoanalytic writings have created parental guilt. Sure, they have added to it and given it substance. But guilt comes from way back when, way back deep down. If you are secure within yourself, nothing anybody writes is going to give you guilt feelings . . . I have been saying for years that the worst you can do is to feel guilty about what you did to your kids, because this is such a tempting weapon in their hands to act out all their oedipal resentment that they practically cannot help using it. And then, they feel miserable about having done so, and you invited them with your guilt to do so. But here I go again making the parents feel guilty, so what's the end?[37]

In the year after Trude's cancer was diagnosed, Bettelheim was continually ill himself. A first operation, followed by a serious allergic reaction, put him out of action for two months; he lost over twenty pounds. Shortly afterward, he required treatment for a lung infection, caused by the diverticulum in his esophagus that was to plague the last part of his life.[38] He ended 1980 with his right leg in a cast for a month, after a fall on the front steps of the San Francisco Opera House. In the spring, he had caught a nasty case of bronchitis in Vienna's main library, where he had loved to study in his youth. On that occasion he was a guest of the Austrian government, for ceremonies marking the twenty-fifth anniversary of the treaty that finally settled Austria's postwar status. In spite of the honors bestowed upon him, the trip to the city of his birth was not a pleasant one. Trude, who had not been back since 1938, was outraged at how much the

Austrians were denying their Nazi past. During a TV interview, Bruno was asked not to mention Hitler in a discussion of fairy tales; the name should be used only in historical programs, he was told. On the same trip, however, Bettelheim was pleasantly surprised by his meeting with Manfred Rommel, the mayor of Stuttgart, who spoke about his father's relationship with Hitler. On the whole, Bettelheim found the Germans much readier to face up to their past than the Austrians were.

He was also rereading Freud, and asking himself iconoclastic questions about psychoanalysis—which he mentioned only to Carl Frankenstein, but which others have discussed publicly since then. "I have come to see to what degree Freud's work is a defense against his pathology, the work of a true genius, but at the same time full of reactions against his own pathology. And I believe psychoanalysis will become what it could be only after these two elements have become separated," he wrote.[39] Or again:

> Will psychoanalysis survive Jewry? . . . Maybe it takes millennia of persecution to have enough compassion with man's deep misery to be a good analyst, I do not know. But in my latest work [Freud and Man's Soul] I was continually appalled [to see] how America made a therapy of adjustment and adaptation out of it, and how the British simply do not understand it, because to them it is but a rather questionable method of therapy . . . They still are convinced that decent Englishmen simply do not have any of these dirty problems. So we are back [with the idea] that only Jews have such dirty minds.[40]

In 1981, the Bettelheims spent another month in Europe, notably in England with Naomi ("We found Britain in very bad shape, but still probably the most civilized country in the world," he wrote.)[41] He had reread Arthur Schnitzler's novel *Der Weg ins Freie*, and had been surprised to discover in it so many new insights into the world around him.[42] As both Bruno and Trude were by now feeling better, they made plans to travel to Israel the following spring.

In mid-October, however, Trude suddenly collapsed, unable to move. She had been complaining of back pains for some time; now the doctors diagnosed bone cancer, which had caused one of her vertebrae to crumble. With radiation treatment plus chemotherapy on a permanent basis, she could hope to live a few more years. Just before Christmas she was able to leave the hospital for home. She could sit up for a few minutes at a time, and the doctors assured her that within two months she would be walking again, although only with the aid of a frame. But her suffering was such that she still had to take painkilling drugs all the time.

At the beginning of March 1982, Bettelheim wrote:

> Despite it all we are in pretty good spirits. The reason is that the first month of it was so horrible, that everything since has been such an improvement (little as it is, seen objectively) that we are quite cheerful. The last two weeks we even went out for dinner a couple of times . . . I work a little, we play music and watch a little TV, and so the days pass. Last week we were able to take Trude to a heated pool for swimming which helps her a lot. Since then, she has been able to walk a few steps in the house without cane or help. As she says, one measures her improvements like those of a baby.[43]

The next two and a half years were thus dominated by Trude's fierce struggle against terrible pain—aggravated at times by the aggressive way her husband expressed his own panic at the possibility of being left on his own. Sometimes his outbursts reduced her to tears, but she never let herself slide into depression. Among the people who knew her, Trude's courage is legendary, and there remains at least one trace of it: the three autobiographical audiotapes she recorded, at her children's request, when she learned that her days were numbered.

The tapes are heartbreaking in their precision and clarity. In them, Trude is obviously carrying out a mission: that of handing down to her children, who live in such a totally different world, some of the memories that will disappear with her, about their ancestors and the city she came from. So she gives a host of striking concrete details about her family and education, and what it was like to be a young woman growing up in Vienna at that time. She is less forthcoming about her feelings, but behind her matter-of-fact tone, the listener quickly senses a lively human being, full of emotions. The effect is heightened by the way this dying woman tells her story, without faltering or hesitating over a single word. When her voice breaks, she switches off the machine until she has regained her breath. To produce an account of such clarity, she must have stopped and rewound the cassette hundreds of times. And even though it obviously cost her dearly to do so, she carried her mission out to the end.

On hearing of Trude's relapse, Naomi returned from England to spend a few weeks in Portola Valley. The remoteness of the couple's home made life very difficult under such circumstances, particularly for a man as incapable of performing the simplest household task as Bettelheim was. To accommodate home help, he had an extra room built on to the house. But when they finally found somebody they considered suitable, cohabiting with a stranger proved to be unlivable for everyone concerned. Eric traveled from San Francisco each weekend to help out. Both Ruth and Naomi offered to put the couple up in their homes, but Trude and Bruno did not want to infringe on their family lives. They preferred in any case to remain independent for as long as possible. Bettelheim inquired about retirement homes in the area, but none of them seemed suitable. Either he was too old, or Trude was too ill, or there was a five-year waiting list.

Hardly had Trude gotten back on her feet again, walking a little each day, than Bettelheim resumed his activities. *On Learning to Read* and a *New Yorker* article on Freud[44] came out within two months of each other, and he was in demand for interviews and lectures. At Eric's urging, he even agreed to play a small role in a Woody Allen film, *Zelig*. And starting in January 1982, he got seriously down to work on the writing of *A Good Enough Parent*. It was to contain "no advice: on the contrary, a warning [to parents] not to look for it, nor to accept it, but an effort to show them how they could and should go about analyzing each situation as it comes about."[45] In April, he spent a few days in Chicago, the first visit during which he did not set foot in the Orthogenic School. In June, however, he was obliged to stop work. He underwent an operation for a detached retina, and the anaesthetic caused a serious blockage of his prostate. A second operation a few days later lasted seven hours, and took a heavy toll on him. "Only now, two months after it all, have I somewhat recovered. I can now walk for some ten minutes without pain, although in a snail's tempo . . . So right now both Trude and I are more or less crippled. We manage to take care of each other and ourselves, but our life and what we can do has become severely limited. Still, we manage, and only hope it'll stay this way for a while," he wrote in mid-August.[46]

Around this time, Bettelheim made a first contact with the Hemlock Society, set up two years earlier in Los Angeles by a Briton, Derek Humphry, to promote assisted suicide and the right to die with dignity. Bruno and Trude agreed on the issue; neither of them ever wanted to find themselves helplessly forced to stay alive when they had lost all ability to act for themselves. They had seen too many of their friends reduced to the status of vegetables. And, in spite of his deep affection for Fritz Redl, Bettelheim had not been able to bring himself to visit his friend since a stroke had incapacitated him a few months earlier.

What is most striking about this whole period, however, is the way the Bettelheims would bounce back as soon as a respite in their health problems allowed them to. For despite his tendency to dramatize his own ailments, Bruno also showed great courage, his correspondence shows. As his strength gradually faded, as simple everyday acts became more and more difficult, he would go through the same cycle: initial discouragement and bitterness, followed rapidly by an attempt to accept the new situation, to compare it to others that were even more harrowing, and then to overcome it by plunging into something interesting. That year, following a visit from Naomi and her husband, a chess enthusiast, Bettelheim discovered the joys of playing against a computer ("which lacks compassion—it beats me all the time," he lamented). He marveled at the progress he was able to make in a game he had not played since his teens. He also enjoyed rereading the novels of Jane Austen and Anthony Trollope: "Their quiet irony, combined with their gentle acceptance of the foibles of man, touch me more than the qualities of other writers."[47]

Around the time Anna Freud died, in 1982, he read Aldo Carotenuto's *A Secret Symmetry*, based on the letters of the psychoanalyst Sabina Spielrein, who had been Carl Jung's patient and for a time his lover before embarking on a dialogue with Sigmund Freud that played a role in his elaboration of the death instinct concept.[48] The previously unknown story of the relations between this unsung pioneer of psychoanalysis (who was to be Piaget's analyst for nine months) and the two giants inspired Bettelheim to write a long essay, in which he expressed some of his ideas on Freud's weaknesses—and therefore his humanity—and also showed what a poor opinion he had of Jung. "I would not trust anything Jung says about Freud. Unfortunately . . . neither of them was open to the other, both dissimulated, only Jung much worse. The friendship with Jung is a sad chapter in Freud's development, while Jung lies outright," he wrote in a letter to Ruth Marquis.[49] The *Atlantic Monthly*, which had commissioned the article, turned it down. This did not surprise Bettelheim: "Since the New York intellectual establishment is in the hands of either Jungians or Freudians, the only chance one has to be published is to side with one

against the other—not to criticize both," he remarked,[50] only to be
forced to eat his words three months later, when his article appeared
in the *New York Review of Books*![51] His sarcasm, however, was probably triggered above all by the frosty reception given to *Freud and
Man's Soul* in the psychoanalytic community, which, while it was to
be expected, hurt him. He was understandably amused, a few months
later, when Hogarth Press, the British publisher of the Standard Edition of Freud's works, contacted him to seek his advice on how the
translations could be improved.

On March 22, 1983, in San Francisco, Bettelheim also had the pleasure of receiving the Goethe Medal, an annual award for service to
German culture. In telling his friends of the honor, he usually mentioned Sigmund Freud's great pride at being awarded the Goethe
Prize, bestowed on the best writers in the German language. While
pointing out that the two honors were not at all comparable, he never
forgot to mention that the president of the Goethe Institutes was at
that time a descendant of Bismarck.

Their determination to live life to the utmost right to the end led the
Bettelheims to undertake, at the end of August 1983, a European tour
that proved to be too much for Trude. "A few days in New York to
break the long trip, then on to London for a long week and another
in Venice, and then a few days to visit with old friends in Basel. That's
all," Bettelheim announced modestly, just before leaving.[52] What he
neglected to say was that the couple had decided to cross the Atlantic
aboard the *Queen Elizabeth II* rather than by plane. His eightieth
birthday was coming up, and in order to avoid the inevitable festivi-
ties, they had arranged to be in mid-ocean at the time. Naomi, who
was in New York, gave them a Sacher torte for the crossing; as it
turned out, it was the only thing they could eat on the whole trip,
which was marred by a huge storm. It was an ordeal for Trude, but a
reunion with Eric and a few days of rest in London put her back on
her feet. When the couple arrived in Basel, after Venice, however, her
friend Emmi Vischer-Radanowicz was shocked to see what efforts
Trude was making to keep up with her husband and avoid disappointing him. The couple were in a taxi in Zurich, on their way to see
a movie after visiting Emmi's daughter, when Trude collapsed with
a heart attack. At the hospital the doctor asked Bettelheim: "You're

opposed to extraordinary measures, I believe?" After a moment's hesitation, Bruno muttered: "Yes, I am."

"You'll be sorry for this!" Emmi, who had rushed from Basel, thought to herself. Bettelheim had to be helped with everything, while Trude's condition was critical. Then, having met up by chance at the airport even though they were all coming from different directions, their three children joined them. Emmi was struck at how instantly Trude perked up when Eric arrived. She sat up in bed and smiled; an outside observer would never have guessed what an ordeal she had just been through.

About a year before that trip, Sandy Lewis, who had been one of Dr. B's favorite students at the Orthogenic School, had written to tell him of his success on Wall Street since leaving the school. He wanted to thank Bettelheim and see whether he in turn could do anything for him. From Zurich, Bettelheim now sent him an SOS; Lewis offered to send his corporate plane over for Trude, but the Swiss authorities would not allow her to travel home on it. Instead, she was flown to Frankfurt on a Red Cross plane, nine days after her heart attack. From there she returned to San Francisco, accompanied by Bruno, Eric, a doctor, and a nurse, arriving at the Stanford University hospital on a stretcher. A few days later she was allowed to return home, and a month after that Bettelheim told his friends that Trude was recovering her strength and morale. "We are determined to try and live as well as we can and try not to let things get us down," he added.[53]

"Trude never believed she was as ill as she was really—it's often the case with cancer patients . . . Three months before she died, she told me about a trip they had made to New York, where she went to see four plays, went shopping, etc. After Zurich, even Bruno thought she would live for another two years," says Emmi.[54] It was not to be. Trude Bettelheim struggled on for just over a year, in spite of agonizing pain, with the times when she could sit out on the terrace and enjoy the sun in relative comfort becoming progressively rarer. Their children took turns coming to see them. In April 1984, the Bettelheims traveled to New York to see Naomi, who was leaving for Vienna; her husband had been given a four-year assignment there. At the theater, in spite of what Trude wrote to Emmi, they never made it to the end of the play, as she could not remain sitting for such long periods. A little later, they spent a week in a seaside resort. Bettelheim was working on his book about child rearing, and writing letters. He too had tried to commit his memoirs to tape, but had soon given up. He could not talk to Trude about her approaching death, and how he would manage without her. His will, and all the plans he had made up to that point, had been based on the assumption that she would outlive him. He had not changed anything, and she resisted all his attempts to broach the subject.

In mid-September, Trude underwent a new course of radiation treatment. The cancer had spread, and now affected her back and one of her feet. She was now in continuous pain. "Please, keep all this to yourself, but I have almost no-one to discuss it with. Here, we don't have any very close friends and, even if we had, I would not tell them anything, for fear Trude would hear how sick she really is," Bettelheim wrote to a friend, after summing up the medical situation.[55] On Thursday, October 25, Trude turned seventy-three, and Eric came over to spend a few days with his parents. On the Sunday evening, after he had left, the couple started a game of Scrabble, but Trude felt too unwell to complete it. Shortly afterward she had another heart attack, and Bruno accompanied her to the hospital in the ambulance. "But even there she made plans with me for the next morning. A few hours later she died. The end was relatively easy and relatively painless, and one must be grateful for that."[56]

As soon as he could summon the strength to do so, Bettelheim wrote to Carl Frankenstein.

> We had been loving each other for the last fifty years. Ours has been a very good life, despite the horrid experiences we shared under Hitler. Despite it, our life turned out much better than we had any reason to hope. I owe to her all I am. It was she whose love encouraged me finally to finish my doctorate and which made it possible for me to overcome my latent depression to make a success here in the U.S. She was a wonderful wife and mother. I do not know how I shall be able to carry on without her . . . but I shall try since this is what she would have wanted.[57]

And to Candy Hilldrup, to whom he usually mentioned Trude less often, he added: "We were the center of each other's lives much more than anybody knew, because we kept what we had gone through together to ourselves."[58]

Unlike her husband, Trude Bettelheim did not wish to be cremated. She had picked out the Skylawn Memorial Park, where both of them are buried. Located in the town of Half Moon Bay, some twenty miles north of Portola Valley, on a hilltop overlooking the Pacific, it is a place of strange beauty: stark, like the eucalyptus forests that surround it, abrupt, like the steep fall to the ocean, yet calm. There the two exiles have found a suitable resting place. Every evening at sunset, when the fast-moving fingers of fog that are the region's hallmark slide in menacingly off the ocean, this little corner of California looks for all the world like an Austrian forest.

On the day of Trude's funeral, Wanda Willig called from New York: Bettelheim's sister, Margarethe, was in a deep depression. She suggested that Naomi stop off in New York on her way back to Vienna to spend a little time with her aunt. But Bettelheim instructed his daughter to fly directly to her husband. Two months later he had to make the trip to New York himself: Margarethe had tried to kill herself, and was now in a semi-coma. He spent Christmas week trying to persuade the doctors to let her die. She was in pain, and complaining continually.

Since Margarethe's arrival in New York, some six months after her brother's, the two siblings had kept in touch, but from afar most of the time. They got along well at a distance, never forgetting each other's birthdays and other holidays. But their lives and interests were very different. Whenever Bettelheim was in New York he would have dinner with Margarethe, but he often asked the Willigs to join the party. For he felt that Margarethe lived in the past, which depressed him. She had never managed to build in the United States the kind of social life she had enjoyed in Vienna. Early on, she had tried working in radio, but her strong accent and declamatory style did not go over well. This left her bitter. She and her husband lived well, but they had no children and opted very early on to move into a retirement home. Since his death in 1974, Margarethe had taken to complaining a great deal about her rheumatism in particular and life in general.

During the week he spent watching her suffer, with death as her only possible escape, Bettelheim felt guilty, according to Wanda Willig, who helped him get over this new trial coming so soon after Trude's death. He no doubt recalled all the things his sister had done for him in the past, for he made a point of telling his children about them. When he was a young man, he had been both proud and a little jealous of her successes on the stage. He remembered how she had introduced him to all her friends in the press and the theater world, and how she always arrived just in time to drag him away from the gaming table when he was about to lose more than he could afford. And of course he remembered all the efforts she had made to obtain his release from the concentration camp.

A story came back to him concerning his brother-in-law, a Hungarian who had served as an officer in the imperial army during World War I. He had been engaged at the time, but with the collapse of the empire his fiancée's family no longer considered him a good match and the marriage was called off. In despair, he resolved to take his own life. He rented a room in a grand hotel, put on his best uniform, and shot himself in the heart. He was still conscious when a chambermaid burst into the room and found him lying in a pool of blood. "My God—and that beautiful shirt completely ruined!" she cried. Having thus realized how little a life could be worth, he pulled through and survived. He met Margarethe later, and dated her for almost twenty years in Austria before finally marrying her in the United States. He died from heart failure, probably caused by the bullet, which had never been removed.

On New Year's Eve, Bettelheim arrived late at a party hosted by Maria Kramer, a psychoanalyst who had been one of Richard Sterba's patients in Vienna before practicing in Chicago and then moving to California.[59] He was obsessed with his sister's fate, and could talk of nothing else throughout the evening. Two years earlier his cousin Edith Buxbaum had died in Seattle, only shortly after getting in touch with him after a long silence. A few days after that New Year's party his friend Hans Willig was to suffer a serious heart attack. One by one, his last childhood companions were deserting him.

It is nearly six months that Trude died—I can still not believe it, but with the passing of that much time . . . patterns slowly begin to adjust. Unpleasant and sad as such adjustments are, they no longer cut so deeply and so acutely. It is rather a general depressive feeling that life has become utterly pointless. I am glad you can write, and write heretical articles. I still cannot write. As I sit down and try to do so, sadness floods me to the degree that I become incapacitated. But one goes to bed in the evening, and hesitantly but nevertheless gets up in the morning, although I do not know what for.

"And so the days pass," Bettelheim wrote to Carl Frankenstein in April 1985.

After Trude's death, he seemed suddenly to have lost the ability to bounce back, to counter his pessimism and attacks of anxiety with the certainty, acquired through years of experience, that out of every catastrophe a new strength can be gained. Up until that point, even when he was very depressed, his letters always reflected such a movement. In fact, writing them probably offered him the best opportunity for it. During the day, Bettelheim was not able to hold back his flashes of anger, the hurtful phrases that earned him a bad reputation, and also made him feel guilty (which usually pushed him to behave even more provocatively). But late in the evening, when he sat down to write, he could at last break out of this vicious circle, returning to the world of ideas and lofty feelings that calmed him down.

As time went by, Bettelheim became more and more aware of the role Trude had played in that process. A year after her death, he wrote:

> Trude knew how to enjoy life so much better than me. Despite all my analyses, I was never able to overcome the depression which followed me all my life. The fact that, relatively late in life, I fully understood its origin helped me to master things intellectually, but not on a deeper emotional level. It was Trude who helped me the most to pull out of my depression at times and it was she alone who, despite all my self-doubts, made it possible for me to achieve what is known as the work of a lifetime (I try to continue working, because when I work, I think of nothing else).[60]

By the end of 1985, Bettelheim had completed the first draft of *A Good Enough Parent*. Despite his depression, he had never been completely inactive. During that year, in addition to the book, he had notably produced four articles, including "Freud's Vienna," written for the catalogue of the "Paris–Vienne" art exhibition at the Pompidou Center in Paris. He had also composed a short preface for the British paperback edition of *The Informed Heart*, dipping into the essays written for *Surviving* to reuse the passage in which he stressed that the death instinct gets the upper hand when one no longer feels desired by others. That was indeed his problem. Although handling ideas and giving a meaning to things helped calm him down, his own work did not have enough value in his own eyes to revive his love of life. He had admitted as much to Ruth Marquis one day, when he encouraged her to send a note to the author of a book she admired: "That's why one writes, you know."

In August, Bettelheim spent a month with Alvin Rosenfeld in Bellagio, in northern Italy. Rosenfeld had been appointed director of child psychiatry training at the Stanford Medical School in 1977, and it was he who had invited Bettelheim to hold a seminar there. Now he had undertaken to produce a book from the resulting material. He was by then based in New York, but his respect for Bettelheim had grown as his work in child psychiatry brought him daily confirmation of the usefulness of his teaching. There was real affection between the two men, although Rosenfeld was forty-two years Bettelheim's junior. The book was his idea. Bettelheim did not believe that collections of dialogues had much sales potential, and cited *Dialogues with Mothers* as a case in point. As the project was lagging, Rosenfeld had obtained an invitation from the Rockefeller Foundation to spend a month in the Villa Serbelloni, a retreat for writers at Lake Como.

The trip to Europe did Bettelheim good. On his way to Italy he stopped off for two weeks in London to stay with Eric, and then went on to Vienna to visit Naomi. He could not get over the fact that she was living in the city of his youth, and took her on a tour of his old haunts. "But as soon as I returned to the empty house where everything reminds me of my terrible loss, I am back in a depression, maybe not as deep as before, but still serious enough so that nothing I do makes any sense . . . Still, I try to keep busy," he wrote later.[61]

Not only was he still teaching a little, he was constantly being invited to take part in conferences or run seminars. He was called on for interviews and for advice, and universities lined up to bestow honors on him. The conservative Hoover Institution on War, Revolution, and Peace, based at Stanford, offered him a fellowship. In the spring, he traveled to New York State to receive yet another honorary doctorate and spend a weekend with his son. From there he went to New England, where two renowned boarding schools wanted his advice on how to deal with their drug and sexual delinquency problems.

Such activities were a welcome distraction for Bettelheim, and also flattering. In each case, he did what he could to help. At the boarding schools, for instance, "I tried to convince them that a disciplinary board would only be recognized by the children if they were part of it, and also that they should think about the causes, and ask themselves why these children are so desperate that they choose to poison themselves."[62] But nothing could shake off for very long the feeling of solitude and uselessness that now plagued him. Only the weekly consultations that he gave in the Child and Adolescent Psychiatric Inpatient (CAPI) Unit of San Jose Hospital still gave him an occasional feeling of being useful. The first time he had met Saul Wasserman, the head of the unit, Bettelheim had called him naive. But over the years a relationship had grown up between them, which in many ways resembled those he had enjoyed with the Orthogenic School counselors. CAPI, which until Wasserman's arrival functioned according to behavioral punishment–reward principles, took in a lot of severely abused children, and Bettelheim's teaching proved providential with them. This brought about a complete rethinking of methods by the staff.[63] "We were very well-meaning and we were convinced that the kids knew it. He helped us to see through their eyes, to understand the deep mistrust they felt towards all adults—including us!" Wasserman says.[64] But the young doctor also got the old man to talk about his life, his love of art, the concentration camps, and his youth.

When considering Bettelheim's final years, it is striking to see how this man who had previously surrounded himself with women, finding in his exchanges with them the energy and the desire to keep going, now relied mainly on young men, in whom he seemed to be seeking, paradoxically, the strength of a father: Sandy Lewis, who was protective in one of the fields through which Bettelheim's anxiety often expressed itself, money; his literary agent, Theron Raines, who shielded him in the publishing world; Alvin Rosenfeld, Saul Wasserman, and a few other spiritual heirs, whose turn it was to act and to heal. And, of course, his son, Eric.

After Trude's death, memories of the Orthogenic School returned to haunt Bettelheim even more frequently, and he was no longer able to combat the feelings of loss and resentment that came with them. When Karen Zelan paid him a visit with her children one day, she was shocked to find that he could talk of nothing else. On his trip east, he had stopped off for two days in Chicago to give a lecture. "Since it was known all over Chicago that I would be there, Jacqui more or less forced me to pay a visit to the School, mostly to give the world the impression that we are on the best of terms. It was an ordeal," he reported to Candy Hilldrup.[65] He got the impression that the only people pleased to see him again were the domestic staff.

His increasing inability to distance himself from his emotions even affected his view of former Orthogenic School students. On learning that a few had said publicly that they should never have been sent to the school, Bettelheim—who only a few years earlier would have viewed this as a healthy reaction—now saw it only as ingratitude. What allowed him to overcome such bitterness were the marks of affection he received from other former patients, and they were numerous. One brought him an academic distinction; another, Sandy Lewis, made a large donation to the University of Chicago; Myles Gordon was to contribute $10,000 to the funding of the 1986 conference in his honor; a former anorexic came by to show him photos of her children; and so on. Hardly a week went by without either a phone call or a visit from a former student or staffer, reminding him that his work had not been in vain. And perfect strangers wrote him from all over the world, either to ask for advice or to thank him for the effect one of his books or lectures had had on their lives. In France, a psychologist whom he did not even know had undertaken to write a book about him; this at first irritated him greatly, then touched him.[66]

But on each such occasion, the soothing effect quickly wore off. The death of his wife had also left Bettelheim even more aware of the ravages of aging. This returned again and again in his letters. "So, you are reaching eighty years of age. You'll see how everything becomes difficult," he wrote to one friend.[67] He found it profoundly humiliating that so many of his everyday acts, previously taken for granted, had now become difficult or impossible. Simply to wash or get dressed took a long time. He could no longer tie his shoelaces, as he could not bend down. He also suffered from the obstruction in his esophagus, which now prevented him from eating practically any solid food. Even with help from his neighbors, Bettelheim soon realized there was no way he could go on living in the remote Portola Valley aerie. Less than a month after Trude's death he was writing: "I've just got over a pretty nasty case of 'flu . . . and it made it obvious that I need to change my living conditions. This is very painful to me, as I am very attached to everything which reminds me of our life together. But here I'm really a long way away from everything."[68]

His daughter Ruth reiterated the offer she had made before her mother's death. As the grounds of her house in Pasadena were large, she proposed to add on a wing in which her father could live. He would thus remain independent, while no longer being alone. Bettelheim hesitated before accepting. He did not like Los Angeles, and he was aware that he would be a burden for his daughter. He once again considered entering a retirement home, but he was not enthusiastic about it: "As for the possibility of living over there with three hundred other old people who like me are awaiting death, it's not very pleasant, but of course it would be more reasonable."[69] He soon found out, however, that the Palo Alto establishment he had in mind could not accept him, on account of his liquid diet.

His daughter's offer was all the more attractive in that, in the months following Trude's death, Ruth had sought to replace her as the family's pole of stability. Physically, she indeed resembled her mother.[70] By the end of February 1985, Bettelheim's mind was made up: he would move in next to Ruth. Not without misgivings; when announcing the decision to his friends, he also listed the proposals he had recently received (a fellowship at the Hoover Institution, the chair of a committee set up to study the working of high schools), all of which would have required his continued presence in San Francisco or its environs. But the architect was already at work on the Pasadena house, and when Eric joined him there at Christmas (Naomi, who had just had a baby, stayed in Vienna that year), the blueprints were ready. "Of course the children miss their mother a great deal, as it was always Trude who gave us a marvelous Christmas. But Ruth tries to emulate her, and she is also a wonderful mother to her children. So one generation follows on from the next, and one must try to hold on to that to avoid losing all courage," he wrote.[71] Bettelheim suddenly seemed ready to emerge from his depression: "I'm finally getting a grip on myself and beginning to try and go on living, mainly for the children's sake. I can't replace their mother, but I can at least try and put off the day when they also lose their father."

A month later, his tone had changed dramatically. He had gone down to Pasadena to make final arrangements for the construction work, and heard from Ruth that she wanted to divorce her husband. The couple's relationship had been shaky for some time. And yet, "had it not been for my project, the marriage would have gone on for a while. But her husband, who at first was in favor, didn't want to know about it after a while. This implicates me in the break-up, which is something that weighs heavily on my heart . . . If Ruth obtains her divorce and custody of the children, then I'll go to help her."[72] That is Bettelheim's version of events. Although it probably exaggerated his role in the couple's separation, it heralded the last act of the drama: his feeling accused of having destroyed Ruth's marriage. Such is the implacable logic of family feuds. This view of things also gave Bettelheim an altruistic excuse for not choosing the exile of an old people's home. And it provided Ruth with a place to live, as her husband was refusing to move out of their house in Pasadena.

Everyone tried to dissuade Bettelheim from setting up house with his elder daughter. They were too alike, in both their demands and their needs. Initially, Eric and Naomi managed to persuade their father not to move right away. Then, as he appeared more and more determined to do so, Naomi enlisted his old friends, notably Wanda Willig and Gina, to try to get him to see reason. "We all knew it was going to be a disaster," she says. Gina, who saw similarities between Bettelheim's relationship with Ruth and the one he had had with his sister, Margarethe, suggested that he instead move into a retirement home in San Francisco. That way, she added, they could go to concerts together and she would be able to take care of him. Bettelheim had been to see the establishment, but the visit only strengthened his determination to move in with Ruth.

By the end of 1985 he was feeling somewhat better. He had been moved by the birth of Naomi's first child, his second grandson, in Vienna, which he mentioned in all his letters. He was also pleased because Eric had gotten engaged. He believed that the timing of the two events, like that of Ruth's divorce, was no coincidence. "The death of a parent triggers a psychic revolution in children. Naomi, who had been wanting a child for a long time, became pregnant only after her mother's death. Our lives are so strangely woven with that of our parents," he wrote.[73] He had another, more down-to-earth reason for feeling better: the white Mercedes that Sandy Lewis had offered him for Christmas. He may have feigned indifference, but he was clearly proud of it.

While waiting for Ruth's divorce to go through, he had a busy schedule. In April 1986 he went to Europe, starting with four days in London. The BBC had organized a debate, "For or Against Psycho-analysis," between him and the writer George Steiner. It was a tax-ing experience for Bettelheim. "Steiner's arguments against psycho-analysis were really silly. He even stooped down to say that the Oedipus theory can't be true, because he never had sexual desires for his mother. This I hadn't heard since World War I. It was so obvious that he is scared to death to discover his unconscious that one can only have *Mitleid* [compassion] with his towering neurosis—if he would just not be so intellectually arrogant. So I was sorry that the debate proceeded on such a low level."[74] Although in full possession of his intellectual powers, Bettelheim had lost some of his nimbleness in outmaneuvering debating opponents. The day after the BBC discussion, he was due to lecture in Stuttgart, at the invitation of the Robert Bosch Foundation. Feeling upset, and suffering from an intestinal ailment, he took too many pills before leaving London, with the result that he had to stop in the middle of his address. The incident turned out not to be very serious, but it shook him. He then went on to Vienna, where his memories and the election posters for president-to-be Kurt Waldheim marred his pleasure at meeting his Viennese grandson—whom, as he liked to point out, his father had named Immanuel, after Kant.

In May, Bettelheim traveled to Chicago for the university's conference in his honor. Despite the tensions with Jacquelyn Sanders, he found it a heartwarming experience to see so many of the people who had made up his life for thirty years. And yet he had a hard time getting close to people. Adrian Kuypers, who held a party for him, found herself spending most of the evening by his side: people would come over to him full of effusive enthusiasm, but after chatting for a while, they drifted away. Bettelheim seemed to have lost his ability to reach out to others. He did not even go over to greet his friend George Perkins, who had been the school's consultant psychiatrist for years, even though a stroke had left him paraplegic and he had to be carried up in his wheelchair. Former staffers and students had indeed flocked to see Dr. B again, but they did not have with him the kind of relationship that could have given them an insight into his depression. He had been their father figure, their ultimate source of authority for so long that they were unable to see things the other way around. They could not possibly imagine how deep the feelings of solitude and loss ran in him, or the ever stronger sensation of slipping into physical decay; that humiliation of the body that ends up by also enslaving the mind. He had witnessed it happening to his father, Anton, in the Tulln clinic; it had threatened him when he was in the hands of the Nazis. It was happening then to Morris Janowitz, who at age sixty-seven was in the final stages of Parkinson's disease. After seeing him delirious and helpless, Bettelheim kept saying to Gayle: "It can't be. He's too young, too young. I'm the one who should be dying, not him."

Once back in California, Bettelheim started sorting through his possessions, and this depressed him even more. "With each piece of paper that one throws away goes a bit of one's life, or so at least it feels."[75] He was apprehensive at having to meet new people in his new home. "True friends, one makes only relatively early in life, and best before and during adolescence. It seems after puberty things become frozen, at least emotionally, to the degree that one can no longer give so freely of oneself, nor take the other into oneself, as true friendship requires."[76] He was convinced that he owed to Trude the few acquaintances he still had in Palo Alto. In deciding how to divide up his possessions among his children, he also betrayed his apprehension at the prospect of living with his daughter in Los Angeles, a city whose weather he feared, and which he saw as superficial and materialistic: "As for Ruth, she does not want anything that she cannot put in the dishwasher!"[77] Meanwhile, he was correcting the manuscript of *A Good Enough Parent*, and reading the proofs of Robert Jay Lifton's *The Nazi Doctors: Medical Killing and the Psychology of Genocide*, which he had been assigned to review for the *New York Times*.

In mid-June 1986 he went to visit the house that Ruth had found in Santa Monica. It was beautiful. But, with its tiled roof, its large, arched windows with leaded panes, and its sculptured door in reddish wood, it looked more like the home of some latter-day Mexican grandee than that of an aging Viennese psychoanalyst. The immense foyer and double staircase would have suited a movie star. In other words, it was, as Bettelheim would later admit, anything but *gemütlich* (cozy). "Everything for show, and nothing for a comfortable life; all of California only worse."[78] Needless to say, it was also very expensive; much more so than Bettelheim had anticipated, particularly as he was going to have to pay for it on his own. Being unable to sell her Pasadena home, still occupied by her husband, Ruth could not pay her share.

It would be pointless to list the financial squabbles which from that point on were to poison relations between the old man and two of his children (Naomi remained outside the fray, except for trying from time to time to find a solution—just as she had preferred to stay out of family conversations as a child). Bettelheim himself said and wrote on many occasions that when people quarrel about money, the real reason lies elsewhere. He would see that principle at work here, attributing his son's warnings against the investment he was making to jealousy over the fact that he had chosen to live with his elder daughter. But it was too late. All the time that Bruno Bettelheim had failed to devote to his children in the past was to be counted out, in dollars and cents, each child convinced he or she was being cheated.

What Bettelheim appears to have had difficulty grasping clearly, judging from his letters, is the complexity of his own relationship to money, beyond his legendary generosity. Money: For the lack of it, the beautiful city of his youth had been ravaged; to it, as a young man, he had had to sacrifice his most noble dreams; without it, he would almost certainly have died at the hands of the Nazis. Money that he would one day be stripped of, or so said the family curse. He may have despised it, but he was always terrified of it. And he had spent his life trying to dominate it—that is, trying not to let himself be dominated by it—because he was all too aware of its destructive power.

At a time when he feared that his health might require major outlays, in a country where serious illness could mean financial ruin, Bettelheim was understandably nervous about pouring all his resources into this opulent house, which he knew was not meant for him. His anxiety was aggravated by the fact that the Hoover Institution fellow to whom he had sold the house in Portola Valley was having a hard time getting together the sum. Eric, whom he had asked to watch over his financial security, advised him against the purchase. But Bettelheim went ahead and signed, accusing his son of selfishness.

He finally moved in to the house on Adelaide Place at the end of September 1986. Two weeks earlier, he wrote: "I am naturally somewhat apprehensive at the thought of moving and living with Ruth. Of course, she too has anxiety. But we are both determined to try and make it work. It will not be easy, but one can assume that it is not for a very long time."[79] Yet on the very day of his arrival, Bettelheim understood that living with his daughter would be even more difficult than he had expected. Ruth and her children had already been settled in for a month. She had taken the master bedroom, on the second floor, leaving the other large room to her father. It was just like the arrangement in the old days, in Chicago, except that she was not Trude, and her children were not Bettelheim's children. And he no longer had the Orthogenic School in which to spend his days and evenings.

"Ruth is trying, but there is no doubt that she feels I am an imposition on her life," he wrote to Gayle Janowitz, two weeks after his arrival.[80] From that point on, the tone of his letters becomes more and more poignant, showing him sliding inexorably into the deepest depression. It was at this time that he started telling Carl Frankenstein about the origins of his anxiety, referring implicitly to his father's syphilis, and stressing how much his childhood fears had been reawakened when Trude was dying. These letters are moving also because in them Bettelheim never tried to put all the blame on his daughter. On the contrary, he stressed how tough Ruth's life was, and how, after a yearlong process of divorce, she had to rebuild it completely. He always mentioned the efforts she was making to help him. But as he told Candy Hilldrup: "There was a misunderstanding right from the start. Ruth thought I was going to come and take care of her. Instead, she saw a tired old man show up who himself needed to be taken care of." He felt like an intruder in his own home. He thought that his grandchildren held him responsible for their parents' divorce. He felt bad about that, but at the same time had little in common with them, finding them noisy and intrusive. The two small rooms that his daughter had assigned him on the first floor were located on either side of the main entrance, and separated from it only by heavy curtains; he had no place where he felt comfortable working. Ruth complained that he frightened her young patients; he was afraid of disturbing someone each time he moved from one room to the other.

Having been unable to obtain Ruth Bettelheim's version of events, it would be dishonest for me to try to describe their quarrels in greater detail. It is indeed easy to imagine how impossible Bettelheim was to live with. How, torn between love and dashed hopes, both father and daughter could be convinced they were doing their utmost, and resent the other for what they saw as ingratitude. How much each must have felt wronged and betrayed.

Bettelheim was to live there twenty months, with some ups and some terrible downs, a lot of illness, a few trips, and even some brief moments when he thought the arrangement might work out. In spite of his antipathy toward Los Angeles, he had found there a lot of acquaintances and even some friends. Within a few months of his arrival he was running a training seminar at a clinic for psychotic children. A little later Seymour Feschback, a professor of psychology at UCLA, invited him to come and discuss psychoanalysis twice a month in his classes. Bettelheim was regularly being asked to teach on other campuses in the region. And he went on giving lectures, running workshops, and replying to the dozens of requests for help he received each month. ("The parents' despair is really terrible . . . I spend almost all my time answering them, so that they feel that one has at least a little compassion for them," he wrote.)[81]

Eric came to spend Christmas with him, helping him settle in and unpack his books and papers from the cartons in which they had been left. Bettelheim was happy at the closeness he felt to his son;

the two discussed politics, art, and literature and felt they understood each other. Another piece of good news cheered him up: Naomi and her husband were returning to the United States, to settle in Washington, D.C. Nevertheless, Bettelheim had by now realized that his life was over. "My children are good children, but we have brought them up to have full lives which occupy them fully. So I don't really feel I serve much purpose any more. We all live too long for our own good."[82]

This was when he seriously started to look into ways of ending his life before it became too late—before a stroke or some other such accident reduced him to helplessness, which he feared most of all. The memory of his father's last two years was now haunting him and, as he told his son-in-law one day, he was determined to ensure that his children did not go through what he had endured. At first, he discussed the issue only with a few friends who were able to understand, such as the psychoanalyst Heda Bolgar, a fellow-Viennese whom he had known in Chicago, and with whom he enjoyed socializing in Los Angeles. "He was very rational about it. What he wanted was to know what to do when the time came. Because the most striking thing was that he didn't actually want to die. He was depressed, but not suicidal. If someone had been able to guarantee that, when the time came, he would be there to help him go without suffering, I don't think he would have killed himself," she says.[83] Al Flarsheim had once made that promise to Bettelheim but, in 1980, he had taken his own life.

Because of Bettelheim's eating problems, the slightest ailment now took on alarming proportions. In February 1987 a bout of influenza, complicated by bronchitis and the aftereffects of a fall on his hip, kept him in bed for two months. ("This illness has shown me that I was right to come here, for Ruth did all she could to assist me."[84]) After a new series of tests, one of his doctors now recommended an operation on his esophagus. He nevertheless pushed ahead with his travels and speaking engagements, notably going to Detroit in June to be the key speaker at a dinner held to mark Richard Sterba's ninetieth birthday. The following month found him in Ramat Gan, in the suburbs of Tel Aviv, for an international congress on "Childhood in the Technological Era." On that occasion, unconcerned by possible charges of sexism, he questioned the role of day care centers in an infant's development.

The lull in his relations with Ruth was short-lived. Each time he returned to "what I now must call home, although it does not feel like one,"[85] he soon was invaded by the same impression of being of no use to anyone or anything. In the outside world, he was feted, respected, and thanked. At home, his life was empty. But it was now taking him progressively longer to get over the strain of each trip. On his return from Israel he was hospitalized for a serious attack of gastroenteritis, and fed through a drip for four days.

In October 1987, Bettelheim nevertheless resumed his travels, this time for a heavily booked tour. After a dozen or so lectures across the United States, he flew to Vienna for a major conference on "Fifty Years of Exile," attended by prominent Austrian expatriates from the whole range of scientific and cultural disciplines. He spoke on "the transfer of culture from Austria to the United States," and as the two other participants older than he had declined the honor, it was he who gave a reply to the chancellor's address on behalf of the gathering. The Austrian minister of universities awarded him a "Cross of Honor" to mark the fiftieth anniversary of his doctorate. And Vienna's Freud Society invited him to address a gathering of its members. Bettelheim's fame being what it was, however, the small room in the *Rathaus*, or city hall, that was generally used for such gatherings soon proved too small, and the organizers had to get the main meeting room specially opened. It was thus that, without realizing it immediately, the author of *The Informed Heart* spoke under a large portrait of Karl Lueger, the famously anti-Semitic politician who had been Vienna's mayor at the time of his birth.

Very much in form, Bettelheim described his first contacts with psychoanalysis. After evoking his rivalry with Otto Fenichel for the favors of Lisl Lazarsfeld, and his first encounter with Richard Sterba, he told the story of little "Johnny," the metaphor that best sums up what a life spent in the service of psychoanalysis had taught him.[86] Johnny, he said, was a young psychotic being treated by Editha Sterba, and Bettelheim used to meet him in the Sterbas' common waiting room.[87] He had tried on several occasions to strike up a conversation with him, but without success; the child would either remain silent or reply with incomprehensible mumblings. Johnny had an obsession that disturbed Bettelheim: On arrival he would rip a leaf off a prickly cactus on a windowsill and start chewing it. He did not appear to feel any pain, even when drops of blood appeared on his lips. One day, unable to stand it any longer, Bettelheim blurted out: "I don't know how long you have been seeing Dr. Sterba, but it must be at least two years . . . and here you are still chewing these awful leaves!" Whereupon the child looked at him and said: "What are two years compared with eternity?"[88] Bettelheim felt humbled.

He drew a first lesson from the incident immediately, which was that his apparent concern for Johnny in fact expressed a very personal worry: He was afraid that his own analysis was not progressing quickly enough. He felt guilty at the hypocrisy, but it took him much longer to decipher the little boy's deeper message. This was that physical pain over time is nothing when compared to psychological suffering, which knows no time limit. Johnny had also showed him in his own way that when people are in deep distress they care nothing for making polite conversation. When suffering is great, the only exchanges worth having are those in which the speaker is truly implicated, those that convey meaning, not conventions.

After Vienna, Bettelheim spent a weekend at a psychoanalytic seminar in the Tyrol, and then flew to London for three more lectures. He then went on to give a week of courses in Florence, before returning to the United States. It had been, he wrote, "a beautiful journey. It does one good to be celebrated in old age, and . . . I was truly pleased with it. It is the first time since Trude's death that I felt good, even though I missed her all the time."[89] Bettelheim next spent a few days in Washington with Naomi and her family. He felt dizzy a couple of times and, the last morning, had some trouble holding up his right arm. But he paid no attention to those symptoms and flew on to Orlando, Florida, where he was due to give a last address. The next morning, he woke up with his right arm and hand paralyzed. It was a mild stroke, and he would never fully recover the use of his hand. The incident fed his anxiety: What if the next stroke were to leave him completely paralyzed?

Once again, Ruth rushed to her father's bedside, bringing her children with her on the night flight to Orlando. It was to be the last time they would return together to Adelaide Place. A month later, Eric came from London to spend Christmas with his father, while Naomi stayed behind in Washington. Discussions about the house had become impossible between father and daughter, and Bettelheim had repeatedly asked for Eric's help. Ruth had finally sold the Pasadena property and, for tax purposes, she had to reinvest her money in another home. Since an agreement on Adelaide Place proved impossible, Eric agreed to arrange for the sale of the house. A few months later Bettelheim once again had to be hospitalized, for a pancreatic infection. The day he was due to come out, his daughter, tied up by her obligations, didn't come to get him until midafternoon, rather than in the morning as he had expected. In the meantime, he had become severely depressed.

"After much thought, I have come to the conclusion that life with Ruth is too difficult, for her as well as for me. I feel physically constrained and psychically overwhelmed by being such a burden for her. I am convinced that she will live much better without me."[90] Once again Bettelheim was putting a good face on his hurt. He had done the same with Gina's rejection: Their divorce had been "by mutual consent" and for material reasons, he generally explained. And he had done so with Paula: His mother had abandoned him to a wetnurse because of her important social obligations.

"I am stuck between Scylla and Charybdis," Bettelheim wrote to Carl Frankenstein in January 1988. The idea of ending up in a retirement home, making conversation with people he had not chosen to be with, horrified him, but he was by now afraid of living alone. He wondered whether he should not move closer to Naomi. He recalled that before dying, Trude had exclaimed: "Poor Bruno!" and the thought tugged at his heartstrings. He felt guilty at not having done enough for her; he missed her more and more. "Your last letter expressed your anguish and desperation about things in Israel . . . My own desperation is with this flesh of mine which will not die," he wrote in March, apologizing for no longer being able to take an interest in world events.[91] He was reading Primo Levi.

At the end of May 1988, Bettelheim finally moved into a small, elegant building on Ocean Avenue, about a mile from Adelaide Place. Through the large bay windows of his apartment he could see the eternally blue sweep of the Pacific, dotted with many-hued funboards. He hardly ever went out any more; he was in a terrible state, being cared for by a nurse. "I now have more peace, but no desire to live," he wrote to Candy Hilldrup.[92] His letters were now very short, around ten lines. And indeed, what could he tell his friends? "My life is my work, Trude and the children," he had written in 1954. He had lost almost all those things, and in that same order. He did not even know that his daughter's new house was located three streets away.

"So intricately, so inextricably interwoven are death and life's meaning that when life seems to have lost all meaning, suicide seems the inescapable consequence . . . Very few suicides are due to the wish to end insufferable pain . . . More frequently suicides are the consequence of an unalterable conviction that the person's life has completely and irremediably lost all meaning," he had written ten years earlier.[93] Now, suicide was constantly on his mind. He mentioned it to all the people who took turns helping him; to Josette Wingo, who on his arrival in Santa Monica had thrown a party to introduce him to people he could work with, and who deployed all the energy of a former Orthogenic School counselor to try and pull him out of his depression; to George and Cathy Kaiser, who lunched with him on a visit to LA; and to many others. He even put his son in an impossible position by asking him whether he would accompany him to the Netherlands, where a doctor had promised to assist him with his suicide. He finally got his friend and former student Connie Katzenstein, who often went with him on outings, to make the promise.

Among the people he saw frequently, the most knowledgeable on the question was undoubtedly Edwin Shneidman, professor of thanatology at UCLA. A former student and friend of Henry Murray at Harvard, Shneidman was fifteen years younger than Bettelheim, but they shared several interests. He was Jewish, conservative, and iconoclastic, and he too had begun his career by working on personality tests, notably Murray's TAT. Shneidman's first patient as a therapist had been a psychotic veteran who was so violent that he had been scheduled for a lobotomy. Shneidman had cured him by convincing him that he respected him. But his reputation had been made by a study of several hundred suicide notes he had stumbled across somewhat by accident in the early 1950s in a forensic pathologist's archives. Edwin Shneidman had since become an authority on the psychological mechanisms associated with death, a subject he was teaching in UCLA's Department of Psychiatry and Biobehavioral Sciences at the time he met Bettelheim in 1987. He had soon had Bettelheim hired as a visiting professor and invited him to join the regular informal Wednesday lunches he held with around a dozen elderly, high-level professors (including two former university presidents, he points out), for free-ranging discussions.[94] Somewhat in the manner of a confidant, or a therapist, Shneidman refuses to divulge the content of his conversations with Bettelheim. But it is clear that they saw a lot of each other, particularly after Bettelheim had left Adelaide Place. Shneidman speaks of him with affection and a lot of respect. He was struck by the large portrait of Trude hanging over Bettelheim's bed.[95]

But the most worried of Bettelheim's friends in Los Angeles was no doubt the psychoanalyst Rudolf Ekstein. He was ten years younger, and had trained in Vienna as a Montessori teacher at the same time as Trude, although he didn't know Bettelheim then. A committed Socialist, Ekstein had emigrated to the United States in 1938. Later, he had worked for some ten years at the Menninger Foundation. During that period a solid friendship, built on both complicity and rivalry, had grown up between him and Bettelheim. They exchanged their articles, and on Ekstein's bookshelves Bettelheim's works are lined up just beside his own. "He was always one book ahead of me," he said, clearly brimming with emotion, in December 1990. He had then just published a new book, thereby evening up the score after his friend's death. Each year, Bettelheim would invite Ekstein to visit the Orthogenic School, and after asking him to speak during a staff meeting, he would cross swords with him in a lively debate. One of their favorite jokes was to argue about which of them had been married to the most beautiful woman in Vienna.

It was notably thanks to Ekstein that Bettelheim was for once in his life well received by a psychoanalytic society, that of Los Angeles. Warm and nostalgic, and a collector of objects once owned by Freud, Ekstein had introduced Bettelheim to the society of which Otto Fenichel had once been a prominent member. As he was not an MD, Bettelheim became only an honorary member. But that ceremony, on May 18, 1989, saw the inauguration of a bust of Bettelheim by the Swedish sculptor Jane Ullman, financed by a donation from Sandy Lewis.[96] Ekstein was deeply concerned by Bettelheim's deteriorating state when he was living on Adelaide Place. As a Freudian analyst fully aware of the complexities of family ties, he was not interested in assigning blame to anyone. But he could see how ill and miserable his friend was, spending his days wandering between two small rooms. He often took him out to lunch at a small deli close by. There, while Bettelheim would eat a bowl of soup, which was practically the only thing he could swallow by then, they would talk about Vienna, about what America had done to psychoanalysis, and also about death. "Rudi is like me, he believes in Thanatos," Bettelheim used to say.

Ekstein often discussed his friend's plight with David James Fisher, a former patient who had become a colleague. Fisher, who was very interested in the history of psychoanalysis, had first made contact with Bettelheim in 1982, on the publication of *Freud and Man's Soul*, which he had reviewed. When Bettelheim moved to Los Angeles, Fisher had offered to help. He visited Bettelheim on weekends. They went for walks and talked a great deal, Bettelheim of his problems and Fisher of his difficult cases. At one point he had even considered asking Bettelheim to be his supervisor. After he had left Adelaide Place, Bettelheim would finally agree to let Fisher record five hours of interviews, on condition that nothing be published before his death. Well before the break with Ruth, Ekstein and Fisher had been wondering who could help pull Bettelheim out of his depression. They finally opted for a woman who had trained as a psychoanalyst with Anna Freud in London. Bettelheim followed their advice, and visited this colleague for several months, once or twice a week, sometimes more in times of crisis. Psychologically, it was once again a struggle for survival. He was so lacking in self-love, so full of resentment against himself—for not having done more for Trude, not having been as good, as disinterested, as considerate as he wished he had been. He spoke of women he had known, who had desired him when he was married but were no longer interested now that he was alone. And he continually returned to his homeliness, to the body that he hated.

One day Bettelheim got a call from Hans Bandler, whom he had not seen since the latter had left Buchenwald and emigrated to Australia. Bandler was passing through California for a meeting, and he longed to see his former fellow-inmate. He had already tried once to contact Bettelheim, during a visit to London, after reading in the newspaper that he had given a lecture in the city. He had telephoned Eric, but it was too late. This time, too, Bandler's efforts were in vain. "I don't feel well enough to see you," Bettelheim said, obviously very depressed. Bandler insisted, feeling sure he could bring some cheer to the person who had once helped him to recover his own human dignity. He called back the next day, but to no avail.

Around the middle of July 1988, Bettelheim was feeling somewhat better. He was taking a daily half-hour walk along the oceanfront, and speaking on the phone every evening with Naomi, who was about to give birth to her second child. On his doctor's advice, he had finally decided to risk the operation on his esophagus. He had resumed his correspondence with several of his friends. He was even working on some of the seminars he and Alvin Rosenfeld had selected, and thinking about the essays to be included in one last book, a more personal work, as his publisher had asked.

"Our job is to help the patient to feel anger." He had repeated this axiom to a group of psychologists only a few months previously; now he seemed to have succeeded in applying the therapy to himself. He finally accepted his own anger toward Ruth, which he had previously always sought to fight with understanding. Hints of this appear for the first time in his letters, and also in his interviews with David James Fisher. To express it, he often linked it to his contempt for Los Angeles, which he saw as an artificial city. "Here so many people live in opulence and without any goal; it's really awful to see how empty they are."[97] To Fisher, he said: "I saw changes in my own daughter from the girl she was in Chicago to the woman she became once she made her home in Los Angeles, which in terms of my values, were undesirable ones. Now, I cannot blame it on the city. It might be her personally. It might be what drove her to move here. I cannot sort it out. I'm much too close to her. There is a concern with possessions which I consider external. But I would have liked to see her develop other qualities."[98] To a very close friend, he gave a detailed description of his clashes with Ruth, adding that in the end she did not even talk to him or visit him in his room when he was "mortally ill."[99] He had decided to disinherit his elder daughter.

The operation on his esophagus was fully successful. But although his vocal cords were not affected, he caught pneumonia in the hospital, due to his weakened state. On returning home, early in September, to replace his nurse he hired a Polish refugee named Wanda, who did everything in the house for him. He found her a little strange, and complained about her cooking, but acknowledged that she was devoted to him. As she spoke little German and even less English, he would on occasion call Wanda Willig in New York to ask her to play the interpreter. While he was in the hospital, the psychoanalytic division of the American Psychology Association had awarded him its Distinguished Scientific Award. He continued to receive a large number of invitations, and at the beginning of October he gave his first lecture after the operation. The next day, however, he was so exhausted that he could not do anything all day.

Physically, Bettelheim was by now extremely weak. He had become very thin, and could walk only with a stick. Getting up, shaving, bathing, and dressing took him all morning; typing even a short letter left him worn out. He was going to the hospital three times a week for rehabilitation sessions, but they took a huge toll on his energy. He was no longer able to control completely a tremor that had developed in his right hand. And at the beginning of November 1988 after two minor accidents, he had to face the fact that he could no longer drive his beautiful Mercedes; his foot did not respond quickly enough. Around the same time, Naomi visited, bringing his new granddaughter.

His relations with his second daughter were much simpler than those with Ruth, but also more brusque. When he started talking of suicide again, she interrupted him to say: "I can't stop you from killing yourself if you want to. But I don't condone it. And, so long as you live, I'll try to convince you not to." She had been horrified to find out that he had disinherited her sister and she tried very hard to make him change his mind, but to no avail. Her efforts at bringing about a reconciliation between her father and sister also proved unsuccessful. After speaking to Bettelheim on the phone, Ruth asked Naomi not to give him her address. Bettelheim's disappointment comes through in his letters, although he kept adding: "If that's the way she wants it, I'll have to come to terms with it."[100] It was the year when he blurted out his statement about his father's syphilis, at Connie Katzenstein's Thanksgiving party.[101] That Christmas he traveled to Washington to be with Naomi, as did Eric. He returned from the trip feeling contented, regretting only that he lived so far away from Washington, not to mention London.

The lull in his depression was to last around six months, during which Bettelheim resumed his seminars, gave a few more classes, and fulfilled several speaking engagements. At the end of March 1989 he addressed a group of nine hundred people in San Francisco. He was amusing, incisive, and thought-provoking. Daniel Karlin was there with a small TV crew; Bettelheim had contacted him to suggest one last interview. It lasted five hours, stretched over two days. Although the old man tired quickly, he had lost none of his verve. When the Frenchman asked him why, given his age and condition, he had not yet committed suicide, since he often thought of doing so, Bettelheim smiled and said: "As long as I can still do things that interest me, such as talking to you, I'll keep going." When Karlin mentioned the nickname "Brutalheim," which had made the rounds among his former students, Bettelheim replied frankly: "It's true I've always been very irritated by stupidity. It's one of my failings. But whenever I was brutal with a student or counselor, it was always to try and make him grasp something. There was always love behind it. To mean something, an experience has to be forceful." Karlin pushed the question further: "But didn't you ever get a kind of pleasure from such brutality?" After pausing to think, Bettelheim murmured: "Yes, certainly. There is always pleasure in dominating intellectually—not physically." He also acknowledged that such brutality may have been a way of getting even for the physical oppression he had once suffered.

In May 1989, Bettelheim finished compiling *Freud's Vienna and Other Essays*, and as always when he completed a book, felt empty. This time around, the sensation was amplified by his uncertainty over his future. Loneliness weighed on him, yet he found it harder and harder to put up with Wanda's constant presence. He complained that she was treating him like a baby, he was furious at having to let her drive the car, and he accused her of spying on him. His oldest friend, Hans Willig, had just died, leaving him the only survivor of his trio from the *Gymnasium*. Being so far from his family was another source of anxiety; Eric was urging him either to come and live in London or to move to the East Coast to be nearer to Naomi. The young lawyer was now traveling to New York from London on business five or six times a year. He repeated both suggestions in Washington that April.

As for Naomi, while she was ready to help her father as much as she could, she wanted to avoid making the same mistake as her sister. She knew that with two small children to care for, she could never devote the amount to time to him that he would want. She therefore did not suggest that he move in with her, but offered instead to inquire about lodgings in her vicinity. Bettelheim hesitated. Although he carped at California's perpetual blue skies, he appreciated their effects on him. And while he gave his distant correspondents the impression that he was very alone, he had in fact built up a good circle of friends in Los Angeles. Why become an exile yet again, and risk yet more disappointments?

As soon as he had moved in with Ruth, he had realized that "although both my daughter and I try to do our best to make living together possible and bearable, it is a most difficult and complex task, given the feelings of a daughter for her father and those of a father for his first-born daughter. I think Freud and his daughter [Anna] managed, because she was the last born, and his favorite had been the oldest daughter who died early, at which point he transferred his attachment to his youngest daughter."[102] His trip to Washington had shown him just how busy Naomi was. But he was also touched to see how, behind her brusque tone and detached manner, she was concerned about him. He felt at ease with his son-in-law, found the couple harmonious and their children charming, even though he was too taken up with his own problems to pay much attention to them. By mid-July, he had finally made up his mind; he would move to Washington in the fall. "The decision to move to an old people's home is a hard one to make, but I can no longer look after myself alone . . . For the moment, though, these are only dreams—or rather nightmares," he wrote.[103]

His friend Wanda Willig could tell, when they spoke by phone, that Bettelheim did not really want to make this new move, and that he was not really all that miserable in Los Angeles. She strongly advised him to stay put. He replied: "But the children want . . ." Rudolf Ekstein also did all he could to dissuade his friend from leaving, even suggesting that he move into the apartment he had arranged for his own father, on the second floor of his house. But Bettelheim declined the invitation. In the fall, he went to visit some of the places Naomi had selected for him in the Washington suburbs.[104]

> Each one has its pros and cons . . . It is a painful blow to have to give up one's independence . . . but I do not know how long I still have to live . . . The moving worries me greatly, and I also wonder whether I will not regret having left here . . . It will very much depend . . . on whether I find somebody with whom I can develop some kind of a friendship over there. My requirements on that score are very modest . . . I have thought many times about suicide, but I decided against it on account of the children, and I have made up my mind to try and live in Washington for a while, however difficult it may be.[104]

At the end of October, Bettelheim granted an interview to the writer Celeste Fremon.[105] She noted how his shoulders were hunched, and how he shuffled when, courteous as ever, he showed her to a chair. His right hand, the writing one, trembled and jerked a little. She was, however, struck by the clarity of his ideas. The interview, which was supposed to deal with previously unknown aspects of Bettelheim's life, such as his marriage, his psychoanalysis, and his friendship with Wilhelm Reich, had not gotten off to a very good start. He was clearly preoccupied. He answered her questions (on Reich: "Few people were as stubborn as he was"), but his mind was clearly elsewhere. "It was as if asking him to talk about his life and ideas was equivalent to asking him to look through a scrapbook from a now-inconsequential journey," Fremon wrote. After a while, exasperated, she asked him in a somewhat aggressive tone: "Are you afraid of dying?"

"No," he said, "I fear suffering. The older one gets, the greater the likelihood that one will be kept alive without purpose." Having noted how the question had made him perk up, she tried to get him to elaborate, but Bettelheim dodged her questions. She had switched off her tape recorder and was getting ready to leave when he suddenly turned to her. "There is something you should know," he said. "I am planning to take a trip to Europe from which I may or may not come back." From that point on, a real dialogue began. Celeste Fremon was to go three times to 515 Ocean Avenue, recording a total of six hours of conversation, of which at least half was devoted to death and suicide.

Clearly touched by Bettelheim's distress, Fremon found herself torn between "the illogical and unjournalistic urge to bring him a dozen brightly colored balloons in the childish hope of cheering him up" and her respect for both the ideas he discussed with her—paradoxical, thought-provoking, and always interesting—and for his considered decision to die at a time of his own choosing—a dilemma that everyone who sought to help Bruno Bettelheim at the end will recognize.

In his interviews with Fremon, the psychoanalyst touched on a multitude of subjects, but his most incisive comments were those on old age, mourning, and depression. They were remarkably frank. For example, after running through the list of his physical ailments, he remarked: "I always found that I understood a problem much better after I began to write about it. I can no longer do that." He stressed that in other countries, old people could still make themselves useful, that they were not shunted off to specialized institutions in which to await death, either in opulence or poverty, as they were in the United States. When Fremon pointed out that a lot of people still came to him for advice, Bettelheim admitted: "People do seek me out . . . perhaps not as much as I would like. But there are some to whom I am important and to whom I feel I make a contribution. That certainly is what is attractive about life."

"Let's not talk about depression. It's depressing," said the old man, almost gaily, at the start of the third interview. His doctor had just prescribed a new antidepressant, which appeared to be working wonders. But then a few sentences further on, the names of Primo Levi and Paul Celan came up. "I don't think that one ever really fully masters this experience of having been a prisoner in a German concentration camp," he said. He went on to reflect at length on the specificity of the camps. "It is an experience that makes one lose one's belief in mankind." He then started talking about Eros and Thanatos: not, Fremon says, as psychoanalytical concepts, but as living forces within himself. "I believe that Freud is right that we have both a life drive and also a death drive. As long as the life drive, or the libido, is in ascendancy—certainly as long as we are sexually active and we want to procreate—we are going to live. But it can also reach a point in old age where one must accept that one withdraws the libido from the world because otherwise one couldn't face death." The reporter probed him further: "Then is the waning of the libido, the waning of life, a consequence of the loss of love?" Bettelheim started to reply. "Loving and being loved . . ." he said. Then, his face flooded with emotion, he turned away. "Maybe we could talk about some other topic," he concluded.

In November 1989, Bettelheim went to Washington to spend Thanksgiving with two of his children, and visit some more retirement homes in the area. As one of the homes selected by Naomi agreed to take people on a trial basis, he decided to stay there for the duration of his visit. Naomi had carefully prepared things. A chauffeured car was available to take her father wherever he wanted to go, notably between the home, located north of the city in Bethesda, and her place in Virginia, to the west. She had also inquired about the house next to hers, which was for sale. Well laid out, with all the basic amenities on the same floor, it seemed ideal for her father. He could be at once independent and close by, as initially planned with Ruth. But he did not seem very interested. Her neighborhood was pleasant but somewhat distant from the city. Naomi had also contacted as many of her father's friends as possible. She had even found work for him: As soon as he moved to Washington he could start training social workers for the Jewish Social Services, giving two or three seminars a week, as he wished.

During the visit, Naomi was dismayed at the state her father was in. He even seemed to have lost his legendary courtesy. When they passed by a florist's, she suggested that he buy a bunch of flowers for the friend of a friend who, at her request, had managed in two days to get together a large dinner in his honor, to be held that evening. "There's no need. I'm past that," Bettelheim replied. He was indeed in a gloomy mood. The more retirement homes he visited, the more awful he found them all. And Naomi had to threaten never to have him in her house again to make him stop discussing his suicide plans in front of his grandson, now age four and able to understand. She also informed him that if he insisted on disinheriting Ruth, she would side with her sister to contest his will after his death. Bettelheim finally gave in and had the document amended. On the evening before Thanksgiving, Eric arrived, and Bettelheim returned to the subject of his death. Feeling uncertain that Connie Katzenstein would go ahead with their plan, he had found another couple who had agreed to accompany him to the Netherlands. But, he explained, they wanted to have his children's consent before committing themselves. Naomi replied that if they asked her, she would advise them to check with a lawyer on the risks they were taking for themselves; Bettelheim was furious. Finally, Alvin Rosenfeld, who had been exercising a pacifying influence during the holiday, told him: "Listen, kill yourself if you really have to. But don't try and get your children to approve."

"I have now decided to move at the end of January," Bettelheim wrote on his return to California.[106] The Dutch doctor he had been counting on to help him to die had just succumbed to a heart attack. That was one more reason for leaving Los Angeles, as he was convinced that his Polish housekeeper would prevent him from killing himself. He complained that she got up in the middle of the night to spy on him. This was not to say that he was about to make an attempt; for the time being, he was waiting for his book to be published, and to make the move east. In the letters he had written for Christmas and the New Year he even used the future: "We'll see . . . "; "Perhaps it might be possible to . . . "; "I hope to receive better news from you there"—the latter to Carl Frankenstein, who had been hospitalized following a heart attack and was to die before reading his letter. In early January, on hearing that Tübingen University in Germany had awarded him its prestigious Lukas Prize, Bettelheim expressed great pride, and added: "I don't think I will be able to attend the ceremony . . . But maybe the move will give me new strength and I will be able to go."[107]

He spent that Christmas in Los Angeles with Eric and his new girlfriend. She made a very good impression, and revived an old dream of attending his son's wedding before he died. Then, at Rudi Ekstein's request, he agreed to be interviewed with Ekstein for UCLA's archives on the history of psychoanalysis. He finally left Los Angeles for Washington on January 19, 1990, after several farewell dinners. A few days previously, David James Fisher had dropped in with a bottle of champagne to celebrate the publication of *Freud's Vienna and Other Essays*. Bettelheim was happy. He found the book handsome, with its dust jacket featuring a black-and-white photo of Freud's building at Berggasse 19 on a rainy day, set off by a border in a brown Art Nouveau pattern found in the Austrian Museum for Applied Arts. But Fisher could not help noticing the effort it cost him to scribble a few words of dedication.

His furniture took two weeks to follow him across the country, and on February 2, 1990, he finally moved into his new apartment, in the Silver Spring residence, Charter House. The place was roomy and comfortable, with a spacious living room, two bedrooms, a large terrace, two bathrooms, and a kitchen. Naomi and her husband had spared no effort to fit it out to the old man's liking. Eric had hired an interior decorator. Curtains, carpeting, bookshelves—everything had been done up or replaced with Bettelheim's tastes in mind. They had hung the engravings and lithographs and arrayed his books on the shelves themselves; they had also bought him a personal computer. Naomi had made sure that her father would have all necessary medical assistance on hand, and that when he took his meals in the common dining room his special needs would be catered to. Charter House, a select establishment for the affluent, was proud to be taking in such a well-known guest. A party had been arranged for Bettelheim's arrival.

"I am terribly disappointed. I cannot find one person to talk to here and I am very lonely, much lonelier than in Santa Monica. The moving has been very traumatic, several pieces of my old furniture were damaged on arrival and I regret very much having left California," he wrote only ten days later.[108] His signature was now little more than a shaky scribble, with only the "B" vaguely legible. The few lines typed under the letterhead of his new home were full of typographical errors. They show clearly that the "cowardly old lion," as Bettelheim had once described himself to Alvin Rosenfeld, had hardly any life left in him. All that remained was his "terrible roar."

At Charter House, it did not take long for Bettelheim to acquire the reputation of an appalling old grump who complained about everything. In the dining room, he could not stand any of the people who proposed to share his table. He railed against the food, the service, and all the rest. After much effort, the management started to despair of the situation. The other residents were turning away from Bettelheim. Charter House was not the Orthogenic School, and nobody had explained to them that, like disturbed children, desperate old people often express their suffering only through unpleasant behavior.

Elsewhere, his hangdog look did not always inspire compassion either. "What's your excuse for being here?" he was asked at a Washington dinner, by a woman he did not know.

"I've just moved to this area," he replied.

"How do you like it?"

"I'm not happy," said Bettelheim.

"How old are you?" she asked.

"Eighty-six."

"Well, then, you might like to be introduced to my friends at the Society for the Right to Die."

Shocked silence around the table.[109]

Bettelheim did not need any such advice. He knew exactly what to do. He had had the pills since Trude's death. And since he would have to act on his own, he had to make sure that neither vomiting nor the arrival of another person would "save" him at the last minute. He wanted to end it all painlessly, and had finally found the answer in a book by the founder of the Hemlock Society. In 1985, Derek Humphry had explained how he himself would commit suicide when the time came.[110] To speed up the process and vastly increase the chances of success, he would put a plastic bag over his head after taking the required dose of sleeping pills. As an added bonus, the carbon dioxide thereby inhaled was said to have a soporific effect.

It took over a month for Bettelheim finally to throw in the towel, even though everything in his new life seemed hopeless. He had traded in the California sunshine for Washington's rain and fog, and his view over the Pacific for the sight of a few trees, scattered among buildings and a parking lot. Having so often condemned the way American society treated its senior citizens, he found himself surrounded by people his age, in a place that, in spite of its flowers and neatness, was for all of them a last stop before the grave. He who so feared illness and infirmity was surrounded by wheelchairs and walkers, and he who hated small talk found himself without anyone with whom to exchange the ideas that he could no longer work on through writing.

The few friends he had in the Washington area all lived far away, and Naomi's house was even farther. He no longer had someone to drive him around; a bitter price to pay for his past carping at Wanda. But as he pointed out in his letters, there was now no turning back. He tried to come to terms with his new life. He agreed to give a few lectures, and there were even plans for a meeting with mothers. As news of his presence in the city spread, invitations began to flood in. And when his agent, Theron Raines, visited toward the end of February, the phone was ringing so often that they hardly managed to talk.

Raines was there to hear his life story. For in 1984, Bettelheim had finally agreed to his requests to let his biography be written. Until that point, he had rejected all such proposals. When Geneviève Jurgensen, whom he respected, had suggested it in 1974, he had backed his refusal by an explanation.

> In truth, I am a very private man. All the world has a right to know is my work, my ideas about matters on which I feel I can speak with confidence. My own children and the rest of my family have suffered enough from the fact that I am fairly well known . . . I do not wish them to suffer from the fact that their father, and as far as my wife is concerned, her husband, becomes known as a person. To them I always was and wish to remain just another father, just another husband, and not somebody who is public property.
>
> There are many aspects of my life and personality—though nothing I am ashamed of, or have any reason to be—which persons who did not have the same experience would not, could not, should not understand . . . It would have to be a work of fiction, a work of art, and of those there are enough around. As a person, I belong to another century and world, but not in my work. There are factors in my life of a most private nature which made me go into my work, and made me good at it. I do not wish that these should become public—in order not to become an actor, or conceited, or self-important, one must keep private things private. Accepting to be interviewed for a book about myself, I would feel a cheater if I didn't speak about those things which were most important in my life. But these very things I wish to keep to myself . . . So, I would have either to do things which I did not want to, or to pretend to say all, while not doing so.'''

By 1984, things were very different. His children were grown up. Trude was in the terminal stages of her illness. And Theron Raines was far more than simply an agent; he was a loyal friend who for close to fourteen years had done a great deal to defend Bettelheim's rights and his works. Bettelheim therefore let himself be persuaded, on condition that Raines do the work himself. He wrote to his friends and oldest colleagues to ask them to take part in the project, and at irregular intervals he began telling Raines his life story.

Theron Raines for obvious reasons did not want to answer my questions on the subject. It seems to me, however, that although Bettelheim may at some point have enjoyed the project, by early 1990, plunged into a depression on which no drug appeared to have any effect, he was finding it a burden. Theron Raines was the last person on whom he could unload the "dark secrets" that had led him to try to heal others. What Bettelheim thought this devoted admirer expected from him was his legend—the stories with the happy endings, which inspire love of life. And yet, coming at a time when he could think of nothing but death, how could such an exercise not confront him once again with the awful feeling of fraud that had plagued him since childhood? "What a bore!" he muttered on Sunday, March 11, when he was due for another session of recollections with Raines.

Bettelheim spent that Sunday with Naomi and her family. In the afternoon, he took a brief walk with his son-in-law. Passing by the house next door, he asked: "Is it still for sale?" As the answer was no, he dropped the subject. Later, Naomi offered him a new ribbon for his typewriter (he had not tried to use his computer), but he did not take it: "Keep it," he said. "I won't need it." His physical condition was no better or no worse than it had been in the preceding weeks. What really surprised Naomi, to the point that she decided to take a picture, is that Bettelheim sat reading and rereading a little book called *Just Me and My Dad* to his granddaughter. Then he went back to Silver Spring.

He could no longer read very much. He was too depressed, and his attention wandered. There were exceptions; he had reread *Moby-Dick*. The opening line of Melville's novel, "Call me Ishmael," still fascinated him. He felt that, by implying the depth of an unrevealed past, it summed up to perfection the attitude of the foreigner, the outsider. He was also rereading Goethe, particularly *Faust*, which took on a meaning completely different from the one he had found in it in his youth. At the beginning of March, Ruth Marquis sent him *Soumchi*, a children's story by Amos Oz, an Israeli writer Bettelheim was fond of.[112] It was the kind of tale that makes adults think; he got through it in two hours and enjoyed it greatly.

He often spoke with Ruth Marquis by phone. But before calling her, he would take some Ritalin, a stimulant, in order to sound cheerful.[113] He knew she could not bear to hear him so utterly depressed. When he moaned "I'm nothing but an ugly old Jew," it upset her so much that she did not know what to say. She was no more able than any of his other friends to understand how this man whom she had seen display such strength and accomplish such miracles, and to whom she owed so many of the ideas that had helped her to live, could have sunk so far, why he was so difficult, demanding and miserable, or why he so needed reassurance.

———— ❈ ————

Two years after Bruno Bettelheim's death, one fine summer afternoon on Long Island, I was sorting out what I had learned about him with his old friend Wanda Willig. After exhausting the specifics, we were down to trading impressions and interpretations. Although she had known him better than most, Wanda was puzzled and cautious in her judgments. Looking back, what particularly baffled her was the extraordinary gap in Bettelheim between the man eager to cut a fine figure, in constant need of admiration, and the almost embarrassing humility he could sometimes display. She had been especially struck by his miserable tone of voice on his answering machine shortly before his death: "He sounded so self-effacing," she kept on saying. The remark stuck in my mind—maybe because it took a while for me to realize that he had indeed "effaced" himself, in the most literal sense.

That fault line in Bruno Bettelheim's personality, that lack of love for himself, which was apparent to everyone who ever cared for him without falling under his spell, is called shame by some psychoanalysts. They say the yawning chasm in the self-image originates in a wound suffered before the personality becomes structured, a wound caused by the mother's disappointed look upon first seeing her baby. She does not recognize him; he is not the child of her dreams; she looks away from him. Sometimes, feeling guilty, the mother tries to make up for that unconscious antipathy with impressive displays of devotion.

The baby is not beautiful ("Thank God it's a boy!"), not worthy of interest (or at least not as interesting as the "social obligations" requiring that she abandon him to the care of a wetnurse). Yet he cannot even be angry at her—she is so devoted, even spending the whole night at his bedside when he is sick. So there can be no doubt in his mind: If he cannot get her to give her full attention to him, it must be his fault, a consequence of what he fails to be. He is obviously unworthy of the love he misses so much that he could die. And this lack, this self-doubt, this shame rooted deep in the child's psyche before he has developed the means to overcome it, to turn it into something else, is almost impossible to cure.

Later, during the oedipal phase, the child discovers guilt, under which he sometimes manages to bury his shame; in other words, he begins to hope that he can "repair" it. He no longer feels the lack of love as resulting from what he is, but from what he does (or does not do). In the best of cases, he will then spend his life trying to lift the curse, to turn the shadow under which he has lived into light— in Bettelheim's case, for example, by identifying the shame in his young patients' hearts early enough to hope that it could be erased at least there, or else by helping them to develop guilt, thus giving them the means to live.

But it is a gigantic mission, because shame begets self-contempt. It happens all the faster when the self-imposed goals set for the "repair" are unattainable. When merely helping incurable patients is not enough, actually curing them is required to silence the self-doubt. And any relief is short-lived. To proceed with one's life, to give that life meaning, shame must be silenced over and over again; it is always ready to spring back, at the first mistake, at the first shortfall between what one has wanted (to be) and what one has managed (to do), between the image of the magician one has held out as a promise and the too-often disappointing results of one's most determined efforts.

In that gap, that "abyss," as Bettelheim himself called it, depression looms, the kind of depression that makes it impossible to get out of bed, that makes one hate the dawn, and only dare to express oneself—to write, that is, to bare the bottom of one's soul—when everybody else is asleep, in the reassuring dark of night, the time of dreams, the time stolen from the gaze of others, when there is nothing to prove. It is the kind of depression that kills all desire to struggle, to build, to live.

We shall never know how far Bruno Bettelheim's own psychoanalysis helped him recognize those mechanisms in himself. He often said that although it revealed the reasons for his depression, it did not help him to overcome it. The way he chose to die seems to confirm this. But the way he lived, and his life's work, also show that, whether it was on Dr. Sterba's couch or at Buchenwald, he had discovered what he most needed to go on: in someone else's eyes, the look that could erase his shame.

At Buchenwald, he had found it in the eyes of Hans Bandler, and of others for whom his listening and storytelling had restored their self-respect and appetite for life. But there, paradoxically, things were simpler, since reality came down to a stark choice between life and death. Later, in his "second life," Bettelheim was able to validate his existence in the eyes of some students, counselors, and readers. And each of his books, each of his essays, was new evidence not only that he deserved to be, since it bore his name, in black and white, but also that his ideas and exemplary tales could earn him even more than admiration—love.

Above all, he found the look he so much needed, the look that effaces shame, in Trude's eyes. By replacing Gina's critical stare with Trude's reassuring and constructive gaze, Bettelheim displayed his instinct for survival; he showed that his love of life was stronger than his fascination with his internal chasm. It was no easy task. For the shame so deeply engraved on the child's soul by the "not good enough" mother [14] cannot be erased by an outpouring of empty flattery. On the contrary, that only makes things worse, by adding the suspicion of fraud to the initial self-doubt. ("Not only am I unworthy of love, but that I managed to win her love for the wrong reasons only goes to show how bad I really am"—monstrous or even mad, depending on the form of self-contempt involved. "And, incidentally, this shows that she isn't worth much either, and I can turn my contempt on her, since she couldn't see through me.")

Bettelheim was immediately ready to trust Gina, because the contempt he saw floating in her eyes merely mirrored the contempt he knew only too well; it was forever echoing inside him. But that Trude managed, with patience and perseverance, to get Bruno to accept the validity of her vision of him shows not only her love but also her great intelligence. And if his outbursts of harshness when she was dying reflected his pain at being reminded of his father's agony, they above all expressed his panic at the thought of seeing Trude's eyes close, of losing the image of himself he had come to trust more than his own. That loss was more than unbearable, it was literally unlivable, as he would write to his children just before his death.

That admission was to be the last little white pebble, the one that brought Bruno Bettelheim, like little Hansel, back home—where the good but fallen father had never succeeded in standing between him and his mother. True, she had not abandoned him deep in a hostile forest. On the contrary, she had done all that she could to save him from the deadly world where he had one day found himself because of the origins she had passed on to him without pride, rather like his face. In that world, he had nevertheless learned "to stand up on his own two feet." And he had summoned the courage to reject a protective blindness, which he had perhaps embraced to spare himself above all from the sight of his own plainness—a plainness he could never forget he had discovered "when his mother first beheld him."

———✸———

On Tuesday, March 13, 1990, at 8:15 A.M., the Charter House janitor called down to reception for help. On using his passkey to enter apartment 1007, he had found Bruno Bettelheim lying in the hallway, behind the door, with a plastic bag over his head. He was shirtless, and a pair of glasses lay on the gray carpet next to his body. The bag was secured around his neck with elastic bands. In the bedroom, the old man had left a brief note to his children on the typewriter. He bade them farewell, and reiterated that he simply could not go on living without their mother.

Two police officers arrived shortly after 9 A.M. to confirm the death. Bruno Bettelheim had apparently died around 2 A.M. He had taken barbiturates and a small amount of liquor.

The same day fifty years earlier, Wehrmacht tanks had rolled into Vienna flying Nazi flags, greeted by a crowd chanting "Death to the Jews." The coincidence was probably not intentional—that, at any rate, is the view of Bruno Bettelheim's children, and others close to him then. But the memory of the unconscious works that way. Coincidences are no accidents.

Notes

Preface

Unless otherwise indicated, the Bettelheim letters referred to here were made available to the author by private individuals.

1. Karlin later published a transcript of the film, plus his comments on the shooting, under the title *Un autre regard sur la folie* (A Different View of Insanity) (Paris: Stock, 1975), with an afterword by Bettelheim.
2. Paris: Robert Laffont, 1973.
3. Reviews published in the *American Journal of Sociology*, January 1957, and in the *New Leader*, May 1, 1958, both of which were later reworked and included in *Freud's Vienna and Other Essays* (New York: Knopf, 1990).
4. Freud referred to this in a letter to his fiancée, Martha Bernays, dated April 1885.
5. When Bert Cohler, Bettelheim's former student and successor at the Orthogenic School, who went on to head the Committee on Human Development at the University of Chicago, looked up Bettelheim's file to write an obituary for the in-house magazine, he commented: "His must have been the shortest résumé in the history of the university!"

Prologue: The "Bettelheim Affair"

The voices at the opening of the chapter are an attempt on my part to reproduce the feelings that were communicated to me along with the actual words when I talked with some of Bettelheim's former charges.

1. *New York Times.*
2. *Washington Post.*
3. Interview published in the *New Haven Register* on April 8, 1984, on the publication of Tom Wallace Lyons's novel *The Pelican and After* (see chapter 14).
4. *Newsweek,* September 10, 1990.
5. Bettelheim often used the term "the shock of recognition," coined by Herman Melville and made famous by the literary critic Edmund Wilson.
6. Jacquelyn Seevak (Sanders's maiden name), "A Case Study of a Brilliant Autistic Boy with Total Reading Disability: An Investigation of the Causes of This Condition and the Steps That Led to His Being Able to Overcome It" (University of Chicago Department of Education, September 1964).
7. In keeping with Bettelheim's philosophy and practice, I have opted to use masculine singular pronouns when referring to an unidentified child.
8. A small boy who forgets to put hands on the drawing of a person may be unconsciously seeking to hide an activity that he believes to be reprehensible. A psychotherapist would think in particular of masturbation.
9. On this extraordinary affair, see Janet Malcolm, *In the Freud Archives* (New York: Knopf, 1984), the book that made Masson widely known, but over which he later sued Malcolm for libel. See also what Masson himself has written about it, particularly *The Assault on Truth: Freud's Suppression of the Seduction Theory* (New York: Farrar, Straus and Giroux, 1983), as well as his comments in *The Complete Letters of Sigmund Freud to Wilhelm Fliess* (Cambridge, Mass: Belknap Press of Harvard University Press, 1985), which he published in unexpurgated form for the first time, and which were the origin of his falling-out with the psychoanalytic community.
10. *Washington Post,* October 6, 1990.
11. *On Learning to Read: The Child's Fascination with Meaning* (New York: Knopf, 1982).
12. Interview with the author in Chicago, November 1990.
13. *Journal of American Folklore* 104, no. 411 (Winter 1991).
14. *Los Angeles Times,* February 7, 1991.

Chapter 1. Vienna: Once Upon a Time . . .

1. *Freud's Vienna and Other Essays* (New York: Knopf, 1990), 133.
2. In *Moses and Monotheism* (1939).
3. In his doctoral dissertation in art history, submitted in 1937, Bettelheim cited the study by Kris, which had been published in 1934 as *Die Legende vom Künstler* (*Legend, Myth, and Magic in the Image of the Artist* [New Haven, Conn.: Yale University Press, 1981]).
4. Budapest was created in 1873 from the merger of Pest with Buda, on the other side of the Danube.

5. See *Die Juden und die Judenmeinde Bratislava* (Brno, Czechoslovakia, 1932), in which one Samuel Bettelheim, a native of Budapest, wrote the chapter titled "History of the Yeshiva of Bratislava."

6. The Yiddish word *shtetl* means "village." The word *ghetto* is, strictly speaking, incorrect in this context, since it implies an obligation to live in a certain place. In fact, in the Austro-Hungarian Empire at least, there was no law obliging Jews to live in the shtetl, even though their material conditions made it very difficult for them to live anywhere else.

7. See Léon Poliakov, *The History of Anti-Semitism* vol. 2 (New York: Vanguard, 1965).

8. Thirty-four percent in 1910, according to Michael Pollak, *Vienne 1900* (Paris: Gallimard/Juillard, 1984).

9. Stefan Zweig, *The World of Yesterday* (New York: Viking, 1943).

10. *Freud's Vienna*, 133.

11. Ibid., 134.

12. It was customary among the Rothschilds to reward with more powerful jobs men who had proved themselves trustworthy by educating the family's children. In France, for example, Georges Pompidou, who became president after Charles de Gaulle, served in his youth as a tutor to Guy de Rothschild's son, and was then appointed head of Banque Rothschild, before going into politics.

13. This post carried more responsibility in the Rothschild bank than it would have elsewhere, since unlike other bank owners, the Rothschilds generally declared their private fortune as security for their liabilities.

14. Although Morris's death certificate mentions tuberculosis, there is in this case every reason to believe the family's version of the cause of death. As was confirmed to me by the official in charge of the Vienna Israelitische Kultusgemeinde, disguising the cause of a death was a common practice at the time, and in Jewish families there was no glory attached to being killed in a duel.

15. In March 1883, a month after Morris Bettelheim's death, Herzl was to resign from the prestigious Albia club as a result of a violently anti-Semitic speech delivered there by the writer Hermann Bahr, one of his fraternity brothers, on the occasion of Wagner's death. Herzl thereby avoided the indignity of being thrown out of the club.

16. Lueger, who was to remain mayor until 1910, made a lasting impression on the young Adolf Hitler, who saw him as a model. Hitler arrived in the city in 1907 in the hope of gaining admission to the Fine Arts Academy. Although he failed in both his attempts, he was to remain in Vienna until 1913.

17. Arthur Schnitzler, "My Youth in Vienna."

18. Converting to Catholicism was a fashionable thing to do at the time. Before the young Theodor Herzl drew up his theory of Zionism, one of his dearest wishes was to see the emperor presiding over mass conversions of Jews in Saint Stephen's Cathedral!

19. See especially Carl E. Schorske, *Fin-de-Siècle Vienna* (New York: Knopf, 1979), and William Johnston, *The Austrian Mind* (Berkeley: University of California Press, 1972). The list of books devoted to this question is too long to be presented in full here. In addition to Stefan Zweig's *World of Yesterday* and the works of Arthur Schnitzler and Martin Buber, I made considerable use of two studies published in France: the regrettably brief *Vienne 1900* by Michael Pollak and the erudite *Modernité viennoise et crises de l'identité* by Jacques Le Rider (Paris: Presses Universitaires de France, 1990). Both books were invaluable in explaining the complexity and ambiguity of the world in which Bettelheim grew up. Also worth mentioning is the very rich catalogue to the Pompidou Center's "Paris–Vienne" exhibition (Paris, 1986), for which Bettelheim first wrote the essay that opens *Freud's Vienna*. Other works, such as *Freud: A Life for Our Time* by Peter Gay (New York: Macmillan, 1988), *Anna Freud* by Elizabeth Young Bruehl (New York: Summit, 1985), and *Les Rothschilds* (Paris: Stock, 1989) gave insights into particular historical issues.

20. One example: When the Austrians chose Kurt Waldheim as their president, in spite of his wartime service in Nazi uniform, Bettelheim snapped: "Bah! They deserve each other!" (interview in *Illustrierte Neue Welt*, November–December 1987).

21. *Freud's Vienna*, 46.

22. To quote the title of the pamphlet Wagner was to publish, first anonymously in 1850, then under his own name in 1869. In it Wagner, who according to his autobiography had agitated for the emancipation of the Jews during an earlier revolutionary period, expressed his anti-Semitism openly for the first time. For more on this question, see Jacob Katz, *Wagner et la question juive* (Paris: Hachette, 1986).

23. Quoted in Poliakov, *History of Anti-Semitism*, vol. 2.

24. There is a huge corpus of work devoted to this question also, among which the study by Poliakov stands out.

25. See the remarkable *La rime et la raison: Savoir et fiction chez Robert Musil* (Paris: Presses Universitaires de Vincennes, 1994) by Laurence Dahan, to whom I am indebted for much of the material in this chapter.

26. As Jean Clair points out in his subtly argued introduction to the catalogue of the "Paris–Vienne" exhibition (see note 19), there is a considerable difference between the artistic movements of the period in the two cities. Rebellious artists in Paris organized the Salon des Indépendants, while the comparable phenomenon in Vienna was labeled the Secession. In the first case, independence implied breaking out of chains to push ahead, in an outward-looking movement. Secession, on the other hand, meant turning in on oneself, breaking away while remaining within existing boundaries.

27. See, for example, Michel Herszlikowicz, *Philosophie de l'antisémitisme* (Paris: Presses Universitaires de France, 1985).

28. "Class, Color and Prejudice," *The Nation*, October 19, 1963.

29. Lessing's book of that name, *Der Jüdische Selbsthass*, was published in 1930. It was hated by most assimilated Viennese Jews, including Sigmund Freud, who was to write, however, in a letter to Lessing's biographer Kurt Hiller dated 1936: "Don't you think that the type of self-hatred depicted by Theodor Lessing is a typically Jewish phenomenon? I really think it is" (quoted in Le Rider, *Modernité viennoise*).

30. See Jean-Paul Sartre's *Réflexions sur la question juive* (Reflections on the Jewish Question) (Paris: Gallimard, 1946); its central idea is that the "Jew" is essentially defined by the anti-Semite.

31. Robert Musil, *The Man Without Qualities*, trans. Eithne Wilkins and Ernst Kaiser (London: Secker & Warburg), vol. 3, chap. 20. It is somewhat ironic to note that Germans, then as now, tend to look down on the Viennese accent, which is somewhat singsong in tone. It would be tempting to conclude that the entire Viennese population, like that of New York, in fact "talks Jewish" without realizing it.

32. See Jacques Le Rider, *Le cas Otto Weininger* (Paris: Presses Universitaires de France, 1982). Practically all the works devoted to turn-of-the-century Vienna discuss the Weininger case, seen as symbolic of the period as a whole. A particularly subtle analysis is to be found in Michael Pollak's *Vienne 1900*.

33. *Sex and Character* was in fact to serve as the catalyst for the split between Freud and his confidant Wilhelm Fliess, who claimed to have originated the concept of bisexuality; he accused Freud of having divulged the idea to a friend of Weininger's.

34. Poliakov, *History of Anti-Semitism*.

35. On this point, see Arthur Schnitzler's fine novel *Der Weg ins Freie* (The Road into the Open) (1908). For a particularly interesting analysis of the different forms that this self-hatred could take, see Le Rider, *Modernité viennoise*.

36. *Freud's Vienna*, 47.

37. For more on this, see chapter 13.

38. *Illustrierte Neue Welt* interview.

39. *Freud's Vienna*, 108.

Chapter 2. One Big Family

1. This information is drawn from a letter of recommendation sent to the chamber of commerce in 1921 by another lumber merchant, in support of Anton Bettelheim's application to be elected to the status of *Kommerzialrat*, as his father had been before him. The application was unsuccessful.

2. The essay, written for the catalogue of the 1986 "Paris–Vienne" exhibit at the Pompidou Center in Paris, was republished as the title piece of *Freud's Vienna and Other Essays* (New York: Knopf, 1990).

3. Stefan Zweig, *The World of Yesterday* (New York: Viking, 1943).

4. *A Good Enough Parent* (New York: Knopf, 1987), 304.

5. Ibid., 307–8.

6. The title of this book is derived from the English psychoanalyst Donald Winnicott's concept of a "good enough mother," as Bettelheim explains in his acknowledgments, the idea being, as he also notes, that "perfection is not within the grasp of ordinary human beings," and that "efforts to attain it typically interfere with that lenient response to the imperfections of othrs, including those of one's child, which alone make good human relations possible."

7. *A Good Enough Parent*, 40–41.

8. Letter to ER, September 1980. This old friend of Bettelheim's prefers not to be identified.

9. *A Good Enough Parent*, 348.

10. Bettelheim told this recollection to Denise Bombardier, who included it in an article in the French magazine *Le Point*, May 28, 1988.

11. *A Good Enough Parent*, 340.

12. Ibid., 304.

13. Letter to Carl Frankenstein, November 19, 1986.

14. *A Good Enough Parent*, 306.

15. "Women: Emancipation Is Still to Come," *New Republic*, November 7, 1964.

16. Edith Buxbaum, unpublished memoirs.

17. Initially, most of the reports I heard of the knitting incident were secondhand, along the lines of "A friend who attended one of Bettelheim's lectures told me . . . " I was beginning to think the whole thing might be a myth until I met Professor Al Reiss Jr., who stated he had been present at a lecture during which Bettelheim rebuked a woman student for knitting, and referred to masturbation. The young woman did not reply, however.

18. One anecdote Bettelheim mentions was reported by Lou Andreas-Salomé around 1912, and is cited in H. F. Peters's biography of her, *My Sister, My Spouse*. Andreas-Salomé was knitting while attending one of the first psychoanalytic gatherings. One of the other participants remarked jokingly that Salomé "seemed to enjoy herself by indulging in continuous coitus, as symbolised by the movement of the knitting needles. She just smiled, and kept on knitting," Bettelheim writes, quoting Peters.

19. Letter to the *New York Times Magazine*, February 8, 1970.

20. Unpublished memoirs.

21. *A Good Enough Parent*, 120.

22. Ibid., 112.

23. Ibid., 187.

24. "Learning to Read: A Primer for Literacy," *Harper's*, April 1978.

25. Interview published in the French magazine *Alma*, in December 1986.

26. The opening sentence of *On Learning to Read: The Child's Fascination with Meaning* (New York: Knopf, 1981).

27. *Dialogues with Mothers* (Free Press, 1962), 165. Bettelheim's handwriting firm, regular, and also elegant, in the old-fashioned European style.

28. *On Learning to Read*, 30.

29. Conversation with the present headmaster.

30. See "Segregation: New Style," *School Review*, April 1958, and "Sputnik and Segregation," *Commentary*, October–November 1958. See also "German Schools Revisited" in the Chicago-based *Elementary School Journal*, November 1955, written after a three-month teaching stint in Germany.

31. In *Freud's Vienna* he gives his age as thirteen, but according to his friend Wanda Willig, he was a little older.

32. *Freud's Vienna*, 24.

33. Interview with Wanda Willig in New York, November 1990.

34. *A Good Enough Parent*, 80.

35. Ibid., 84.

36. He could in fact have been slightly older. When telling his children of the incident, he gave his age as fourteen or fifteen.

37. Zweig, *World of Yesterday*, 98.

38. Edith Buxbaum, unpublished memoirs.

39. J. P. Bardet, ed. *Peurs et terreurs face à la contagion* (Paris: Fayard, 1988), 331.

40. Ibid., 425.

41. "The Social Studies Teacher and the Emotional Needs of Adolescents," *School Review*, December 1948. The quotations in this and the next paragraph are drawn from this source.

42. Zweig, *World of Yesterday*.

43. *Saturday Evening Post*, March 11, 1967.

44. *Peurs et terreurs face à la Contagion*, p. 322.

45. The essay, published in *Freud's Vienna*, was originally a lecture Bettelheim gave at the University of Southwestern Louisiana. In a shorter form, it was also published as the preface to an American edition of Korczak's book *King Matt the First* (New York: Farrar, Straus and Giroux, 1986).

46. Henryk Goldszmit was Korczak's original Jewish name. He changed it to the Gentile Janusz Korczak at the age of twenty in order to enter a literary competition.

47. *Freud's Vienna*, 196.

48. Betty Jean Lifton, *The King of Children: A Biography of Janusz Korczak* (New York: Farrar, Straus and Giroux, 1988).

49. *A Good Enough Parent*, 86.

50. Edith Buxbaum, unpublished memoirs.

51. *The Empty Fortress: Infantile Autism and the Birth of the Self* (New York: Free Press, 1967), 6.

52. Zweig, *World of Yesterday*.

53. Published in the Swiss magazine *Le Temps Stratégique* in 1987–88 and reprinted in *Freud's Vienna*.

54. In particular in his book *Geschichte als Sinngebung des Sinnlosen* (History as Projecting Meaning into the Meaningless).

55. Paul Watzlavik, of the Palo Alto Mental Research Institute, offers a splendid example of how fiction can thus be used to help resolve a real-life problem. Before dying, a father tells his three sons that he wants the eldest to have half of his estate, the second a third, and the youngest a ninth. As his estate amounts to seventeen camels, they see no other way to carry out his wishes than to cut some of them up. They are about to do so when a mullah passes by on camelback. They ask him for advice. "I give you my camel," he says. "Now that you have 18, you the eldest can take nine, i.e. half of them. The second brother can take six, or a third. And the youngest can take two, or a ninth of the estate. They add up to 17. So one is unaccounted for. It is mine, and I take it back!"

56. After writing these lines, I learned that the Folklore Studies Center at the University of Tel Aviv had carried out a comparative study of Jewish tales and fairy tales. The team, under Dov Noy, found that in 80 percent of cases there was a similarity of themes between the two genres.

57. Out of a total Austrian population of 8 million, 1.2 million were to be killed and 3 million injured during World War I.

58. *Larousse Mensuel Illustré*, August 1919, 866.

59. *The Informed Heart: Autonomy in a Mass Age* (Glencoe, Ill.: Free Press, 1960), 5.

60. In regard to workplace legislation, Austria had already proved itself progressive in comparison with other empires. As early as 1883, a labor inspectorate was set up by law to ensure respect for restrictions on working hours, including a ban on Sunday work and limits on the employment of women and adolescents. And in 1887, Austria created an early form of health insurance, including measures to compensate employees for accidents at work.

61. A similar suspicion was voiced in countries allied to Austria. As Léon Poliakov notes in *The History of Anti-Semitism*, in October 1916, with the war in full swing, the Ministry of War in Berlin ordered a census of all Jews serving in the armed forces, with information on whether they were at the front or in the rear. The official reason for the survey, the results of which were never published, was to disprove the widely believed rumor that most Jewish soldiers managed to get themselves cushy noncombat postings in offices or in the rear.

62. As Bettelheim himself was to point out in "Class, Color and Prejudice," *The Nation*, October 19, 1963.

63. It is worth noting that the father of the Austrian Social Democratic party, Victor Adler, who was Jewish, was in his youth a supporter of the Pan-German party of Georg von Schönerer, only changing his opinion when the latter openly declared himself an anti-Semite.

64. Letter to Carl Frankenstein, November 19, 1986.

Chapter 3. Gina

1. Interviews with the author, December 1990, July 1991, and May 1990.
2. In *Freud's Vienna and Other Essays* (New York: Knopf, 1990), 25.
3. Bettelheim was to confirm his romance with Lisl Lazarsfeld much later, during a lecture given in 1987 in Vienna, at the invitation of the Freud Museum. Paul Lazarsfeld was later to emigrate to the United States, where he became a leading proponent of social psychology.
4. Quoted by Russell Jacoby in *The Repression of Psychoanalysis: Otto Fenichel and the Political Freudians* (New York: Basic Books, 1983), 59.
5. *Freud's Vienna*, 26.
6. According to Naomi, the younger daughter, Bettelheim only informed the two girls of the situation because Gina had told her own daughter about it, and he was afraid that they would learn it from her before he told them.
7. At the end of World War I, when Galicia became part of Poland, there were still some 700,000 Jews recorded as living there, most of them in ghettos.
8. *Freud's Vienna*, 20.
9. The boat salesroom that now occupies its ground floor no doubt makes it look a little more bourgeois than the butcher's store of Freud's day.
10. *Saturday Evening Post*, July 27, 1968. In the same article, Bettelheim tempers the statement by noting: "My own children study best with the door open and the record player going full blast, and in this radically different setting they learn as much and as well as I did."
11. *Freud's Vienna*, 110.
12. The meeting of Gina and Wanda was to be the start of a friendship that was still going strong over sixty years later. Wanda, who like Gina had been born in Lemberg, was studying medicine, which greatly impressed her new friend. While Bruno and Hans were busy deciding how to change the world ("They were the serious types," says Wanda), the two women were discovering the many things they had in common, notably an interest in psychoanalysis and a shared sense of humor.
13. All the references and quotes relating to Bettelheim's reading in this passage are drawn from his essay "Essential Books of One's Life," published in *Freud's Vienna*, 97 and passim. Bettelheim originally wrote the essay in 1987 for the Swiss magazine *Le Temps Stratégique*.
14. Sigmund Freud himself was to spend seventeen years teaching at the lowly rank of *Privatdozent*, a kind of unpaid guest lecturer. It was only thanks to the intervention of one of his patients that he was finally to be awarded the fellowship his standing merited. See Peter Gay, *Freud: A Life for Our Time* (New York: Norton, 1988; Anchor, 1989), 138.
15. Letter to ER, September 10, 1954.
16. Von Jauregg was famed for discovering a treatment for the general paralysis that characterizes the final stage of syphilis. His method, which involved vaccination with malaria bacteria, won him a Nobel Prize.

17. R. Sterba, *Reminiscences of a Viennese Psychoanalyst* (Detroit: Wayne State University Press, 1982), 8, 31.
18. A few years later, Anna Freud would run what has since become known as the Jackson Nursery there.
19. *Freud's Vienna*, 110.
20. Purchased with a loan from the Autokredit Gesellschaft company. It was to be confiscated by the Nazis in 1938.
21. Friedrich Torberg, *Die Tante Jolesch* (Munich: DTV, 1974).
22. Letter to ER, September 10, 1954.
23. *Freud's Vienna*, 197.
24. Letter to ER, September 10, 1954.

Chapter 4. Patsy

1. Edith Buxbaum, unpublished memoirs.
2. The Sterbas were later to co-author the psychoanalytic study *Beethoven and His Nephew*, trans. Willard R. Trask (New York: Pantheon, 1954).
3. Gina does not remember the date, but Bruno Bettelheim mentions the fall of 1932 in *The Empty Fortress: Infantile Autism and the Birth of the Self* (New York: Free Press, 1967). That would be consistent with the documents I was able to find in Vienna, notably the police records on the whereabouts of Patsy's mother, Agnes Piel Crane.
4. Indeed, several times during our interviews, Gina confused the name of Patsy with that of her own daughter, born much later during her second marriage. She herself finally noticed the Freudian slip.
5. Patsy was almost seventy when I interviewed her, in August 1991.
6. In his *Reminiscences of a Viennese Psychoanalyst* (Detroit: Wayne State University Press, 1982), 167, Richard Sterba tells how, shortly before the Anschluss, he had asked for help from a former American patient whose daughter was one of his wife's patients. In a laconic and exquisitely diplomatic footnote, he adds: "I believe that it was this experience with the girl that contributed to Bettelheim's interest in autistic children."
7. Notably in the last television interview he granted to the French journalist Daniel Karlin on March 18, 1989, and during a conference in San Francisco four days later. Karlin included extracts from the interview in his film on Bettelheim (see preface).
8. *A Good Enough Parent* (New York: Knopf, 1987), 199–200.
9. Bettelheim to Daniel Karlin in conversation.
10. *A Good Enough Parent*, 200.
11. In the August 1991 interview.
12. It would seem that she did not, however, take Patsy to see the great Swiss psychologist Jean Piaget, contrary to what Bettelheim was to state in some versions of the story.
13. His daughter Naomi recalls seeing one of them.
14. It is probably to this child that Bettelheim refers (as the cactus-chewing

"Johnny") in his essay "How I Learned About Psychoanalysis," published in *Freud's Vienna*. That story appears to be another example of
Bettelheim's propensity for embroidering the truth.

15. Bettelheim, *The Informed Heart: Autonomy in a Mass Age* (Glencoe,
Ill.: Free Press, 1960), 12.

16. *Freud's Vienna*, 28.

17. Ibid., 29.

18. Ibid., 28.

19. Gina was unaware that Trude had been a patient of Editha Sterba. But
the two women did not know one another well.

20. Unfortunately, I was unable to find out Sterba's side of the story, since
people who were close to him refused point-blank to talk to me. This
of course proves nothing, except maybe that they felt uneasy about discussing Bettelheim.

21. Letter to Carl Frankenstein, December 14, 1986.

22. Here again, what is important from the psychological point of view is
not the literal truth, but the way Bettelheim interpreted it.

23. Interview with Dr. Maria Kramer, May 26, 1993.

24. This expression is widely preferred to the word *patient*, which gives a
too passive impression of the person in analysis.

25. *The Empty Fortress*, 79.

26. None of this is at odds with what Bettelheim himself was trying to
explain about psychotic children in the passage being quoted. For he
wrote that when such children managed to create whole sentences to
communicate with somebody else, in this case the therapist, that in
itself was a sign of improvement, since it constituted an act directed
toward the outside world. But as he refers here to the "secret of psychoanalytic technique," we feel justified in broadening the field of
application of his definition. The formulation of complete sentences
clearly represents an improvement in a child which up to then has been
incapable of communicating with the outside world, but to make the
same criterion the key to the psyche of an adult who is well adapted to
the real world seems to reflect a rather limited view of the analytical
process.

27. In a recording he made for his children.

28. *Freud's Vienna*, 27.

Chapter 5. The Anschluss

1. *Mein Kampf* (London: Hutchinson Press, 1969), 114.

2. This in particular explains the influence Mach exerted on thinkers like
Freud and Musil.

3. In the first part of the dissertation, Bettelheim writes from a historical
viewpoint to show how, with the development of urban culture and
socialization, the natural world gradually became an object of aesthetic
pleasure. He meanwhile deplores the fact that modern aesthetics either

excludes nature altogether or views it as an inferior experience, far less important than art. In part two, Bettelheim questions the distinction between beauty as applied to art and as applied to nature. He proposes to replace the dichotomy by a distinction between human creations, living creatures, and landscapes. He attributes the fact that modern thinkers give precedence to art over nature both to historical factors (the history of art being an older discipline than aesthetics) and to system-related ones (the work of art, being an ordered object, is much more easily apprehended by the subject than nature, which leaves everything to his subjectivity).

Bettelheim goes on to discuss the two prevalent tendencies in modern aesthetics: idealism and formalism. Since idealism pays attention only to the ideational content of the work, it considers nature as a minor aesthetic object (as seen in Hegel or Vischer), in which the manifestation of the Idea is compromised or sullied by purely contingent elements. For the formalists, on the other hand, the only thing that counts is the form of the object (the relationship between its parts, the harmony of its colors, tones and rhythms, and so on). Their aim is to create a science of judgments of taste, based on an analysis of the elementary relations that make up any complex impression. Bettelheim sees a parallel between formalism and experimental psychology, criticizing the latter for taking only the simplest types of aesthetic expressions into account, and for being incapable of drawing up objective criteria for aesthetic values.

He then lists the various strains of formalism, noting that for most of them, the natural world can only attain the rank of an aesthetic object to the extent that the subject projects human feelings onto it, thereby bringing it to life or giving it a soul. This process occurs either directly or via the associations that the natural scene conjures up in the subject. In the case of the strictest type of formalism, the aesthetic effect is seen as springing from laws, such as unity in diversity, eurhythmy, the balance of proportions, harmony, and so on. The aesthetics of nature is thus relegated to the sidelines.

In the next two parts of his dissertation Bettelheim seeks to show on the contrary that enjoyment of the natural world is a full-fledged aesthetic experience. He begins by stressing that aesthetic norms have almost always been deduced from the analysis of existing works of art, and that they cannot therefore lay claim to universal validity. He adds that in any case, the enjoyment of nature corresponds to the main criteria defined by various schools of thought: unity in diversity, specific human content, disinterested (that is, nonutilitarian) stance of the subject, and so on.

For Bettelheim, the reason that nature has been excluded from consideration as a valid aesthetic object has to do with the difficulty of clearly defining it. One's perception of a landscape is indeed dependent on many factors: one's vantage point, the way one frames the scene, the weather, season, and time of day, even the way one is feeling, both physically and psychologically. Furthermore, the experience involves not only vision but hearing, smell, and other sensations, such as reactions to temperature.

In the case of an artwork, it is the artist himself or herself who narrows the field of perceptions, a process that is indispensable if the impression is to have unity. But when the object is a natural scene, that narrowing has to be carried out by the observer alone. For Bettelheim, this proves that the enjoyment of nature is a more authentic aesthetic experience, as it is not mediated by a third party. It is also a more rounded one, since it involves all the senses, not just sight. Lastly, it is closer to the origins of aesthetic experience, since its object has not yet been influenced by the work of an artist.

In the fifth part of his dissertation Bettelheim distances himself from both the idealist and formalist positions in an original way by transposing Reininger's psycho-physical theory of love onto the field of aesthetics. To give aesthetics its full meaning, he writes, one must put the accent on the experience itself, and not on either the subject (idealism) or the object (formalism) alone. The aesthetic experience constitutes an interactive relationship between the ego and the object, in which the object represents the outside world. In the instant when the experience occurs, the ego and the world merge, and it is precisely the transcendence of the ego–world duality that is the source of aesthetic pleasure.

What both idealists and formalists have failed to realize, Bettelheim writes in part six of his dissertation, is that such transcendence inhibits rational thought. As the forces that make up the ego (willpower and thought) dissolve in the aesthetic experience, there is no longer a clear opposition between the interior and the exterior, the subject and the object; the aesthetic experience takes place in a sphere from which the dualistic oppositions of rational thought (animate–inanimate, person–thing, spiritual–material, inside–outside) have been banished. The laws of aesthetics are thus at once objective and subjective; the object has to conform to certain aesthetic norms, and the subject must obey certain psychological laws.

What makes the natural world different from this standpoint is that, in the absence of an artist, the aesthetic object is entirely constructed by the subject. A person looking at a landscape enjoys the same freedom and spontaneity as an artist creating his work from impressions of the outside world—with one difference: Here the object is not simply a representation of that outside world, it is itself part of it.

Bettelheim concludes by stressing that the aesthetic experience is an essential counterweight to the rationalist approach, particularly in a complex social structure in which any kind of unifying view has become more and more elusive. And nature can provide a purer and more complete aesthetic experience than art, because the latter is not freed from all the workings of reason. In the natural world, one does not think the world, one lives it, beyond the contradictions and questions that it raises. Aesthetic experience of nature is thus of fundamental importance for man, since it allows him to rise above his human condition.

4. Cited by Alan Bullock in *Hitler: A Study in Tyranny* (London: Penguin, 1962), 47.

5. *Last Waltz in Vienna: The Destruction of a Family 1842–1942* (London: Macmillan, 1981), part 4.

6. British Prime Minister Neville Chamberlain had refused to get involved in what he considered an inter-German affair. Czechoslovakia, like Italy, had been taken in by Hitler's promises. As for the French government, it had stepped down the previous day.

7. Quoted by the American journalist William Shirer, *The Rise and Fall of the Third Reich* (London: Secker and Warburg Ltd., 1960), 341.

8. Ibid.

9. In the memoir she tape-recorded for her children.

10. Marilyn Garner, interview with the author, May 1993. The second occasion is described in chap. 7.

11. Clare, *Last Waltz*, part 3. This treatment (which Trude's mother was subjected to) was meted out so widely in the weeks following the Anschluss that after the war, when the Vienna city authorities finally decided to erect a monument to the Jewish martyrs of Nazism, the sculpture that was adopted depicted a bowed, kneeling figure. It would be difficult to imagine an emblem more symbolic of Vienna's abiding ambivalence toward Jews!

12. Quoted in Anthony Read and David Fisher, *Kristallnacht: Unleashing the Holocaust* (London: Michael Joseph, 1989).

13. A scene described by, among others, Shirer, *Rise and Fall*.

14. In 1938, $10,000 was equivalent to about six years' wages for a factory worker in the United States.

15. Quoted in Read and Fisher, *Kristallnacht*.

16. *Reminiscences of a Viennese Psychoanalyst* (Detroit: Wayne State University Press, 1981).

17. *Last Waltz*.

18. Quoted by Herbert Rosenkranz in *The Nazi Concentration Camps*, proceedings of the 4th International Yad Vashem Historical Conference, Jerusalem, 1984.

19. *Nazi Conspiracy and Aggression*, vol. 7 (Washington, D.C.: U.S. Government Printing Office, 1946), 818–39.

20. In his *Reminiscences of a Viennese Psychoanalyst*, Richard Sterba states that he accompanied Peter Weinmann to the station March 12, which would mean that Gina and Patsy left that day, as they were on the same train. (However, Sterba gives erroneous dates for several other events, as, for example, when he states that Hitler arrived in Vienna on that same Saturday whereas in fact he came two days later. One can but reflect on the frailty of the human memory in regard to traumatic events.)

21. Once the "final solution" was under way, *Juden-Aktion* became synonymous with extermination. That was not yet the case in the Vienna of 1938, however. In the documents of that period, the term refers simply to the arrests. At the time, the Jewish population of Austria totaled some 192,000, of whom 95 percent lived in the capital. The city was thus home to Europe's third-largest Jewish community, after Warsaw and Budapest. Already at the end of 1938, only 64,000 remained, and six years later, when the Red Army liberated Vienna, records indicate that there were only 200.

22. A striking example of this admiration is to be found in the minutes of the famous Berlin meeting that took place after the Crystal Night pogrom in November 1938. Göring, presiding, heard reports from all the regional governors, with the Vienna *Gauleiter* speaking last. When he had finished, Göring exhorted those present to follow the example set by the Austrians. They had done more in five months than the German Nazis had managed to do in five years, he added.

23. Sterba, *Reminiscences*.

Chapter 6. Dachau: The Making of a Survivor

1. I would in particular like to thank Barbara Distel of the Dachau Memorial and Vidar Jakobson of the Centre de Documentation Juive Contemporaine in Paris for their invaluable help.

2. Freud made Ernst's father, Paul, the de facto head of the Vienna Psychoanalytic Society after 1923, when Freud was diagnosed as suffering from cancer.

3. Ernst Federn described his encounter with Bettelheim in a collection of essays, *Witnessing Psychoanalysis* (London: Karnac, 1990). I interviewed him in Vienna in October 1990 and June 1992.

4. Hans Bandler gave a brief account of his arrest and deportation in *Strauss to Matilda, 1938–1988*, a book on the Austrian community in Australia (Sydney: Wenkart Foundation, 1988). I interviewed him October 9 and 11, 1991, in London.

5. Langbein, *Against All Hope: Resistance in the Nazi Concentration Camps, 1938–1945*, trans. Harry Zohn (New York: Paragon House, 1994).

6. When the other camps were built, former Dachau cadres were used to set an example of how things should be done. In addition to the notorious Auschwitz commander Rudolf Höss, and his successor Karl Baer, the heads of Flossenbürg, Ravensbrück, Bergen-Belsen, Mathausen, Lublin, Sachsenhausen, Natzweiler, and other less well known camps all got their initial training at Dachau.

7. As Olga Wormser-Migot writes, in "Le système concentrationnaire nazi" (Paris: Presses Universitaires de France, 1968, 73), "For camps to be set up for the Jews, for the Nuremberg Laws to take on their full meaning, it was necessary for the war to be under way, and for the

authorities to be able to deport the Jews outside the borders of the Reich, or to seek them out in the countries in which they had found refuge and deport them." One is tempted to add, since Austria is such a special case in this context, ". . . and to eliminate them from the city in which Adolf Hitler had learned to hate them."

8. Notably in "Freedom from Ghetto Thinking," published in *Midstream* in March 1962, and in "Survival of the Jews," a review of Jean-François Steiner's book *Treblinka* which appeared in the *New Republic* on July 1, 1967. Bettelheim was later to recast and merge those two texts to form the last chapter of his *Freud's Vienna and Other Essays*, which constitutes his last word on the subject. This also explains why he uses the concept of an "Informed Heart." See below, chapter 13, for more on that subject.

9. Seven years later, in his testimony before one of Judge Jackson's aides, Bettelheim mistakenly gave the date of his admission to Dachau as early May.

10. It is worth recalling that this annexation was at the time contested by practically nobody. When Bettelheim arrived in New York eleven months later, the U.S. immigration authorities recorded him as having been born in "Vienna, Germany."

11. Decree of February 20, 1933. See Olga Wormser-Migot, op cit.

12. David Rousset, *The Other Kingdom* (New York: Reynal & Hitchcock, 1947).

13. In *Surviving and Other Essays* (New York: Knopf, 1979).

14. In his diary, Freud gave the time of his departure from the city as 3:25 P.M. on June 3. However, his first biographer, Ernest Jones, said this was a mistake, and that the date was in fact June 4. A truly Freudian slip, which Peter Gay, in his *Freud: A Life for Our Time* (New York: Norton, 1988) attributes to the old man's ambivalence at leaving the city. Harald Leupold-Löwenthal, president of the Vienna Freud Society, who sifted through all the evidence with a fine-tooth comb (even establishing the precise minute at which Freud's train left, 3:14 P.M.), said it was Ernest Jones who had got the day wrong, because it was in fact *he* who felt ambivalent about Freud's arrival in London!

15. *Surviving*, 12.

16. According to the Dachau records the train was carrying 595 men on arrival. The average travel time from Vienna to the camp was fourteen hours. An account of a similar journey in the same period can be found in Viktor Frankl's autobiographical *Man's Search for Meaning*, trans. Ilse Lasch (Boston: Beacon Press, 1959).

17. Ernst Federn, who had been taken to Dachau just over a week earlier, reported a similar experience. The abuse lasted until the train arrived at the Salzburg station. There a new team of guards took over, and the rest of the trip was relatively peaceful.

18. *Surviving*, 61.

19. Ibid., 63.

20. Ibid., 62.

21. At this stage, the Nazis' desire to appear respectable was not yet pure bluff: when Ernst Federn was freed from Buchenwald, seven years later, his personal effects were returned to him!

22. *Surviving*, 12–13.

23. *The Informed Heart: Autonomy in a Mass Age* (Glencoe, Ill.: Free Press, 1960), 213–14.

24. A whole string of top Austrian civil servants were to die in that way in the quarries at Buchenwald.

25. *The Informed Heart*, 147–48.

26. *Surviving*, 69.

27. Professor Leni Yahil of Haifa University commented that this was a good example of how, in the camps, the ideas and standards accepted by society in the outside world were stood on their heads. According to several witnesses, he said, professors and other intellectuals in Buchenwald worked in the latrines. They could be seen pushing their barrows along, engaged in philosophical discussion. (*The Nazi Concentration Camps*, proceedings of the 4th International Yad Vashem Historical Conference, Jerusalem, 1984).

28. *The Theory and Practice of Hell: The Concentration Camps and the System Behind Them* (New York: Farrar, Straus, 1950). Originally published in German under the title *Der SS-Staat*, the work includes a report that Kogon drew up for the psychological warfare department of the U.S. Army after the liberation of Buchenwald.

29. *Surviving*, 58, n. 7.

30. *The Informed Heart*, 13.

31. Ibid., 114.

32. Ibid., 112.

33. *Surviving*, 51.

34. Ibid., 13.

35. Ibid., 52.

36. Ibid., 13.

37. In fact, he was misinformed: Norbert Bettelheim had filed the required statement on July 16. In addition to Bruno's car and his stake in his own company, the list mentioned two gold watches (estimated at 200 Reichmarks), a silver platter (RM80), and a picture (RM200). In a second inventory, filed in December, the lawyer referred to RM452 owed by Bettelheim as a result of an order made against him by a court in the district of Heitzing, where he lived. I was unable to find out the reason for that. The only other debts Bettelheim had were the sums outstanding on his car (around RM1,500) and on his life insurance policy (RM189). At that time a Reichmark was worth $2.50.

38. It was not always to be thus. In 1942, War Minister Albert Speer ordered that Buchenwald be downgraded from the status of "concentration camp" to that of simple "labor camp." Before that happened, all but 200 of the Jews at Buchenwald had been transferred to other camps, notably to Auschwitz. Those who remained behind were bricklayers,

retained because of their skills. (This is confirmed by Ernst Federn, who certainly owed his life to the fact that he chose early on to specialize in that much-needed craft.) Buchenwald's change in status also followed the departure of its appalling commander Karl Koch, at a time when the Nazi war effort demanded that the maximum use be made of the prisoners' labor power. At the same time, for reasons of efficiency, the SS put "political" rather than "common-law" prisoners in most key posts in the camp. (It was in the contiguous camp of Dora that the V-1 and V-2 flying bombs, which were to cause such havoc in England in the last months of the war, were built, in an underground factory.) As for the living skeletons found by the U.S. troops who entered Buchenwald at the war's end, and whose pictures shocked the world, they were in fact detainees from Auschwitz who had been moved to Buchenwald because of the advance of the Soviet forces in the east. As Federn explains, a special camp had been built for the Auschwitz prisoners inside Buchenwald at the end of 1944.

39. *Witnessing Psychoanalysis,* 4.

40. See Walter Poller, *Medical Block, Buchenwald* (London: Souvenir, 1961). First published in German by Verlag das Segel, Offenbach am Main.

41. See *Against All Hope: Resistance in the Nazi Concentration Camps,* by Hermann Langbein. First published as *Nicht Wie die Shäfe sur Schlachtbank* (Frankfurt: Fischer Taschenbuch Verlag, 1980).

42. See Olga Wormser-Migot, op cit, 483 and passim.

43. As Bettelheim and other writers have noted, the system also fostered the delusion among many inmates, who had not had much direct contact with the SS, that some of their captors actually disapproved of the ill treatment they were suffering.

44. A note dated May 16, 1945, in the unpublished diary kept by Ernest Thape at Buchenwald (Friedrich Ebert Foundation, Bonn), and quoted in Langbein, *Against All Hope.*

45. From the start, the Nazi regime created a special status for those it deported. They were no longer referred to as *Gefangene* (prisoners), but as *Häftlinge* (detainees).

46. Poller, *Medical Block, Buchenwald,* 30.

47. On November 7, 1938, a young Polish Jew in Paris, shattered at receiving news of his family's persecution at the hands of the Nazis, went to the German embassy and shot third secretary Ernst vom Rath. His death in the hospital two days later was the excuse the Nazis had been waiting for to launch a major operation against Germany's Jewish population. On the night of November 9, Nazi gangs in towns and cities across the Reich torched synagogues and wrecked Jewish shops and stores in what became known as *Kristallnacht* (the "night of crystal") because of the huge number of windows that were smashed. The gangs seized some 30,000 Jews, who were held in ordinary prisons for a few days before being dispatched to Dachau, Buchenwald, and Sachsenhausen.

At the time of Poller's arrival, some ten thousand of the Kristallnacht Jews—Poller gives the figure as 12,000, but the exact number was 9,845 according to Rita Thalmann and Emmanuel Feinermann (*La nuit de cristal* [Paris: Robert Laffont], 167)—were crammed into five crudely built wooden blocks in conditions of extreme overcrowding and squalor. These special barracks, which gave onto the vast *Appelplatz*, or parade ground, were separated from the rest of the camp by a ten-foot-high barbed-wire fence. This ensured that everyone else in the camp could observe the suffering of the Kristallnacht Jews without being able to help them.

48. *The Informed Heart*.

49. Koch was recognized even by the Nazis to be particularly venal, and was later sentenced for corruption.

50. *The Informed Heart*, 234.

51. Written for the *New Yorker*, which published it on August 2, 1976. It was reprinted as the title essay of a collection.

52. A large oak on the camp grounds was known among the detainees as "Goethe's tree." The narrator of Alain Resnais's film *Nuit et Brouillard* (*Night and Fog*) even says "they built the camp around it, but they respected the tree." But Olga Wormser-Migot quotes a conversation during which Goethe refers to a *beech* tree on which he and Schiller had carved their names. As for the famous oak, it was destroyed by bombing in 1944.

53. Thalmann and Feinermann, *La nuit de cristal*, 181.

54. *Surviving*, 62. In *The Informed Heart* (chapter 4), Bettelheim gives practically the same account, only this time in the first person.

Chapter 7. Buchenwald: The Price of Freedom

1. Eugen Kogon, in *The Theory and Practice of Hell: The Concentration Camps and the System Behind Them* (New York: Farrar, Straus, 1950), says that three prisoners tried to escape, but both Bettelheim and Hans Bandler mention only two.

2. This is the figure Bettelheim gives in *Surviving*, his last book on the subject. In *The Informed Heart*, however, he put the toll at fifty. Eugen Kogon says the total was over seventy.

3. The song, "*Moorsoldaten*" (Marsh Soldiers), was officially attributed to the *Kapo* who worked in the camp post office, but in fact it had been written by two Austrian Jews. The words were by Löhner-Beda, who had written librettos for Franz Lehar, the music was by the cabaret singer Leopolodi.

4. In "The Dynamism of Anti-Semitism in Gentile and Jew," *Journal of Abnormal and Social Psychology* 42, no. 2 (April 1947). The article appears in an edited version in *The Informed Heart*.

5. "Gestapoman" was the expression Bettelheim used in 1943. However, when he edited the article for inclusion in *The Informed Heart*, he described the guard as an SS soldier.

6. "The Dynamism of Anti-Semitism in Gentile and Jew."

7. See chapter 10.

8. Unless one is to believe that he remained without glasses from June to December 1938, when he finally got permission to ask for a new pair. Given that he required nine-diopter lenses, plus correction for astigmatism, that seems highly unlikely.

9. *The Informed Heart: Autonomy in a Mass Age* (Glencoe, Ill.: Free Press, 1960), 154, fn.

10. *Surviving and Other Essays* (New York: Knopf, 1979), 12, fn.

11. Primo Levi, *The Drowned and the Saved* (London: Michael Joseph, 1988), chap. 3 (Italian title: *I Sommersi e i salvati*).

12. In one of his letters he referred to it as the "Presse."

13. *The Informed Heart*, 193, fn.

14. Bettelheim makes no allusion to the question in his letters to his mother. It is conceivable, however, that he transposed onto the intellectual plane an incident linked to something else, for example his business affairs. He notably expressed great bitterness towards his partner Hans Schnitzer, who had not been arrested, but this is no more than speculation.

15. "Individual and Mass Behavior in Extreme Situations," in *Surviving*, 54.

16. *Surviving*, 56.

17. Letter to Federn, January 8, 1969.

18. *The Informed Heart*, 157.

19. Quoted by Annette Wieviorka in *Déportation et génocide* (Paris: Plon, 1992).

20. It was written for *Midway* on the occasion of the publication of *Death in Life: Survivors of Hiroshima*, by Robert Jay Lifton (New York: Random House, 1967). The essay, considerably edited, forms the opening chapter of *Surviving*.

21. Starting with his very first article on the camps, published in 1943, Bettelheim had used the expression to refer to the train ride to the camp, and the interminable roll call of December 14, 1938, but he had not given a theoretical definition. Even seventeen years later, in *The Informed Heart*, he contented himself with rounding off a catalogue of abuse suffered by inmates with the phrase "All of which may explain why I speak of them as persons finding themselves in an 'extreme' situation." *The Empty Fortress* in 1967 gives this definition: "This, psychologically, is what constitutes an extreme situation: when we ourselves respond to an external danger—real or imagined—with inner maneuvers that actually debilitate us further" (p. 77).

22. "*Mors ultima linea rerum est,*" from the Epistles, I.

23. He was to return to and further develop this idea a few years later in his introduction to *Surviving*. Quotes are taken from the original version of the article.

24. Written eighteen years earlier, about the patients of the Orthogenic School. Federn was in fact to criticize that title in his own book, *Witnessing Psychoanalysis*.

25. By way of illustration, Bettelheim referred in his letter to the "small child, who has as yet no conception of death, is unable to love, though very much in need of it," and for whom "life is so taken for granted that it has no meaning."

26. Bettelheim's relationship to Freudian thought is discussed in chapter 10.

27. This could be compared, in psychoanalytic parlance, to being dominated by the id, Freud's German term having being rendered in English by the Latin word meaning *that*. See chapter 10.

28. *The Informed Heart*, 38.

29. Ibid., 172.

30. Published in Vienna in 1936. First published in English by the Hogarth Press, London, 1937.

31. See "The Ignored Lesson of Anne Frank," in *Surviving*.

32. *The Informed Heart*, 150.

33. Ibid.

34. Quoted by Thalmann and Feinermann in *La nuit de cristal*.

35. *The Informed Heart*, 165, fn.

36. *Surviving*, 15, fn.

37. Ibid., 14, fn.

38. In particular, the correspondence between Agnes Crane and the head of the State Department's visa section, which are still in the official archives.

39. A daylong search through Mrs. Roosevelt's private correspondence at the Franklin D. Roosevelt library in Hyde Park, New York, persuaded me that the rumor is unfounded. Her remarkable action to save Jewish children had not really begun at the time Bettelheim was interned. From various notes she sent, notably to the State Department, it emerges that in fact Mrs. Roosevelt had not yet overcome the somewhat anti-Semitic prejudices of her social background, nor had she fully realized the extent of the persecution to which German and Austrian Jews were being subjected.

40. Archived at Columbia University, New York.

41. It should be noted that Lehmann's archives contain only postwar correspondence with Paul Federn; as Bettelheim was arrested in 1938, his name might have been found in earlier correspondence.

42. *Surviving*, 14.

43. Aboard the SS *Pennland* from the Belgian port of Antwerp, with a U.S. visa obtained in Vienna on August 24, 1939.

Chapter 8. A Short-Lived Reunion

1. The sum printed next to his name on the ship's manifest.

2. From an address by Bettelheim to the San Jose Holocaust Conference, February 1977.

3. Information provided by Edith Buxbaum in 1978 during an interview with Dr. Lawrence H. Schwartz, published by the Seattle Psychoanalytic Institute in 1990.

4. For instance, during his last interview with the French TV documentary maker Daniel Karlin in June 1989.

5. Interviews with the author, December 1990 and May 1993.

Chapter 9. *From Chicago to Rockford, and Back*

1. Interview with the author, July 25, 1991.

2. I was not able to ascertain, for instance, whether Bettelheim had any knowledge of a test carried out by Charlotte Bühler and her team on "Children and Art," an account of which had been published by Amalie Koerperth-Tippel in 1935, a year before Bettelheim enrolled as a PhD student with Karl Bühler. The test, which was used on two hundred children between the ages of three and fourteen, sought to determine at what age art appreciation appears. Like the test Bettelheim designed at Chicago, it used a comparative method in order to prevent the results from being influenced by the child's verbal skills. But unlike Bettelheim's test, it involved already made-up pairs of images, each one consisting of an art reproduction alongside a "kitsch" representation of the same subject.

3. Interview with the author, July 18, 1991.

4. Bettelheim's report on his test was published in *Appraising and Recording Student Progress*, edited by Eugene R. Smith and Ralph W. Tyler (New York: Harper, 1942), 276–312.

5. Letter to Candace Hilldrup, a former Orthogenic School counselor who was in the process of settling in France, April 1975. Subsequent quotes in this paragraph are from the same source.

6. Surprising though it may seem, in his thirty years at the University of Chicago, Bettelheim was never once asked to produce the slightest documentary evidence of his degrees. I received confirmation of this during my first visit to Chicago, at a time when the most extravagant allegations were being made against him. Learning that I had started my research by going to Vienna the previous month, the university's legal counsel could not resist asking me: "And did you see his dissertation?" My answer was clearly a great relief to him.

7. Interviews with Aimee Horton, Bettylou Pingree Rellahan, and Ronnie Dryvage, May–June 1993.

8. *American Journal of Orthopsychiatry*, 1947.

9. Interview with Betty Lou Pingree Rellahan, May 1993.

10. The TAT, devised by C. D. Morgan and H. A. Murray in 1934, in fact consists of forty cards, from which the psychologist selects twenty depending on the sex and age of the subject.

11. See Freud, *The Poet and Daydreaming*, Collected Papers, vol. 4 (London: Hogarth, 1925).

12. Quote provided by Dr. Erwin Angres, December 1990.

13. Interview with the author, May 1993.

14. Interview with the author, May 1993.

15. It is discussed in chapter 10.
16. As shown by the letter of reference Cheek wrote for him in May 1944, when he applied for a job at a small Connecticut college. The tone was much more reserved than that of her letter to Tyler two years earlier.

Chapter 10. A New Man for the New World

1. When Trude applied for U.S. citizenship, Ruth Eissler was one of her two witnesses.
2. This was not technically a lie, since aesthetics is a branch of philosophy, and the department that granted Bettelheim his PhD was called the Department of Philosophy and Psychology.
3. A good example is provided by a series of interviews Bettelheim granted in the fall of 1988 to the psychoanalyst David James Fisher, published in the *Los Angeles Psychoanalytic Bulletin*, Spring 1990. The interviewer, fascinated by the history of psychoanalysis, plied him with questions about the Vienna Psychoanalytic Society. Bettelheim was evasive: "I don't really have any memories of this Society, but rather of those who attended it. Because, you see, I was not yet a member. I was very friendly with Wilhelm Reich, and . . . Fenichel also became a good friend, and others. I got reports of what happened." On his own analytical training, he also stayed as close as he could to the truth without actually demolishing the legend, replying to three separate questions: "I had just started the training analysis before the Nazis marched in." Then: "I was interviewed, *as all candidates at the time were*, by Anna Freud and Paul Federn." Finally he gave in to his interviewer's curiosity, telling him that on one occasion Sigmund Freud had entered the room and said, "A Bettelheim does not need any introduction to me," and adding that one of his uncles had done his military service alongside Freud. While it is true that a certain Joseph Bettelheim was one of Freud's classmates (although it was not possible to ascertain whether he was any relation), the story appears fantastic for several reasons. Bettelheim's uncle Morris, the one who died in a duel, would have been four years younger than Freud, and he was the eldest of his uncles. And according to Gina Weinmann, Bettelheim had not met Paul Federn in Vienna. Lastly, by well before 1938, the meetings of the Psychoanalytic Society were no longer being held at the Freuds' house.
4. Cohler, a former student of the Orthogenic School, was in 1971 to take over from Bettelheim as its director for a year. See chapter 16.
5. Interview with the author, December 4, 1990.
6. In a tape cassette on which he recorded some recollections for his children.
7. In the French weekly *L'Evénement du Jeudi*, October 28, 1993.
8. Interview with David James Fisher. This is also confirmed by recent research—for example, in *The International Handbook of Traumatic Stress Syndrome* (New York: Plenum, 1993), a collective work pro-

duced under the direction of J. P. Wilson and B. Raphael. An Israeli study published in this work reveals that 80 percent of concentration camp survivors suffer from "repetitive nightmares." The psychiatrist Marc-Antoine Crocq, who writes in the same work, told me: "This post-traumatic symptom never completely disappears, and has a tendency to get worse at the time of retirement. The subject never gets used to it, and his average anxiety level remains considerably higher than that found in the population as a whole. For these subjects, everything in their daily life can generate anxiety or feelings of persecution. Which explains, for example, the rather paranoid attitude of someone like Solzhenitsyn toward the media."

9. He probably did not get official confirmation of this immediately, but all the news he received from Vienna at the time pointed to it.

10. Letter to Candace Hilldrup, February 19, 1975.

11. George Sheviakov, who was well versed in psychoanalysis, outlines the problems he had with his Freudian friends on that issue when he was working on the Eight-Year Study in recollections he tape-recorded for his children.

12. Revealing from this point of view is an exchange of letters between Franz Alexander, founder of the Chicago Psychoanalytic Institute, and Karl Menninger, one of his former patients. (Menninger ran a clinic for disturbed children in Topeka, Kansas, which for a long time was the only institution in the United States that could be compared with the Orthogenic School, even though it was run on different lines.) See *The Selected Correspondence of Karl A. Menninger* (New Haven, Conn.: Yale University Press, 1988).

13. A story he tells in "A Jury Trial of Psychoanalysis," *Journal of Abnormal and Social Psychology*, 1940.

14. The twenty-four letters from Freud to Alexander are in the possession of Dr. George Pollack, a former director of the Chicago Psychoanalytic Institute who is currently writing Alexander's biography.

15. During a symposium on lay analysis held as a prelude to the Innsbruck International Psychoanalytic Congress. The resulting texts were published in the same year, appearing simultaneously in German (in *Internationale Zeitschrift*) and in English (in the *International Journal of Psycho-Analysis*).

16. And also that between the patient and psychoanalysis itself.

17. *Freud et l'âme humaine* (Paris: Robert Laffont, 1984).

18. "Analysis, Terminable and Interminable," Standard Edition, vol. 23, (London: Hogarth, 1937), 229.

19. Daniel Karlin, interview with Bettelheim recorded in June 1989.

20. Notably in his letter to Pastor Oskar Pfister on November 25, 1928.

21. According to the French historian and psychoanalyst Elisabeth Roudinesco (*Lacan and Others* [Chicago: University of Chicago Press, 1990]), two basic conditions are required for psychoanalysis to durably take root in a country: democracy and the existence of a structured

psychiatric (medical) system. She explains the medicalization of psychoanalysis in the United States by the nonfulfillment of the second condition when the first European analysts arrived in the country. Psychoanalysis offered psychiatry a model of the human psyche which it lacked. In other countries, psychiatry had contented itself with integrating the model into its teaching. But in the United States it also in effect incorporated the practitioners. This is why American psychoanalysts are often referred to as psychiatrists, and why those who were not also medical doctors had to be called psychologists, until 1993, when a Supreme Court anti-monopoly ruling stated that non-MD's also had a right to the title of analyst.

22. Letter to Theodor Reik, July 3, 1938, quoted in Gay, *Freud: A Life for Our Time* (New York: Norton, 1988), 633.

23. "Autobiographical Study," Standard Edition, vol. 20, p. 52.

24. Paul Roazen, *Freud and His Followers* (New York: New York University Press, 1984), 5.

25. "Autobiographical Study."

26. In particular, his contribution to *Das Psychanalytische Volksbuch* in 1926 and "The Ego Feeling in Dreams," 1932.

27. The latter film came out only a few weeks before Bettelheim's death. One can only wonder whether he saw it.

28. This was an attempt to bring together psychoanalysis and anthropology by questioning the universal nature of the Oedipus complex. Born from the interest shown in Freud's ideas by certain anthropologists (notably Bronislaw Malinowski, Ruth Benedict, Abram Kardiner, and Margaret Mead), it was to attract a number of dissident Freudians, such as Erich Fromm and Karen Horney.

29. Notably in his book *Essays in Ego Psychology* (New York: International Universities Press, 1964).

30. *Freud and Man's Soul* (New York: Knopf, 1982), 5.

31. Ibid., 7.

32. Bettelheim notes that the French translations of Freud's key terms are much more faithful to the original. *Das Ich* is rendered as *le moi* (the me), *das Es* as *le ça* (the it), and *das Über-Ich* as *le surmoi* (the above-I).

33. I heard such replies in particular from members of the Chicago Psychoanalytic Institute, but also from a few Europeans.

34. On Freud's relations with the United States, see Gay, *Freud* which includes a good bibliography on the question; Roazen, *Freud and His Followers*, and Roudinesco, *Lacan and Others*. For a French view of the debate over lay analysis, see Michael Schneider's commentary in *La question de l'analyse profane* (Paris: Gallimard, 1985), a collection of Freud's writings on the subject of lay analysis.

35. Letter to Arnold Zweig, March 5, 1939.

36. Letter to Carl Frankenstein, August 10, 1981. His exact words were: "I (have) finally finished my long essay on the translations of Freud into English in which I make him sound better than he deserves as a

person. But what a mind! What insights into the foibles of man! and how unable, despite of it, to do something about the obvious limitations of his own personality and his inability to really deal respectfully with his followers, not to speak of his enemies . . . Well, I guess the limitations of a true genius, and one's mentor, are hard to accept."

37. In Vienna, Bettelheim explained, patients ending their analyses were asked to wait around two years before applying to become analysts themselves, so as to be sure that their calling was not simply an effect of the transference (interview with David James Fisher).

38. This has recently been the subject of many symposiums, notably in Israel. Most psychoanalysts who were in the camps thought for a time that they could separate that experience from their professional activities. In France the German-born analyst Anne-Lise Stern, who was a patient of Jacques Lacan after her release from Auschwitz, was the first to show that this was impossible. But that was not before 1968, when, having worked with many drug addicts and otherwise troubled young people, she discovered how traces of the Holocaust remained present—and deadly—in the unconscious of patients who had not even been direct victims.

39. Letter to ER, July 1980.

40. The remark figures in all the different versions of his study on the camps, including his testimony to the Nuremberg Tribunal.

41. *The Informed Heart: Autonomy in a Mass Age* (Glencoe, Ill.: Free Press, 1960), 12.

42. "Nazi Conspiracy and Aggression," U.S. Government Printing Office, Washington, D.C., 1946. Vol VII (818–39).

43. Furthermore, *The Informed Heart*, when it was published in 1960, was still the first psychological analysis of the camps to appear outside specialist publications, aimed at the general public. This is noted by Paul Marcus and Alan Rosenberg in "Reevaluating Bruno Bettelheim's Work on Nazi Concentration Camps: The Limits of His Psychoanalytic Approach," in a special issue of the *Psychoanalytic Review* titled "Bruno Bettelheim's Contribution to Psychoanalysis," Fall 1994.

44. See, for example, the remarkable *Mémoire et personne* by Georges Gusdorf (Paris: Presses Universitaires de France, 1950).

45. *Surviving and Other Essays* (New York: Knopf, 1979), 54.

46. According to Bettelheim's editor, Ruth Marquis, who saw the manuscript when the two of them were working on *The Informed Heart*.

47. "The Ultimate Limit," *Surviving*, 14–15.

48. *Mortal Storm* was not in fact banned. Although it was a failure, its U.S. release provided Goebbels with an excuse to ban all MGM films from Germany.

49. *Surviving*, 16.

50. Readers who find this difficult to believe should bear in mind that up until the start of World War II, the Nazis were very careful to create

a facade of legality to cover up their actions. As Bettelheim points out, they even tried to maintain this fiction inside the concentration camps. Although guards had the right to shoot prisoners, for example, they were officially forbidden to steal from them. In practice, they used blackmail to get the detainees to "give" them whatever they coveted.

51. In the report on Buchenwald he drew up in April 1945 for the Psychological Warfare Division of the U.S. Army, the Austrian journalist Eugen Kogon, for example, describes three phases in the creation of the "hardened" camp inmate: the shock of internment, the selection process of the initial months, and the phase of adaptation. The latter could stretch over years. And, indeed, Kogon's report, which was written six years after Bettelheim's and, enlarged, was later published in English as *The Theory and Practice of Hell: The Concentration Camps and the System Behind Them* (New York: Farrar, Strauss, 1950), only confirms how remarkably insightful Bettelheim's observations had been.

52. George Clare, *Last Waltz in Vienna: The Destruction of a Family 1842–1942,* (London: Macmillan, 1981).

53. To Alvin Rosenfeld, who quotes it in *The Art of the Obvious*, the book he co-authored with Bettelheim.

54. *Surviving*, 16.

55. As is shown by his correspondence, for example, in a letter he wrote on February 19, 1975, to a friend in Paris. She had sent him a large number of press cuttings on the controversy sparked in France by the broadcasting of Daniel Karlin's films. He replied: "All my life, since I began working, I have been accused of much worse things—when I spoke and wrote about the concentration camp at a time when nobody wanted to know about it, I was called psychotic, paranoiac, suffering from persecution neurosis . . . I never defended myself, and five years later Eisenhower ordered all occupation officers to read the paper which had been declared a bunch of psychotic ravings. This was my first big lesson."

56. A few days before the U.S. Army's fourth armored division entered the main Buchenwald camp, on April 12, 1945, the troops stumbled almost by accident on one of its annexes, the small camp of Ohrdruf. There, the SS troops had shot all the detainees before fleeing. The first pictures of Buchenwald to reach the outside world thus showed piles of dead bodies. See Robert H. Abzug, *Inside the Vicious Heart* (New York: Oxford University Press, 1985).

57. As soon as he was freed, Federn also published an analysis of Buchenwald. This appeared first in Belgium, where Federn was then living, as *"Essai sur la psychologie de la terreur"* in *Synthèses* (vol. 7 and 8, Brussels, 1946). It was published in the United States as "Terror as a System: The Concentration Camp" in *Psychiatric Supplement*, Utica, N.Y., 1948.

58. *A Home for the Heart* (New York: Knopf, 1974), 284.
59. New York: Norton, 1942.
60. At the time, Karen Horney had just left the New York Psychoanalytic Society to set up a breakaway group, which diverged from unorthodox Freudianism on several questions, notably the concept of "penis envy" (the repressed wish of a female to possess a penis). Bettelheim's friend Wanda Willig had in fact joined Horney's group.
61. *New York Times Book Review*, October 8, 1961.

Chapter 11. Orthogenic School: The Magical Years

1. In the preface he wrote for the published transcript of Daniel Karlin's film, Bettelheim stated, "No one at the School refers to the children as 'patients.'" He nevertheless does use the term from time to time in *A Home for the Heart*, his last book on the Orthogenic School, written after he had left it.
2. He says so in *The Art of the Obvious*.
3. Whenever I have had to use a pseudonym for a child in the following chapters, this is indicated by quotation marks around the first use of the name.
4. "On the whole, I have felt convinced of the validity of case histories and their authors' conclusions only where so many potentially verifiable data were presented that the individual came alive in my imagination as a three-dimensional person, moving in time and space. In these rare instances I felt that I knew much more than was actually stated," he wrote in *Truants from Life* (New York: The Free Press, 1955), 4.
5. "A Psychiatric School," *Quarterly Journal of Child Behavior*, January 1949, reprinted as part of *Love Is Not Enough*.
6. *Love Is Not Enough*, 35, fn.
7. August Aichhorn, *Wayward Youth* (New York: Viking Press, 1935).
8. "Milieu Therapy: Indications and Illustrations," *Psychoanalytic Review*, January 1949.
9. Interview with the author, May 1993.
10. Several psychoanalysts, notably Paul Federn, had undertaken to cure psychotics, but the treatment had been individual and non-residential. As for the homes for children opened by Anna Freud in England during World War II, while they were of course based on psychoanalytic thinking, they recruited their pupils on the basis not of psychological problems but of separation from their parents by the war.
11. At a meeting August 11, 1944, the Department of Pediatrics had stressed: "The proper function of the OS is to provide resident facilities for adequate treatment of severe behavior problems in children of normal intelligence; and to afford opportunity for the instruction of medical students, social workers, interns, nurses, teachers and play therapists in the care and handling of such children."

12. In May 1986, on the occasion of a conference organized in Bettelheim's honor by the University of Chicago.

13. Interview with the author, May 1993.

14. A pathology identified in 1945 by René Spitz in children who had grown up in institutions and had been deprived of any long-term emotional attachment.

15. Bettelheim, *Truants from Life*, 475.

16. See Bettelheim and Alvin Rosenfeld, *The Art of the Obvious*.

17. A rumor that proved impossible to verify since by the time I started work on this book, Emmy Sylvester had already been diagnosed as having Alzheimer's disease.

18. In the *American Journal of Orthopsychiatry:* "Therapeutic Influence of the Group on the Individual" (October 1947), "A Therapeutic Milieu" (April 1948), and "Notes on the Impact of Parental Occupations" (October 1950). In *Psychoanalytic Study of the Child* (International Universities Press): "Physical Symptoms in Emotionally Disturbed Children" (1949) and "Delinquency and Morality" (1950). And the seminal text on their technique, "Milieu Therapy: Indications and Illustrations," published in the *Psychoanalytic Review* (January 1949).

19. As Patty Pickett McKnight points out, the testimony of Emmy Sylvester's former patients on this issue is less reliable than that of the former counselors; for a young boy with problems it is much more frightening to feel one's inner anxieties or obsessions being probed and revealed by a woman than by a man.

20. Interview with the author, May 1993.

21. Ibid.

22. "Types of Institutional Structure," *Psychiatry* 20 (1957).

23. In 1950, the average yearly salary for workers was $2,800 and for a family of four, $4,230. In 1970, the figures were: $6,400 (workers) and $8,000 (family), according to official statistics. It should be noted that, over the years, the Orthogenic School's counselors' salaries had fallen in real terms.

24. Interview with the author, November 1990.

25. B. Bettelheim and B. Wright, "Staff Development in a Treatment Institution," *American Journal of Orthopsychiatry*, October 1955.

26. Ibid.

27. Karen Zelan points out that, a few years later, Bettelheim's requirements had changed a little: "The facts, he said, have to be sifted through a mind. And that's what's of interest to me."

28. Florence White was a highly regarded social worker with psychiatric training who was a friend of Trude Bettelheim and joined the Orthogenic School in the early days. Bettelheim was very dependent on her. She saw several children in therapy and, unlike the counselors, had some contact with the students' parents.

29. Candace Hilldrup, unpublished memoirs, Paris, 1975. For more on Candy's story at the school, see chapter 16.

30. Interview with the author, May 1993.

31. Some are stored in the Bettelheim collection at the University of Chicago's Regenstein Library. Others are in the care of Dr. Oliver Kerner, the Chicago psychoanalyst who initiated those seminars.

32. Interestingly enough, Bettelheim's son Eric is a lawyer.

33. *Dialogues with Mothers* (Free Press, 1962), 4.

34. In his book *Un autre regard sur la folie* (Paris: Stock, 1975), Daniel Karlin says that the sequence was actually shot on the morning of Bettelheim's last day with the children at the school, before leaving for California and retirement.

35. Interview with the author, May 1993.

36. Letter to Carl Frankenstein, November 19, 1986.

37. *Dialogues with Mothers*, 201, in a chapter titled "Tyrannizing."

38. "Dynamics of Prejudice: A Psychological and Sociological Study of Veterans." See chapter 12 for more on this.

Chapter 12. Dr. B the Enchanter

1. The trend was not confined to right-wing circles. Trotskyite groups in the United States at this time took to referring to their pro-Soviet opponents not as Stalinists but as Stalinoids, basing their jargon on the psychological terminology then in fashion.

2. See Russell Jacoby, *The Repression of Psychoanalysis: Otto Fenichel and the Political Freudians* (Chicago: University of Chicago Press, 1986).

3. Letter to Ernst Federn, September 9, 1945.

4. Interview, July 1991.

5. In 1948, for example, the director's salary came to $4,533 a year. The university was also paying Bettelheim $1,967 for his teaching (for equivalents in today's dollars, see 559, n. 23).

6. The Regensteins themselves, who financed the building of the library, were among the donors to the Orthogenic School.

7. Original title *L'Amour en plus*.

8. December 16, 1981.

9. Letter to Madeleine Chapsal, January 19, 1982.

10. One might, however, question the judiciousness of an explanation that could be seen as encouraging racist attitudes. The reason the neighborhood was changing was that black families were moving into it and white ones leaving.

11. Bettelheim himself tells of such an incident in *Truants from Life*.

12. Jacquelyn Sanders, *A Greenhouse for the Mind* (Chicago: University of Chicago Press, 1989).

13. Interview with the author, May 1993. Once a child overcomes the problems that led to his disturbed behavior, it is normal for him to forget about them.

14. *Children Who Hate: The Disorganization and Breakdown of Behavior Controls*, with David Wineman (Glencoe, Ill.: Free Press, 1951) and

especially *Controls from Within: Techniques for the Treatment of the Aggressive Child* (Glencoe, Ill.: Free Press, 1952).

15. For his other books with Kaplan, Bettelheim followed the same method of only signing a contract when he handed in the manuscript, without any prior agreement.

16. This is especially true of the books comprising case studies: *Truants from Life* and *The Empty Fortress*.

17. A journal founded by Gerard Piel, the nephew of Agnes Piel Crane.

18. The best-known result of which was to be *The Authoritarian Personality* by David Riesman, a friend of Bettelheim's.

19. In their acknowledgements, the authors cite, in addition to Edward Shils, the philosopher and musicologist Theodor Adorno, one of Horkheimer's companions in the Frankfurt School, as having helped them draw up their research plan.

20. His best-known work is *The Professional Soldier*, published in 1960. In addition to numerous treatises, he also produced *Social Change and the Welfare State* (1976), *The Last Half-Century* (1978), and *The Reconstruction of Patriotism* (1983).

21. *Mobility, Subjective Deprivation and Ethnic Hostility* by M. Janowitz, University of Chicago, 1948.

22. From an article by Karen Zelan, published in *Prospects*, Geneva 1993, Vol. 23, no. 1/2.

23. According to Maria Piers, who worked closely with Erikson, he never forgave Bettelheim for the way he had snubbed him in Vienna.

24. "Harry: A Study in Rehabilitation," *Journal of Abnormal and Social Psychology*, April 1949.

25. O. F. Raum, *Chaga Childhood* (London: Oxford University Press, 1940).

26. Bettelheim makes little mention in the main body of his text of circumcision practiced at birth, simply noting that it probably has the same function as that carried out at puberty, since it is in general at the latter stage that boys truly become aware of it. He returns to the question in an appendix to stress that Judaism, as the first monotheistic religion, was the most phallic and the one in which the superego had most completely overruled the id. He concluded that Jewish circumcision, probably inherited from earlier, pagan practices, reflected a greater level of symbolization of the initiation process, with a desire on the part of the men in the tribe to eliminate women from it altogether.

27. *Symbolic Wounds: Puberty Rites and the Envious Male* (New York: Free Press, 1954), 56.

28. It is worth noting that Erik Erikson, as his biographer Paul Roazen points out, also took great care to link his own ideas to Freudian thinking, even when they were in fact far removed from the latter. Bettelheim and Erikson had several things in common, and the relationship between them, based on strong rivalry and a measure of mutual contempt, was abysmal.

29. Readers of the French version (*Les blessures symboliques* [Paris: Gallimard, 1971]) did not have to look far to find the criticism, since the editor of the series in which it appeared decided to include, at the end of Bettelheim's text, a discussion of it by the psychoanalyst André Green and the anthropologist Jean Pouillon. As his private correspondence shows, Bettelheim was furious at this move, which the editor, Jean-Bertrand Pontalis, made without even informing him. He never raised the issue with the French publisher, however, being convinced that any complaint would have no effect (letter to Candace Hilldrup, February 19, 1975).

30. Ruth Marquis, who had by then left Chicago, had not taken part in the final revisions of the first edition of *Symbolic Wounds*, with the result that its tone was much more academic than that of Bettelheim's other books. She resumed her activities as editor in time to supervise the second edition, however.

31. Jean Pouillon, in his appendix to the French edition, described Bettelheim's statement as "ambiguous," noting that "primitive societies, just like our own, contain children, schizophrenics, and adults, and they should not be confused with one another."

32. *Symbolic Wounds*, chapter titled "The Biological Antitheses," 150, 151.

33. And, indeed, not all anorexics reach the state of near starvation that people usually associate with the condition. As a teacher at the Orthogenic School, Adrian was later to display great intuition with her anorexic students.

34. Interview with the author, May 1993.

35. Interview with the author, May 1993.

36. Gayle Janowitz remembers, for example, one deeply disturbed mother who sent her son pornographic pictures of herself and accused Dr. B of wanting to kidnap him. In order to stop her from coming and disturbing the boy on Christmas Eve, the school's social worker had on several successive years spent the holiday with her!

37. Some critics, notably Gina Weinmann, have attacked Bettelheim for the catchy titles he used, considering that such a desire to attract casual readers was unworthy of a serious work.

Chapter 13. The Ultimate Limit

1. Letter to ER, September 10, 1954.

2. Quote provided by Tom Lyons, among others.

3. Letter to Ruth Marquis, March 1973.

4. As Ruth Bettelheim replied with total silence to all my requests, both written by me and passed on by other people, for interviews, all the information I possess about her comes from third parties.

5. Bettelheim's comments to this effect were reported by several people. Their testimony is backed up by his correspondence and interviews he gave at the end of his life.

6. Naomi Bettelheim, who was much too young to remember the incident, later heard a different version of the story, which Bettelheim told to at least two people.

7. *Commentary*, September 1951.

8. From an address delivered at North Shore Hospital on February 14, 1951.

9. "A Home Is to Be Human," written in March 1974, Bettelheim collection, Regenstein Library, University of Chicago.

10. Letter to Ruth Marquis, September 30, 1973.

11. Although I was able to meet only Naomi and Eric, I have little doubt that this is also true of Ruth.

12. "The Helpless and the Guilty," *Common Sense*, July 14, 1945. It should be noted that these visits, initially arranged for the benefit of journalists and U.S. politicians, soon became particularly unpleasant, in spite of the well-meaning ideas behind them.

13. "War Trials and German Re-education," *Politics*, December 2, 1945.

14. "The Dynamism of Anti-Semitism in Gentile and Jew," *Journal of Abnormal and Social Psychology*, April 1947, vol. 42, and "The Victim's Image of the Anti-Semite," *Commentary*, February 1948. See chapter 7.

15. "Exodus, 1947," *Politics*, Winter 1948. The emphasis is Bettelheim's.

16. "Individual and Mass Behavior in Extreme Situations," *Surviving and Other Essays* (New York: Knopf, 1979), 48.

17. "The Concentration Camp as a Class State," *Modern Review*, October 1947.

18. "Schizophrenia as a Reaction to Extreme Situations," *American Journal of Orthopsychiatry*, July 1956. Also included in both *The Informed Heart* and *Surviving*.

19. "German Schools Revisited," *Elementary School Journal*, November 1955.

20. "Returning to Dachau," *Commentary*, February 1956, and later included in *Freud's Vienna and Other Essays*.

21. Bettelheim had filed his first application on August 30, 1954, just ten days after the deadline.

22. In spite of the existence of at least two letters from the bank testifying that the money paid by the Nazi buyer had been confiscated.

23. As noted by Paul Marcus and Alan Rosenberg in "Reevaluating Bruno Bettelheim's Work on the Concentration Camps: The Limits of His Psychoanalytic Approach," *Psychoanalytic Review*, Fall 1994.

24. In his article, which is not aimed at a specialist audience, Bettelheim defines the ego as "the conscious, rational aspects of the personality . . . which mediates between the demands of the instincts, the superego and reality," the superego being seen as the subject's conscience and ideals, and the id as his instincts (or drives, as Bettelheim would later call them).

25. "Individual Autonomy and Mass Control," published in 1955 as part of a special edition of the Frankfurt Institute's review *Sociologica* marking the sixtieth birthday of Max Horkheimer. Among the many bylines

included besides Bettelheim's were those of Theodor Adorno, Raymond Aron, Walter Benjamin, Franco Lombardi, and Herbert Marcuse. The quotes in this and the following two paragraphs are from this source.

26. Miklos Nyiszli, *Auschwitz: A Doctor's Eyewitness Account*, trans. Tibère Kremer and Richard Seaver (New York: Frederick Fell, 1960).

27. *Harper's*, November 1960. Parts of the article were already in *The Informed Heart*, published the same year. The whole article was also to be included, with minor changes, in *Surviving*.

28. Bettelheim was the first one to use the expression "business as usual" in this context. It was subsequently to be widely employed in other works on the Holocaust.

29. *Midstream*, March 1962. Reprinted, with minor alterations, in *Freud's Vienna*.

30. "Eichmann: The System, the Victims," *New Republic*, June 15, 1963. Reprinted in shortened form, with some changes, in *Surviving*. The quotations in the following paragraphs are all from *Surviving*.

31. *Jewish Resistance* (New York: Waldon Press, 1964).

32. Ibid.

33. Phone interview with Nell Pekarsky, May 1993.

34. *The Informed Heart: Autonomy in a Mass Age* (Glencoe, Ill.: Free Press, 1960), 109, fn.

35. D. Karlin, "Dernier entretien avec Bruno Bettelheim" (last interview with Bruno Bettelheim, broadcast in France after the latter's death).

36. *Treblinka* (New York: Simon & Schuster, 1967). First published in French by Librairie Arthème Fayard, Paris, 1966. Reviewed by Bettelheim in *New Republic*, July 1, 1967, in an article titled "Survival of the Jews." The quotations in the following paragraphs are all drawn from that source.

37. Writing in similar vein twelve years later, Bettelheim was to amend his article on "ghetto thinking" for *Freud's Vienna* by including excerpts from this one.

38. *The Informed Heart*.

39. In particular, in *The Drowned and the Saved*, trans. Raymond Rosenthal (London: Michael Joseph, 1988).

40. "Trauma and Reintegration," *Surviving*.

41. *Encounter*, December 1978. Reprinted in revised form as "The Holocaust—One Generation Later" in *Surviving*.

42. "The Ultimate Limit," *Midway*, Fall 1968.

43. Terrence Des Pres, *The Survivor: An Anatomy of Life in the Death Camps* (New York: Oxford University Press, 1976). A few months after the publication of "Surviving" in the *New Yorker*, August 2, 1976, Des Pres hit back with a long article detailing Bettelheim's violations of accepted academic practices, "The Bettelheim Problem," *Social Research*, Winter 1979.

44. Notably Marcus and Rosenberg, "Reevaluating Bruno Bettelheim's Work on Nazi Concentration Camps."

45. Des Pres, *The Survivor.*
46. Ibid., 157.
47. Terrence Des Pres died suddenly in 1987.
48. Letter to Carl Frankenstein, March 13, 1976.
49. See, for example, Paul Roazen, "The Rise and Fall of Bruno Bettelheim," *Psychohistory Review*, Spring 1992.
50. Letter to Carl Frankenstein, November 20, 1978.
51. Des Pres, *The Survivor.*
52. In "How to Arm Our Children Against Anti-Semitism," Bettelheim stresses the feeling of insecurity sparked in a child when some racist remark gives him the impression that his parents, even more than himself, are not "good enough."
53. "The Ultimate Limit," *Midway*, Autumn 1968.
54. Letter to James Farrel, June 7, 1973.
55. *Surviving*, 103.
56. Ibid., 98–99, from Paul Celan, *Speech Grille and Selected Poems* (New York: Dutton, 1971), trans. Joachim Neugroschel; Bettelheim, however, specifies that the final two lines were retranslated by him.
57. *Surviving*, 103.
58. *Freud's Vienna*, 213.
59. *Surviving*, 20.
60. It is worth noting in passing that in the course of his long and painful self-analysis, Bettelheim had little by little moved away from the triumphalist assertions of ego psychology to rediscover the importance of the drives, or instincts. Indeed, his next book after *Surviving* (with the exception of a work on teaching children to read, which he had been engaged in on and off for a decade, and which he was to co-author in 1981 with Karen Zelan) was to be *Freud and Man's Soul.*
61. " 'Owners of Their Faces,' " in *Surviving*, 110–11. Celan poem, op. cit.
62. By Claudine Vegh. Paris: Gallimard, 1980. Published in the United States as *I Didn't Say Goodbye*, trans. Ros Schwartz (New York: Dutton, 1984).
63. "Children of the Holocaust," in *Freud's Vienna.*
64. Letter to Madeleine Chapsal, October 12, 1979.

Chapter 14. The Big Bad Wolf

1. "Joey: A Mechanical Boy," *Scientific American*, March 5, 1959.
2. Telephone conversation on August 7, 1994.
3. In a report to the Wiebold Foundation, which five years earlier had allocated him a grant to study childhood schizophrenia.
4. Bettelheim himself edited the film, shot by Charles Sharp, and used it to illustrate his method with autistic children. He showed it notably to Anna Freud in London. In 1973, he allowed Daniel Karlin to use it in his documentary on the Orthogenic School.
5. Conversation quoted in Bettelheim and Alvin Rosenfeld, *The Art of the Obvious* (New York: Knopf, 1993), 120.

6. B. Bettelheim and D. Karlin, *Un autre regard sur la folie* (Paris: Stock, 1975).

7. Today, the clinical term *schizophrenic* is no longer used before adolescence. These definitions still vary from country to country. For instance, the term *schizophrenia* as used in the United States refers to a much wider range of symptoms than it does in France.

8. The term itself had been coined in 1911 by the Swiss psychiatrist Bleuler to describe adults in *Dementia Praecox or the Group of Schizophrenias* (New York: International University Press, 1950 [reprint]). In a letter to Freud in 1906, Carl Jung, who worked under Bleuler, explained it as a contraction of *auto-eroticism*. Kanner gave *autism* its modern definition in "Autistic Disturbances of Affective Contact," *Nervous Child*, 1943.

9. Mahler, address given at the Amsterdam Congress in 1951, and published as "On Child Psychosis and Schizophrenia: Autistic and Symbiotic Infantile Psychoses," *Psychoanalytic Study of the Child* 7 (1952).

10. Having identified "emotional growth and mental health" as key research themes, the Ford Foundation decided in 1955 to provide $15 million over five years to a Program of Support for Research in Mental Health covering fifteen projects centered on those issues. Three of the grants were assigned to research on "children's disorders," and the applicants were numerous and, in many cases, famous. In addition to Bettelheim, they included Anna Freud and Dorothy Burlingham's Hampstead Child Guidance Clinic in London, plus most of the Americans then working on childhood schizophrenia, notably Bender, Gardner, Rabinovitch, Rank, Loomis, the Menninger Clinic, and even Dr. Spock.

11. Several authors have, for that very reason, paid homage to Bettelheim for the title of his book. "What a good image that is, the 'empty fortress,'" enthuses French psychoanalyst Denys Ribas in *Un cri obscur* (An Obscure Scream), (Paris: Calmann Lévy, 1992). "It warns us not to expect to find treasures hidden behind the autistic barrier! Only mutual exchanges are enriching."

12. *The Art of the Obvious*, 119.

13. Ibid.

14. Letter to Candace Hilldrup, September 17, 1980.

15. Bettelheim was to use her case to illustrate his conviction that so-called feral children were probably autistic children who had been abandoned or lost for a period by their parents. When they were discovered, their behavior was so disturbing that it was easier for people to believe they had been brought up by animals. His article, published in March 1959 in the *American Journal of Psychology*, elicited an enthusiastic reaction from the anthropologist Margaret Mead (July 1959).

16. *The Empty Fortress: Infantile Autism and the Birth of the Self* (New York: Free Press, 1967), 7.

17. Ibid.

18. Ibid., 77.
19. Ibid., 73.
20. The text of his address was published as "Schizophrenia as a Reaction to Extreme Situations," *American Journal of Orthopsychiatry*, July 1956.
21. See chapter 12.
22. "Punishment versus Discipline," *Atlantic Monthly*, November 1985.
23. "Obsolete Youth," *Encounter*, September 3, 1969.
24. *Truants from Life: The Rehabilitation of Emotionally Disturbed Children* (New York: Free Press), 2.
25. On overhearing a new child say to another: "Come, let's kill Johnny," Bettelheim had laid down the school's ground rules as follows: "You're not here to kill Johnny or anybody else. Kids come here to be safe, not to be threatened. Nobody lays a hand on anybody in the school, except me." The last sentence was backed up with a slap.
26. This was during our first interview, in the fall of 1990. Later, he was less categorical: "There were, I believe, one or two times when I was not hit for over a year—certainly not the last two and a half years at the school," he wrote me in 1995.
27. For obvious reasons, specific details of the case histories or the pathologies of former Orthogenic School students cannot be revealed. A sketchy description of events will have to suffice.
28. Freud is very clear on that point. "In our unconscious we are today still a band of murderers. In our silent thoughts, we eliminate all those who stand in our way, those who have insulted or harmed us, every day and at each moment. The 'To the devil with him' that so often crosses the threshold of our lips like a weakened interjection, and which in reality means 'To death with him,' is for our unconscious something totally serious. It is really lucky that all of these ill wishes have no power whatsoever. Humanity would have disappeared long ago, the best and the wisest of men, the most beautiful and sweetest of women, would no longer exist." (S. Freud, "Death and Ourselves," a little-known speech made to the Vienna branch of B'nai Brith on February 16, 1915.)
29. *The Empty Fortress*, 71.
30. Ibid., 69.
31. Tom Wallace Lyons, *The Pelican and After: A Novel About Emotional Disturbance* (Richmond, Va.: Prescott, Durrell, 1983), 24.
32. Ibid., 24.
33. Each dormitory at the school had its own name, chosen by the children themselves.
34. The fax is dated September 14, 1994, and the phone conversation was a few weeks before that.
35. When this happened, between 1970 and 1972, Bettelheim's friend and first publisher, Jeremiah Kaplan, had become the head of Macmillan, after the big publishing group had bought out the Free Press. Lyons's manuscript had been accepted and was in the hands of Robert Markel,

editor-in-chief, when Kaplan learned of its existence. He demanded that the author obtain written permission from Bettelheim as a precondition to publishing it.

From what Kaplan himself told me in 1993, he had not read the novel when he gave that order, but he had been told that it slandered his friend. Whatever the case, a period of around three months elapsed between the time Bettelheim first heard of the novel and the time he actually got a copy of the manuscript. During that period, at Macmillan's request, Lyons called him. "I was eager to talk to BB. I actually believed the book would be a source of satisfaction to him." But Bettelheim was not at all pleased. "I don't appreciate that you want to libel me," he said, adding that it was a "very poor reward" for having rescued Lyons. Following this conversation, Augusta Wallace Lyons, Tom's mother, who had always been on friendly terms with Bettelheim and was one of the school's benefactors, intervened on her son's behalf. In the course of a lengthy phone discussion, Bettelheim told her that he would sign the required authorization on condition that Tom dedicate the book to him and add an introduction making clear what state he was in when he entered the Orthogenic School. There followed a series of phone calls and letters, amid mounting tension, all before Bettelheim had even set eyes on the manuscript. During that period, a young teacher, Nina Helstein, happened to be in Bettelheim's office when he took a call, during which he said in an irritated voice: "Publish it if you want. But remember it is based on the recollections of a psychotic child."

As soon as he had actually read the manuscript, in April 1971, Bettelheim wrote directly to Tom Lyons and congratulated him. He repeated that he had no intention of opposing the book's publication and once again raised the idea of a dedication and an introduction. On the same day, he wrote to Mrs. Lyons to say that, having realized to what extent his own relationship with Tom was at the heart of the book (something he had not understood until then, he stressed), he preferred from then on to discuss it only with the young man himself. In passing, he remarked that he felt Tom's portrayal of both himself and the school was unfair. He seemed very irritated at the mounting suspicions of him and stressed that Mrs. Lyons was in possession of several letters in which he had promised not to oppose publication of the book.

A week later, however, Tom Lyons was informed that Macmillan had rejected his manuscript without any real explanation. In subsequent correspondence with both Tom and his mother, Bettelheim expressed regret, but refused to intervene: For personal reasons, he had decided to change publishers, he explained, but he had refrained from telling Kaplan this as long as Tom's manuscript was still under discussion.

In June 1971 he finally signed the required authorization after Tom Lyons showed him a (somewhat exaggerated) draft introduction in which he mentioned the initial diagnosis of childhood schizophrenia, paid homage to Bettelheim, and emphasized that the school portrayed in the novel was only loosely based on the one he had grown up in. A year later, having changed publishers, Bettelheim released Lyons from all the conditions he had initially laid down for his book's publication. The novel was finally published in 1983 by a small company in Virginia.

36. *New Haven Register*, April 8, 1984.
37. Letter to Tom Lyons, April 21, 1971.
38. This point is well illustrated in Tom Lyons's novel.
39. Interview with the author, Chicago, May 1993.
40. Ibid.
41. Karen Carlson Zelan, "The Intellectual Development of an Autistic Girl" (master's thesis, University of Chicago, 1974).
42. Interview with the author, Paris, September 1993.
43. The grant was originally to end in February 1961, but as Bettelheim had not spent all the funds by that date, he had asked for, and obtained, a two-year extension.

Chapter 15. Israel: Understanding Is Not Enough

1. Thanks to a grant from the Federal Delinquency Control Fund, obtained for him by Morris Janowitz.
2. In 1937, members of the kibbutz were to translate Freud's works into Hebrew, in exchange for psychoanalytic treatment that they could not otherwise have paid for.
3. See Walter Laqueur, *A History of Zionism* (London: 1972). Laqueur also wrote *Young Germany: A History of the German Youth Movement* (London: Routledge & Kegan Paul, 1962).
4. The following year, his cousin Edith Buxbaum was to work for a year at the Oranim kibbutz teacher-training center, apparently quite independently of Bettelheim, since at the time they were no longer in contact.
5. The proceedings of the conference were published as *Children in Collectives*, ed. Peter B. Neubauer (Springfield, Ill: Charles C Thomas, 1965).
6. Interview with the author at Ramat Yohanan, August 1992.
7. Melford E. Spiro, *Children of the Kibbutz* (Cambridge, Mass.: Harvard University Press, 1958). Bettelheim's review appeared under the title "Nakhes Fun Kinder," in *The Reconstructionist*, April 1959.
8. "Does Communal Education Work?" *Commentary*, February 1962.
9. In the early 1930s the Hashomer Hatzair movement experienced deep divisions over their position toward the Soviet Union, resulting in an exchange of residents between the two kibbutzes. The hard-core pro-Communists all settled in Bet Alpha, while the moderates went to Ramat Yohanan, which became a kibbutz of the Mapai, or Labor Party. See Laqueur, *A History of Zionism*.

10. Interview with the author, August 1992.
11. The Foundation is the New World Foundation, which had financed his trip.
12. Letter to Ruth Marquis, March 13, 1964.
13. Letter to Ruth Marquis, March 24, 1964.
14. "Personally I felt suffocated by the lack of privacy when I visited a kibbutz," he wrote in "The Right to Privacy Is a Myth," *Saturday Evening Post*, July 27, 1968.
15. Sharp, whom Bettelheim had called in to film the progress of some very sick children at the Orthogenic School, notably "Marcia," made two films during his stay in Israel. The first, *The Kibbutz*, won several prizes, including the top award at the 1966 International Film and Television Festival in New York. The second, *Children of the Dream*, is a report on Bettelheim's research at the kibbutz.
16. "Institutional Care of Problem Children," *Megamot*, no. 2, Spring 1951.
17. Interview with the author, Jerusalem, August 1992.
18. George Clare, *Last Waltz in Vienna: The Destruction of a Family 1842–1942* (London: Macmillan, 1981).
19. *The Children of the Dream* (New York: Macmillan, 1969), 33.
20. Interview with Haim Hadoumi's widow Leah Hadoumi, August 1992, London.
21. Letter to Carl Frankenstein, January 18, 1986.
22. Letter to Carl Frankenstein, April 30, 1987.
23. "It was a religion that viewed (women's) very femininity as a curse, that condemned her to apartheid in its places of worship, that even forbade her to wear her own hair, and required her to shave it off at marriage" (*The Children of the Dream*, 34).
24. Ibid., 39–40.
25. Interview with the author, Israel, August 1992.
26. *Children of the Dream*, 190.
27. Ibid., 28.

Chapter 16. The Bad Guy

1. According to the *Directory for Exceptional Children* for 1965, annual fees at the Orthogenic School that year were between $7,200 and $8,000.
2. Geneviève Jurgensen, *La folie des autres* (Paris: Robert Laffont, 1973).
3. Philip Pekow's daughter, who had also been a student at the Orthogenic School, had left it by the time Bettelheim was appointed director.
4. I found the file in May 1993 among documents turned over to the University of Chicago's Regenstein Library by the Orthogenic School. It may well have been removed since then, however, as the cards bore the real names of all children involved, and should therefore have remained confidential.
5. The Bettelheim and Rimland letters are at the Regenstein Library.

6. *The Empty Fortress: Infantile Autism and the Birth of the Self* (New York: Free Press, 1967), 3.

7. Ibid., 74.

8. In the opening chapters of *The Empty Fortress*, Bettelheim indeed devotes himself to the development of the child's "self" rather than that of the ego. He describes the self as including not just the ego, but the id and superego as well. This is an essentially post-Freudian concept, the contours of which vary from author to author. (Donald Winnicott, for example, speaks of the "false self" that is developed by a child whose mother is not "good enough.") At the time Bettelheim was writing, the self was just beginning a brilliant career in the United States. It was to appear as a kind of bridge between ego psychology and Freudian psychoanalysis. Its main theoretician, Heinz Kohut, was a friend of Bettelheim's, a fellow Viennese exile and an eminent member of the Chicago Psychoanalytic Institute.

9. From a footnote in Winnicott's essay "The Use of an Object in the Context of 'Moses and Monotheism,'" dated January 16, 1969, in his *Psychoanalytic Explorations* (London: Karnac, 1989). The passage is quoted by Elio Frattaroli, a psychoanalyst who worked at the Orthogenic School from 1970 to 1973, in "Bruno Bettelheim's Unrecognized Contribution to Psychoanalytic Thought," *Psychoanalytic Review* (Fall 1994).

10. He believed that transference and counter-transference set in right from the first meeting, and that anything the therapist had previously read about his patient could only serve to obscure the intuitive knowledge he could draw from that encounter. For more on this point, see Bettelheim and Alvin Rosenfeld, *The Art of the Obvious* (New York: Knopf, 1993).

11. France had until June 1967 been one of Israel's staunchest allies and, with the United States, its main supplier of arms. But President de Gaulle was adamant that Israel should not initiate war against Egypt in spite of the mounting threats from that country. Feeling that his message was not being heard in Tel Aviv, he imposed an embargo on the sales of arms to "all countries in the region" just three days before Israel launched its air raid against the Egyptian fleet.

12. The decision not to renew her contract was apparently not due to her ideas, but to the fact that she had failed to fit in with the team, and had not published very much. But Bernice Neugarten, who was in charge of the Committee on Human Development, where the young woman also taught, disagrees. She accuses her colleagues of sexism, and also says they failed to show a minimum of academic courtesy by not even informing the committee of their intention to let her contract lapse.

13. Comment reported by Marc Lubin, Kathy's husband, in December 1990.

14. *Chicago Sun-Times*, February 16, 1969. The quotes in this paragraph are all from that source.

15. The word printed in the newspaper is *cares*, not *chaos*, but given the context and other statements by Bettelheim, it seems likely that this was the result of a transcription error.
16. "Obsolete Youth," *Encounter*, September 3, 1969.
17. *Chicago Sun-Times*, February 16, 1969.
18. Interview with the author, Paris, February 1991.
19. Interview with the author, Paris, July 1994.
20. Interview with Augusta Wallace Lyons, Paris, September 1992.
21. Letter to Candace Hilldrup, January 29, 1971.
22. Letter to Ruth Marquis, September 1971.
23. From a manuscript Bettelheim gave as a gift to Candace Hilldrup. It is undated, and does not contain the final part of the book. This quote does not appear in the published edition.
24. Letter to Candace Hilldrup, August 7, 1971.
25. He had undergone an operation on his left leg. Letter to Candace Hilldrup, January 19, 1972.
26. Ugo Formigoni remembers how, as a senior counselor, she had him rewrite his first dictation seven times, only to hear Bettelheim judge it not spontaneous enough! The result was that it was also to be his last report: Formigoni refused to ever write another—and got away with it.
27. Letter to Ruth Marquis, January 1973.
28. Letter to Ruth Marquis, March 1973.
29. Letter to Ruth Marquis, January 1973.
30. Daniel Karlin, *Un autre regard sur la folie* (Paris: Stock, 1975).
31. Karlin, *Un autre regard sur la folie*. The preface was initially published as an afterword and then, in a subsequent printing, reinstated as the preface it was originally meant to be.
32. *"Le roi se meurt"* is both a saying that was traditional at the French court and the title of a play by Eugène Ionesco.
33. Letter to Candace Hilldrup, March 27, 1974.
34. Interview with the author, New York, August 3, 1991.
35. Sartre, *Réflexions sur la question juive* (Reflections on the Jewish Question) (Paris: Gallimard, 1946).
36. This may be less true in the United States than elsewhere, but Bruno Bettelheim remained a European.
37. Hitler himself, in *Mein Kampf*, was quite explicit on that point.
38. The slogan was chanted in response to the decision of the government to expel from France one of the student leaders, Daniel Cohn-Bendit, who happened to be a German national. It is also worth noting that the link between the Holocaust and the events of the late 1960s was made from the outset in Germany itself. During one of the first anti–Vietnam War protests, the Red Army Faction leader Ulrike Meinhoff said, referring to the Bonn government: "How can we trust these people? They are the ones who created Auschwitz."
39. Literally "Under the cobblestones, the beach," a popular slogan of the May 1968 revolt in France, where huge numbers of cobblestones were

ripped up from Paris streets to make barricades and to be thrown at the police.

40. Karlin, *Un autre regard sur la folie.*
41. Letter to Candace Hilldrup, June 29, 1973.
42. Letter to Candace Hilldrup, March 20, 1976.
43. Interview with the author, May 1993.
44. Karlin, *Un autre regard sur la folie*, 225. Bettelheim is obviously referring to Ben Wright.
45. J. Seevak Sanders, *A Greenhouse for the Mind* (Chicago: University of Chicago Press, 1989). It is worth noting that five years earlier, Bettelheim had published *Freud and Man's Soul*, in which he explained why the word *mind* betrayed the essential tenets of psychoanalysis.
46. The archives are in Regenstein Library, University of Chicago. The letter was an attempt at reconciliation written in 1987, at the time when Jacquelyn Sanders was about to bring out her own book, of which, as she herself underlines, Bettelheim was likely to be called on to give his opinion.
47. In addition to Bert Cohler and Sanders herself, who spoke in other forums in their capacities as academics.

Epilogue. Trude and the Children

1. What he actually said is: "I know how I trembled and still tremble for my children, how I always worried that something might happen to one of the children at the School." Letter to Geneviève Jurgensen, June 30, 1980.
2. Published in *Elle* (French ed.), May 16, 1988.
3. Letter to Ruth Marquis, September 30, 1973.
4. Ibid.
5. Letter to Carl Frankenstein, January 13, 1975.
6. Letter to Ruth Marquis, September 30, 1973.
7. Letter to Carl Frankenstein, January 13, 1975.
8. See in particular Alison Lurie, in a review of the book published in *Harper's* in June 1976, and Joan Blos, writing in the *Merrill-Palmer Quarterly* in 1978.
9. Although she refused to edit the final draft of *A Home for the Heart*, Ruth Marquis had in fact edited many of the texts Bettelheim incorporated into it.
10. Alan Dundes, "Bruno Bettelheim's Uses of Enchantment and Abuses of Scholarship," *Journal of American Folklore*. Some of the similarities mentioned by Dundes had previously been cited by Joan Blos, op. cit.
11. J. Heuscher, *A Psychiatric Study of Fairy Tales* (New York: Charles C. Thomas, 1963). Here are two examples. Referring to Snow White, Heuscher writes: "Not wishing to deprive any one too much, she eats just a little from each of the seven plates and drinks just a drop from each glass (how different from Hansel and Gretel who, rather disrespectfully,

start eating the gingerbread house)"; Bettelheim's version is "Though very hungry, she eats just a little from each of the seven plates, and drinks just a drop from each of the seven glasses, so as to rob none of them too much. (How different from Hansel and Gretel, the orally fixated children, who disrespectfully and voraciously eat up the gingerbread house!)" And discussing Hansel and Gretel's first return to their home, "Hansel and his sister Gretel appear successful at first. But the frustrations at home continue. The mother seems to be more shrewd in her plans for rejecting her children . . . " (Heuscher); "The children's successful return home does not solve anything . . . The frustrations continue, and the mother becomes more shrewd in her plans for getting rid of the children" (Bettelheim).

12. See Erich Fromm, *The Forgotten Language: An Introduction to the Understanding of Dreams, Fairy-Tales and Myths* (New York: Rinehart & Winston, 1951).

13. Letter to Carl Frankenstein, January 13, 1975.

14. Letter to Candace Hilldrup, February 19, 1975.

15. Letter to Carl Frankenstein, August 16, 1975.

16. "My trip to France worried me even more than the one to Germany, because the French intellectuals are all communists, of the most naïve type. Highly sensitive and intellectual, full of goodwill, they are convinced because they are French, once the communists take over, it will be all different from Russia and China. And since they know little about China, they are convinced that things there are ideal, or in Cuba. One could cry if it were not so ridiculous . . . It seems people are only motivated by what they are against, and hardly by what they are for. They still fight De Gaulle so as not to have to realize that there was hardly any French resistance, and that . . . the communists contributed greatly to the collapse of France." Letter to Carl Frankenstein, November 4, 1974.

17. Letter from Carl Frankenstein, January 22, 1975.

18. The full quote appears as an epigraph to this chapter.

19. Interview with Charles Walton, July 1991.

20. As was noted by the French psychoanalyst Thierry Braconnier when he visited the United States in the early 1980s. His trip included a visit to the Orthogenic School.

21. Letter to Candace Hilldrup, September 4, 1980.

22. Letter to Carl Frankenstein, August 21, 1977.

23. Letter to Carl Frankenstein, December 28, 1977.

24. Ibid.

25. Letter to GR, October 26, 1977. Translated from German.

26. Letter to Carl Frankenstein, August 2, 1978.

27. Letter to Carl Frankenstein, February 27, 1978.

28. Letter to Madeleine Chapsal, October 12, 1979.

29. Letter to ER, September 1979. Translated from German.

30. Ibid.

31. Of Karen Zelan, Bettelheim wrote in January 1973: "Her observations are excellent; only she can't criticize me," to Ruth Marquis, adding: "But who can, other than you?"
32. Letter to Carl Frankenstein, January 15, 1979.
33. Letter to Carl Frankenstein, May 24, 1978. The "defeat" referred to was a U.S. contract to supply fighter bombers to Saudi Arabia.
34. Letter to Carl Frankenstein, March 1, 1979.
35. When Naomi Bettelheim visited her parents, she slept in a room that was next to her father's study. She often complained that the sound of his typing late at night kept her from sleeping.
36. Letter to Ruth Marquis, September 30, 1973.
37. Letter to Ruth Marquis, March 1973.
38. This slow-developing ailment had first surfaced many years earlier, with the appearance of a growth inside his throat. As it grew bigger, the diverticulum started pressing against his lungs, causing inflammation, secretions, and a series of attacks of pneumonia. Bettelheim's doctors nevertheless advised against an operation; as the growth was just behind his vocal cords, he risked losing his voice.
39. Letter to Carl Frankenstein, May 10, 1981.
40. Letter to Carl Frankenstein, July 10, 1981.
41. Letter to Carl Frankenstein, October 14, 1981.
42. Published in the United States as *The Road into the Open* (Berkeley: University of California Press, 1992).
43. Letter to Candace Hilldrup, March 2, 1982.
44. "Freud and Man's Soul," *New Yorker*, March 1982.
45. Letter to Carl Frankenstein, January 28, 1982.
46. Letter to Gayle Janowitz, August 12, 1982.
47. Letter to Ruth Marquis, December 28, 1982.
48. Aldo Carotenuto, *A Secret Symphony* (New York: Pantheon Books, 1982).
49. Letter to Ruth Marquis, December 28, 1982.
50. Letter to Carl Frankenstein, February 10, 1983.
51. "Scandal in the Family," *New York Review of Books*, June 3, 1983.
52. Letter to Carl Frankenstein, August 24, 1983.
53. Letter to Carl Frankenstein, October 4, 1983.
54. Interview with the author, November 1990.
55. Letter to ER, September 10, 1984. Translated from German.
56. Letter to Carl Frankenstein, November 10, 1984.
57. Ibid.
58. Letter to Candace Hilldrup, December 18, 1984.
59. Maria Kramer is the widow of Paul Kramer, whom Bettelheim knew well and who was a consulting psychiatrist at the Orthogenic School.
60. Letter to ER, January 2, 1986. Translated from German.
61. Letter to Carl Frankenstein, November 20, 1985.
62. Poison themselves with drugs, of course. Letter to ER, June 1, 1985. Translated from German.
63. Saul Wasserman and Alvin Rosenfeld recounted their work in *Healing*

the Heart, a booklet published by the Child Welfare League of America (Washington, D.C., 1990). It was Rosenfeld, a consultant for CAPI, who had introduced Bettelheim to Wasserman.

64. Interview with the author, July 1991.

65. Letter to Candace Hilldrup, June 3, 1985.

66. Geneviève Bersihand, *Bettelheim* (Paris: Robert Jauze, 1977). It is a slim volume with no new information about Bettelheim but a reflection on his writings.

67. Letter to ER, January 6, 1990. Translated from German.

68. Letter to ER, December 4, 1984. Translated from German.

69. Ibid.

70. This assertion is based solely on statements by other sources and on photographs, as Ruth Bettelheim responded with complete silence to all my letters and requests for interviews.

71. Letter to ER, January 2, 1986. Translated from German.

72. Letter to ER, February 3, 1986. Translated from German.

73. Ibid.

74. Letter to Carl Frankenstein, May 6, 1986.

75. Letter to Carl Frankenstein, June 26, 1986.

76. Letter to Carl Frankenstein, March 11, 1985.

77. Letter to ER, August 3, 1986. Translated from German.

78. Letter to ER, January 25, 1988.

79. Letter to ER, September 1, 1986. Translated from German.

80. Letter to Gayle Janowitz, October 2, 1986.

81. Letter to ER, February 22, 1987. Translated from German.

82. Ibid.

83. Interview with the author, December 1990.

84. Letter to ER, March 9, 1987. Translated from German.

85. Letter to Candace Hilldrup, March 18, 1987.

86. The tale is told in "How I Learned About Psychoanalysis," in *Freud's Vienna and Other Essays* (New York: Knopf, 1970).

87. Editha Sterba wrote an essay about "Johnny" that attracted attention at the time, *"Ein abnormes Kind," Zitschrift für psychoanalytische Pedagogie* (1933); published in English in 1936 in *Psychoanalytical Quarterly*.

88. *Freud's Vienna*, 32.

89. Letter to ER, December 8, 1987. Translated from German.

90. Letter to ER, January 28, 1988. Translated from German.

91. Letter to Carl Frankenstein, March 6, 1988.

92. Letter to Candace Hilldrup, June 16, 1988.

93. *Surviving and Other Essays* (New York: Knopf, 1979), 4.

94. Interview with the author, July 1991.

95. That portrait had been commissioned for him by Eric.

96. A second cast was donated to the Orthogenic School.

97. Letter to ER, January 25, 1987.

98. Interview published in *Society* 28, no. 3 (March–April 1991).

99. Letter to ER, June 12, 1988. Translated from German.
100. Letter to ER, December 31, 1988. Translated from German.
101. See chap. 2.
102. Letter to Carl Frankenstein, October 19, 1986.
103. Letter to ER, July 8, 1989. Translated from German.
104. Letter to ER, October 23, 1989.
105. Published under the title "Love and Death" in the *Los Angeles Times Magazine*, January 27, 1991, almost a year after Bettelheim's death. All the quotes and other details concerning Celeste Fremon's discussions with him are from that source.
106. Letter to ER, December 3, 1989.
107. Letter to ER, January 6, 1990. Bettelheim was to receive the Lukas Prize posthumously, during a memorial ceremony for him on May 15, 1990.
108. Letter to ER, February 12, 1990.
109. Conversation reported in the *Washington Post*, April 24, 1990.
110. In *Let Me Die Before I Wake: Hemlock's Book of Self-Deliverance for the Dying* (Los Angeles: Hemlock, 1985).
111. Letter to Geneviève Jurgensen, January 20, 1974.
112. Amos Oz, *Soumchi* (New York: Harper & Row, 1980).
113. Ritalin has a paradoxical effect on children, for whom it is prescribed as a sedative. In the past, Bettelheim had frequently denounced the abuse of such drugs.
114. In the meaning given by Donald Winnicott to this expression. As the reader will no doubt have understood, this is not intended as criticism of Paula Bettelheim, who, from the little I know about her, always behaved in an exemplary manner to her son. And yet, Bettelheim devoted an entire book, which cost him much time and pain to write, to proving—maybe to himself first of all—that his parents had been "good enough."

*Bruno Bettelheim's Works**

BOOKS

Love Is Not Enough: The Treatment of Emotionally Disturbed Children. New York: Free Press, 1950.

Symbolic Wounds: Puberty Rites and the Envious Male. New York: Free Press, 1954.

Truants from Life: The Rehabilitation of Emotionally Disturbed Children. New York: Free Press, 1955.

The Informed Heart: Autonomy in a Mass Age. Glencoe, Ill.: Free Press, 1960.

Dialogues with Mothers. New York: Free Press, 1962.

The Empty Fortress: Infantile Autism and the Birth of the Self. New York: Free Press, 1967.

The Children of the Dream. New York: Macmillan, 1969.

A Home for the Heart. New York: Knopf, 1974.

The Uses of Enchantment. New York: Knopf, 1976.

Surviving and Other Essays. New York: Knopf, 1979.

Freud and Man's Soul. New York: Knopf, 1982.

A Good Enough Parent. New York: Knopf, 1987.

Freud's Vienna and Other Essays. New York: Knopf, 1990.

In Collaboration

With Morris Janowitz: *Dynamics of Prejudice: A Psychological and Sociological Study of Veterans.* New York: Harper, 1950. Republished as a part of *Social Change and Prejudice.* New York: Free Press, 1964 and 1975.

---

*Initially, this was intended to be the first comprehensive listing of all Bettelheim's published writings. However, he wrote so much and for such diverse publications that I had to curtail my ambition. Despite the efficient assistance of the American Library in Paris and a few others, it proved impractical to find some of the books or other publications to which he contributed. While not claiming to be exhaustive, the present list can only hope to be "good enough."

With Daniel Karlin: *Un autre regard sur la folie*. Paris: Stock, 1975.

With Karen Zelan: *On Learning to Read: The Child's Fascination with Meaning*. New York: Knopf, 1981.

With Alvin A. Rosenfeld: *The Art of the Obvious*. New York: Knopf, 1993.

CHAPTERS, PREFACES, AND AFTERWORDS

"The Evaluation of the Appreciation of Art," *Appraising and Recording Student Progress*, ed. Eugene R. Smith, Ralph W. Tyler, and the Evaluation Staff, Adventure in American Education series, vol. 3. New York: Harper, 1942.

"Concentration Camps, German," *Ten Eventful Years*, vol. 2. Chicago: Encyclopaedia Britannica, 1947.

"The Special School for Emotionally Disturbed Children," *Yearbook of the National Society for the Study of Education*, Part I, Chicago, 1948.

"A Therapeutic Milieu," *Psychopathology: A Source Book*, ed. Charles F. Reed, Irving E. Alexander, and Silvan S. Tomkins. Cambridge, Mass.: Harvard University Press, 1958.

Foreword, *Auschwitz: A Doctor's Eyewitness Account*, by Miklos Nyiszli, trans. Tibère Kremer and Richard Seaver. New York: Frederick Fell, 1960.

"The Real Lesson of the Concentration Camp," *The Open Form: Essays for Our Time*, ed. Alfred Kazin. New York: Harcourt, Brace & World, 1961.

"Self-Realization for the Educated Woman," *The Role of the Educated Woman*, Rice University Symposium, 1963.

"The Commitment Required of a Woman Entering a Scientific Profession," *Women and the Scientific Professions*, ed. Jacquelyn A. Mattfeld and Carol G. Van Aken. Cambridge, Mass: MIT Press, 1965.

"How Much Can Man Change?" *Profile of the School Dropout*, ed. Daniel Schreiber. New York: Random House, 1967.

Postscript, *The Third Reich of Dreams*, by Charlotte Beradt. Chicago: Quadrangle Books, 1968.

"Alienation and Autonomy," *Changing Perspectives on Man*, ed. Ben Rothblatt. Chicago: University of Chicago Press, 1968.

"Autonomy and Inner Freedom, Skills of Emotional Management," *Life Skills in School and Society*. Washington, D.C.: ASCD 1969 Yearbook Committee, 1969.

"The Education of Emotionally and Culturally Deprived Children," *From Learning for Love to Love of Learning: Essays on Psychoanalysis and Education*, ed. Rudolf Ekstein and Rocco L. Motto. New York: Brunner/Mazel, 1969.

Preface, *Infantile Autism*, by Gerhard Bosch. New York: Springer-Verlag, 1970.

"Education and the Reality Principle," *Moral Education: Five Lectures*, ed. James M. Gustafson et al. Cambridge, Mass.: Harvard University Press, 1970.

"About Summerhill," *Summerhill: For and Against*, by Harold H. Hart. New York: Hart, 1970.

"Growing Up Female," *Starting Over: A College Reader*. New York: Random House, 1970.

"Infantile Autism," *The World Biennal of Psychiatry and Psychotherapy*, vol. 1, ed. Silvano Arieti. New York: Basic Books, 1970.

"The Change in Woman's Role in Home and Society," *What Is Happening to American Women*. Atlanta: Southern Newspaper Publishers Association Foundation, 1970.

"About the Sexual Revolution," *Sexual Latitude: For and Against*, by Ronald Atkinson et al., ed. Harold H. Hart. New York: Hart, 1971.

"Mental Health in Slums," *The Social Impact of Urban Design*. Chicago: University of Chicago Center for Policy Study, 1971.

"The Future of Residential Treatment in the Society of the Future," *Healing Through Living*. Springfield, Ill.: Charles C Thomas, 1971.

"The Anatomy of Academic Discontent," *In Defense of Academic Freedom*, ed. Sidney Hook. New York: Pegasus, 1971.

Preface, *Faces of Authority*, by William T. Kulik. Scott, Foresman, 1972.

"To Nurse and to Nurture," *The Psychodynamics of Patient Care*, by L. Schwartz. Englewood Cliffs, N.J.: Prentice Hall, 1972.

"Regression as Progress," *Facts and Techniques in Psychoanalytic Therapy*, ed. Peter Giovacchini. New York: Science House, 1972.

"Middle-Class Teacher and Lower-Class Child," *Rethinking Urban Education*, ed. Herbert J. Walberg and Andrew T. Kopan. San Francisco: Jossey-Bass, 1972.

Preface, *La folie des autres*, by Geneviève Jurgensen. Paris: Robert Laffont, 1973.

Preface, *Les mille et une nuits*, ed. T. Carlier. Paris: Seghers, 1978.

Afterword, *Je ne lui ai pas dit au revoir*, by Claudine Vegh and Louis Evrard. Paris: Gallimard, 1979. U.S. edition: *I Didn't Say Goodbye*, trans. Ros Schwartz. New York: Dutton, 1984.

"The Child's Perception of the City," *Literature and the Urban Experience: Essays on the City and Literature*, ed. Michael C. Jaye and Ann Chalmers Watts. New Brunswick, N.J.: Rutgers University Press, 1981.

Preface, *The Words to Say It*, by Marie Cardinal. Cambridge, Mass.: Van Vector & Goodheart, 1983.

"La Vienne de Freud," *Catalogue de l'Exposition Paris–Vienne*. Paris: Editions du Centre Pompidou, 1986.

"Lionel Trilling on Literature and Psychoanalysis," *Explorations: The Twentieth Century*, vol. 3. Lafayette: University of Southwestern Louisiana, 1989.

ARTICLES AND ESSAYS

1943

(October) "Individual and Mass Behavior in Extreme Situations." *Journal of Abnormal and Social Psychology*.

1944

(August 1) "Behavior in Extreme Situation." *Politics.*

(November 4) Review: *New Bearings in Aesthetics and Art Criticism* by Bernard C. Heyl. *College Art Journal.*

1945

(January 2) Review: *Diagnosis of Our Time: Wartime Essays of a Sociologist* by Karl Mannheim. *Politics.*

(July 14) "The Helpless and the Guilty." *Common Sense.*

(December 2) "War Trials and German Re-Education." *Politics.*

1946

(September) "A Scientific Approach to the Problem of Prejudice." Public Relations Workshop Summary, American Council on Race Relations.

1947

"What Students Think About Art." General Education in the Humanities, American Council on Education.

"The Concentration Camp as a Class State." *Modern Review*, vol. 1.

(January) "Self-Interpretation of Fantasy." *American Journal of Orthopsychiatry.*

(April) "The Dynamism of Anti-Semitism in Gentile and Jew." *Journal of Abnormal and Social Psychology*, vol. 42.

(October) With E. Sylvester, "The Therapeutic Influence of the Group on the Individual." *American Journal of Orthopsychiatry.*

1948

(February) "The Victim's Image of the Anti-Semite." *Commentary.*

(April) With E. Sylvester, "A Therapeutic Milieu." *American Journal of Orthopsychiatry.*

(June) "Some Concomitants of Prejudice." *Intercultural Educational News.*

(July) "Closed Institutions for Children?" *Bulletin of the Menninger Clinic*, vol. 12, no. 4.

(October) "Somatic Symptoms in Superego Formation." *American Journal of Orthopsychiatry.*

(November) Review: *Myths of War* by Marie Bonaparte. *American Journal of Sociology.*

(November) Review: *Essays on Anti-Semitism* by K. L. Pinson. *American Journal of Sociology.*

(December) "Exodus, 1947." *Politics.*

(December) "The Social-Studies Teacher and the Emotional Needs of Adolescents." *School Review.*

1949

With E. Sylvester, "Physical Symptoms in Emotionally Disturbed Children."

Psychoanalytic Study of the Child, vol. 3–4. New York: International Universities Press.

(January) With E. Sylvester, "Milieu Therapy: Indications and Illustrations." *Psychoanalytic Review*, vol. 36, no. 1.

(January) "A Psychiatric School." *Quarterly Journal of Child Behavior*, vol. 1, no. 1.

(April) "Harry: A Study in Rehabilitation." *Journal of Abnormal and Social Psychology*, vol. 44.

(May) Review: *Resolving Social Conflicts: Selected Papers on Group Dynamics* by Kurt Lewin. *American Journal of Sociology*.

(September) With M. Janowitz, "Ethnic Tolerance: A Function of Social and Personal Control." *American Journal of Sociology*.

Review: *Doctors of Infamy: The Story of the Nazi Medical Crimes* by Alexander Mitscherlich. *American Journal of Sociology*.

(December) "On the Rehabilitation of the Offender." *Federal Probation*, vol. 13.

1950

With E. Sylvester, "Delinquency and Morality." *Psychoanalytic Study of the Child*, vol. 5.

With M. Janowitz, "Dynamics of Prejudice." *Harper's*.

"Przypadek Harry's Ego." *Psychological Abstracts*, vol. 25.

Review: *Searchlights on Delinquency* ed. K. R. Eissler, *American Journal of Sociology*.

(January) "Love Is Not Enough." *University of Chicago Magazine*.

(Spring) With M. Janowitz, "Reactions to Fascist Propaganda: A Pilot Study." *Public Opinion Quarterly*.

(June) "The Relief of Understanding." *University of Chicago Magazine*.

(September) "The Psychoanalysis of Anti-Semitism" (review: *Anti-Semitism and Emotional Disorder* by N. Ackerman and M. Johoda). *Complex*, vol. 3.

(October) With M. Janowitz, "Prejudice." *Scientific American*.

(October) With E. Sylvester, "Notes on the Impact of Parental Occupations." *American Journal of Orthopsychiatry*.

(November) Review: *The Autobiography of Wilhelm Stekel* ed. Emil A. Gutheil. *American Journal of Sociology*.

1951

Review: *Character Assassination* by Jerome Davis. *University of Chicago Law Review*, vol. 18.

(February) Discussion: *Family Structure and Psychic Development* by Jules Henry. *American Journal of Orthopsychiatry*.

(March) Review: *The Lonely Crowd* by David Riesman. *University of Chicago Magazine*.

(April) "Institutional Care of Problem Children." *Megamot* (Jerusalem), vol. 2.

(July) "Love Is Not Enough." University of Chicago Round Table.

(September) "How Arm Our Children Against Anti-Semitism." *Commentary*.

(October) "Does Your Child Fight Sleep?" *Parents.*

(October) "Helping Jewish Children to Face Prejudice." *Jewish Affairs.*

(November) Review: *Children in Conflict* by Margaret L. Lambert. *Marriage and Family Living.*

(November) Review: *Personal Aggressiveness and War* by E. F. M. Durbin and John Bowlby. *American Journal of Sociology.*

(December) Review: *Personality and Psychotherapy* by John Dollard and Neal Miller. *Elementary School Journal*, vol. 52.

"The Case of Michael." Institute for Juvenile Research.

1952

(January) "Mental Health and Current Mores." *American Journal of Orthopsychiatry.*

(April) "Schizophrenic Art: A Case Study." *Scientific American.*

(October) "Mental Health and the Child." *Elementary School Journal.*

(October) "Remarks on the Psychological Appeal of Totalitarianism." *American Journal of Economics and Sociology.*

(December) Review: *Sex Education as Human Relations* by Lester Kirkendall. *Federal Probation*, vol. 16.

1953

(January) "Securing Our Children Against Prejudice." *Jewish Center Worker*, vol. 14.

(June) Review: *An Autobiographical Study* by Sigmund Freud. *American Sociological Review*, vol. 18.

(December) Review: *Children in Play Therapy* by C. E. Moustakas. *Elementary School Journal.*

1954

"Governor's Conference on Mental Health." *Elementary School Journal.*

(April) Review: *The Step-Child* by W. C. Smith. *University of Chicago Magazine.*

1955

"Individual Autonomy and Mass Control." *Frankfurter Beiträge zur Soziologie.*

(January) Review: *Seduction of the Innocent* by Frederic Wertham. *Library Quarterly*, vol. 25.

(March) "Don't Deny Them Discipline." *National Parent Teachers*, vol. 49.

(June) "Death Life's Purpose?" (review: *The Psychiatrist and the Dying Patient* by K. R. Eissler). *Chicago Review.*

(September) "Early Ego Development in a Mute Autistic Child." *Bulletin of the Philadelphia Association for Psychoanalysis*, vol. 15.

(October) With B. Wright, "Staff Development in a Treatment Institution." *American Journal of Orthopsychiatry.*

(November) "Educational News, German Schools Revisited." *Elementary School Journal.*

1956

(February) "Returning to Dachau." *Commentary.*

(April) "Discrimination and Science" (review: *Prejudice and Your Child* by Kenneth B. Clark). *Commentary.*

(July) "Childhood Schizophrenia as a Reaction to Extreme Situations." *American Journal of Orthopsychiatry.*

(October) "Fathers Shouldn't Try to Be Mothers." *Parents.*

1957

(January) Review: *The Life and Work of Sigmund Freud* by Ernest Jones. *American Journal of Sociology.*

(March) Review: *Promise of Youth: Exploring Psychiatric Research in Juvenile Delinquence. Federal Probation,*

(March) With B. Wright, "Professional Identity and Personal Rewards in Teaching." *Elementary School Journal.*

1958

"Psychiatric Consultation in Residential Treatment: The Doctor's View." *American Journal of Orthopsychiatry.*

(May 19) Review: "Ernest Jones' Freud: A Dissenting Opinion." *New Leader,* vol. 19.

(Autumn) "Segregation: New Style." *School Review.*

(October) "Sputnik and Segregation." *Commentary.*

(November) "Toward a New School." *Elementary School Journal.*

1959

Review: *Motility in Infants,* a film by B. Mittelman. *Contemporary Psychology,* vol. 4.

(March) "Reading the Signs of Mental Health." *National Parent Teachers,* vol. 53.

(March 5) "Joey: A Mechanical Boy." *Scientific American.*

(March) "Feral and Autistic Children." *American Journal of Sociology.*

(April) "Nakhes Fun Kinder." *Reconstructionist,* vol. 25.

(May) Review: *Sigmund Freud's Mission* by Erich Fromm. *New Leader,* vol. 42.

(August) "A Note on the Concentration Camps" (review: *From Death-Camp to Existentialism: A Psychiatrist's Path to a New Therapy* by Viktor Frankl). *Chicago Review.*

(November) "Help for our Troubled Children." *Think,* vol. 25.

1960

(May) "Emotional Blocks to Learning: A Problem Learner." *Parents.*

(November) "The Ignored Lesson of Anne Frank." *Harper's.*

1961

"The Decision to Fail." *School Review.*

(April) "Delusions for Moderns." *University of Chicago Magazine.*

(April) "Comment": Letter to the editor responding to the review of *The Informed Heart. Midstream*, vol. 7.

1962

(Winter) "The Problem of Generations." *Daedalus.*

(February) "Does Communal Education Work? The Case of the Kibbutz." *Commentary.*

(Spring) "Freedom from Ghetto Thinking." *Midstream*, vol. 8.

(March) "Facing the Full-View Mirror." *WFMT Perspective*, vol. ii.

(May) "Talks with Mothers." *Redbook.*

(October) "Growing Up Female." *Harper's.*

1963

"A Noncontribution to Educational Research" (review: *Educating Emotionally Disturbed Children* by N. G. Haring and E. Lakin Phillips). *Harvard Educational Review.*

(January) "Conversations with Parents." *University of Chicago Magazine.*

(February) "How to Ask the Right Question About Your Child." *Parents.*

(March) "Roadblocks to Learning." *NEA Journal*, vol. 52.

(May) "Finding Identity in Mass Movements." *McCormick Quarterly Special Supplement.*

(June 15) "Eichmann: The System, the Victims." *New Republic.*

(October 19) "Class, Color and Prejudice." *The Nation.*

(November) "Parents versus Television." *Redbook.*

1964

"Art and Art Education: A Personal Vision." *Art.*

(February 7) "Why Does a Man Become a Hater?" *Life.*

(April) "The Class of '84." *Toronto Education Quarterly*, vol. 3.

(April 11) "Speaking Out: Stop Pampering Gifted Children." *Saturday Evening Post.*

(May) "Sex and Violence in Books, Magazines and Television." *Redbook.*

(May 9) Letter to the Editor on "Segregating the Gifted." *New Republic.*

(July) "What Children Learn from Play." *Parents.*

(September) "How Much Can Man Change?" (review: *Stability and Change in Human Characteristics* by Benjamin Bloom). *New York Review of Books.*

(November 7) "Women: Emancipation Is Still to Come." *New Republic*, 50th anniversary special issue.

1965

(March) "Grouping the Gifted." *NEA Journal*, vol. 54.

(March) "How Mothers-in-Law Disrupt Marriages: An Old Problem in New Forms." *Redbook.* The article triggered a reply in the April issue: "What Our Daughters-in-Law Didn't Tell You," to which Bettelheim responded.

(June) Review: *Psychiatric Aspects of the Prevention of Nuclear War* by the Committee on Social Issues. *Bulletin of the Atomic Scientists.*

(June) "The Orthogenic School." *University of Chicago Magazine.*

(September) "Teaching the Disadvantaged." *NEA Journal,* vol. 54.

(October) "When Children Lie or Steal." *Redbook.*

(October) "Young Children's Sex Behavior: Why Can't We Ignore It?" *Ladies' Home Journal.*

(November) "Children's Jealousy: 'We Got the Baby for You.'" *Ladies' Home Journal.*

1966

(January) "Am I Ruining My Child for Life?" *Ladies' Home Journal.*

(March) "Violence: A Neglected Mode of Behavior." *Annals of the American Academy,* vol. 364.

(March) "Why Working Mothers Feel Guilty." *Redbook.*

(July) "Training the Child-Care Worker in a Residential Center." *American Journal of Orthopsychiatry.*

(September) "The Danger of Teaching Your Baby to Read." *Ladies' Home Journal.*

(October 6) "Children Without Parents" (review: *Children in Collectives: Rearing Aims and Practices in the Kibbutz* ed. Peter B. Neubauer). *New York Review of Books.*

1967

(February) Review: *Microcosm: Structural, Psychological and Religious Evolution in Groups* by Philip E. Slater. *American Sociological Review,* vol. 32.

(February 12) "Parent and Child: Where Self Begins." *New York Times Magazine.*

(March 11) "Speaking Out: Children Should Learn About Violence." *Saturday Evening Post.*

(July 2) "Survival of the Jews" (review: *Treblinka* by Jean-François Steiner). *New Republic.*

1968

A reply to Prof. Gary Merritt's review of *The Empty Fortress. American Journal of Orthopsychiatry.*

(July 27) "Speaking Out: The Right to Privacy Is a Myth." *Saturday Evening Post.*

(September) "The High Calling of a University Student." *Rochester Review,* vol. 31.

(Autumn) "The Ultimate Limit." *Midway.*

1969

Review: *Death in Life: Survivors of Hiroshima* by Robert Jay Lifton. *Political Science Quarterly*, vol. 84.

"Personality Formation in the Kibbutz." *American Journal of Psychoanalysis*, vol. 29.

(January) "The Anatomy of Courage." *Barat Review*, vol. 4.

(February) "Where Do Nightmares Come From?" *Ladies' Home Journal.*

(March) Dialogue with Bruno Bettelheim: "How Can Elementary Schools Help Boys." *Instructor.*

(April) Discussion of Dr. Flarsheim's Paper. *Bulletin of the Chicago Society for Adolescent Psychiatry*, vol. 2.

(April 7) "Too Many Misfits in College" (excerpts from a statement made to the House Special Subcommittee on Education). *U.S. News & World Report.*

(April 13) "Children Must Learn to Fear." *New York Times Magazine.*

(May) "The Anatomy of Academic Discontent." *Change in Higher Education.*

(May 4) "On Campus Rebellion: A New and Potentially Dangerous Rite of Manhood." *Chicago Tribune Magazine.*

(June) "Portnoy Psychoanalyzed." *Midstream.*

(June) "Psychoanalysis and Education." *School Review.*

(September 3) "Obsolete Youth: Towards a Psychograph of Adolescent Rebellion." *Encounter.*

(October) "Psychoanalysis and Education." *Education Digest.*

(December) "Deviancy in Children." *Boston University Journal*, vol. 17.

1970

"The Kibbutz: Dream and Reality." *Histradut Round Table Series*, no. 1.

(January) "The Right and Wrong Way to Teach Sex." *Ladies' Home Journal.*

(February) "Young People Who Hate the Police." *Ladies' Home Journal.*

(February 8) "Knitting: Its Role in the Life of Dr. Bruno Bettelheim" (letter to the editor). *New York Times Magazine.*

(March) "It Wasn't Me Who Wet." *Ladies' Home Journal.*

(April) "The Perils of Overexposing Youth to College." *Education Digest*, vol. 35.

(April) "What Sleepwalking Means." *Ladies' Home Journal.*

(May) "Oldest, Middle, Youngest Child—Which Is Better Off?" *Ladies' Home Journal.*

(June) "Why Working Mothers Have Happier Children." *Ladies' Home Journal.*

(July) "Why Parents Should Take a Firm Stand." *Ladies' Home Journal.*

(August) "How to Say No Without Guilt." *Ladies' Home Journal.*

(September) "Meddling Grandmothers." *Ladies' Home Journal.*

(October) "What Adoption Means to a Child." *Ladies' Home Journal.*

(November) "Mothers and Daughters." *Ladies' Home Journal.*

(November) "What Psychoanalysis Can Do for Education." *The Critic.*

(December) "Redundant Youth." *Realities.*

1971

(January) "What Does Independence Really Mean?" *Ladies' Home Journal.*
(February) "Expressing Anger: The Right and Wrong Way to Discipline Children." *Ladies' Home Journal.*
(March) "The Roots of Radicalism." *Playboy.*
(March) "When Should Parents Push?—'I Can't Do It.'" *Ladies' Home Journal.*
(April) "Learning Blocks." *Ladies' Home Journal.*
(May) "What's Happening to the Family." *Ladies' Home Journal.*
(September) "Why School Lunch Fails." *Family Health.*
(October) "The Need for Roots." *Ladies' Home Journal.*
(November) "The Meaning of Play." *Ladies' Home Journal.*
(November) "Ten Who Don't Belong." *The Critic.*
(December) "Should Parents Encourage Their Children to Believe in Santa Claus?" *Ladies' Home Journal.*

1972

"The Impatient Treatment of Psychotics." *Science and Psychoanalysis*, vol. 20.
"Psychotherapy and Psychopedagogy." *Psychotherapy and Psychosomatics*, vol. 20.
(January) "Our Children's Friends." *Ladies' Home Journal.*
(February) "Divorce." *Ladies' Home Journal.*
(March) "Teaching Your Child to Tell the Truth." *Ladies' Home Journal.*
(March) "Why School Lunch Fails." *School Foodservice Journal.*
(April) "Sibling Rivalry." *Ladies' Home Journal.*
(May) "Bed-wetting." *Ladies' Home Journal.*
(July) "When Should Parents Seek Professional Psychiatric Help for Their Child?" *Ladies' Home Journal.*
(August) "Some Unexpected Problems Between Mothers and Daughters in These Days of Women's Lib." *Ladies' Home Journal.*
(September) "Helping the Handicapped Child." *Ladies' Home Journal.*
(October) "Misplaced Anger and How to Deal with It." *Ladies' Home Journal.*
(November) "Teaching Children How to Make Decisions." *Ladies' Home Journal.*
(November) "Play and Education." *School Review.*
(December) "Teaching Self-Control to a Screaming Two-Year-Old." *Ladies' Home Journal.*

1973

(January) "Reading Problems and Dyslexia." *Ladies' Home Journal.*
(February) "The Hyperactive Child." *Ladies' Home Journal.*
(March) "Advice on Raising Children of Divorce." *Ladies' Home Journal.*
(April) "A Look into Your Future: Child Raising." *Today's Health*, vol. 51.
(April) Review of books on the treatment of psychotic children. *Journal of Child Psychiatry*, vol. 12.
(April) "Who's Afraid of the Big Bad Wolf—And Why?" *Ladies' Home Journal.*

(May) "Does Your Child Throw Screaming Tantrums in Public?" *Ladies' Home Journal.*

(June) "Teaching Children That Males and Females Should Be Complementary, Not Competitive, Often Means That the Parents Have to Learn the Lesson First Themselves." *Ladies' Home Journal.*

(July) "Teaching Children to Make Decisions: When Should You Let Them Choose?" *Ladies' Home Journal.*

(August) "Child Identification at Age Four When Child's Parents Are at Odds About Basic Beliefs." *Ladies' Home Journal.*

(September) "Children Succeeding: Difference Between Encouraging and Pressuring a Child." *Ladies' Home Journal.*

(October) "In Praise of Fairytales." *Ladies' Home Journal.*

(November) "What Can Such Fairytales as Hansel and Gretel and Little Red Riding Hood Teach Children About the Real World?" *Ladies' Home Journal.*

1974

(November) "Janet and Mark and the New Illiteracy: Reading and the Emotions." *Encounter.*

1975

(February) "Some Further Thoughts on the Doll Corner." *School Review.*
(December 8) "Reflections: The Uses of Enchantment." *New Yorker.*

1976

(August 2) "Reflections: Surviving." *New Yorker.*
(September) "Untying the Family." *Center Magazine*, vol. 9.
(October) "Recreating Family Life: The Means Are in Our Hands." *Parents.*

1977

(January 2) "Where Psychoanalysis Was Born" (review: *Sigmund Freud's Home and Offices: The Photographs of Edmund Engelman*). *New York Times Book Review.*

1978

(April) "Learning to Read: A Primer for Literacy." *Harper's.*
(December) "The Holocaust, a Generation later." *Encounter.*
(December 23) "Lessons for Life: The Uses of Enchantment." *Opera News.*

1980

(January 2) "Children, Curiosity and Museums." *Child Today*, vol. 9.
(July 8) "The Child's Perception of the City." *Humanities.*

1981

(October) "The Art of Motion Pictures: Man, Superman and Myth." *Harper's.*

(November) With Karen Zelan, "Why Children Don't Like to Read." *Education Digest* and *Atlantic Monthly*.

1982

(March) "Freud and Man's Soul." *New Yorker*.
(May 13) "Scandal in the Family." *New York Review of Books*.

1983

(June 30) "Scandal in the Family" (follow-up). *New York Review of Books*.

1985

(September 10) "A Child's Garden of Fantasy." *Channels Commun*, vol. 5.
(October 28) "TV Stereotypes 'Devastating' to Young Minds." *U.S. News & World Report*.
(November) "Punishment versus Discipline: A Child Can Be Expected to Behave Well Only If His Parents Live by the Values They Teach." *Atlantic Monthly*.

1986

"The Illustrated Fable." *The Advocate*.
(October 5) "Their Specialty Was Murder" (review: *The Nazi Doctors: Medical Killing and the Psychology of Genocide* by Robert Jay Lifton). *New York Times Book Review*.

1987

(March) "The Importance of Play." *Atlantic Monthly*.
(July 12) "A Return to the Land of Fairy Tales." *New York Times*.

1988

(Winter and Spring issues) "Les livres essentiels de Bruno Bettelheim." *Le Temps Stratégique* (Geneva).
"The Holocaust in the Undermind of the West." *Dimension*, vol. 4.

1989

(Summer) "Lionel Trilling on Literature and Psychoanalysis." *Explorations*, vol. 3.

1990

(Spring) "The Birthplace of Psychoanalysis." *Wilson Quarterly*, vol. 14.

Index